REBECCA MOORE HOWARD

D0202271

SECOND EDITION

WRITING MATTERS

A **HANDBOOK** FOR WRITING AND RESEARCH

ACCESS Matters

Powered by **Connect Composition Plus 2.0**, **mcgrawhillconnect.com**, *Writing Matters* is the most accessible handbook available.

- **Easy Content Search** Locate what you need in the brief table of contents to the right, the complete table of contents on the inside back cover, the contents on the back of each tab, or the index on easy-to-find tinted pages at the back of the book.

- **Quick Flip** Use the colored tabs to flip to the section you need and to locate checklists of key responsibilities.

- **Citation and Common Sentence Problems** Interactive online animations and foldouts accompanying tabs 6, 7, and 10 show you how to document your sources and to correct common sentence problems such as comma splices and fused sentences.

- **Writing Responsibly** *Writing Responsibly* notes (listed on the back flap) keep you focused on your responsibilities to other writers, your topic, your audience, and yourself.

- **Chapter Highlights** *Quick Reference* boxes highlighting key content appear throughout the book and are listed on the back flap.

- **Learn More, Online and Elsewhere** *More about...* guides in the margins of the print book use page numbers to lead you to related topics; online, click the links to jump directly to what you need to know.

- **Student Projects** 21 student writing models and other examples appear in the book, and over 30 more, in a variety of genres, are available on *Connect Composition Plus 2.0*.

P9-DNC-368

Dear Colleagues:

Thank you for taking the time to consider *Writing Matters!*
I started this project as a way of giving back to the composition
community and helping students with their development as
writers. Working on this handbook has also been a source
of my own development: My life and teaching have been
immeasurably enriched by the students and instructors I
have met during my travels to discuss *Writing Matters* and my
responsibilities-focused approach to writing.

Rebecca Moore Howard
is Professor of Writing
and Rhetoric at Syracuse
University. Her recent work on
the Citation Project is part of
a collaborative endeavor to
study how students really use
resources.

While developing on the second edition of *Writing Matters*,
I have also been working on the Citation Project, a nationwide
study of the researched writing of 174 students for their
composition classes. Some of the results of that research are
available on the Citation Project website: citationproject.net.
There you will see a variety of signs that students may not be
reading their sources carefully and completely and that their
research projects suffer accordingly. This edition includes newly
developed materials that teach concrete skills, such as marking where the source material ends
and the writer's own voice begins. On a larger scale, these materials encourage students to invest
themselves in their writing.

In *Writing Matters*, I draw on three decades' worth of teaching, writing, and research—as well as
on my recent travels—to focus sustained attention on **writers' responsibilities to other writers,
to their readers, to their topics,** and most especially, **to themselves.** The result is a teaching
and learning framework that unites research, rhetoric, documentation, grammar, and style into a
cohesive whole, helping students to find consistency in rules that might otherwise confound them.
Students experience responsible writing not only by citing the work of other writers accurately but
also by treating those writers' ideas fairly. They practice responsible writing by providing reliable
information about a topic at a depth that does the topic justice. Most importantly, they embrace
responsible writing by taking their writing seriously and approaching writing assignments as
opportunities to learn about new topics and to expand their scope as writers.

Students are more likely to write well when they think of themselves as writers rather than as
error-makers. By explaining rules in the context of responsibility, I address composition students
respectfully as mature and capable fellow participants in the research and writing process.

Sincerely,

Rebecca Moore Howard

REBECCA MOORE HOWARD
Syracuse University

SECOND EDITION

WRITING
MATTERS

A HANDBOOK FOR WRITING AND RESEARCH

McGraw Hill

Connect
Learn
Succeed™

WRITING MATTERS: A HANDBOOK FOR WRITING AND RESEARCH, SECOND EDITION (TABBED)

Published by McGraw-Hill, a business unit of The McGraw-Hill Companies, Inc., 1221 Avenue of the Americas, New York, NY 10020. Copyright © 2014 by The McGraw-Hill Companies, Inc. All rights reserved. Printed in the United States of America. Previous edition © 2010. No part of this publication may be reproduced or distributed in any form or by any means, or stored in a database or retrieval system, without the prior written consent of The McGraw-Hill Companies, Inc., including, but not limited to, in any network or other electronic storage or transmission, or broadcast for distance learning.

Some ancillaries, including electronic and print components, may not be available to customers outside the United States.

This book is printed on acid-free paper.

3 4 5 6 7 8 9 0 QTN/QTN 1 0 9 8 7 6 5 4

Comb: ISBN: 978-0-07-784028-0
        MHID: 0-07-784028-3

Spiral: ISBN: 978-0-07-750597-4
          MHID: 0-07-750597-2

Senior Vice President, Products & Markets: *Kurt L. Strand*
Vice President, General Manager, Products & Markets: *Michael Ryan*
Vice President, Content Production & Technology Services: *Kimberly Meriwether David*
Managing Director: *David S. Patterson*
Director: *Susan Gouijnstook*
Senior Brand Manager: *Nancy Huebner*
Senior Director of Development: *Dawn Groundwater*
Senior Development Editor: *Michael O'Loughlin*
Executive Market Development Manager: *Nanette Giles*
Senior Marketing Manager: *Kevin Colleary*

Digital Product Analyst: *Janet Byrne Smith*
Content Project Manager: *Sandy Wille*
Buyer: *Nicole Baumgartner*
Cover/Interior Design: *Preston Thomas, Cadence Design Studio*
Cover Illustration: *Lachina Publishing Services*
Content Licensing Specialist: *Shawntel Schmitt*
Photo Researcher: *Deborah Anderson*
Compositor: *Thompson Type*
Typeface: *10.5/12 Garamond Premier Pro*
Printer: *Quad/Graphics*

All credits appearing on page or at the end of the book are considered to be an extension of the copyright page.

Library of Congress Cataloging-in-Publication Data

Howard, Rebecca Moore.
    Writing matters : a handbook for writing and research / Rebecca Moore Howard, Syracuse University.—Second edition.
        pages cm
    This is a Howard TABBED edition.
    Includes index.
    ISBN-13: 978-0-07-750597-4—ISBN-10: 0-07-750597-2 (hard copy)
    1. English language—Rhetoric. 2. Report writing. I. Title.
    PE1408.H685247 2013b
    808'.042-dc23   2012039211

The Internet addresses listed in the text were accurate at the time of publication. The inclusion of a website does not indicate an endorsement by the authors or McGraw-Hill, and McGraw-Hill does not guarantee the accuracy of the information presented at these sites.

www.mhhe.com

Writing Matters is dedicated
to the memory of my sister, Sandy

Change the Conversation . . .

Writing Matters offers instructors and students a four-part framework that focuses the rules and conventions of writing through a lens of responsibility, ultimately empowering students to own their ideas and to view their writing as consequential.

Writing Matters helps students see the conventions of writing as a network of responsibilities . . .

> **to other writers** by treating information fairly and accurately, and crafting writing that is fresh and original
>
> **to the audience** by writing clearly, and providing readers with the information and interpretation they need to make sense of a topic
>
> **to the topic** by exploring a topic thoroughly and creatively, assessing sources carefully, and providing reliable information at a depth that does the topic justice
>
> **to themselves** by taking writing seriously, and approaching the process as an opportunity to learn about a topic and to expand research and writing skills

Make It your Own!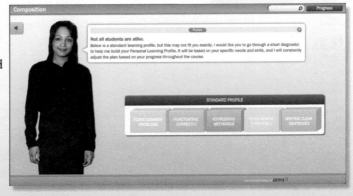

McGraw Hill **connect** plus+ | COMPOSITION

WRITING MATTERS eBook

The CONNECT COMPOSITION PLUS 2.0 eBook provides *Writing Matters* content in a digital format that is accessible from within Connect and Blackboard. In support of the engaged learning experience, students can link directly to activities and assignments within **CONNECT** from the eBook. Students can have all the resources from *Writing Matters* right on their desktops!

Personal Learning Plan (PLP)

Through an intuitive, adaptive diagnostic that assesses proficiencies in five core areas of grammar and mechanics, students generate a personalized learning plan tailored to address their needs within the timeframe students determine they want to study. The personalized program includes contextualized grammar and writing lessons, videos, animations, and interactive exercises and provides immediate feedback on students' work and progress. Based on metacognitive learning theories, the **PERSONAL LEARNING PLAN** continually adapts with each interaction, while built-in time management tools keep students on track to ensure they achieve their course goals. The Personal Learning Plan is designed to improve student writing, allow classroom instruction to focus on critical writing processes, and support the goals of writing programs and individual instructors with reports that present data related to progress, achievement, and students who may be at risk.

Change, Rearrange, Exchange . . .

Your courses evolve over time—shouldn't your course material? With **McGraw-Hill Create™**, you can easily arrange and rearrange material from a variety of sources, including your own. You can select content by discipline or collection, including 4,000 textbooks, 5,500 articles, 25,000 cases, and 11,000 readings. When you build a **CREATE** book, you will receive a complimentary print review copy in 3 to 5 business days or a complimentary electronic review copy (eComp) via e-mail in about one hour. Go to mcgrawhillcreate.com and register today.

With Create you can:

choose which chapters in the handbook you want from

- *Writing Matters* Comprehensive with exercises
- *Writing Matters* Tabbed with or without exercises
- *Writing Matters* Pocket
- McGraw-Hill texts

choose which resources you want from

- other McGraw-Hill collections, such as *The Ideal Reader* (800 readings by genre, mode, theme, discipline, and author), *Annual Editions* (5,500 articles from journals and periodicals), *Traditions* (readings in the humanities), *Sustainability* (readings with an environment focus), and *American History and World Civilization Documents* (primary sources including maps, charters, letters, memoirs, and essays)

- your own works, such as syllabi, institutional information, study guides, assignments, diagrams, and artwork; and student writing, art, and photos

choose which format you want

- print
- electronic

Make It Your Own!

Connect Composition Plus 2.0

When you draw upon **CONNECT COMPOSITION PLUS 2.0 with *WRITING MATTERS*** to implement your curriculum, you use digital tools developed by composition experts to create a state-of-the-art teaching and learning environment that engages your students with their course assignments, including:

- group assignments
- blog assignments
- discussion board assignments
- writing assignments with accurate formatting

The flexible content and powerful tools found in **CONNECT COMPOSITION PLUS 2.0 with *WRITING MATTERS*** work well in traditional course settings as well as in online or hybrid courses.

Peer Review

CONNECT COMPOSITION PLUS 2.0 offers writing assignments with superior peer reviewing capability that helps instructors easily assign and manage groups and peer review exercises. This program gives students an engaging space in which to collaborate online, benefit from their classmates' comments, and participate in a crucial step in the writing process. Managed through an efficient and fun-to-use online system, this collaborative experience prepares students for the group writing projects they will encounter throughout their college careers and in the workplace.

Outcomes-Based Assessment of Writing

CONNECT's powerful **OUTCOMES-BASED ASSESSMENT** tool generates clear, simple reports—suitable for program evaluation or accrediting bodies—allowing a variety of stakeholders a view of student progress toward program goals. Prebuilt, customizable grading rubrics, written specifically for composition programs, can be adapted to your unique assignments and objectives to make the set-up, management, and reporting of outcomes-based writing assessment efficient, professional, and useful.

Make It Your Own!

Blackboard® and MH Campus®

All the content of *Writing Matters*—writing instruction, readings, assignments, documentation flowcharts—is integrated with your program's course management system to offer single sign-on, seamless use of all **CONNECT COMPOSITION PLUS 2.0** assets and synchronization for all assignment and grade book utilities.

Tegrity

TEGRITY CAMPUS is a service that makes class time available all the time. It automatically captures every lecture in a searchable format, allowing students to review course material when they study and complete assignments. With a simple one-click start-and-stop process, you capture all computer screens and corresponding audio. Students replay any part of any class with easy-to-use, browser-based viewing on a PC or Mac.

McGraw-Hill Makes Change Easier

McGraw-Hill is firmly committed to the success and professional growth of our customers as they use our digital course solutions. We understand that incorporating new systems and technologies into your programs can feel daunting. But we know it also can be transformative. The following programs support instructors of all proficiencies in a variety of formats, with the goal of helping every one of our customers exceed their expectations.

- **Digital Success Academy**—The Digital Success Academy offers a wealth of training resources and course creation tips for instructors. Presented in easy-to-navigate, easy-to-complete sections, the Digital Success Academy includes the popular *Connect 100* and *Connect 200* video shorts, step-by-step *Clickthrough Guides*, and *First Day of Class* materials that explain how to use both the Connect platform and its course-specific tools and features.

http://create.mcgraw-hill.com/wordpress-mu/success-academy

- **Digital Success Team**—The Digital Success Team is a group of McGraw-Hill professionals dedicated to working online with instructors—one-on-one—to demonstrate how the Connect platform works and to help incorporate Connect into a customer's specific course design and syllabus. You can request a Digital Success Team personal consultation through your McGraw-Hill sales representative or by visiting our Digital Products Support Center. **http://mpss.mhhe.com/orientation.php**

- **Digital Learning Consultants**—Digital Learning Consultants are local resources who work closely with your McGraw-Hill sales representative. They can provide face-to-face faculty support and training. You can request a Digital Learning Consultation through your McGraw-Hill sales representative. **http://catalogs.mhhe.com/mhhe/findRep.do**

- **Digital Faculty Consultants**—Digital Faculty Consultants are experienced instructors who have utilized Connect in their classroom. These instructors are available to offer suggestions, advice, and training about how best to use Connect in a real classroom. To request a Digital Faculty Consultant to speak with, please e-mail your McGraw-Hill sales representative.

- **National Training Webinars**—McGraw-Hill offers an ongoing series of webinars for instructors to learn and master the Connect platform as well as its course-specific tools and features. We hope you will refer to our online schedule of national training webinars and sign up to learn more about Connect! **https://mhhe.webex.com/mhhe/onstage/g.php?p=280&t=m**

- **Customer Experience Group (CXG)**—McGraw-Hill is dedicated to making sure instructors and students can reach out and receive help with any of our digital products. To contact our customer support team, please call us at 800-331-5094 or visit us online at **http://mpss.mhhe.com/contact.php**. Hours of operation are Sunday 6 p.m.–11 p.m., Monday–Thursday 8 a.m.–11 p.m., and Friday 8 a.m.–6 p.m. Please note that all times are Central.

  > McGraw-Hill is focused on delivering a memorable and rewarding service experience to instructors and students using our digital products. Our Customer Experience Group is a dedicated support team available to assist all faculty and students with support questions and inquiries as they relate to McGraw-Hill digital products.

- **The Connect Community**—The Connect Community brings together faculty from across the country to discuss critical issues, answer questions, and share best practices. As a member, you can participate in lively conversations, lead new groups and forums based on the issues you would like to explore, and get up-to-date news and information about Connect. Join the Community today and engage. **http://theconnectcommunity.com**

Components of *Writing Matters*

Writing Matters includes an array of resources for instructors and students. Under the leadership of Rebecca Moore Howard, experienced instructors created supplements that help instructors and students fulfill their course responsibilities.

Instruction Matters

Instruction Matters includes teaching tips and learning outcomes. It connects each instructor and student resource to the core material and makes the exercises relevant to instructors and students.

Assessment Matters

Assessment Matters offers more than a thousand test items.

Practice Matters offers three sets of grammar and ESL activities and exercises to practice writing well.

Exercises for ESL Students

Exercises for Students

Grammar Exercises for Students

Presentation Matters

This PowerPoint deck is designed to give new teachers confidence in the classroom and can be used as a teaching tool by all instructors. The PowerPoint slides emphasize key ideas from *Writing Matters* and help students take useful notes. Instructors can alter the slides to meet their own needs.

Acknowledgments

The creation and evolution of *Writing Matters* has been an exciting and humbling experience. I began in the belief that I knew what I was doing, but I quickly realized that I had embarked upon a path not only of sharing what I know but also of learning what I should know. *Writing Matters* lists a single author, Rebecca Moore Howard, but that author is actually the central figure in a collaboration of hundreds of students, teachers, and editors.

I thank the instructors who have provided invaluable insights and suggestions as reviewers and members of the board of advisors. Talking with instructors at all sorts of institutions and learning from them about the teaching of writing has been an unparalleled experience. As a result of this project, I have many new colleagues, people who care deeply about teaching writing and who are experts at doing so. I also thank the many students who have shared their thoughts with us through class tests and design reviews. I particularly thank the students who have shared their writing with me and allowed me to publish some of it in this book. *Writing Matters* has been improved greatly by their contributions.

Manuscript Reviewers

Abraham Baldwin Agricultural College: Jeff Newberry

Allen County Community College: Tracy R. Lee (*Board of Advisors*), Bruce Symes,

Baton Rouge Community College: Rosemary Mack, Jaimie Stallone (*Board of Advisors*)

Boise State University: Gail Shuck

Bowie State University: Stephanie Johnson, Sidney Walker

Brigham Young University: Brian Jackson, Brett McInelly

Butler Community College: John Buaas, Sheryl LeSage, Troy Nordman (*Board of Advisors*)

Butte College: Molly Emmons, John Osbourne

Caldwell Community College: Paula Rush

Cameron University: William Carney, John Hodgson, Carolyn Lindsey Kinslow

Catawba Valley Community College: Polly Watson

Central Piedmont Community College: Amy Bagwell, Brad Bostian, Patricia Bostian (*Board of Advisors*), Jack Summers, Barbara Urban

Clark State Community College: Laurie Buchanan, Cecilia Kennedy, Kathryn Ward

Clayton State University: Mary Lamb, Dan Mills

Community College of Allegheny County: Pamela Jean Turley

Delaware Technical and Community College Dover: Bonnie Ceban, Nicholas David, Theodore A. Legates

Eastern Arizona College: Ida Nunley, Margaret Simonton

Florence-Darlington Technical College: Marjory Hall, Mark Rooze, Alan M. Trusky

Florida International University: Andrew Golden, Kimberly Harrison, Ben Lauren, Robert Saba, Andrew Strycharski

Frederick Community College: Kenneth P. Kerr, Kelly Trigger

Georgia College and State University: Craig Callender, Robert Viau

Georgia Gwinnett College: A. Keith Kelly, Scott Reed

Georgia State University: Lynee Lewis Gaillet, Marti Singer

Greenville Technical College: Julie Gibson

Harding University: Nicholas Boone, Terry Engel (*Board of Advisors*)

Hutchinson Community College: Bonnie Feeser, Trudy Zimmerman

Indian River State College: Camila Alvarez, Ray Considine, Roderick Hofer, Tammy Powley (*Board of Advisors*), Donald Skinner, April Van Camp

Indiana University-Northwest-Gary: Pat Buckler, William K. Buckley, Lou Ann Karabel, Doug Swartz

Indiana University-Purdue University Indianapolis: Steve Fox

John Jay College: Tim McCormack

Jones County Junior College: David Lowery, Patti Smith, Tammy Townsend, Cheryl Windham

KCTCS Western Kentucky Community and Technical College: Kimberly Russell

Kent State University: Andrea Adolph, Charles Douglas Baker, Robert Miltner, Stephen E. Neaderhiser, Beverly Neiderman, Lindsay Steiner

Kent State University-Stark: Brooke Horvath

Lamar State College: Andrew Preslar, Arlene Turkel, Gwen Whitehead

Loyola University of Chicago: Victoria Anderson, Margaret Loweth, Sherrie Weller

Luzerne County Community College: Stephen Housenick, Mary Stchur

Marist College: Joseph Zeppetello

Marquette University: Virginia Chappell

Marshalltown Community College: Connie Adair, Carolyn Briggs

Metropolitan State College of Denver: Jane Chapman Vigil, Elizabeth Kleinfeld; Mikkilynn Olmstead, Jessica Parker, Jim Sundeen

Miami University of Ohio: Heidi McKee, Jason Palmeri, James E. Porter (*Board of Advisors*)

Morehouse College: Consuella Bennett, Albert Turner, Corey Stayton

Mount Hood Community College: Jonathan Morrow

New England College: Susan Nagelsen

New Jersey Institute of Technology: Mark Arnowitz, Norbert Elliot

Northern Virginia Community College-Alexandria: Shonette H. Grant (*Board of Advisors*)

Northwest Florida State College: Vickie Hunt, Julie Nichols

Norwalk Community College: Cindy Casper (*Board of Advisors*), Lisa Dresdner

Olympic College: Sonia Begert, Ian Sherman

Palo Alto College: Ruth Ann Gambino, Caroline Mains, Diana Nystedt

Purdue University-Calumet-Hammond: Karen Bishop-Morris, Susan Roach

Robert Morris University: Diane Todd Bucci, Tracy Gorrell, Edward Karshner, Sylvia Pamboukian, Connie Ruzich, Scott Wyatt

Rutgers University-Camden: William FitzGerald

Saint Johns River State College: Paul Robert Andrews, Melody Hargraves, Jeannine Morgan, Roger Vaccaro

Salisbury University: Elizabeth Curtin, Loren Loving Marquez (*Board of Advisors*), Nicole Munday

San Diego State University: Candace Boeck (*Board of Advisors*), Chris Werry

Seton Hall University: Gita Dasbender, Edmund H. Jones, Judith Pike

Shawnee Community College: Susan Woolridge

Snow College: Melanie Jenkins

Southwestern Oklahoma State College: Jill T. Jones, Kelly S. Moor, Valerie A. Reimers

Syracuse University: Patrick Williams

University of Cincinnati-Blue Ash College: Sonja Andrus

University of Illinois-Urbana-Champaign: Courtney Caudle, Cara Finnegan, Grace Giorgio, Greg Webb, Jessica Wong

University of Miami: Andrew Green, Gina Maranto
University of Utah: Jay Jordan
University of Wisconsin-River Falls: Kathleen Hunzer
US Air Force Academy: Andrea Van Nort
Waynesburg University: Jill Moyer Sunday
Wayne State University: Jeff Pruchnic
Weatherford College: Sarah Lock
Weber State University: Sylvia Newman, Scott Rogers
Wichita State University: Darren DeFrain
York College of Pennsylvania: Julie S. Amberg

Personal Acknowledgments

Writing Matters is the result of rich collaboration with a creative, supportive, knowledgeable team who have a deep understanding of both teaching and publishing: Tom Howard, senior lecturer in University Studies at Colgate University, has worked with me from the beginning to the end, and his intelligence and ingenuity are evident everywhere in this project. Colleagues have also drafted sections of *Writing Matters:* Amy Rupiper Taggart from North Dakota State University drafted "Designing in Context: Academic and Business Documents"; Ted Johnston, formerly of El Paso Community College, and Maggie Sokolik, University of California, Berkeley, drafted "Language Matters: Issues for Multilingual Writers" and the ESL Notes that appear throughout *Writing Matters;* and Sandra Jamieson, Drew University, and Bruce R. Thaler, drafted many of the exercises.

McGraw-Hill has supported the project from beginning to end. My thanks go out to David Patterson, Managing Director; Susan Gouijnstook, Director; Dawn Groundwater, Director of Development; Nanette Giles, Executive Market Development Manager; Nancy Huebner, Brand Manager; and Kevin Colleary, Marketing Manager. My special thanks go to Michael O'Loughlin, my brilliant Senior Development Editor, whose energy, patience, and intelligence have made a second edition that shines.

In addition, *Writing Matters* has benefited greatly from the efforts of an extended editorial team: Christopher Bennem, David Chodoff, Paul Banks, Janet Byrne Smith, Elizabeth Murphy, Dana Wan, and Stephanie Lippitt. It has been a pleasure to work with an outstanding production team: Terri Schiesl, Debra Hash, Preston Thomas, Shawntel Schmitt, Nicole Baumgartner, Lenny Behnke, Deborah Anderson, Kay J. Brimeyer, Debra DeBord, and Nancy Ball. In particular, I would like to thank Jennifer Gordon, the copyeditor, whose careful eye saved me from many embarrassing errors, and Sandy Wille, our fabulous production editor, who juggled schedules and personalities with aplomb.

1

Writing
Responsibly
Tools for the Information Age

Use tab 1 to learn, practice, and master these writer's responsibilities:

❏ **To Audience**

Focus on a topic readers will find engaging, provide persuasive reasons and evidence, choose reliable sources, fulfill readers' expectations of the genre, avoid bias and treat others with respect, and use language clearly, correctly, logically, and with flair.

❏ **To Topic**

Support your claims with logical reasons and solid evidence from relevant and reliable sources and consider alternative viewpoints and evidence, even when they undermine your claims.

❏ **To Other Writers**

Acknowledge borrowed words and ideas, and represent the ideas of others fairly and accurately.

❏ **To Yourself**

Select a topic you find engaging, synthesize information from sources to produce fresh ideas, and create a persona that reflects your best self.

Writing Responsibly

1

1 Writing Today

In 2004, the National Commission on Writing published a report called "Writing: A Ticket to Work ... Or a Ticket Out," surveying 120 of the largest corporations in America. Among the results: American corporations expect their salaried employees to be able to write clearly, correctly, and logically. Eighty percent of finance, insurance, and real estate employers take writing skills into consideration when hiring salaried employees. For these employers, good writing is a "threshold skill." To get a good job, to keep that job, or to get promoted, you must write clearly, logically, and accurately; for the appropriate audience; and with the necessary level of support and documentation. As you write projects for your college courses, you are, in effect, standing before the elevator of your own future. You decide whether the elevator will take you up.

But writing well is more than a skill needed for a good job. Whether drafting business e-mails or making PowerPoint presentations, texting friends or commenting on a Facebook page, posting a tweet, or composing a paper for a college course, we write to develop and evaluate beliefs and ideas, to move others, to express ourselves, and to explore possibilities. For all these reasons and more, writing matters!

1a The Expanding Definition of Literacy

Long before Johannes Gutenberg introduced the printing press, in the fifteenth century, a *page* was seen as a sheet of paper covered with text, and *literacy* meant the ability to read and write a text, whether written on the page or carved in stone. With the spread of literacy has come the spread of information, which has led to improvements in health and productivity. The ability to read is needed to understand the safety warnings on medication inserts and to check the ingredients on a jar of baby food. The ability to write is needed to craft and convey everything from emergency plans to instructions for assembling shelving from Ikea. More importantly, the spread of literacy has strengthened our democratic institutions. Without news reports and a wide audience to read them, the decisions of politicians could go unchallenged, and voters would have little idea of a candidate's positions. These are just a few of the many reasons our society values print literacy.

But as the Internet revolution changes our understanding of what a page is, it also expands our concept of literacy (Figure 1.1). Today, a page can be a sheet of paper, but it can also be a screen in a website or an e-mail message on a

FIGURE 1.1 The media revolution In the fifteenth century, few could read (or had access to) the Gutenberg Bible. Today, readers can view its pages on their phones, but to do so they must be multiliterate: Not only must they be able to read and write, but they must also know how to access multiple media online.

Droid. It can include not only words, but also images and sound files, links to other web pages, and Flash animations.

1b Multiliteracies and Print Literacy

Like most people reading this book, you are probably already multiliterate: You "code shift," switching from medium to medium easily, because the "literacies" required for each medium are not entirely separate. Whether penning a thank-you note, searching a library database, composing a college paper, or texting your best friend, you adjust your message in response to your purpose, audience, context, and medium: When texting a friend you may ignore the conventions of punctuation and capitalization, for example, but you would not do so when writing a résumé.

This handbook focuses on print literacy because it remains central, yet the handbook also addresses digital, visual, oral, and information literacies because they have become impossible to separate from one another and from traditional print literacy. As a reader, you must be able not only to decipher written language but also to interpret visuals, drawing meaning from advertisements, for example, and subjecting them to the scrutiny of a careful shopper. As a writer, you may incorporate graphics into papers in economics and psychology, contribute to class blogs or Twitter discussions, search online databases and electronic library catalogs, or create presentations using Prezi and Jing. As both a reader and a writer, you will be expected to manage all the information you receive and transmit. Being multiliterate *means* being information literate.

> **More about**
Writing business documents, 56–59
Creating Power-Points, 64–65
Creating websites, 59–60
Writing in literature, 87–96
Reading critically, 7–15
Interpreting visuals, 10–13
Incorporating visuals, 54–55
Searching online databases, 104–06
Searching library catalogs, 110–11
Searching the Internet, 107–10

2 The Writer's Responsibilities

With opportunities to express and even create yourself in words come responsibilities. Like the palm fronds being woven into a basket in the photograph, your responsibilities as a writer are intertwined and difficult to tease apart. They include the responsibilities you have to your readers, to the topics you address, to the other writers from whom you borrow and to whom you respond, and perhaps especially to yourself as a writer with ideas and ideals to express.

2a Understanding Your Responsibilities to Your Audience

Audience members make a commitment to you by spending their time reading your work. To make your readers feel that this commitment was worthwhile, you can do the following:

- Choose a topic that your audience will find interesting and about which you have something you want to say.
- Make a claim that will help your audience follow your thoughts.
- Support your claim with thoughtful, logical, even creative evidence drawn from sources that you have evaluated carefully for relevance and reliability.
- Write clearly so that your audience (even if that audience is your composition teacher) does not have to struggle to understand. To write clearly, build a logical structure, use transitional techniques to guide readers, and correct errors of grammar, punctuation, and spelling.
- Write appropriately by using a tone and vocabulary that are right for your topic, audience, context, and genre.
- Write engagingly by varying sentence structures and word choices, avoiding wordiness, and using repetition only for special effect.

More about
List of Writing Responsibly boxes, back flap
Devising a topic, 19–22, 98–99
Finding information, 103–14
Using supporting evidence, 25, 31–35, 137–38
Evaluating sources, 114–23
Organizing, 24–25, 136–37
Providing transitions, 29–30
Correcting grammar, 319–94
Correcting punctuation and mechanics, 421–70
Writing with flair, 277–318

Writing Responsibly | Your Responsibilities as a Writer

When you write, you have four areas of responsibility:

1. To your audience
2. To your topic
3. To other writers
4. To yourself

3

Most writers cannot accomplish all this in a first draft. They must revise thoughtfully and edit and proofread carefully to fulfill their responsibilities to their readers.

2b   Understanding Your Responsibilities to Your Topic

You treat your topic responsibly when you explore it thoroughly and creatively, rely on trustworthy sources, and offer supporting evidence that is accurate, relevant, and reliable. You treat your topic responsibly when you provide enough evidence to persuade readers of your claims and when you acknowledge evidence even when it does not support your position. In a college writing project, not fulfilling your responsibilities to your topic might lead to a bad grade. In the workplace, it could have great financial, even life-and-death consequences: The Merck pharmaceutical company, for example, was accused of suppressing evidence that its drug Vioxx could cause heart attacks and strokes. As a result, Merck faced a host of lawsuits, trials, and out-of-court settlements.

2c   Understanding Your Responsibilities to Other Writers

You have important responsibilities to other writers whose work you may be using.

More about
When to quote, paraphrase, or summarize, 127–31
Using quotation marks, 436–43
Formatting block quotations, 153, 190, 437–38
Adjusting quotations using brackets and ellipses, 448, 450–52
Citing and documenting sources, 149–276
Avoiding plagiarism and patchwriting, 126–31, 139–48
Common knowledge, 125–26

1.   Acknowledge your sources.

Writing circulates easily today, and vast quantities of it are available online, readily accessible through search engines such as Google and databases such as JSTOR. It may seem natural, then, simply to copy the information you need from a website and paste it into your own text, as you might if you were collecting information about a disease you were facing or a concert you hoped to attend. But when you provide readers with information, ideas, language, or images that others have collected or created, you have a responsibility to *acknowledge* those sources. Such acknowledgment gives credit to those who contributed to your thinking, and it allows your audience to read your sources for themselves. Acknowledging your sources also protects you from charges of plagiarism, and it builds your authority and credibility as a writer by establishing that you have reviewed key sources on a topic and taken other writers' views into consideration.

To acknowledge sources in academic writing, you must do *all three* of the following:

1. When quoting, copy accurately and use quotation marks or block indention to signal the beginning and end of the copied passage; when paraphrasing or summarizing, put the ideas fully into your own words and sentences.

Quick

> **Reference** **Your College's Plagiarism Policy**
>
> Most colleges publish their plagiarism policies in their student handbook, which is often available online. **Find your plagiarism policy** by searching the student handbook's table of contents or index. Or search your college's website, using key terms such as *plagiarism, cheating policy, academic honesty,* or *academic integrity.* Before writing a research project, **read your school's plagiarism policy** carefully. If you are unsure what the policy means, talk with your adviser or instructor. In addition to the general policy for your college, **read your course syllabi** carefully to see what specific guidelines your instructors may provide there.

2. Include an in-text citation to the source, whether you are quoting, paraphrasing, or summarizing.
3. Document the source, providing enough information for your readers to locate the source and to identify the type of source you used. This documentation usually appears in a bibliography (often called a list of works cited or a reference list) at the end of college research projects.

Writing Responsibly around the World Concepts of plagiarism vary from one culture to another. Where one may see cooperation, another may see plagiarism. Even if borrowing ideas and language without acknowledgment is a familiar custom for you, writers in the United States (especially in academic contexts) must explicitly acknowledge all ideas and information borrowed from another source.

2. Treat other writers fairly.

Your responsibility to other writers does not end with the need to acknowledge your use of their ideas or language. You must also represent *accurately* and *fairly* what your sources say: Quoting selectively to distort meaning or taking a comment out of context is irresponsible. So is treating other writers with scorn.

> *More about*
> Bias, 297–99
> *Ad hominem,* 81

It is perfectly acceptable to criticize the ideas of others. In fact, examining ideas under the bright light of careful scrutiny is central to higher education. But treating the people who developed the ideas with derision is not. Avoid *ad hominem* (or personal) attacks, and focus your attention on other writers' ideas and their expression of them.

2d Understanding Your Responsibilities to Yourself

You have a responsibility to yourself as a writer. Writers represent themselves on paper and screen through the words and images (and even sounds) they create and borrow, so submitting as your own a paper that someone else has written is a form of impersonation—it does not represent you. Make sure that

Many students enter writing classes thinking of themselves as "bad writers." This be-lief can be a self-fulfilling prophecy—students fail to engage because they already believe they are doomed to fail. You can escape from this vicious circle by remember-ing that writing is not an inborn talent but a skill to be learned. Instead of thinking of yourself as a bad writer, think of yourself as a writer-in-progress, someone who has something to say and who is learning how to say it effectively. If you speak or have studied another language, think of yourself as someone who is learning to draw on that experience.

to SELF

> **More about**
> Synthesis, 11–12, 137
> Common sen-tence problems, foldout following tab 10
> Style, 277–318
> Sentence gram-mar, 319–94
> Punctuation and mechanics, 421–70

the writing "avatar," or *persona,* you create is the best representation of yourself it can be. Encourage readers to view you with respect by treating others—not only other writers but also other people and groups—without bias. Earn your audience's respect by synthesizing information from sources to produce new and compelling ideas and by using language clearly, correctly, logically, and with flair.

If you graduate from college having learned to be an effective writer, you will have learned something employers value highly. More importantly, though, you will have fulfilled a key responsibility to yourself.

2

Writing
Matters

Planning, Writing, Editing

Use tab 2 to learn, practice, and master these writer's responsibilities:

❏ **To Audience**

Choose language that readers will find appropriate and compelling; craft paragraphs and writing projects that readers will find relevant, unified, and coherent; integrate source material fully; and revise, edit, and proofread to provide readers with a worthwhile reading experience.

❏ **To Topic**

Fully engage with texts so that you can put source material in context and respond creatively, devise thesis statements that encourage insight into your topic, develop solid reasons of your own, and provide evidence from sources to support your ideas.

❏ **To Other Writers**

Understand fully what you have read in other sources, and represent the ideas of other writers accurately.

❏ **To Yourself**

Get as much as you can from your reading, consider your writing situation and assignment so you can meet your goals, choose a topic that engages your interest, and manage your time to create a text that is a reflection of your best self.

AIR MAIL
PAR AVION

Writing Matters

3 Reading Critically

When you read critically, you peel back a text to uncover its meaning. You begin with comprehension, just getting the gist of a text. Next comes reflection, when you annotate and analyze the text. As you prepare to write, you explore not only what is written but also what is left unstated, and you draw on your own experience and other texts to hone your evaluation. The process of peeling back a text, as you would the layers of an onion, is what drives and deepens the intellectual process.

3a Comprehending the Text

Most of the texts you read in college were written to inform or educate you about an issue or topic. They may also have a secondary purpose: to persuade you to accept a position on that issue or topic. Because most college-level reading assignments attempt to engage you in the complexities of an issue, you should read the text several times. In your first reading, focus on getting the gist of, or *comprehending,* the text:

- Preview the text by noting the title, subtitle, and headings; reading the abstract (or *summary*), introduction, and conclusion; noting the key terms, usually indicated in italic or boldface type; and scanning illustrations and captions.

- Read the text, circling words or phrases to look up later, determining the author's main claim, or ***thesis,*** and identifying key supporting evidence.

- Summarize the text by restating the thesis and major supporting points accurately in your own words and sentences.

> *More about*
> Summarizing,
> 129–31
> Drafting a thesis,
> 22–24, 134–35

3b Reflecting on the Text

For many readers, the first step in coming to terms with a text is to ***annotate*** it, to read it with a pencil in hand, making notes and adding responses directly on the page. For others, taking notes in a notebook or computer or discussing the text with a classmate or friend works best. Whatever techniques work for you, focus on the following when rereading a text:

- Look up unfamiliar words.

- Underline the most important, interesting, or difficult concepts, and return to these passages to consider their significance.

Writing Responsibly / **Engaging with What You Read**

When conducting research, you have a responsibility to engage with the texts you read. If you are struggling, begin by determining what barrier is keeping you from making a connection with the text: Is the language too challenging? Is the topic unfamiliar or too familiar? Is your concentration poor because you did not eat lunch? Then try to overcome the barrier: Use a dictionary to acquaint yourself with the unfamiliar vocabulary; consider the material as a primer or a recapitulation of an important topic; eat a sandwich.

to TOPIC

Tech   **Annotating Online Texts**

As you conduct research, take notes on what you learn. Then use Track Changes or footnoting options to comment and the highlighting function to mark key ideas.

- Note the writer's attitude, or *tone*—sarcastic, sincere, witty, shrill—and circle the words and phrases that convey it.

- Consider what surprised or impressed you, whether the logic was sound, and what challenged your own assumptions. Note specifics in the text that prompted your reaction.

> **More about**
> Tone, 17–18, 75,
>   302–03, 306–07
> Bias, 297–99

The annotations to the following newspaper article reflect one student's thoughts, insights, and struggles with the text. Betsy Smith's annotations define vocabulary, note reflections, and make connections.

Professional Model Newspaper Article

Tiny Bat Pits Green against Green

By MARIA GLOD

Washington Post, October 22, 2009

GREENBRIER COUNTY, W.VA.—Workers atop mountain ridges are putting together 389-foot windmills with massive blades that will turn Appalachian breezes into energy. Retiree David Cowan is fighting to stop them.

Because of the bats.

Cowan, 72, a longtime caving fanatic who grew to love bats as he slithered through tunnels from Maine to Maui, is asking a federal judge in Maryland to halt construction of the Beech Ridge wind farm. The lawsuit pits Chicago-based Invenergy, a company that produces "green" energy, against environmentalists who say the cost to nature is too great.

The rare green vs. green case went to trial Wednesday in U.S. District Court in Greenbelt.

It is the first court challenge to wind power under the Endangered Species Act, lawyers on both sides say. With President Obama's goal of doubling renewable energy production by 2012, wind and solar farms are expanding rapidly. That has sparked battles to reach a balance between the benefits of clean energy and the impact on birds, bats, and even the water supply.

At the heart of the Beech Ridge case is the Indiana bat, a brownish-gray creature that weighs about as much as three

Annotations (margin notes):

Standard size for windmills?

Main claim

Why Maryland if the area in question is in West Virginia?

Rare? My instructor passed out 2 news articles about similar cases from other newspapers.

What is the Endangered Species Act? I will have to look it up!

Bats are dying regardless of windmills.

pennies and, wings outstretched, measures about eight inches. A 2005 estimate concluded that there were 457,000 of them, half the number in 1967, when they were first listed as endangered.

"Any kind of energy development is going to have environmental impacts that are going to concern somebody," said John D. Echeverria, a Vermont Law School professor who specializes in environmental law and isn't involved in the suit. "This has been an issue for the environmental community. They are enthusiastic; at the same time, they realize there are these adverse impacts."

adverse— unfavorable

Indiana bats hibernate in limestone caves within several miles of the wind farm, which would provide energy to tens of thousands of households. The question before the judge: Would the bats fly in the path of the 122 turbines that will be built along a 23-mile stretch of mountaintop?

Eric R. Glitzenstein, an attorney for the plaintiffs, said in his opening statement that both sides agree the windmills will kill more than 130,000 bats of all types over the next 20 years.

How many bats of all types will die of natural causes over the next 20 years? Some context would be helpful.

"The question comes down to whether there is some reason to think Indiana bats will escape that fate," he said. "The position of the defendants is, 'Let's roll the dice and see what happens.' We believe that the rolling-the-dice approach to the Endangered Species Act is not in keeping with what Congress had in mind."

This is the plaintiffs' argument.

Cowan and other plaintiffs, including the D.C.-based Animal Welfare Institute, support wind power as one way to mitigate climate change. But they say this setting, a lush rural area where coal and timber industries

mitigate—to make less harsh or hostile

once dominated, is the wrong one.

They say Indiana bats are likely to fly near the turbines in the fall as they migrate to caves from forests, where they spend spring and summer. Some biologists who analyzed recordings at the site say they are nearly certain that Indiana bats made some of the calls.

Which biologists? How many of the calls are from Indiana bats? Sentence seems vague.

Any deaths would be a blow to a species that has been slow to rebound from the damage caused by pollution and human disturbance of their caves, partly because females have only one baby each year, the plaintiffs say.

Invenergy argues there is no sign that Indiana bats go to the ridge. When a consultant put up nets at or near the site in summer 2005 and 2006 to search for bats, no Indiana bats were captured. Some bat experts say that the females prefer lower areas when they have their young and that the ridge is too high. The company also stresses that there is no confirmed killing of an Indiana bat at any wind farm nationwide.

The "consultant" was paid by Invenergy and therefore could be biased.

Does that mean that other types of bats were captured?

"A $300 million, environmentally friendly, clean, renewable energy project waiting to serve 50,000 households is in limbo over a rare bat nobody has ever seen on the project site," Clifford J. Zatz, a lawyer at Crowell & Moring, which represents the wind farm, said in court.

Argument of the defense. Article reports both sides of the issue.

In an area scarred by mountaintop coal mining, company officials say, the wind farm is a friend to the environment. It also is bringing jobs to the region.

"We're a clean, green energy company," said Joseph Condo, vice president and general counsel. "The project will be able to deliver clean energy for years."

> *Why now being heard in Maryland? Because it's the "Greenbelt court"? What does "Greenbelt court" mean?*

> *Opinion of a person who is affected by, but not involved in, the lawsuit.*

> *A bit patronizing, maybe?*

The project has twice survived challenges in the West Virginia Supreme Court, including complaints that it would mar the picturesque view. If the Greenbelt court does not intervene, the first set of 67 turbines is expected to be running next year. The state has required that bat and bird fatalities be tracked for three years. . . .

Brad Tuckwiller, a county commissioner who manages his family's 1,700-acre cattle farm not far from the ridge, is a supporter of the wind farm. When the project was proposed, he visited one of Invenergy's farms in Tennessee.

"I know some of our citizens are upset, but I don't think it's about the bats. I think it's about the viewshed or fear," Tuckwiller said. "If America is going to have energy independence, we have to look at these alternative sources—solar, wind, geothermal—in addition to nuclear and coal."

To Cowan, the risk is too great. The house he and his wife built to be near West Virginia's caves has bat profiles on the windows. The napkin holder on the dining table is decorated with a bat. Their car has a bat bumper sticker.

"I think if the turbines kill one Indiana bat, that ought to end it," he said. "That ought to shut it down."

3c Preparing to Write about the Text

To evaluate a text, you must analyze how it works by considering the following:

> **More about**
> Analysis, 34, 89
> Purpose, 16, 22–24
> Tone, 17–18, 75,
>   302–03, 306–07
> Writer's credibility,
>   303
> Appeals to intellect and emotions, 75–77
> Audience, 17,
>   97–98
> Style, 277–318
> Evaluating sources,
>   116–21
> Making claims,
>   22–24, 74–75
> Patterns of development, 31–35

- The major claims and whether they are backed by evidence
- The type and quality of the evidence offered to support the claims
- The presence or absence of counterevidence
- The sources the author draws on (if any) and their reliability
- The organizational or rhetorical patterns (such as comparison-contrast or cause-effect) and their possible effects on the audience
- The rhetorical appeals used in the text: *logos* (rational, logical claims or evidence), *ethos* (showing the expertise or credibility of the author or the sources), or *pathos* (drawing on the audience's emotions or sympathy)
- The logical pattern, which provides information about the author's purpose. Exploratory arguments are likely to use ***inductive logic,*** citing particular examples and then drawing a general conclusion. Persuasive arguments are likely to use ***deductive logic,*** offering generally accepted truths from which conclusions can be drawn about specific instances.
- The style or tone and what that reflects about the author's purpose or attitudes

After analyzing the text, ***interpret*** it by considering its significance or meaning and drawing conclusions about what may be below the surface. Use the following questions to help guide your interpretation:

- What assumptions does the writer make about the subject or audience? Why are such assumptions significant?

- What does the text omit (evidence, opposing views), and what might these omissions indicate?

- What conclusions can you draw about the author's attitude from the tone? What motives can you infer from the author's background or previous publications?

- Who published this text or sponsored the research, and what influence might these sponsors have on the way the information, arguments, or evidence is presented?

- In what context was the text written—place, time, cultural environment—and how might this context have influenced the writer?

College assignments often ask you to *synthesize*—to connect what you have read to ideas you have discussed in class or read about in other texts. To synthesize, ask yourself the following questions:

- What outside forces (historical events, socioeconomic forces, cultural shifts) might influence or underlie the text?

Writing Responsibly   **Drawing Conclusions**

A conclusion is only as good as what it is based on. Conclusions based on facts are fair; those based on personal values and beliefs or on a faulty understanding of the text are apt to be one-sided and unfair. Aim for the former and avoid the latter.

to TOPIC

> *More about*
> Identifying bias and vested interests, 117–118
> Interpreting, 87–90
> Synthesizing, 137

Self Assessment   **Evaluating Visuals**

When evaluating visuals, consider the following questions. Return to these questions as you evaluate your draft and revise as needed.

Analysis

- ☐ What does the image depict in the foreground, background? When was the work created? Who produced or sponsored it? How do accompanying words (if any) affect your understanding?
- ☐ What is the artist's purpose, or goal?
- ☐ Who is the intended audience?
- ☐ What is the artist's attitude toward the subject?
- ☐ What values does the image assume or promote? Do they challenge or reinforce the values of the intended audience?
- ☐ Is something missing? Has the visual been cropped, for example, to eliminate background? If so, how does this affect your understanding?

Synthesis

- ☐ What do you know about the time or place in which the image was created, and how does this affect your understanding?
- ☐ How is this image similar to or different from others that you know? Have you read or studied anything that could help you understand this visual?
- ☐ What knowledge or personal experiences do you have that might deepen your understanding?

Critique

- ☐ What, based on your analysis, were the artist's aims?
- ☐ Were the artist's aims achieved? Why or why not?

Writing
Responsibly   **Understanding** *Criticism*

In everyday speech, *criticism* is often used simply to mean "finding fault." But in academic disciplines, *criticism* means "evaluating a work's merits based on a careful and fair analysis." The ideal critic approaches a text skeptically yet with an open mind and provides evidence for the judgments she makes. You may be used to thinking about published texts as absolutely authoritative sources of information, but it is important for you to realize that *all* texts present only partial views that can always be challenged.

to AUDIENCE

- What else have you read or experienced that this text may explain, illustrate, clarify, complicate, or contradict?
- What claims could these texts, taken together, provide evidence for?
- How is your understanding of a topic enhanced or your thinking changed by putting these texts together? What might others gain by seeing these texts together?
- What expertise or life experience does the writer bring to the topic?

A *critique* is a well-informed evaluation. It may be positive, negative, or a bit of both. A movie review, for example, is a critique; it provides readers with an evaluation, supported by evidence from the film, to help them decide whether to see it. As you prepare to critique a text, consider the following issues:

- What are the author's goals? Does she or he achieve them? Are they worth achieving?
- What are the writer's claims? Are you persuaded by them? Why or why not?
- How credible is the evidence? Is the evidence verifiable and relevant? Is the author's reasoning sound?

Student Model Critique of an Advertisement

More about
Claims, 22–24,
   74–75
Evidence, 35–36,
   39, 75–77, 91
Authority, 75
Relevance, 114–16
Reliability, 116–21
Audience, 17,
   97–98

Betsy Smith uses analysis, interpretation, and synthesis as well as critique in her assessment of an advertisement designed to encourage energy conservation. As you read, consider whether Smith fulfills her responsibility to her topic by analyzing the visual thoroughly and by supplying accurate and persuasive evidence to support her claim.

Betsy Smith

Professor Locke

Composition 102

27 Sept. 2012

Critique of an Advertisement

The explicit claim of the Keep America Beautiful ad from 1971 (Fig. 1) is that "Pollution hurts all of us," so everyone should "get involved" in helping to lessen it. The bold white letters set against the black background give the message force and a sense of urgency, and the photograph of a Native American shedding a tear for the degeneration of the land adds an emotional appeal.

Fig. 1. Advertisement for the Keep America Beautiful Campaign, 1971 ("Historic Campaigns," *Ad Council*. Advertising Council, n.d. Web. 26 Sept. 2010)

The implied connection between the Native American and his concern about pollution is implicitly contrasted with the attitude of most Americans, those people who have not yet gotten involved in the fight against pollution. (The television spot we saw in class makes this contrast explicit; it shows the Native American in traditional Indian dress weeping over pollution, while a white American man on a car-choked highway throws garbage out his car window.) Aldo Hendricks, my environmental studies teacher, called this ad a major influence in heightening awareness and generating support for the environmental movement.

By today's standards, the use of a Native American, wearing a feather in his long pigtails, seems stereotypical, and the assumption that Native Americans have a closer connection to the Earth also seems like bias (even though it's a positive bias). Despite this depiction, however, the ad is still powerful. The tear shed by Iron Eyes Cody reinforce the personal responsibility we each have to protect our environment.

Writing **Responsibly**
Understanding and Representing the Entire Source

Make It Your Own! For a research project to be worthwhile, it should represent the overall arguments of its sources—more than just a few sentences—so that readers can understand what the sources were saying and how they fit together.

Each time you write from sources, push yourself to work with them in more substantial ways. Take the time to read each source—the entire source—carefully. Next, **summarize** it, as a way of processing the information: Restate, concisely and in fresh language, the main claims (and the most important supporting evidence) of an entire source. Then when you draft your research project, blend in summaries of your important sources, so that your readers understand how they, too, contribute to your discussion.

You can also draw from sources by quoting or paraphrasing brief passages. But if you simply paste a quotation into your draft, how much do you or your audience actually understand the source or even the passage you are quoting? **Paraphrasing** is a better alternative, because it pushes you to think about the passage: to know the material well enough to restate it in your own words. Changing just a few words in the passage, however, is not paraphrasing; it is **patchwriting**: a mixture of your words and the source's. This is an error interpreted by most readers as plagiarism.

Because quoting and patchwriting do not require much comprehension and are easy to do, inexperienced college writers rely on them too heavily. Frequently, too, the quotations come from the first few pages of the source—which some students feel is all they have to read. Researchers with the Citation Project found that the majority of college writers' citations came from the first two pages of the source (see chart) and felt the quality of these papers suffered. That is because, in most sources, the first few pages discuss only general findings, while the insightful, detailed examples and evidence that are important to a good analysis or argument are deeper in the text.

When a writer provides only isolated quotations from sources ("dropped quotations"), the result may be uninformative, like this passage from a paper about social media and individual identity:

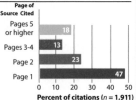

Page Cited
DATA FROM **The Citation Project**

Page of Source Cited	Percent of citations
Pages 5 or higher	18
Pages 3-4	13
Page 2	23
Page 1	47

0   10   20   30   40   50
Percent of citations (n = 1,911)

Researchers found that although most college writers quote from the first pages of a source, the best research projects drew from the entire source.

First draft

> Student's voice
>
> People value their personal lives and try to separate their private and public selves. Many are aware of being different people in the workplace, in school, on a date.
>
> All this may be changing, though. "The fact that the Internet never seems to forget is threatening, at an almost existential level, our ability to control our identities; to preserve the option of reinventing ourselves and starting anew; to overcome our checkered pasts"
>
> Quotation
>
> (Rosen).
>
> Parenthetical citation

Notice how, in this draft, readers are given no information about the source; they are presented only with one sentence from it. This causes the reader to wonder: Does the writer understand the source, or has she simply found a "killer quote" that supports her argument? Because the writer provides only the isolated quotation, it is not even clear what her purpose is in including it.

Now consider how this passage is transformed by adding a summary and contextualized quotations:

Revised draft

People value their personal lives, and many deliberately work to keep their private and public selves separate. Many of us are aware, too, of being different people in the workplace, in school, on the athletic field, on a date. Some value these differences, happy to switch from dedicated intellectual in the classroom to enthusiastic player on the soccer field.

> **Student's voice**

All this may be changing, though. Writing in the *New York Times*, journalist Jeffrey Rosen points out that we may no longer be in control of the multiple identities that were previously taken for granted. In our online lives, what we post on Facebook and Twitter can easily merge with what we post on a school blog, in our comments on a news story, or in our pictures on Flickr. Rosen explains that even in untagged pictures, our faces can be identified through facial-recognition technology. He also describes the privacy-protecting laws that are in development and the companies that offer services to clean up our online reputations. Most central to my research, though, is his explanation for this claim: "The fact that the Internet never seems to forget is threatening, at an almost existential level, our ability to control our identities; to preserve the option of reinventing ourselves and starting anew; to overcome our checkered pasts."

> **Signal phrase providing information about the author**

> **Summary of the remainder of the source**

> **Summary of the parts of the source relevant to the student's argument**

> **Student's voice**

> **Quotation (no page reference because source is unpaginated)**

Source: Rosen, Jeffrey. "The Web Means the End of Forgetting." *New York Times* 21 July 2010: n. pag. Web. 1 Feb. 2011.

The writer has shown responsibility to her source, her topic, and her audience. Because she has taken the time to read and understand the source, she is able to summarize it to show what its main claims are. Her audience now knows how the quotation was used in the source and how it supports her argument. With this brief summary, the writer has also explained her ideas clearly and established a "conversation" between herself, her source, and her audience—that is, rather than just "using" sources, she is thinking about them, interacting with them, and giving her audience enough information that they can do the same.

Self Assessment

Review and revise your work with each source. Have you done the following?

☐ Read, understand, and accurately represent the whole source: Did you look for the details deeper in the source material?

☐ Summarize the main ideas of the source: Did you put the source's ideas in your own words, fairly and accurately? ▶ *Paraphrasing, 127–29*

☐ Incorporate your summary into your source analysis: Did you use the best examples and evidence?

☐ Locate the most relevant passages: Did you cite from *throughout* the source? ▶ *Critical reading, 7–13*

4 Planning and Drafting Your Project

Before producing a new line of clothing or an automobile, designers sketch the product, planning and arranging the shapes before dressing them in colors and textures. Writers, too, begin with a plan. They take into account the writing situation (purpose, audience, topic, context, and genre), then sketch their ideas in words and arrange them in sentences and paragraphs. Both designers and writers sometimes erase initial ideas and revise early efforts. For both, until that first sketch is penned, the finished work is merely an idea.

4a Analyzing Your Writing Situation

The first step in planning a writing project is analyzing the ***writing situation:***

- What is your *purpose?* What do you hope to accomplish with the text?
- Who is your *audience?* Who will be reading the text you produce, and why?
- What *topics* will interest them?
- What *tone* is appropriate to your purpose and audience?
- What is the *context* (academic, business, personal) of your writing project, and what ***genre*** (or type) of writing will you produce (research report, résumé, Facebook status update)? How will your context and genre affect the way you write this project?

Student Models
Informative writing projects:
First Draft: "Is Alternative Energy Really Good for the Environment?" Betsy Smith, 25–27
"The Power of Wardrobe," Heather DeGroot, 231–38

> ***More about***
> Analyzing and crafting arguments, 73–86

1. Purpose

The classical reasons, or ***purposes,*** for writing are to entertain, to express your feelings or beliefs, to inform, and to persuade your audience. The most common purposes in college and business writing are to inform and to persuade. Entertaining or expressing your feelings are unlikely to be primary, but they may well play a secondary role.

An ***informative*** (or ***expository***) text may explain a concept, describe a sequence of events or a process, or analyze a relationship. Scientific, technical, journalistic, and business writing are typically informative.

A ***persuasive*** (or ***argumentative***) text tries to convince readers to adopt beliefs or opinions or to take action. Editorials, book and movie reviews, grant proposals, and much academic writing have a persuasive purpose.

Writing Responsibly   Seeing and Showing the Whole Picture

As a writer, you have a responsibility to look beyond your own experiences, beliefs, and self-interest. As you explore an issue, give thorough, respectful attention to interpretations that contradict or conflict with yours. Figure out what motivates the support-ers of opposing positions. Consider whether your own opinion should be revised. Then, as you write, no matter which position you support in your text, let your audience see all the viewpoints and the rea-sons for them.

to AUDIENCE

2. Audience

A text is seldom written for the writer alone. Rather, it is intended for an ***audi-ence.*** Before putting fingers to keyboard, consider the characteristics of your audience, such as age and gender, occupation and interests, educational back-ground, political or cultural affiliations, and ethnic or religious background. Then consider what will make your writing most effective for this audience:

- What information will your audience need to understand and appreci-ate what you are saying?

- What kinds of language, examples, evidence, or reasons will be most effective?

3. Topic

Frequently in college writing, a ***topic,*** or subject, will be assigned. When you are expected to devise your own topic, however, consider not only what will sustain your interest, but also what you have special insight into and what your reader will find intriguing and relevant.

4. Tone

When you speak, your tone of voice, gestures, facial expressions, and body language all convey your attitude. Are you patient, annoyed, angry, pleasantly surprised? Writers also convey their attitude toward their readers and their subject through their ***tone.*** In writing, tone is conveyed primarily through ***level of formality*** and the ***connotation*** (emotional resonance) of the words you choose. To write at a formal level, use standard American English; avoid regionalisms (such as *y'all*), colloquial language (such as *what up*), and slang (such as *hot* rather than *good* or *exciting*); and write in complete sentences (*Are you coming?* rather than just *Coming?*).

Recognizing Differences in Connotation A word in your first language may share a literal meaning with a word in another language but have a very different connotation. The word *ambition* ("eagerness for success"), for example, can be positive or negative in English; in Spanish, *ambición* is generally negative. If you are not sure how specific words are used by your prospective readers, consult a cross-language or bilingual dictionary or check with classmates, a writing tutor, or your instructor.

Student Models
Persuasive writing projects:
"Alternative Energy: Does It Really Offer an Alternative?" Betsy Smith, 44–47
"Why Students Cheat," Tom Hackman, 82–86
"Holy Underground Comics, Batman!" Lydia Nichols, 192–200
"My View from the Sidelines," Rita McMahan, 93–96

> ***More about***
> Level of diction, 302–07
> Connotation and denotation, 302–03, 306
> Regionalisms, colloquial-isms, slang, online shortcuts, 294–96

> ***More about***
> Dictionaries for English-language learn-ers, 309, 311
> Writing in college, 67–72
> Considering alternative view-points, 77–78
> Business writing, 56–59

Writing Responsibly

Choosing an Engaging Topic

When devising a topic, ask yourself the following questions:

1. Is my topic timely or relevant?
2. Do I have something to add?
3. Is it worth reading (and writing) about?

Thinking critically about saturated topics (such as abortion and gun control) is difficult. Instead of articulating your own reasons, you can easily wind up offering a rehash of other people's.

The topics about which you can write most interestingly are those on which you have a distinctive perspective. Almost any eighteen-year-old can write passionately about the drinking age, for example, but to justify resuscitating tired topics, you must have something original to add. Whatever topic you choose, you will have your best shot at engaging your readers and doing justice to your topic when you write about something you and your readers find compelling.

to TOPIC

Most instructors will expect you to write at a fairly formal level and to adopt a measured tone. Shrill or sarcastic prose will suggest to your audience that your opinions spring from your heart and not your head. This does not mean that emotional topics are off limits in college writing or that you may not express your beliefs, but look at all sides of an issue carefully before drawing a conclusion, and show respect for those with whom you disagree.

5. Context and genre

The **context** (or setting) in which your text is to be read will affect all your writing decisions. So, too, will the **genre** (or type) of writing you produce. The contexts in which you are likely to write, now and in the future, are academic, business, public, and personal. Like academic writing, business and public writing generally adopt a formal level of diction. In business writing, use words with neutral connotations. In public writing, which ranges from letters to the editor to press releases and reports, you may sometimes use more impassioned language.

Whether you are writing a business e-mail, a scientific report, a grant proposal, or a letter to the editor, the expectations readers have for this type, or genre, of writing will affect every choice you make, from whether to use the first person (*I*) to how to structure the text. If you are unfamiliar with the

Quick Reference   Analyzing the Purpose of an Assignment

If the assignment asks you to ...	The purpose is ...	The approach is ...
describe, explain	informative (expository)	to put into words what something looks, sounds, feels, smells, or tastes like; to discuss how something functions
assess, evaluate, argue	persuasive	to make a judgment based on evidence or offer an interpretation based on close reading, and to explain why
analyze, consider, discuss	informative or persuasive	to break a topic, reading assignment, or issue into its component parts and explain how it works; to reflect critically on the pros and cons of an issue, offer an interpretation based on a close reading, and sometimes explain why you have reached this conclusion

context and genre in which you will be writing, read several examples to determine what they have in common.

4b   Analyzing the Assignment and Setting a Schedule

Recognizing the purpose of an assignment is crucial to success. If you are asked to *argue* for or against the goals of the plain speech movement of the 1920s, for example, and, instead, you *describe* those goals, you will probably not get an *A*. When analyzing an assignment, look for words that indicate purpose. (See the Quick Reference box on the previous page.)

> *More about*
> Argument, 73–86
> Analysis, 10–12, 34,
>   89, 91, 137
> Critique, 12, 137,
>   145–47

The audience for an assignment is, of course, your instructor, and the instructor's goal in assigning the project is to be reassured that you have done the reading, understood the issues, and synthesized information from classroom lectures and discussions with assigned reading. In addition, most instructors want to see that you can express yourself clearly and correctly in writing.

Frequently, an assignment will specify the approach you should take. If you are asked to analyze, for example, your instructor will expect you to break the topic, issue, or text into its component parts and determine how those parts work together. If your instructor asks you to evaluate a text, you will be expected to identify the writer's claims and evidence and to assess their credibility.

Sometimes, an assignment will specify the genre, although the genre may be taken for granted. A biology instructor teaching a laboratory class may assume that you understand that a laboratory report is required. If you are not sure what the genre of the assignment is, or what it requires, ask your instructor.

Finally, writing assignments will generally include a due date. To create a realistic schedule, list the steps in the writing process (from drafting a thesis and generating ideas to revising, editing, proofreading, and formatting) in reverse order on your calendar, working back from the due date. (Remember that writing is not a linear process: You may go back to generate ideas while revising, for example, so leave some extra time.) Be sure to take into consideration your other obligations, such as other assignments and exams, work, rehearsals or team practices, and family and social obligations.

> *More about*
> Scheduling a
>   writing project,
>   97–98
> Online assignment
>   calendar, 99
> Avoiding plagia-
>   rism, 124–33,
>   139–48

4c   Generating Topics and Ideas

When you are required to come up with a topic on your own, ask yourself these questions:

- What topics are appropriate to the assignment?
- What topics will interest, exasperate, or intrigue me *and* my reader?
- What topics do I have special access to or knowledge about? You can create special knowledge by doing research and by thinking critically about your topic.

> *More about*
> Finding informa-
>   tion, 103–14
> Reading critically,
>   7–13

Invention techniques, like those that follow, can help you devise and develop a topic. No single strategy will work for everyone, and most writers use several methods.

Writing Responsibly

Plagiarism and Time Management

Few writers begin a project with the intention of plagiarizing, but many who buy papers do so because they have not budgeted the time needed to write an effective paper themselves. Even those who write their own essays tend to copy more from their sources when they are pressed for time.

Keep yourself out of danger by starting work as soon as you receive an assignment, figuring out what steps will be necessary to complete the project well and on time (including multiple drafts), and setting aside chunks of time to work on the project at a steady pace.

to SELF

 Generating Ideas in English or Your First Language? If English is not your first language, you might find it helpful to keep a journal, freewrite, or brainstorm in English. If you get stuck, try using words and phrases from your first language. But be careful when returning to your notes to translate not merely your *words* but also your *ideas* into English that is appropriate for your readers.

1. Freewrite.

Freewriting is writing the first thing that enters your head and then continuing to write nonstop for ten to fifteen minutes or for a set number of pages. To be useful, freewriting must be fast and spontaneous. If you find that you cannot resist correcting and revising, turn the brightness down until your screen is very dim or even black. Once the time has elapsed, read through what you wrote and looking for usable ideas.

A variation of freewriting is *focused freewriting.* Instead of starting from the first idea to pop into your head, start from something specific: your topic, a quotation, a memory, an image, an idea from your freewriting.

2. Brainstorm.

Brainstorming (or *listing*) is writing down everything you can think of on a topic. Brainstorming helps get ideas percolating and provides a record of that percolation. Below is a snippet of brainstorming on the environmental movement, the topic of Betsy Smith's essay.

Student Models
"Alternative Energy: Does It Really Offer an Alternative?" Betsy Smith, 25–27 (first draft), 44–47 (revised draft)

Student Model Brainstorm

	The green movement has been around for a while but has been gaining in recognition in recent years.
	Many aspects of the green/environmentalist movement: climate change, preservation, endangered species, alternatives to fossil fuels, etc.
	People can feel very strongly about these issues. Some modify how they eat and what they buy; some join groups like Greenpeace and are willing to be arrested and/or put themselves in danger to fight for change.
	Are there conflicts within the green movement? What might they entail?

3. Cluster.

Clustering, or *mapping* (Figure 4.1), is a visual method for identifying relationships among ideas. To create a cluster or idea map, write your topic in the

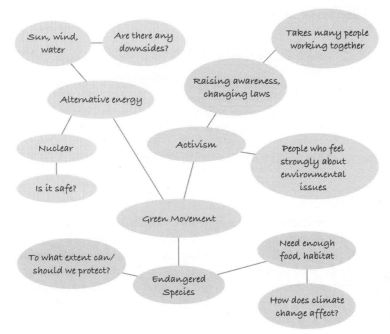

FIGURE 4.1 A sample cluster diagram

middle of the page and circle it. Write other ideas related to your topic around the central idea bubble, and circle each of them. Then draw connecting lines from the word bubbles to the central topic or to the other word bubbles to show how the ideas fit together.

4. Answer the journalists' questions.

The *journalists' questions*—*who, what, where, when, why,* and *how*—not only can help you generate ideas about your topic but also can help you figure out what you need to learn to write your project. When considering a topic, ask yourself questions like those Betsy Smith asked herself (Figure 4.2).

5. Discuss your topics with friends and classmates.

Sometimes, just batting ideas around with friends or classmates can help you generate ideas. This can be as casual as a late-night chat with your roommate ("What do you think about . . . ?") or as formal as a scheduled brainstorming session with a collaborative writing group. A blog can open up the discussion to others interested in your topic.

6. Use the Internet, the library, and classroom tools.

Surfing the Internet can provide direction and stimulate ideas when you are faced with a new topic. For very current topics, searching a news site or locating a specialized blog can also be useful.

Specialized reference sources can give you a sense of how your topic is usually discussed. Turn to specialized dictionaries or encyclopedias for a more

> **More about**
> Blogs, 106–07
> Evaluating online
> sources, 115–21
> Reference sources,
> 103–04
> Using databases,
> 107–10

Student Model Journalists' Questions

• Who is affected by the building of wind farms? Who will benefit from their being built?
• What other sources of energy do we have? What impact do they have on the environment? What impact will the wind farms have?
• Where are wind farms being built?
• When will the wind farms go online? When will the courts rule on the challenges to these wind farms?
• Why is there disagreement within the environmental community about whether wind farms should be built?
• How will the issues be resolved? How can animals be protected?

FIGURE 4.2 The journalists' questions

detailed introduction. Searching a library database, like PsycArticles or CQ Electronic Library, can help you devise or narrow a topic.

Because you will often be writing about topics that were introduced in class, look for ideas in your textbook, class notes, and any handouts your instructor has distributed. All can provide context or help you identify a topic that interests you, is relevant, or would benefit from further exploration. Betsy Smith used some articles her instructor had distributed as a jumping-off point for her essay.

4d   Narrowing Your Topic and Drafting an Effective Thesis

A *thesis* is a brief statement (one or two sentences) of the central claim you will make. To begin drafting possible thesis statements, ask yourself probing questions about your topic and then answer them. Review your answers, looking for ones that identify your topic and make a claim about it. Choose one that will allow you to bring insight to the topic, and use that as your preliminary thesis. Your thesis should do four things:

> **More about**
> Generating ideas,
>   19–22
> Devising a thesis,
>   134–37
> Purpose, 16, 97
> Claims, 74–75

1. Identify your topic
2. Indicate your purpose (informative or persuasive)
3. Make a claim (or assertion) that you can support—a *claim of fact* (a verifiable issue) for an informative project, or a *claim of judgment* or *value* (a belief or opinion that can be supported by reasons and evidence) for a persuasive project
4. Engage your readers

Only rarely does a writer accomplish all four of these objectives in the first draft of the thesis. Most writers need to revise the thesis, either before drafting or during revision.

 Stating the Main Idea In some contexts and cultures, it is appropriate to imply the main idea rather than state it explicitly. However, readers in the United States, especially in academic and business contexts, will usually expect you to express your thesis clearly and directly, usually at the beginning of your written project.

1. Purpose: Informative

The thesis of an informative essay makes a ***claim of fact,*** an assertion that can be verified. To be engaging, an informative thesis must make a claim of fact that is not yet widely known to or accepted by the audience, and it must be specific enough that the writer can explore it in depth:

Student Model
Informative essay:
25–27, 231–38

DRAFT THESIS

This paper is about conflicts within the environmental movement.

Topic

This draft thesis establishes a topic, but it does not make a claim of fact, and it is far too general to explore in depth.

REVISION 1—FOR AN INFORMATIVE PROJECT

There are many conflicts within the environmental movement.

Topic

This thesis statement establishes the topic and makes a claim of fact, but the claim is too broad. Because the writer has not specified which conflicts she has in mind, she would potentially have to explain all possible conflicts within the environmental movement to satisfy the promise of the thesis.

REVISION 2—FOR AN INFORMATIVE PROJECT

Among the conflicts within the environmental movement is that between those who want to reduce global warming by replacing fossil fuels with alternatives, like wind energy and solar energy, and those who fear that new energy generating plants will harm local wildlife.

Topic

The thesis statement now narrows the claim—makes it specific—so that it focuses solely on one area of conflict within the environmental movement. It will intrigue readers interested in environmental issues and inform those who know little about the conflicts.

2. Purpose: Argumentative

The thesis of a *argumentative* writing project must make a *claim of value* (a belief about the way the world should be) or *judgment* (an opinion or a provisional decision that is not widely shared). The claim must be one that can be supported with evidence. The revised informative thesis above clearly specifies a topic and will probably intrigue readers, but it is not appropriate for an argumentative project because it makes a claim of fact, not a claim of value or judgment:

REVISION 3—FOR AN ARGUMENTATIVE PROJECT

As serious and time sensitive as the issue of climate change is, alternative energy is not a solution if it will be just as harmful to wildlife as conventional energy.

Topic

This thesis still specifies the topic, but it now also makes a claim of judgment ("alternative energy is not a solution"). Because it is narrow, focusing on just one issue ("alternative energy [that] is . . . harmful to wildlife"), it can be explained in a brief essay. Because it demonstrates the importance of the topic ("As serious and time-sensitive as the issue of climate change is"), it is likely to interest readers.

When drafting your thesis statement, make sure that it focuses on a claim you can support and that it will interest your reader. When revising your thesis statement, make sure that the reasons and evidence you provide support your claim directly. If they do not, either replace the irrelevant reasons and evidence, or revise your thesis so that the support you offer is pertinent.

4e Organizing Your Ideas

Outlines, whether formal or informal, not only guide you as you draft, but they also allow you to experiment with ways of sequencing your supporting paragraphs. The type of outline you choose depends entirely on your own preferences, the complexity of your essay, and your instructor's expectations. For a brief writing project, an *informal outline* may be all you need. An informal (or *scratch*) outline is simply a list of your ideas in the order you want to present them. You can jot down your ideas in words, phrases, complete sentences, even pictures—whatever you need to jog your memory about what to put next. Here is a sample informal outline for Betsy Smith's draft essay on conflicts within the environmental movement.

Student Model Informal Outline

> *Intro*
> *Green/environmental movement: brief explanation*
> *Growing importance and awareness in recent years → conflict within the movement about how to handle these issues*
> *Thesis: A major goal of the green movement is to find fossil fuel alternatives, but some members are concerned that wind, solar, and nuclear power sites will also harm the environment.*
>
> *Body*
> *Benefits/importance of alternative energy; types of alternative fuel being proposed: wind, solar, nuclear*
> *Problems with alternative energy sources: harmful to animals, scenic views, safety for humans*
>
> *Conclusion*
> *Conflicts might be inevitable, but we have to move forward, find creative compromises, use less energy*

A *formal outline* is helpful when drafting longer, more complex writing projects. In a formal outline, roman numeral headings indicate your main ideas and capital letters and arabic numbers indicate your supporting points. Each point in your outline must support the idea at the level above it and must be supported by the points in the level below it.

A *topic outline* uses words and phrases to indicate the ideas to be discussed. A *sentence outline* uses complete sentences. Some writers prefer a topic outline because it is easier to construct. Others prefer a sentence outline because it provides a starting point for drafting. Compare a section of a topic outline with a section of a sentence outline for a later draft of Betsy Smith's essay:

Thesis: A major goal of the green movement is to find fossil fuel alternatives, but some environmentalists are concerned that wind, solar, and nuclear power sites will also harm the environment.

Topic Outline	**Sentence Outline**
I. Divisions within environmental movement over alternative energy	I. When it comes to alternative energy sources, environmentalists are divided.
A. Benefits of alternative fuel	A. There are numerous potential benefits of using alternative fuel sources.
1. Fewer greenhouse gas emissions/ less warming	1. Alternative energy produces fewer carbon dioxide and other greenhouse gas emissions, improving air quality and slowing the rate of global warming.
2. Sustainable renewable energy sources: the sun, wind, and water	2. Renewable energy sources, including the sun, wind, and water, are sustainable; they cannot be depleted and therefore can be used for the foreseeable future.
B. Drawbacks	B. Although there are many advantages to alternative fuel sources, there are drawbacks as well.
1. Bad for environment: scenery, humans	1. New structures can have negative consequences on their surroundings, ranging from ruining picturesque views to endangering human health.
2. Destruction of animal habitats, extinction	2. Habitats may be destroyed, leading to extinction of species.
3. Future problems unknown without tests	3. The long-term effects of building new facilities are still largely unknown and could present even greater problems in the future.

4f Drafting Your Writing Project

When the moment comes to combine words and sentences into paragraphs and paragraphs into a writing project, set aside some time and find a place where you can concentrate. Begin drafting by reviewing the writing you have done while generating ideas, drafting your thesis, and creating an outline. Even in the best circumstances, you may encounter writer's block, but by using the appropriate techniques—write what you can, in parts rather than all at once; take breaks; avoid perfection—you should be able to get past it.

> **More about**
> Topic sentences, 28–29
> Developing paragraphs, 28–38

Your project should explain *why* you believe that your thesis statement is true and why your readers should agree with you. The topic sentence (or main idea) in each supporting paragraph will form the backbone of your essay, and the reasons and evidence you supply will be the flesh that covers the skeleton. Some kinds of evidence you can draw on to convince your readers include facts and statistics, expert opinion, examples and anecdotes, observations and case studies, and passages from the text you are studying. The chapter that follows describes how to write well-developed and compelling paragraphs for the introduction, conclusion, and body of your writing project.

> **Tech** **Protecting Your Work**
>
> Because terrible things happen to computer files all the time, it is important to **save early and often,** and to **save your file in multiple locations:** Burn it to a disc, save it on a flash drive, or send a copy to your e-mail account. Remember to date each version of a file so you know which is the most recent.

> **Student Models**
> Development of "Is Alternative Energy Really Good for the Environment?"
> Brainstorming, 20
> Clustering, 20–21
> Journalists' questions, 22
> Draft thesis, 23
> Revised thesis, 23
> Outlines, 24, 25
> Final draft, 44–47

Student Model First Draft

Read the first draft of Betsy Smith's essay on conflict within the environmental movement. Note that she does not worry about polished writing or perfect grammar and spelling. She knows she can make changes as she revises. For now, her focus is on getting her ideas down in a logical order and supporting her thesis. Consider what she will need to do as she revises to fulfill her writer's responsibilities.

Betsy Smith

Professor Locke

Composition 102

4 Oct. 2012

Is Alternative Energy Really Good for the Environment?

The Environmental, or Green, Movement has been around for many years. Although the movement includes many areas (politics, economics, agricultureetc.), most environmentalists want to create and maintain a healthy planet. But the green movement is made up of many different individuals with different opinions about how to best preserve nature. The result is conflict. Recently, with the growing attenention to global warming in recent years, these agreuments have tended to involve alternitive fuel sources. A major goal of the green movement is to find fossil fuel alternitives, but some environmentalists are concerned that wind, solar, and nuclear power sites will also harm the environment.

One example of this green vs. green debate was recently featured in *The Washington Post*. In this case, the company Invenergy is trying to build a wind power facility on Beech Ridge in West Virginia, but it is being fought by David Cowan, a nearby resident who is a bat enthusiast. He argues that the wind turbines that spin as part of the process are harmful to the surrounding wildlife, namely the endangered Indiana Bat. Even though "Cowan and other plaintiffs, including the D.C.-based Animal Welfare Institute, support wind power as one way to mitigate climate change." These members of the environmental movement are also worried about the dangers of the new technology alternitive energy requires (Glod).

The Beech Ridge case is not the only example of this debate. In Imperial County, CA, near San Diego, environmentalists are fighting the construction of a solar energy project. They claim that the project's location would hurt the bighorn sheep there and also be harmful to the flat-tailed horned lizard. Another solar project in the Mojave Desert is being opposed because it will threaten California desert tortoises and endangered cacti (Breen).

When it comes to using alternitive energy, greenies disagree. There are numerous environmental benefits of using alternitive fuel sources. Alternitive energy produces fewer carbon dioxide and other greenhouse gas emissions, which improve air quality and reduce pollution. Renewable energy sources, including the sun, wind, and water, are sustainable; they can't be depleted and therefore can continue to be used ("Environmental Benefits . . .").

Margin annotations:

First draft, so not concerned with spelling, style, grammar

Thesis statement makes a claim of fact, appropriate if purpose is informative but not if purpose is persuasive.

Topic sentence introduces first example of conflict.

Sentence fragment; quotation not especially vivid

Sources cited even in first draft

Topic sentence introduces second example of conflict

Abbreviations generally avoided in prose

Sentence 1 introduces contrasting views of environmental movement (discussed in next 3 ¶s); sentence 2 introduces topic of this ¶

Contractions may be too informal for college writing.

While there are many advantages to alternitive fuel sources, there are drawbacks as well. New structures can hurt their surroundings ranging from ruining picturesque views to endangering some species of animal to, in the case of nuclear, poisoning human beings (Breen, Glod, Mark). Due to the fact that the long term effects of new facility production are still largely unknown and could present even greater problems that we do not yet comprehend.

Another source of alternitive energy now being reexamined is nuclear. Now that climate change has become such a dominant factor, some environmentalists feel that increasing nuclear power production is better than burning fossil fuels. Nuclear power has divided the movement more than wind and solar power, largely because "more than 50 years after the establishment of the civilian atomic energy program, the country still lacks a way to safely handle the radioactive waste formed during the fission process." But even some of the most invested environmentalists believe that in the face of climate change, we may have to turn to nuclear power (Mark).

Even though these issues are complex, there are efforts being made to find solutions. In West Virginia, there is research being done to reduce the number of bats the wind turbines will harm, "including stopping the turbines at certain times or using sound to deter the bats" (Glod). New locations for construction are being explored, and all over the world, new theories about how to safely handle nuclear waste are being proposed and tested. Our planet is in it's current bad situation because of our recklessness with natural resources, and as serious and time-sensitive as the issue of climate change is, alternitive energy is not a solution if it will be just as harmful to wildlife as conventional energy. Until we make wind, solar and nuclear power sites that are safe for the living things surrounding them, there will continue to be conflict within the green movement.

-- [new page] --

Works Cited

Breen, Steve. "Green vs. green," *The San Diego Union Tribune.* Oct. 21, 2009.

"Environmental Benefits of Renewable Energy," *Clean Energy.* Union of Concerned Scientists, 2009.

Glod, Maria. "Tiny Bat Pits Green against Green," *The Washington Post.* Oct. 22, 2009

Mark, Jason. The Fission Division: "Will nuclear power split the green movement?" *Earth Island Journal* 22.3 (2007).

Annotations (right margin):

- Topic sentence introduces discussion of drawbacks to alternative fuel sources
- Sentence fragment
- Topic sentence introduces discussion of nuclear fuel, with its advantages, disadvantage
- Quotation not cited
- Conclusion
- Quotation does not offer an example of "research" as claimed in first half of sentence
- Cites sources even in first draft
- Citations need revision to follow MLA style

5 Crafting and Connecting Paragraphs

American architect Frank Lloyd Wright claimed that "[t]rue ornament is not a matter of prettifying externals. It is organic with the structure it adorns. . . ." Wright believed that each element—even the furniture and windows (like the one here)—should be an essential part of the overall structure. Similarly, a writing project will be most effective when each paragraph is essential to the whole. When is a paragraph essential? It is essential when it is relevant, unified, coherent, well developed, interesting, and carefully connected to the paragraphs that come before and after it.

Frank Lloyd Wright, stained glass window, 1912

5a Writing Relevant Paragraphs

A paragraph is *relevant* when it contributes to the reader's understanding of or belief in the main idea of the paper (the *thesis*). Compare the paragraph below (from Betsy Smith's revised essay at the end of chapter 6) to her essay's thesis:

> **Thesis:** Although environmentalists might agree on this overarching objective [to establish and maintain a healthy planet], groups within the movement have different opinions about how best to preserve nature.

Topic sentence

Evidence for supporting alternative energy sources

Evidence for opposing alternative energy sources

Student Model
Final draft, 44–47

> When it comes to using alternative energy, environmentalists are divided. There are those who see the numerous environmental benefits of using alternative fuel sources. Alternative energy reduces greenhouse gas emissions, improving air quality and slowing the rate of global warming. Renewable energy sources—namely, the sun, wind, and water—are sustainable; they cannot be depleted and therefore can be used in the foreseeable future ("Environmental Benefits"). But even if they acknowledge these advantages, opposing environmentalists point out that there are drawbacks as well. New structures can have negative consequences on their surroundings, causing problems that range from ruining picturesque views to endangering some species of animals to, in the case of nuclear energy, poisoning human beings (Breen, Glod, Mark).

5b Writing Unified Paragraphs

Paragraphs are *unified* when they focus on a single main idea. Unifying a paragraph is easiest when it includes a *topic sentence,* a single sentence (sometimes two) that clearly states the main idea of the paragraph. The following paragraph would be more unified if its writer pruned the sentences that do not relate to working on an organic farm in Costa Rica.

Topic sentence

Relevant

> Last summer, I traveled to Costa Rica to work on an organic farm. I had always wanted to experience Central America, and this was a perfect opportunity to truly

get to know the land. Thailand and Cambodia also fascinate me. I worked eight hours each day on the farm, helping to care for the animals and learning how to raise organic vegetables. After a day outside, I would help my host family prepare dinner, with food fresh from the land. Breakfast is actually my favorite meal because I like to eat eggs and hash browns. As I ate, I knew that I had played a part in the food I was eating. Though I only stayed in Costa Rica for the summer, I came back with much higher expectations for my food. I think I'm going to go back to Costa Rica next summer to work with a nonprofit to build houses in San Jose.

Irrelevant

Topic sentences typically appear at the beginning of a paragraph so that readers can see immediately the relationship between the main idea and the supporting reasons and evidence that follow.

Environmentalists paint a bleak picture of aquaculture. The David Suzuki Foundation, for example, maintains that fish waste contained in the fishery pens kills organisms living in the seabed. Yvon Gesinghaus, a manager of a tribal council in British Columbia, Canada, also notes that the scummy foam from the farms collects on the beaches, smothering the clams that provide the natives with food and money. George K. Iwama, Biksham Gujja, and Andrea Finger-Stich point to the destruction of coastal habitats in Africa and Southeast Asia to make room for shrimp ponds.
—Adrianne Anderson, Texas Christian University

Topic sentence

Occasionally, writers may place the topic sentence at the end of a paragraph to draw a conclusion based on the evidence presented and to enhance dramatic effect or in the middle of the paragraph, where the topic sentence acts as a linchpin. Some paragraphs (especially descriptive and narrative ones) may even leave the main idea unstated if it is clearly conveyed by the details and the word choices.

5c Writing Coherent Paragraphs

A paragraph is *coherent* when readers can understand the relationships among the sentences without having to pause or ponder. Readers are most likely to find a paragraph coherent when writers use transitional strategies to link sentences.

Transitional words and phrases alert readers to the significance of what the writer is saying and point up the relationships among ideas. The paragraph below uses transitional words and phrases indicating contrast, cause and effect, emphasis, and time to guide readers through a comparison of two books.

Baron's book, which is written in the relentlessly melodramatic style of *Jaws*, describes cougars spreading inexorably eastward. By contrast, Elizabeth Marshall Thomas, in *The Tribe of Tiger: Cats and Their Culture*, argues that cougars were never fully exterminated in the East and instead survived in remote areas by being especially stealthy around humans. The difference is significant. If you accept Marshall Thomas's argument, then the eastern seaboard sounds

Contrast

Cause-effect

Emphasis

Time

a great deal like pre–cougar-resurgence Colorado. Indeed, the herds of deer plaguing the-unbroken strip of Eastern suburbs makes a replay of the Boulder situation likely—but on a far larger scale. Already, bears and coyotes are invading the Eastern suburbs. Can cougars and wolves be far behind?

—Peter Canby, "The Cat Came Back," *Harper's*

The Quick Reference box below lists other types of transitional words and phrases. The number of possibilities is great, so choose transitions that convey the relationship you are trying to express and vary your selection.

Repetition of keywords and sentence structures, when used judiciously, can also knit sentences together into a unified paragraph, as can replacing keywords with pronouns, synonyms (words that mean the same thing), and equivalent expressions. The paragraph below provides an example of how these strategies can be used effectively:

Repeated structure

Keyword

Pronouns

Equivalent expressions

The first law of gossip is that you never know how many people are talking about you behind your back. The second law is thank God. The third—and most important—law is that as gossip spreads from friends to acquaintances to people you've never met, it grows more garbled, vivid, and definitive. Out of stray factoids and hesitant impressions emerges a hard mass of what everyone knows to be true. Imagination supplies the missing pieces, and repetition turns these pieces into facts; gossip achieves its shape and amplitude only in the continual retelling. The best stories about us are told by perfect strangers.

—Tad Friend, "The Harriet-the-Spy Club," *New Yorker*

Quick Reference Sample Transitional Words and Phrases

To add to an idea: *again, also, and, and then, besides, further, furthermore, in addition, incidentally, likewise, moreover, next, still, too*

To indicate cause or effect: *accordingly, as a result, because, consequently, hence, since, then, therefore, thus*

To indicate chronology (time sequence): *after, afterward, as long as, as soon as, at last, before, earlier, finally, first, formerly, immediately, in the first place, in the interval, in the meantime, in the next place, in the last place, later, latter, meanwhile, next, now, often, once, previously, second, shortly, simultaneously, since, sometime later, subsequently, suddenly, then, third, today, tomorrow, until, until now, when, years ago, yesterday*

To conclude: *all in all, finally, in brief, in conclusion, in other words, in short, in sum, in summary, that is, to summarize*

To compare: *alike, also, in the same way, like, likewise, resembling, similarly*

To concede: *certainly, granted, of course*

To contrast: *after all, although, and yet, but, conversely, despite, difference, dissimilar, even so, even though, granted, however, in contrast, in spite of, instead, nevertheless, nonetheless, notwithstanding, on the contrary, on the other hand, otherwise, regardless, still, though, unlike, while this may be true, yet*

To emphasize: *after all, certainly, clearly, even, indeed, in fact, in other words, in truth, it is true, moreover, of course, undoubtedly*

To offer an example: *as an example, for example, for instance, in other words, namely, specifically, that is, thus, to exemplify, to illustrate*

To indicate spatial relationships: *above, adjacent to, against, alongside, around, at a distance from, behind, below, beside, beyond, encircling, far off, farther along, forward, here, in front of, inside, nearly, near the back, near the end, next to, on, over, surrounding, there, through, to the left, to the right, to the north, to the south, up front*

Writing Responsibly / Guiding the Reader

As a writer, you have a responsibility to guide your reader from point to point, highlighting the relationships among your words, sentences, and paragraphs. Do not leave readers to puzzle out the relationships among your ideas for themselves. Few academic readers in the United States will think explicit claims and transitions insult their intelligence.

to AUDIENCE

5d Developing Paragraphs Using Patterns of Organization

To be effective, a writing project must offer enough "meat" to satisfy readers. How much is enough? There are no hard-and-fast rules, but you should provide enough support to explain your ideas fully. Consider the paragraph below:

> One of the most important . . . features of American life in the late twentieth century was the aging of the American population. After decades of steady growth, the nation's birth rate began to decline in the 1970s and remained low through the 1980s and 1990s. In 1970, there were 18.4 births for every 1,000 people in the population. By 1996, the rate had dropped to 14.8 births.

Topic sentence

Left as is, the paragraph above would be inadequately developed: The topic sentence discusses the aging of the population, but the supporting sentences discuss only the birth rate—a factor in the aging of a population, but not the whole story.

Now consider the complete paragraph:

> One of the most important . . . features of American life in the late twentieth century was the aging of the American population. After decades of steady growth, the nation's birth rate began to decline in the 1970s and remained low through the 1980s and 1990s. In 1970, there were 18.4 births for every 1,000 people in the population. By 1996, the rate had dropped to 14.8 births. The declining birth rate and a significant rise in life expectancy produced a substantial increase in the proportion of elderly citizens. Almost 13 percent of the population was more than sixty-five years old in 2000, as compared with 8 percent in 1970. The median age in 2000 was 35.3, the highest in the nation's history. In 1970, it was 28.0.
>
> —Alan Brinkley, *American History: A Survey*

Topic sentence

Compares birth rates

Compares life expectancies

Compares median ages

Here, the writer compares the population in 1970 with the population in later periods on not one but three traits—birth rate, life expectancy, and median age—and he provides concrete evidence (facts and statistics) to convince readers that the population was aging. Some other kinds of evidence you can draw on to support your claims include expert opinion, examples, observations, case studies, anecdotes, passages from a text you are studying, and your own analysis.

Patterns of organization, such as comparison-contrast (as in the example paragraph above), description, narration, and exemplification, can help you flesh out your paragraphs (and your writing projects) fully. They lend a structure to your paragraphs, and they suggest the types of evidence that will be most effective.

1. Use comparison-contrast: Show similarities and differences.

A paragraph that is developed using comparison-contrast points out similarities or differences (sometimes both) of two or more items. The example paragraph on the previous page, for instance, compares the US population in 1970 with the US population in later periods. Note that this paragraph compares the US population on each of three traits, using facts and statistics to support its claims. The paragraph uses the *alternating pattern* of organization, switching back and forth between 1970 and the last decade of the twentieth century.

Another option for organizing comparison-contrast paragraphs is to discuss all the traits of the first item before moving on to all the traits of the second item. The paragraph below follows the *block pattern* of organization.

> Europeans interpreted the simplicity of Indian dress in two different ways. Some saw the lack of clothing as evidence of "barbarism." André Thevet, a shocked French visitor to Brazil in 1557, voiced this point of view when he attributed nakedness to simple lust. If the Indians could weave hammocks, he sniffed, why not shirts? But other Europeans viewed unashamed nakedness as the Indians' badge of innocence. As remnants of a bygone "golden age," they believed, Indians needed clothing no more than government, laws, regular employment, or other corruptions of civilization.
> —James West Davidson et al., *Nation of Nations,* 5th ed.

Topic sentence

First item of comparison

Second item of comparison

This paragraph uses examples as support. In general, the block pattern works best with fewer points of comparison.

2. Use description with details.

When describing, include details that appeal to the senses (sight, sound, taste, smell, touch) and organize them spatially (from left to right, top to bottom, near to middle to far) to mimic how we normally take in a scene. Spatially organized paragraphs rely on indications of place or location to guide the reader by the mind's eye (or ear or nose).

Sensory description

Indications of place or location

> A few moments later French announces, "Bottom contact on sonar." The seafloor rolls out like a soft, beige carpet. Robison points to tiny purple jellies floating just above the floor. Beyond them, lying on the floor itself, are several bumpy sea cucumbers, sea stars with skinny legs, pink anemones, and tube worms, which quickly retract their feathery feeding arms at *Tiburon*'s approach. A single rattail fish hangs inches above the bottom, shoving its snout into the sediments in search of a meal.
> —Virginia Morell, "OK, There It Is—Our Mystery Mollusk,"
> *National Geographic*

3. Tell a story or describe a process.

A paragraph that tells a story or describes a process unrolls over time. Include each step or key moment, and describe it in enough detail that readers can envision it.

The very first trick ever performed by Houdini on the professional stage was a simple but effective illusion known generally as the "Substitution Trunk," though he preferred to call it "Metamorphosis." Houdini and his partner would bring a large trunk onto the stage. It was opened and a sack or bag produced from inside it. Houdini, bound and handcuffed, would get into the sack, which was then sealed or tied around the neck. The trunk was closed over the bag and its occupant. It was locked, strapped, and chained. Then a screen was drawn around it. The partner (after they married, this was always Mrs. Houdini) stepped behind the screen which, next moment, was thrown aside—by Houdini himself. The partner had meanwhile disappeared. A committee of the audience was called onstage to verify that the ties, straps, etc. around the trunk had not been tampered with. These were then laboriously loosened; the trunk was opened and there, inside the securely fastened bag, was—Mrs. Houdini!

Step 1

Step 2

Step 3

Step 4

Step 5

Step 6

Step 7

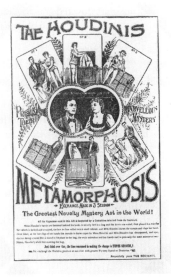

The sequence of events in the Substitution, or Metamorphosis, trick is depicted in Figure 5.1.

FIGURE 5.1 A visual process analysis

4. Exemplify: Explain through example.

Exemplification works by providing examples to make a general point specific:

For many years I believed that women had only one thing to learn from men: how to get the attention of a waiter by some means short of kicking over the table and shrieking. Never in my life have I gotten the attention of a waiter, unless it was an off-duty waiter whose car I'd accidentally scraped in a parking lot somewhere. Men, however, can summon a maître d' just by thinking the word "coffee," and this is a power women would be well-advised to study. What else would we possibly want to learn from them? How to interrupt someone in midsentence as if you were performing an act of conversational euthanasia? How to drop a pair of socks three feet from an open hamper and keep right on walking? How to make those weird guttural gargling sounds in the bathroom?

Example 1

Example 2

Example 3

—Barbara Ehrenreich, "What I've Learned from Men: Lessons for a Full-Grown Feminist," *Ms.*

5. Give reasons and consequences.

A cause-and-effect paragraph explains why something happened or what its consequences are:

<table>
<tr><td>Causes</td><td rowspan="2">When we exhibit these [positive] emotions, society showers us with positive reinforcement; we learn this even before we get out of diapers. When, as children, we hug our rotten little puke of a sister and give her a kiss, all the aunts and uncles smile and twit and cry, "Isn't he the sweetest little thing?" Such coveted treats as chocolate-covered graham crackers often follow. But if we deliberately slam the rotten little puke of a sister's fingers in the door, sanctions follow—angry remonstrance from parents, aunts, and uncles; instead of a chocolate-covered graham cracker, a spanking.</td></tr>
<tr><td>Effects</td></tr>
</table>

—Stephen King, "Why We Crave Horror Movies," Playboy

6. Analyze by dividing a whole into its parts.

Analysis divides a single entity into its component parts:

<table>
<tr><td>United States</td><td rowspan="3">The central United States is divided into two geographical zones: the Great Plains in the west and the prairie in the east. Though both are more or less flat, the Great Plains—extending south from eastern Montana and western North Dakota to eastern New Mexico and western Texas—are the drier of the two regions and are distinguished by short grasses, while the more populous prairie to the east (surrounding Omaha, St. Louis, and Fort Leavenworth) is tall-grass country. The Great Plains are the "West"; the prairie, the "Midwest."</td></tr>
<tr><td>Great Plains</td></tr>
<tr><td>Prairie</td></tr>
</table>

—Robert D. Kaplan, An Empire of Wilderness

7. Define a word by explaining its meaning or concept.

Like those in a dictionary, a definition explains the meaning of a word or concept by grouping it into a class and then providing the distinguishing characteristics that set it apart from other members of that class:

Term to Be Defined	Class	Distinguishing Characteristics
Argument is	a way to discover truth	by examining all sides of the issue.

Extended definitions (definitions that run to a paragraph or more) analyze in detail what a term does or does not mean. They go beyond a desktop dictionary, often using anecdotes, examples, or reasons for using the word in this particular way:

<table>
<tr><td>Term to be defined</td><td rowspan="3">The international movement known as theater of the absurd so vividly captured the anguish of modern society that late twentieth-century critics called it "the true theater of our time." Abandoning classical theater from Sophocles and Shakespeare through Ibsen and Miller, absurdist playwrights rejected traditional dramatic structure (in which action moves from conflict to resolution), along with traditional modes of character development. The absurdist</td></tr>
<tr><td>Class</td></tr>
<tr><td>Distinguishing characteristics</td></tr>
</table>

play, which drew stylistic inspiration from dada performance art and sur-
realist film, usually lacks dramatic progression, direction, and resolution.
Its characters undergo little or no change, dialogue contradicts actions, and
events follow no logical order. Dramatic action, leavened with gallows humor,
may consist of irrational and grotesque situations that remain unresolved at
the end of the performance—as is often the case in real life.

—Gloria Fiero, *The Humanistic Tradition,* 5th ed.

5e Writing Introductory Paragraphs

Introductory paragraphs shape readers' attitudes toward the rest of the text, so
they are an important part of the writing project. Yet writers often have a hard
time producing these paragraphs. Many find it helpful to draft the body of the
essay before tackling the introduction.

Whether you write it first or last, the introduction should prepare the
reader for what follows. In many cases, this means including the thesis in the
introduction, often at the end of the introductory section or paragraph.

Regardless of where you place your thesis, your introduction should identify and convey your stance toward your topic, establish your purpose, and
engage readers to make them want to read on. Some strategies for writing an
effective introduction include the following:

- Begin with a vivid quotation, a compelling question, or some interest-
  ing data.
- Start with an engaging—and relevant—anecdote.
- Offer a surprising but apt definition of a key term.
- Provide background information readers will need.
- State a commonly held belief and then challenge it.
- Explain what interesting, important, conflicting, difficult, or misun-
  derstood territory the essay will explore.

In the introductory paragraph that follows, the writer uses several effective
strategies: She begins with a question that challenges the audience to examine
some common assumptions about the topic, she provides background information that her readers may lack, and she concludes with a thesis statement
that explains why reading her text should be important to the audience.

> Many people enjoy sitting down to a nice seafood dinner, but how many of
> those people actually stop to think about where the fish on their plate came
> from? With many species of wild fish disappearing because of overfishing,
> increasingly the answer will be a fish farm. But while fish farming can help
> to supply the demand, it can threaten the environment and cause problems
> with wild fish. It can also threaten the health of consumers by increasing the
> risk of disease and increasing the quantity of antibiotics consumed. In fact,
> as a careful and conscientious consumer, you would do well to learn the risks

Student Models
Introductions: 26, 35,
    45, 83–84, 94, 193,
    233–34, 257

Opening question

Answer that provides
background
information

Thesis

involved in buying and eating farm-raised fish before one winds up on your dinner plate.

—Adrianne Anderson, Texas Christian University

Brief essays may require only a one-paragraph introduction, but longer texts often need more. A text of twenty pages may have an introduction that runs several paragraphs, and introductions to books are generally the length of a short chapter. There are no firm rules about the length of the introduction, but it should be in proportion to the essay's length.

 Avoid Praising the Reader in Your Introduction In some contexts and cultures, writers attempt to win the approval of readers by overtly praising their taste, character, or intelligence. Generally, however, this is considered inappropriate for a college paper, and academic and professional writers in the United States avoid referring directly to the reader and occasionally will actually challenge the reader's beliefs.

5f Writing Concluding Paragraphs

As with the introduction, the conclusion is a part of the essay that readers are likely to remember. In fact, because it is the last thing the audience will read, it is what they will probably remember best. Thus, it demands a writer's best work.

Student Models
Conclusions: 27, 37, 47, 85–86, 95, 199, 236, 260

Conclusions often start out specific, with a restatement of the thesis (in different words), and then broaden out. The purpose of the conclusion is to provide readers with a sense of closure and also to provide them with a sense that reading the text was worthwhile. Some ways to achieve closure and to convey the importance of the essay include the following:

- Recur to the anecdote, question, or quotation with which the project began.

- Summarize your findings (especially in long or technical projects).

- Discuss how what you have learned has changed your thinking.

- Suggest a possible solution (or solutions) to the problems raised in the text.

- Indicate additional research that needs to be conducted or what the reader can do to help solve the problem.

- Leave the reader with a vivid and pertinent image, quotation, or anecdote.

Makes reader feel time reading was well spent by showing importance of American dream

Restates thesis (American dream = hope for greater security, opportunity)

The concluding paragraph below provides an example of an effective conclusion.

The farmers of nineteenth-century America could afford to do here what they had not dared to do in the Old World: hope. This hope—for greater economic security, for more opportunity for themselves, their children, and their grandchildren—is the optimism and idealism that has carried our country forward and that, indeed, still carries us forward. Although the American dream has evolved across the centuries, it survives today and is a cornerstone of American philosophy. It is what underlies our Constitution and our laws, and it is a testimony to the vision of the farmers who founded this nation.

—Leonard Lin, University of Southern California, "The Middle Class Farmers and the American Philosophy"

> Achieves closure by recurring to introduction with mention of American dream

5g Connecting Paragraphs

Readers need to know not only how sentences connect to one another but also how paragraphs are connected. You can link paragraphs using the same techniques you use to link sentences:

- Providing transitional expressions (and sentences)
- Repeating words and phrases strategically
- Using pronouns, synonyms, and equivalent expressions to refer back to words and ideas introduced earlier
- Creating parallel sentence structures

You can also create coherence among paragraphs by referring back to the writing project's main idea.

The essay excerpted below, by former vice president and 2007 Nobel Peace Prize recipient Al Gore, uses all of these strategies to create a cohesive—and powerful—text.

Professional Model Editorial

An Inconvenient Truth

By AL GORE

> Keywords, phrases

Some experiences are so intense while they are happening that time seems to stop altogether. When it begins again and our lives resume their normal course, those intense experiences remain vivid, refusing to stay in the past, remaining always and forever with us.

> ¶ 2 provides an example of the intense experiences mentioned in ¶ 1.

> Transitional words, expressions

Seventeen years ago my youngest child was badly—almost fatally—injured. ... Thankfully, my son has long since recovered completely. But it was during that traumatic period that I made at least two enduring changes: I vowed always to put my family first, and I also vowed

to make the climate crisis the top priority of my professional life.

Unfortunately, in the intervening years, time has not stood still for the global environment. The pace of destruction has worsened and the urgent need for a response has grown more acute. ...

The climate crisis is, indeed, extremely dangerous. In fact it is a true planetary emergency. ... But along with the danger we face from global warming, this crisis also brings unprecedented opportunities. There will be plenty of new jobs and new profits—we can build clean engines;

> Adjective *that* in "that interlude 17 years ago," "that traumatic period" refers back to period of child's injury, introduced in ¶ 2.

> "Time has not stood still" refers back to "time seems to stop" (¶ 1).

we can harness the sun and the wind; we can stop wasting energy; we can use our planet's plentiful coal resources without heating the planet. . . .

But there's something even more precious to be gained if we do the right thing. The climate crisis also offers us the chance to experience what very few generations in history have had the privilege of knowing: a generational mission; the exhilaration of a compelling moral purpose, a shared and unifying cause; the thrill of being forced by circumstances to put aside the pettiness and conflict that so often stifle the restless human need for transcendence; the opportunity to rise.

When we do rise, it will fill our spirits and bind us together. Those who are now suffocating in cynicism and despair will be able to breathe freely. Those who are now suffering from a loss of meaning in their lives will find hope.

When we rise, we will experience an epiphany as we discover that this crisis is not really about politics at all. It is a moral and spiritual challenge. At stake is the survival of our civilization and the habitability of the Earth. . . .

I began with a description of an experience 17 years ago that,

for me, stopped time. During that painful period I gained an ability I hadn't had before to feel the preciousness of our connection in our children and the solemnity of our obligation to safeguard their future and protect the Earth we are bequeathing to them.

Imagine with me now that once again, time has stopped—for all of us—and before it starts again, we have the chance to use our moral imaginations and to project ourselves across the expanse of time, 17 years into the future, and share a brief conversation with our children and grandchildren as they are living in the year 2023.

Will they feel bitterness toward us because we failed in our obligation to care for the Earth that is their home and ours? Will the Earth have been irreversibly scarred by us? Imagine now that they are asking us: "What were you thinking? Didn't you care about our future? Were you really so self-absorbed that you couldn't—or wouldn't—stop the destruction of Earth's environment?" What would our answer be?

We can answer their questions now by our actions, not merely with our promises. In the process, we can choose a future for which our children will thank us.

Marginal notes:

Transitional sentence refers to list of opportunities in previous ¶.

Uses *chance* as synonym for *opportunity*.

Repetition of *rise* and sentence structure ("When we . . .") ties these three ¶s together.

Repetition of "children," "Earth," "17 years ago," "time has stopped" or "stopped time," and so on, tie the last four ¶s together and harken back to the opening anecdote.

Emphasis on pronouns contrasts *we* and *they* and connects final ¶ with previous ¶s.

6 Revising, Editing, and Proofreading

As writers revise, they chisel meaning from their first words and sentences, they erase and redraw parts of the broad outline, they carve out details from generalities, and they sand down rough edges. Only through revising, editing, and proofreading carefully can a writer transform a rough-hewn draft (like a sculpture emerging from stone) into a polished work.

6a Revising Globally: Analyzing Your Own Work

Revising globally means looking at the big picture to address issues like thesis, evidence, audience, context, genre, and ethical responsibilities. The first step toward assessing these aspects of your writing is to take a step backward to gain the distance needed for being objective about your own work. The second is to dive in, adjusting thesis and evidence, making changes to address your audience more effectively, and organizing your ideas more logically. You may find it possible to revise for thesis, evidence, audience, and organization simultaneously, but most writers focus on one issue at a time.

1. Thesis and introduction

Because writers often discover and develop their ideas as they draft, the draft thesis may no longer capture the project's main idea. (Often, the true thesis appears in the conclusion of the first draft.) This might mean you should adjust your evidence to match your thesis. More frequently it means that you should revise your thesis to match the evidence offered in your draft. Check your draft, too, to be sure that the introduction indicates your purpose—your reasons for writing—and your attitude toward your material.

> **More about**
> Drafting and
> revising a thesis,
> 22–24, 134–35

2. Evidence and counterevidence

In rereading your text, you may have had concerns about the evidence you offered in support of your thesis. Perhaps you noticed something weak, irrelevant, or overly general, or that you just did not supply enough evidence. If you need more or better evidence, go back to the idea-generating stage or return to the library to do additional research. Perhaps your draft talked only about the reasons for believing your thesis, while ignoring conflicting information and alternative interpretations. An effective argument shows both evidence and counterevidence and explains why the writer believes the evidence is more valid or useful than the counterevidence.

> **More about**
> Effective arguments: classical, Rogerian, Toulmin models, 78–80

39

Writing Responsibly

The Big Picture

Another way to think about revising is to focus on your responsibilities to your audience, your topic, other writers, and yourself:

- Have you provided your audience with a worthwhile reading experience?
- Have you explored your topic fully and creatively?
- Have you represented borrowed ideas accurately and acknowledged all your sources, whether you have quoted, summarized, or paraphrased?
- Have you developed a stance that readers will find credible, represented your ideas clearly and powerfully, and written in a voice that is a reflection of your best self?

to SELF

3. Audience

> **More about**
> Audience, 17
> Introduction,
>   35–36
> Development, 25,
>   31–35
> Connotation, 17,
>   302–03
> Level of formality,
>   17–18
> Conclusions, 36–37

After rereading your text, consider how your readers will react. Have you won them over? Think about your introduction: Does it make your audience want to keep reading? Next, consider the evidence in your body paragraphs. Will it persuade the people who will be reading your project? Is the language appropriate to those people? Finally, review your conclusion. Does it provide readers with a feeling of closure?

4. Organization

> **More about**
> Unity, 28–29
> Coherence, 29–31

Rereading your text may have alerted you to problems with organization. When revising, make sure that all the paragraphs support the thesis and that all the details in each paragraph support the paragraph's main idea. Make sure, too, that your ideas are presented in a logical order, with smooth transitional words and phrases, and that no steps are missing.

6b Reconsidering Your Title

Once you have revised your draft globally, revisit your title. It should prepare the audience for what they will read in your essay. In most college projects, your title should accurately reflect not only the topic but also your approach to the topic:

Topic
Approach

- The Power of <u>Wardrobe</u>: An Analysis of <u>Male Stereotype Influences</u>

Some writers use a clever turn of phrase, a quotation, or a question to intrigue their readers and draw them into the project:

Clever phrase
Descriptive phrase

- <u>Holy Underground Comics, Batman!</u> <u>Moving Away from the Mainstream</u>

However, this may not be appropriate in all disciplines.

6c Gaining Insight from Peers

Writers frequently feel a sense of "ownership" that helps them produce an authentic voice and a commitment to the ideas they express. This sense of ownership, however, can sometimes hold a writer back from making the kinds of changes needed for the success of a writing project. Outlining your draft to check its organization, or allowing time between drafts, can help you gain the distance you need. You can also gain perspective by having a friend read your draft aloud to you or by asking readers for feedback in peer review.

1. The writer's role

When it is your turn to get feedback, adopt an engaged and receptive stance:

- **Talk.** Explain what you are trying to accomplish and what you would like help with.

- **Listen.** Listen instead of arguing or defending. If readers seem confused or careless, figure out how you can revise the text so that even a confused or careless reader can understand what you are trying to say.

- **Question.** Ask readers to point to specific passages to support their claims or to explain points you find unclear.

- **Write.** Take notes as group members talk so that you have a record when it is time to revise.

- **Evaluate.** Be open to advice, but consider whether there may be a better way of solving a problem.

 Peer Review with Multilingual Students Many students are nervous about working in peer groups, but participation can reduce people's fears by showing that everyone makes mistakes and benefits from their experience with diversity. Group work helps non-native speakers of English become more familiar with the rules and idiosyncrasies of English—resolving difficult issues of idiom and word choice, for example—and more trustful of native speakers' natural abilities with their language.

> **More about**
> Mastering idioms,
> 306
> Effective word
> choice, 302–07

Native English-speaking students may also be hesitant to work in groups with peers from different language backgrounds. However, workplaces, like college, are increasingly diverse, and just as it is excellent practice for students to hear responses to their writing, it can be especially valuable coming from classmates who have diverse experiences with language. Your multilingual peers may have perspectives on your topic, organization, and style that you have not considered.

2. The reviewer's role

When giving feedback to a classmate, keep the following guidelines in mind:

- **Stay positive.** Praise the writer, pointing to specific aspects of the text that work (an effective example, a powerful turn of phrase).

- **Respond to the writer.** Listen to the writer's concerns, whether conducting the session face-to-face or electronically.

- **Look at the big picture, but be specific.** Start by stating what you take to be the writing project's main idea. Support general comments by pointing to specific passages in the text and explaining as best you can why they do not work for you.

- **Be a reader and a fellow writer—not a teacher, editor, or critic.** Remember that your job is not to judge the text or to rewrite it, but rather to help the writer recognize and resolve issues.

Here is an example of a portion of Betsy Smith's essay, with comments from peer reviewers:

Comment [td1]: This sentence seems too general with all the "many"s and "different"s. Can you be more specific?

Comment [jh1]: I like this short, punchy sentence. It might work better at the end of the paragraph to give "closure" (as our prof. says).

Comment [pb1]: This is an important topic. Isn't our purpose supposed to be persuasive, though? I think this makes a claim of fact, not a claim of value or judgment.

> Is Alternative Energy Really Good for the Environment?
>
> The environmental, or green, movement has been around for many years. Although the movement includes many areas (politics, economics, agriculture, etc.), most environmentalists want to create and maintain a healthy planet. But the green movement is made up of many different individuals with different opinions about how to best preserve nature. The result is conflict. Recently, with the growing attention to global warming in recent years, these agreements have tended to involve alternative fuel sources. A major goal of the green movement is to find fossil fuel alternatives, but some environmentalists are concerned that wind, solar, and nuclear power sites will also harm the environment.

NOTE Many colleges and universities sponsor writing centers that offer free tutoring. When planning your schedule, include time to take advantage of these services.

6d Revising Locally: Editing Your Words and Sentences

Your writing is a reflection of you—your ideas and your attitude toward your topic and audience. Revising locally means making sure that your individual words and sentences reflect your meaning and create a *persona* that is appropriate for your writing situation.

persona The apparent personality of the writer as conveyed through tone and style

1. Words

More about
Denotation, 17, 302–03
Connotation, 17, 302–03

First, be sure that each word reflects your intended meaning, that it has the right *denotation.* Readers may sometimes be able to guess your intent, but you should not expect them to be charitable. Also consider the emotional associations, or *connotations,* that words carry. These indicate the writer's attitude.

Compare *freedom fighter* with *terrorist*. Both refer to people who use violence to achieve political ends, but the connotative difference is enormous.

Next, consider the level of formality that is appropriate to your writing situation. A text message to a friend may be filled with slang and acronyms, but this informality is rarely appropriate in a business or academic context. Writers who intend to sound sophisticated by trotting out a word like *progenitor* to mean *parent* or even *mom* or *dad* may instead make themselves sound pompous. All writing, though, benefits from avoiding biased language—language that unfairly or offensively characterizes groups or individuals.

Finally, consider whether you have combined general, abstract language with specific, concrete words. Explaining broad issues requires abstract language, but specific words will make your writing more compelling.

> **More about**
> Levels of formality,
> 17–18, 296–97
> Biased language,
> 297–99
> General and spe-
> cific language,
> 303–04

2. Sentences

When revising, ask yourself these three questions about your sentences:

1. Are they grammatically correct?
2. Are they varied, and do they emphasize the most important information?
3. Are they as concise as they can be without losing meaning or affecting style?

> **More about**
> Common sen-
> tence problems,
> foldout following
> tab 10
> Sentence prob-
> lems, 319–94
> Variety, 284–94
> Emphasis, 291–94,
> 294–97
> Writing concisely,
> 277–80

NOTE Instructors often use symbols to indicate the most common mistakes. A list of commonly used editing symbols appears at the end of this book.

Compare the first paragraph in the revised version of Betsy Smith's writing project (page 44) with the version that appears on page 42. How do the changes Betsy made improve the reading experience?

6e Proofreading Your Project Carefully

When revising, you concentrate on your ideas and how you express them; when you proofread, you pull back from the content of the writing project to concentrate on correcting errors. An effective way to achieve the distance you

Writing
Responsibly   **Beware the Spelling Checker!**

While spell-check software can be very helpful in catching typos, it cannot distinguish between homonyms (*they're, their*) or other frequently confused words (*lay, lie; affect, effect*). Spelling checkers may even lead you astray, suggesting words that are close to the word you mistyped (*defiant* for the misspelled *definate*) but worlds away from the word you intended (*definite*). As a writer, you have a responsibility not to leave your reader guessing. Do not merely run your computer's spell-check software; also use a dictionary to double-check the spelling checker's suggestions, check usage in the usage glossary in this book, and proofread your text carefully. Only you can know what you *meant* to say!

to SELF

Self Assessment A Checklist for Proofreading

Before you submit your text to your instructor, check your work. If you did not do the following, revise as needed.

Spelling
- ☐ Spell-check your project using your word processing software.
- ☐ Read through the text carefully, looking for misused words.
- ☐ Check specifically for words you frequently confuse or misspell.

Punctuation
- ☐ Check sentence punctuation, especially use of the comma and the apostrophe.
- ☐ Double-check, in a text with dialogue or in a research project, that all quotations have quotation marks and that end punctuation and in-text citations are correctly placed.

- ☐ Check specifically for errors you regularly make (for example, comma splices or fused sentences).

Other Errors
- ☐ Check to make sure that remnants of previous corrections—an extra word, letter, or punctuation mark—do not remain.
- ☐ Check that you have included all in-text citations where needed (for summaries, paraphrases, quotations, or ideas you have borrowed) for a research project.
- ☐ Check that all in-text citations are included in the reference list or list of works cited, and make sure that documentation formatting is correct and consistent.

> **More about**
> Using a dictionary,
> 308–11
> Usage glossary,
> 311–18

need to proofread effectively is to print out your draft and read the hard copy line by line from the bottom up. Mark each correction on the printout as you read; enter them one by one, and then check to make sure that you have made each correction without introducing additional errors. Another option for proofreading is to work in teams: One person reads the text (including punctuation marks) out loud, while the other person marks errors on the printout.

A proofreading checklist appears in the Self-Assessment box above. Adjust it to your own needs by adding the errors you make most frequently.

 Proofreading If you have difficulty proofreading a project, try reading it aloud; whatever your background and culture, you will find this helps you recognize errors. If you are a non-native speaker of English, ask your instructor if you can have a friend or classmate help you proofread. A visit to the writing center may help, too.

Student Model Final Draft

You have seen Betsy Smith's writing project as it developed, from brainstorm to outline to initial draft. Now consider her final draft. Notice how she has revised her thesis—her purpose has changed from informative to persuasive. She has also worked to provide a better reading experience for her audience by making her introduction and conclusion more compelling. Notice, too, how she has developed her ideas more fully and provided additional reasons to support her claims. Has she now successfully fulfilled her responsibilities to her audience, topic, other writers, and herself? Why or why not?

Header (last name and page number) appears on all pages

Identifying information on p. 1

Betsy Smith

Professor Locke

Composition 102

18 Oct. 2012

Alternative Energy: Does It Really Offer an Alternative?

Descriptive title (centered)

In general, members of the environmental, or green, movement work toward a common goal: to establish and maintain a healthy planet. Although environmentalists might agree on this overarching objective, groups within the movement have different opinions about how best to preserve nature. Some focus on the big picture—stopping climate change—and so they work to reduce our carbon emissions by providing alternatives to fossil fuels; others focus on local issues, and so they work to preserve habitats for local plants and animals. Often, the result is conflict.

Introduction

When it comes to alternative energy, environmentalists are divided. There are those who see the numerous environmental benefits of using alternative fuel sources. Alternative energy reduces greenhouse gas emissions, which improves air quality and slows the rate of global warming. Renewable energy sources—namely, the sun, wind, and water—are sustainable; they cannot be depleted and therefore can be used for the foreseeable future ("Environmental Benefits"). But even if they acknowledge these advantages, opposing environmentalists point out that there are drawbacks as well. New structures needed to generate this energy can have negative consequences on their surroundings, causing problems that range from ruining picturesque views to endangering some species of animals to, in the case of nuclear energy, poisoning human beings (Breen, Glod, Mark). As serious and time-sensitive as the issue of climate change is, alternative energy is not a solution if it will be just as harmful to wildlife as conventional energy.

Paragraph developed using comparison-contrast

Thesis statement makes claim of judgment

Topic sentence introduces example 1

One type of alternative energy that seems safe on the surface is wind energy: It relies on a clean, renewable resource that will have little effect on the local environment. Or will it? Wind turbines reach hundreds of feet into the air (Glod), endangering

Transition

any bird or bat that flies through this air space. Eric Glitzenstein, an attorney with a public-interest law firm and president of the Wildlife Advocacy Project, testified before Congress that a 44-turbine wind farm in West Virginia killed dozens of migrating birds in a single night (6). The *New York Times* reported that both parties to a lawsuit over construction of a wind farm in Greenbrier County, West Virginia, acknowledge that more than 100,000 bats will be killed over twenty years by the 122 proposed turbines. Some of those killed might be the endangered Indiana bat, whose population has already fallen by half since 1967 (Glod). Opponents to this wind farm recognize that alternative energy sources, like wind power, are necessary if we are to slow global warming, but they are also concerned about the hazards the new technology creates.

> Body

Solar energy plants , too, are an alternative to more polluting fossil fuels, but they may also threaten local wildlife. The *San Diego Union Tribune* reports that some environmentalists in Imperial County, California, are fighting the construction of solar energy facilities. They argue that the facility will endanger both flat-tailed horned lizards and peninsular bighorn sheep (Breen). Another solar project in the Mojave Desert is being opposed on the grounds that it will threaten California desert tortoises and endangered cacti (Breen).

> Topic sentence introduces example 2

> Transition

Nuclear energy is also being touted as a clean alternative to fossil fuels. With the looming threat of global warming, some environmentalists now feel that increasing nuclear power production is preferable to burning fossil fuels. According to Stewart Brand, the founder and editor of the *Whole Earth Catalog,* "Climate change . . . changes priorities. Suddenly, worrying about radiation 6,000 years from now kind of goes down the list" (qtd. in Mark). Antinuclear activists, however, remind us of the accidents that occurred at nuclear power plants in Three Mile Island, Pennsylvania, and Chernobyl, Ukraine, in the 1970s and 1980s; they also warn that there is still no safe way to dispose of radioactive fuel rods and that, since we have not yet found a way to store nuclear waste safely, using even more nuclear energy will increase the environmental damage (Mark).

> Topic sentence introduces example 3

> Transition

Restates thesis

Transition

Clearly, it is important that we reduce our carbon footprint, but it is also important that we protect the living things with which we share the planet. In the face of green versus green conflicts, we must look for realistic solutions. In some cases, that is already being done. Wind-power company Invenergy, for example, has proposed several compromises with Greenbrier County residents to reduce the number of bats killed, including using sound to keep bats away from the turbines (Glod). In the Imperial County and Mojave Desert cases, new locations for construction are being considered (Breen). In terms of nuclear power, new theories about how to store nuclear waste safely are being proposed and tested (Mark). More importantly, however, we must change the way we approach the problem. Yes, we will continue to need energy, but shouldn't we also consider how we can reduce our energy demands as well? We are faced with the prospect of climate change today because of our recklessness with natural resources. It is time to consider how we can do more with less.

Refers back to examples to show compromises to protect animals

Suggests possible solution, calls attention to importance of issue

Conclusion

-- [new page] --

Works Cited

List of works cited follows MLA style

Breen, Steve. "Green vs. Green." *SignonSanDiego.com.* San Diego Union Tribune, 21 Oct. 2009. Web. 6 Oct. 2012.

Glitzenstein, Eric. "Testimony of Eric R. Glitzenstein before the House Subcommittee on Fisheries, Wildlife, and Oceans, House Committee on Resources, May 1, 2007." *Wildlife Advocacy Project.* Meyer, Glitzenstein, & Crystal, n.d. Web. 6 Oct. 2012.

Glod, Maria. "Tiny Bat Pits Green against Green." *Washington Post.* Washington Post, 22 Oct. 2009. Web. 6 Oct. 2012.

Mark, Jason. "The Fission Division: Will Nuclear Power Split the Green Movement?" *Earth Island Journal* 22.3 (2007): n. pag. Web. 6 Oct. 2012.

Writing **Responsibly**

Explaining Your Choice of Sources

Make It Your Own! When college writers share their opinion of their sources, their text is more interesting and convincing. Rather than just quoting from your sources, tell *why* you are quoting them, and your writing will be more persuasive.

In much of your college writing, you select and work with sources: You decide how to use sources to help convey your thesis. Your basic responsibility is to acknowledge those sources, cite them correctly, and provide full publication information about them at the end of your paper. When you talk *about* your sources—tell what you think of your source and its information—you invite your audience into your thinking processes and portray yourself as an experienced academic writer.

When college writing instructors involved in the Citation Project studied research papers from US colleges, they noticed how few students talked about their sources. Most of the papers just pulled out information—usually a brief quotation—from sources, as if all the sources were alike. The nature of the sources and the student's thoughts about them remained invisible to the audience. The following example, from a paper on sexism and sexual violence, shows the drab result:

First draft

Student's voice	Hostility toward women can be seen even in the ancient West. Stevenson observes,	Citation
Quotation	"Livy's underlying message, it would seem, is that Roman men have to regulate public	
	contributions by prominent women, and not accept female advice too easily, without	
	prolonged consideration" (189).	

The material from the Stevenson source is accurately quoted and cited, and the sentences flow. But the passage provokes questions rather than insights. Who are Stevenson and Livy? Where did this source come from? Why did the writer choose it? Why should the writer's audience respect Stevenson's opinions? What else did the source say? What was the context in which the quotation appeared? These are the kinds of questions readers ask, and answering them will bring your text to life:

Revised draft

Student's voice	Hostility toward women can be seen even in the ancient West. Tom Stevenson, a clas-	Citation
Credentials of author and publisher	sics scholar at the University of Queensland, writes in the scholarly journal *Classical World*	
	that the Roman historian Livy described women who supported their menfolks' success,	Summary of the remainder of the source
	which might seem to be a compliment to the women. But notice that the women aren't hav-	
	ing their own successes. Furthermore, all of Livy's women are either described too briefly,	
	or they are flawed. Even as Stevenson provides this analysis, he also cautions against	

Revised draft continued

Counter-evidence	being too simplistic about Livy's portrayal of women; some of their faults were because their men were flawed. Still, Stevenson concludes, "Livy's underlying message, it would seem, is **[Quotation]**
Citation	that Roman men have to regulate public contributions by prominent women, and not accept female advice too easily, without prolonged consideration" (189).

Source: Stevenson, Tom. "Women of Early Rome as *Exempla* in Livy, *AB Urbe Condita,* Book 1." *Classical World* 104.2 (Winter 2011): 175–189. Print.

Now, not only is the material from the source accurately quoted and cited, but Levy has been identified, and Stevenson's credentials and the authority of the publication have been established, along with a description of his argument.

Sometimes you choose to use a source because you like its argument or presentation of information, even if it may not be particularly scholarly. In these cases, too, you should let your audience know why you have chosen the source:

Information about why the writer chose this source	One good way to understand the treatment of women in contemporary society is to consult newsmedia. They are not reports of research written by experts, but rather are sources that reflect and shape popular opinion. *Time* magazine publishes an article on date rape because it believes this is an issue that readers will or should care about. It also reports on current events. So it is *Time* that reports on a congressional bill intended to reduce sexual
Summary of some information in the source	violence in colleges. Why is the bill needed? The answer is in the shocking numbers the **[Student's voice]** magazine cites: "One in five college women will be the victim of a sexual assault (and 6% of **[Quotation]**
Citation	men)" (Webley).

Source: Webley, Kayla. "It's Not Just Yale: Are Colleges Doing Enough to Combat Sexual Violence?" *Time.com* 18 Apr. 2011: n. pag. Web. 20 Apr. 2011.

Self Assessment

Review and revise your work with each source. Have you done the following?

☐ Identify the author of the source and his or her credentials: Did you show what makes you trust this person? ▶ *Analyzing and crafting arguments, 73–86*

☐ Identify the publisher of the source and evaluate its credentials: Did you show what makes you trust this organization? ▶ *Finding information, 103–14*

☐ Consider the date of publication: Did you provide and comment on the publication date, if it affects your trust in the source?

☐ Summarize the source: Did you indicate how the selection you have drawn from contributed to the argument the source was making? ▶ *Evaluating information, 114–21*

☐ Provide additional discussion: Did you help your audience understand the reasons you chose this source and your selections from it?

3 Design Matters

Designing in Multiple Media

Use tab 3 to learn, practice, and master these writer's responsibilities:

❏ **To Audience**

Guide readers by using the principles of design, fulfilling readers' design expectations by formatting in accordance with academic expectations, and using language and presentation techniques that will help you connect with your audience.

❏ **To Topic**

Use design to create an impression that is appropriate to your topic, use associations and color combinations that are appropriate, and use visuals and multimedia to aid understanding (when they are appropriate to your context and genre).

❏ **To Other Writers**

Treat sources with respect and acknowledge your sources, including when you are making a presentation.

❏ **To Yourself**

Show pride and commitment by using design to reflect and reinforce what you want to express, adopting positions you believe in, and preparing fully for all projects and presentations.

3

Design Matters

7 Designing Printed and Electronic Documents

The early Peruvians wove this design to represent and honor their sun god. They used proximity (to connect the head and tail to the figure's torso), alignment and repetition (of lines and shapes, to create a background against which the figure stands out), and contrast (of white outline against brown background) to define the figure and attract the eye. According to renowned designer Robin Williams, these four principles—proximity, alignment, repetition, and contrast—are the pillars on which effective design rests.

7a Planning Your Design Project

To figure out the best way to apply the four principles of design, begin with a careful consideration of your writing situation:

- **Topic.** What is your topic, and how can you reflect that topic through your design?
- **Audience.** Who will your audience be, what kind of expectations do readers bring with them, and what kind of relationship do you have (or want to have) with them?
- **Purpose.** Is your purpose to inform, to persuade, to express yourself, or to entertain, and how should this be reflected in your design?
- **Context.** In what context (academic, business, public) or setting (over the Internet, in person) will your project be received, and how might this affect its design?
- **Genre.** What genre (résumé, business letter, essay, lab report) will best fulfill your purpose, and what design conventions are associated with this genre?

> *More about*
> Purpose, 16,
> 22–24, 97
> Audience, 17,
> 97–98
> Topic, 17, 19–24,
> 98–99
> Context and genre,
> 18–19

Then determine how the pieces of information you want to convey relate to one another, and organize them accordingly. Ask yourself the following questions:

- What information is most and least important?
- Does some of the information support a broader claim or provide evidence for this claim?
- How might you convey or reinforce your ideas visually?

> *More about*
> Organizing, 24–25,
> 136–37

7b Laying Out and Formatting Your Document

Once you have assessed your writing situation and organized your project, you are ready to begin designing it.

More about
Formatting college projects, 56
Formatting business projects, 56–59

1. Create an overall impression.

Start by considering the overall impression you want to give the reader: Should the design be conservative or trendy, serious or playful? Let your own sense of style and the nature of your project guide you in your choice of colors, fonts, and visuals.

2. Plan the layout.

Next consider the overall *layout,* the visual arrangement of text and images. An effective layout should use proximity, alignment, repetition, and contrast to make the relationships among the elements clear. Keep your layout simple, and use it to direct the reader's eye to the most important pieces of information.

3. Format the document.

Create a cohesive and attractive design by using the following elements:

Fonts Word processors give writers a wide range of fonts (or typefaces) to choose from. Serif fonts (fonts with a little tail on the ends of letters, like Cambria and Times New Roman) are easier to read when printed on paper, while sans serif fonts (such as Arial and Calibri) are easier to read on screen and are preferred for web publishing.

More about
Using italics and underlining, 456–59

In addition to selecting the font family, you can set your font in a variety of styles, including **boldface,** *italics,* underlining, or color. Use color or **boldface** for emphasis and contrast, but do so consistently and sparingly: The more they are used, the less attention they will call to themselves. Because *italics* and underlining often have specific meaning, avoid using them except when required.

When choosing a font size, make sure it will be easy to read (especially if you are using it for the body of your project). Generally, a 10- or 12-point type will be legible to most readers, but print out a page of text to check the font size: 10-point type in one font may look larger than 12-point in another.

The font you choose can also add contrast, or it can group items through repetition: If most of your text is in a serif font, a sans serif font (or the same font in bold or a different color) can call attention to a heading.

Writing Responsibly

Selecting Fonts with Readers in Mind

Not all readers have perfect vision. If your audience includes members over forty (or under twelve), use a font size of at least 12 points to make the reading experience easier and more pleasant. If your audience includes visually impaired people, increase your font size even more.

to AUDIENCE

Writing Responsibly

Establishing a Consistent Font

When you copy material from a source, you have the responsibility of citing the source, indicating that it is a direct quotation, and providing full information about the source in a bibliography. When you cut and paste your direct copy from an electronic source, you also have the responsibility of converting its font to the one you are using for your main text. Otherwise, when the font suddenly shifts from black to blue, or from Times to Arial, the audience may be distracted from your message.

to OTHER WRITERS

NOTE For college writing, check the style guide for your discipline to determine the most appropriate font and style.

> **More about**
> Using information
> responsibly,
> 125–33

White space The portion of a page or screen with no text or images, the **white space,** does not literally have to be white (Figure 7.1). Margins provide white space, as does the extra space before a paragraph and around a heading. Extra white space can group elements into a section or lend emphasis through contrast. Ample white space makes a page inviting and easy to read; without it, a page looks crowded, and the eye has difficulty knowing where to focus.

> **More about**
> Page layout:
> MLA style, 188–200
> APA style, 227–38
> Chicago style,
>   255–62
> CSE style, 274–76

Lists Another strategy for grouping related items (and for adding white space) is to use lists. Keep lists succinct to allow readers to skim them for information. They can be particularly effective in web pages, as Figure 7.1 demonstrates.

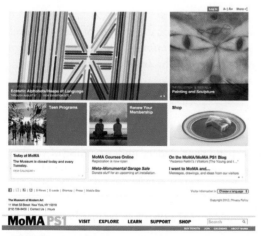

FIGURE 7.1 Formatting a web page The web pages from the museum (*left*) and the newspaper (*right*) use font size, style, color, and white space to highlight information and make the page attractive. A news page is by necessity crowded with information, so it also adds lists, boxes, and bullets to make the page easier to navigate.

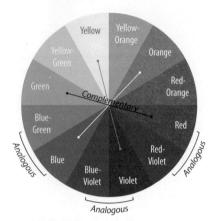

FIGURE 7.2 The color wheel Colors opposite each other on the color wheel are complementary; colors adjacent to each other are analogous.

Color Color, through contrast, calls the reader's attention to what is important in the text, but use color judiciously:

- Use a limited color palette to avoid a hodge-podge effect.

- Use analogous colors, those adjacent to each other on a color wheel (Figure 7.2), to create a softer, more harmonious look; use complementary colors, those opposite each other on the color wheel, to contrast with each other and make the other color look brighter.

- Make sure that color combinations are readable, that they contrast sufficiently with their background.

- Consider the associations colors and combinations of colors carry: pastel pinks and blues for new babies, bright yellow and black for warnings, green for nature.

- Repeat colors to group items of the same type.

Headings The principles of repetition and contrast are crucial with headings:

- Set all headings of the same level in the same font, style, and color, and align them in the same way on the page or screen:

  First-level heading

  Second-level heading

  Third-level heading

> **More about**
> Parallelism, 281–84

- Use the same grammatical structure for all headings of the same level. For example, use all *-ing* phrases (*Containing the Economic Downturn, Bailing Out Wall Street*) or all *noun* phrases (*Economic Downturn Ahead, Wall Street Bailout*).

7c Adding Visuals

> **More about**
> Visuals in academic writing, 69

To be effective, images must expand your readers' understanding of your text, and they must be appropriate to your writing situation. When including visuals, be sure to place them as soon as possible after the text discussion that refers to them. Make sure, too, that you choose the visual that is most appropriate to the information you are conveying. (See the Quick Reference box on the next page.)

Quick

Reference   **Matching Your Evidence to the Correct Type of Visual**

TABLE 7.1	PROJECTED ENROLLMENT IN DEGREE-GRANTING INSTITUTIONS, 2010–2014 (IN HUNDREDS OF THOUSANDS)				
	2010	**2011**	**2012**	**2013**	**2014**
Men, full time	53.22	53.41	53.55	53.83	54.20
Men, part time	29.30	29.46	29.64	29.76	29.82
Men, total	**82.52**	**82.88**	**83.19**	**83.59**	**84.02**
Women, full time	65.77	66.63	67.56	69.07	70.15
Women, part time	42.97	43.35	43.87	44.44	45.10
Women, total	**108.74**	**109.98**	**111.43**	**113.51**	**115.26**
Total enrollment	**191.26**	**192.86**	**194.62**	**197.10**	**199.28**

Tables. Use tables to display large amounts of data, data that include decimals, or data on multiple variables that are difficult to convey in a graph.

Source: US Department of Commerce, Census Bureau, Current Population Reports, "Social and Economic Characteristics of Students," various years.

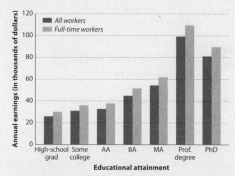

Bar graphs. Use bar graphs to compare two or more variables.

Pie charts. Use pie charts to convey significant divisions in a single entity that add up to 100 percent.

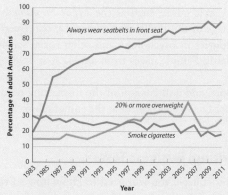

Line graphs. Use line graphs to show changes among variables over time.

Photographs and other images. Use photographs and other images, such as movie stills and screenshots, to provide an example or other reference point or to depict a process.

8 Designing in Context: Academic and Business Documents

If you were meeting friends for a casual dinner or to see a band, many outfits might be appropriate, but few would be right for the world of business, where your appearance can be a strike against you. Just as an outfit sends a message to a potential employer about whether you would be a good fit, the texts you write also represent you. To be successful, your words must be tailored to the context in which they are going to be read. Such tailoring allows readers to focus on the ideas, not on the appearance of your writing project.

8a Formatting (and Writing) Academic Texts

As with any other type of writing, writing in an academic context requires that you consider the expectations of your reader. Because your reader (usually, your instructor) will be focusing mainly on your content—your ideas and how you express them—keep formatting simple, and focus on presenting your text clearly, using a standard font (such as Times New Roman or Arial) in 10- or 12-point type and leaving 1- to 1.5-inch margins. Include identifying information on the first page or on a title page and in a header that appears on each page (in case pages get separated). Double-space the text to provide a comfortable reading experience.

More about
MLA format,
149–200 (tab 6)
APA format,
201–38 (tab 7)

In most academic areas, a style guide, such as the *MLA Handbook* for courses in literature and language or the *Publication Manual of the American Psychological Association* for courses in psychology and other social sciences, will provide formatting standards. Sample pages from an MLA-style project appear in Figure 8.1.

For a sample research report, and a discussion of the formatting requirements of APA style, see Heather DeGroot's project at the end of tab 7.

8b Formatting (and Writing) Business Texts

Regardless of what you do after college, you will need to know how to write business letters and e-mail messages, résumés, and letters of application. All these business communications share an emphasis on getting to the point quickly and conveying information clearly, directly, and concisely.

Student Models MLA-style Writing Project and Works Cited

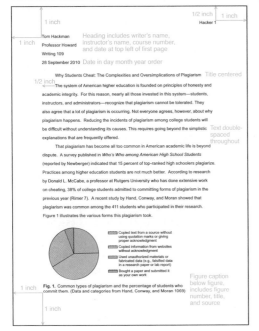

Tom Hackman — Heading includes writer's name,
Professor Howard — instructor's name, course number,
Writing 109 — and date at top left of first page

28 September 2010 — Date in day month year order

Why Students Cheat: The Complexities and Oversimplications of Plagiarism — Title centered

The system of American higher education is founded on principles of honesty and academic integrity. For this reason, nearly all those invested in this system—students, instructors, and administrators—recognize that plagiarism cannot be tolerated. They also agree that a lot of plagiarism is occurring. Not everyone agrees, however, about why plagiarism happens. Reducing the incidents of plagiarism among college students will be difficult without understanding its causes. This requires going beyond the simplistic explanations that are frequently offered. — Text double-spaced throughout

That plagiarism has become all too common in American academic life is beyond dispute. A survey published in *Who's Who among American High School Students* (reported by Newberger) indicated that 15 percent of top-ranked high schoolers plagiarize. Practices among higher education students are not much better. According to research by Donald L. McCabe, a professor at Rutgers University who has done extensive work on cheating, 38% of college students admitted to committing forms of plagiarism in the previous year (Rimer 7). A recent study by Hand, Conway, and Moran showed that plagiarism was common among the 411 students who participated in their research. Figure 1 illustrates the various forms this plagiarism took.

Copied text from a source without using quotation marks or giving proper acknowledgment

Copied information from websites without acknowledgment

Used unauthorized materials or fabricated data (e.g., falsified data in a research paper or lab report)

Bought a paper and submitted it as your own work

Fig. 1. Common types of plagiarism and the percentage of students who commit them. (Data and categories from Hand, Conway, and Moran 1069) — Figure caption below figure, includes figure number, title, and source

Works Cited — Heading centered, double-space between heading and first entry

Baty, Phil. "Plagiarist Student to Sue University." *Times Education Supplement [London]* 28 May 2004: n. pag. *TimesOnline.* Web. 15 Sept. 2010.

Birchard, Karen. "Canada's Simon Fraser U. Suspends 44 Students in Plagiarism Scandal." *Chronicle of Higher Education* 53.8 (2004): 46. EbscoHost. Web. 21 Sept. 2010. — List of works cited double-spaced

Hard, Stephen F., James M. Conway, and Antonia C. Moran. "Faculty and College Student Beliefs about the Frequency of Student Academic Misconduct." *Journal of Higher Education* 77.6 (2006): 1058–80. Print.

Howard, Rebecca Moore. "A Plagiarism Pentimento." *Journal of Teaching Writing* 11.3 (1993): 233–46. Print.

Hunt, Russell. "Four Reasons to Be Happy about Internet Plagiarism." *Teaching Perspectives* 5 (Dec. 2002): 1–5. St. Thomas University, Canada. Web. 15 Sept. 2010.

Jiang, Xueqin. "Chinese Academics Consider a 'Culture of Copying.'" *Chronicle of Higher Education,* 48.36 (2002): A45–46. EbscoHost. Web. 21 Sept. 2010.

Leland, John. "Beyond File Sharing: A Nation of Copiers." *New York Times* 14 Sept. 2003, sec. 9: 1. Lexis-Nexis. Web. 15 Sept. 2010.

Newberger, Eli H. "Why Do Students Cheat?" *School for Champions.* School for Champions, 6 Dec. 2003. Web. 16 Sept. 2010.

Rimer, Sara. "A Campus Fad That's Being Copied: Internet Plagiarism Seems on the Rise." *New York Times,* 3 Sept. 2003: 7. Lexis-Nexis. Web. 15 Sept. 2010.

FIGURE 8.1 The first page of an MLA-style writing project (*left*) and an MLA-style list of works cited

1. Business letters and e-mail messages

Readers of business letters (Figure 8.2, p. 58) and e-mail messages expect you to state your purpose in your first paragraph, keep your paragraphs short, and be clear and specific so that they can skim your communications and grasp the main points immediately. Adopt a positive and somewhat formal tone. (IM abbreviations such as IMO, for "In my opinion," are out of place in business communications.)

Business letters should include a date, a return address (unless you are using letterhead stationery), the address of the recipient (or *inside address*), and a formal salutation ("Dear Ms. Grayson:") and closing ("Sincerely," "Yours truly," "Best wishes,"). Include a formal salutation and closing only in the most formal e-mails. Business e-mail should include a Subject line that accurately summarizes the content of the message. Include in the To line only those recipients who need to take action on the message; include in the Cc (or "carbon copy") line anyone who must be kept informed but from whom you do not need a reply.

Both business letters and e-mail messages usually use ***block style,*** in which all text aligns with the left-hand margin. Instead of indenting paragraphs, an extra line of space is inserted between them.

> **More about**
> Abbreviating titles, 459–60

Student Model Business Letter

FIGURE 8.2 **Block-style business letter**

More about
Document design,
51–55

Creating Task-oriented E-mail In formal settings in the United States, e-mail messages are task oriented, and they frequently dispense with formalities and personal touches. In some cultures such messages would be considered rude, but US readers view them as efficient and timesaving.

2. Résumés and cover letters

A *résumé* (Figure 8.3) is a brief document that summarizes your work and educational experience for a prospective employer. A résumé is usually accompanied by an *application* or *cover letter* (Figure 8.4), which is essentially a sales letter—an opportunity to sell yourself to prospective employers. In drafting your résumé and cover letter, keep your audience and purpose in mind: What will your readers want to know? What will persuade them to put your application at the top of the pile?

Your résumé should indicate the position for which you are applying, a listing of the degrees you hold (college and above) and when you received them, and any honors or certifications you have attained. Especially for those new to the workforce, the résumé should focus on the skills you have acquired from any work experience. For example, you might explain that you "maintained good customer relations" and "presented a positive corporate image" in your job at a fast-food restaurant. Be sure to list your employers in reverse chronological order (most recent first). Include any specific skills (such as proficiency in Excel or Dreamweaver or fluency in another language), and include references or indicate that they are available on request. Limit your résumé to one page unless your work experience is extensive. Figure 8.3 shows the sections included in most résumés.

Writing
Responsibly | **Maintaining Confidentiality in E-mail**

You may have noticed the Bcc (or "blind carbon copy") option in the header of your e-mail messages. Any recipient you list in this line will receive a copy of your message but will not be identified to other recipients. Sending blind copies to keep the e-mail addresses of recipients private is ethical, but blind-copying a recipient to deceive your correspondent into believing a message is confidential is not. So your readers will not mistakenly believe they are the only recipient of a message, mention in the body of the message that it is being shared with others. If you wish to forward another's e-mail, first obtain permission.

to SELF

Student Models Résumé and Cover Letter

FIGURE 8.3 **Résumé**

FIGURE 8.4 **Cover letter**

Address your cover letter to a specific person, even if you have to phone the company to determine who that is. Start your letter by mentioning the specific job for which you are applying. In subsequent paragraphs, explain what qualifies you for the job, pointing out items on your résumé that are a good fit for this position but not just repeating the résumé. Conclude your letter by asking for an interview and providing information about how you can be reached. Throughout your résumé and cover letter, you need to walk a fine line: Do not be too modest about your accomplishments, but do not exaggerate your qualifications, either.

8c Creating Websites and Web Pages

Writing for the web generally means creating a *website,* a collection of files located at a single address, or URL, on the World Wide Web.

Every website begins with a *home page,* the page designed to introduce visitors to the site. The home page should include the website's title, the date the site was created or last updated, and links to a site map (or table of contents), contact information, and a copyright or Creative Commons notice. Most sites also have additional *web pages*—documents that, like the home page itself, may include text, audio and video, still images, and database files.

To make your website useful to others, plan the overall structure of the site carefully. Unlike print documents in which reading proceeds *linearly* (the

Reference Consider Your Writing Situation When Creating a Website

Purpose and Focus

Readers scan websites quickly, so keep your sentences brief and clear and your focus tight. Images, sound files, and design should reflect your purpose and capture readers' attention.

Context and Audience

Consider any restrictions of your host or site sponsor as you plan your site. Consider, too, the needs and expectations of your readers, but remember that unintended readers may also see what you post on the open web, so avoid language or content that you or others might find embarrassing or offensive.

Genre

If the information you are providing will remain current for a long time, create a website that you update once or twice a year; if your site requires daily or weekly updates, create a *blog;* if you want readers to participate in the creation of the site's content, create a *wiki.*

document is arranged so that all readers begin at page 1 and read through to the end) most websites are *hypertextual* (users may enter the site at any page and follow their own path through it). A site that includes a home page and a handful of web pages with loosely related content may work best with a hub-and-spoke structure, where each page links back to the home page (Figure 8.5). If your website will offer a series of pages with related content, a hierarchical arrangement, with links from the home page to lower-level pages and from page to page, may be more useful (Figure 8.6).

Since users frequently move from page to page in search of information, make navigation easy by providing links within a web page and *menus* at the top or side of the page. Include a link to the site's home page on every web page.

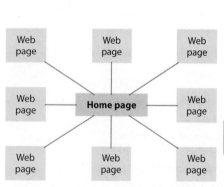

FIGURE 8.5 A hub-and-spoke structure

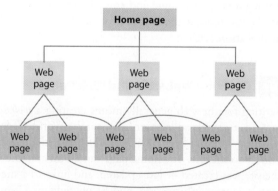

FIGURE 8.6 A hierarchical, treelike structure, with additional links

Writing Responsibly · Flaming

The quick interactivity and the anonymity of online media present a special challenge: keeping your temper. *Flaming*—writing a scathing response to someone with whom you disagree—is a great temptation, but it shuts down reasoned discussion, instead encouraging *ad hominem* (or personal) attack. Flaming may impart a sense of power for your having found a biting way to put down an opponent, but it also minimizes the likelihood of anyone's listening to or being influenced by you.

to OTHER WRITERS

> *More about*
> Ad hominem and
>   other logical fal-
>   lacies, 80–82

8d   Writing Responsibly in Interactive Media

With the rapid spread of broadband access, online communication has become an increasingly familiar part of our lives: Instant messaging and chat rooms, bulletin boards and discussion groups, and wikis and blogs are now common additions to the classroom, newsroom, and living room. The very familiarity of these media can lull writers into making errors that they later regret. In particular, be sure to think about your purpose and to tailor your writing style and tone to your intended audience, considering carefully how your readers might interpret your message *before* you send or post it.

When participating in online discussions, focus on responding directly to the comments of other participants and summarizing the discussion before moving on. Your online voice can be casual, but strive to keep your comments clear and to maintain a voice that is friendly and polite, even when you disagree.

When participating in a discussion in *asynchronous media* (media that do not require participants to sign on at the same time, like e-mail and blogs), reflect on and proofread your comments before posting them. In *synchronous media,* such as instant messaging and chat, reflection and careful proofreading are not possible, but synchronous discussions are useful for brainstorming and for developing a sense of community.

9 Designing a Multimedia Presentation

Hurricane Katrina
August 29, 2005

Photo: NOAA

Al Gore's presentation on global warming, captured in the documentary *An Inconvenient Truth,* has been seen by millions of viewers worldwide. Very few of us ever have an opportunity to reach such a large audience on a topic of global importance. Still, we are often called upon to present our ideas at school, at work, and in our communities. If we can present them clearly and compellingly, using multiple media when they will help us reach listeners, we, too, can effect change.

9a Identifying Your Writing Situation

More about
Purpose, 16,
22–24, 97
Audience, 17, 40,
97–98
Topic, 17, 19–24,
98–99
Context and genre,
18–19

As with any writing project, begin planning a presentation by considering your *purpose, audience, topic, context,* and *genre.* In an academic or business context, your primary *purpose* is likely to be the same as for a written text: to present information or to persuade others to accept your position or to take action. Even more so than a written text, an oral presentation is likely also to have a secondary purpose: to engage the imagination or emotions of the audience so that members can more readily identify with and remember the key points.

When addressing classmates or colleagues, you will probably have a sense of the needs and expectations of your *audience.* When addressing an unfamiliar group, ask yourself why the group has assembled and what topics they would be interested in. It may be useful to ask the event organizers about audience characteristics and interests.

The *context,* or setting, in which you deliver your presentation will affect the kinds of equipment you will need, the types of multimedia aids you create, and the relationship you can establish with your audience. When addressing a small group in a college classroom, for example, you will probably not need any special equipment, whereas in larger settings you may need a projector, a sound system, and special lighting.

Finally, consider the *genre* of your presentation. As a college student, you are most likely to be asked to contribute to or lead a class discussion, or to give a presentation online or in person to a class, student group, or social service organization. In business, you may be asked to train colleagues or make a sales pitch to potential customers.

Contributing to Class Discussion In US schools, active participation in class is an important part of the learning experience, and it often plays a role in instructors' grades. If you are uncomfortable with the idea of speaking in class, let your instructor know. If students in your class seem uncomfortable when they speak, remember that you are responsible for being an effective listener as well as a speaker. That means listening patiently and respectfully at all times.

9b Devising a Topic and Thesis

A presentation, like a written text, begins with an appropriate topic and a well-focused thesis. Your topic and approach should engage you and your audience and offer special insight. Craft a thesis that conveys your purpose and that will engage and guide your audience.

> **More about**
> Devising a topic,
> 19–22, 98–99
> Crafting a thesis,
> 22–24, 99

9c Organizing the Presentation

It is more difficult for people to understand and remember ideas they have heard than ideas they have read. Organize your talk to help your audience hold your main points in memory while the presentation unfolds.

1. Introduction

Use your introduction (10–15 percent of your presentation) to develop a rapport with your audience and to establish the key points of your presentation. Your introduction should specify your topic and approach, convey the topic's importance, engage your audience, establish your credentials, and provide a brief overview of your main points.

> **More about**
> Introductions,
> 35–36

2. Body

The body (75–85 percent of your presentation) should explain the points that you previewed in your introduction. For each claim you make, supply appropriate, relevant evidence, such as specific examples drawn from your reading or your experience. Facts and statistics can be very effective as long as you do not burden your audience with more numbers than it can process. Use transitions such as "first," "second," and "third" to guide your audience, and provide a brief summary of the main points you made earlier ("As I explained a few minutes ago . . .") and a preview of the points you are about to discuss ("Next I will show how . . ."). Presenting statistics in graphs or charts can also help.

> **More about**
> Organizing, 24–25,
> 40, 136
> Explaining and
> supporting
> ideas, 25, 31–35,
> 40, 91, 137–39
> Finding informa-
> tion, 103–114
> Transitions, 29–30
> Adding visuals,
> 54–55

3. Conclusion

Keep your conclusion brief (5–10 percent of your presentation). Use it to reinforce the main point of the presentation: Repeat the main idea and key points,

> **More about**
> Conclusions, 36–37

end with a brief but powerful statement, or return to the opening anecdote, example, or statistic.

9d   Rehearsing the Presentation

For an oral presentation, you may speak off-the-cuff or read a presentation aloud, but generally, speaking from notes will be most effective. The notes will keep you organized and prevent you from forgetting important points while allowing you to make eye contact with the audience.

1. Prepare a speaking outline.

> *More about*
> Topic outlines, 25,
> 136–37

When speaking from notes, create a speaking outline by jotting notes on a topic outline about where to pause, when to increase the urgency in your voice, and when to advance to the next slide or visual aid. Add content notes, too, but keep them brief, including only as much information as you need to remind yourself of the point you want to make.

2. Use language effectively.

> *More about*
> Abstract versus
> concrete lan-
> guage, 303–04
> Eliminating wordi-
> ness, 277–80
> Figures of speech,
> 304–05
> Parallelism, 281–84
> Repetition (inten-
> tional), 293

Well-chosen language can help listeners understand and remember your main points. When you can, use familiar, concrete words; support abstract words with concrete examples and vivid figures of speech such as metaphors and similes; keep your sentences concise; and use parallelism and repetition to emphasize your points.

3. Use visual, audio, and multimedia aids.

When using visual, audio, or multimedia aids during a presentation, make sure the aids are relevant, that you explain them clearly and succinctly, and that you do not provide so many that the audience pays attention to them rather than to you. Be sure, too, that you speak to your audience, not to your visual aids.

Quick | **Reference**   Overcoming Presentation Anxiety

If you get anxious before making a presentation, you are in good company. The following tips may help you get through your presentation with a minimum of nerves.

- Envision your success: Picture yourself calm and relaxed at the podium; imagine your sense of accomplishment at the end of the presentation.
- Take several slow, deep breaths, or tighten and relax your muscles just before you take the podium.

- Ignore your racing heart or clammy hands. Instead, use the adrenaline surge to add energy to your presentation.
- Focus on your message: Get excited about what you have to say, and you will bring the audience with you.
- Accept the fact that you may stumble, and be prepared to go on.

Assessment   Using Presentation Software Effectively

When preparing a presentation, reflect on your work. If you answer no to any of the following questions, revise as necessary.

☐ **Did you review your outline to determine where slides would enhance your presentation?** Do not overwhelm your presentation by creating a slide for every moment.

☐ **Did you begin with a title slide?** This slide should include the title of your presentation, your name, and any other useful identifying information.

☐ **Did you keep text brief, design uniform, and contents varied?** The audience should be listening to you, not reading your slides. To make slides easy to absorb, maintain a consistent design and keep text brief. To enhance interest, vary the other components (images, information graphics, video clips).

☐ **Did you add blank slides?** Go to a blank slide when no illustration is relevant.

☐ **Did you check that slides are visually pleasing?** Keep slides uncluttered and balanced; limit your use of animations (the way text or images enter a slide).

☐ **Did you proofread your slides?** Correct all misspellings and mistakes of grammar, punctuation, and mechanics.

☐ **Did you learn your software's commands?** Keystroke commands allow you to advance or return to slides, use the animation effects, and end the slide show.

☐ **Did you practice your presentation with your slides in advance?** Use animations to bring information forward, and do not leave slides up after you have moved on to the next topic.

☐ **Did you check your equipment in advance?** Make sure that cords are long enough, that you can lower the lights and cover windows, and so forth.

☐ **Did you practice giving your presentation without your slides?** Murphy's Law—whenever something *can* go wrong, it *will* go wrong—applies to presentation software. If the power fails or your computer dies, you should still be able to go on with the show.

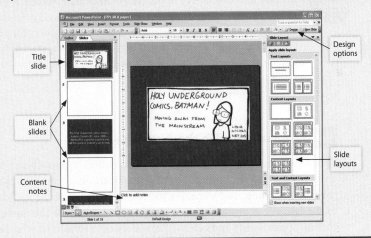

Presentation software such as Microsoft PowerPoint or Apple Keynote usefully projects visual, audio, and multimedia aids. However, overuse of presentation software or poor preparation of slides can cause "death by PowerPoint." (For advice on effective use of presentation software, see the Self-Assessment box above.)

More about
Visual design,
  51–55
Using visuals
  appropriately,
  54–55

Writing Responsibly

Remembering the Speaker's Responsibilities

In addition to your responsibilities as a writer, keep these additional responsibilities as a speaker in mind:

- Know your material and your purpose. For an informative speech, be sure your information is current and your examples pertinent. For a persuasive speech, adopt a position that you believe in, one for which you can offer compelling, concrete evidence.
- Acknowledge counterevidence and alternative interpretations. Do not alter quotations unfairly or misuse statistics. Avoid words and images that manipulate your audience or that rely on logical fallacies.
- Since readers will not have access to your written text, acknowledge sources with signal phrases such as "Alison Ling's research shows . . ." and be prepared to provide a list of works cited if requested.
- Respect the time and attention of your audience by practicing your presentation until you can deliver it with confidence and grace and without overreliance on notes.

to AUDIENCE

4. Rehearse.

More about
Logical fallacies,
80–81

Practice your presentation out loud in front of a mirror, a group of friends or family, or a video camera. Plan at least two or three practice sessions to become comfortable with the content of your presentation and to polish your delivery.

Adjusting Your Gestures to Appeal to a Multicultural Audience Gestures vary from culture to culture. As you prepare to give formal presentations, pay attention to the gestures commonly made by classmates or other peers who represent your prospective audience. How do they differ from gestures you are accustomed to? Are you aware of any gestures you should not use while speaking to a multicultural audience?

9e Connecting with the Audience

When the time comes to make your presentation, approach the podium and wait for your audience to settle down. Then introduce yourself, thank the audience for attending, and smile. As you speak, look out at the audience, turning to the left, the right, and the center, so all members of the audience feel included. Speak slowly and clearly. Pause between sections of your presentation, and vary the tone of your voice. If you sense that you are losing your audience, slow your pace, increase your volume, or step closer to the audience.

4

Genre
Matters
Writing in College

Use tab 4 to learn, practice, and master these writer's responsibilities:

❏ To Audience

Adjust your approach, your language, your citation style, and your use of visuals in response to the expectations of academic readers; reason logically, and appeal to the intellect and (when appropriate) the emotions of the audience.

❏ To Topic

Choose topics that are appropriate to your discipline, that are debatable when writing an argument, and that go beyond summary when analyzing literature.

❏ To Other Writers

Treat alternative viewpoints fairly and opponents with respect, and cite and document sources fully, using the style guide that is appropriate to the discipline in which you are writing.

❏ To Yourself

Establish your credibility, by adopting a reasonable tone, using sound logic, and treating opposing views fairly; take the time to think deeply about your topic and to write about it creatively and thoughtfully.

Genre
Matters

4

10 Writing in College: Comparing the Disciplines

Academic studies are classified into groups, or *disciplines*: communities of scholars who share a subject, approaches, and resources (types of evidence) for answering questions. The traditional disciplines are the humanities, the social sciences, and the natural sciences. Just as we eat from all four food groups (meat and beans, fruits and vegetables, dairy, grains) to maintain a balanced diet, so do many colleges require students to taste each of the disciplines to achieve a balanced education. Whether you focus on a single discipline or take a bite from them all, understanding the academic approach and tools of each discipline is crucial to college success.

10a Adopting an Academic Approach

The disciplines differ in what counts as good evidence. A biologist, for example, is likely to test claims by producing laboratory data, a sociologist might administer a survey, and a literature scholar might read a novel or poem closely. The disciplines also vary according to the types of sources they use, the ways they use language, the way they cite and document their sources, the way they use visuals, and the kinds of questions they ask on exams. One thing they all require, however, is that students adopt an analytical approach to the subject matter and that they fulfill their responsibilities by doing the following when writing:

> **More about**
> Analysis, 10–12, 34, 89, 133, 137

- Crafting a thesis that represents the writer's own insights or a synthesis of sources

- Presenting an unbiased assessment of evidence

- Depicting honestly any shortcomings in their research or alternatives to their claims

- Representing and citing ideas, information, and images accurately

Writing Responsibly Writing Responsibly across the Disciplines

Most disciplines not only have their own subjects and approaches, they also have specific ethical expectations for researchers and writers. As you learn the research methods of a discipline, take the time to locate its ethical code and learn what that discipline most values in its writing and research.

to TOPIC

10b Using the Sources of the Discipline

More about
Specialized reference works, 104
Scholarly versus popular sources, 116–17
Finding articles, 107–10
Primary versus secondary sources, 89, 112–14

Researchers may use discipline-specific reference works to begin their study of a topic, but they continue their research with *scholarly sources*—peer-reviewed journal articles and books by experts, often published by university presses. To find scholarly articles, use discipline-specific databases, such as the MLA International Bibliography (for literature) or PsycArticles (for psychology). A librarian can help you determine which databases are most appropriate for your discipline.

For researchers, the scholarly books and articles they use are *secondary sources.* These sources describe, evaluate, or interpret primary sources, and they *synthesize* information from primary and secondary sources. Academic researchers also rely on *primary sources.* In the humanities, those may be works of literature, art, or film, or they may be historical documents or speeches. In the natural sciences and social sciences, primary data come from observational studies, surveys, interviews, and laboratory or field experiments.

Academic Expectations in the United States Academic expectations vary from culture to culture. In some cultures, students are expected to memorize and report the information the instructor conveys in class. In the United States, most instructors also expect students to express their own ideas and to think critically about what they are learning. If you find this difficult, you are not alone. Most college students, regardless of their national origin or native language, find these expectations challenging.

10c Using the Language of the Discipline

Each time you enter an academic discipline, you enter a new language group. Courses may be taught in English, but the vocabulary is specialized. Consider, for example, the following passage from an article in a linguistics journal:

> My corpus data largely supports these arguments, although there are also early instances of YOU that do not occur in ambiguous contexts. . . . In accusative plus infinitive constructions with verbs such as *pray,* there is a great deal of variation in the choice of the pronoun form. . . . Variation between the two pronoun forms was quite prolonged in optative sentences . . . (58).
> —Helena Raumolin-Brunberg, "The Diffusion of Subject YOU: A Case Study in Historical Sociolinguistics," *Language Variation and Change*

More about
Specialized encyclopedias and dictionaries, 104, 308–09

Corpus data? Accusative constructions? Optative sentences? What does it all mean? To understand this paragraph, readers have to learn specialized vocabulary. Fortunately, most instructors (and textbook authors) explain specialized vocabulary as they introduce new words and concepts. If they do not, ask your instructor for an explanation or consult a specialized encyclopedia or dictionary. (Some may be available online through your college library.) Remember that every reader of articles like this—even your instructor—once had to master this vocabulary.

Not only must you learn a new vocabulary, but you must also learn the language group's expectations:

- Do writers use the past tense, the present tense, or a combination? In literature and the humanities, most writers use the present tense to discuss the work and the past or present tense to discuss actual events. In the natural sciences and social sciences, writers use the past tense to discuss the research they have conducted; they use the present tense to discuss their conclusions.

- Is it acceptable to write in the first person (*I*) or must you use the third person (*she, he, it*)? In most disciplines, writers tend to use the third person, unless they are emphasizing their own experience.

- Should you use the active voice, the passive voice, or a combination? In the humanities, writers tend to use the active voice (*Snyder uses symbolism and rhythm . . .*). In the natural sciences and social sciences, writers often use the passive voice to describe how research was conducted (*The participants were randomly assigned to one of three groups . . .*).

More about
Writing about
  literature, 87–96
First person versus
  third person,
  346–47
Active versus
  passive voice,
  279–80, 293–94,
  329

To learn the expectations of your new language communities, read assigned texts and listen to lectures, paying close attention to how language is used.

10d Citing and Documenting Information Borrowed from Sources

Every discipline expects writers to acknowledge borrowed ideas and information, and each discipline has its own style manual to guide this process. In literature and language, the most commonly used style guide is the *MLA Handbook for Writers of Research Papers*. Writers in the other humanities tend to use the *Chicago Manual of Style*. The most commonly used style guide in the social sciences is the *Publication Manual of the American Psychological Association*. In the natural sciences, writers tend to use *Scientific Style and Format: The CSE Manual for Authors, Editors, and Publishers*. Models for citing sources in the text and providing bibliographical information in the list of references or works cited appear in tabs 6, 7, and 8. Always use the latest edition of these texts.

More about
MLA style, 149–200
APA style, 201–38
Chicago style,
  239–62
CSE style, 263–76

10e Using Visuals in the Disciplines

When considering the use of visuals as supporting evidence for your project, think carefully about the needs of your subject and the expectations of your audience. Although writers in some academic disciplines (such as anthropology, biology, geology, and history) regularly use information graphics (tables, graphs) and other visuals (photographs and schematic drawings) to explain and support their ideas, others (such as those writing in English literature and philosophy) rarely do so, unless the subject of the project is visual (as when writing about a film or a work of art).

More about
Using visuals,
  54–55

10f Preparing for and Taking Examinations

Writing appropriately for the disciplines also requires flexibility in test-taking strategies as you move from a short-answer exam in your management class to an essay exam in anthropology.

Prepare for the Exam

The most successful preparations begin long before the exam as you stay on schedule with assigned readings, take notes and listen attentively in class, and work on assignments throughout the term. As you take notes, focus on the major points; do not try to write down every detail. Pay special attention to ideas in the text or lecture that strike you as crucial or interesting, and connect them to ideas you are learning in other classes.

> *More about*
> Reading critically, 7–15, 87–90
> Taking notes, 126–33
> Synthesis, 11–12, 137

Before the exam, identify essential terms, concepts, issues, and patterns that have arisen repeatedly. Then draft—and answer—possible questions based on them.

Quick

Reference   Common Verbs on Essay Exams

What is the question?

1. **Analyze** the architectural style of Frank Lloyd Wright.

2. **Compare and contrast** the major economic problems of the North and South during the Civil War.

3. **Define** the terms *denotation* and *connotation,* and discuss these terms in regard to the word *brother.*

4. **Describe** how bees build a hive.

5. **Evaluate** John F. Kennedy's performance as commander in chief during the Cuban missile crisis.

6. **Illustrate** the effects of global warming on mammals of the Arctic, including the walrus and the polar bear.

7. **List** and **explain** the four main causes of an economic recession.

8. **Summarize** Carl Rogers's humanist approach to psychology.

What am I supposed to do?

1. **Identify** the elements of his style, and then **critically examine** those elements and the style as a whole.

2. State the economic problems and explain how they were **similar and different** in the North and South.

3. Give the **main characteristics** of the terms. **Show that you understand** the definitions by applying them to *brother.*

4. Create, in words, a **step-by-step picture** of what bees do.

5. State **what you think** of Kennedy's performance, and give specific **reasons** and concrete **evidence** for your opinion(s).

6. Give specific **examples** of the effects on the animals named and at least one additional animal.

7. **Jot down** the causes and **tell clearly** how each results in a recession.

8. Give the **main points** of his approach, and keep your answer **concise.**

Approach the Exam Strategically

When you take the exam, look it over before beginning to write. Determine how many points are assigned to each question, and set a time limit for answering each part.

Next, analyze each question. Consider what it asks you to do: *Compare* is quite different from *define* or *summarize,* so pay close attention to verbs, and do what they tell you. (See the Quick Reference box on the previous page for analyses of sample essay questions.)

Then, write an outline and *thesis statement* that responds directly to the question. As you write your answer, incorporate evidence and connect it back to your thesis. Devote most of your time to supporting your thesis, but try to wrap up your answer with a concluding statement or paragraph.

Finally, check your work: Does your thesis answer all parts of the question precisely and fully? Did you support all of your major points sufficiently? Did you include any irrelevant material? Did you make any mistakes of grammar or spelling? Are any words illegible?

> **More about**
> Analysis, 10, 34, 89,
>   133, 137
> Comparison-
>   contrast, 32
> Definition, 34–35
> Summary, 7,
>   129–31
> Outlining, 24–25,
>   136–37
> Thesis statements,
>   22–24, 90–91,
>   134–35
> Proofreading,
>   43–44

Student Model **Effective Essay Exam Response**

The sample answer on page 72 responds directly to the exam question by comparing *The Big Lebowski* and *The Big Sleep* and by including the core concept "film noir" in the answer. Notice that this writer fulfills his responsibility to his reader (and to himself) by demonstrating that he understands the issues discussed in class and can synthesize information from films he has seen to support his claims.

Essay Exam Question

Identify and compare/contrast the films from which the stills below are taken. Be sure to include in your discussion at least one of the core concepts we have discussed in class, such as genre, dialogue, film noir, etc.

Thesis answers question

Thesis: Big Lebowski is new kind of film noir, main difference is kind of hero

Core concept discussed in class

Though The Big Lebowski is generally considered a parody of film noir detective stories such as The Big Sleep, it might also be categorized as a contemporary variation on the style. As the still photos show, the differences are obvious: gonzo comedy aside, Lebowski chiefly differs in the nature and quality of its hero. Instead of the occasionally superhuman wit and capability of Philip Marlowe, we have The Dude, called by the film's narrator "one of the laziest people on the planet Earth." However, though The Dude's ineptitude is largely played for laughs, much of the humor derives from discomfort and even dread; his insufficiency as a hero only heightens the sense of alienation.

Emphasizes contrast between heroes

Supports claims with details about heroes from these films

    At the beginning of The Big Sleep, Marlowe is made to sit in an orchid hothouse, where he proceeds to grow more physically uncomfortable with every passing moment, but he is able to speak his client's language, anticipate his interests and needs, and ultimately earn the general's quiet admiration. The Dude, in contrast, is so out of his depth that he seems incapable of scoring a single point against anyone he meets. When The Dude finds himself in a shadow-drenched room, the viewer may not feel an immediate sense of dread, but it does seem clear that the protagonist has little hope of prevailing. In a particularly revealing scene, The Dude's "client" taunts him with the failure of his generation's ideals, and our hero has no real answer.

Conclusion compares/ contrasts heroes

Returns to key concept and how these heroes display it

    These two scenes reveal the core of the typical noir hero: the individual who loses, over and over again, and who is compelled to absorb these defeats and continue on, often with a diminished sense of self. The hero responds by creating a persona to act as surrogate for this loss—one as the hard-boiled detective (Marlowe), and the other as the hyper-passive Dude.

11 Analyzing and Crafting Arguments

This advertisement uses text and a visual to argue that drinking and driving is wrong because of the harm drunk drivers can cause to others. Visually, the ad is powerful because the symbol, a broken heart, shows a human profile in red, suggesting the absence of a loved one. The white type on a stark black background adds drama and highlights the message. The placement of the advertisement is also persuasive: That it is on the back of a bus stop bench suggests an alternative to driving under the influence.

Arguments like this one are all around us—from television and Facebook, to editorials and blogs. As readers, we have a responsibility to think critically about whether such arguments are logical, provide evidence to support their claims, and are underlain by assumptions we share. As writers, we have a responsibility to explore issues with an open mind and to support our positions with sound reasoning and compelling evidence.

11a Persuading and Exploring

Arguments may be *persuasive* (claim based) or *exploratory* (inquiry based). In a persuasive (or thesis-driven) argument, the writer's purpose is to convince readers to agree with or at least to respect a position on a debatable issue (Figure 11.1). In an exploratory (or thesis-seeking) argument, the writer's purpose is to consider a wide range of evidence and eventually to arrive at the most plausible claim.

Academic writing is frequently exploratory in its early stages and becomes persuasive as the essay develops. Betsy Smith, whose first draft and revised draft appeared in tab 2, started by considering conflicts within the environmental movement (first draft) before deciding which position she held and revising her draft to reflect that conclusion (final draft). Moving from exploration to

Takeout can eat up your savings.

Pack your own lunch instead of going out. $6 saved a day x 5 days a week x 10 years x 6% interest = $19,592. That could be money in your pocket. Small changes today. Big bucks tomorrow. Go to feedthepig.org for free savings tips.

FIGURE 11.1 Arguing to persuade This advertisement argues that taking your lunch to work saves money over time; it first asserts this claim, then backs it up with evidence.

Student Models
"Alternative Energy:
"Does It Really Offer
an Alternative?" Betsy
Smith, 25–27 (first
draft), 44–47 (final
draft)

persuasion often yields a more thoughtful, considered argument than does beginning from a predetermined position.

 Exploratory versus Persuasive Approaches to Argument For personal or cultural reasons, you may be more comfortable seeking consensus than asserting an opinion. Seek help in formulating an argument, or if you want to take an exploratory approach, check with your instructor to be sure this is acceptable.

11b Making Claims

More about
Purpose, 16, 97

Most texts—speeches, websites, journal or magazine articles—have a main point or thesis that makes a claim. Informative (or expository) writing projects make claims of fact; persuasive and exploratory writing projects make claims of judgment or value.

1. A claim of fact can be verified.

Claims of fact are statements that are either true or false:

TRUE   Susan B. Anthony and Martha Carey Thomas worked for women's voting rights in the United States.

FALSE   Denmark became a constitutional monarchy in 1848.
        [No, Denmark became a constitutional monarchy in 1849.]

Because they are either true or false, claims of fact are not debatable. They cannot be the central claim in a persuasive or exploratory writing project. When writing or revising an argument, make sure you have taken a position on which reasonable people could disagree.

2. A claim of value is based on moral or religious beliefs.

More about
Warrants, 78

Claims of value are statements of fundamental moral or religious principles that individuals or groups hold to be inarguably true:

All people should be treated fairly under the law.

Stealing is unjustifiable.

People tend to defend firmly held beliefs with great passion, and claims of value, like the statements above, are frequently at the heart of arguments. However, since claims of value rest on shared assumptions, they can be difficult to support with objective evidence. As you craft your own argument or read the arguments of other writers, carefully assess the relationship between claims of value and the assumptions (or warrants) underlying them. Will readers who do not share your beliefs be persuaded to accept your claim?

Writing Responsibly   The Well-Tempered Tone

In public discourse, especially in public blogs, an insult or clever put-down is often used to trump an opponent. Sarcasm also thrives: Some bloggers take a sarcastic tone toward whatever they oppose. However, if you want your argument (and yourself) to be taken seriously—especially in academic and business circles—and if you want to persuade people who do not already agree with you, establishing a fair, even-tempered tone and avoiding sarcasm are crucial. Use logic and sound evidence, not snide comments, to make your point.

to SELF

> **More about**
> Ethos (credibility), 76

3. A claim of judgment reflects a reasoned opinion.

Claims of judgment are opinions based on available information:

> The healthiest diet is low in carbohydrates.

> The Adam Ezra Group is destined to have a number-one hit song.

Supplied with identical facts, not everyone will hold the same opinion, so claims of judgment are debatable. Because holders of an opinion regard it as the most plausible answer *for now,* based on an evaluation of the available facts, they can be persuaded to change their minds. When opinions are not provisional or temporary, they become *prejudices:*

> Women are too emotional to be president.

> Blondes are dumb.

11c Choosing Evidence Rhetorically

An argument will be only as persuasive as the evidence, or *grounds,* that support the claim. Support can appeal to your readers' intellect, it can draw on the authority of a figure they respect, or it can appeal to their emotions. Each of these is a *rhetorical appeal.* The ancient Greeks called these appeals *logos, ethos,* and *pathos.* Each has a place in responsible writing. As you develop your evidence, you have a responsibility, to your audience and yourself, to make rhetorical appeals that your audience will find appropriate and persuasive.

> **More about**
> Evaluating reliability, 116–23

Writing Responsibly   Preparing Oral Arguments

When you write formal arguments for college courses, rational appeals are usually more appropriate to your context and genre, but when you deliver a speech, presentation, or other form of oral argument, supplement logical appeals with vivid emotional appeals that your audience will remember. Be sure to support emotional appeals with logical evidence: After telling a moving story about an individual, use statistics to show how the issue affects others. Without logical evidence, an emotional appeal merely manipulates your audience.

to AUDIENCE

1979   2003

FIGURE 11.2 Shrinking area of Arctic permafrost, 1979–2003 These photographs make a logical appeal: They provide factual (verifiable) evidence for global warming.

1. Appeal to your readers' intellect (logos).

Logos refers to evidence that is rational and relevant; it appeals to readers by engaging their logical powers. Academic writing relies heavily on reasoned support and concrete evidence (facts, statistics, examples) for its persuasive power.

Visuals can also provide concrete evidence. This evidence may be displayed in a graph, chart, or map, or, as in Figure 11.2, in a before-after photo pair.

2. Appeal to your readers by establishing your credibility (ethos).

Establishing a credible *ethos*—good character, sound knowledge, or good reputation—encourages readers to have confidence in what you say. Maxine Paetro, for example, establishes her credentials before she expresses her judgments:

Background

Experience

> As the executive recruiter for several major ad agencies, I've eyeballed more than 40,000 cover letters. Some were winners. Some should have been deleted before ever seeing the light of print.
> —Maxine Paetro, "Mission: Employable," *Mademoiselle*

3. Appeal to your readers' emotions (pathos).

Using *pathos* to support a claim means stirring the audience's emotions in an effort to elicit sympathy and, thus, agreement. Pathos often relies on examples, stories, or anecdotes to persuade readers. It also uses a tone that stimulates readers' feelings. Visuals that appeal to the readers' emotions or beliefs

Writing Responsibly (Establishing Yourself as a Responsible Writer

As a writer, you can establish your ethos not only by offering your credentials, but also by providing readers with sound and sufficient evidence drawn from recognized authorities on the topic, thereby demonstrating your grasp of the material. By adopting a reasonable tone and treating alternative views fairly, you demonstrate that you are a sensible person. By editing your prose carefully, you establish your respect for your readers.

to SELF

FIGURE 11.3 Loss of sea ice poses a threat to the polar bear This photograph makes an emotional appeal—we fear for the safety and well-being of the polar bear—but it would be out of place without statistics that show, for example, a clear relationship between dropping polar bear populations and reduced ice coverage caused by global warming.

(Figure 11.3) make an emotional (or *pathetic*) appeal. Use pathos cautiously: Arguments that appeal solely to readers' emotions can be manipulative, even unethical, unless they are backed by strong logical evidence. In addition, many academic disciplines respect only logos and ethos as rhetorical appeals.

> *More about*
> Making a presentation, 62–66
> Tone, 17–18, 75, 296–97, 302–03

Logos and Ethos in the United States In academic and business writing in the United States, argument relies primarily on rational appeals. Mentioning highly revered traditional authorities or sources (such as important political figures or religious works) is not considered a sufficient form of support. Instead, evaluate the arguments and supporting evidence of these authorities, and include their work as support only if it directly contributes to your argument.

11d Considering Alternative Viewpoints

To consider an issue in all its complexity, you must consider alternative viewpoints. When writing an argument, consider *counterevidence:* the doubts you or other reasonable people might have or the objections that opponents might raise. Ask friends or colleagues to help you brainstorm alternative positions or search for alternative voices in printed and online sources. When assessing an argument, consider whether the writer has taken alternative viewpoints into consideration and how well the writer responds to critics' concerns.

> *More about*
> Finding information, 103–14

Responses to alternative viewpoints can take several approaches:

- They can provide counterevidence that refutes the opposition.

  To reject all hip-hop because gangsta rap espouses violence is unfair to performers like Kanye West and Lauren Hill, who offer a positive message to listeners.

  > Counterevidence

- They can acknowledge alternative views and explain why the writer's position is still the most reasonable *despite* this counterevidence.

  Clearly, some of the most popular hip-hop songs do revolve around violent or sexist themes. Still, it is important to remember that these themes draw attention to conditions in the communities out of which hip-hop developed.

  > Acknowledgment of alternative views

  > Support despite counterevidence

- They can make concessions, using qualifiers such as *some* or *usually.*

Qualifiers

The lyrics of some rap songs are violent, but most listeners are mature enough to realize that these are works of art, not strategies for living in society.
—Alea Wratten, SUNY-Geneseo, "Reflecting on Brent Staples Editorial 'How Hip Hop Music Lost Its Way and Betrayed Its Fans'"

11e Discovering Assumptions and Common Ground

To persuade an audience of the truth of a claim, the writer must persuade readers to accept certain common assumptions, or **warrants.** In 1963, when Martin Luther King, Jr., said, "The nations of Asia and Africa are moving with jet-like speed toward gaining political independence, but we still creep at horse-and-buggy pace toward gaining a cup of coffee at a lunch counter," he assumed that American progress should not lag behind that of Africa and Asia. Is this assumption fair? Your answer will likely depend on whether you share it. Dr. King knew that most people in his audience—US citizens—would. An African or Asian audience, on the other hand, might be less likely to share this assumption about American progress.

As you read and write arguments, consider carefully the assumptions that underlie the claims being made: On what common ground must both reader and writer stand before they can discuss a topic productively? What must both writer and audience agree is true without argument or evidence?

11f Organizing Arguments: Classical, Rogerian, and Toulmin Models

> **More about**
> Organization,
> 24–25, 136–37
> Purpose, 16,
> 22–24, 97
> Audience, 17, 40,
> 97–98

As with any writing, an argument is most effective when it is carefully organized. The following are three widely used models for organizing arguments. Each one serves certain purposes of argument.

1. The classical model

The *classical model* of argumentation derives from the work of ancient Greek and Roman orators. It is well suited to persuasive arguments and is composed of five parts, usually presented in this order:

1. **Introduction.** Acquaint readers with your topic, give them a sense of why it is important and why you are qualified to address it, suggest your paper's purpose, and state the essay's main claim (or thesis) in one or two sentences.
2. **Background.** Provide information to help your audience understand and appreciate your position. You might include a brief review of major sources or a chronology of relevant events.

3. **Evidence.** Offer logical, well-chosen examples and data to support your claims. Appeal to readers through their intellect and (if appropriate) through their emotions.
4. **Counterevidence.** Concede facts that undermine your position and refute counterevidence with which you disagree, but treat alternative viewpoints fairly and opponents with respect.
5. **Conclusion.** Leave readers with a strong sense of why they should agree with you by suggesting solutions, calling for action, or re-emphasizing the value of your position.

2. The Rogerian model

The *Rogerian model* builds common ground on complex issues, not to "win" an argument. It was developed by Carl Rogers, a twentieth-century psychologist, who hoped this method would make discussion more productive. The Rogerian model is composed of the same five parts as the classical model, but in a different order:

1. **Introduction**
2. **Background**
3. **Counterevidence**
4. **Evidence**
5. **Conclusion**

In a Rogerian argument, the counterevidence appears before the evidence because the presentation of counterevidence helps establish the complexity of the issue. Instead of refuting the counterevidence, the writer explores its legitimacy first and then explains why he or she nevertheless believes the thesis. Tom Hackman's essay at the end of this chapter follows the Rogerian model.

3. The Toulmin model

The *Toulmin model* for arguments, developed by philosopher Stephen Toulmin, includes five parts, but the parts are somewhat different from those of classical and Rogerian argument:

1. **Claim:** your thesis, the central argument
2. **Grounds:** the reasons you believe the claim and the evidence supporting your claim
3. **Warrants:** any assumptions that explain how the grounds support the claim
4. **Backing:** supporting evidence for the warrants, which require their own supporting evidence because they are themselves claims
5. **Rebuttal:** counterevidence and your response

Like classical argument, the Toulmin model is persuasive, and like classical argument it presents the main claim and evidence before counterevidence. One distinctive feature of Toulmin argument is that it places counterevidence

Writing
Responsibly | **Visual Claims and Visual Fallacies**

In academic writing, you might use a visual to *support* a claim, but you should be cautious about using a visual to *make* a claim. Visual claims are effective sales tools (they are common in advertisements), but they are likely to commit a visual fallacy, such as *hasty generalization*—drawing a conclusion based on too little evidence. (Is it reasonable to assume that *all* women using a certain brand of soap or shampoo will look like a movie star simply because one celebrity claims to use the product?)

to TOPIC

> **More about**
> Revising, 39–44
> Claims of value,
>   judgment, 23,
>   74–75
> Evidence, 25,
>   31–35, 39, 91
> Counterevidence,
>   77–78
> Persuading and
>   exploring, 73–74
> Ethos, 76, 82

last, and it also refutes the counterevidence, leaving less doubt that the main claim is the best perspective. It also recognizes that assumptions underlie all claims and brings those assumptions to the surface, making the search for common ground easier (or at least clarifying the terms of the discussion).

11g Avoiding Logical Fallacies

When assessing an argument or writing one, keep an eye out for logical *fallacies.* Because inductive arguments depend on examples and the conclusions you draw from them, fallacies like the following can creep in:

- **Hasty generalization (jumping to conclusions).** *Look at her, running that stop sign! She's a terrible driver!*

  A hasty generalization occurs when a general conclusion is based on insufficient evidence: Since even the best drivers occasionally make mistakes, this one piece of evidence is not enough to incriminate this driver.

- **Sweeping generalization.** *She's a typical woman driver—terrible!*

  A sweeping generalization applies a claim to *all* cases when it actually applies to only a few or maybe to none. Stereotypes are often based on sweeping generalizations.

- **False analogy.** *Bob's victories over his enemies during the war will ensure his victory over his political opponents in this election.*

  A false analogy draws a connection between two items or events that have few or no relevant common characteristics. This false analogy does not explain why previous military victories would guarantee a political victory. Is the political process really like a military campaign? Are opposition candidates really like enemy soldiers?

- **Bandwagon appeal.** *"Mom and Dad, I really need an iPhone. All my friends have one!"*

The bandwagon appeal implies that the majority opinion is the right opinion and invites you to climb aboard. Some bandwagon appeals may be based on poll results, lending them the impression of reliability. Poll results, however, merely report what the majority of respondents *believe* to be true. Many Americans in 1860 might have believed that holding other people in slavery was perfectly acceptable, which goes to show that the majority can be wrong.

The power of deductive arguments depends on the strength of your premises and the relationship between your premises and your conclusion, so watch out for arguments based on dubious, hidden, or missing premises or conclusions that do not follow from the premises:

- **Begging the question (circular reasoning).** *You must believe me because I never lie.*

  An argument that begs the question uses the conclusion (in a disguised form) as one of the premises in the argument. In this example, the second half of the sentence repeats the conclusion rather than offering a premise from which the conclusion can be derived.

- **Non sequitur (irrelevant argument).** *You can solve a lot of problems with money, so the rich must be much happier than we are.*

  A non sequitur (which means "it does not follow" in Latin) draws a conclusion from a premise that does not follow logically. The conclusion in the statement above equates money with happiness, but anyone with money will tell you that the two do not necessarily go hand in hand.

- ***Post hoc, ergo propter hoc* (false cause).** *This ring must be lucky: I wore it for the first time today, and I pitched a perfect game.*

  Post hoc, ergo propter hoc means "after this, therefore, because of this" in Latin. In a *post hoc* fallacy, the speaker wrongly assumes that the first event caused the second: Just because the player wore a ring while pitching a perfect game does not mean that the ring is "lucky."

- **Either-or fallacy (false dilemma).** *You're either for us or against us!*

  The either-or fallacy allows, misleadingly, for only two choices or sides in an argument, never acknowledging compromise or complexity (Figure 11.4, p. 82).

- **Ad hominem (personal attack).** *His views on the campus parking problem are ridiculous! What would you expect from a member of a frat that has its own parking lot?*

  An ad hominem (personal attack) attempts to undermine an opposing viewpoint by criticizing the motives or character of the individual holding the position, without connecting character flaws to the issues in question. (*Ad hominem* means "to the man" in Latin.)

FIGURE 11.4 Either-or fallacy in a visual This image suggests that there are only two ways to protect yourself. A third option might be to call the police. Source: http://bbvm.wordpress.com/2009/03/12/two-ways-to-shield-yourself-from-a-violent-attack-see-women-of-caliber/

As you revise your argument, consider the following issues. If your answer to any of these questions is no, revise as necessary.

☐ **Claim.** Do you take an arguable position based on an opinion or belief on which reasonable people could disagree? Have you modified the claim to avoid making it stronger than you can effectively support?

☐ **Evidence.** Do you supply evidence in support of your claim? Do you use rational appeals that are appropriate to your topic, purpose, and audience? Where appropriate, do you make emotional appeals that are supported by evidence and use visuals to support your claim?

☐ **Counterevidence.** Have you acknowledged alternative interpretations of your evidence? Have you explained why your position is the most reasonable despite these objections?

☐ **Organization.** Have you followed an appropriate model of argument, such as classical, Rogerian, or Toulmin? Is the organizational structure appropriate to your overall aim—persuasion or exploration?

☐ **Ethos.** Have you established your credibility by avoiding fallacies and providing evidence from reliable sources, treating those with whom you disagree respectfully, and revising, editing, and proofreading with care?

Student Model Exploratory Essay

In the following essay, Tom Hackman, a student at Syracuse University, argues that universities should take differences in motivation into consideration when devising their plagiarism policies. As you read, consider whether Hackman demonstrates responsibility by treating those who disagree with him fairly and by supplying enough evidence to be persuasive.

Tom Hackman

Professor Howard

Writing 109

28 September 2010

Why Students Cheat: The Complexities and Oversimplifications of Plagiarism

The system of American higher education is founded on principles of honesty and academic integrity, yet plagiarism on college campuses is common. According to research by Donald L. McCabe, a professor at Rutgers University who has done extensive work on cheating, 38% of college students admitted to committing forms of plagiarism in the previous year (Rimer). A recent study by Hard, Conway, and Moran corroborates McCabe's research. Their study showed that plagiarism was common among the 421 students who participated. Fig. 1 illustrates the various forms this plagiarism took.

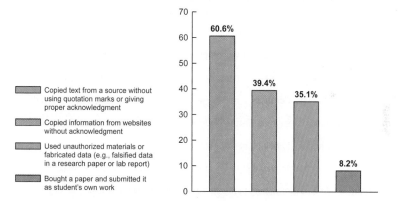

Introduction and background

Fig. 1. Common types of plagiarism and the percentage of students who commit them. (Data and categories from Hard, Conway, and Moran 1069)

One result of this plagiarism epidemic is "zero tolerance." A dean at Canada's Simon Fraser University voices a typical view: "We have a zero tolerance policy for cheating. . . . And we hope the severity of the penalties sends a strong message to other students who might be tempted to cheat or cut academic corners" (Birchard). A quick Google search shows penalties ranging from an F on the assignment (University of California–Berkeley) to expulsion (West Point).

But is this approach fair? The severity of such penalties seems to assume that students are knowingly appropriating the work of others and submitting it as their own. For students who inadvertently omit quotation marks or accidentally "patchwrite," these severe penalties seem out of proportion to the offense, and they don't discourage plagiarism among students who commit it by accident or out of ignorance. A better way to solve the problem of plagiarism among college students is for instructors and administrators to recognize that the word "plagiarism" is used for a whole variety of activities and to adjust the penalties to reflect the intention of the student.

> **Claim (thesis): Claim of value**

Of course, some students are guilty of intentional plagiarism. High-achieving students, for example, fear what a bad grade will do to their otherwise stellar GPA. Such students treat high grades as a necessity and will betray the very academic system they revere in order to sustain their average. Other students plagiarize more from lack of interest in a particular course than from general laziness. Students who view writing papers as hoops they must jump through to graduate, for example, are more likely simply to download a paper from an online "paper mill" than to write one themselves. For them, a college writing class is something to be endured, rather than an opportunity for learning. Russell Hunt, a professor at St. Thomas University in Canada, explains this attitude in point 2 of his article:

> **Counter-evidence**

> If I wanted to learn how to play the guitar, or improve my golf swing, or write HTML, "cheating" would be the last thing that would ever occur to me. It would be utterly irrelevant to the situation. On the other hand, if I wanted a certificate saying that I could pick a jig, play a round in under 80, or produce a slick webpage (and never actually expected to perform the activity in question), I might well consider cheating. . . .

Students draw a distinction between their interests and their academic assignments. They rationalize their plagiarism as a way to escape an "unfair" academic obligation. Websites such as essaytown.com, which will write a paper to order, cater to students like these, who consider at least some aspects of academia essentially useless.

However, many other instances of plagiarism are committed by students with honest intentions who are ignorant of citation methods. Michael Gunn, a British student, copied quotations from Internet sources in numerous papers over several years and was shocked to learn that this qualified as plagiarism (Baty). Even students who recognize the importance of citation may not know how to cite their sources correctly. A student who omits the source of a paraphrase in a paper would probably be surprised to learn that he or she is often considered as guilty of plagiarism as the student who downloads an entire essay.

Evidence

The Internet has made citation even more confusing. The Internet is a place of free exchange, where information moves from computer to computer with the click of a mouse. In this environment, ownership and citation become hazy. As John Leland, a reporter for the *New York Times,* writes, "Culture's heat now lies with the ability to cut, paste, clip, sample, quote, recycle, customize, and re-circulate." Many students find it "natural" to copy and paste text from an online source into a word processing document. Because it can be hard to keep track of everything they have read, the chances of accidental plagiarism (forgetting to cite the copied text) increase. So, too, does the likelihood of "patchwriting," inserting synonyms or moving sentences around, but not really putting the text into your own words (Howard 233).

To add to the complexity of the plagiarism issue, societal norms play a significant role in students' and even scholars' views about fair use of another's work. Unlike in the West, Chinese culture largely accepts appropriating others' ideas and holds that private property is less important than the needs of the people. Professors copy from other professors, and students follow their lead. The "culture of copying" is prevalent throughout Chinese academia (Jiang A45).

Conclusion

There is a common myth about how most plagiarism occurs. Late at night, a student sits staring at a computer screen. A paper is due the following morning, research needs to be done, notes need to be taken, and, in the end, an essay needs to be written and edited. Instead of completing this immense task, the student succumbs to the temptations of plagiarism—"cutting and pasting" from sources found on the Internet or simply buying a paper from a website. According to this myth, students are too apathetic and slothful to complete their assignments on their own; instead, they cheat.

Undeniably, some plagiarism occurs because students find it easier to copy than to do the work required. In many cases, however, students commit plagiarism by accident. A student who buys a paper from a paper mill has far different attitudes than a Chinese student who doesn't cite a source. The various categories of plagiarism also threaten academic integrity to varying degrees and, therefore, demand a flexible response tailored to each specific incident. Only through a combination of education and punishment will plagiarism, in all its forms, be reduced.

> Restatement of claim (thesis)

Works Cited

Baty, Phil. "Plagiarist Student Set to Sue University." *TimesOnline.* Times Higher Education Supplement [London], 28 May 2004. Web. 15 Sept. 2010.

Birchard, Karen. "Cheating Is Rampant at Canadian Colleges." *Chronicle of Higher Education* 53.8 (2006): 46. *EbscoHost.* Web. 15 Sept. 2010.

Hard, Stephen F., James M. Conway, and Antonia C. Moran. "Faculty and College Student Beliefs about the Frequency of Student Academic Misconduct." *Journal of Higher Education* 77.6 (2006): 1058–80. Print.

Howard, Rebecca Moore. "A Plagiarism Pentimento." *Journal of Teaching Writing* 11.3 (1993): 233–46. Print.

Hunt, Russell. "Four Reasons to Be Happy about Internet Plagiarism." *Teaching Perspectives.* St. Thomas University, Canada, Dec. 2002. Web. 15 Sept. 2010.

Jiang, Xueqin. "Chinese Academics Consider a 'Culture of Copying.'" *Chronicle of Higher Education* 48.36 (2002): A45–46. *EbscoHost.* Web. 21 Sept. 2010.

Leland, John. "Beyond File Sharing: A Nation of Copiers." *New York Times* 14 Sept. 2003, sec. 9: 1. *LexisNexis.* Web. 15 Sept. 2010.

Rimer, Sara. "A Campus Fad That's Being Copied: Internet Plagiarism Seems on the Rise." *New York Times* 3 Sept. 2003: 7. *LexisNexis.* Web. 15 Sept. 2010.

12 Writing about Literature

There is rarely one right way to interpret or appreciate literature. Instead, novels, poems, and plays offer readers multiple doors to understanding. At first glance, these doors may seem confusing, but they actually offer rewarding opportunities to explore the many ways of being human.

12a Reading and Analyzing Works of Literature (Novels, Poetry, Plays)

Whether focused solely on the text or on its social, historical, or cultural contexts, writing about literature is an act of interpretation. While those who study literature produce multiple meanings, each interpretation must be based on a careful analysis of the text and use evidence from the text to persuade others to accept the writer's position.

1. Read actively and reflectively.

Understanding works of literature is not merely a matter of extracting information, but it does begin with reading to gain a basic understanding of the text. Begin by writing a summary: What is the main point of the work? In literature, this is the ***theme.*** A summary will help you get to the heart of the matter, but keep in mind that literary analysis must do more than summarize what the text says.

> **More about**
> Summary, 7,
> 127–31
> Annotation, 7–10

Next, annotate or make notes about the work. Some of your notes may provide perspectives on the work that you can use later when writing. The notes in Figure 12.1, for example, show the beginnings of themes that Rita McMahan explores in her analysis of Gary Snyder's poem "Front Lines."

> **Student Model**
> "My View from the
> Sidelines," Rita
> McMahan, 94–96

Writing Responsibly / Reading with Study Guides

SparkNotes and similar study guides, long a staple of college bookstores and now available online, may tempt struggling students to substitute the guide for the text itself. Do not succumb! You not only deprive yourself of a learning experience, but you may also find that the study guide leaves you unprepared for the sophisticated level of understanding your instructor expects. If you are having difficulty making sense of a text, discuss the work with classmates, read essays about or reviews of the work at your college library, watch a reading or a performance of the work, or seek advice from your instructor.

to SELF

Finally, enjoy what you are reading. If you make an effort to appreciate the language, note insights, or make connections to something in your own experience, you will get more out of your reading.

Student Model Textual Analysis

Battlelines? Reminds me of a Buffalo Springfield song my parents used to play—"For What It's Worth"—from sort of the same period, I think— "Battlelines being drawn..."

FRONT LINES
Gary Snyder

The edge of the cancer   *A tumor, sickness, death...*
Yuck! Swells against the hill—we feel   *scary*
A foul breeze—
Sounds like "stinks" And it sinks back down.
The deer winter here
A chainsaw growls in the gorge.   *Animal noise*

Ten wet days and the log trucks stop,   *Not a real*
The trees breathe.   *breather*
Sunday the 4 wheel jeep of the
Realty Company brings in
Landseekers, lookers, they say   *Pornography?*
To the land,
Rape!? Prostitution? Spread your legs.

The jets crack sound overhead, it's OK here;   *Hard to read this line out loud*

Rhythm Every pulse of the rot at the heart
Heart disease? In the sick fat veins of Amerika   *Why with a "k"?*
Edge of what? The cancer? Pushes the edge up closer
Amerika?

A bulldozer grinding and slobbering   *Human sounds—gross!*
Sideslipping and belching on top of
Makes the bushes The skinned-up bodies of still live bushes   *Bushes = victims*
seem human In the pay of a man   *Bulldozer = mercenary*
From town.

Same rhythm Behind is a forest that goes to the Arctic
And a desert that still belongs to the Piute
And here we must draw
Our line.   *Relates to title?*

FIGURE 12.1 Notes from a close reading of the poem "Front Lines" by Gary Snyder

2. Analyze the text.

Understanding a work of literature involves analysis, dividing the work into its component parts to see how they work together. The Quick Reference box below lists some of the elements that a literary analysis should take into consideration. Usually you will need to study the text again (and again) to identify the elements from which it is constructed and to determine how these parts work together.

> *More about*
> Analysis, 10–12, 34,
> 133, 137

3. Adopt a critical framework.

In introductory classes in literature, students are often expected to take a *formalist approach,* looking closely at the work itself (the primary source) to understand how it functions. Other critical approaches are outlined in the Quick Reference box on the next page.

Before adopting a critical approach, consider the issues you have discussed in class or in other classes you are taking. A psychology class, for example, may provide a theory that will help you explain the behavior of a character; an economics class may help you understand the market forces affecting the plot; a women's studies class may provide methods of interpretation that will give you new perspectives on historical events.

Secondary sources—works about the author, period, text, or critical framework—may provide you with needed background about the primary

> *More about*
> Synthesis, 11–12,
> 133, 137
> Searching a library
> catalog, 110–11
> Searching a peri-
> odical database,
> 107–10

Quick **Reference**   **Elements of Literature**

When writing about a work of literature, consider the following elements and ask yourself these questions:

Genre. Into what broad category, or genre (fiction, poetry, drama), does the work fit? Into what narrower category (mystery, sci-fi; sonnet, ode; comedy, tragedy) does the work belong? What expectations are set up by the genre, and how does the work adhere to or violate these expectations?

Plot. What happens? Does the plot unfold chronologically (from start to finish), or does the text use flashbacks or flash-forwards? Does the plot proceed as expected, or is there a surprise?

Setting. Where and when does the action occur? Is the setting identifiable? If not, what hints does the text give about the where and when? Are time and place consistent, or do elements from other times or places intrude?

Character. Who is the *protagonist,* or main character? Who are the supporting characters? How believable are the characters? Do they represent types or individuals?

Point of view. Who is telling the story—one of the characters or a separate narrator? What point of

view does the narrator take—the first-person (*I*) or third-person (*she, he, it*)? Does the narrator have special insight into the characters or recount events as an outsider?

Language/style. What level of diction (formal, informal, colloquial, dialect) does the text use, and why? How are words put together? Does the text contain long, complex sentences or short, direct ones? Does the text contain figurative language (such as metaphor and simile), or is the writing more literal?

Theme. What is the main point? If you were to tell the story as a fable, what would its moral be?

Symbol. Do any of the characters, events, or objects represent something more than their literal meaning?

Irony. Is there a contrast between what is said and what is meant, between what the characters know and what the reader knows?

Allusion. Does the work contain references to literary and cultural classics or sacred texts?

Quick

Reference Critical Approaches

Biographical approach. Focus on the author's life to understand the work. Does the work reflect the trajectory of the author's own life or perhaps depict a working out in literature of something the author was unable to work out in reality?

Feminist approach. Focus on the power relations between men and women (or elements in the work that take on gender traits). Does the work reinforce traditional power relations or challenge them?

New historicist approach. Focus on the social-historical moment in which the work was created. How does the work reflect that historical moment?

Postcolonial approach. Focus on the power relations between colonizing and colonized peoples (or on elements in the work that reflect colonial power dynamics). Does the work reinforce or challenge those power relations?

Queer approach. Focus on the power relations between "normal" and "deviant." How differently can a text be read when the reader rejects this dichotomy?

Reader response approach. Focus not on the author's intentions or the text's meaning but on the experience of the individual reader. How does the individual reader construct meaning in the act of reading the work of literature?

source you are studying. Use secondary sources to develop and support, not substitute for, your own interpretation. To find secondary sources, search your library's catalog and specialized databases such as the MLA International Bibliography, the Book Review Digest, and Literature Criticism Online.

12b Devising a Literary Thesis

More about
Devising a thesis,
22–24, 99,
134–35

Narrow your focus to an idea you can develop fully in the assigned length. To devise a topic in literature, ask yourself questions about the elements of the work:

- What are the central conflicts among or within characters?
- What aspects of the plot puzzled or surprised you, and why?
- How might the setting (time and place) have influenced the behavior of the characters?
- Did the writer use language in a distinctive (or difficult or obscure) way, and why?
- What images recurred or were especially powerful, and why?
- What other works did you think about as you were reading this one, and why?

Then answer one of your questions. Your answer can be your *working thesis.*

As you draft your paper, you should analyze or interpret (not merely summarize) the text, as these contrasting examples demonstrate:

SUMMARY THESIS   In this poem, Snyder shows that development destroys nature.

INTERPRETIVE/
ANALYTICAL THESIS

In this poem, Snyder uses symbolism and rhythm to urge readers to see the conflict between "development" and ecological sustainability.

To support the first thesis, the writer could merely report the poem's main point. To support the second thesis, however, the writer must analyze the poem's symbolism and rhythm and then use that analysis to explain her interpretation of the poem's central conflict.

12c Supporting Your Claims with Reasons and Evidence from the Text

As with any writing project, you can use idea-generating techniques like brainstorming, freewriting, and clustering to figure out what your thesis is and why you believe it. Then turn back to the text: What details from the work illustrate or support your reasons? These are the *evidence* your readers will need. Although your paper may draw on secondary sources (works about the author, text, or period), your main source of supporting evidence is from your analysis of, interpretation of, or response to the novel, poem, or play itself.

> **More about**
> Idea-generating techniques, 19–22

Consider this passage from Rita McMahan's essay:

The title, "Front Lines," implies that a battle (or perhaps multiple battles) is occurring—wars are fought on the front lines. A first reading suggests a conflict over property on a hillside between two opponents, but a closer look reveals that the war is between the developers (and their technology) and the hillside, or Earth, itself. The juxtaposition of the deer and the chainsaw in the first stanza—"The deer winter here / A chainsaw growls in the gorge" (lines 5–6)—pits them on opposite sides of this battle, as does the placement of the log trucks and trees (7–8), the bulldozer and bushes (18–20).

> Topic sentence: States claim

> Evidence: Uses quotations and summary from the poem and explains their relevance

McMahan argues that Snyder uses the symbolism of war between the developers and nature, and she offers concrete evidence from the text—some quoted, some summarized—to support the claim. Note that McMahan does not merely drop the evidence from the poem into her essay but instead explains its relevance.

> **More about**
> Incorporating evidence, 25, 43–44, 137–39

12d Using the Appropriate Tense, Point of View, and Voice

Each discipline uses language distinctively. Some of the conventions for writing about literature are discussed below.

1. Use past and present tense correctly.

In literature, writers use the present tense when writing about the work being studied (the events, characters, and setting) or the ideas of other scholars,

> **More about**
> Tense, 362–66

and they use the present or past tense (as appropriate) when discussing actual events, such as the author's death or a historical or cultural event from the time that the work was published.

Present Tense

> Uses present tense to discuss the work studied

These witches and ghosts are real, and often present, for Haun's characters, and "witch doctors" have busy practices fending them off.

—Lisa Alther, "The Shadow Side of Appalachia:
Mildred Haun's Haunting Fiction"

Past Tense

> Uses past tense to discuss earlier events

Margaret Lindsey, defamed as a sorceress (incantatrix) by three men in 1435, successfully purged herself with the help of five women; her accusers were warned against making further slanders under pain of excommunication.

—Kathleen Kamerick, "Shaping Superstition in Late Medieval England"

2. Use first and third person correctly.

> **More about**
> Person, 346–47

In literary studies, the emphasis is on the work of literature, so writers use the third person whenever reasonable. Compare these two versions of a sentence from Rita McMahan's essay on the poem "Front Lines":

First Person	Third Person
When I first read the poem, I thought the conflict was over property on a hillside, . . . but a closer look revealed to me that the conflict was a war between the developers (and their technology) and the hillside, or Earth, itself.	A first reading suggests a conflict over property on a hillside, . . . but a closer look reveals that the war is between the developers (and their technology) and the hillside, or Earth, itself.

The version in the third person shifts the emphasis from the writer to the poem and is thus less personal and more persuasive. (Notice also that it shifts to the present tense.)

3. Use the active voice.

> **More about**
> Active versus passive voice, 279–80, 293–94, 329

In literature, writers typically use the active voice:

ACTIVE   Snyder employs another symbol to represent the nature of this conflict: cancer.

PASSIVE   Another symbol—cancer—is employed by Snyder to represent the nature of this conflict.

Use the passive voice only when the "who" is unknown or when you want to emphasize the action rather than the actor.

4. Use the author's full name at first mention and surname only thereafter.

In writing about literature, provide the author's complete name (*Gary Snyder*) the first time it is mentioned and thereafter use the surname (*Snyder*) only, unless this will cause confusion. (When writing about the Brontë sisters, for example, you may need to specify whether you are discussing Charlotte, Emily, or Anne.)

5. Include the work's title in your title.

When writing about a work of literature, provide the title of the work in the title and first paragraph of your project.

> *More about*
> Capitalizing titles,
> 455–56
> Quotation marks
> versus italics for
> titles, 438–39,
> 455–56, 456–57

12e Citing and Documenting Sources in MLA Style

Whenever you quote, paraphrase, summarize, or borrow ideas or information from a work, you must cite your source in the text and document it in your list of works cited. Writers in literature usually follow the *MLA Handbook for Writers of Research Papers*.

> *More about*
> Citing and docu-
> menting sources
> in MLA style,
> 149–200

Student Model Explication

The essay that begins on the next page was written by Rita McMahan, a student at Eastern Oregon State University. McMahan draws evidence from a close reading of the poem "Front Lines" (see Figure 12.1) to support her claim that poet Gary Snyder uses symbolism and rhythm to persuade readers to accept his view of development. To build her case, McMahan also draws on other primary sources, including a video showing Snyder reading his poetry and information gleaned from an e-mail interview with the poet. As you read, consider whether McMahan has fulfilled her responsibility to her audience by using the conventions of writing about literature appropriately.

Rita McMahan

Professor Meneelly

English 110

2 May 2012

My View from the Sidelines: Gary Snyder's "Front Lines"

Gary Snyder might be classified not only as a poet and free thinker but also as an agent for change—a visionary. One of the Beat generation writers of San Francisco, Snyder has worked as a logger, seaman, trail crew member, and firewatcher (Maxwell). His poetry can be seen as an intersection between his alternative cultural viewpoints and his experiences in nature. In fact, many of Snyder's works focus on maintaining Earth's ecological balance, and "Front Lines," in particular, expresses his passionate feelings on the subject. In this poem, Snyder uses symbolism and rhythm to urge readers to see development and ecological sustainability in a new light.

The title, "Front Lines," implies that a battle is occurring—wars are fought on the front lines. A first reading suggests a conflict over property on a hillside between two opponents, but a closer look reveals that the war is between the developers (and their technology) and the hillside, or Earth, itself. The juxtaposition of the deer and the chainsaw in the first stanza—"The deer winter here / A chainsaw growls in the gorge" (lines 5–6)—pits them on opposite sides of this battle, as does the placement of "log trucks" and "trees" (7–8) and "bulldozer" and "bushes" (18–20).

Snyder employs another symbol to represent the nature of this conflict: cancer. "The edge of the cancer" (1) creates fear in the reader, since cancer strikes without warning, spreading quickly and unpredictably. Likewise, Snyder implies that no one is safe from the ravages of unchecked, exploitive growth. Snyder's use of cancer to communicate the destruction of the environment raises what may be perceived as a benign issue—the protection of trees or deer habitat—to something more obviously dangerous, possibly fatal.

In addition to the cancer symbolism, Snyder conjures up the fearful image of rape: "To the land / Spread your legs" (12–13). This appears as a direct order, unlike any other line in the poem, and it is aggressive, not erotic. Because of its consequences to the victim, no restitution can ever be made; what is lost in the act is lost for all time. Similarly, the land can never be returned to its original state after its exploitation by developers. Like the battlefield and cancer, Snyder chooses rape as a symbol for the attack on the land, and as the images accumulate, a feeling of danger and damage overtakes the reader.

In addition to symbolism, Snyder employs rhythm to convey this sense of danger. In a 1989 video of Snyder reading his poetry and discussing his techniques with students (*Writers Uncensored*), the way he enunciated each word and gave certain phrases special emphasis made it obvious that he wanted us to notice the sound of each syllable. Snyder explains in the video that "Sometimes driven behind the origin is the rhythm. . . . Rhythm is in a very real sense, primary" (*Writers Uncensored*). Reading "Front Lines," one can infer that Snyder tries to make the reader *feel* the "pulse of the rot at the heart" (15–16) through the way the words themselves are chosen and arranged, with the stress on *pulse, rot,* and *heart.*

There is no single rhythmic pattern at work in the poem, but the second, fourth, and fifth stanzas all end in short, choppy lines, which themselves end in one-syllable words that draw the reader's attention. Furthermore, lines 21–22 ("In the pay of a man / From town") and 25–26 ("And here we must draw / Our line") have a marching cadence, a rhythm that reinforces the battlefield symbolism. Snyder's words and lines are short and easy to read, but their rhythmic impact makes the reader sit up and take notice that something important is being communicated.

Line 14 ("The jet crack sounds overhead, it's OK here") contains a similar choppy rhythm. In an e-mail, Snyder explained that he chose words to communicate exactness or precision. He said that the printed version of the poem is actually wrong—"jet" should be plural, and "sounds" should be singular, referring to the sound barrier. He explained that the line is meant to convey the sound of jets making sonic booms while going faster than the speed of sound. The rhythm of the line echoes the startling sounds of the sonic booms. As with Snyder's symbolism, his use of rhythm is not simply for decoration but helps reinforce and make vivid his activist message.

Throughout the poem, Snyder uses symbolism and rhythm to compel the reader to defend the natural world, rather than to "develop" or destroy it, and his use of these techniques generates strong feelings and associations—especially if you have the chance to hear him read his own work, when his words seem even more particular and expressive. The fight to protect the environment continues, as does Snyder's advocacy. At 79, he serves as a professor emeritus at the University of California–Davis, where he continues to influence a new generation of writers and motivate readers to meet the challenges of the modern world (Maxwell).

Marginal annotations:

- Topic sentence (begins second half of essay body)
- Integrates quotation as support
- Links Snyder's commentary to poem under discussion
- Topic sentence
- Uses information from e-mail interview with poet as support
- Topic sentence
- Conclusion: Thesis restated, importance of poem's theme reiterated
- Provides closure by circling back to poet

Works Cited

Maxwell, Glyn. "About Gary Snyder." *Modern American Poetry: An Online Journal and Multimedia Companion to the* Anthology of Modern American Poetry. Ed. Cary Nelson. Dept. of English, University of Illinois at Urbana-Champaign, 2002. Web. 15 Apr. 2010.

Snyder, Gary. "Front Lines." *No Nature: New and Selected Poems.* New York: Pantheon, 1992. 218. Print.

Snyder, Gary. E-mail interview. 15 Apr. 2010.

Writers Uncensored: Gary Snyder. Prod. Lewis MacAdams and John Dorr. Perf. Gary Snyder. Lannan Foundation, 1989. MPEG.

5 Research Matters

Finding, Evaluating, and Citing Sources

Use tab 5 to learn, practice, and master these writer's responsibilities:

❏ **To Audience**

Understand your assignment, draft a thesis that will focus readers' attention on your main point, contextualize sources so that readers understand why the evidence is relevant and reliable, and organize your project so that readers can follow your logic.

❏ **To Topic**

Answer research questions using relevant and reliable library resources, whether printed or digital; evaluate all sources carefully; use media sources when they are relevant and appropriate; and generate information through field research as needed.

❏ **To Other Writers**

Build a working bibliography to keep track of sources, avoid plagiarism and patchwriting by taking careful notes, and cite sources to show where source information begins and ends.

❏ **To Yourself**

Set a schedule that takes all your responsibilities into account; select a challenging topic that you want to learn about; analyze sources to enhance your understanding; support your own ideas with sources; and revise, edit, proofread, and format your project carefully.

5

Research
Matters

13 Planning a Research Project

To create this collage, the artist had to devise a plan, gather the right materials, and assemble them to create a unified whole. Yet it took more than just the right materials; it took an idea that would unify them and engage the viewer. Similarly, when you write a research project, you not only must devise a plan and gather supporting information, but you must also have a vision. Your goal should be to present the research in your text in a way that engages and even enlightens the reader. The first stage of the research process—planning—is crucial to the success of this endeavor.

Jan Cartwright, collage, *Self-Portrait*, 2001

13a Analyzing the Research Assignment and Setting a Schedule

Most research projects have one of two purposes:

- **To inform:** to explain an issue, compare proposed solutions, or review the research on a specific topic
- **To persuade:** to argue for a claim or to propose a solution to a problem

The purpose of Lydia Nichols's research project, which appears at the end of tab 6 (pp. 192–200), is persuasive; the purpose of Heather DeGroot's research project, which appears at the end of tab 7 (pp. 231–38), is informative.

Figure out the purpose of the assignment by looking closely at the words it uses:

If the assignment asks you to . . .	your purpose is likely to be . . .
describe, discuss, review	informative (expository)
assess, evaluate, argue	persuasive

> **More about**
> Purpose, 16, 22–24
> Argument, 73–86
> Methods of development, 31–35, 90
> Interpretation, analysis, synthesis, and critique, 10–12, 34, 89, 133, 137

Sometimes, college research assignments specify the method of development to use: comparison-contrast, cause-effect, and so on. One of the most frequently used methods of development is *analysis*—the writer divides the issue, proposal, or event into its component parts; explains how the parts work together; and discusses the implications.

As a writer, you have a responsibility to shape your project with the needs and expectations of your audience in mind, so consider who that audience will be. For most college assignments, your audience will include your instructor and perhaps your fellow students. Your instructor will want to see not only

97

Student Models
"Holy Underground
   Comics, Batman!"
   Lydia Nichols,
   192–200
"The Power of Ward-
   robe," Heather
   DeGroot, 231–38

that you understand the material covered in class, but also that you can interpret it, analyze it, and think creatively and critically about it. Fellow students may need you to define terms or provide background.

To set a realistic schedule, ask yourself not only when your research project is due and how extensive it is to be but also what other responsibilities you have to fulfill, such as other assignments you must complete, tests for which you must study, and family, work, and personal responsibilities you must meet. Then work back from your due date, filling in dates for the intermediate tasks. Crafting an effective research project usually includes these tasks:

- Devise and narrow a topic.
- Draft research questions and a thesis.
- Develop a working bibliography, reference list, or list of works cited.
- Conduct research.
- Evaluate potential sources and take notes on them.
- Develop an outline.
- Draft the project.
- Revise and edit your draft.
- Proofread and format your draft.

Remember that the writing process is *recursive*. This means that you may complete these tasks in a different order (by drafting, say, before you develop an outline) or that you may need to return to a step along the way. You may decide, for example, to revise your thesis, which may lead you to conduct additional research. Leave extra time in your schedule in case you need to return to an earlier stage in the process.

13b Choosing and Narrowing a Research Topic

When the choice is up to you, select a topic that will interest your readers as well as you, ideally one about which you already have some knowledge and insight. Idea-generating techniques such as freewriting and brainstorming can help you devise a topic that will be of interest to your readers, and they can help you narrow your topic so that you can write about it specifically and

Writing
Responsibly **Using Printed Sources**

With so much information available online, you might think that you no longer need to consult printed materials. However, many classic and scholarly books are not (yet) available digitally, and your library may not subscribe to the electronic versions of important newspapers, magazines, and scholarly journals. Dedicate yourself to finding the best information available, whether you access it through a search engine like Google or Bing, through an online database like Academic Search Complete or Web of Science, or through trips to your library's stacks.

to TOPIC

> **Tech**   **Using an Assignment Calculator**
>
> To set a realistic schedule, try using an online assignment calculator. Such tools divide the writing process into steps and suggest a date by which each step should be completed. Check your library's web- site to see whether a time management calculator is provided, or search for one by typing "assignment calculator" into the search box of a search engine such as Google or Bing.

insightfully. For college research projects, conducting preliminary research or reviewing assigned reading or class notes may be the most helpful in choosing and narrowing your topic. You might try putting your general topic into the search box of a library catalog or database to see what topics arise in the results that are returned. A search in the database PsycINFO on "peer influence" generated topics from smoking and group initiation to copycat crime among juvenile offenders.

13c Drafting the Thesis with Research Questions

Once you have chosen a topic and narrowed it to a subtopic that you can explore fully in the assigned length, ask yourself some intriguing questions that you can answer through research. Remember that the best questions will not lead you on a search for facts but rather on an exploration of complex issues for which there is no easy, obviously right answer. Notice that dull questions tend to be overly broad or overly narrow:

> *More about*
> Devising a thesis, 22–24, 90–91, 134–35
> Taking notes to avoid plagiarism, 124–33
> Patchwriting, 125, 127–31
> Annotating, 7–10, 87–88

DULL QUESTIONS	INTRIGUING QUESTIONS
What are the characteristics of superhero comics?	What makes underground comics so much more compelling than superhero comics?
How do teenagers influence one another?	Are men more likely to be influenced by a stereotypically "male" man than by an average or counterstereotypical man?

When you have crafted questions to research, write the answers you expect to find. These answers are the ***hypotheses*** that your research will test. As you conduct research, your questions and answers will change. The ***thesis*** for your research paper will probably come from your answer to one of these questions.

13d Choosing Research Sources

Your research project must reflect real research, instead of just creating the appearance of it. The sources you choose are key to fulfilling your responsibilities to your reader, your topic, and yourself. When choosing sources, ask yourself these questions:

- Have you visited your library and its academic databases (not just Google) to see what kinds of resources are available?

- Have you consulted, for background, general reference sources that provide basic facts about your topic?

- Have you consulted, for an authoritative overview, specialized reference sources that discuss the debates and issues about your topic?

- Have you found in-depth analyses and arguments written by experts on your topic?

- Have you located—after finding a journalist, blogger, or website discussing research findings—the research report itself, instead of settling for secondhand information?

- Have you chosen sources that are either up-to-date or are classics that established the principles for studying the topic you are researching?

- Have you consulted enough sources to develop a broad understanding of your topic?

- Have you consulted sources that offer a variety of perspectives on your topic, rather than just searching for sources that agree with your hypothesis?

- Have you consulted the best sources, even if they are not available online?

- Have you conducted experiments, observations, surveys, or interviews, when relevant, to develop information of your own?

You may need help to determine whether a source is up-to-date or reliable or to locate sources online or in your library's print collection. When you do, consult a research expert—a reference librarian.

13e Building and Annotating a Working Bibliography

Start your research by gathering potential sources and reviewing them to discover whether they are relevant and reliable. Then set up a *working bibliography* to record those that might be useful. Annotate each entry so that you can remember why you thought the source was worth examining.

Writing Responsibly Avoiding Accidental Plagiarism

The ease with which you can cut and paste material from sources into a digital file makes it easy to fall into unintentional plagiarism. If you are taking notes electronically, it is especially important to keep precise records about what you have copied from a source and what you have paraphrased, summarized, or commented on. Consider supplementing your electronic notes with a folder for printouts and photocopies so that you can double-check your draft against your sources.

to SELF

1. Components of a working bibliography

A working bibliography should include the information you will need for locating and documenting your sources:

To locate and document . . .	include in the working bibliography . . .
a printed book or an article or chapter in a printed book	the call number, the name of the author or editor, the title of the book, the title of the article or chapter (if relevant), the publisher, the place of publication, the date of publication, and the medium of publication (*Print*).
an e-book or an article or chapter in an e-book	all of the above minus the call number, plus the DOI (digital object identifier) or URL (uniform resource locator); include the e-book format (for example, *Kindle e-book, Nook e-book*) as the medium.
a printed article	the name of the author, the title of the article, the title of the journal, the volume and issue number of the journal, the year of publication, the page numbers of the article, and the medium of publication (in this case, *Print*).
an article accessed through a database	all of the above, plus the name of the database, the DOI or, if there is no DOI, the URL for the journal's home page, and the date you last accessed the file. If no page numbers are provided, include paragraph numbers or section name. (The medium will be *Web*.)
an article in an online journal	all of the above. (The medium will be *Web*.)
a web page, wiki entry, or entry in a blog or discussion list	the name of the author, the title of the web page or entry title, the title of the website or blog, the sponsor, and the publication date or the date you last accessed the file. (The medium will be *Web*.)

As you construct the entries in your working bibliography, follow the documentation style that you will use in your project. Writers in literature typically use MLA style (tab 6), writers in psychology and other social sciences typically use APA style (tab 7), writers in the humanities (except for literature) typically use *Chicago* style (tab 8), and writers in the sciences typically use CSE style (tab 8). (If you are not sure which documentation style to use, consult your instructor.) Using the appropriate style in the planning stage will save you time later, when you are formatting your finished project.

Saving a copy of an e-file or photocopying a printed document is prudent in case the source becomes unavailable later. Some instructors may also require

> *More about*
> Documenting books, foldouts following tabs 6 and 7, 164–73, 210–217, 240–46, 265–68
> Documenting articles in periodicals, foldouts following tabs 6 and 7, 173–77, 217–21, 247–51, 268–72
> Documenting websites and other sources, foldout following tabs 6 and 7, 177–86, 221–26, 251–55, 272–74
> Digital object identifier (DOI), 211, 218, 248

DOI (digital object identifier) A permanent tag that does not change over time or from database to database

Tech **Citation Management Software**

Citation management software—such as the proprietary EndNote and RefWorks and the open source Zotero—can format the entries in your bibliography no matter what documentation style you choose. Your library may make such software available to you for free. Use the documentation chapters in this handbook to test your program for accuracy; not every program performs to perfection, and you are the writer and the person responsible for providing your audience with error-free documentation that does not cause confusion.

Student Model
Research essay: "Holy Underground Comics, Batman!" Lydia Nichols, 192–200

you to submit copies of your sources with your final project. A PDF generally captures an article as it looked (or would have looked) in print, while an HTML copy provides the text, but not the formatting or illustrations. If both a PDF and an HTML file are available, select the PDF, which will enable you to cite the page numbers of the article and see any illustrations.

2. Annotate the working bibliography.

In addition to the information needed for documenting and locating a source, an *annotated bibliography* includes a brief summary or evaluation of the source. Below is a sample entry with annotation for an article from Lydia Nichols's research project.

authors   article title
Fenty, Sean, Trena Houp, and Laurie Taylor. "Webcomics: The Influence
                                                        journal title   no.   year
and Continuation of the Comix Revolution." *ImageTexT* 1.2 (2004):
paragraphs   access date   journal home page
22 pars. Web. 8 April 2012. <http://www.english.ufl.edu/imagetext>.
        medium

This article appeared in a peer-reviewed online journal. It provides a definition of underground comics and a good history of the movement. It compares print comics and web comics, concluding that online comics are more experimental than printed comics.

14 Finding Information

A simple Internet search can provide ready access to information—some excellent, much unreliable. It will not, however, help you strike a good balance among the types of sources you consult in your research. Searching on the web can easily become an issue of quantity, collecting "enough sources." The inexperienced researcher may tend to choose brief, quickly available online resources that are easy to read but that lead to a shallow paper that relies only on general facts or pieces that do not fit. Experienced researchers use advanced techniques that yield a good balance between general reference sources, specialized reference sources, popular opinion, and expert insight. And they go beyond the open web to find scholarly resources—the print, electronic, and multimedia gems.

> **More about**
> Relevance, 28,
>   115–16
> Reliability, 116–23
> Scholarly versus
>   popular sources,
>   68, 116–17

14a Finding Reference Works

Unless you are already an expert on your research topic, your search for sources should include both general and specialized reference works such as dictionaries, encyclopedias, biographical sources, bibliographies, almanacs, yearbooks, and atlases. General reference sources, written for newcomers to the topic, can do the following:

- Introduce you to your topic and help you determine whether it will sustain your interest
- Provide an overview and basic facts

Writing Responsibly / Using Wikipedia Responsibly

Wikipedia (www.wikipedia.org) is an online encyclopedia created and revised by users. Its ongoing updates make its entries more up-to-date than those in most other encyclopedias. Most Wikipedia updates, however, are done by a relatively small number of people whose average age is 27, which means most entries are not validated by experts—unlike a source such as the *Encyclopedia Brittanica*. Approach Wikipedia with care, and verify the information you find there. Wikipedia is not an authoritative source for most college-level research projects, and its use in your project could subject you to the sort of ridicule that a US presidential candidate encountered when she cited Wikipedia in a campaign ad.

> **More about**
> Reliability, 116–23

to TOPIC

More about
Searching the
   library catalog,
   110–11
Selecting a diction-
   ary, 308–09
Relevance, 28,
   115–16

Your search should also include specialized, subject-specific reference works written for researchers wanting in-depth understanding of the topic; these can:

- Introduce you to the issues and debates on your topic
- Help you get a sense of subtopics you might want to explore
- Provide lists of reliable sources on the topic
- Introduce and define special terminology, which will help you develop a list of keywords that you can use in further searching for sources

Specialized dictionaries such as the *Blackwell Dictionary of Political Science* or the *Dictionary of American History* can help you develop your list of keywords by introducing and defining the special terminology used in your discipline. Specialized encyclopedias such as the *McGraw-Hill Encyclopedia of Science and Technology* or the *Encyclopedia of Bioethics* can introduce you to the main issues in a debate. Bibliographies can provide a list of reliable sources on your topic, and they often include an abstract, or brief summary, that will help you determine whether a source is relevant to your project. If your library makes Reference Universe or Credo available, you can search across all the library's reference works, both online and in print.

> **Quick**
> ## Reference   General Reference Works
>
> *American National Biography*
> *CIA World Fact Book*
> *Concise Columbia Electronic Encyclopedia*
> *Dictionary of National Biography (British)*
> *New Encyclopedia Britannica*
> *Oxford English Dictionary*
> *Webster's Third New International Dictionary*
> *World Almanac and Book of Facts*

You will find reference works listed in your library's catalog. You may also be able to link to electronic reference sources through your library's home page or database portal.

14b   Finding Information on the Web

When most of us want to find out something, we turn to the web. To learn where a movie is playing nearby or when to move the clocks back to standard time, a simple Google search is appropriate. For college research, too, a web

> **Quick**
> ## Reference   Accessing Government Documents Online
>
> The websites for the following all provide access to government documents and databases online:
>
> Europa: europa.eu/index_en.htm
> FedStats: www.fedstats.gov
> Government Printing Office: www.gpo.gov/fdsys
> Library of Congress: www.loc.gov/index.html
>
> National Institutes of Health: www.nih.gov
> United Nations: www.un.gov
> US Census Bureau: www.census.gov
> US government: www.usa.gov

Writing Responsibly   **Going beyond Reference Sources**

Because both general and specialized reference works provide background information to orient you to your topic, they are an essential starting point in your research.
For a college-level research project, however, reference works are only the beginning; to fulfill your responsibilities to your topic and audience, you must go beyond
these sources to find books, articles, and websites that treat your topic in depth.

to TOPIC

search can be a good starting point. Often, however, when researchers limit
themselves to a keyword search on the web, they are deluged with more results
than they can thoughtfully consider. A Google search using the term *underground comics*—the topic of Lydia Nichols's paper at the end of tab 6—yielded
more than 2 million hits. Many of these results were unreliable, and most were
irrelevant.

There are ways to narrow search results to more relevant websites and web
pages. You can group terms using quotation marks or combine terms. A search
on *history "underground comics"* reduced the number of hits from almost
2 million to 30,600—still too many but a definite improvement. (See the
Quick Reference box on the next page to learn more about techniques for customizing a search.)

Using a search engine's *advanced search options* can limit results further by
pulling up only those sites that are in English, for example, or only those with
a specific domain (.edu, .gov, .org, .net, .com). Limiting the search *history "underground comics"* to sites with the domain *.edu* reduced the number of hits to
1,150 (Figure 14.1).

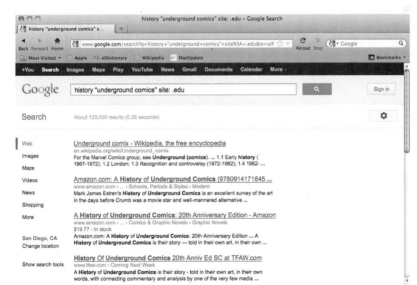

**FIGURE 14.1 Nar-
rowing a search by
combining terms
and limiting the do-
main to .edu** Limit-
ing the search to .edu
sites results in no
"sponsored" (adver-
tising) sites.

Reference   Customizing a Search

Most search engines and library databases use Boolean operators to narrow or expand a search.

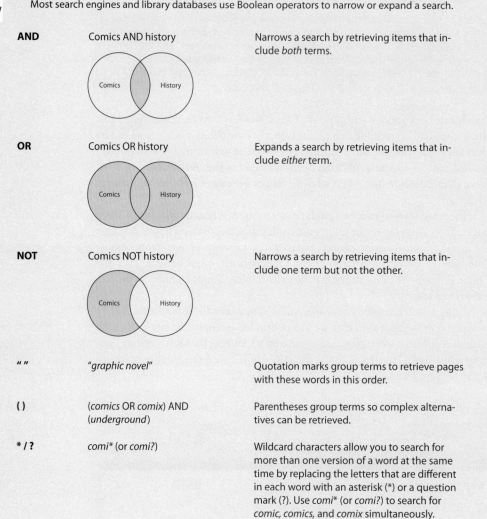

AND	Comics AND history	Narrows a search by retrieving items that include *both* terms.
OR	Comics OR history	Expands a search by retrieving items that include *either* term.
NOT	Comics NOT history	Narrows a search by retrieving items that include one term but not the other.
" "	*"graphic novel"*	Quotation marks group terms to retrieve pages with these words in this order.
( )	(*comics* OR *comix*) AND (*underground*)	Parentheses group terms so complex alternatives can be retrieved.
* / ?	*comi** (or *comi?*)	Wildcard characters allow you to search for more than one version of a word at the same time by replacing the letters that are different in each word with an asterisk (*) or a question mark (?). Use *comi** (or *comi?*) to search for *comic, comics,* and *comix* simultaneously.

14c Finding Reliable Interactive Media

In addition to conventional websites, a variety of other electronic sources, including blogs, discussion lists, and groups on social networking sites like Facebook, can be useful if you are researching a popular topic or if your topic is so up-to-the-minute that conventional scholarly sources are not available (Figure 14.2). To find a blog or discussion list on your topic, add the word *blog, listserv, newsgroup,* or *chat room* to your search term.

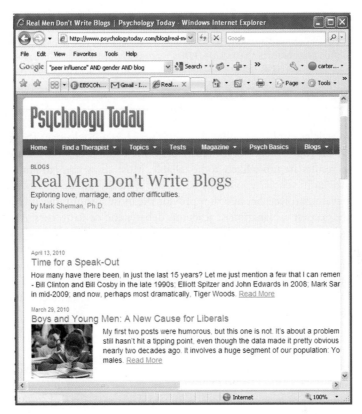

FIGURE 14.2 A blog on gender issues
A blog on gender issues might provide up-to-the-minute information for Heather DeGroot's topic: peer influence and social stereotyping among men.

News alerts and RSS feeds collect news stories on topics you specify. Registering for alerts at sites such as Google (www.google.com/alerts) will bring daily updates on your chosen topics to your e-mail box. To read RSS feeds you can use the integrated RSS reader in your web browser or download mobile applications such as Instapaper or Byline; then you can register at sites to have stories "clipped" and saved to your desktop or phone.

NOTE Not all blogs, discussion lists, groups, and even news sites are equally authoritative. Evaluate the reliability of such sites carefully, and verify the information you glean from such sources.

> **More about**
> Documenting a blog, 178 (MLA), 222 (APA), 252 (*Chicago*), 273 (CSE)
> Documenting a discussion list, 178 (MLA), 222 (APA), 252 (*Chicago*), 273 (CSE)
> Reliability, 116–23

14d Finding Articles in Journals and Other Periodicals Using Databases and Indexes

A *periodical* is a publication like a magazine, newspaper, or scholarly journal that is issued at regular intervals—daily, weekly, monthly, quarterly. Articles in periodicals are listed in *databases,* which index them by author, title, subject, and other categories. Search engines such as Google or Yahoo! can point you

Tech **HTML versus PDF**

Articles accessed through a database are often available in both HTML and PDF versions. The HTML (often called *full text*) version will download much more quickly, but the PDF (often called *full text PDF*) version may be a duplicate of the article as it appears in the publication, including illustrations and page numbers, which you can then include in your reference list or list of works cited.

to articles published online, but their search is not selective. The databases to which your college library subscribes limit a search to reputable publications, so results are more likely to be reliable. Most allow users to limit a search to articles in scholarly journals, which are typically the best sources for college research projects because they provide the most authoritative information and the deepest explanation of academic debates and controversies. Also, many articles you locate through Google will require a fee or subscription for access, whereas the databases available through your college library will typically provide access to articles for free, in either a PDF or HTML file. Databases also provide an *abstract,* or summary, of the articles indexed. (Such abstracts are useful for determining the relevance of articles, but remember that they are no substitute for the articles themselves.)

More about
Relevance, 28,
115–16

1. Choose a database.

More about
Writing situation,
16–19
Reliability, 116–23

Student Models
Research essays:
"The Power of Wardrobe," Heather
DeGroot, 231–38
"Holy Underground
Comics, Batman!"
Lydia Nichols,
192–200

Most college libraries provide a wide variety of databases, including an all-purpose database like ProQuest Central, Academic Search Complete, or Academic OneFile, which indexes both popular magazines and scholarly journals. Libraries also typically provide discipline-specific databases, such as Education FullText, PsycARTICLES, and Science Direct. They may also offer LexisNexis Academic, which indexes news reports from around the world. A reference librarian can help you learn which databases available at your library will best suit your research needs. For Heather DeGroot, writing on stereotyping and social influence for her psychology class, PsycARTICLES was a good starting place for her periodicals search. For Lydia Nichols, researching underground comics, a general database such as ProQuest Central or Academic Search Complete was a good place to start.

Writing Responsibly *Really* Reading *Real* Sources

As you choose your sources, it may seem efficient to select only those that are short and easy to read. Resist this temptation; fulfill your responsibility to your topic by pushing beyond easy, basic information. If you consulted only brief sources, you would be basing your research project only on basic facts and would produce a shallow, less thoughtful paper. Instead, when your source selection is finished, include substantial sources that treat complex questions in complex ways. Reading these sources will be a greater challenge, but the writing you produce from them will be richer and more successful.

to TOPIC

2. Search a database.

Searching a database is much like using a search engine such as Google or Yahoo! You type in a search term and hit Return to generate a list of articles that include your keywords. Unlike a search engine, however, the database uses a preset list of subject headings to index articles. If your keywords turn up few relevant articles, try a synonym (*comics* instead of *cartoons*) or ask a librarian for help.

To make sure the results are relevant, narrow your database search by combining search terms. (See the Quick Reference box on p. 106 for tips on customizing a search.) Typing *comics* in the search box of a database like Academic Search Complete generates a list of more than 17,000 items—fewer than with a Google search but still far too many to be helpful. Combining terms using Boolean operators (*comic books AND underground*) narrows the search. The search could be narrowed further by using the database's search options. The menu bars on the left and right in Figure 14.3 show some of the options for narrowing a search. If narrowing your search by combining terms and using the database's narrowing options is not producing useful results, try running your search on another database. Remember, too, that databases differ from vendor to vendor and are updated frequently, so checking the Help screens or asking a librarian for advice is a good idea.

> **More about**
> Relevance, 28, 115–16
> Customizing a search, 106

3. Find copies of articles.

Once you have generated a list of articles from your database search, you are ready to retrieve copies of the articles. Some articles you can access directly

FIGURE 14.3 Search results for *comics*

from the database search page. (The first two articles from the search screen in Figure 14.3—a PDF and an HTML file, respectively—are available online.) Not all articles are available electronically, however. To access articles, consult your library's website (or a librarian) for a list of journals your library subscribes to or can obtain through interlibrary loan.

14e Finding Books for In-Depth Information Using Your Library's Catalog

Books provide the most sustained and in-depth treatments of your topic, so they can be very useful sources, especially in the humanities and some social sciences, where up-to-the-minute information is not crucial. To find books on your topic, search your library's online catalog.

> **More about**
> Keyword searching, 104–06

Most library catalogs allow users to search for resources by author, title, and subject. Some also allow users to search by call number (Figure 14.4). Because catalogs differ from library to library, check the Help or Search Tips screen before beginning a search. If your library's catalog allows keyword searching, you may find it useful to conduct a "keyword anywhere" search, using your search terms. Most library catalogs include tables of contents for anthologies and edited books, so a keyword search may yield useful results.

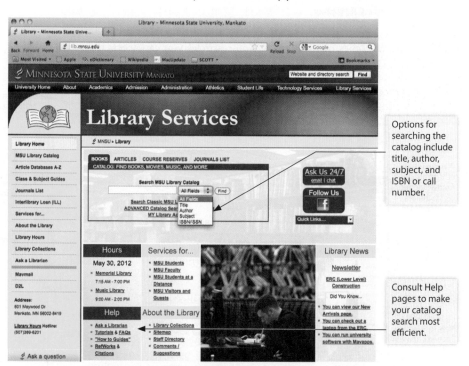

FIGURE 14.4 A library website Many students can now search their library's catalog directly from the library's home page.

2. Search a database.

Searching a database is much like using a search engine such as Google or Yahoo! You type in a search term and hit Return to generate a list of articles that include your keywords. Unlike a search engine, however, the database uses a preset list of subject headings to index articles. If your keywords turn up few relevant articles, try a synonym (*comics* instead of *cartoons*) or ask a librarian for help.

To make sure the results are relevant, narrow your database search by combining search terms. (See the Quick Reference box on p. 106 for tips on customizing a search.) Typing *comics* in the search box of a database like Academic Search Complete generates a list of more than 17,000 items—fewer than with a Google search but still far too many to be helpful. Combining terms using Boolean operators (*comic books AND underground*) narrows the search. The search could be narrowed further by using the database's search options. The menu bars on the left and right in Figure 14.3 show some of the options for narrowing a search. If narrowing your search by combining terms and using the database's narrowing options is not producing useful results, try running your search on another database. Remember, too, that databases differ from vendor to vendor and are updated frequently, so checking the Help screens or asking a librarian for advice is a good idea.

> **More about**
> Relevance, 28,
> 115–16
> Customizing a
> search, 106

3. Find copies of articles.

Once you have generated a list of articles from your database search, you are ready to retrieve copies of the articles. Some articles you can access directly

FIGURE 14.3 **Search results for** *comics*

from the database search page. (The first two articles from the search screen in Figure 14.3—a PDF and an HTML file, respectively—are available online.) Not all articles are available electronically, however. To access articles, consult your library's website (or a librarian) for a list of journals your library subscribes to or can obtain through interlibrary loan.

14e Finding Books for In-Depth Information Using Your Library's Catalog

Books provide the most sustained and in-depth treatments of your topic, so they can be very useful sources, especially in the humanities and some social sciences, where up-to-the-minute information is not crucial. To find books on your topic, search your library's online catalog.

> **More about**
> Keyword searching, 104–06

Most library catalogs allow users to search for resources by author, title, and subject. Some also allow users to search by call number (Figure 14.4). Because catalogs differ from library to library, check the Help or Search Tips screen before beginning a search. If your library's catalog allows keyword searching, you may find it useful to conduct a "keyword anywhere" search, using your search terms. Most library catalogs include tables of contents for anthologies and edited books, so a keyword search may yield useful results.

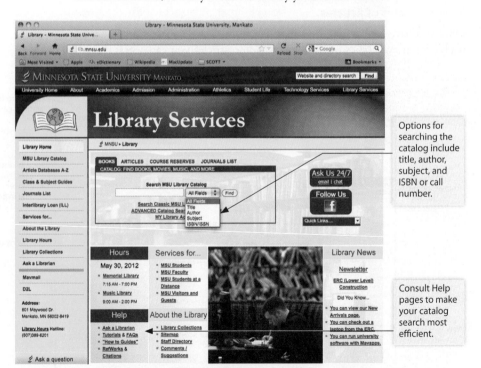

FIGURE 14.4 A library website Many students can now search their library's catalog directly from the library's home page.

FIGURE 14.5 Finding subject headings in a library record Subject headings are usually listed in the book's full record.

As with library databases, library catalogs use preset subject headings to index books. If your keywords turn up only a few relevant books, try a synonym (*comics* instead of *cartoons*) or ask a librarian for help. Once you have located a relevant book, check the subject headings you find in the full record of that book for keywords you can use in a fresh search (Figure 14.5).

Since books on a topic share the first part of a call number, they are shelved close together. If you are free to wander in your library's stacks, check for other books on your topic shelved close to those you have identified as relevant. If your library catalog allows it, search for other books on your subject by inserting the first part of a relevant book's call number in the catalog's search box. Or you might find sources on related topics by checking the results page in an online catalog search on your library's website.

14f Finding Government Information

Although you will usually rely on books and articles in your college research, government documents and datasets can provide you with rich resources, including congressional records, government reports, and legal documents. Local, state, and federal government agencies make thousands of publications available online, free of charge. To locate government documents and datasets, conduct an advanced web search limited to the domain .gov or search databases such as CQ Press Electronic Library and LexisNexis Congressional. Some useful sites for accessing government publications are listed in the Quick Reference box on page 104.

Quick Reference **Multimedia Resources**

Academy of American Poets
Archive.org
American Rhetoric: The Power of Oratory in the United States
Library of Congress
MIT Open Courseware
National Aeronautics and Space Administration (NASA)
National Park Service
New York Public Library
Perry Castañeda Library Map Collection, University of Texas
Smithsonian Institution

14g Finding Multimedia Sources

Besides the video clips you can find on YouTube or the pictures you find on Google Images, you may also find appropriate multimedia resources through your library's catalog or online at the sites hosted by the organizations listed in the Quick Reference box on this page. Use them when they are appropriate to your writing situation.

14h Conducting and Reporting Field Research

Field research is often part of a research project in which the writer begins by reviewing information from secondary sources (reports of others' research) and then adds to the body of information by conducting primary, firsthand research. The most common types of field research are interviews, observational studies, and surveys.

1. Interviews

Student Model
Literary analysis:
"My View from the Sidelines: Gary Snyder's 'Front Lines,'"
Rita McMahan, 93–96

Expertise and the knowledge that comes with experience can often be gained only through an interview. Media such as e-mail, text messaging, and even the telephone extend your range of possible interviewees. (Rita McMahan used e-mail to interview the poet Gary Snyder for her project on his poem "Front Lines.") However, face-to-face interviews give you an opportunity to read the other person's body language—facial expressions and bodily gestures—which can provide insight and direction for follow-up questions.

Interviews will be most useful if you do the following:

- Conduct background research on the topic and on the person whom you are interviewing.

- Develop a number of questions, more than you will probably have time to ask, and list them from most to least important.

- Ask questions that will prompt a thoughtful reply, and avoid simple yes-or-no questions.

- Ask your prepared questions, but also listen for surprises and ask follow-up questions.

- Listen carefully to answers and take good notes or, if permitted, record the interview.

- Reflect on your notes while the interview is still fresh. Jot down your thoughts and any additional questions you would like to ask; then phone or e-mail the interviewee *once* for follow-up. (Multiple follow-up calls are likely to annoy.)

- Send a thank-you note within a day of your interview, and send a copy of your finished project with a note of thanks.

2. Observational studies

Observational studies are common in the social sciences, particularly in psychology, sociology, and anthropology. Consider the following before beginning an observational study:

- **Your hypothesis.** What do you expect to learn? Use your tentative answer, or *hypothesis,* to guide your observations. Refine your hypothesis as your observations continue, but start out with a hypothesis to guide your observations and note taking.

- **Your role.** Will you participate in the group or observe from outside? The role you play will influence your perspective and affect your observations. Consider the steps you can take to minimize bias.

- **Your methods.** Establish categories for the observations you expect, and adjust them in response to your observations. Make notes immediately after a research session rather than during it, so your presence will be less obtrusive.

3. Surveys

Surveys are used frequently in politics and marketing, but they are useful in any type of research in which the beliefs, opinions, and behaviors of large groups are relevant. When developing a survey, ask yourself these questions:

Tech   **Online Surveys**

A variety of web-based survey tools allow you to conduct surveys online. The following are popular:

- Google Docs
- SurveyGizmo
- SurveyMonkey
- Zoomerang

Each allows users to create and send out a basic survey to a limited number of respondents for free. You might also consider conducting your survey with the help of social media such as Facebook or Twitter.

Researchers may also locate respondents using social networking sites, but be sure that the participants are representative of your target group.

Writing Responsibly

Reporting Results Fairly

As you integrate the results of your field research into your larger project, explain how you chose your research participants, how many you invited, and how many agreed to participate. Do not, however, name or indirectly identify your participants unless they have agreed to their identity being made public. When you quote from an interview or survey, indicate how typical the quotation is. Did you choose it just because it supports your thesis, or is it typical of the majority of responses?

to AUDIENCE

- **Your hypothesis.** What do you expect to learn?
- **Your participants.** What group will you reach and how will you contact them? Strive to include a broad and representative range of respondents.
- **Your questions.** What type of questions will you ask, how many questions will you include, and how will you administer the survey? Most questions should be true-false, yes-no, and multiple-choice because these are easier to tabulate, but a few open-ended questions may deepen your sense of the respondents' feelings. Because respondents are not likely to spend more than a few minutes answering questions, surveys should be brief; one to two pages is a reasonable limit.

Most surveys conducted for a college research project cannot meet the high standards of statistical accuracy, but if designed with care, they can provide tentative insights into local situations.

15 Evaluating Information

CLOTHING

"Do you have this in sheep?"

In Aesop's fable "The Wolf in Sheep's Clothing," the wolf uses a sheep's skin to lull his intended dinner into a false sense of security. Texts, too, can be a kind of wolf in sheep's clothing. They can appear to be wonderful resources, full of interesting facts and persuasive arguments, while hiding misinformation and faulty reasoning. For this reason, it is crucial that researchers dig below the surface to evaluate their sources carefully for relevance and reliability. Just as a wolf can hide under a sheep's clothing, a book should not be judged by its cover!

15a Evaluating the Relevance of Potential Sources

A source is *relevant* when it furthers your investigation not only by providing evidence to support your thesis but also by supplying useful background information or alternative perspectives on your topic. Start your search with your library's catalog or one of its periodical databases, rather than the open web. The books in your library's collection and the databases to which your library subscribes have been chosen selectively, which means your library search will yield a greater proportion of reputable publications than will a Google search.

To determine whether a source is likely to be relevant, examine its title and date of publication. The title usually indicates the topic and suggests the author's approach. The date of publication indicates how recent the source is. In general, recent sources are likely to be more relevant than older sources, especially in the sciences, but you should not discount older sources entirely. They can be helpful in disciplines such as history and philosophy, and they may be classics, sources that contain information or ideas on which researchers still rely. One sign of a classic is that it is cited frequently by other sources. Your instructor or a reference librarian can also help you identify them. Databases that list periodicals (scholarly journals, magazines, and newspapers) provide an *abstract,* or summary, which will give you an overview of the source. Figure 15.1 shows how to assess the likely relevance of a source using one of the periodicals databases provided by your library.

> **More about**
> Previewing the text, 7
> Using a library catalog to find books, 110–11
> Using a library database to find articles in periodicals, 107–10

NOTE Reading an abstract can help you determine whether a source is relevant, but it is not a substitute for reading the source itself.

If a source looks promising from a scan of its entry in the library catalog or database, retrieve the source and peruse the following:

- **Foreword or introduction and conclusion.** Usually, the first few paragraphs of an article and the foreword or first chapter of a book provide an overview of the source's topic and approach; the conclusion (the last few paragraphs of an article or the last chapter of a book), too, may summarize the main points in the source.

- **Headings and subheadings.** Headings and subheadings provide an outline of the source.

- **Figures and illustrations.** Figures and illustrations signal important ideas.

- **List of works cited.** A list of works cited or reference list may lead you to other relevant works; you can sometimes also judge relevance by assessing whether the source's references seem relevant and reliable.

- **Index.** Check the index for key terms in your research.

Ultimately, you will need to read the source to determine its relevance, but a careful scan will help you narrow your selection.

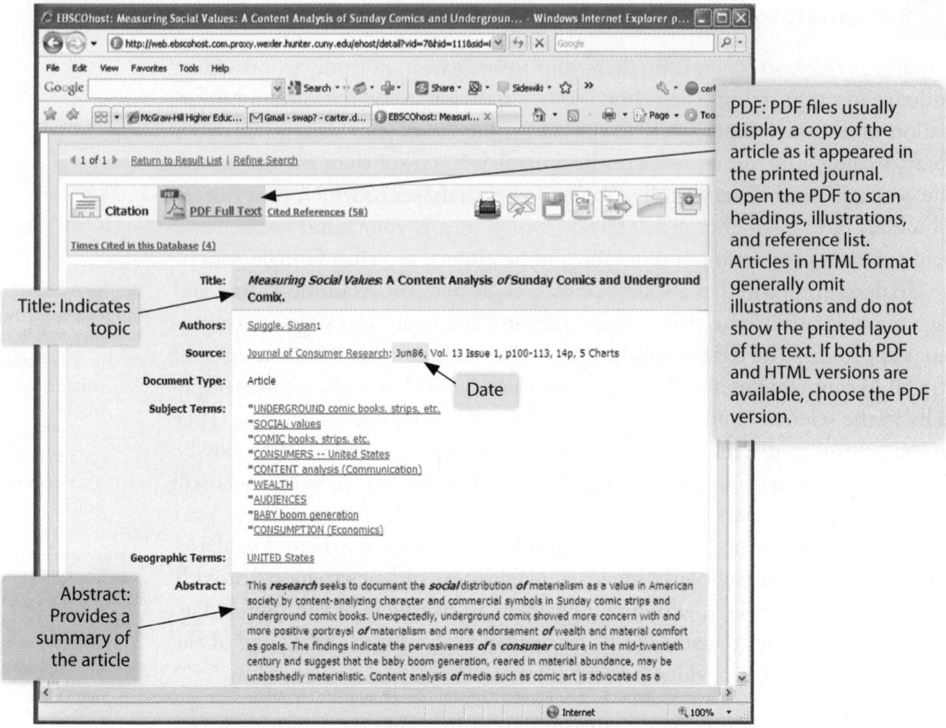

FIGURE 15.1 Assessing relevance You can determine the title and date of a publication from your database's search results screen, but you will need to click on the article's record (shown here) to read the abstract summarizing it. Note that this article's topic was pertinent, but because the article was published in June 1986, it may have been too old to be relevant to Lydia Nichols's project, which appears at the end of tab 6.

15b Evaluating the Reliability of Potential Sources

Judging reliability is not a simple, yes-or-no litmus test. Instead, it is a balancing act: You rate a source on a variety of criteria; the more criteria on which you can rate the source highly, the more reliable it is likely to be. Several criteria to consider follow.

1. Scholarly versus popular

Scholarly sources include articles published in academic journals and books published by scholarly presses (Figure 15.2). They typically include citations of their own sources and full bibliographic information for them. They are written by subject-matter experts, not for profit but as a contribution to knowledge, and reviewed by other subject-matter experts ("peer review") before being accepted for publication.

In contrast, articles in magazines and books published by the popular press are commercial; among other reasons, they were selected because an editor believed that an audience would be interested enough in the material to buy it.

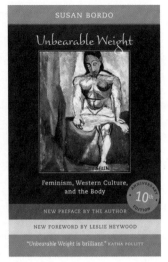

FIGURE 15.2 **Popular versus scholarly books** *The South Beach Diet* (Rodale) is a popular-press book aimed at a general audience: people wanting to lose weight. *Unbearable Weight: Feminism, Western Culture, and the Body* (University of California Press), on the other hand, is a scholarly book about our culture's obsession with women's weight; its target audience is scholars in fields such as women's studies and cultural studies.

Popular sources are often fact-checked, but they are not usually reviewed by experts. Popular sources tend to be easier to understand than scholarly sources because they avoid specialized terminology and high-level vocabulary but also because they often simplify complex controversies and debates. Of course, there are a range of popular sources. Well-respected magazines, like the *Atlantic* or the *New Yorker,* are more likely to be reliable than are supermarket tabloids, like the *National Enquirer.*

2. Expertise

Expertise is special knowledge, training, or experience in a specific field. Consider this: In a 2008 poll by the Yale Project on Climate Change, 66 percent of respondents said that their most trusted source of information about climate change was their television weather reporter. The poll respondents were confusing *weather* (short-term changes in the atmosphere) with *climate* (long-term changes). Weather reporters may be expert predictors of whether it will rain tomorrow, but they rarely have expertise in determining how the climate will change over the coming decades. When deciding whether your source was written by an expert, consider the author's background: Does the writer have a degree in an appropriate field? Do others consider the author an expert: Has he or she been cited in other reliable sources?

3. Objectivity

Objectivity means making observations or decisions uninfluenced by personal opinion or benefit. It has long been a goal of research, but it is often regarded as unachievable. Still, striving for objectivity is important, and authors who make an effort to treat all sides of an issue fairly are more likely to be reliable than those who do not make this effort. An author who characterizes groups unfairly or offensively, who makes sweeping generalizations, who ignores

Quick Reference | Distinguishing between Scholarly Journals and Popular Periodicals

Articles in scholarly journals ...	Articles in popular magazines ...
... are written by scholars, specialists, and researchers.	... are written by journalists or professional writers.
... use technical terminology.	... avoid technical terminology.
... tend to be long—typically, ten pages or more.	... tend to be brief—as little as one or two pages.
... include citations in the text and a list of references.	... do not include citations or a list of references.
... are reviewed by other scholars before publication.	... may be fact-checked but are not reviewed by experts.
... acknowledge any conflicts of interest (such as research support from a pharmaceutical company).	... are unlikely to acknowledge conflicts of interest.
... generally look serious; they are unlikely to include decorative color photographs, but they may include charts, graphs, and tables	... are often published on glossy paper with a lot of color and images.
... are published by professional organizations.	... are published by commercial companies.

counterevidence and competing claims, or who treats individuals comprising a group as if they are all the same is unlikely to be reliable.

Also consider whether the author has a ***vested interest*** in the topic. Most authors will benefit in some way, either through sales of the book or through the prestige of publishing. But reflect on whether the author or publisher will benefit in some other way: Is the author promoting a product or process from which she will benefit financially? Will the author or publisher gain adherents to a political position? Check the author's or publisher's website for advertisements and to see whether a mission statement reveals an agenda.

> **More about**
> Bias, 297–99
> Sweeping general-
> ization and other
> fallacies, 80–81
> Opinion versus
> belief, 74–75

To determine whether an author or a publisher has a vested interest in a topic, check the author's or publisher's website for advertisements or for a mission statement, and check the first page of research reports for conflict-of-interest disclosures.

4. Source citations

A bibliography, or list of works cited, can provide a way to gauge reliability. If the works cited are reputable, then the source is likely to be reliable. Most

Writing Responsibly   Keeping an Open Mind

As a researcher, you also have a responsibility to avoid bias: Read sources with an open mind, use reliable sources, avoid exaggerated claims and logical fallacies, and criticize unreasonable or poorly supported conclusions but not the people who hold them. Make sure to consider all sides of an argu-ment, especially those that challenge the positions you hold. Use difficult sources, too: Do not reject a source because it is written to a more expert audience than you. Find the time to study it carefully and gain at least a preliminary understanding of it.

to OTHER WRITERS

scholarly articles and books and some popular books include a bibliography, and some journal databases list the sources of the articles they index. Reputable magazines and newspapers check a writer's sources, though they often go unnamed, identified only as a "White House source" or a "source close to the investigation."

Also important is the number of times a source has been cited by other scholarly works. Google Scholar, Microsoft Academic Search, and some journal databases, such as Web of Knowledge, Scopus, and Academic Search Complete, indicate the number of times an article has been cited by other articles indexed by the database (Figure 15.3).

5. Access point

Sources accessed through your college library are more likely to be reliable than are sources located through a Google search because library sources are

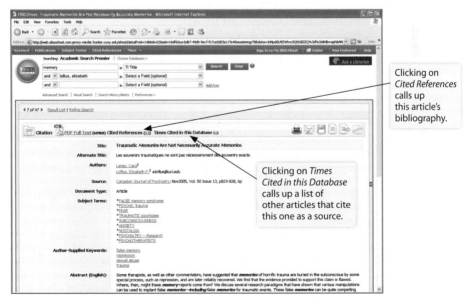

FIGURE 15.3 Determining reliability by assessing citations Both the number of times an article has been cited and the citations in the article itself are useful ways of determining an article's reliability.

selected in consultation with subject-matter experts, in response to reviews, or after considering where the source was published. A source accessed through the web is not likely to have been subjected to the same level of scrutiny. Google searches will return such sites, but library databases will not. Finding a source on a library database is not a guarantee of reliability, but it is one indicator.

6. Quality of editing

Sources are more likely to be reliable when the writer or publisher takes seriously the responsibility to write, organize, edit, and proofread carefully. A source filled with grammatical and spelling errors is likely to be unreliable.

15c Evaluating Online Texts: Websites, Blogs, Wikis, and Discussion Forums

Anyone can create a website, post a blog, or contribute to an open wiki or discussion forum. This freedom makes the web exciting, but it also means that sites may be biased, erroneous, deceptive, and even dangerous. For these reasons, researchers must evaluate online sources with special care. In addition to the general criteria listed above for evaluating sources, consider the following factors when evaluating websites.

1. URL

Every item on the web has a *URL* (universal resource locator, its web address), and all URLs end with an extension, or *domain,* that indicates the type of site it is. The most common domains are these:

- **.com** (commercial): sites hosted by businesses
- **.edu** (educational): sites sponsored by colleges and universities
- **.gov** (governmental): sites sponsored by some branch of government, federal, state, or local
- **.net** (network): typically sites sponsored by businesses selling Internet infrastructure services (such as Internet providers) but also sometimes chosen by businesses that want to appear technologically sophisticated or organizations that want to indicate that they are part of a network
- **.org** (organization): usually, sites sponsored by nonprofit groups (although sometimes the nonprofit status of these groups may be questionable)

Sites sponsored by educational, governmental, and nonprofit organizations are likely to be reliable, but your evaluation of a website should never end with its URL. Although businesses usually offer information intended to sell products or services, commercial sites can nevertheless be highly informative. A site ending in .edu may just as easily have been constructed and posted by a student as by an expert.

Writing Responsibly — Online Plagiarism

The ease with which users can cut and paste information from one site into another means you must be wary of online sites, especially if they are self-sponsored. Unreliable sites frequently copy directly from other, more reliable sites. If you suspect plagiarism, copy a passage and paste it into a search engine's search box. Do any of your hits use the same (or very similar) language? The best way to avoid using material plagiarized from another site is to evaluate sites carefully for reliability.

to SELF

2. Sponsor

As with any publication, the credentials of a website's creator are an important factor in assessing reliability, but websites frequently lack an identified author. Instead, they have *sponsors*—corporations, agencies, and organizations that are responsible for creating content and making it available. To determine who sponsors a site, jump to the home page, link to pages called "About" or "Contact us," or click on the website's logo. Often, deleting the portion of the URL following the domain (.com, .edu, .org) will take you to the home page. If the website yields little information, try conducting a web search on the site's name; you might even try including the word *scam* or *fraud* in that search. You can also go to the Whois site (www.whois.net) to search for information about your website.

3. Open versus moderated

The reliability of online discussion forums depends in large part on their contributors. Sources to which anyone can contribute should be screened carefully. Wikis and web forums in which prospective contributors are screened by the site's owner, or moderator, are more likely to be reliable.

> **Tech**   **Identifying Personal Websites**
>
> A URL that includes a personal name (jsmith) plus a tilde (~) or percent sign (%) or words like *users* or *members* is likely to be personal (not sponsored by a larger organization). Before using information from a personal site, investigate the author's credentials carefully.

4. Links

An additional step in assessing the reliability of a website is to determine the number and type of sites that link to it. From the Google search page, you can determine the number of times a site has been linked to, and you can then review the linked sites. Type "link:" plus the URL in the search box and click Search or hit Return. Popularity alone does not guarantee reliability—the site may just be fun to read or authored by a celebrity—but when coupled with other criteria, it can be an indication of reliability.

5. Last update

The most current sources tend to be the most relevant. To determine whether a website is current, check its copyright date or when it was last updated. This information usually appears at the bottom of the home page, but you may have to look around for it. Broken links may also indicate that a web page is outdated.

> **More about**
> Relevance, 28,
> 115–16

Writing **Responsibly**
Choosing and Unpacking Complex Sources

Make It Your Own! Research projects that rely heavily on short, simple sources tend to be simplistic and awkward. If you find, read, and write about lengthy, complex sources, you will produce superior scholarship.

Everyone wants to be efficient, yet college writers trying to save time may inadvertently do themselves and their audience a disservice when they write. While incorporating research into their papers, too many writers choose only short, simple sources that can be read quickly (see chart), and the quality of their papers suffers.

Researchers with the Citation Project were struck by the extent to which the quality of students' research projects was reduced by the shallowness of their sources. More than half of the papers' citations were to a source no longer than five pages, resulting in projects that were simplistic and unimpressive. They lacked the complex information and in-depth opinions that are essential to good research and interesting writing.

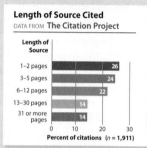

Length of Source Cited
DATA FROM **The Citation Project**

Researchers found that while most college research writers choose short, simple sources, the best writers work from lengthy, complex sources that bring details and insight—and not just basic facts—to the topic.

Writers relying on short sources work with too small a toolbox. Their papers will have very little to say if there is very little to draw on. Sources that are more extensive, in contrast, explore the interesting complexities and important debates about their topic. Such sources give writers—and the writers' audience—things to think about and talk about. They provide essential research material that leads to rich analysis and well-grounded argument.

Simply choosing lengthy sources is not enough, however. You should also "unpack" your sources—share with your audience the complexities and insights of your sources. Note how, in the following example, from an article on unnecessary medical procedures, complexity is lacking when the writer simply drops a quotation into his text and lets it speak for him:

First draft

Student's voice

Every time a person goes to the doctor, he or she should be aware of the risks of unnecessary medical testing. A doctor from San Francisco says, "[M]ost experts agree that overuse needs to be curbed. If it isn't, we could face a future public health problem of rising cancer rates, thanks to our medical overzealousness" (Parikh).

Quotation

Signal phrase

Parenthetical citation

The writer offers a quotation that supports his argument, and he has cited the quotation correctly. He has also provided some information about the writer of the source. However, because this quotation stands alone, readers of this student's paper may think that the source made this statement as a simple directive: *Overuse of CT scans should stop.* In fact, the source offered a detailed review of the reasons for the overuse of CT scans, as well as a thoughtful set of recommendations.

Such information deserves to be represented. It is part of your responsibility to your audience and topic to show the whole picture that the source offers. Consider how much more interesting, informative, and persuasive the passage becomes when it provides more information and context:

Revised draft

Student's voice	Every time a person goes to the doctor, he or she should be aware of the risks of un-
Signal phrase	necessary medical testing. San Francisco Bay Area pediatrician Rahul Parikh says that CT — **Summary that clarifies the argument of the source**
	scans are a dangerously overused test, putting children in particular risk for cancer due
Quotation	to the radiation levels in the procedure. "[M]ost experts agree that overuse needs to be
	curbed. If it isn't, we could face a future public health problem of rising cancer rates, thanks
Signal phrase	to our medical overzealousness," says Parikh. He notes, though, that the test is quick and — **Summary of the source's complex treatment of the topic**
	easy. Moreover, television medical shows give people a general awareness of tests like
	the CT scan, and thus patients may demand it even when it is not medically necessary.
	Doctors, too, have a reason for overusing the test: It is financially profitable. In addition to
	recommending that the test be administered less often, Parikh advocates adjusting the — **Signal phrase**
	radiation dose when the CT scan is administered to children.

Source: Parikh, Rahul. "How TV Illustrates a Disturbing Medical Trend." *Salon* 18 Apr. 2011: n. pag. Web. 18 Apr. 2011.

Notice that in the first draft, it sounds as if the doctor quoted is talking about all medical testing; the second draft shows that in fact Parikh was talking about a specific test, the CT scan. Choosing extensive sources, paying attention to the complexity of the material, and incorporating that complexity into your paper not only increases the sophistication of your own writing; it can also save you from misrepresenting the source.

Self Assessment

Review your work with each source, revising as necessary, to be sure you:

- ☐ Choose lengthy, detailed sources. Did you find material that provides insights and debates on the topic? ▶ *Finding information, 108*
- ☐ Discuss the complexities of your sources' treatment of their topic. Did you go beyond simple, basic facts? ▶ *Analyzing, interpreting, synthesizing, and critiquing, 137; "Understanding and Representing the Entire Source," 14–15*
- ☐ Explain any material you quote. Did you give background on every source? ▶ *Relevance and reliability, 115–20*

16 Using Information Responsibly: Taking Notes and Avoiding Plagiarism

Doris Kearns Goodwin

Plagiarism makes news. In 2002, historian Doris Kearns Goodwin was accused of plagiarizing portions of her book *The Fitzgeralds and the Kennedys*. She admitted that she had carelessly included some sentences word for word from her sources without putting those sentences in quotation marks. Her publisher was forced to make a financial settlement with the writer whose sentences she lifted, and Goodwin's credibility was severely undermined.[1] The next year, the British government "borrowed" information from Ibrahim al-Marashi's doctoral thesis to make its case for war against Iraq—without citing the author of the thesis. Exposure of the appropriation undermined the British government's credibility.[2] Then in 2007, Mounir Errami and Harold Garner (University of Texas Southwestern Medical Center) used text-matching software to test a portion of the abstracts in Medline, a database listing reports of medical research. They came up with some 420 potential duplicates, of which 73 were written by different authors, leading them to suspect widespread plagiarism. Errami and Garner conducted their research because they were concerned that the publication of plagiarized drug-safety studies gives practitioners a false assessment of the risk associated with the drugs tested.[3]

Ibrahim al-Marashi

Harold Garner

Plagiarism involves the presentation of another person's work—a paper or story, a photograph or graphic, a speech or song, a web page or e-mail message—without indicating that it came from a source. Buying a paper or "borrowing" a sentence (without citation and quotation marks) are both classified as plagiarism.

---

[1] Mark Lewis, "Doris Kearns Goodwin and the Credibility Gap," *Forbes* 27 Feb. 2002. Web. 30 Dec. 2012.

[2] Gaby Hinsliff, Martin Bright, Peter Beaumont, and Ed Vulliamy, "First Casualties in the Propaganda Firefight," *Guardianco.uk [Manchester, Eng.]* 9 Feb. 2003. Web. 14 Dec. 2012; "The Plagiarism Plague," *BBC News Online.* BBC, 7 Feb. 2003. Web. 17 Dec. 2012.

[3] Mounir Errami and Harold Garner, "Commentary: A Tale of Two Citations," *Nature* 451.7177 (2008): 397–99. *Academic Search Premier.* Web. 30 Dec. 2012.

Sometimes plagiarism may be inadvertent—Kearns Goodwin, for example, claimed that she had copied passages word for word into her notes and then forgot that these passages were not her own.[4] Whether intentional or not, such borrowings are still considered unacceptable.

Student plagiarism may not be reported in the *New York Times,* but to many instructors it is even more objectionable than the cases discussed here, because when students are given a writing assignment, they are expected to learn something about the topic and about writing itself, and plagiarism prevents this learning.

Also be alert to the possibility of *patchwriting,* copying and only partially changing the language of a source. The National Council of Writing Program Administrators defines patchwriting as a misuse of sources. Sometimes, though, instructors and college policies categorize it as plagiarism. In either case, patchwriting is not good writing. It often results not from an intention to present another's words and ideas as one's own but, rather, from inaccurate note taking, misunderstanding the source, incorrect use of or omission of quotation marks, or incomplete paraphrasing.

> **More about**
> Patchwriting,
> 127–30

Inform yourself in detail about what your instructor and your college (or your employer) define as ethical writing; although everyone rejects plagiarism, the definition of what constitutes plagiarism can vary subtly from one discipline or profession to another. Still, as you follow the guidelines for writing described in this chapter (and throughout this book), you can be confident that the work you produce represents its sources responsibly.

> **citation** The acknowledgment of sources in the body of a research project **documentation** Information in a footnote, bibliography, reference list, or list of works cited that allows readers to locate the source cited in the text

Plagiarism and Culture Attitudes toward and definitions of plagiarism vary from one culture to another. Some individualist cultures, like that of the United States, see words and ideas as personal property that can be "stolen" by plagiarists. Some collectivist cultures view information as a shared good. Whether your home culture tends to be individualist or collectivist, when writing for a US academic audience, be especially careful to mark borrowed language as quotation, to provide a citation whenever you borrow language or ideas, and to document sources fully.

> **More about**
> Using quotation marks, 436–43
> Block indention for long quotations, 153, 190 (MLA), 227 (APA)
> Citing sources, 149–64 (MLA), 201–10 (APA), 239–55 (*Chicago*), 263–64 (CSE)
> Documenting sources, 164–86 (MLA), 201–26 (APA), 239–55 (*Chicago*), 265–74 (CSE)
> Using signal phrases, 141–42, 149–50, 202

16a Learning What You Do and Do Not Have to Acknowledge

The Earth is approximately 93 million miles from the sun on average; US women won the right to vote on August 26, 1920; the Beatles' song "I Want to Hold Your Hand" was that band's first number-one hit in the United States. Information like this—incontestable facts available in three or more

---

4 David Kirkpatrick, "Historian Says Borrowing Was Wider Than Known," *New York Times.* New York Times, 23 Feb. 2002. Web. 30 Dec. 2012.

Writing Responsibly — Using Illustrations and Avoiding Plagiarism

The web contains a variety of images, videos, and sound files that you can download to your word processor: A click of the mouse, and they are yours. Or are they? Keep full records of who created them, where you found them, and on what date you downloaded them so that you can cite them fully.

to OTHER WRITERS

More about
Citing media illustrations, 179–84
(MLA), 223–24
(APA), 252–54
(*Chicago*)

sources—is *common knowledge.* You do not have to document common knowledge (unless it is included in a quotation). Everything else—surprising facts, interpretations, quotations even from well-known works of literature—must be cited in the text of your research project and documented in a footnote, bibliography, reference list, or list of works cited, regardless of whether you are quoting, paraphrasing, or summarizing from the source.

NOTE What counts as common knowledge can differ from one group of people or one academic discipline to another. If you are unsure whether a fact is common knowledge, err on the side of safety by citing and documenting it.

16b Making Notes That Help You Avoid Plagiarizing

More about
Working bibliography, 100–02

Inadvertent plagiarism is a growing problem for researchers today because cutting and pasting material from online sources into notes is so easy. As Doris Kearns Goodwin knows only too well, it is easy to lose track of which material has been borrowed and which material came from which source. The following strategies for maintaining good research notes can help you avoid problems:

- **Keep a working bibliography.** For every source you consult, add a complete entry to your working bibliography.

- **Make a fresh computer file, notebook section, or card for notes on each source, and include the author and page number in each note.** Separating notes helps you avoid confusing one source with another.

More about
Annotation, 7–10,
87–88

- **Use columns or different colored fonts or note cards to distinguish borrowed material from your own ideas.** If done consistently, using one column or color for your own comments and another for quota-

Writing Responsibly — Highlighting versus Making Notes

While highlighting is a useful way to signal important information in a source, it is not a substitute for writing your own notes about a text. Highlighting can help you mark what is important, but annotating will push you to engage with the text and save you from leafing through page after highlighted page, looking for a passage that you faintly recall having read. So even though it may seem more time-consuming than highlighting, making notes will actually serve you better in the long run.

to SELF

tions, summaries, and paraphrases can provide a useful visual cue for identifying source material and avoiding unintentional plagiarism.

> **Tech**   **Bookmarking and Listing Favorites**
>
> If you will not always be working from a single computer, set up bookmarks on a social bookmarking site like Pinterest or Digg, which allows you to store, tag, and share bookmarks.

- **Create a favorites list or bookmark useful web pages.** When taking notes on a computer, bookmarking or creating a favorites list can help you keep track of your sources.

- **Photocopy sources or download PDFs from which you borrow information or ideas.** You will be able to check quotations, paraphrases, and summaries against these copies after you have drafted your research project.

16c Paraphrasing and Summarizing Sources without Patchwriting

Paraphrasing and summarizing force you to understand your sources and to capture their meaning accurately in original words and sentences. They allow you to maintain a consistent voice—yours—throughout the research project. However, paraphrasing and summarizing accurately are difficult. Often, inexperienced writers *patchwrite*: They replace some terms with synonyms, delete a few words, or alter the grammar or sentence structure slightly, but they do not put the passage fully into their own words and sentences. The sections that follow will show you how to paraphrase and summarize without patchwriting.

1. Paraphrase.

A *paraphrase* restates someone else's ideas in fresh words and sentences. Paraphrase a source when you want to do the following:

- Understand the logic of complex passages
- Convey the main idea and key supporting points from a source in your own words
- Mention examples and details from the source

Because a paraphrase includes all of the writer's main ideas, it is often as long as, and sometimes even longer than, the original. Like a summary, a paraphrase must not use the same language as the source (except for keywords), and the order of ideas and the sentence structures must be new as well. To paraphrase *without* patchwriting, follow these steps:

1. Read the source until you feel you understand it. Think about the overall meaning of the passage. Figure out whether there are any key terms that must be retained in your paraphrase.

More about
Varying sentence length and structure, 284–85
Bookending a paraphrase, 142–43
Using signal phrases, 141–43

2. Close the text and walk away. Do something else for a few minutes or a few hours.
3. Come back to your desk and write down what you remember. If you cannot remember anything, repeat steps 1 and 2.
4. Check your paraphrase against the source to make sure you have correctly represented what it said. If you have closely followed the language or sentence structure of the source, revise your notes.

Where possible, use synonyms (words with a similar meaning) rather than the words of the source. If no synonym makes sense, then use key terms from the source. Rearrange the ideas of the source so that they make sense in your own text, use different sentence structures from those in the original passage, and omit details that are not relevant to your main point. Introduce the paraphrase with a signal phrase by mentioning the author's name ("MacDonald argues . . . "), and include a page reference (in parentheses) at the end of the borrowed passage; then document the source in your bibliography, reference list, or list of works cited. The examples below show passages that have been paraphrased with and without patchwriting.

Passage from source

With these caveats, we argue more limitedly that digital technology offers new avenues of aesthetic experimentation for comic artists and that the internet has given some comic artists a modest prosperity that they would not have without the internet as a means of distribution. (Sean Fenty, Trena Houp, and Laurie Taylor, "Webcomics: The Influence and Continuation of the Comix Revolution," *ImageTexT* 1.2 [2004]: par. 2. Web. 18 Mar. 2007.)

Authors

Picks up language from source

Uses synonym or word in another form

Paragraph reference (use only when source numbers its paragraphs)

Note with patchwriting

Fenty, Houp, and Taylor argue that digital technology provides comic artists with an opportunity for artistic experimentation and that some have more success than they would have without the Internet (par. 2).

Note without patchwriting

According to Fenty, Houp, and Taylor, comic artists use the computer to experiment and the Internet to publish their works, allowing them more creative options and earning them more money than they made in the pre-Internet era (par. 2).

Notice that the patchwritten note relies heavily not only on the language but also on the sentence structure of the source. The note without patchwriting captures the main ideas of the passage without borrowing sentence structures or more than a few keywords from the original.

Here is another example:

Passage from source

Until recently, the Church was one of the least studied aspects of the Cuban revolution, almost as if it were a voiceless part of Cuban society, an institution and faith that had little impact on the course of events. (Super, John C. "Interpretations of Church and State in Cuba, 1959–1961." *The Catholic Historical Review* 89.3 [2003]: 511–529. Print.)

Note with patchwriting

> Super 511
>
> According to Super, the Catholic Church until recently was not much studied as an aspect of the Cuban revolution. It was as if the Church was voiceless in Cuban culture, as if it had little influence on events (511).

Authors
Picks up language from source
Uses synonym or word in another form
Page reference

Note without patchwriting

> Super argues that scholarship on the Cuban revolution is only beginning to recognize the influential role of the Church (511).

The revised note still retains key terms from the source: "Cuban revolution" and "Church" appear in both the original passage and the revised note because there can be no synonyms for proper nouns (names). But the passage no longer draws heavily on the source's sentence structure, organization, or word choices.

If you find yourself leaning heavily on the wording of the source, work for greater comprehension of the text by looking up unfamiliar words or thinking about concepts you do not understand. Then turn away from the source, and write from your head rather than the source.

2. Summarize.

An effective *summary* briefly captures the major claims (and, if space permits, the key evidence) of a source while omitting the details. A summary is usually at least 50 percent shorter than the material you are summarizing. Summarize a source when you want to do the following:

- Push yourself to a complete understanding of a complex source
- Demonstrate to your reader that you have read and fully engaged with the source
- Help your reader understand a text that is key to your project

More about
Transitions, 29–30
Using signal
phrases, 141–42
Citing and docu-
menting sources,
149–200 (MLA
style), 201–38
(APA style),
239–62 (*Chicago*
style), 263–76
(CSE style)

To summarize a source, follow these steps:

1. Read the source, underlining key terms and looking up words that you do not know.
2. Annotate the source. Underline or highlight the thesis or main idea of the source, and identify the key supporting ideas. For a longer source, creating an outline may be helpful.
3. Write down—without looking at the source—the thesis or main claim in your own words.
4. Write a one- or two-sentence summary for each group of supporting paragraphs.
5. Combine your restatement of the thesis and your summary of the source's main ideas into a paragraph. Edit to eliminate repetition, and insert transitions to emphasize logical connections among sentences.
6. Check your summary against the source. Have you used fresh words and sentence structures? If not, this may be a sign that you do not yet understand the source. Go back and read the material again, and revise your summary to avoid patchwriting.
7. Record source information.

When you incorporate your summary into your paper, cite the original source and include a page reference at the end of the summary. Below is an example of an effective summary of an original source:

Student Model Summary

Passage from source

Before exploring these connections, however, webcomics must be more clearly defined. Many people are only familar with webcomics through Scott McCloud's explanation of them in *Reinventing Comics,* where he took on the role of a spokesperson for webcomics. While McCloud offered an initial study on webcomics, this paper does not operate within a McCloudian definition of comics, where he expounds upon their potential to revolutionize all comics production. In this paper, the term webcomics must be distinguished from hyperbolic proclamations about the internet as an inevitable site of radical aesthetic evolution and economic revolution for comics. The problems with McCloud's claims about the liberatory and radical properties of the internet have been addressed by others, like Gary Groth in his article for *The Comics Journal,* "McCloud Cuckoo Land." Our argument does not claim that the internet is a superior comic medium, free of those "tiny boxes" and "finite canvases" that seem to trouble McCloud (online). Further, we recognize that the internet has not offered a level playing field, free of corporate domination, "a world," to quote McCloud's *Reinventing Comics,* "in which the path from selling ten comics to selling ten thousand comics to selling ten million comics is as smooth as ice" (188, Panel 1). With these caveats, we argue more limitedly that digital technology offers new avenues of aesthetic experimentation for comic artists and that the internet has given some comic artists a modest prosperity that they would not have without the internet as a means of distribution. (Sean Fenty, Trena Houp, and Laurie Taylor, "Webcomics: The Influence and Continuation of the Comix Revolution," *ImageTexT* 1.2 [2004]: par. 2. Web. 18 Mar. 2007.)

Summary

Scott McCloud claims that the Internet will free underground comic artists from the restrictions of print distribution and make it possible for underground comic artists to reach huge audiences. Fenty, Houp, and Taylor, on the other hand, focus on the possibilities for experimentation on the web and argue that the web provides better opportunities to make money publishing underground comics than does print. (Fenty, Houp, and Taylor par.2)

Notice that the writer of the summary captures the main idea of the source in her own words and sentence structures. Her summary is about one quarter the length of the original material.

 Making Notes in English If you are a non-native writer of English, you may want to save time by copying passages in English into your notes word for word or by copying your own translation of the material into your notes. However, your English language skills will improve more quickly if you make an effort to paraphrase, and you will also be less likely to commit unintentional plagiarism. Remember that writing with sources in US academic and professional settings often means using your sources critically—another reason to avoid simply copying them.

16d Capturing Quotations in Your Notes

A *quotation* is someone else's words transcribed exactly, with quotation marks or block indention to signal that it is from a source. Since readers are interested in what the writer of the research project has to say, you should use quotations sparingly. Quote from a source only for the following reasons:

- To reproduce particularly vivid or engaging language
- To convey a subtle idea or technical passage that might be distorted by a paraphrase or summary
- To lend credibility to your position through an expert's words
- To analyze or highlight the specific language of a source (as when studying a work of literature or a historical document)

If you find that you are quoting frequently but paraphrasing little and summarizing even less, you may not be fully comprehending what you are reading. Slow down. Read the source again, looking up words you do not understand, consulting reference sources that can provide background information, and discussing the source with your instructor, classmates, or friends. Then summarize or paraphrase the source.

Good scholarship requires that you work to understand the whole source rather than just quoting from the sections that you believe you understand or that you think sound authoritative. Understanding the difficult parts is important, for they may change the meaning of what you thought at first you understood.

The following reading note correctly uses quotation marks to signal material taken word for word from the source, yet it indicates that the writer does not fully understand what she is writing about.

Student Model Reading Note

Draft note

Authors

Quotations

Page reference

> According to Milne, the "free-black community . . . of Five Points" is not reflected in "the areas of Block 160 that were excavated." "All that survived . . . were the remains of their ancestors interred in the mostly forgotten burying ground, a few intriguing and unusual items discarded in the defunct privies and cisterns, and a handful of church addresses." But "it is probable that many members of this community remained in the neighborhood, living 'off-the-grid'. . ." (140).

This note is merely a string of quotations, sewn together with a few of the note-taker's own words. Using these notes as is would produce a research paper that would similarly be a mosaic of quotation, difficult to read and lacking the researcher's insight and critical judgment. Rereading the source in order to gain a better understanding of it enabled the writer to summarize with much less quotation. The following revision is much easier to read as well:

Revised note

> According to Milne, very few items belonging to members of the African American population in Five Points have been excavated, most likely because members of this community were not part of mainstream society—they were "living 'off the grid'" (140)—not because they had all moved away.

More about
Integrating borrowed ideas and words, 147–48
Using quotation marks, 436–43
Analysis, interpretation, synthesis, and critique, 10–13, 89, 137

Other chapters in this text discuss the mechanics of using quotation marks and integrating quotations into your text. Consult these sections before you begin your research, as you make notes on sources, and as you draft and revise your text.

16e Including Analysis, Interpretation, Synthesis, and Critique in Your Notes

In addition to recording information from sources, the note-taking stage is also the time to start analyzing, interpreting, synthesizing, and critiquing what you read. The Self-Assessment box lists questions to ask yourself as you read and take notes on your sources, and the next chapter provides examples of analysis, interpretation, and synthesis in a student's research project.

Self Assessment

When analyzing, interpreting, synthesizing, and critiquing a source, ask yourself the following questions. If the answer is not clear, reread and reevaluate the source, as necessary.

Analysis
- ☐ What is the purpose of the source?
- ☐ Who is the intended audience?
- ☐ What major claims does the source make?
- ☐ What evidence (reasons, facts, statistics, examples, expert testimony) does the source use to support these claims?

Interpretation
- ☐ What assumptions does the author make about the subject or audience, and why are such assumptions significant?
- ☐ What does the source omit (evidence, opposing views), and what might these omissions indicate?
- ☐ What conclusions can you draw about the author's attitude from the tone of the source? What motives can you infer from the author's background?
- ☐ Who published this text or sponsored the research, and what influence might these sponsors have had on the way the information, arguments, or evidence is presented?
- ☐ In what context was the text written—place, time, cultural environment—and how might this context have influenced the author?

- ☐ What expertise or life experience does the author bring to the subject, and is it relevant to the topic?

Synthesis
- ☐ Do any other sources make a similar (or opposing) claim, reach a similar (or opposing) conclusion, or offer similar (or opposing) evidence?
- ☐ Do any other sources identify similar causes or effects?
- ☐ What else do you know about this topic?
- ☐ How does this source support your claims?

Critique
- ☐ Are the aims of the source worthwhile, and have they been achieved?
- ☐ What claims does the source make? Are you persuaded by them? Why or why not?
- ☐ How credible is the evidence? Is the evidence based on verifiable facts? How relevant is the evidence?
- ☐ How logical is the source? Does the author commit any fallacies?
- ☐ How fairly does the source treat alternative viewpoints?

17 Writing the Research Project

Writing a research project is much like entering a conversation. When you first join the conversation, you hang back to learn what the conversation is all about. As you become more comfortable, you overcome your shyness and find your voice. When you first start work on a research project, you "listen in" on your sources by summarizing, paraphrasing, and quoting from the experts. As you come to grips with the topic, through analysis, interpretation, synthesis, and critique of your sources, you develop insights that you will share with your partners in the conversation—your readers.

17a Drafting a Thesis Statement Based on Your Research Question

You started work on your topic by planning and conducting research. You join in on the discussion that will become your research project by drafting a thesis that states your main claim and serves as the focus of your project. Your thesis should be a one- or two-sentence statement that grows out of your research questions. It should be a statement that you will explain in the body of your research project, using information you have gleaned from sources and your own ideas, and it should convey your *purpose* (typically, for academic and business projects, to persuade or inform). For illustration, read the research question and thesis statement for the student project by Lydia Nichols, which appears at the end of tab 6.

Thesis statement makes purpose clear: uses comparison of comic types to persuade readers that underground comics are more innovative and sophisticated.

> **Research question:** What makes underground comics so much more compelling than superhero comics?
>
> **Thesis statement:** While far less well-known than their superhero counterparts, underground comics offer an innovative and sophisticated alternative to mainstream titles.

Quick

Reference   Drafting the Research Paper

- **Thesis.** Draft a one- or two-sentence thesis statement that grows out of your research questions and answers. Revise your thesis as you draft your project.
- **Organization.** List and explain the reasons you believe your thesis statement or why you think it is the most reasonable way to address a difficult issue. Sort research notes into separate piles for each of your reasons. Draft an outline that organizes your material so that readers can follow your logic and maintain interest to the end.
- **Analysis, interpretation, synthesis, critique.** Divide ideas into their component parts (analysis), and think about what they mean (interpretation). Then combine ideas from sources with your own ideas to come up with something fresh (synthesis). Decide whether sources have achieved their goals and whether their goals were worthwhile (critique).
- **Evidence and counterevidence.** Incorporate evidence, making sure it is relevant. Use summaries, paraphrases, and a few well-chosen quotations as support. Acknowledge opposing or contradictory evidence, and explain why your position is reasonable despite this. (If your position does *not* seem reasonable in light of counterevidence, revise your thesis.) Make sure you provide enough evidence—and the appropriate types of evidence—to influence your readers.
- **Citation and documentation.** Cite sources in the text, using the style that is appropriate for your discipline (MLA style for literature and languages, APA style for psychology and other social sciences, *Chicago* style for history and other humanities, and CSE style for the sciences). Double-check that you have used quotation marks where needed and that paraphrases have not slipped into patchwriting. Document sources in a list of works cited (MLA), reference list (APA, CSE), or footnotes and bibliography (*Chicago*).

> *More about*
> Assessing the writing situation, 16–19, 97–98
> Crafting research questions, 99–100
> Devising a thesis, 22–24, 99
> Organizing, 24–25, 78–80, 136–37
> Drafting, 25, 28–38, 137–39
> Finding information, 103–14
> Acknowledging alternative views, 17, 77–78
> Citing and documenting sources, 149–200 (MLA style), 201–38 (APA style), 239–62 (*Chicago* style), 263–76 (CSE style)

Just as a conversation partner may say something that changes your perspective, you may discover as you draft your project that the counterevidence is overwhelming or that the body of your draft offers a different answer to your research question than the one in your thesis. (Frequently, the true thesis takes shape in the conclusion of the first draft.) If this happens to you, be prepared to revisit your thesis, revising or even replacing it as the evidence necessitates.

Writing
Responsibly   Acknowledging Counterevidence

While sorting your notes, be sure to retain *counterevidence*—evidence that *undermines* your claims. If some of your research contradicts or complicates your thesis or supporting reasons, do not suppress it. Instead, revise your thesis or supporting reasons on the basis of this counterevidence, or acknowledge the counterevidence and explain why the reasons for believing your thesis are more convincing than those that challenge it. Your readers will appreciate your presentation of multiple perspectives.

to AUDIENCE

17b Organizing Your Notes and Outlining Your Project

More about
Generating ideas,
19–22
Making notes,
126–33

More about
Scratch outlines,
24
Sentence outlines,
24–25
Topic outlines,
24–25

Student Model
Research project:
"Holy Underground
Comics, Batman,"
Lydia Nichols,
192–200

Start organizing your project by listing the reasons you believe your thesis is true. While these reasons may be derived from your research, they should be *your* reasons, stated in your own words.

Next, review the notes you took while conducting research. Do they provide background information your readers will need? Do they provide evidence for believing your thesis? Separate index cards into piles, or cut and paste notes into separate computer files according to the role they play in your research project.

Then assess your stock of evidence: If your notes look skimpy, find more supporting evidence, revise your thesis, or delve deeper into your reasons for believing your thesis.

After you have organized your notes, consider writing an outline to help you determine the most effective order for your ideas. Some writers use a scratch (informal) outline, which lists the reasons and major supporting points of the project in order of presentation. A scratch outline is quickest to draft, but it can be too sketchy for a complex project. Others prefer a sentence outline because it aids drafting—each sentence in the outline becomes the topic sentence of a paragraph—and because the formal structure of numerals and letters makes the structure of the draft clear. Still others prefer a topic outline; it is quicker to draft than a sentence outline, but its formal structure (the topic outline, too, uses numbers and letters) makes the structure of the draft clear. Some writers do not use an outline at all, or they create an outline only after they have written a draft, to help them see the structure of their project. A portion of a topic outline for Lydia Nichols's research project appears below.

Student Model Topic Outline

Overall organiza-
tion: Chronological
(1930s, 1950s)

Uses definitions,
facts, examples to
support claim

> Thesis: While far less well-known than their superhero counter-
> parts, underground comics offer an innovative and sophisticated
> alternative to mainstream titles.
>
> I. Success of superhero comics in the late 1930s led to
>   homogenization
>   A. Superhero defined
>   B. Superman debuted June 1938
>   C. Copycat superheroes
> II. Further homogenization in the 1950s, with creation of Comics
>   Code Authority (1954)
>   A. Specific rules of CCA code—letters of the word "crime"
>   cannot be bigger than other letters on the cover

B. General rules of CCA code

   1. Respect for parents, morality (good triumphs over evil)

   2. Criminals, crimes portrayed negatively

   3. Religion treated respectfully

   4. No profanity

Student Model
Sentence outline, 25

17c Supporting Your Claims with Analysis, Interpretation, Synthesis, and Critique of Sources

Your goal in a research project is to draw on information from sources to support your own ideas. Use analysis, interpretation, synthesis, and critique of sources to make sense of your claims for the reader. The paragraph below from Lydia Nichols's essay on underground comics shows how she uses these techniques to support her claim.

Underground artists not only push the envelope in terms of content, but they also incorporate experimental visual devices, earning critical praise for breaking away from traditional comic layouts in favor of more artistic perspectives. Artists such as Daniel Clowes argue that comic art can be more evocative than film, especially in the use of nonlinear storytelling techniques (Hignite 18). *New York Times* columnist John Hodgman agrees: Discussing a moment of existential crisis in Kevin Huizenga's *Ganges* #1, he writes, "I have never seen any film . . . that gets at that frozen moment when we suddenly feel our mortality, when God is seen or denied, as effectively as a comic panel." Artist Chris Ware manipulates the borders and frames in his comics so extensively that even reading his works can feel like an art to be mastered (see fig. 3). The demands his comics place on the reader create an interaction between viewer and artist that is unheard of in the pages of superhero titles.

Sentence 1: Nichols's claim (topic sentence).

Sentences 2 and 3 synthesize information from sources to support her claim.

Sentences 4 and 5 provide her own analysis to support her claim.

Fig. 3. Cover from Chris Ware's *Jimmy Corrigan: The Smartest Kid on Earth* (New York: Pantheon, 2000). Critically acclaimed *Jimmy Corrigan* comics use visual storytelling techniques, pushing the limitations of comics and forcing the reader to work to achieve understanding.

Figure and caption: Illustration provides an example that supports Nichols's claim, and caption offers interpretation.

Quick

Reference　Writing the First Draft

As you begin writing, keep in mind that you are composing a draft—what you write will be revised—so do not worry whether you are saying it "right." A few writers' tricks will help you produce that first draft:

- Keep your thesis statement (and your outline, if you have devised one) in front of you to help you stay focused.
- Start with the sections that are easiest to write, and then fill in the gaps later.
- Begin writing *without* consulting your sources. Only add evidence from sources *after* you have sketched out your own ideas.

- When incorporating quotations, paraphrases, or summaries in your draft, note which source the material comes from (including the page number) so that you will not need to track down this information later and, perhaps, plagiarize inadvertently.
- Draft with a notepad next to you or another file open on your computer so that you can jot down ideas that come to you while writing another section.
- Include visuals when they support your points or help your reader understand what you are writing about.

17d Supporting Your Claims with Summaries, Paraphrases, and Apt Quotations from Sources

When you are drawing on sources, use quotations sparingly. In most cases, you should put borrowed information and ideas into your own words, using either paraphrase or summary. In the sample paragraph on page 137, Nichols uses a combination of quotation and summary to support her claims. She quotes Hodgman because the quotation is especially vivid, but she summarizes Clowes's ideas to convey his argument concisely.

NOTE When summarizing or paraphrasing, work to avoid patchwriting, and, when quoting, use quotation marks or indent longer quoted passages as a block.

> *More about*
> Drafting, 25–27,
> 　28–38
> Summarizing, 7,
> 　127–31
> Paraphrasing,
> 　127–29
> Quoting, 131
> Avoiding patch-
> 　writing, 127–31
> Quotation marks,
> 　436–43
> Incorporating
> 　visuals, 54–55,
> 　190–91 (MLA
> 　style), 229–30
> 　(APA style),
> 　252–54 (*Chicago*
> 　style)

17e Revising, Editing, Proofreading, and Formatting Your Project

Once you have composed a first draft, however rough it may be, you can begin the process of shaping and polishing it—the process of *revision.* First, attend to big-picture or global issues, such as clarifying your purpose, making sure your essay is cohesive and unified, and ensuring that your ideas are fully developed. Next, attend to local issues, such as making sure your word choices reflect your meaning and are at the appropriate level of formality, that you have varied your sentences, and that your prose is concise. This is the time, too, to double-check your in-text citations against your list of works cited or reference list to make sure that you have documented all the sources from which you have borrowed ideas or information (except for common knowledge).

Writing Responsibly   Owning the Proofreading Process

While spell-check software can be helpful, it cannot identify words you have misused, such as *it's* (*it is*) for *its* (possessive) or *infer* (*surmise*) for *imply* (*suggest*). Nor will it identify citations that do not appear in your list of works cited. To fulfill your responsibility to yourself and your readers, be sure to proofread your project carefully before submitting it, to check that in-text citations are included in your list of works cited and that all items in that list are referenced in the text of your project, and to check that you have formatted accurately the entries in your list of works cited.

to SELF

Once revision is complete, edit your text to correct errors of grammar, punctuation, and mechanics. Then proofread carefully, checking not only your spelling and punctuation but also the entries in your list of works cited or references. Finally, double-check that the formatting of your project follows the requirements of your discipline.

18 Citing Expertly

When you research a topic, you work with sources with multiple viewpoints, settling on those that further the conversation on your topic, and then present your sources' ideas in ways that allow readers to see your text clearly.

Source citations are necessary in a researched paper, yet simple citations do not help readers see the clarity of your thinking. For your readers, the clarity of your project comes when you go beyond simply naming the source. When you cite expertly, you use accurate signal verbs, show source boundaries, emphasize your own voice, provide context for the source, and accurately integrate altered quotations. Expert citation makes your conversation with sources, like the image or message in a glass paperweight, "transparent": Others can see how your ideas developed and how you are relating to your sources and the information in them.

Citations are an essential part of academic writing. They name the sources you are using—the other writers with whom you are talking. At more expert levels of researched writing, ***rhetorical citations*** accomplish this task and more: They provide helpful information about your sources; they reveal your attitude toward, and judgment of, your sources; and they highlight your own contributions to the "conversation" that takes place between you and your sources.

18a Integrating Source Material Responsibly

More about
Using information responsibly,
124–33
In-text citation,
14–15, 149–200
(MLA style,
ch. 19), 442–43
Ethos, 76

When writing from sources, your most basic responsibility is to let your audience know whenever your text is drawing on a source. This protects you from charges of plagiarism. It also fulfills a responsibility to your audience, by letting readers know who is speaking in your text. It fulfills a responsibility to yourself, as well: Careful citation increases your writerly *ethos*; it makes you a more credible, respected writer. In MLA style, ***in-text citation***—whether through parenthetical references, signal phrases, or a combination of the two—accomplishes all of this.

Having a Conversation with Sources You may consider published sources to be authorities, but an important aspect of academic writing is learning how to be critical even of authoritative material. You are free to agree or disagree with any source, but it is important that you use sources to support your claims, rather than simply repeating a source's language and ideas.

1. Use parenthetical citations.

You can cite your sources by using the author's last name and relevant page number(s) in a ***parenthetical citation.***[1] Place that reference at the end of the material from your source:

> Quotation marks indicate the beginning and end of the source's exact words

"His name was Mark Zuckerberg, he was a sophomore, and although Eduardo had spent a fair amount of time at various Epsilon Pi events with him, along with at least one prepunch Phoenix event that Eduardo could remember, he still barely knew the kid"

> Source author (last name only)

(Mezrich 15).

> Page in source

When you are paraphrasing or summarizing material, you should also use parenthetical citation to acknowledge that your material comes from a source:

---

[1] The terms *parenthetical citation, parenthetical note,* and *parenthetical reference* are often interchangeable.

> Who wouldn't envy the genius and wealth of the person who
> invited Facebook? But who wouldn't pity a person who has no
> close friends? Mark Zuckerberg may have great wealth, but he
> has few confidantes (Denby 98).

Source author (last name only)

Page in source

2. Use signal phrases.

To incorporate borrowed material smoothly into your prose, introduce it with a *signal phrase.* One part of the signal phrase is an identification (usually the name) of the writer from whom you are borrowing. The other part is a verb; choose one that conveys your sense of the writer's intention.

In choosing your signal verb, consider the attitude or position of the writer you are quoting. Is the writer making a claim? Is she or he agreeing or disagreeing or even conceding a point? Or is the writer's position neutral? It is easy to choose a neutral verb, such as *writes, says,* or *comments.* Whenever possible, though, go beyond these neutral verbs to indicate the writer's attitude:

> *More about*
> Verb tense, 362–66

Oscar Wilde quipped, "A poet can survive everything but a misprint."

Quick

Reference   Signal Verbs

Neutral Signal Verbs		Signal Verbs That Indicate:		
analyzes	introduces	**Concession**		**Claim/Argument**
comments	notes	acknowledges	argues	finds
compares	observes	admits	asserts	holds
concludes	records	concedes	believes	maintains
contrasts	remarks	grants	charges	points out
describes	reports		claims	proposes
discusses	says		confirms	recommends
explains	shows		contends	suggests
focuses on	states		demonstrates	
illustrates	thinks			
indicates	writes	**Agreement**		**Disagreement**

Writers in literature and the other humanities typically use present tense verbs in signal phrases; writers in the sciences use the present or past tense, depending on the context.

Agreement	**Disagreement**	
agrees	complains	questions
concurs	contradicts	refutes
confirms	criticizes	rejects
supports	denies	warns
	disagrees	

For the Wilde quotation, *quipped* (which means "uttered a witty remark") is clearly appropriate, given the cleverness of the sentence quoted. *Snarled,* on the other hand, would not be appropriate: Although Wilde's quip may have an edge to it, few would agree that the comment conveys the anger or viciousness associated with the verb *snarl.*

To maintain your audience's interest, vary the signal words you use, while avoiding verbs that might misrepresent the writer's intentions. (A list of signal verbs appears in the Quick Reference box on p. 141.) You can also vary your placement of the signal phrase:

> E. M. Forster asked, "How do I know what I think until I see what I say?"

> "How do I know what I think," E. M. Forster asked, "until I see what I say?"

> "How do I know what I think until I see what I say?" E. M. Forster asked.

18b Showing Source Boundaries

More about
Paraphrasing,
127–29
Summarizing,
127–31
Using quotation
marks, 436–43

When the material from your source is a quotation, it is easy for the audience to see the source boundaries: The quotation marks indicate where your use of source material begins and ends. When you are paraphrasing or summarizing the source, the place where you begin to use source material may not be clear. Signal phrases help solve the problem; you can place a signal phrase at the beginning of the source material and a parenthetical citation at the end.

Consider this example:

Who wouldn't envy the genius and wealth of the person who invented Facebook? But who wouldn't pity a person who has no close friends? [Signal phrase includes source author (full name on first reference)] David Denby describes Mark Zuckerberg as having great wealth, but he has few confidantes. ["Quotation marks indicate the beginning and end of the source's exact words] *The Social Network* is shrewdly perceptive about such things as class, manners, ethics, and the emptying out of self that accompanies a genius's absorption in his work" (98). [Page in source]

In the example above, it is clear that the first two sentences are the writer's statement of her own ideas, the third sentence is a paraphrase from the Denby source, and the fourth a quotation from Denby. Notice that when the author's name is included in the signal phrase, it does not need to be included in the parenthetical citation.

1. Unpaginated source material

Many sources are accessed electronically and have no page numbers. For an unpaginated source, include only the author's last name in the parenthetical citation:

> "Facebook, which surpassed MySpace in 2008 as the largest social-networking site, now has nearly 500 million members, or 22 percent of all Internet users, who spend more than 500 billion minutes a month on the site" (Rosen).

Source author
(last name only)

When you are quoting from the source, the quotation marks show where the source use begins and ends.

When you are paraphrasing or summarizing from an electronic source with no page numbers, however, you must work subtly with the material to show your audience where the source use begins and ends. Usually you can do this by using the author's name in the parenthetical citation and describing the author in a signal phrase:

Signal phrase
describes source
author

A writer for the *New York Times* explains how damaging Facebook material can be when one searches for a job (Rosen).

Parenthetical reference identifies source author
(last name only)

18c Emphasizing Your Voice

Just as important as signaling source boundaries is the need to signal your own voice. Your readers want to know clearly when it is *you* talking. In the following example it is not clear where the student writer stops drawing from the Rosen source and begins to state his own ideas:

Signal phrase

Rosen explains, "Seventy percent of U.S. recruiters report that they have rejected candidates because of information found online, like photos and discussion-board conversations and membership in controversial groups." With 500 million people on Facebook, the dangers are widespread. It is ironic that this phenomenon of personal data revealed to the world was begun by a person who himself had poor social skills.

The use of a signal phrase with a parenthetical citation shows the boundaries of the information from Rosen:

> **Signal phrase describes source author**
>
> A writer for the *New York Times* explains, "Seventy percent of U.S. recruiters report that they have rejected candidates because of information found online, like photos and discussion-board conversations and membership in controversial groups." With 500 million people on Facebook, the dangers are widespread
>
> **Parenthetical reference identifies source author (last name only)**
>
> (Rosen). It is ironic that this phenomenon of personal data revealed to the world was begun by a person who himself had poor social skills.

The final sentence in this passage is an interesting one, and the student writer wants to emphasize that it is his own insight. That could be done with first-person singular phrases such as "I believe" or "in my opinion."

> **More about**
> First-person pronouns, 369–76

Yet in some genres and writing situations (including many college assignments), first-person singular is inappropriate. Fortunately, there are more sophisticated ways to handle the task. One option is to speak in the first-person plural, subtly drawing the audience into the conversation:

> A writer for the *New York Times* explains, "Seventy percent of U.S. recruiters report that they have rejected candidates because of information found online, like photos and discussion-board conversations and membership in controversial groups." With 500 million people on Facebook, the dangers are widespread
>
> **Parenthetical reference shows end of source material**
>
> (Rosen). We cannot escape the irony that this phenomenon of personal data revealed to the world was begun by a person who himself had poor social skills.
>
> **First-person plural suggests shift to student writer's voice**

It is even better to comment upon the source or its information:

> A writer for the *New York Times* explains, "Seventy percent of U.S. recruiters report that they have rejected candidates because of information found online, like photos and discussion-board conversations and membership in controversial groups." With 500 million people on Facebook, the dangers are widespread (Rosen). Such information suggests an irony: This phenomenon of personal data revealed to the world was begun by a person who himself had poor social skills.

Parenthetical reference shows end of source material

Transition to student writer's interpretation of source material

In this version, the writer's voice is implicitly clear. He uses the adjective *such* to point to the previous material and then provides his interpretation. Demonstrative pronouns (*this, that, these, those*) can also be used as a transition to the student writer talking about the source material.

18d Providing Context

Readers appreciate knowing not only when it is your voice they are reading and when it is the voice of your sources, but also *who* your sources are and why you have chosen them. Rhetorical citations provide this information smoothly: Your citations can explain why you chose the source, what kind of source it is, when the source was published, and what its argument was.

1. Explain your choice of sources.

Unless your readers are familiar with your sources, they may have no reason to respect them and thus no reason to believe your claims. You can avoid this problem with rhetorical citations that not only name your source but also indicate why you respect the source, as this writer does:

Signal phrase includes student writer's opinion of the source

> Gary Wolf provides a helpful, wide-ranging overview of our motivations for gathering and sharing data about ourselves, offering examples like this: "*Foursquare,* a geo-tracking application with about one million users, keeps a running tally of how many times players 'check in' at every locale, automatically building a detailed diary of movements and habits; many users publish these data widely."

In the example above, the writer establishes that the source can be respected for its thorough treatment of the topic.

> **More about**
> Evaluating sources,
> 114–123 (ch. 15)

The selection below acknowledges the shortcomings of the source while also asserting its usefulness:

> Signal phrase becomes extended explanation of student writer's opinion of the source

Mezrich has made up parts of his story about Zuckerberg's rise, while claiming he is sticking as closely as possible to reality. Yet his fiction is worth reading; it shows how people perceive Harvard and its geniuses: "There was something playful about those eyes—but that was where any sense of natural emotion or readability ended. His narrow face was otherwise devoid of any expression at all. And his posture, his general aura—the way he seemed closed in on himself, even while engaged in a group dynamic, even here, in the safety of his own fraternity—was almost painfully awkward" (15).

> Page in source

2. Identify the type of source.

Is your source a newspaper column? A blog? A scholarly article? The differences between types of sources are important. If you want up-to-the-minute information, a newspaper or blog is likely to have it. If you want carefully researched, accurate information, a scholarly journal article is a good choice. Your readers want to know that you have made appropriate source choices, and you can provide such information in rhetorical citations:

> Signal phrase describes and identifies source author and his credentials

Writing in the *New York Times*, journalist Gary Wolf provides a wide-ranging overview of our motivations for gathering and sharing data about ourselves, offering examples like this: "*Foursquare,* a geo-tracking application with about one million users, keeps a running tally of how many times players 'check in' at every locale, automatically building a detailed diary of movements and habits; many users publish these data widely."

3. Identify the date of publication.

For many topics, the date of publication is important. The number of people who use the Foursquare application, for example, changes constantly. Providing the date on which such information is published helps readers know how fresh the numbers are and how accurate they might still be:

<table>
<tr>
<td>

Signal phrase includes publication date of time-sensitive information

</td>
<td>

In a 2010 article in the *New York Times,* journalist Gary Wolf says, "*Foursquare,* a geo-tracking application with about one million users, keeps a running tally of how many times players 'check in' at every locale, automatically building a detailed diary of movements and habits; many users publish these data widely."

</td>
</tr>
</table>

4. Identify the larger discussion in the source.

For the most successful, persuasive writing from sources, you need to *read* the sources, rather than just pulling sentences from them. That allows you not only to position the quotation, paraphrase, or summary in your text, but also to indicate how it contributed to the source text's discussion. Build brief source summary into rhetorical citation:

<table>
<tr>
<td>

Extended signal phrase includes summary of the source

</td>
<td>

In a 2010 article in the *New York Times*, journalist Gary Wolf provides a wide-ranging overview of our motivations for gathering and sharing data about ourselves, offering examples like this: "*Foursquare,* a geo-tracking application with about one million users, keeps a running tally of how many times players 'check in' at every locale, automatically building a detailed diary of movements and habits; many users publish these data widely."

</td>
</tr>
</table>

The phrase "overview of our motivations for gathering and sharing data about ourselves" summarizes the source.

Citation is not only ethical but rhetorical; in addition to protecting you against charges of plagiarism, it also creates a sophisticated, readable document that audiences are likely to trust.

> **More about**
> Critical reading,
> 7–15
> Avoiding plagiarism, 124–33
> (ch. 16)

18e Integrating Altered Quotations

Sometimes you may need to alter a quotation so that it fits into your sentence. In her draft on page 137, Nichols deletes words from the Hodgman quotation because those words do not help her make her point. As long as the meaning is not significantly changed, writers may do any of the following to fit quoted material more fluidly into their own sentences:

- Quote short phrases rather than full sentences
- Add or change words for clarity

- Change capitalization
- Change grammar

More about
Using ellipses
in quotations,
450–51
Using square
brackets in
quotations, 448,
451

All added or changed words should be placed in square brackets; deleted words should be marked with ellipses. The example below shows a responsible alteration of a quotation:

Quotation integrated into student text	Original quotation
Certain portions of the Comic Book Code were incredibly specific and controlling, such as the rule that forbade "[t]he letters of the word 'crime' on a comics magazine . . . [to] be appreciably greater in dimension than the other words contained in the title" (qtd. in "Good Shall Triumph over Evil").	The letters of the word "crime" on a comics magazine shall never be appreciably greater in dimension than the other words contained in the title.

A capital letter was changed to a lowercase letter, double quotation marks were changed to single, one word was added and a couple of others were omitted, but the overall meaning of the passage remains the same.

Imagine, however, that the writer had made these changes instead:

Quotation unfairly altered	Original quotation
Certain portions of the code allowed some flexibility. Consider, for example, the rule that allowed "[t]he letters of the word 'crime' on a comics magazine . . . [to] be appreciably greater in dimension than the other words contained in the title" (qtd. in "Good Shall Triumph over Evil").	The letters of the word "crime" on a comics magazine shall never be appreciably greater in dimension than the other words contained in the title.

Clearly this alteration of the quotation is not acceptable, as it changes the meaning of the passage completely.

Self Assessment

As you revise projects that use sources, review your draft with the following questions in mind:

- ☐ Did you cite your sources? Name any from which you are paraphrasing, summarizing, or quoting.
- ☐ Did you use signal verbs? Convey the attitude of your source.
- ☐ Did you use signal phrases and parenthetical citations? Show where each source use begins and ends, even when it is unpaginated.
- ☐ Did you emphasize your own insights? Comment on or analyze the source, rather than just repeat it.
- ☐ Did you provide relevant contextual information? Identify the type of source, its date of publication, and its publisher.
- ☐ Did you reveal your reasoning? Explain why you chose and trusted your sources.

6
Documentation
Matters
MLA Style

Use tab 6 to learn, practice, and master these writer's responsibilities:

❏ To Audience

Cite and document sources so that readers can see where each use of sources begins and ends in your project; format your research project using MLA style, in keeping with readers' expectations.

❏ To Topic

Cite and document sources to demonstrate that you have explored your topic fully.

❏ To Other Writers

Provide citations for all borrowed ideas and information, whether quoted, paraphrased, or summarized; document all sources cited in the research project in a list of works cited at the end of the project.

❏ To Yourself

Use sources to build knowledge, and cite them to show readers where your ideas begin and end; to enhance your ethos, or credibility; and to present your ideas effectively.

6

Documentation
Matters

Journal Article from an **Online Database**

author · title and subtitle (article)

Decker, Alicia, and Mauricio, Castro. "Teaching History with Comic Books: A Case Study of

journal · issue

Violence, War, and the Graphic Novel." *History Teacher:* 45.2 (2012): 169-188.

database · medium · access date · vol. · year · pages

Academic Search Elite. Web. 17 Dec. 2012.

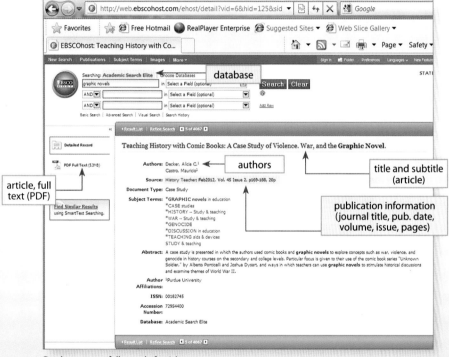

Database screen: full record of article

Look for the information you need to document an article you accessed through an online database on the search results screen, the full record of the article, or the first and last pages of the article itself. The access date is the date you last consulted the source; record this date in your notes. (For more about documenting an article accessed through an online database, see pp. 174–176.)

Short Work on a Website

author   web page title   website title
Esposito, Joseph. "E-books and the Personal Library." The Scholarly Kitchen.
              sponsor/publisher   medium   access date
Society for Scholarly Publishing, Aug. 20, 2012. Web. 17 Dec. 2012.
©date/last update

Web page

Frequently, the information you need to create a complete entry in the list of works cited is missing or difficult to find on web pages. Look at the top or bottom of the web page or home page or for a link to an "About" or "Contact Us" page. If no sponsor or publisher is listed, use *n.p.*; if no publication date is available, use *n.d.* (For more about documenting online sources, see pp. 177–79.)

19 Creating MLA-Style In-Text Citations

Developed by the Modern Language Association (MLA), MLA style guidelines are used by many researchers in the humanities—especially in languages and literature—to cite and document sources and to format papers in a uniform way. *The MLA Handbook for Writers of Research Papers* (7th ed.) requires that sources be acknowledged in two ways:

- **Citation:** In the body of your project, provide an in-text citation for each source used.
- **Documentation:** At the project's end, provide a list of all the works you cited in the project.

In-text citations appear in the body of your paper. They mark each use you make of a source, regardless of whether you are quoting, paraphrasing, summarizing, or drawing ideas from it. They also alert readers to a shift between *your* ideas and those you have borrowed.

> **More about**
> Popular academic styles per discipline, 69
> APA style, 201–38 (tab 7)
> *Chicago* style, 239–62 (tab 8)
> CSE style, 263–76 (tab 8)

19a Using a Signal Phrase and Page Reference or a Parenthetical Citation to Alert Readers to Borrowed Material in Your Research Project

You can cite a source in your text by using a signal phrase and page reference (in parentheses) or a parenthetical note:

- *Signal phrase.* Include the author's name and an appropriate verb in your sentence before the borrowed material, and put the page number(s) in parentheses after the borrowed material. Often you will use just the author's surname, and you should never use the author's first name alone.

> **More about**
> Signal verbs, 139–48 (ch. 18)

Writing Responsibly   Citing and Documenting Sources

When you cite and document sources, you demonstrate how thoroughly you have researched your topic and how carefully you have thought about your sources, which encourages your audience to believe you are a credible researcher. In your citations and documentation you acknowledge any material that you have borrowed from a source and you join the conversation on your topic by adding your own interpretation. Accurate entries in the body of your project and list of works cited allow your audience to find and read your sources so that they can evaluate your interpretation and learn more about the subject themselves. Accurate entries also demonstrate the care with which you have written your research project, which further reinforces your credibility, or ethos.

to AUDIENCE

Qualifications of
source author

> While encouraging writers to use figurative language, journalist
> *signal phrase*
> Constance Hale cautions that "a metaphor has the shelf life of a fresh
> *page no.*
> vegetable" (224), illustrating the warning with her own lively metaphor.

Using a signal phrase allows you to integrate the borrowed material into your sentence, to put the source in context by adding your own interpretation, and to describe the qualifications of the source author. For these reasons, most summaries, paraphrases, and quotations should be introduced by a signal phrase.

- *Parenthetical note.* Include in parentheses the author's surname plus the page number(s) from which the borrowed material comes:

> While figurative language can make a passage come alive, be aware
> *parenthetical note*
> that metaphors have "the shelf life of a fresh vegetable" (Hale 224).

Parenthetical notes are useful when you are citing more than one source, when you are establishing facts, or when the author's identity is not relevant to the point you are making.

More about
Creating works-cited entries, 164–86

NOTE The works-cited entry is the same whether you use a signal phrase or a parenthetical note:

author   *title*   *publication info.*   *medium*
Hale, Constance. *Sin and Syntax.* New York: Broadway, 2001. Print.

More about
What you do and do not need to cite, 125–26
Signal phrases, 141–42
Signal verbs (list), 141
Integrating borrowed material into your text, 147–48

Quick Reference   **General Principles of In-Text Citation**

- Cite not only direct quotations but also paraphrases, summaries, and information gathered from a source, whether printed or online.
- In most cases, include the author's surname and a page reference. For one-page and unpaginated sources (such as websites), provide only the author's name.
- Place the name(s) either in a signal phrase or in a parenthetical note. A signal phrase makes it easier to integrate borrowed information or the author's credentials into your own prose. A parenthetical citation is appropriate when establishing facts or citing more than one source for a piece of information.
- For two or more sources by the same author, include the title—either a complete title in the text or an abbreviated title in the parenthetical note.
- Whenever you add a title or abbreviated title, insert a comma between the surname and the title, but not between the title and the page number. In parenthetical citations, do not insert punctuation between the author's surname and the page number.

Tech	**Page References and Web Pages**

Despite the term *web page*, most websites do not have page numbers in the sense that printed books do. Your browser may number the pages when you print a web page from a website, but this numbering appears only on your printed copy. Different computers and printers break pages differently, so your printed page 5 might be someone else's page 4 or 6. For this reason, in-text citations of most web pages include only the author's name. If a website numbers its paragraphs, provide that information in place of a page reference.

19b Including Enough Information to Lead Readers to the Source in Your List of Works Cited

Whether you are using a signal phrase or a parenthetical note, in-text citations should provide enough information for readers to locate the source in the *list of works cited.* In most cases, providing the author's surname and a page reference is enough. Occasionally, however, you may need to provide more information:

- If you cite more than one source by the same author, mention the title of the work in the text or include a shortened form of the title in the in-text citation. (You may also want to mention the title of the work, if it is relevant to the point you are making.)

  > Example 6, 156

- If you refer to sources by two different authors who have the same surname, mention the authors' first names in the text, or include the authors' first initials in the in-text citation.

  > Example 7, 156

Occasionally, you may need to include less information. For example, you would omit a page number when you are summarizing an entire source, when your source is just one page long, or when your source, such as a web page, is not paginated.

> Example 8, 156
> Example 16a, 161

19c Placing In-Text Citations to Avoid Distracting Readers and to Show Them Where Borrowed Material Starts and Stops

When you incorporate a quotation, paraphrase, summary, or idea from a source into your own text, carefully consider the placement of the in-text citation, keeping the following goals in mind:

- To make clear exactly which material is drawn from the source
- To avoid distracting your reader

Signal phrase When using a signal phrase, bookend the borrowed information: Insert the author's name *before,* and the page number *after,* the cited material.

Signal phrase

Page number

> Daniels, who has written several books about DC Comics' creations, notes that underground comics artists are not controlled by corporate interests that discourage daring material (165).

More about
Phrases, 330–32
Clauses, 332–34,
  341–43
Sentences, 334–35

Parenthetical note When using a parenthetical note, place the note at a natural pause—at the end of a phrase, clause, or sentence—right after the borrowed material and before any punctuation.

Following a sentence

> Common themes of underground comics include sex and sexual identity, politics, and social issues (Daniels 165).

Following a clause

> Other common themes of underground comics include sex and sexual identity, politics, and social issues (Daniels 165), as shown in Robert Crumb's *Snarf* comics.

Following a phrase

> The themes of underground comics, such as sex and sexual identity, politics, and social issues (Daniels 165), are all demonstrated in Robert Crumb's *Snarf* comics.

Writing Responsibly

Using Signal Phrases to Demonstrate Your Relationship with Sources

More about
Integrating supporting material, 140–42
When to use signal phrases, 141–42

As you consider using a source, think about *why* you want to use it. Does it provide a supporting reason or illustration? Does it provide an authoritative voice? Does it make a point that contrasts with your own? Then include a signal phrase that reflects your answer to that question.

> Tom Bergin, who covers the oil and gas industry for Reuters, provides one example of the consequences of offshore drilling.

> Neurobiologist Catherine Levine agrees with this point of view.

> The views of meteorologist John Coleman contrast dramatically with those of the majority of climate scientists.

to TOPIC

Block quotations When the text you are quoting takes up more than four lines of your project, indent the borrowed material as a block by one inch from the left margin, and place the parenthetical note one space *after* the closing punctuation mark. No quotation marks should be used when indenting quoted material as a block.

> *More about*
> Block quotations,
> 158–59, 190,
> 437–48

Example

> signal phrase
> Howard and Kennedy assert that parents and school officials tend to ignore
> hazing until an incident becomes public knowledge. They describe a concrete
> incident that demonstrates their claims:
>
> ←——→ In general, the Bredvik school community (parents, teachers,
> 1"
> coaches, and students) condoned or ignored behaviors that could
> be called "hazing" or "sexual harassment." However, when the
> incident was formally brought to the attention of the larger, public
> audience, a conflict erupted in the community over how to frame,
> understand, and react to the event. (347-48)

19d Adjusting In-Text Citations to Match Your Source

The exact form of an in-text citation depends on the source. Does it have one author, several authors, or no authors? Is the source paginated? Is the source a novel, a story in an anthology, or a PowerPoint presentation? The examples below cover the most common source types. (A list of in-text citation examples in MLA style appears on the next page.) For more unusual sources, study the general principles as outlined here and in the *MLA Handbook for Writers of Research Papers,* 7th ed. (available in any library), and adapt them to your special circumstances.

1. One author

a. Signal phrase

> Cahill cautions responsible historians against disparaging the Middle
> Ages. Medieval Europe's reputation as a time of darkness, ignorance,
> page no.
> and blind faith is "largely (if not wholly) undeserved" (310).

MLA In-Text
Citations Index

1. **One author**
2. Two or three
   authors
3. More than
   three authors

MLA In-Text Citations Index

b. Parenthetical note

> The Middle Ages are often unjustly characterized as a time of darkness, ignorance, and blind faith (Cahill 310).

2. Two or three authors Include the surnames of all the authors in your signal phrase or parenthetical note; use *and*, not an ampersand (&), in the parenthetical note.

> To write successfully about their families, authors must have motives beyond merely exposing secret histories (Miller and Paola 72).

3. More than three authors For sources with more than three authors, you may either list each author by surname (following the order in the text) or insert the Latin phrase *et al.* following the first author's surname.

et al. Abbreviation of the Latin phrase *et alii,* "and others"

NOTE *al.* is an abbreviation, so it requires a period; *et* is a complete word, so it does not. There should be no punctuation between the author's name and *et al.*

all authors in signal phrase

Visonà, Poynor, Cole, Harris, Abiodun, and Blier stress that symbols used in African art are not intended to be iconic but instead to suggest a wide variety of meanings. The authors liken this complexity to "a telephone line that carries multiple messages simultaneously" (19).

Symbols used in African art are not intended to be iconic but rather to

1st author + et al.

suggest a complex range of meanings (Visonà et al. 19).

Whichever you choose, do the same in your list of works cited.

> Example 3, 165

4. Group, government, or corporate author When a government agency, corporation, or other organization is listed as the author, use that organization's name in your in-text citation. The MLA suggests incorporating names into your sentence in a signal phrase to avoid long parenthetical notes.

government agency as author

The Federal Emergency Management Agency indicates that Kansas City is located in a region of frequent and intense tornado activity (4).

If a parenthetical note makes more sense in the context, use common abbreviations ("US" for *United States,* "Corp." for *Corporation*) to shorten the name where you can.

5. Unnamed author If the author is unnamed and the work is alphabetized by title in the list of works cited, use the title in your in-text citation. Abbreviate long titles in parenthetical citations.

One nineteenth-century children's book vows that "when examined by the microscope, the flea is a pleasant object," and the author's vivid description of this sight—a body "curiously adorned with a suit of polished armor, neatly jointed, and beset with a great number of sharp pins almost like the quills of a

title

porcupine"—may win readers' curiosity, if not their sympathy (*Insects* 8).

> Example 4, 165

If you do abbreviate the title, start your abbreviation with the word by which the title will be alphabetized in your list of works cited. Also, only if the author is listed specifically as "Anonymous" should you use that designation.

6. Two or more sources by the same author When you draw on two or more sources by the same author, differentiate between those sources by including titles.

book title

In her book *Nickel and Dimed*, social critic Barbara Ehrenreich demonstrates

that people cannot live on the then-current minimum wage (60). Perhaps, as

blog entry title

she notes in her blog entry "'Values' Voters Raise Minimum Wages," they will

be a little better able to hold their own in the six states (Arizona, Colorado,

Montana, Missouri, Nevada, Ohio) that have recently raised their minimum

wage.

7. Two or more authors with the same surname When you cite sources by two different authors with the same surname, differentiate them by including their first names (the first time you mention them in a signal phrase) or by including their first initials (in a parenthetical reference or subsequent in-text citations).

Including citations is important not only because they give credit but

also because they "organize a field of inquiry, create order, and allow for

accountability" (S. Rose 243). This concern for acknowledging original sources

dates back to the early eighteenth century: Joseph Addison was one of

the first to argue for "the superiority of original to imitative composition"

(M. Rose 114).

8. Entire source (including a one-page source) Mention an entire source—whether it is a film or a website, a book or an article, a painting or a graphic novel—in your text using the information that begins the entry in your list of works cited.

> The film *The Lady Eve* asks whether love is possible without trust.

Example 41b, 180

9. Selection from an anthology If your source is a selection from an anthology, reader, or other collection, your citation should name the author of the selection—not the editor of the anthology. In the example below, Faulkner is the author of the selection "A Rose for Emily," a story that appears in a literature anthology edited by Robert DiYanni.

Example 10, 168

MLA In-Text
Citations Index

> Southern fiction often explores the marked curiosity that women of stature
>
> author of selection
> and mystery inspire in their communities. Faulkner's "A Rose for Emily," for
>
> example, describes the title character as "a tradition, a duty, and a care; a
>
> sort of hereditary obligation upon the town . . ." (79).

10. Multivolume source If you use information from more than one volume of a multivolume work, your in-text citation must indicate both the volume and the page from which you are borrowing. (This information can be omitted if you use only one volume of the work, since your works-cited entry will indicate which volume you used.)

Example 15b, 171

> author
> Tarbell writes that in 1847 Abraham Lincoln was a popular man of
>
> "simple, sincere friendliness" who was an enthusiastic—though awkward—
>
> vol. no. pg. no.
> bowler (1: 210).

The words *volume* and *page* (or their abbreviations) are not used.

11. Literary source Because many classics of literature—novels, poems, plays—are published in a number of editions (printed and digital) with pagination that varies widely, your citation should provide your readers with the information they will need to find the passage, regardless of which edition they are reading.

a. Novel Include the chapter number (with the abbreviation *ch.*) after the page number (or location reference for digital books) from your edition.

> Joyce shows his protagonist's dissatisfaction with family, faith, and country
>
> through the adolescent Stephen Dedalus's first dinner at the adult table, an
>
> pg. no. ch. no.
> evening filled with political and religious discord (274; ch. 1).

Use arabic (*2, 9, 103*), not roman (*ii, ix, ciii*), numerals, regardless of what your source uses.

If the novel has chapters grouped into parts or books, include both the part or book number and the chapter number, using the appropriate abbreviation (*pt.* for *part* or *bk.* for *book*).

> Even though New York society declares the Countess Olenska beyond her
>
> prime, Newland Archer sees in her the "mysterious authority of beauty"
>
> (Wharton 58; bk. 1, ch. 8).

b. Play When citing plays, use act, scene, and line numbers (in that order), not page numbers or location numbers (used in digital editions). Do not label the parts. Instead, separate them with periods.

> When the ghost of Hamlet's father cries, "Adieu, adieu, adieu! remember
>
> me," Hamlet wonders if he must "remember" his father through vengeance
>
> (1.5.91).

Use arabic (*1, 5, 91*), not roman (*i, v, xci*), numerals for act, scene, and line numbers, and omit spaces after periods between numbers.

c. Poem For poetry, use line numbers, rather than page or location numbers. With the first reference to line numbers, use the word *line* or *lines;* omit it thereafter.

> In Audre Lorde's poem "Hanging Fire," her fourteen-year-old frets, "What if
>
> I die / before morning" (lines 7-8), making me remember my own teenage
>
> *1st ref.*
>
> worries of just a few years ago. Each of the three stanzas ends with "and
>
> momma's in the bedroom / with the door closed" (9-10, 20-21, 32-33),
>
> *later refs.*
>
> bringing me back to my "now": I am that mother who does not understand.

MLA In-Text
Citations Index

For long poems that are divided into sections (books, parts, numbered stanzas), provide section information as well, omitting the section type (such as *book* or *part*) and separating the section number from the line number(s) with a period.

David Mason's *Ludlow* (2007) begins with a description that captures Luisa's life:

> Down below
>
> the mesa, smells of cooking rose from shacks
>
> in rows, and there Luisa scrubbed the pot
>
> as if she were some miner's wife and not
>
> a sapper's daughter, scrawny, barely twelve. (1.5-8)

sec.
lines.

> Use arabic (*1, 5, 8*), not roman (*i, v, viii*), numerals, and omit spaces.

12. Sacred text Cite sacred texts (such as the Bhagavad-Gita, the Talmud, the Qur'an, and the Bible) not by page number but by book title (abbreviated in parenthetical notes), chapter number, and verse number(s), and separate each section with a period. Do not italicize book titles or put them in quotation marks, and do not italicize the name of the sacred text, unless you are referring to a specific edition.

sacred text
In the Bible's timeless love poetry, the female speaker concludes her description of her lover with this proclamation: "This is my beloved and this is my friend, / O daughters of Jerusalem" (Song of Sol. 5.16).

book   ch.verse

— No space

specific edition
The *New Oxford Annotated Bible* offers a moving translation of the
book
timeless love poetry in the Song of Solomon. The female speaker concludes her description of her lover with this proclamation: "This is my beloved and this is my friend, / O daughters of Jerusalem" (5.16).

ch.verse

13. Motion picture, television or radio broadcast The information you include in an in-text citation for a motion picture or for a television or radio broadcast depends on what you are emphasizing in your project. When you are emphasizing the work itself, use the title; when you are emphasizing the director's work, use the director's name; when you are emphasizing an actor's work, use the actor's name. Start your works-cited entry with whatever you have used in your in-text citation.

> Example 41b, 180

title
While *The Lady Eve* is full of slapstick humor, it is mainly remembered for

its snappy dialogue, at once witty and suggestive.

actor's name
Barbara Stanwyck's portrayal of Jean Harrington is at once sexy and

wholesome.

14. Indirect source When you can, avoid quoting from a secondhand source. When you cannot use the original source, mention the name of the person you are quoting in your sentence. In your parenthetical note, include *qtd. in* (for *quoted in*) plus the name of the author of the source in which you found the quotation.

Handel's stock among opera-goers rose considerably over the course of the

author quoted
twentieth century. In 1912, an English music critic, H. C. Colles, maintained

that "it would be difficult, if not impossible, to make any one of Handel's

source of quotation
operas tolerable to a modern audience" (qtd. in Orrey 62). Today, however,

Handel's operas are performed around the world.

In your list of works cited, include the *indirect* source (*Orrey*), not the source being quoted (*H. C. Colles*).

15. Dictionary or encyclopedia entry In the citation of a dictionary or encyclopedia entry, omit the page number on which you found the item. For a dictionary entry, place the defined word in quotation marks, followed by the abbreviation *def.* Follow this with the letter or number of the definition you wish to reference.

Another definition of *honest* is "respectable" ("Honest," def. 6), but what, if

anything, does truth have to do with respectability?

In the parenthetical note for an encyclopedia entry, include the entry's full title in quotation marks.

More about
Parts of a dictionary entry, 310–11

> The study of ethics is not limited to philosophers, as its "all-embracing
>
> practical nature" makes it an applicable or even necessary course of study in
>
> a wide variety of disciplines, from biology to business ("Ethics").

If you are citing two entries with the same title from different reference sources, add an abbreviated form of the reference work's title to each entry.

> While the word *ethics* is commonly understood to mean "moral principles"
>
> ("Ethics," def. 4, *Random House Webster's*), to philosophers it is "the
>
> evaluation of human conduct" ("Ethics," *Philosophical Dict.*).

MLA In-Text Citations Index

14. Indirect source
15. Dictionary or encyclopedia entry
16. **Website or other online source**
17. Personal communication
18. Table, chart, or figure

16. Website or other online source Cite electronic sources such as websites, online articles, e-books, and e-mails as you would print sources, even though many of these sources do not use page numbers.

a. Without page, paragraph, screen, or slide numbers Unless there is another numbering system at work (such as numbered paragraphs, screens, or slides), cite the author without a page reference.

> When first published in 1986, Alan Moore's *Watchmen* revolutionized the
>
> comic book. Today, even its harshest critics acknowledge the book's
>
> author only
> landmark status (Shone).

You may credit your source more elegantly by mentioning the author in a signal phrase and omitting the parenthetical citation altogether.

> signal phrase
> Reading Alan Moore's *Watchmen* in 2005, critic Tom Shone found it
>
> "underwhelming," but he admitted that in 1986 the comic book was
>
> "unquestionably a landmark work."

b. With paragraph, screen, or slide numbers If an electronic source numbers its paragraphs, screens, or slides, you can reference these numbers as you would pages (with an appropriate identifying abbreviation—*par.* or *pars., screen* or *screens*).

> The Internet has also become an outlet for direct distribution through artist
>
> websites, making independent titles not only more accessible to consumers
>
> but also more affordable for individual artists to produce and market (Fenty,
>
> Houp, and Taylor par. 1).

More about
PDF files, 102, 108

c. In a PDF file Online documents offered as a PDF (portable document format) file include all the elements of the printed document, including the page number. Since pages are fixed, you can and should cite page numbers.

MLA In-Text Citations Index

17. Personal communication (e-mail, letter, interview) As with other unpaginated sources, when citing information from a letter, e-mail message, interview, or other personal communication, you should include the author's name in a signal phrase or parenthetical citation. Also indicate the type of source you are citing.

> Many people have asked why teachers cannot do more to prevent school
>
> source type
> shootings; in an e-mail to this author, one instructor responds: "As creative
>
> writing teachers untrained in psychology, can we really determine from a
>
> student's poetry whether he or she is emotionally disturbed—even a threat
>
> author of e-mail
> to others?" (Fox).

Examples 47–51,
183–84

18. Table, chart, or figure If a copy of the visual you are discussing is *not* included in your project, include relevant information in the text (artist's name or table title, for example), and include an entry in your list of works cited.

> There is no experience quite like standing in front of a full-size painting by
>
> Jackson Pollock. His paintings have an irresistible sense of movement to
>
> them, the particular quality of which is unique to his work. This is especially
>
> evident in *One (Number 31, 1950),* which currently hangs on the fourth floor of
>
> New York's Museum of Modern Art.

If a copy of the visual *is* included in your project, reference it in your text and include the source information in a table's source note (Figure 19.1) or in a figure's caption (see the figure caption on p. 195 in the project at the end of chapter 22).

19. Government document Because government documents are alphabetized in the list of works cited by the name of the nation that produced them, mention the country as well as the agency in your text.

TABLE 1	THE DEMISE OF THE THREE-DECKER NOVEL
Year	**No. of 3-deckers published**
1894	184
1895	52
1896	—
1897	4
1898	0

Source: Information from John Feather, *A History of British Publishing* (Clarendon: Crown Helm, 1988; print; 125).

FIGURE 19.1 Table in MLA style

Just as the nation was entering World War II, the United States War Department published a book outlining what it had learned about reading aerial photographs.

> Example 52, 184

20. Legal source Laws, acts, and legal cases are typically referred to by name either in your sentence or in a parenthetical citation. Laws and acts are neither italicized nor enclosed in quotation marks.

> Example 53, 185

In 2008 the US Congress passed the Combat Bonus Act.

Legal cases are italicized in your text, but not in the list of works cited.

In 1963 the Supreme Court ruled that poor defendants should receive legal representation, even if they could not pay for it themselves (*Gideon v. Wainright*).

21. Multiple sources in one sentence When you use different information from multiple sources within a single sentence, give separate citations in the appropriate place.

Other common themes of underground comics include sex and sexual identity, politics, and social issues (Daniels 165), as shown in Crumb's work, which is well known for its satirical approach to countercultural topics (Heller 101-02).

22. Multiple sources in one citation When you draw information from more than one source, follow the borrowed material with a list of all relevant sources, separated by semicolons.

> Jamestown was once described as a failed colony populated by failed
>
> colonists, but new findings suggest that the colonists were resourceful
>
> survivors (Howard; Lepore 43).

20 Preparing an MLA-Style List of Works Cited

The list of works cited, which comes at the end of your research project, includes information about the sources you have cited in your text. (A bibliography that includes sources you read but did not cite in your research project is called a *list of works consulted*.) Your list of works cited provides readers with the information they need to locate the material you used in your project. The format of each entry depends in part on the type of source it is. (See the Quick Reference box on pp. 166–67 for a list of MLA-style examples included in this chapter.)

Annotated visual of where to find author, title, and publication information, on foldout accompanying tab 6

Books—Printed and Electronic

In a printed book, most or all of the information you need to create an entry in the list of works cited appears on the title and copyright pages, which are located at the beginning of the book. In an online or e-book, print and electronic publication information often appears at the top or bottom of the first page or screen or is available through a link.

1. One author

a. **Printed** The basic entry for a printed book looks like this:

> Author's surname, First name. *Title: Subtitle*. Place of publication: Publisher
>
> (shortened), date of publication. Medium of publication.

Here is an example of an actual entry in the list of works cited:

> author   title   publication information medium
> Morrison, Toni. *Home*. New York: Knopf, 2012. Print.
>   place   pub.   date

b. Database Some books are available in online, full-text archives, or databases, such as *Bartleby.com*. When you are documenting a book you accessed through a database, add the name of the database and change the medium of publication from *Print* to *Web*. Also, add the date (day, month, and year) on which you accessed the work.

> Wharton, Edith. *The Age of Innocence.* New York: D. Appleton, 1920.
>
> database   date accessed
> *Bartleby.com.* Web. 5 July 2007.
>   medium

c. E-book The citation for an electronic version of a book is the same as for a printed book except that the medium of publication changes from *Print* to the specific type of e-book file you read: Nook file, Microsoft Reader file, Kindle file, and so on.

>   medium
> Morrison, Toni. *Home.* New York: Knopf, 2012. Kindle file.

2. Two or three authors List authors in the order in which they appear on the title page. Only the first author should be listed with surname first.

> author 1   author 2
> Miller, Brenda, and Suzanne Paola. *Tell It Slant.* New York: McGraw-Hill,
>
>   2004. Print.

> author 1   author 2   author 3
> Fullagar, Simone, Kevin W. Markwell, and Erica Wilson. *Slow Tourism:*
>
>   *Experiences and Mobilities.* Bristol: Multilingual Matters, 2012. Print.

3. More than three authors Either list all the authors, or just list the first and add *et al.* Whichever you choose, do the same in your in-text citation.

> Visonà, Monica Blackmun, Robin Poynor, Herbert M. Cole, Michael D. Harris,
>
>   Rowland Abiodun, and Suzanne Preston Blier. *A History of Art in Africa.*
>
>   New York: Abrams, 2001. Print.

> Visonà, Monica Blackmun, et al. *A History of Art in Africa.* New York: Abrams,
>
>   2001. Print.

4. Unnamed (anonymous) author Start the entry with the title.

>   title
> *Terrorist Hunter: The Extraordinary Story of a Woman Who Went*
>
>   *Undercover to Infiltrate the Radical Islamic Groups Operating in America.*
>
>   New York: Ecco-HarperCollins, 2003. Print.

MLA Works-Cited Entries

1. One author
2. Two or three authors
3. More than three authors
4. Unnamed (anonymous) author
5. Author using a pen name
6. Two or more works by the same author

More about et al., 154–55

Example 3, 154

Quick

Reference   Examples of MLA-Style Works-Cited Entries

MLA Works-Cited Entries

Alphabetize the entry in your list of works cited using the first significant word of the title (not an article like *a, an,* or *the*). Only if the author is listed specifically as "Anonymous" should you use that designation in the works-cited entry (and in your text).

> Anonymous. *Go Ask Alice.* Englewood Cliffs: Prentice, 1971. Print.

5. Author using a pen name (pseudonym) If the author is using a pen name (or *pseudonym*), document the source using the author's pen name and insert the author's actual name in brackets following the pseudonym.

> Keene, Carolyn [Edward Stratemeyer]. *The Secret of the Old Clock.* New York:
>
> Grosset, 1930. Print.

6. Two or more works by the same author Alphabetize the entries by the first important word in each title. Supply the author's name only with the first entry. For subsequent works, replace the author's name with three hyphens.

> Lethem, Jonathan. *The Ecstasy of Influence: Nonfictions, Etc.* New York:
>
> Doubleday, 2011. Print.
>
> ---. *Gun, with Occasional Music.* Philadelphia: Harvest, 2003. Print.

7. Group or corporate author Treat the sponsoring organization as the author.

> corporate author
> Blackfoot Gallery Committee. *The Story of the Blackfoot People:*
>
> *Nitsitapiisinni.* Richmond Hill: Firefly, 2002. Print.

MLA Works-Cited Entries

8. Edited book or anthology (printed or online) When citing the book as a whole, treat the editor as the author and insert the abbreviation *ed.* (or *eds.* if there is more than one editor) after the name.

> Furman, Laura, ed. *The O. Henry Prize Stories: The Best Stories of the Year.*
>
> New York: Anchor, 2011. Print.

> Delbanco, Nicholas, and Alan Cheuse, eds. *Literature: Craft and Voice.* New
>
> York: McGraw-Hill, 2009. Print.

9. Author and editor or translator List the author first. After the title, include the abbreviation *Ed.* or *Trans.* (as appropriate) before the editor's or translator's name. If the book was accessed online, add the information shown in item 1b–c.

> Larsson, Asa. *Sun Storm.* Trans. Marlaine Delargy. New York: Delacorte, 2006.
>
> Print.

NOTE When the abbreviation appears before the editor's or translator's name, it means *edited by* or *translated by,* so use the same abbreviation regardless of whether there is one editor or translator or many. When the abbreviation *ed.* appears after the name, it means *editor,* so add an *-s* (*eds.*) if more than one editor is listed. The abbreviation *trans.* does not change.

---

10. One or more selections from an edited book or anthology (printed or online) If you are citing a selection from an edited book or anthology, start the entry with the selection's author and title. Include the page numbers for the entire selection (even if you used only part).

> author   title (selection)
> Faulkner, William. "A Rose for Emily." *Literature: Reading Fiction, Poetry,*
>
> *and Drama.* Ed. Robert DiYanni. 6th ed. New York: McGraw-Hill, 2009.
>
> pages (selection)
> 79-84. Print.

When documenting a longer work, such as a novel or a play, that is included in the anthology or collection, italicize the work's title.

> title (selection)
> Ives, David. *Sure Thing. Literature: Reading Fiction, Poetry, and Drama.* . . .

Example 8, 168

If you are citing more than one selection in the anthology or collection, include an entry for the collection as a whole.

DiYanni, Robert D., ed. *Literature: Reading Fiction, Poetry, and Drama.* 6th ed.

New York: McGraw-Hill, 2009. Print.

Then, for each selection you use from the anthology, include only the author and title of the selection, the surname of the anthology's editor, and the page numbers of the selection.

Faulkner, William. "A Rose for Emily." DiYanni 79-84.

For a scholarly article included in an edited book, include the article's original publication information first, the abbreviation *Rpt. in* for *reprinted in,* and then the publication information for the anthology.

Example 24 a–c, 173–74

original publication info.
Stock, A. G. "Yeats and Achebe." *Journal of Commonwealth Literature*
reprint publication info.
5.3 (1970): 105-11. Rpt. in *Things Fall Apart.* By Chinua Achebe.

Ed. Francis Abiola Irele. New York: W.W. Norton, 2008. 271-77. Print.

If the book was accessed online, add the information shown in item 1b–c.

11. Edition other than the first Insert the edition number (*2nd ed., 3rd ed.*) or edition name (*Rev. ed.* for "revised edition") before the publication information. The edition number or name should appear on the title page.

Feather, John. *The Information Society: A Study of Continuity and Change.* 5th

ed. London: Facet, 2008. Print.

12. Imprint (division) of a larger publishing company Name both the imprint and the publisher, separating them with a hyphen.

Betcherman, Lita-Rose. *Court Lady and Country Wife: Two Noble Sisters in*
imprint
Seventeenth-Century England. New York: William Morrow-
publisher
HarperCollins, 2005. Print.

13. Introduction, preface, foreword, or afterword Begin with the name of the person who wrote this section of the text. Then provide a descriptive label (such as *Introduction* or *Preface*), the title of the book, and the name of the book's author. (If the author of the section and the book are the same, use only the author's surname after the title.) Include the page numbers for the section.

author of intro.   label   title of book   author of book
Camuto, Christopher. Introduction. *The Shenandoah.* By Julia Davis.
pages (intro.)
Morgantown: West Virginia UP, 2011. 7-30. Print.

If this section has a title, include it before the descriptive label.

afterword's title
Burton, Larry W. "Countering the Naysayers: Independent Writing

Programs as Successful Experiments in American Education."

label
Afterword. *A Field of Dreams: Independent Writing Programs and the*

Future of Composition Studies. Ed. Peggy O'Neill, Angela Crow, and

Larry W. Burton. Logan: Utah State UP, 2002. 295-300. Print.

14. Entry in a reference work Format an entry in a dictionary or encyclopedia as you would a selection from an edited book or anthology. For signed articles, include the author's name. (Articles in reference works often carry the author's initials only, so you may need to cross-reference the initials with a list of contributors in the front or back of the book.) If an article is unsigned, begin with its title.

a. Printed For familiar reference works, omit publication information other than the edition, year of publication, and medium. If the entries are arranged alphabetically, omit a page reference.

"Culture." *Oxford English Dictionary.* Compact 2nd ed. 1991. Print.

Green, Michael. "Cultural Studies." *A Dictionary of Cultural and Critical Theory.*

Cambridge: Blackwell, 1996. Print.

b. Online For online reference works, add the site's sponsor, change the medium of publication to *Web,* and add the date you accessed the site.

sponsor
"Culture." *Merriam-Webster Online Dictionary.* Merriam-Webster Online,

medium access date
2008. Web. 3 Mar. 2010.

c. CD-ROM or DVD-ROM Although CD-ROMs have largely been replaced by the Internet, you may still need to use them. If the CD-ROM or DVD-ROM is published in versions rather than editions, use the abbreviation *Vers.* and include the version number before the publication information. Change the medium of publication to *CD-ROM* or *DVD-ROM.*

Cooley, Marianne. "Alphabet." *World Book Multimedia Encyclopedia.*

version   medium
Vers. 6.0.2. Chicago: World Book, 2002. CD-ROM.

15. Multivolume work

a. Multiple volumes Indicate the total number of volumes, followed by the abbreviation *vols.,* and indicate the span of years in which the volumes were pub-

lished. Specify the volume from which you borrowed a particular passage or   Example 10, 157
idea in your in-text citation.

> no. of vols.
Tarbell, Ida M. *The Life of Abraham Lincoln.* 2 vols. New York: Lincoln
> pub. dates
      Memorial Assn., 1895-1900. Print.

b. One volume If you used only one volume, include the number of the volume
you used before the publication information, and give only the publication
date of that volume.

> vol. used
Tarbell, Ida M. *The Life of Abraham Lincoln.* Vol. 1. New York: Lincoln
> pub. date
      Memorial Assn., 1895. Print.

16. Book in a series If the book you are citing is part of a series, the series title
will usually be noted on the book's title page or on the page before the title
page. Insert the series title (with no quotation marks or italics) after the medium of publication. If books in the series are numbered, include the number
following the series title.

> Todorov, Tzvetan. *Mikhail Bakhtin: The Dialogical Principle.* Trans. Wlad
> series title
      Godzich. Minneapolis: U of Minnesota P, 1995. Print. Theory and
> no.
Hist. of Lit. 13.

17. Republished book If a book has been republished, its original date of publication will appear on the book's copyright page. If the original publication
date may be of interest to your readers, include it before publication information for the version you consulted. If the book was edited or an introduction
was added, include that information before the republication information.

> orig.
> pub. date   editors
Burroughs, William S. *Naked Lunch.* 1959. Ed. James Grauerholz and
> repub. info.
      Barry Miles. New York: Grove, 2001. Print.

18. Title within a title Omit italics from any title that would normally be italicized when it falls within the main title of a book.

> book title   title within title
Blamires, Harry. *The New Bloomsbury Book: A Guide Through* Ulysses.

      3rd ed. London: Routledge, 2006. Print.

If the title within the title would normally appear in quotation marks, retain
the quotation marks and italicize both titles.

MLA Works-
Cited Entries

13. Introduction,
    preface,
    foreword, or
    afterword
14. Entry in a
    reference work
**15. Multivolume
    work**
**16. Book in a
    series**
**17. Republished
    book**
**18. Title within a
    title**
19. Sacred text
20. Missing
    publication
    information

MLA Works-Cited Entries

❯ Example 1, 164

19. Sacred text Italicize the title of the edition you are using. Editors' and translators' names follow the title.

> *The New Oxford Annotated Bible.* Ed. Michael D. Coogan, Marc Z. Brettler,
>
> Carol A. Newsom, and Pheme Perkins. Augmented 3rd ed. New York:
>
> Oxford UP, 2007. Print. Rev. Standard Vers. with Apocrypha.

> *The Holy Qur'an.* Ed. and trans. Abdullah Yusuf Ali. 10th ed. Beltsville: Amana,
>
> 1997. Print.

20. Missing publication information Replace missing information with an appropriate abbreviation, such as *n.d.* for *no date* or *n.p.* for *no publisher* or *no place of publication.* (The letter *n* is capitalized following a period and lowercased after a comma.)

> Barrett, Edgar, ed. *Football West Virginia 1960.* N.p.: West Virginia University,
>
> n.d. Print.

21. Pamphlet, brochure, or press release Follow the format for book entries. For a press release, include day, month, and year of publication, if available.

> "Family Teams Key to March for Babies." Fargo: March of Dimes, 17 Jan. 2008.
>
> Print.

If the item was e-mailed or published online, document it as you would a book published online.

❯ Example 46, 183

22. Conference proceedings Include the title of the conference, the sponsoring organization (if its name is not cited in the conference title), and the date and location of the conference, if that information is not already included in the publication's title.

> sponsor
> Bizzell, Patricia, ed. *Proceedings of the Rhetoric Society of America:*
> title (conference)   date
> *Rhetorical Agendas: Political, Ethical, Spiritual.* 28–31 May 2004,
> location
> U of Texas—Austin. Mahwah, NJ: Erlbaum, 2005. Print.

For a paper delivered at a conference, follow the format for a lecture.

23. Dissertation Include the abbreviation *Diss.,* the school to which the dissertation was submitted (abbreviate *University* to *U*), and the year it was submitted. For published dissertations, italicize the title.

Agopsowicz, William Joseph. *In Praise of Fantasy: A Study of the Nineteenth Century American Short Story (Poe, Hawthorne, Irving, Melville, Bierce, James).* Diss. Arizona State U, 1992. Ann Arbor: UMI, 1992. Print.

For unpublished dissertations, put the title in quotation marks.

Brommer, Stephanie. "We Walk with Them: South Asian Women's Organizations in Northern California Confront Domestic Abuse." Diss. U of California—Santa Barbara, 2004. Print.

diss. submission info.

Periodicals—Printed and Electronic

A periodical is a publication issued at regular intervals—newspapers are typically published every day, magazines every week or month, and scholarly journals four times a year. Most researchers today find articles in periodicals by searching their library's *databases,* online indexes that provide citation information as well as an abstract (or summary) and sometimes an electronic copy of the article itself, in either PDF or HTML format. (A PDF file shows the article more or less as it would have appeared in print; an HTML file includes the text of the article but not the illustrations or formatting of the print version.) For all periodicals, include not only the title of the article (in quotation marks) but also the title of the periodical (in italics). The other publication information you include depends on the type of periodical you are documenting.

24. Article in a scholarly journal The information you need to create an entry for a printed journal article is on the cover or in the table of contents of the journal and on the first and last page of the article. For articles downloaded from a database, the information you need appears on the screen listing the articles that fit your search terms, on the first and last page of the file you download, or in the full record for the article you select. For articles that appear in journals published solely online, you may find the information you need on the website's home page, in the journal's table of contents, or on the first screen of the article. Access dates for database and online articles should come from your notes.

> Annotated visual of where to find author, title, publication, and other information, on foldout accompanying tab 6

a. Printed The basic entry for an article in a printed journal looks like this:

Surname, First name. "Article Title." *Journal Title* volume.issue (year): pages. Medium of publication.

Here is an example of an actual entry:

author Weaver, Karen. "A Game Change: Paying for Big-Time College Sports." *article title*

journal title *issue* *pages*
Change 43.1 (2011): 14-21. Print.
vol. *year* *medium*

b. Accessed through a database When you document an article from a scholarly journal that you accessed through an online database, add the name of the database (in italics), change the medium of publication to *Web,* and add the date (day, month, year) on which you accessed the work at the end of the entry.

> Weaver, Karen. "A Game Change: Paying for Big-Time College Sports."
>
> database
> *Change* 43.1 (2011): 14–21. *EBSCOhost Education Research*
> medium access date
> *Complete.* Web. 3 Mar. 2010.

c. Online To document an online journal article, follow the model for a printed journal article, change the medium to *Web,* and add the date on which you accessed the article at the end of the entry. Although many journals that are published only online do not provide all the information that is available for printed journals, your entry should include as much of that information as possible. If the article you are documenting omits page numbers, use *n. pag.* in their place. Include the article's URL only if readers will not be able to find the article by searching for the author or title. (The parts that are different from a printed journal article are highlighted.)

> Woolums, Viola. "Gendered Avatar Identity." *Kairos* 16.1 (2011):
> medium access date
> n. pag. Web. 3 Jan. 2012.

25. Article in a magazine (weekly, monthly)

a. Printed Provide the issue's publication date (month and year or day, month, and year) and the page range for the article, but not the magazine's volume or issue number, even when they are available.

> Fuller, Alexandra. "Her Heart Inform Her Tongue: Language Lost and
> pub. date pgs.
> Found." *Harper's* Jan. 2012: 60–64. Print.

> Collins, Lauren. "The King's Meal." *New Yorker* 21 Nov. 2011: 66–71. Print.

If the article appears on nonconsecutive pages (the first part appears on p. 2 but the rest of the article is continued on p. 10), include a plus sign after the first page number (*2+*).

b. Accessed through a database

> Fuller, Alexandra. "Her Heart Inform Her Tongue: Language Lost and
> database medium access date
> Found." *Harper's* Jan. 2012: 60–64. WilsonWeb. Web. 13 Apr. 2012.

c. Online If you are documenting the online edition of a magazine that also appears in print, use the site name (usually a variation on the print title, such as *Progressive.org* or *Vanity Fair Online*).

Carr, Nicholas. "Is Google Making Us Stupid?" *The Atlantic.com.*
website

Atlantic Monthly Group, July/Aug. 2008. Web. 2 Dec. 2008.
site sponsor

Stevenson, Seth. "Ads We Hate." *Slate.com.* Washington Post.Newsweek
website   site sponsor

Interactive, 28 Dec. 2009. Web. 3 Mar. 2010.

26. Article in a newspaper The information you need to create an entry for a printed newspaper article is on the masthead of the newspaper (at the top of the first page) and on the first and last page of the article. For newspaper articles downloaded from a database, the information you need appears on the screen listing the articles that fit your search terms or on the first and last page of the article itself. Articles that appear in online versions of the newspaper usually contain all the information you need at the top of the first screen. Use conventional capitalization of titles even when your original source does not.

a. Printed For an article in a daily newspaper, include the date (day, month, year). If the paper paginates sections separately, include the section number, letter, or name immediately before the page number.

Richtel, Matt, and Julie Bosman. "To Serve the Young, E-Book Fans

Prefer Print." *New York Times* 21 Nov. 2011: B1. Print.
date   sec. & pg.

If the section number or letter is not part of the page number, add the abbreviation *sec.* and the section name, number, or letter. If the section is named, add the section name before the abbreviation *sec.* If no author is listed, begin the entry with the title of the article. If the article continues on a nonconsecutive page, add a plus sign after the first page number (*A20+*). If the newspaper's masthead specifies an edition (such as late edition or national edition), include that information after the date.

Keller, Julia. "Viral Villainy." *Chicago Tribune* 22 Mar. 2009, final ed., sec. 6:
section

1+. Print.
nonconsecutive pg.   edition

If the name of the city in which the newspaper is published does not appear in the newspaper's title, include it in brackets after the title.

Willman, David. "NIH Calls Actions of Senior Researcher 'Serious

Misconduct.'" *Plain Dealer* [Cleveland] 10 Sept. 2006: A15. Print.
newspaper   city

For well-known national newspapers (such as the *Christian Science Monitor, USA Today,* and the *Wall Street Journal*), no city or state is needed. If you are unsure whether the newspaper is well known, consult your instructor or a reference librarian.

> Annotated visual of where to find author, title, publication, and other information, on foldout accompanying tab 6

> **More about** Title capitalization, 455–56

MLA Works-Cited Entries

b. Accessed through a database For a newspaper article accessed through a database, add the database name, change the medium to *Web,* and add the access date.

> Richtel, Matt, and Julie Bosman. "To Serve the Young, E-Book Fans
>   database medium
>   Prefer Print." *New York Times* 21 Nov. 2011: B1. *Factiva.* Web.
>   access date
>   2 Feb. 2012.

c. Online For an online newspaper article, provide the site name and sponsor, and include your date of access.

> Netburn, Deborah. "Theaters Set Aside Tweet Seats for Twitter Users."
>   website   sponsor   access date
>   *LATimes.com.* Los Angeles Times, 6 Dec. 2011. Web. 23 Jan. 2012.

Example 24a, 173
Example 25a, 174
Example 26a, 175

27. Article on microform Many libraries still store some back issues of periodicals on microform, a photograph of a periodical printed on plastic and viewed through a special microform reader. Your entry for an article on microform is the same as for a printed article.

If your source is preserved on microform in a reference source such as NewsBank, change the medium of publication to *Microform* and add the title of the reference source and any access numbers (such as fiche and grid numbers) following the medium of publication.

Example 24a–c,
173–74
Example 25a–c,
174–75
Example 26a–c,
176–76

28. Review (printed or online) Begin with the reviewer's name (if provided), followed by the title of the review (if any) and the label *Rev. of* (for *Review of*). Then include the title and author of the work being reviewed. Finally, include the title of the periodical and its publication information. If the review was accessed online, add information as shown in item 24b–c, 25b–c, or 26b–c.

> reviewer   title (review)   title (book)
> Grover, Jan. "Unreliable Narrator." Rev. of *Love Works Like This: Opening*
>   author
>   *One's Life to a Child,* by Lauren Slater. *Women's Review of Books*
>
>   19.10-11 (2002): 40. Print.

29. Editorial (printed or online) Often editorials are unsigned. When that is the case, begin with the title of the editorial (if any). Then insert the label *Editorial* and follow with the periodical's publication information.

> editorial title
> "Expanding the Horizon: OSU President Seeks to Give Students a New
>   label
>   View of Their Place in the World." Editorial. *Columbus* [OH] *Dispatch*
>
>   12 Mar. 2009: 8A. Print.

If the editorial was accessed online, add information as shown in item 24b–c, 25b–c, or 26b–c.

30. Letter to the editor (printed or online) Begin with the author's name, followed by the label *Letter* and the periodical's publication information.

Example 24a–c,
173–74
Example 25a–c,
174–75
Example 26a–c,
175–76

letter author   label
Park, John. Letter. *Time* 5 Dec. 2011: 9. Print.

If the letter to the editor has a title, add it (in quotation marks) after the author's name. If the letter to the editor was accessed online, add information as shown in item 24b–c, 25b–c, or 26b–c.

Other Electronic Sources

While it is usually easy to find the information you need to create a complete entry for a book or an article in a periodical, websites can be a bit trickier. Most of the information you need will appear on the site's home page, usually at the bottom or top of the page, or on the web page you are documenting. Sometimes you may need to look further: Click on links such as "About us" or "More information." Frequently, websites do not provide complete information, so include as much as you can.

Annotated visual of where to find author, title, and publication information, on foldout accompanying tab 6

31. Website The basic entry for a website looks like this:

Author's surname, First name. *Website title.* Site sponsor, Publication date or

date last updated. Medium. Access date.

Here is an example of an actual entry:

editor   title (website)
McGann, Jerome J., ed. *The Complete Writings and Pictures of Dante Gabriel*

Rossetti: A Hypermedia Archive. Institute for Advanced Technology
site sponsors
in the Humanities, U of Virginia, and Networked Infrastructure for
update   access date
Nineteenth-Century Electronic Scholarship, 2008. Web. 15 Feb. 2012.
medium

If no author or editor is listed, begin with the website's title.

32. Web page or short work on a website Add the title of the web page to the entry for a website.

page title
Bahri, Deepika. "Yehuda Amichai." *Postcolonial Studies.* Dept. of English,

Emory U, 13 Nov. 2002. Web. 17 Feb. 2012.

Personal websites often do not provide all the information needed to create a complete entry. If the site does not have a title, include the identifier "home page" or "website" in its place; if the title includes the author's name, do not restate it.

33. Home page (academic)

a. Course

instructor   title (course)   title (website)   site sponsor
Gray, David. "Introduction to Ethics." *Dept. of Philosophy.* Carnegie
medium   access date
Mellon U, Spring 2006. Web. 17 Apr. 2007.

b. Department

label
English Dept. Home page. *U of California—Santa Barbara.* UCSB, 2010.

Web. 20 July 2010.

34. Discussion list posting Treat the subject line (or *thread*) as the title, and include the name of the list, the sponsoring group, and the date of the posting.

subj. line   list name
Rendleman, Eliot. "Binge Writing and Moderation Writing." *Writing Program*
site sponsor   post date
Administration Discussion List. WPA, 21 Aug. 2011. Web. 27 Sept. 2012.

35. Article on a wiki Since wikis are written and edited collaboratively, there is no author to cite. Instead, begin the entry with the article title.

"Harry Potter—Is It Worth the Hype?" *ChildLitWiki.* 21 July 2007. Web.

12 Dec. 2011.

36. Blog

a. Blog

blogger   title (blog)   sponsor   update
Ebert, Roger. *Roger Ebert's Journal. Chicago Sun-Times,* 2012. Web.
access date   medium
12 June 2011.

b. Blog posting

author (post)   title (post)
Luther, Jason. "Our Failed Writing Center: A Response." *Taxomania!,*
date (post)
11 Nov. 2011. Web. 30 Nov. 2011.

c. Comment on a blog posting

author (comment)   title of entry commented on
Danderson, Mark. "Some Tough Love for Authors." *The Scholarly Kitchen.*
sponsor   date (comment)
Society for Scholarly Publishing, 25 Oct. 2011. Web. 19 Mar. 2012.

If the comment's author uses a screen name, use that; if the actual name is available and of interest to readers, provide that as well, following the screen name, in square brackets.

37. Avatar If the author/speaker uses an avatar with a different name than the writer's actual name, use the avatar's name, but if the writer's actual name is available and of interest to readers (it may lend credibility, for example), provide it in square brackets following the avatar name.

> avatar   actual name
> Reuters, Eric [Eric Krangel]. "*Second Life* on *The Daily Show*." *Second Life*
>
>   *News Center/Reuters*. Second Life, 8 Apr. 2007. Web. 10 Feb. 2008.

38. Source published in more than one medium Some sources may include multiple media. For example, a printed book may come with a supplementary website or CD-ROM. In the entry in your list of works cited, follow the entry format for the part of the source that you mainly used, but list all the media you consulted in alphabetical order.

> Davis, Robert L., H. Jay Siskin, and Alicia Ramos. *Entrevistas: An Introduction*
>
>   *to Language and Culture*. 2nd ed. New York: McGraw-Hill, 2005.
>
>   list of media
> Print, website.

39. Computer software

>   release   download
>   title   vendor   date   date
> *PowerResearcher*. Atlanta: Uniting Networks, 2004. 8 June 2004.

40. Video game

>   game   publisher
> *Rock Band 2*. Wii. Nintendo, 2008.
>   platform   release date

Audio and Visual Sources

The information you need to create an entry for most audio and visual sources will appear on the cover, label, or program of the work or in the credits at the end of a film. The person you list in the "author" position—the director, performer, artist, or composer—will vary depending on what you have emphasized in your research project. If you are writing about a director's body of work, put the director's name first; if you are writing about a performance, put the performer's name first. If it is the work itself that you are writing about, put the title of the work first. (This decision should be mirrored in your in-text citation.) However you choose to organize the entry, indicate the role of those whom you list, using abbreviations such as *perf.* (*performer*), *dir.* (*director*), and *cond.* (*conductor*).

As with any other entry, italicize the titles of complete or longer works (such as albums, films, operas, and original works of art) and place quotation marks around the titles of shorter works or works published as part of a larger whole (such as songs on a CD or a single episode of a television show). Publication information includes the name of the distributor, production company, or network, as well as the date on which the audio or visual was created, recorded, or broadcast. The medium will be *Film, DVD, Television, Radio, Podcast*—however you accessed the work. If you found the audio or visual source online, also include the date on which you last accessed it.

41. Motion picture

a. Film

title   director   distributor   release date   medium
Good Deeds. Dir. Tyler Perry. Lionsgate, 2012. Film.

If other artists besides the director are relevant to your project, list them between the director and the distributor.

performers
Good Deeds. Dir. Tyler Perry. Perf. Tyler Perry and Thandie Newton.

Lionsgate, 2012. Film.

If your project stresses the director, performer, or other contributor, place that information at the beginning of the citation.

Perry, Tyler, dir. *Good Deeds*. Perf. Tyler Perry and Thandie Newton. Lionsgate,

2012. Film.

b. Video or DVD Include the original release date, when relevant, before the distributor, and include the medium you viewed.

The Lady Eve. Dir. Preston Sturges. Perf. Barbara Stanwyck and Henry

orig. release   distributor   medium
Fonda. 1941. Universal Home Entertainment, 2006. DVD.

c. Internet download Include the date on which you accessed the film.

Juno. Screenplay by Diablo Cody. Dir. Jason Reitman. Perf. Ellen Page, Michael

Cera, Jennifer Garner, Jason Bateman. Fox Searchlight, 2007 iTunes,

access date
2008. Internet download. 19 Jan. 2012.

d. Online video clip Cite a video clip on YouTube or a similar site as you would a web page.

performer   video clip title   website
Ok Go. "This Too Shall Pass—Rube Goldberg Machine Version." *YouTube*.

site sponsor   medium
YouTube, 2 Mar. 2010. Web. 4 Mar. 2012.
date posted   date accessed

e. DVD extras Add the title of the extra (in quotation marks).

DVD extra
"The Making of *Winter's Bone*." *Winter's Bone*. Dir. Debra Granik. Perf.

Jennifer Lawrence and John Hawkes. 2010. Lionsgate, 2010. DVD.

42. Television or radio broadcast In most cases, begin with the title of the series or episode. Follow that with a list of the relevant contributors and information about the local station that broadcast the program (omit for cable). Because the director may change from episode to episode, other contributors, such as the creator or producer, may be more relevant. Include the date of the program and the medium in which you accessed it. If your project emphasizes an individual, begin with that person's name. Add any supplementary information at the end of the entry.

a. Series

series title
The Office. Creat. and exec. prod. Greg Daniels, Ricky Gervais, and

Stephen Merchant. Perf. Steve Carell, Rainn Wilson, John

city of local
network   station
Krasinski, and Jenna Fischer. NBC. WNBC, New York,
broadcast dates   call letters
24 Mar. 2005–20 May 2010. Television.
medium

Bridging the Morphine Gap. Host Mukti Jain Campion. BBC. Radio 4, London,

3 Mar. 2008. Radio.

b. Episode

"In Buddy's Eyes." *Desperate Housewives.* Perf. Teri Hatcher, Felicity Huffman,

Marcia Cross, Eva Longoria, and Nicollette Sheridan. ABC. KNXV,
supplementary info.
Phoenix, 20 Apr. 2008. Internet download, television. iTunes, 2008.

c. Single program

Persuasion. By Jane Austen. Adapt. Simon Burke. Perf. Julia Davis and Rupert

Penry-Jones. PBS. WGBH, Boston, 13 Jan. 2008. Television.

d. Podcast For a podcast, replace the original medium of publication with the word *Podcast,* and add the date on which you accessed the file.

"The Giant Pool of Money." Narr. Ira Glass. *This American Life.* Natl. Public
medium   access date
Radio. WBEZ, Chicago, 27 Sept. 2008. Podcast. 3 Oct. 2008.

43. Musical or other audio recording Begin with whichever part of the entry is more relevant to your project—the name of the composer or performer, or the title of the CD or song. Place the title of shorter works, such as a song, in quotation marks. Italicize the titles of longer works, such as the title of an opera, but not the titles of symphonies identified only by form, number, and key, such as Brahms's Symphony no. 1.

a. CD, LP, audiobook

Adamo, Mark. *Little Women.* Perf. Stephanie Novacek, Chad Shelton, Margaret

    Lloyd, and Stacey Tappan. Houston Grand Opera. Cond.

    prod. co. & release date
    Patrick Summers. Ondine, 2001. CD.
                    medium

Brahms, Johannes. Symphony no. 1. Chicago Symphony Orchestra. Cond.

    Georg Solti. Decca, 1992. CD.

b. Song or selection from a CD or LP or a chapter from an audiobook

Los Campesinos. "My Year in Lists." *Hold on Now, Youngster. . . .* Arts & Crafts,

    2008. CD.

c. Compressed music file (MP3, MP4)

Los Campesinos. "My Year in Lists." *Hold on Now, Youngster. . . .* Arts & Crafts,

    supplementary info.   download date
    2008. Download. iTunes, 2008. MP3 file. 16 Dec. 2008.

> Example 32, 177

d. Online sound file or clip For a sound recording accessed online, combine the
format for a web page with the format for a sound recording.

    author   selection title
    Chaucer, Geoffrey. "'The Miller's Tale': Nicholas Seduces Alisoun."

                    title of work   website
    Perf. Alfred David. *The Canterbury Tales.* *"The Criyng and the Soun":*

                                       sponsor
    The Chaucer Metapage Audio Files. VA Military Inst. Dept. of Eng.

            date posted   date accessed
    and Fine Arts, 2009. Web. 20 June 2012.

                  medium

44. Live performance The entry for a performance is similar to that for a film.
Instead of the distributor, year of release, and medium of publication, include
the group (if any), the venue and city of the performance, the date of the performance you attended, and the label *Performance.* If your project emphasizes
the composer, writer, or performer, begin the entry with that information. If
the performance is untitled, include a descriptive label.

a. Ensemble

The Importance of Being Earnest. By Oscar Wilde. Dir. Jerry Chipman. Perf.

                                          group
    Brian Everson, Stephen Garrett, and Bennett Wood. Theatre Memphis.

    venue   city   perf. date
    Lohrey Stage, Memphis, TN. 27 Jan. 2012. Performance.

b. Individual

performer   label
Hartig, Caroline. Clarinet recital. Brigham Young University. 18 Nov. 2011.

Performance.

45. Musical composition To document a musical composition itself rather than a specific performance, recording, or published version of it, include only the composer and the title of the work (in italics unless the composition is identified only by form, number, and key).

composer   untitled symphony
Schumann, Robert. Symphony no. 1 in B-flat major, op. 38.

46. Lecture, speech, or debate Treat the speaker as the author; place the title in quotation marks (if there is one); and indicate the occasion and sponsoring organization (if relevant), location, date, and mode of delivery. If the lecture, speech, or debate is untitled, replace the title with a brief descriptive label.

speaker   title   sponsor
Capri, Frank. "The Peace Movement of the 1960s." 92nd Street Y,
location   date   medium
New York. 14 Mar. 2010. Lecture.

47. Table For a table included in your project, place source information in a note below the table. For a table that you are discussing but that does not appear in your paper, include an entry in your list of works cited following the model below.

Example 18, 162

author   title   label   website
United States. Senate. "Senate Salaries since 1789." Table. US Senate.
sponsor   medium
US Senate, 7 June 2012. Web.

48. Work of art For a work of art included in your project, place source information in the figure caption. For a work that you discuss but that does not appear in your project, include an entry in your list of works cited following the models below.

Example 18, 162

a. Original work

date of
artist   title   production   medium
Pollack, Jackson. One (Number 31). 1950. Acrylic on canvas.
location
Museum of Mod. Art, New York.

b. Reproduction of a work of art

Lichtenstein, Roy. Whaam! 1963. Acrylic on canvas. Tate Gallery, London.

Responding to Art: Form, Content, and Context. By Robert Bersson.

New York: McGraw-Hill, 2004. Print.

MLA Works-Cited Entries

49. Comic or cartoon For a cartoon reproduced in your project, provide source information in the caption. For cartoons that you discuss without providing a copy of the image in your project, include an entry in your list of works cited following the models below.

a. Cartoon or comic strip

artist · title · label · publication information
Thaves, Bob. "Frank and Ernest." Comic strip. *Evening Sun* [Norwich, NY]
medium
9 Dec. 2011: 16. Print.

b. Comic book or graphic novel

authors · title
Pekar, Harvey, and Joyce Brabner, writers. *Our Cancer Year.* Illus. Frank
pub. info. · medium
Stack. Philadelphia: Running Press, 1994. Print.

Example 18, 162

50. Map or chart For a map or chart reproduced in your project, provide source information in the caption. For a map or chart discussed but not included in your project, include an entry in your list of works cited following the model below.

"The Invasion of Sicily: Allied Advance to Messina (23 July-17 August
label
1943)." Map. *The West Point Atlas of American Wars.* Ed.

Vincent J. Esposito. Vol. 2. New York: Praeger, 1959. 247. Print.

51. Advertisement For an advertisement reproduced in your project, provide source information in the caption. For an advertisement discussed but not included in your project, include an entry in your list of works cited following the models below.

label
Earthlink Cable Internet. Advertisement. *Metro* 17 Apr. 2007: 11. Print.

date accessed
Infiniti. Advertisement. *Yahoo.com.* Web. 20 Apr. 2007.

date broadcast
Domino's Pizza. Advertisement. Comedy Central. 2 Aug. 2006.

Television.

Miscellaneous Sources—Printed and Electronic

Example 7, 167
Example 19, 163

52. Government document If no author is listed, use the name of the governing nation and the government department and agency (if any) that produced the document, as you would for a work with a corporate author. Abbreviate Government Printing Office as *GPO*.

MLA Works-
Cited Entries

50. Map or chart
51. Advertisement
**52. Government
document**
53. Legal source
**54. Letter
(published)**
55. Interview
56. Personal cor-
respondence
57. Diary or
journal

nation   department
United States. War Department. *Advanced Map and Aerial Photograph*

Reading. Washington, DC: GPO, 1941. Print.

For congressional documents, include the number and session of Congress and the number and type of document. Common abbreviations in US government documents include the following:

Doc.	Document	**Rept.**	Report
GPO	Government Printing Office	**Res**	Resolution
HR	House of Representatives	**S**	Senate
		Sess.	Session

a. Printed

United States. Cong. House. *Combat Bonus Act.* 110th Cong., 2nd sess. HR

6760. Washington, DC: GPO, 2008. Print.

b. Online

United States. Cong. House. *Combat Bonus Act.* 110th Cong., 2nd sess.

website   sponsor
HR 6760. *Thomas.gov.* Lib. of Cong., 31 July 2008. Web.

access date
16 May 2012.

53. Legal source

legal case   case number   court   decision yr
Gideon v. Wainwright. 372 US 335. Supreme Court of the US. 1963.

website   sponsor   medium   access date
FindLaw. Thomas Reuters, 2010. Web. 16 Dec. 2008.

update

54. Letter (published)

a. Single letter Cite a single letter as you would a selection from an edited book or anthology but add the recipient's name, the date the letter was written, and the letter number (if there is one).

Example 10, 168

author   recipient   date written
Brooks, Phillips. "To Agnes." 24 Sept. 1882. *Children's Letters: A Collection*

of Letters Written to Children by Famous Men and Women. Ed. Elizabeth

Colson and Anna Gansevoort Chittenden. New York: Hinds, 1905. 3-4.

Print.

b. Collection of letters Cite as you would an edited book or anthology.

Example 8, 168

55. Interview Treat a published interview as you would an article in a periodical. Treat an interview broadcast on radio or television or podcasted as you

Examples 24–26,
173–76
Example 42, 181

would a broadcast. For an unpublished interview you conducted, include the
name of the person interviewed, the label *Personal interview, Telephone interview,* or *E-mail interview,* and the date on which the interview took place.

person
interviewed   label   date
Harberg, Amanda. Personal interview. 11 Feb. 2012.

56. Personal correspondence To document personal correspondence, such
as a letter or e-mail message you received, include a descriptive label such as
Letter to the author or *Message to the author,* as well as the medium (*MS* for
"manuscript," *E-mail*).

a. Letter

letter writer   label   date written
Gould, Stephen Jay. Letter to the author. 13 Nov. 1986. MS.
medium

b. E-mail

e-mail author   subject line   label
Elbow, Peter. "Re: bibliography about resistance." Message to the author.
date sent   medium
12 Apr. 2004. E-mail.

A mass e-mail or electronic memo should include a label describing recipients,
such as *E-mail to ENG 204 students.*

c. Memorandum Very few institutions send out printed memos anymore, but if
you need to document one, treat it as you would an e-mail message, replacing
the word *e-mail* with the word *memo* at the end of your entry.

d. Instant message (IM)

Grimm, Laura. Message to the author. 14 June 2012. Instant message.

Example 10, 168

57. Diary or journal

a. Single entry, published Treat an entry in a published diary or journal like an
article in an edited book or anthology, but include a descriptive label (*Diary
entry*) and the date of composition after the entry title.

b. Single entry, unpublished

author   title
Zook, Aaron. "Sketches for *Aesop's Foibles* (new musical)."
label   entry date   medium
Journal entry. 1 May 2007. MS.

Example 8, 168

c. Diary or journal, published Treat a complete diary or journal as you would an
edited book or anthology.

21

Using MLA Style for Informational Notes

In addition to in-text citations, MLA style allows researchers to include informational notes to provide relevant, but potentially distracting, content or to provide bibliographic information about one or more sources. MLA style recommends using a list of endnotes at the end of the project. To identify informational notes in the text, include a superscript (above-the-line) arabic number that corresponds to the note number in the list of endnotes. Include an entry for each source in your list of works cited.

> Beneath the crude humor of *Zap* and similar comics lay insightful commentary on society and its principles, which many readers found to be a refreshing change from mainstream superhero titles.[1] . . . Comics like Tomine's provide a subject or situation that readers can identify with more easily than, say, Superman's battles with Brainiac.[2]

> **Notes**   Heading (centered), new page
>
> ½″ 1. According to Schnakenberg, more than two million copies of *Zap* comics were in print by 1999.
>
>   2. For an intriguing argument that the world of classic comic book superheroes is not so different from our own—including a discussion of how comics before World War II commented on then current events—see Wright 1-28.

Use ***content notes*** to provide information that clarifies or justifies a point in your text, but avoid notes that include interesting digressions that could distract your readers. You can also use content notes to acknowledge the contributions of others (tutors, classmates, and so on) to the preparation of your paper.

Bibliographic notes can add information about a source or point readers to other sources on the topic. If several sources provide the same information, cite the most valuable source in your text, and list the others in a bibliographic note. Then include the full citation of all these sources in your list of works cited.

22 Formatting a Paper in MLA Style

The care with which you cite and document your sources reflects the care you have taken in writing your research project. Continue that care by formatting your project in the way your readers expect. For most writing projects in literature and composition, follow the MLA's formatting guidelines.

22a Margins and Spacing

Student Model
Research project, MLA style, 192–200

Set one-inch margins at the top, bottom, and sides of your paper. Double-space the entire paper, including long quotations, the list of works cited, and any endnotes. Indent the first line of each paragraph by half an inch, and do not add an extra space between paragraphs. Use a hanging indent for each entry in the list of works cited: The first line should be flush with the left margin with subsequent lines indented half an inch. (For more on creating a hanging indent in a word processing program, see the Tech box on the next page.)

22b Typeface

More about
Choosing a typeface and type size, 52–53

Choose a standard typeface, such as Times New Roman or Arial, in an easily readable size (usually 12 points).

22c Header

MLA style requires that each page of your project include a header, consisting of your surname and the page number. Place the header in the upper right-hand corner, a half inch from the upper edge and one inch from the right edge of the page.

Tech   **Creating a Header**

Most word processing programs allow you to insert a header. In Microsoft Word, select "Header" from the Insert tab. Any information you type into the header space will then appear at the top of every page of your manuscript. You can also choose to insert page numbers to paginate your project automatically.

The major style guides (MLA, APA, *Chicago*, CSE) were initially written before the widespread use of personal computers, when most writers still worked on typewriters. To create a paragraph or hanging indention on a typewriter, the typist would hit the space bar five times or set a tab. Now, just about everyone creates writing projects on a computer, where paragraph and hanging indentions are created using the Ruler or Paragraph Dialog box.

Ruler

Paragraph Dialog Box

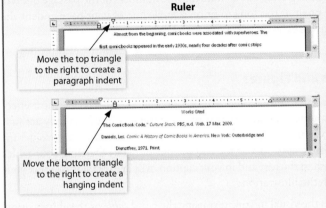

Move the top triangle to the right to create a paragraph indent

Move the bottom triangle to the right to create a hanging indent

22d Identifying Information

No title page is required in MLA style. Instead, include the following identifying information in the upper left-hand corner of the first page of your research project, one inch from the top and left edges of the paper:

- Your name
- Your instructor's name
- The number of the course in which you are submitting the paper
- The date

If your instructor requires a title page, ask for formatting instructions or follow the model on page 231.

22e Title

Center the title of your project and insert it two lines below the date. Do not put quotation marks around your title or italicize it. Drop down two more lines before beginning to type the first paragraph of your research project.

> **More about**
> Crafting a title, 40

22f Long Quotations

More about
Block quotations,
153, 158–59,
437–38
Sample block
quotations, 153
(prose), 159
(poetry)

Set quotations of prose longer than four lines of your text as a block: Omit the quotation marks, and indent the entire quotation one inch from the left margin of your text. When quoting four or more lines of poetry, indent all the lines one inch from the left margin; keep the same indention and line breaks that were in the original poem, and include the line numbers of the passage quoted. If a line of the poem is too long to fit on a single line of your page, indent the continuation by an extra quarter of an inch.

22g Tables and Figures

Sample tables and
figures, 162–63
(table); 195, 197,
198

Tables and figures (photographs, cartoons, graphs, and charts) are most effective when they appear as close as possible after the text in which they are first discussed. (If placing figures and tables appropriately is awkward, consider including them in an appendix at the end of your project.) Labeling your tables and figures, both in the text and in your caption, will help readers connect your discussion with the illustration:

- Refer to the visual in your text using the word *table* or the abbreviation *fig.*, and number tables and figures in a separate sequence using arabic numerals (table 1, table 2; fig. 1, fig. 2). MLA style uses lowercase for in-text references to tables and figures unless they begin a sentence: "Table 1 presents 2010 data, and table 2 presents 2012 data."

- Accompany each illustration with the word *Table* or the abbreviation *Fig.*, the appropriate number, and a brief, explanatory title. Customarily, table numbers and titles appear above the table, and figure numbers and titles appear below the figure. Generally, they use the same margins as the rest of the paper.

- If additional information is needed, provide an explanatory caption after the number and title. (Remember that your text should explain what the figure or table demonstrates. That information should not be repeated in the caption.)

Writing Responsibly | Of Deadlines and Paperclips

Instructors expect students to turn in thoughtful, carefully proofread, and neatly formatted papers on time—usually in class on the due date. Another expectation is that the writer will clip or staple the pages of the paper *before* it is submitted. Do justice to yourself by being fully prepared.

to SELF

- If you borrow the illustration or borrow information needed to create the illustration, cite your source. Any photographs or drawings you create yourself should identify the subject but do not need a citation. Citations usually appear below the table in a source note or in the figure caption. If you document the illustration in a figure caption or source note, you do not need to include an entry in your list of works cited.

22h Printing and Binding

If you are submitting a hard copy of your project, print it using a high-quality printer (make sure it has plenty of ink), on opaque 8½ × 11–inch white paper. Most instructors do not want you to enclose your project in a binder. Unless your instructor tells you otherwise, staple or paperclip the pages together in the upper left-hand corner.

22i Portfolios

Many instructors ask students to submit the final draft of the research project in a portfolio, which may include an outline, preliminary notes and drafts, a working or annotated bibliography, and a personal statement describing their writing process and what they have learned from the experience (Figure 22.1).

More about
Outlining, 23–25,
136–37
Note taking, 7–10,
126–32
Writing a first draft,
25
Working or anno-
tated bibliogra-
phy, 100–02

FIGURE 22.1 Page 1 of Lydia Nichols's personal statement Nichols created a visual personal statement to explain how her interest in underground comics developed.

Student Model Research Project: MLA Style

In the sample student research project that follows, Lydia Nichols fulfills her responsibilities to topic and audience. She uses comparison-contrast to support her claim that underground comics are more innovative than their mainstream cousins, and she provides a historical overview to fill in the background her readers lack. Her research draws on a variety of print and online sources, and she uses visuals to support some of her points.

Lydia Nichols

Prof. Concannon

Writing 205

6 April 2012

Holy Underground Comics, Batman! Moving Away from the Mainstream

When most people think of comic books, predictable images usually come to mind: caped heroes, maniacal villains, deeds of incredible strength, and other typical elements of super-powered adventures. Undeniably, characters like Batman, Superman, and Spider-Man are the most prominent features of the comic book landscape, in terms of both popularity and revenue (Wright xiv). However, there is more to comic books than superpowers and secret identities. Underground comics (also known as *comix*), printed by small publishers or by individual artists, are very different from what is usually expected in the genre. While far less well-known than their superhero counterparts, underground comics often offer an innovative and more sophisticated alternative to mainstream titles.

Almost from the beginning, comic books were associated with superheroes. The first comic books appeared in the early 1930s, nearly four decades after comic strips such as *Yellow Boy* began appearing in the major newspapers. However, Les Daniels, who has written extensively on conventional and underground comics, points out that comic books did not gain widespread popularity until June of 1938, when writer Jerry Siegel and artist Joe Shuster debuted their character Superman in *Action Comics* #1 (9). Daniels reports that Superman was an immediate success, and the character quickly inspired the creation of copycat superheroes in other comic books. The protagonists of these comics each had their own strengths and vulnerabilities, but the stories all shared a basic formula: individuals with extraordinary abilities battling against evil and struggling to maintain a secret identity. These superhero comics, though similar to each other, set the comic book industry on its feet, paving the way to profits and sustained success. Over the decades and even today, superhero comics are what are typically seen on store shelves.

193

Topic sentence: Claim supported by quotation and summary

While artists and writers over the years have certainly done inventive work in superhero comics, some similarity in mainstream titles was for many years unavoidable due to the creation in 1954 of the Comics Code Authority (CCA), an organization formed by a number of the leading comic publishers to regulate the content of comics ("Good Shall Triumph"). It set very explicit standards, dictating what content was allowed in comic books and what content was expected. Some parts of the code were incredibly specific and controlling:

Block indention for long quotation; ellipses mark cut

> The letters of the word "crime" on a comics magazine shall never be appreciably greater in dimension than the other words contained in the title. The word "crime" shall never appear alone on a cover. . . . Restraint in the use of the word "crime" in titles or subtitles shall be exercised. (qtd. in "Good Shall Triumph")

Indirect source: Author unknown, so title used

Other rules were more general—vague enough to allow the CCA a free hand in shaping content. One read, "Respect for parents, the moral code, and for honorable behavior shall be fostered" (qtd. in "Good Shall Triumph").

Quotation marks for brief quotation

The CCA also regulated the presentation of criminals and criminal acts, themes of religion and race, and dialogue, especially profanity.

Paragraph uses combination of summary, paraphrase, and quotation

While the CCA had no legal authority, major magazine distributors refused comics that did not have CCA approval. Many comic publishers, such as EC Comics (*Vault of Horror, Tales from the Crypt*), were virtually forced out of business as a result of the CCA, though the banned titles would eventually gain the appreciation of collectors and aspiring comic artists such as Art Spiegelman, author of the graphic novel *Maus* (1986) ("Comic Book

Websites: no page numbers

Code"). Other publishers, including DC Comics, made their artists abide by CCA rules in order to continue selling to a wide audience ("Good Shall Triumph"). The result was that the comics with the largest distribution were those that conformed to the CCA's strict rules about appropriate language, subjects, and tone.

In the 1960s, in contrast to mainstream CCA-approved superhero comics, alternatives began to appear.

Signal phrase identifies source and establishes credibility

According to Steven Heller, an art director at the *New York Times* and a founder of the Masters in Graphic Arts Program at the School for Visual Arts in New York, Robert Crumb's *Zap* (1968) initiated the "underground comix revolution" (101). Crumb and other like-minded artists did not submit their comics for CCA approval. Though this limited

Fig. 1. Mainstream versus Underground Comics. Spider-Man (left) extols (and exhibits) his prowess as superhero, while (right) a less conventional comic book "hero" struts his stuff. (Left: Cover from Jack Kirby and Steve Ditko, *Amazing Fantasy* #15. [New York: Marvel Comics, 1962; print]; right: Cover from Robert Crumb, *Snarf* #6 [Amherst: Kitchen Sink Enterprises, 1976; print])

> Figure number links visual to text discussion

> Source information in caption

the distribution of their work, it allowed them artistic freedom. From its first issue, *Zap* satirized mainstream, conservative beliefs and did not shy away from sexual or political content (Heller 101-02). Beneath the crude humor of *Zap* and similar comics lay insightful commentary on society and its principles, which many readers found to be a refreshing change from mainstream superhero titles, so refreshing that more than two million copies of *Zap* comics were in print by 1999 (Schnakenberg).

To see the contrast between these mainstream and underground comics, compare the two covers in fig. 1 (above). The *Amazing Fantasy* cover (left) includes the Comics Code Authority approval stamp in its upper right corner, while the *Snarf* cover (right) does not. The *Snarf* cover actually pokes fun at covers like the one at left; on the *Amazing Fantasy* cover, superhero Spider-Man dangles from a high building by a thread, proclaiming his "awesome might" to the world, while on the *Snarf* cover, a geeky guy in an unwieldy

> Topic sentence: Claim supported by visual, analysis; figure number links discussion to visual

> Figures analyzed in text

homemade contraption wants to save the world by fighting "the big companies," which include oil companies (the "Gas" industry this inventor is trying to boycott) and probably DC Comics, too.

Topic sentence: Claim supported by examples

Underground comics continue to be less well-known than superhero comics, but they are better-respected among mature readers for their bold and inventive content. Graphic novels, such as Spiegelman's *Maus* and Harvey Pekar and Joyce Brabner's *Our Cancer Year* (1994), have successfully addressed some of the most highly charged and sensitive subjects in modern society. Both of these show the subtlety and wide range of topics that underground comics explore. Daniels notes that underground comics frequently explore themes of sex and sexual identity, politics, and social issues (165), as shown in Crumb's work, which Heller describes as taking a satirical approach to countercultural topics (101-02).

Topic sentence: Claim supported by example, visual, quotation

Mainstream superhero comics are set on an epic scale—depicting amazing feats, heroic battles between good and evil, and the like—while underground comics tend to focus on everyday life. Steven Weiner, who reviews graphic novels for *Library Journal,* called Adrian Tomine, for example, "a master of pseudorealistic stories" due to his ability to present an ordinary situation as profoundly interesting and complex (58; see fig. 2, next page). Comics like Tomine's provide a subject or situation that readers can identify with more easily than, say, Superman's battles with Brainiac.

The quirky perspectives of underground artists would be impossible in mainstream comics because the structure for producing and publishing mainstream comics limits the input of the artists working on them. The modern comic book industry is a huge business, selling not only comics but also related merchandise such as T-shirts, toys, and video games, not to mention tickets to comic book–inspired movies. Story decisions involving major characters such as Batman and the Hulk have to be made with profits in mind. Because mainstream comic publishers often change the creative teams working on their titles (Herndon 23) and because teams can include dozens of members (McCloud 180),

Citation: Placement clarifies which information comes from which source

individual artists can have only so much impact on a particular character or story. Most mainstream comics are the result of work done by many different people.

Fig. 2. Comic whose characters face realistic challenges—the loss of a loved one, parental guilt—that readers can easily relate to. From Adrian Tomine, *Optic Nerve* #6 (Montreal: Drawn and Quarterly, Feb. 1999; print; 22).

In contrast, the individual artist in the underground realm has almost total control in creating his or her comic book. The creative teams working on underground titles are usually very small, and they rarely change (Herndon 23). Daniels notes that underground comic artists are not controlled by corporate interests that discourage daring material that might not sell (165, 180). This freedom allows for the uninhibited creativity that distinguishes underground comics from their more commercially oriented counterparts.

Underground artists not only push the envelope in terms of content but they also incorporate experimental visual devices, earning critical praise for breaking away from traditional comic layouts in favor of more artistic perspectives. Artists such as Daniel Clowes

Transition

Signal phrase

Information from two passages, same source

Topic sentence: Claim supported by summary, quotation, visual example

Fig. 3. Cover from Chris Ware's *Jimmy Corrigan: The Smartest Kid on Earth* (New York: Pantheon, 2000; print). Critically acclaimed *Jimmy Corrigan* comics use visual storytelling techniques, pushing the limitations of comics and forcing the reader to work to achieve understanding.

Caption explains how visual supports claim

argue that comic art can be more evocative than film, especially in the use of nonlinear storytelling techniques (Hignite 18). *New York Times* columnist John Hodgman agrees: Discussing a moment of existential crisis in Kevin Huizenga's *Ganges* #1, he writes, "I have never seen any film or read any prose that gets at that frozen moment when we suddenly feel our mortality, when God is seen or denied, as effectively as a comic panel." Artist Chris Ware manipulates the borders and frames in his comics so extensively that even reading his works can feel like an art to be mastered (see fig. 3, above). The demands his comics place on the reader create an interaction between viewer and artist that is unheard of in the pages of superhero titles.

Signal phrase identifies source and establishes credibility

While Ware and Clowes demonstrate how the page can be used to create innovative and complicated layouts, other underground artists excel at creating simple, striking visuals. Unlike mainstream comics, which depict dynamic scenes through loud, flamboyant colors, underground comics often achieve their effects through simplicity. Frequently, they are printed in black and white or with limited colors, with characters rendered in clean, bold lines. The clarity and lack of clutter in such art allows for immediate, striking storytelling (see fig. 2, page 5).

Reference to earlier figure

Obviously, most underground comics are not intended for young children. Yet because of the childish connotations of the term "comic," most adults overlook the fascinating work that underground comic artists do. The association of comics with superheroes and children has made reading comics a source of shame or embarrassment for many adults. As Clowes comments, "I think that the average reader is far more open to a well-designed book than a standard comic book. . . . Very few would feel comfortable reading a standard comic book pamphlet" (qtd. in Hignite 17). Artists such as Scott McCloud have changed this perception of comic books by offering a broader definition of what a comic is. According to McCloud, comics are "juxtaposed pictorial and other images in a deliberate sequence" (12). This definition includes not only what one might find in the latest Spider-Man comic, but also all the experimental work that McCloud and his underground colleagues are creating.

McCloud and others have succeeded in bringing underground comics to a wider audience. Since the 1980s, underground comics have been finding their way into gallery and museum exhibitions, where the craftsmanship of the individual comic book artist can be better appreciated (Hignite 18). Major newspapers like the *New York Times* have begun featuring underground comics in their pages, including serialized graphic novels such as *George Sprott (1894-1975)* and *Watergate Sue*. The market for underground comics has also expanded through Internet venues such as *eBay*, where interested readers can find not only new titles but also classic comix otherwise available only in specialty shops. The Internet has also become an outlet for direct distribution through artists' websites, making independent titles not only more accessible to consumers but also more affordable for individual artists to produce and market (Fenty, Houp, and Taylor, par. 1). While underground comics may never sell as well or be as large a part of popular culture as Superman and his ilk, their creators will likely continue to be heroes to anyone seeking courage, creativity, and artistic quality in their comics.

Establishes credibility

Signal phrase and parenthetical page reference bookend apt quotation

Conclusion: Provides closure

Revisits thesis, states why underground comics provide more sophisticated alternative

Works Cited *Heading (centered), new page; entries alphabetized by author (or title if no author)*

Web page: No author, no date — "The Comic Book Code." *Culture Shock*. PBS, n.d. Web. 17 Mar. 2009.

Daniels, Les. *Comix: A History of Comic Books in America*. New York: Outerbridge, 1971. Print.

More than one author; order of names reversed for first author. Journal article published only online; paragraphs numbered — Fenty, Sean, Trena Houp, and Laurie Taylor. "Webcomics: The Influence and Continuation of the Comix Revolution." *ImageTexT* 1.2 (2004): 22 pars. Web. 18 Mar. 2009.

Online scholarly project: No authors—alphabetized by title — "'Good Shall Triumph over Evil': The Comic Book Code of 1954." *History Matters: The U.S. History Survey Course on the Web*. American Social History Project/Center for Media and Learning, CUNY, and the Center for History and New Media, George Mason University, 2006. Web. 22 Mar. 2009.

Heller, Steven. "Zap Comics." *Print* May/June 2000: 100-05. *Academic Search Complete*. Web. 26 Mar. 2009.

Herndon, L. Kristen. "Mainstream Culture Is in Trouble, and Superman's Not Gonna Save It. But the Simpsons Might." *Art Papers* 21.1 (1997): 22-25. *Art Index*. Web. 10 Mar. 2009.

Journal article: Accessed through database — Hignite, M. Todd. "Avant-Garde and Comics: Serious Cartooning." *Art Papers* 26.1 (2002): 17-19. *Art Index*. Web. 10 Mar. 2009.

Newspaper article: Accessed through database — Hodgman, John. "Comics Chronicle." *New York Times* 4 June 2006, late ed., sec. 7: 18. *LexisNexis*. Web. 19 Mar. 2009.

Book (printed): Popular press — McCloud, Scott. *Understanding Comics, the Invisible Art*. New York: Harper Perennial, 1994. Print.

Specialized reference work: Accessed through database — Schnakenberg, Robert E. "Zap Comix." *St. James Encyclopedia of Popular Culture*. Detroit: St. James Press, 2002. *Find Articles*. Web. 17 Mar. 2009.

Weiner, Stephen. "Beyond Superheroes: Comics Get Serious." *Library Journal* 7.2 (2002): 55-58. *Academic Search Complete*. Web. 10 Mar. 2009.

Book (printed): Scholarly press, University Press abbreviated to UP — Wright, Bradford W. *Comic Book Nation: The Transformation of Youth Culture in America*. Baltimore: Johns Hopkins UP, 2001. Print.

7

Documentation
Matters

APA Style

Use tab 7 to learn, practice, and master these writer's responsibilities:

❏ **To Audience**

Cite and document sources so that readers can see where each use of sources begins and ends in your project; format your research project using APA style, in keeping with readers' expectations.

❏ **To Topic**

Cite and document sources to demonstrate that you have explored your topic fully.

❏ **To Other Writers**

Provide citations for all borrowed ideas and information, whether quoted, paraphrased, or summarized; document all sources cited in the research project in a reference list at the end of the project.

❏ **To Yourself**

Use sources to build knowledge, and cite them to show readers where your ideas begin and end; to enhance your ethos, or credibility; and to present your ideas effectively.

Documentation
Matters

Journal Article from an **Online Database**

author   year   article title and subtitle

Fancher, R. E. (2009). Scientific Cousins: The relationship between Charles Darwin and Francis Gallon.

       publication information   digital object identifier

American Psychologist 64, 84–92. doi:10.1037/a0013339

        journal title   volume pages

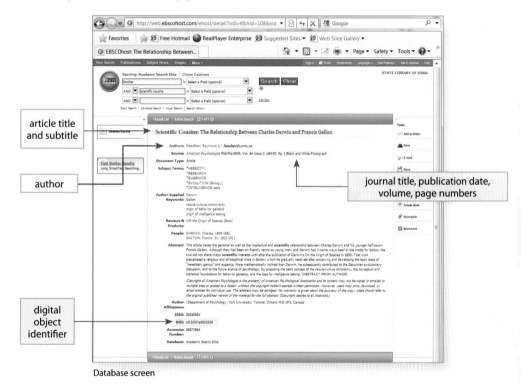

Database screen

Look for the information you need to document an article you accessed through an online database on the search results screen, the full record of the article, or the first and last pages of the article itself. When there is a subtitle, include this information. Include a digital object identifier (DOI) if one is provided. No access date is needed. (For more about documenting an article accessed through an online database, see pp. 219–21.)

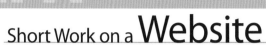

Short Work on a Website

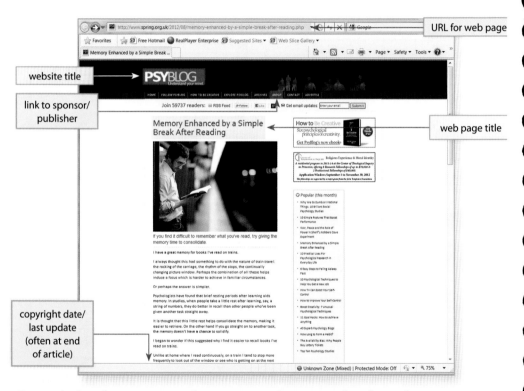

corporate author/ / ©date/
publisher / last update / web page title (and subtitle when available) / retrieval statement

PsyBlog (2012, August 28). Memory enhanced by a simple break after reading. Retrieved from

URL for web page

http://www.spring.org.uk/2012/08/memory-enhanced-by-a-simple-break-after-reading.php

URL for web page

website title

link to sponsor/ publisher

web page title

copyright date/ last update (often at end of article)

Frequently, the information you need to create a complete entry in the reference list is missing or difficult to find on web pages. Look at the top or bottom of the web page or home page or find the link to an "About" or "Contact Us" page. If no author is cited, move the title to the author position. If the web page is untitled, add a description (in brackets) in place of the title. If the page was created and published by the same group, omit the publisher name from the retrieval statement; if not, add the publisher's name before the URL (*Retrieved from APA website:*). (For more about documenting online sources, see pp. 221–23.)

23 Creating APA-Style In-Text Citations

Developed by the American Psychological Association, APA style is used by researchers in psychology and many other social science disciplines, such as education, social work, and sociology. The *Publication Manual of the American Psychological Association* (6th ed.) requires that sources be cited in two ways:

- **Citation:** In the body of your project, provide an in-text citation for each source used.
- **Documentation:** At the project's end, provide a reference list.

In-text citations appear in the body of your project. They mark each use you make of a source, regardless of whether you are quoting, paraphrasing, or drawing on an idea. In-text citations should include just enough information for readers to locate the source in your reference list, which appears at the end of the project. They should also alert readers to shifts between *your* ideas and those you have borrowed from a source.

> **More about**
> Popular academic documenta-
>   tion styles, per
>   discipline, 69
> MLA style, 149–200
>   (tab 6)
> *Chicago* style,
>   239–62 (tab 8)
> CSE style, 263–76
>   (tab 8)

23a Placing In-Text Citations So That Readers Know Where Borrowed Material Starts and Stops

When you incorporate a quotation, paraphrase, summary, or idea from a source into your own prose, carefully consider the placement of the in-text citation, keeping the following goals in mind:

- To make clear exactly which material is drawn from the source
- To avoid distracting your reader

> **More about**
> What you do and
>   do not need to
>   cite, 125–26
> Signal phrases,
>   141–42
> Integrating bor-
>   rowed material
>   into your text,
>   147–48

Writing Responsibly — Citing and Documenting Sources

When you cite and document sources, you demonstrate how thoroughly you have researched your topic and how carefully you have thought about your sources, which encourages your audience to believe you are a credible researcher. In your citations and documentation, you acknowledge any material that you have borrowed from a source, and you join the conversation on your topic by adding your own interpretation. Accurate entries in the body of your project and list of references allow your audience to find and read your sources so that they can evaluate your interpretation and learn more about the subject themselves. Accurate entries also demonstrate the care with which you have written your research project, which further reinforces your credibility, or ethos.

to AUDIENCE

Reference General Principles of In-Text Citation

- Cite not only direct quotations but also paraphrases, summaries, and information gathered from a source, whether printed or online.
- Include the author's surname and the year of publication. You may place the name(s) in a signal phrase or in a parenthetical note.
- Place parenthetical citations after the borrowed material; if the author is named in a signal phrase, insert the year of publication, in parentheses, immediately following the author's name and the page reference at the end of the borrowed passage.
- For works with no author, use the first few words of the title in the author position.
- For works with multiple authors, use the word *and* before the last author in a signal phrase; replace the word *and* with an ampersand (&) in a parenthetical citation.
- Include a page or paragraph number when borrowing specific information but not when summarizing an entire source.

You can cite a source in your text in two ways:

- ***Signal phrase.*** Include the author's name (often just the surname) and an appropriate verb in your sentence, and place the date of publication, in parentheses, immediately following the author's name.

Psychologist G. H. Edwards (1992) found that subtypes or subcategories of beliefs emerge from within gender categories.

A signal phrase often makes it easier for readers to determine where your ideas end and borrowed material begins. It also allows you to integrate the borrowed material into your sentence and to put the source in context by adding your own interpretation and the qualifications of the source author. For these reasons, most of your summaries, paraphrases, and quotations should be introduced by a signal phrase.

- ***Parenthetical note.*** In parentheses, provide the author's surname, followed by a comma and the year in which the source was published. Place the note immediately after the borrowed material.

Subtypes or subcategories of beliefs emerge from within gender categories (Edwards, 1992).

Parenthetical notes are most appropriate when citing more than one source or establishing facts.

NOTE The reference list entry is the same, regardless of whether you use a signal phrase or a parenthetical note:

More about
Creating reference list entries, 210–26

author   pub. year   title
Edwards, G. H. (1992). The structure and content of the male gender role

publication info.
stereotype: An exploration of subtypes. *Sex Roles, 27*, 553–561.

Provide enough information in your in-text citation for readers to locate the source in the reference list. In most cases, the author's surname and the date of publication are sufficient. Occasionally, you may need to provide more information. When citing works by authors with the same surname, also include the authors' initials.

Examples 1–2, 203–05

Example 11, 208

Example 7, 214

> While subtypes or subcategories of beliefs may emerge from within gender categories (Edwards, G. H., 1992), broader categories of beliefs emerge from within cultural groups (Edwards, C. P., 1988).

When quoting from a source, include page numbers.

Example 2, 204

> The stereotype effect occurs when "individual members . . . are judged in a direction consistent with group-level expectations . . ." (Biernat, 2003, p. 1019).

APA In-Text Citations

1. **One author, paraphrase or summary**
2. One author, quotation
3. Two authors

23b Adjusting In-Text Citations to Match Your Source

The exact form of an in-text citation depends on the type of source you are citing. The examples that follow cover the most common types. For more unusual sources, study the general principles outlined here and adapt them to your special circumstances or consult the *Publication Manual of the American Psychological Association,* 6th ed. (available in any library).

1. One author, paraphrase or summary The APA does not require that writers include a page reference for summaries and paraphrases, but your instructor may. If your instructor does want you to include a page reference, follow the model for a quotation on the next page.

Example 2, 204

Quick

Quick Reference **Examples of APA-Style In-Text Citation Entries**

1. One author, paraphrase or summary 203
   a. Signal phrase 204
   b. Parenthetical note 204
2. One author, quotation 204
   a. Signal phrase 204
   b. Parenthetical citation 205
3. Two authors 205
4. Three to five authors 205
5. Six or more authors 206
6. Group or corporate author 206
7. Unnamed (anonymous) author 207
8. Two or more sources in one citation 207
9. Two or more sources by the same author in one citation 207
10. Two or more sources by the same author in the same year 208
11. Two or more authors with the same surname 208
12. Reprinted or republished work 208
13. Sacred or classical source 208
14. Indirect source 209
15. Website or other online source 209
16. Personal communication (e-mail, letter, interview) 210

a. Signal phrase

> signal phrase
> Plummer (2001) indicates that boys begin pressuring one another to conform in childhood, telling each other to toughen up or to stop acting like a baby.

b. Parenthetical note

APA In-Text Citations

1. **One author, paraphrase or summary**
2. **One author, quotation**
3. Two authors
4. Three to five authors

> This pressure to conform to recognized masculine norms typically begins at a very young age, and boys may tell each other to toughen up or to stop acting like a baby (Plummer, 2001).

2. One author, quotation If you are borrowing specific language from your source, include the author's name, the year of publication, and a page reference.

NOTE The APA suggests, but does not require, that writers include a page reference for summaries and paraphrases when readers may need help finding the cited passage. Your instructor may require that you always include one, so be sure to ask. If your instructor *does* want you to include a page reference, follow examples 2a–b.

a. Signal phrase In a signal phrase, insert the year of publication immediately after the author's name and a page reference at the end of the cited passage. This not only provides source information but also makes clear what part of your text comes from the source.

Plummer (2001) argues that an overt pressure to conform to recognized

norms of masculinity typically begins at a very young age, with boys

discouraging one another from being "soft" or "artistic" (p. 18).

b. Parenthetical note In a parenthetical note, include all three pieces of information at the end of the passage cited.

This overt pressure to conform to recognized norms of masculinity typically

begins at a very young age, with boys discouraging each other from being

"soft" or "artistic" (Plummer, 2001, p. 18).

3. Two authors List two authors by surnames in the order listed by the source; be sure to use this same order in your reference list entry. In a signal phrase, spell out the word *and* between the two surnames; in a parenthetical citation, replace the word *and* with an ampersand (&).

signal phrase (*and* spelled out)
Carpenter and Readman (2006) define physical disability as "the restriction

of activity caused by impairments, for example, the loss of a limb, involuntary

movements, loss of speech or sight" (p. 131).

Medical doctors define the word *disability* as "an individual problem of

parenthetical citation (ampersand)
disease, incapacity, and impairment" (Carpenter & Readman, 2006, p. 131).

APA In-Text Citations

1. One author, paraphraase or summary
2. **One author, quotation**
3. **Two authors**
4. **Three to five authors**
5. Six or more authors
6. Group or corporate author

4. Three to five authors When a source has three, four, or five authors, list them all in your first in-text citation.

The research of Oller, Pearson, and Cobo-Lewis (2007) suggests that

bilingual children may have a smaller vocabulary in each of their languages

than monolingual children have in their sole language.

et al. Abbreviation of the Latin phrase *et alii*, "and others"

In subsequent citations, list only the first author, representing the others with the abbreviation *et al.* In APA style, this abbreviation should not be underlined or italicized.

> The bilingual children in the study were all Spanish-English speakers
>
> (Oller et al., 2007).

NOTE *al.* is an abbreviation, so it requires a period; *et* is a complete word, so it does not. There should be no punctuation between the author's name and *et al.*

5. Six or more authors If the source has six or more authors, use only the surname of the first author plus *et al.* unless confusion will result.

> The researchers note that "there is less direct experimental evidence for the effect
>
> of grazing animal species on biodiversity" (Rook et al., 2003, p. 141).

APA In-Text Citations

3. Two authors
4. Three to five authors
5. **Six or more authors**
6. **Group or corporate author**
7. Unnamed (anonymous) author
8. Two or more sources in one citation

6. Group or corporate author Provide the full name of the group in your signal phrase or parenthetical note. If you are going to cite this source again in your project, use the group's name in a signal phrase and insert an abbreviation of the name in parentheses. In subsequent in-text references, use only the abbreviation.

> full name
> In 2003 the National Commission on Writing in America's Schools and
> acronym
> Colleges (NCWASC) demanded that "the nation's leaders . . . place writing
>
> squarely in the center of the school agenda, and [that] policymakers at the
>
> state and local levels . . . provide the resources required to improve writing"
>
> (p. 3). The NCWASC also noted that . . .

Alternatively, include the full name in a parenthetical citation, and insert the abbreviation in square brackets afterward.

> If writing is to improve, our society "must place writing squarely in the center
>
> of the school agenda, and policymakers at the state and local levels must
>
> provide the resources required to improve writing" (National Commission on
> full name   abbreviation
> Writing in America's Schools and Colleges [NCWASC], 2003, p. 3).

7. Unnamed (anonymous) author When no author is listed for a source, use the first few words of the reference list entry (usually the title) instead.

> On average, smokers shave about 12 minutes off their life for every
>   title
> cigarette smoked ("A Fistful of Risks," 1996, pp. 82–83).

More about
Quotation marks with titles, 438–39
Italics with titles, 456–57

Set titles of articles or parts of books in quotation marks and titles of books and other longer works in italics.

8. Two or more sources in one citation When the information you are drawing on comes from more than one source, follow the borrowed material with a list of all relevant sources, separated by semicolons. List the sources in alphabetical order, the same order in which they appear in the reference list.

> When placed in well-structured rehabilitative programs, juvenile offenders—
>
> even those who commit serious crimes such as murder—can become more
>
> mature thinkers, more involved and loving members of their families, and more
>
> successful workers and learners (Beyer, 2006; Burns & Hoagwood, 2002).

9. Two or more sources by the same author in one citation When citing two or more sources by the same author in a single citation, name the author once but include all publication years, separating them with commas.

> Wynn's work explores the ability of human infants to perform mathematical
>   pub.   pub.
>   year 1   year 2
> functions, such as addition and subtraction (1992, 2000).

APA In-Text Citations

5. Six or more authors

6. Group or corporate author

7. Unnamed (anonymous) author

8. Two or more sources in one citation

9. Two or more sources by the same author in one citation

10. Two or more sources by the same author in the same year

11. Two or more authors with the same surname

Human infants have shown surprising abilities to perform mathematical

pub. pub.
year 1 year 2
functions, such as addition and subtraction (Wynn, 1992, 2000).

Example 6, 213

10. Two or more sources by the same author in the same year When your reference list includes two or more publications by the same author in the same year, add a letter following the year (*2006a, 2006b*). Use these year-and-letter designations in your in-text citations and in your reference list.

The brain not only controls the senses of sight and sound, but it also plays an

important role in associating emotions such as fear with particular situations
letter assigned
(Barinaga, 1992b).

11. Two or more authors with the same surname If your reference list includes works by different authors with the same surname, include the authors' initials to differentiate them.

Rehabilitation is a viable option for many juvenile offenders, whose

immaturities and disabilities can, with institutional support and guidance,
first initial + surname
be overcome as the child matures (M. Beyer, 2006).

If a source has more than one author, include initials for the first author only.

12. Reprinted or republished work Include both dates in your in-text citation, with the original date of publication first.

orig. year
Danon-Boileau (2005/2006) takes a cross-disciplinary approach to the study
reprint year
of language disorders in children.

13. Sacred or classical source Cite sacred texts, such as the Bible, the Talmud, or the Qur'an (Koran), in the body of your research project using standard book titles, chapter numbers, and verse numbers, and indicate the version you used.

> In the Song of Solomon, the female speaker concludes her description of
> her lover with this proclamation: "His mouth is sweetness itself, he is all
> delight. / Such is my lover, and such my friend, O daughters of Jerusalem"
> ch.   version
> (5:16, Revised Standard Version).
> verse

APA In-Text
Citations

12. Reprinted or
    republished
    work
13. Sacred or
    classical
    source
**14. Indirect
    source**
**15. Website or
    other online
    source**
16. Personal com-
    munication
    (e-mail, letter,
    interview)

For classical works, cite the year of the translation or version you used: (Plato, trans. 1968).

14. Indirect source When you can, avoid quoting from a secondhand source (source material you have learned about through its mention in another source). When you cannot locate or translate the original source, mention the original author's name in a signal phrase. In your parenthetical note, include *as cited in* followed by the name of the author of the source in which you found the information, and conclude with the year of that source's publication.

> Choy, Fyer, and Lipsitz (as cited in King, 2008) make the distinction that
> people with phobias, unlike those with general anxiety, can identify specific
> causes for their feelings of nervousness and dread.

In the reference list, provide only the source you used: For the example above, include a reference list entry for King, not Choy, Fyer, and Lipsitz.

15. Website or other online source Frequently, the information you need to create a complete in-text citation is missing. Electronic sources may lack fixed page numbers: Page 5 in one printout may be page 4 or 6 in another. Use page numbers only when they are fixed, as in a PDF file. When paragraph numbers are provided, include those (with the abbreviation *para.*) instead of a page number.

> *More about*
> PDF files, 102, 108

> The Internet has also become an outlet for direct distribution of underground
> comics through artist websites, making independent titles more affordable to
> market (Fenty, Houp, & Taylor para. 1).

Examples 27–28, 221

When paragraphs are not numbered, include the title of the section and number of the paragraph in which the material you are citing appears. If the author is unnamed, use the first few words of the title.

> Cell-phone use while driving can impair performance as badly as drinking
>
> alcohol does ("Driven to Distraction," 2006, para. 1).

APA In-Text Citations

14. Indirect source
15. Website or other online source
16. **Personal communication (e-mail, letter, interview)**

If no date is provided, use *n.d.* for *no date.*

> Barrett (n.d.) unwittingly reveals the sexism prevalent on college campuses in
>
> the early 1960s through his account of a football game.

16. Personal communication (e-mail, letter, interview) For sources such as personal e-mail messages, interviews, and phone calls that your readers cannot retrieve and read, mention the communication in your text or provide a parenthetical note, but do not include an entry in the reference list.

> The scientist himself was much more modest about the development
>
> (S. J. Gould, personal communication, November 13, 1986).

24 Preparing an APA-Style Reference List

The reference list, which comes after the body of your research project, lists the sources you have cited in your text. The format of each entry in the list depends in part on the type of source you are citing, such as a printed book, an article in an electronic journal or accessed through a database, or an audio recording. (See the Quick Reference box on pp. 212–13 for a list of APA-style reference list examples.)

Books—Printed and Electronic

In a printed book, the information you need to create a reference list entry appears on the title and copyright pages at the beginning of the book. In an online book or e-book, print and electronic publication information appears at the top or bottom of the first page or is available through a link.

Annotated visual of where to find author, title, and publication information, on foldout accompanying tab 7

1. One author

a. Printed The basic entry for a printed book looks like this:

> Author's surname, Initial(s). (Year of publication). *Title: Subtitle*. Place of
>
> publication (city, state [abbreviated]): Publisher.

Here is an example of an actual citation:

> Pollock, J. (2012). *Crime and justice in America: An introduction to criminal*
>
> *justice*. Maryland Heights, MO: Anderson Publishing.

For books, only first word of title and subtitle (plus names) are capitalized.

b. E-book Works published electronically or made accessible online are now frequently tagged with a digital object identifier (DOI). Unlike a URL that may change or stop working, a DOI is a permanent identifier that will not change over time or from database to database. If the e-book you are documenting is tagged with a DOI, use that identifier instead of publication information or URL, and add a description of the source type in brackets after the title. If no DOI has been assigned, replace publication information with the URL from which the electronic file can be obtained. If you accessed the source on a device such as a Kindle or Nook, no URL should be included.

More about
Digital object identifiers, 101, 211
URLs, 120–21, 221–22

> Carter, J. (2003). *Nasty people: How to stop being hurt by them without stooping*
>
> *to their level* [Adobe Digital Editions version]. doi:10.1036/0071410228

> von Hippel, E. (n.d.). *Democratizing Innovation*. Retrieved from http://web.mit
>
> .edu/evhippel/www/democ.htm

If no publication date available, use *n.d.*

2. Two authors
When there are two authors, list them in the order in which they appear on the title page.

> author 1   author 2
> Raskin, H., & Rabiner, D. (2012). *College drinking and drug use*.
>
> New York, NY: Guilford.

Use an ampersand (&) between names.

APA Reference List Entries

Tech   **Citing Electronic Sources: Digital Object Identifiers (DOIs) and URLs**

Because URLs change and links break, the APA now recommends using a digital object identifier (DOI), a permanent identifying code, whenever available; use a URL, or web address, only when no DOI is available. Most electronic books and articles in academic journals now include a DOI. When your citation ends with a DOI or URL, do *not* add a period after it. Break a DOI or URL (if necessary) only after a slash or before a dot or other punctuation mark; do not add a hyphen.

1. **One author**
2. **Two authors**
3. Three to seven authors
4. Eight or more authors

3. Three to seven authors When the book has three to seven authors, list all their names.

Use an ampersand (&) between the last two names.

James, J., Burks, W., & Eigenmann, P. (2011). *Food allergy.* Philadelphia, PA:

Saunders.

4. Eight or more authors When the book has eight or more authors, list the first six authors followed by three ellipsis points and the last author's name.

Masters, R., Skrapec, C., Muscat, B., Dussich, J. P., Pincu, L., Way,

L. B., . . . Gerstenfeld, P. (2010). *Criminal justice: Realities and challenges.*

New York, NY: McGraw-Hill.

5. Unnamed (anonymous) author Start the entry with the title followed by the publication date. Alphabetize the entry in the reference list using the first significant word in the title (not an article such as *a, an,* or *the*).

And still we conquer! The diary of a Nazi Unteroffizier in the German Africa

Corps. (1968). University, AL: Confederate Publishing.

6. Two or more books by the same author For multiple books by the same author (or authors), arrange the entries in order of publication (from least to most recent).

> Rose, G. (1993). *Feminism and geography: The limits of geographical*
>
> *knowledge.* Minneapolis: University of Minnesota Press.
>
> Rose G. (2011). *Visual methodologies: An introduction to researching with visual*
>
> *materials.* Thousand Oaks, CA: Sage.

When books were written by the same author(s) in the same year, alphabetize the entries by title and add the letter *a* following the publication date of the first entry, *b* following the publication date of the second entry, and so on.

> Dobrin, S. I. (2011a). *Ecology, Writing Theory, and New Media: Writing Ecology.*
>
> New York, NY: Routledge.
>
> Dobrin, S. I. (2011b). *Postcomposition.* Carbondale: Southern Illinois University
>
> Press.

APA Reference
List Entries

5. Unnamed
   (anonymous)
   author
6. **Two or more
   books by the
   same author**
7. Two or more
   authors with
   the same
   surname and
   first initial

Example 10, 208

APA Reference List Entries

5. Unnamed (anonymous) author
6. Two or more books by the same author
7. Two or more authors with the same surname and first initial
8. Group or corporate author
9. Author and editor or translator
10. Edited book or anthology
11. Selection from an edited book or anthology

Works written by a single author should be listed *before* sources written by that same author plus a coauthor, regardless of publication dates.

> Morrison, J. R. (2007). *Diagnosis made easier: Principles and techniques for*
>
> *mental health clinicians.* New York, NY: Guilford.

> Morrison, J. R., & Anders, T. F. (1999). *Interviewing children and adolescents:*
>
> *Skills and strategies for effective* DSM-IV *diagnosis.* New York, NY:
>
> Guilford.

When citing multiple sources by an author and various coauthors, alphabetize entries by the surname of the second author.

> Clarke-Stewart, A., & Allhusen, V. D. (2005). *What we know about childcare.*
>
> Cambridge, MA: Harvard University Press.

> Clarke-Stewart, A., & Brentano, C. (2006). *Divorce: Causes and consequences.*
>
> New Haven, CT: Yale University Press.

7. Two or more authors with the same surname and first initial When your reference list includes sources by two different authors with the same surname and first initial, differentiate them by including their first names in brackets.

> Cohen, A. [Andrew]. (1994). *Assessing language ability in the classroom.*
>
> Boston, MA: Heinle.

> Cohen, A. [Anne]. (1973). *Poor Pearl, poor girl! The murdered girl stereotype in*
>
> *ballad and newspaper.* Austin: University of Texas Press.

No state abbreviation if state included in name of university press

8. Group or corporate author List the sponsoring organization as the author. Use the full name, and alphabetize it in the reference list according to the name's first significant word (ignoring articles such as *a, an,* or *the*). If the same group or corporation is also listed as the publisher, replace the name of the publisher with the word *Author.*

> Fabian Society, Commission on Life Chances and Child Poverty. (2006).
>
> *Narrowing the gap: The final report of the Fabian Commission on Life*
>
> *Chances and Child Poverty.* London, UK: Author.

9. Author and editor or translator If the source originally appeared earlier than the edited or translated version, add the date of original publication at the end of the entry. If the work has an editor, use the abbreviation *Ed.* For a translator, use the abbreviation *Trans.*

> Alvtegen, K. (2010). *Shame* (S. Murray, Trans.). New York, NY: Felony and
>
> Mayhem. (Original work published 2006)

10. Edited book or anthology Put the editor's name in the author position.

> Ghosh, R. A. (Ed.). (2005). *CODE: Collaborative ownership and the digital*
>
> *economy.* Boston, MA: MIT Press.

For a book with multiple editors, change the abbreviation to *Eds.*

11. Selection from an edited book or anthology Begin with the selection's author, followed by the publication date of the book and the selection's title (with no quotation marks or other formatting). Then insert the word *In,* the editors' names, and the title of the book or anthology (italicized). Next include page numbers for the entire selection (even if you used only part of it). Conclude the entry with the publication information for the book in which the selection appeared.

> selection author   selection title   editors
> Smither, N. (2000). Crime scene cleaner. In J. Bowe, M. Bowe, & S.
>
> selection pg. nos.
> Streeter (Eds.), *Gig: Americans talk about their jobs* (pp. 96–103).
>
> New York, NY: Crown.

12. Edition other than the first Insert the edition number (*2nd ed., 3rd ed.*) or edition name (*Rev. ed.* for "revised edition") after the book's title. (The edition number or name usually appears on the title page.)

> Nier, J. A. (2013). *Taking sides: Clashing Views in Social Psychology* (4th ed.).
>
> New York, NY: McGraw-Hill.

13. Introduction, preface, foreword, or afterword The sixth edition of the *Publication Manual of the APA* does not provide an example of an entry for an introduction, preface, foreword, or afterword, but based on other examples, such an entry might look like the one below:

> foreword's author   label   book's author   book's title
> Andretti, M. (2008). Foreword. In D. Daly, *Race to win: How to become a*
>
> pg. nos. (foreword)
> *complete champion* (pp. 2–3). Minneapolis, MN: Quayside-Motorbooks.

14. Entry in an encyclopedia or other reference work Format an entry in a reference work as you would a selection from an edited book. For signed

Example 11, 215

APA Reference List Entries

articles, include the author's name. (Articles in reference works often carry the author's initials only, so you may need to cross-reference the initials with a list of contributors in the front or back of the book.) If an article is unsigned, begin with its title.

a. Printed

entry author   entry title

Treffert, D. A. (2000). Savant syndrome. In A. E. Kazdin (Ed.), *Encyclopedia*
      entry page nos.
     of psychology (pp. 144–148). New York, NY: Oxford University Press.

b. Online

Depression, reactive. (2001). In E. Reber & A. Reber (Eds.), *Penguin*
                 URL
     dictionary of psychology. Retrieved from http://www.credoreference.com

15. Multivolume work

Tomasello, M. (Ed.). (1998–2003). *The new psychology of language: Cognitive*

     and functional approaches to language structure (Vols. 1–2). Mahwah, NJ:

     Erlbaum.

16. Republished book

Huxley, E. (2006). *Red strangers.* New York, NY: Penguin. (Original work

     published 1939)

17. Title within a title The sixth edition of the *Publication Manual of the APA* does not provide an example of an entry for a book with a title within the book's title, but based on other examples, such an entry might look like the one below:

              —— title within title ——

Porter, L. (1987). The interpretation of dreams: *Freud's theories revisited.*

     Boston, MA: Twayne.

Omit italics from any title that would normally be italicized when it falls within the main title of a book. If the title within the title would normally appear in quotation marks, retain the quotation marks and italicize both titles.

Example 13, 208

18. Sacred or classical source No entry in the reference list is needed for a sacred source, such as the Bible, the Talmud, or the Qur'an, or a classical source, such as Plato's *Republic.*

19. Dissertation or thesis Indicate whether the work is a doctoral dissertation or a master's thesis. If the dissertation or thesis was accessed through a database service, include the name of the database from which it was obtained and provide any identifying number. If it was obtained from a university or personal website, include the URL.

a. Published

> Song, L. Z. (2003). *Relations between optimism, stress and health in Chinese and American students* (Doctoral dissertation). Available from ProQuest Dissertations and Theses database. (UMI No. AAI3107041)

> Lillie, A. S. (2008). *MusicBox: Navigating the space of your music* (Master's thesis, Massachusetts Institute of Technology). Retrieved from http://thesis.flyingpudding.com/documents/Anita_FINAL_THESIS.pdf

b. Unpublished

> Luster, L. (1992). *Schooling, survival and struggle: Black women and the GED* (Unpublished doctoral dissertation). Stanford University, Stanford, CA.

c. Abstracted in DAI If you used the abstract in the *Dissertation Abstracts International* database, include that information in the entry. Remember, though, that reading the abstract is no substitute for reading the actual source.

> Kelley, E. (2008). Parental depression and negative attribution bias in parent reports of child symptoms. *Dissertation Abstracts International: Section B. Sciences and Engineering, 69*(7), 4427.

Periodicals—Printed and Electronic

A periodical is a publication issued at regular intervals—newspapers are generally published every day, magazines every week or month, and scholarly journals four times a year. For periodicals, include not only the title of the article (with no quotation marks or italics) but also the title of the periodical (in italics, all important words capitalized). Other publication information you include depends on the type of periodical you are citing.

20. Article in a scholarly journal The information needed to create a reference list entry for a printed journal article appears on the cover or in the table of contents of the journal and on the first and last page of the article. For articles downloaded from a database, the information appears on the search results screen, in the full record of the article, or on the first and last page of the downloaded file. For articles that appear in journals that are published solely online, the needed information may be on the website's home page, in the journal's table of contents, or on the first page of the article.

APA Reference List Entries

17. Title within a title
18. Sacred or classical source
19. **Dissertation or thesis**
20. **Article in a scholarly journal**
21. Special issue of a journal
22. Article in a magazine

> Annotated visual of where to find author, title, publication, and other information, on foldout accompanying tab 7

More about
Formatting author
information:
Examples 1–11,
203–08

a. Printed The basic citation for an article in a printed journal looks like this:

> Author's surname, Initial(s). (Year of publication). Article title. *Journal Title, vol*
>
> *no.,* pages.

Here is an example of an actual citation:

> Wright, S. (2011). Invasive species and the loss of beta diversity. *Ethics*
>
> *and the Environment, 16,* 75–98.

If the article is published in a journal that starts each issue with page 1, provide the issue number after the volume number (not italicized, in parentheses).

> Sui, C. (2007). Giving indigenous people a voice. *Taiwan Review, 57*(8), 40.

More about
Digital object
identifiers (DOIs),
PDFs, 101, 108,
211

b. Online or accessed through a database More and more, researchers access journal articles electronically, either through online journals or through databases that provide access to articles in PDF or HTML format. Articles accessed electronically now frequently include a digital object identifier (DOI). The DOI is a permanent code that does not change from library to library or from database to database. The DOI makes URLs unnecessary. Whenever a DOI is provided, include it at the end of your reference list entry. The basic citation for an article in an online journal or accessed through an online database that has a DOI is the same as for a printed journal article except that the DOI appears at the end of the citation.

APA Reference
List Entries

> Luo, Y. (2011). Do 10-month-old infants understand others' false beliefs?
>
> DOI
> *Cognition, 121,* 289–298. doi:10.1016/j.cognition.2011.07.011

For an article in an online journal that does *not* provide a DOI, include the phrase *Retrieved from* followed by the URL for the journal's home page.

> Janyam, K. (2011). The influence of job satisfaction on mental health of factory
>
> workers. *Internet Journal of Mental Health, 7*(1). Retrieved from http://www
>
> .ispub.com/journal/the_internet_journal_of_mental_health/

21. Special issue of a journal

> special issue title
> Leong, F. (Ed.). (2009). History of racial and ethnic minority psychology
>
> label
> [Special issue]. *Cultural Diversity and Ethnic Minority Psychology, 15.*

22. Article in a magazine

Example 20, 217

a. Printed or accessed through a database Provide the full publication date of the issue (year, month, and day or year and month). If the volume and issue number of the magazine are available, include that information as you would for a journal article.

> Greene, K. (2011, December). Our data, ourselves. *Discover,* 42–47.

> Pelusi, N. (2009, January/February). The appeal of the bad boy. *Psychology
>
> Today, 42*(1), 58–59.

b. Online Include the URL for the magazine's home page.

> Fairhall, D. (2011, December 10). Welcome to the new Arctic. *Salon.* Retrieved
>
> from http://www.salon.com

If the magazine is available in a printed edition but the article is only available online, include the phrase *Supplemental material* in brackets after the article's title.

> Daniller, A. (2007, December). Psychology research done right [Supplemental
>
> material]. *GradPSYCH.* Retrieved from http://gradpsych.apags.org

23. Article in a newspaper The information you need to create a reference list entry for a printed newspaper article is on the masthead of the newspaper (at the top of the first page) and on the first and last page of the article. For newspaper articles downloaded from a database, the information you need appears on the search results screen, the full record of the article, or the article itself. For articles that appear in online versions of the newspaper, the information you need is usually at the top of the first page of the article.

a. Printed or accessed through a database

> author   pub. date   title
> Ritter, M. (2011, December 1). Mouse study offers hope for new HIV
>
>   newspaper   sec./pg. no.
> protection. *Atlanta Journal-Constitution,* p. A7.

If the title of a newspaper does not include its place of publication, supply the city and state, in square brackets, following the title.

> Esch, M. (2011, July 1). New York may ban gas drilling in watersheds, state
>
> land. *Evening Sun* [Norwich, NY], pp. 1, 3.

If the pages of the article are not continuous, provide all page numbers.

> Vergano, D. (2011, July 3). Shuttles proved humans could work together in
>
> space. *Press & Sun-Bulletin* [Binghamton, NY], pp. A1, A4.

To cite a newspaper article downloaded from a database, follow the model for a printed newspaper article, but omit the page numbers, and change the comma after the newspaper's title to a period.

b. Online Follow the format for a printed newspaper article, but omit the page reference and include the words *Retrieved from* and the URL for the newspaper's home page.

> Smyth, J. C., & Thompson, D. (2011, December 10). Public retirement ages come
>
> under greater scrutiny. *Denver Post.* Retrieved from http://www.denverpost.com

24. Review (printed or online) Follow the model for the type of periodical in which the review appeared. In the author position, insert the name of the author of the review; if the review is titled, insert that title in the title position (no italics or quotation marks); and add in brackets the label *Review of the book* (or *Review of the film,* and so forth) followed by the title and author of the reviewed work. End with publication information for the periodical in which the review appeared.

> review author ⎯⎯⎯⎯⎯⎯ review title ⎯⎯⎯⎯⎯⎯ label
> Balk, D. E. (2007). Diamonds and mummies are forever [Review of the

Comma between title, author

> book *Remember me,* by L. T. Cullen]. *Death Studies, 31,* 941–947.
>
> doi:10.1080/07481180701603436

If the review is untitled, substitute the label *Review of the book,* the book's title, and the book's author in brackets.

> Hurdley, R. (2011, September). [Review of the book *Gripes: The little*

Comma between title, author

> *quarrels of couples,* by J. Kaufmann]. *Cultural Sociology, 5,* 452–453.

25. Letter to the editor (printed or online) Follow the model for the type of periodical in which the letter appeared, and insert the label *Letter to the editor* in brackets following the letter's title.

> letter author ⎯⎯⎯⎯⎯ letter title ⎯⎯⎯⎯⎯ label
> Richmond, A. (2009, May). Miracle drug? [Letter to the editor].
>
> *The Atlantic, 303*(4), 14.

If the letter is untitled, put the label *Letter to the editor,* in brackets, in the title position.

26. Abstract (printed or online) It is always better to read and cite the article itself. However, if you relied only on the abstract, or summary, cite only the abstract to avoid misrepresenting your source and your research.

> Loverock, D. S. (2007). Object superiority as a function of object coherence and
>
> task difficulty [Abstract]. *American Journal of Psychology, 120,* 565–591.

Tebeaux, E. (2011). Technical writing and the development of the English

paragraph 1473–1700. *Journal of Technical Writing and Communication,*

41, 219–253. Abstract retrieved from http://www.ebscohost.com

Other Electronic Sources

While it is usually easy to find the information you need to create a complete citation for a book or an article in a periodical, websites can be a bit trickier. Most of the information you need will appear on the site's home page, usually at the bottom or top of that page, or on the web page you are citing. Sometimes, however, you may need to look further. Click on links with titles such as "About us" or "More information." Frequently, websites do not provide complete information, in which case include as much information in your entry as you can.

> Annotated visual of where to find author, title, and publication information, on foldout accompanying tab 7

27. Website   In general, when mentioning an entire website in a research project, you do not have to include an entry in your reference list. However, if you quote or paraphrase content from the site or interact with it in a substantial way, include it, following this model:

> Example 15, 209

Author's surname, Initial(s). (Copyright date or date last updated). *Website title.*

Retrieved from + URL

Here is an example of an actual citation:

Gilbert, R. (2001). *Shake your shyness.* Retrieved from http://shakeyourshyness

.com

If no author is cited, move the title to the author position. If the web page is untitled, add a description in brackets. If no date is provided, insert *(n.d.)* following the author's name.

> Example 5, 212

28. Web page   Provide the title of the page (with no formatting) and the URL for the specific page you are citing.

web page title

American Psychological Association. (2011). Treatment for binge eating.
URL for web page
Retrieved from http://www.apa.org/

29. Discussion list posting   Treat the subject line (or *thread*) as the title, and include the label *Discussion list post* (in brackets).

date posted   subj. line   label

Arendes, L. (2008, July 9). Objectivity [Discussion list post]. Retrieved
URL
from news://sci.psychology.research

> **Tech** **Checking URLs and DOIs**
>
> **DOIs.** If your entry includes a DOI, check it before submitting your project by visiting crossref.org and inserting the DOI into the search box.
>
> **URLs.** Just before submitting your paper, test all the URLs. Sometimes web addresses change or content is taken down.
>
> If the URL you provided no longer works, search for the work online by title or keyword; you may find it "cached" on the web even though the owner of the original site has taken the work down. Then use the URL for the cached version in your bibliographic entry.

If the name of the list is not included in the URL, add it to the retrieval statement: *Retrieved from Early Childhood Education Discussion List: http://www.dmoz.org/Reference/Education/Early_Childhood*

30. Article on a wiki Cite a wiki article as you would a web page. Because wikis are written and edited collaboratively, there is no author to cite; begin with the article's title. If the date of the most recent update is not noted, include the abbreviation *n.d.* (*no date*) in its place. Always include a retrieval date and direct URL.

APA Reference List Entries

retrieval date
Battered person syndrome. (n.d.). Retrieved April 22, 2012, from http://
URL
psychology.wikia.com

31. Blog Include a screen name if the author's name is not provided.

a. Blog posting

post author   post date   post title
Dean, J. (2009, January 1). Gratitude enhanced by focusing on end
                                    label
of pleasurable experience [Web log post]. Retrieved from
                          URL (post)
http://www.spring.org.uk/2009_01_01_blogarchive.php

More about
Reliability, 116–21

b. Comment on a blog posting

comment author   date posted   subject line (thread title)
Carosin, R. (2011, December 11). Re: An untranslatable mind [Web log
                                    URL
comment]. Retrieved from http://mindhacks.com/

32. Computer software Provide an entry for computer software only if it is unfamiliar to your readers and it is necessary to a computation you have made.

title   label
Power Researcher [Computer software]. Atlanta, GA: Uniting Networks.

If the software you are citing is available in more than one version, add a version number in parentheses between the title of the software and the identifying label.

33. Presentation slides The sixth edition of the *Publication Manual of the APA* does not provide an example of an entry for presentation slides, but based on other examples such an entry might look like the one below:

> Doyle, T. (2009). *Privacy, free expression, and compromising images*
> label
> [PowerPoint slides]. Retrieved from http://library.hunter.cuny
> .edu/pdf/Privacyfreeexpression.ppt

Audio and Visual Sources

The information you need to create an entry for most audio and visual sources appears on the cover, label, or program of the work or in the credits at the end of a film or television show. As with other citations, italicize the titles of longer works, such as CDs and films, and do not format or add quotation marks to the titles of shorter works, such as single songs or single episodes of television programs.

34. Motion picture

> release   title
> Grazer, B. (Producer), & Howard, R. (Director). (2001). *A beautiful mind*
> distributor
> [Motion picture]. United States: Warner Bros.

35. Online video or video blog (vlog)

> ATTC Network. (2007, July 12). Michael–Clinical psychologist [Video file].
> Retrieved from http://www.youtube.com/watch?v=4OAYT5P6xaQ

36. Television or radio broadcast

a. Series

> Garcia, R. (Executive producer). (2008–2009). *In treatment* [Television series].
> New York, NY: HBO.

b. Episode

> Reingold, J. (Writer), & Barclay, P. (Director). (2009). Mia: Week three
> [Television series episode]. In R. Garcia (Executive producer), *In*
> *treatment*. New York, NY: HBO.

c. Podcast

> Mitchell, N. (Producer). (2008, March 15). The psyche on death row. *All in*
> *the mind* [Audio podcast]. Retrieved from http://www.abc.net.au/rn/
> allinthemind/default.htm

37. Musical or other audio recording

a. CD, LP, or audiobook

> Gore, A. (Writer), & Patton, W. (Narrator). (2007). *The assault on reason*
>
> [CD]. New York, NY: Penguin Audio.

b. Selection or song on a CD, LP, or audiobook

> writers   © date   performers
> Dilly, D., & Wilkin, M. (1959). The long black veil [Recorded by H. Dickens &
>
> A. Gerrard]. On *Pioneering women of bluegrass* [CD]. Washington,
>
>   recording date
> DC: Smithsonian/Folkways Records. (1996).

38. Lecture, speech, conference presentation, or poster session

> Krauss, S. A., & Dahlsgaard, K. K. (2011, May 21). *Work after war: National*
>
> *Guard soldiers' experience of the postdeployment return to civilian*
>
> *employment.* Paper presented at the Conference on Work, Stress, and
>
> Health, Orlando, FL.

> Ferandi, Alan B. (2009, April). *The effect of stable unions on child health,*
>
> *nutrition, and development.* Poster session presented at the annual
>
> meeting of the Population Association of America, Detroit, MI.

39. Work of art
The sixth edition of the *Publication Manual of the APA* does not provide an example of an entry for a work of art such as a painting or a sculpture, but based on other examples, such an entry might look like the one below.

>   date   title of
> artist   completed   artwork   label   location
> McElheny, J. (2008). *Island universe* [Sculpture]. White Cube, London, UK.

40. Advertisement
The sixth edition of the *Publication Manual of the APA* does not provide an example of an entry for an advertisement, but based on other examples, such an entry might look like the one below:

> company or product   label   source of advertisement
> Regal Cinemas [Advertisement]. (2010, March 10). *Los Angeles Times.*
>
> Retrieved from http://www.latimes.com/

41. Map

> U.S. Census Bureau, Geography Division (Cartographer). (2001). Mean center
>
> of population for the United States: 1790 to 2000 [Demographic map].
>
> Retrieved from http://www.census.gov/geo/www/cenpop/meanctr.pdf

Miscellaneous Sources—Printed and Electronic

42. Government publication

a. Printed

U.S. Department of Health and Human Services, National Institutes of

    Health, National Institute of Mental Health. (2008). *Bipolar disorder*

    (NIH Publication No. 3679). Washington, DC: Government

    Printing Office.

U.S. Department of Health and Human Services. (2005). *Steps to a*

    healthier US. Washington, DC: Author.

Example 8, 214

b. Online

U.S. General Accounting Office. (1993, September 21). *North American Free*

    Trade Agreement: A focus on the substantive issues

    (Publication No. GAO/T-GGD-93-44). Retrieved from http://www

    .gpoaccess.gov/gaoreports/search.html

43. Report (nongovernmental)

American Psychological Association, Task Force on Gender Identity and

    Gender Variance. (2008). *Report of the Task Force on Gender Identity*

    and Gender Variance. Retrieved from http://www.apa.org/pi/lgbc

    /transgender/2008TaskForceReport.pdf

44. Data set

U.S. Department of Justice, Federal Bureau of Investigation. (2007, September).

    2006 Crime in the United States [Data set]. Retrieved from http://www

    .data.gov/raw/310

45. Fact sheet, brochure, pamphlet

Department of Health and Human Services, Centers for Disease Control and

    Prevention. (2005, May 3). Basic information about SARS [Fact sheet].

    Retrieved from http://www.cdc.gov/ncidod/SARS/factsheet.htm

APA Reference
List Entries

40. Advertisement
41. Map
42. **Government
   publication**
43. **Report (non-
   governmental)**
44. **Data set**
45. **Fact sheet,
   brochure,
   pamphlet**
46. Conference
   proceedings
47. Legal source
   (printed or
   online)

If no author is listed, move the title to the author position. If no publication date is available, insert *n.d.* (for *no date*) in its place.

Example 10, 208
Example 21, 218

46. Conference proceedings Cite conference proceedings either as an edited book or as the special issue of a journal, depending on how they were published.

47. Legal source (printed or online)

      case title   *U.S. Reports* decision
    (abbreviated)   *vol.*   *no.* date
Lynn v. Alabama, 493 U.S. 945 (1989). Retrieved from *Open Jurist* website:
                   URL
    http://openjurist.org/493/us/945/lynn-v-alabama

48. Interview (published or broadcast)

interview subject   broadcast date
Cameron, J. (2009, December 18). James Cameron, a king with a soft

    touch. Interview by M. Norris [Digital download]. National Public

    Radio, Washington, DC. Retrieved from http://www.npr.org

Example 16, 210

49. Personal communication (e-mail, letter, interview) Cite personal communications that are not available to the public in the body of the research project, but do not include an entry in the reference list.

25 Using APA Style for Informational Notes

In addition to in-text citations, APA style allows researchers to include informational notes. These notes may provide supplementary information, acknowledge any help the writer received, or call attention to possible conflicts of interest.

    To add supplementary information, include a superscript (above-the-line) arabic number in the text and at the beginning of the note (either at the bottom of the page for a footnote or in a list of notes at the end of the project).

The participants in each condition were told at the beginning of the experiment that they were

participating in a memory-recall task. They were to identify what they could remember from a clip

from the movie *Pretty Woman* (Milchan, Reuther, & Marshall, 1990),[1] a stereotypical "chick-flick."

Notes

←—½"—→ [1]This romantic comedy starring Julia Roberts and Richard Gere (dir. Garry Marshall) was

extremely popular, grossing nearly $464 million worldwide, according to the site Box Office Mojo

(http://www.boxofficemojo.com/movies/?id=prettywoman.htm). Nevertheless, participants had not

seen the film before participating in the experiment.

Add notes to acknowledge help or possible conflicts of interest to the title page, four lines below the date.

> Sample title page, 231

26 Formatting a Paper in APA Style

The care with which you cite and document your sources reflects the care you have taken in writing your research project. Continue that care by formatting your project in the way your readers expect. For most writing projects in the social sciences, follow the APA's formatting guidelines. The *Publication Manual of the APA* (6th ed.) offers guidance for writers submitting projects for publication in scholarly journals, so not all its formatting requirements are appropriate for student projects. Ask your instructor about making reasonable modifications.

> **Student Model**
> Research project (APA style): "The Power of Wardrobe," Heather DeGroot, 231–38

26a Margins and Spacing

- Set margins of at least one inch at the top, bottom, and left- and right-hand sides of your paper.

- Indent the first line of each paragraph half an inch.

- Indent quotations of forty or more words as a block, half an inch from the left margin.

> ***More about***
> Block quotations, 437–38

- Double-space the entire paper, including the abstract, title page, block quotations, footnotes, figure captions, and the reference list. Set the text so that the right margin is uneven (ragged), and do not hyphenate words at the ends of lines.

- Insert two spaces after punctuation at the end of a sentence.

- Use a hanging indent for each reference list entry: The first line should be flush with the left margin with subsequent lines indented half an inch.

> Sample reference list, 237

The major style guides (MLA, APA, *Chicago,* CSE) were initially written before the widespread use of personal computers, when most writers still worked on typewriters. To create a paragraph or hanging indention on a typewriter, the typist would hit the space bar five times or set a tab. Now, just about everyone creates writing projects on a computer, where paragraph and hanging indentions are created using the Ruler or Paragraph Dialog box.

Ruler   **Paragraph Dialog Box**

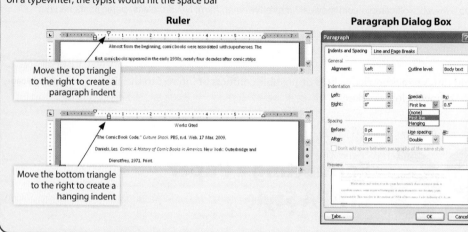

26b Typeface, Header, and Page Number

More about
Choosing a typeface and type size, 52–53

Use a standard typeface such as Times New Roman or Arial in a readable size (usually 12 points). Include a header, or *running head,* consisting of the first two or three words of the title (no more than fifty characters) in the upper left-hand corner of the page, half an inch from the upper edge. Include the page number half an inch from the top and one inch from the right edge of the page. Use your word processor's header feature to insert the running head and number the pages automatically.

26c Title Page

More about
Crafting a title, 40
Notes acknowledging help or conflicts, 226–27, 231

- Insert the title, typed in upper- and lowercase letters, centered on the top half of the page.

- Insert a blank line and then type your name.

Word processing programs allow you to insert a header automatically. In Microsoft Word, select "Header and Footer" under the View menu. If you have any questions about creating a header, consult your program's Help directory.

- Papers for submission to a scholarly journal include the author's university or college affiliation; student writers usually include the course number, the name of the instructor to whom the project will be submitted, and the date of submission, each centered on separate lines.

- If you need to acknowledge help you received—for example, in conducting your research or interpreting your results—include a note on the title page, four lines below the identifying information.

❯ Sample title page, APA style, 231

26d Abstract

The abstract generally includes a one-sentence summary of the most important points in each section of the project:

❯ Sample abstract, APA style, 232

- Introduction—problem you are investigating

- Methods—number and characteristics of the participants and your research methods

- Results—your outcomes

- Discussion—implications of your results. This section concludes your text.

The abstract follows the title page and appears on its own page, headed with the word *Abstract* centered at the top of the page. The abstract should be no more than 150–250 words.

26e Tables and Figures

- Refer to tables and figures in the text, using the word *Table* or *Figure* followed by the number of the table or figure in sequence. (The first figure is Figure 1; the first table is Table 1.) Discuss the significance of tables and figures in the text, but do not repeat the information that appears in the table or figure itself.

- Include a caption with each figure. The caption should begin with the word *Figure* and the number assigned in the text (both in italics). The caption, which follows the figure, should describe the figure briefly but not repeat the information in your text. If you borrowed the figure or the data to create the figure, include the source information at the end of your caption.

❯ Sample figure captions, APA style, 238

- Include the word *Table* and the table number (no italics) on one line and, on the next line, the table title (in italics). The table itself should appear below the table number and title. If you borrowed the table or the data to create the table, include source information below the table, preceded by the word *Note* (in italics, followed by a period).

Sample figures,
APA style, 238

- In research projects submitted for publication, tables should appear, each on a new page, after the reference list or endnotes (if any). Figures (graphs, charts, photographs, maps, and so on) should appear, each on a new page, following the tables. In college research projects, however, your instructor may prefer to see tables and figures in the body of your research project, as close as possible following their first mention in the text. Check with your instructor before formatting your project.

26f Reference List

- Center the heading "References" at the top of the page.

- Use a hanging indent for each reference list entry: The first line should be flush with the left margin, with subsequent lines indented half an inch.

- Alphabetize the entries in the reference list by the surname of the author or, if no author is listed, by the first important word in the title (ignoring *A, An,* or *The*).

More about
Italics with titles,
456–57

- Italicize all titles of books and websites, but do not enclose titles of articles or book chapters in quotation marks.

More about
Capitalization,
452–56
Proper nouns, 320

- Capitalize the first word, the first word following a colon or a dash, and proper nouns in titles of books, articles in periodicals, websites and web pages, films, and so on. Capitalize all major words in journal titles: *Psychology, Public Policy, and Law; Monitor on Psychology.*

26g Printing, Paper, and Binding

Print your project using a high-quality printer (make sure it has plenty of ink), on opaque, 8½ × 11–inch white paper. Most instructors do not want you to enclose your paper in a binder, but if you are in doubt, ask. If it is not submitted in a binder, paper-clip or staple the pages together.

Writing Responsibly Of Deadlines and Paperclips

Instructors expect students to turn in thoughtful, carefully proofread, and neatly formatted papers on time—usually in class on the due date. Another expectation is that the writer will clip or staple the pages of the paper *before* the paper is submitted. Do justice to yourself by being fully prepared.

to SELF

Student Model **Research Project: APA Style**

In the sample student research project that follows, Heather DeGroot examines the influence that gender stereotypes can have on behavior. She fulfills her responsibilities to topic and audience by drawing on a variety of relevant and reliable sources to provide the background that her readers will need, by including visuals that help her readers understand her project, and by following the format for an APA-style research project, the format her readers expect. By acknowledging her sources, she fulfills her responsibility to the other writers from whom she has borrowed information. By conducting her primary research with care, by thanking Patrick Brown for the assistance he provided, by acknowledging the limitations of her project, and by revising, editing, and proofreading her project carefully, she demonstrates her own credibility as a researcher and writer.

> *More about*
> Writing in college,
> 67–72

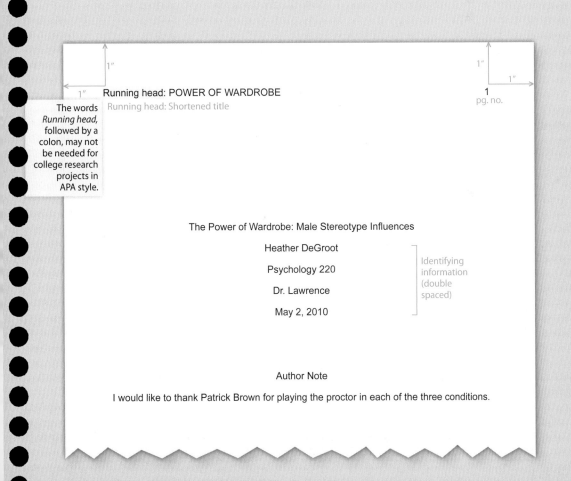

1"

1"

1"

1"   Running head: POWER OF WARDROBE   1
                                              pg. no.
The words   Running head: Shortened title
Running head,
followed by a
colon, may not
be needed for
college research
projects in
APA style.

The Power of Wardrobe: Male Stereotype Influences

Heather DeGroot

Psychology 220

Dr. Lawrence

May 2, 2010

Identifying
information
(double
spaced)

Author Note

I would like to thank Patrick Brown for playing the proctor in each of the three conditions.

½" 1" 1" ½" 1"

Abstract   Heading (centered, 1" from top), new page

This study explores the potential influence of stereotypical appearances on male subjects'
stated opinions regarding entertainment perceived as "feminine." Results are based on responses from 26 undergraduate males. Data were analyzed using one-way variance tests
and Tukey HSD post hoc tests. The findings show that participants were more likely to give
a favorable rating to a "chick-flick" in the presence of a counterstereotypical male ($M = 8.67$,
$SD = 1.53$) than in the presence of a stereotypical male ($M = 5.31$, $SD = 1.97$) or control
proctor ($M = 5.20$, $SD = 1.99$). Results suggest that participants may have experienced
gender role conflict.

Abstract: Sum-
mary of problem,
methods, results,
discussion

The Power of Wardrobe: Male Stereotype Influences   Title (centered)

¶ indent: ½″

Stereotypes—expectations placed upon people because of their gender, race, or

religion—may be discouraged in their most overt forms, but they continue to flourish in the

Text:
Double-
spaced media. In contemporary American culture, this sort of bias places an exaggerated emphasis

on physical appearance. Such attitudes are not isolated features of media programming;

rather, they influence many interactions in everyday life. Sontag, Peteu, and Lee (1999)

indicate that this is especially true among adolescents and young adults, for whom clothing,

personal image, and identity tend to be inextricably bound.

Signal phrase with parenthetical citation for date; the word *and* used before last author's name

Impressions of other people can be classified into two categories: stereotypes and

individuating information. Stereotypes focus on social categories, while individuating

information is the focus of other factors, including personality, actions of the individual, and

so forth (Kunda & Thagard, 1996). The stereotype effect, as defined by researcher Monica

Biernat (2003), is "a finding that individual members (comparable in all ways except their

category membership) are judged in a direction consistent with group-level expectations or

stereotypes" (p. 1019). Under such circumstances, people are judged more by the category in

which one can group them than by their qualities or skills as individuals. However, according

to Kunda and Thagard (1996), the division of these types of judgment is not always clear.

This was the influence for their impression-formation theory in which stereotypes, traits, and

behaviors are all constrained by positive and negative associations. In their research, they

found that appearance was crucial in this process.

Introduction: De-Groot provides background, definitions, hypothesis.

Signal phrase with parenthetical citation for date, page number included with quotation

The influential power of stereotypes is particularly interesting when gender

boundaries are crossed. In a 2003 study, researchers Vescio, Snyder, and Butz found that

while membership in a socioeconomic class or "power position" (p. 1062) tended to give

participants a biased or predetermined opinion about the beliefs and behaviors (such as

work ethic) by which a person in another category lived, gender exerted at least as great an

influence on the manner in which people were categorized. Mansfield (2006) demonstrated

that males in power positions were likely to be viewed differently than females in the same

positions.

Date of publication in text, so not in parentheses following author names

1″

1″

   Would these findings remain consistent if only one gender were used in the study? That is, can we identify intra-gender roles or stereotypes that similarly affect perception and beliefs about individuals? A study by G. H. Edwards (1992) found that beliefs regarding men and women transcend gender, with subtypes or categories (such as for men, businessman, athlete, or loser) emerging within each sex. Typically, such seeming variations represent varying degrees of a supposed normative "masculinity," rather than truly distinct expressions of a male gender role. Rudman and Fairchild (2004) write that "for men, a lifetime of experience observing one's peers being teased or ostracized for 'effeminate' behavior may evoke strong normative pressures toward highly masculine self-presentations" (p. 160). Plummer (2001) indicates that boys begin pressuring one another to conform in childhood, telling each other to toughen up or to stop acting like a baby.

Direct quotation from PDF; page number included

   The purpose of this study is to observe whether male participants are likely to be influenced by a stereotypically "male" opinion. Are college-aged males more swayed by the "jock" or "cool guy on campus" than by those with an "average Joe" or a "metrosexual" appearance? Hypothetically, male participants should more likely be swayed by the opinions of the stereotypical male than by those of the control group ("average Joe") or the experimental group (counterstereotypical).

Hypothesis

Methods
First-level heading (centered, boldface)

Methods: DeGroot explains how study was conducted.

Participants
Second-level heading (left, boldface)

   Twenty-six undergraduate males from a large southeastern university (mean age = 19) participated in this study in order to fill a course requirement in their general psychology classes.

Procedure

Projects for publication: Tables and figures follow reference list or endnotes. College projects: Ask your instructor—tables and figures may be included in the text, following the first reference to them. Figures for this project appear on p. 238.

   The participants were randomly assigned to one of three conditions in the study: the stereotypically "male" proctor group, the counterstereotypical proctor group, and the control group. The proctor was the same person in each condition, but his appearance was different in each (Figure 1). In the stereotypically male proctor condition, the proctor wore an outfit consisting of team sports apparel: a baseball cap, a basketball jersey, shorts, and sneakers. In the counterstereotypical condition, he wore a long-sleeved, light pink button-down shirt (tucked in), creased khaki pants, and dress shoes. In the control condition, the

proctor wore a short-sleeved blue polo shirt (not tucked in), khaki shorts, and sneakers.

The participants in each condition were told at the beginning of the experiment that they

were participating in a memory-recall task. They were to identify what they could remember

from a clip from the movie *Pretty Woman* (Milchan, Reuther, & Marshall, 1990), a stereotypical

"chick-flick." During the ten-minute film clip, which was constant for each of the three

conditions, the proctor read scripted lines such as "Oh! I love this part!" and "I'm seriously such

a sap, but this film is just so good!" The script was a constant in each of the three conditions.

After the clip was viewed by all, the proctor handed out a questionnaire to conduct

the "memory-recall task." The questionnaire contained diversion questions such as "What

color is the dress that Vivian (Julia Roberts's character) wears in the scene?" and "What

game do Edward and Vivian play after the performance?" At the end of the questionnaire,

the participants rated the movie on an opinion scale from 1 to 10, with 10 being the highest

overall liking.

After the experiment was over, participants in each condition were debriefed as a

group and were dismissed from the study.

Results

A one-way analysis of variance (ANOVA) was conducted on the data in order

to determine whether males are more influenced by a stereotypically "male" proctor

in comparison to the counterstereotypical and control-group proctors. The analysis

demonstrated that at least one group was significantly different from the others, $F(2, 23) =$

4.08, p < .05. Tukey HSD post hoc tests were performed to measure the difference between

the groups individually. The Tukey HSD revealed that the participants were more likely to give

a favorable movie rating under the influence of the counterstereotypically masculine proctor

($M = 8.67$, $SD = 1.53$) than the stereotypically masculine proctor ($M = 5.31$, $SD = 1.97$) or the

control proctor ($M = 5.20$, $SD = 1.99$) (see Figure 2).

There were no significant differences in movie ratings between those in the

stereotypically masculine proctor's group and those in the control proctor's. These results

Ampersand used in parenthetical citation

Results: DeGroot summarizes data and research findings; includes figures, p. 238.

were contrary to the study's initial hypothesis, and they suggest that male participants are more likely to defy gender roles in the presence of a counterstereotypical proctor than in the presence of a stereotypically masculine proctor.

Discussion

Discussion: DeGroot interprets data, draws conclusions, expresses concerns, and raises questions for further study.

The study elicited something beyond stereotypical responses from the participants. In fact, the participants may have experienced gender role conflict. Instead of scoring favorably when the masculine male proctor said he enjoyed the film, the participants scored the film lower than initially expected. The presence of a highly or moderately "masculine" male, though he made favorable comments in each condition, may have caused the participants to adhere more rigidly to socialized male gender roles and thus rate the movie lower than subjects in the atypically "masculine" proctor group, who did not feel the pressure to assert masculinity in their rating of *Pretty Woman*. (See McCreary et al., 1996.)

Citations of six or more authors: First author plus *et al.*

Certain irregularities in the study provoked questions that might be investigated in future research. Due to factors beyond the researcher's control, each condition had a different number of participants. The counterstereotypical condition, which had significant findings, had the smallest number of participants; as a result, those scores are subject to greater statistical variation due to strong individual opinion. However, one might also question whether the number of males present influences a subject's tendency to admit to a counterstereotypical opinion or value judgment. If the study were to be replicated to find for stereotype differences alone, it would be crucial for the number of participants in each condition to be the same. On the other hand, a separate study might use multiple viewing groups of varying individual sizes to determine the effect of group size in gender-stereotype-determined valuations.

Another issue to consider is the effect of the fictional nature of the film to which the male viewers were asked to react. A study reported in *Business Week* suggests that men are more willing to show empathy when they know the stories eliciting their emotional response are fictional. Jennifer Argo, one of the authors of the study, is quoted as saying that fictional works provide "an excuse to relax gender stereotypes" (as cited in Coplan, 2008, p. 17). This factor was not considered in the study reported here.

References

Biernat, M. (2003). Toward a broader view of social stereotyping. *American Psychologist,*

58, 1019–1027. doi:10.1037/0003-066X.58.12.1019

Coplan, J. H. (2008, January 28). When it's all right for guys to cry. *Business Week, 4068,*

17. Retrieved from http://www.businessweek.com

Edwards, G. H. (1992). The structure and content of the male gender role stereotype: An

exploration of subtypes. *Sex Roles: A Journal of Research, 27,* 553–551.

Kunda, Z., & Thagard, P. (1996). Forming impressions from stereotypes, traits, and behav-

iors: A parallel-constraint-satisfaction theory. *Psychological Review, 103,* 284–308.

Mansfield, H. C. (2006). *Manliness.* New Haven, CT: Yale University Press.

McCreary, D. R., Wong, F. Y., Wiener, W., Carpenter, K. M., Engle, A., & Nelson, P. (1996).

The relationship between masculine gender role stress and psychological adjustment:

A question of construct validity? *Sex Roles: A Journal of Research, 34,* 507–516.

Milchan, A. (Producer), Reuther, S. (Producer), & Marshall, G. (Director). (1990). *Pretty*

woman [DVD]. USA: Touchstone Home Video.

Plummer, D. C. (2001). The quest for modern manhood: Masculine stereotypes, peer cul-

ture and the social significance of homophobia. *Journal of Adolescence, 24,* 15–23.

Rudman, L. A., & Fairchild, K. (2004). Reactions to counterstereotypic behavior: The role

of backlash in cultural stereotype maintenance. *Journal of Personality and Social*

Psychology, 87, 157–176.

Sontag, M. S., Peteu, M., & Lee, J. (1999). *Clothing in the self-system of adolescents:*

Relationships among values, proximity of clothing to self, clothing interest, anticipated

outcomes and perceived quality of life. Retrieved from Michigan State University

Extension website: http://web1.msue.msu.edu/msue/imp/modrr/rr556098.html

Vescio, T. K., Snyder, M., & Butz, D. A. (2003). Power in stereotypically masculine domains:

A social influence strategy X stereotype match model. *Journal of Personality and*

Social Psychology, 85, 1062. doi:10.1037/0022-3514.85.6.1062

Heading (centered), new page; entries alphabetized by author

½″

Journal article: Accessed through database, DOI included

Magazine article: Accessed through a website—URL of home page provided

Book: Scholarly press

Film: Medium in brackets

Journal article: PDF accessed through database, no DOI—page numbers included, no URL

Research report on website: URL of report included; sponsor named in retrieval statement

(a) **(b)** **(c)**

Figure caption: Label *(Figure)* and number in italics; caption below illustration

Figure 1. Male proctor in three conditions: (a) stereotypical, (b) counterstereotypical, and (c) control.

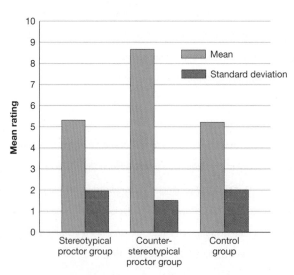

Figure 2. Tukey HSD post hoc test results for the three groups: Group with the stereotypical proctor, group with counterstereotypical proctor, and control group.

8

Documentation Matters

Chicago and **CSE** Styles

Use tab 8 to learn, practice, and master these writer's responsibilities:

❏ To Audience

Cite and document sources so that readers can see where each use of sources begins and ends; format your research project using *Chicago* or CSE style, in keeping with readers' expectations.

❏ To Topic

Cite and document sources to demonstrate that you have explored your topic fully.

❏ To Other Writers

Provide citations for all borrowed ideas and information, whether quoted, paraphrased, or summarized; document all sources cited in the research project in notes and a bibliography or reference list at the end of the project.

❏ To Yourself

Use sources to build knowledge, and cite them to show readers where your ideas begin and end; to enhance your ethos, or credibility; and to present your ideas effectively.

Documentation

Matters

27 Documenting Sources: *Chicago* Style

Written by editors at the University of Chicago Press, the *Chicago Manual of Style* (16th ed.) provides advice to help writers and editors produce clear and consistent copy for their readers. Many writers in the humanities and social sciences (in history, economics, and philosophy, for example) follow the guidelines provided by the *Chicago Manual* for citing and documenting sources.

Editors at the University of Chicago Press recognize that readers from different disciplines may have different expectations about how in-text citations and bibliography entries should look, so the *Chicago Manual* provides an author-date system similar to that of the American Psychological Association (APA) and the Council of Science Editors (CSE) for writers in the sciences. It also provides a note and bibliography system for writers in the humanities and social sciences. If your readers (including your instructor) expect you to use the author-date system, consult the *Chicago Manual* itself or follow the style detailed in the APA tab and CSE chapter in this book.

This chapter includes examples of the most common types of *Chicago*-style notes and bibliography entries. For more information or for examples of less common types of sources, consult the *Chicago Manual* itself. You can also subscribe to the *Chicago Manual* online.

> **More about**
> Popular academic documentation styles per discipline, 69
> MLA style, 149–200 (tab 6)
> APA style, 201–38 (tab 7)
> CSE style, 263–76 (ch. 28)

27a Creating *Chicago*-Style Notes and Bibliography Entries

The note system offered by the *Chicago Manual* allows you to include full bibliographic information in a footnote or endnote or to use an abbreviated footnote or endnote with a bibliography. The University of Chicago Press recommends using abbreviated notes with a bibliography.

> **footnote** Note that appears at the bottom of the page

> **endnote** Note that appears in a list of notes at the end of the project

Writing Responsibly   Citing and Documenting Sources

When you cite and document sources, you demonstrate how thoroughly you have researched your topic and how carefully you have thought about your sources, which encourages your audience to believe you are a credible researcher. In your citations and documentation, you acknowledge any material from which you have quoted, paraphrased, summarized, or drawn information, and you join the conversation on your topic by adding your own interpretation. Accurate entries in the body of your project and bibliography allow your audience to find and read your sources so that they can evaluate your interpretation and learn more about the subject themselves. Accurate entries also demonstrate the care with which you have written your research project, which further reinforces your credibility, or ethos.

to AUDIENCE

Examples of the *complete* form of notes and bibliography entries for different types of sources appear in the next section. An *abbreviated* note typically includes enough information for readers to recognize the work and find it in the bibliography. It usually includes the author's surname, a shortened version of the title that includes the title's key words in the same order as they appear on the title page, and the page number you are citing. Here is an example of an abbreviated note and a bibliography entry for the same book:

NOTE (ABBREVIATED)	1. Vancouver, *Voyage of Discovery*, 283.
BIBLIOGRAPHY	Vancouver, George. *A Voyage of Discovery to the North Pacific Ocean and Round the World, 1791–1795*. Edited by W. Kaye Lamb. London: Hakluyt Society, 1984.

A complete bibliographic note or bibliography entry includes three parts: the author's name, the title of the work, and the publication information (print, electronic, or both). The information you include in each of these parts will differ depending on the type of source you are citing. There are many models, but every variation cannot be covered, so be prepared to adapt a model to your special circumstances.

Annotated visual of where to find author and publication information, on foldouts accompanying tabs 6 and 7

Books—Printed and Electronic

In a printed book, the information you need to create a note and bibliography entry (with the exception of the page numbers) is on the title and copyright pages, at the beginning of the book. In an online or e-book, print and electronic publication information often appears at the top or bottom of the first screen or is available through a link.

Chicago Note & Bibliography Entries

1. **One author**
2. Two or three authors
3. More than three authors

1. One author

a. Printed The basic note for a printed book looks like this:

> Ref. No. Author's first name Surname, *Title: Subtitle* (Place of Publication: Publisher, date of publication), page(s).

More about
Formatting notes (*Chicago* style), 255–56
Formatting bibliographies (*Chicago* style), 256

Tech **Creating Footnotes and Endnotes**

Most word processing programs, including Microsoft Word and Google Docs, allow you to insert footnotes and endnotes easily. This automated system for inserting footnotes will automatically renumber all the notes in your project if you add or delete one. However, the software for managing notes may not provide many formatting options, so check with your instructor in advance to make sure the software's default format is acceptable.

Quick Reference · Examples of *Chicago*-Style Note and Bibliography Entries

Books—Printed and Electronic

1. One author 240
   a. Printed 240
   b. Database 242
   c. E-book 242
2. Two or three authors 242
3. More than three authors 243
4. Unnamed (anonymous) author 243
5. Two or more works by the same author 243
6. Group or corporate author 243
7. Editor (no author) 244
8. Author and editor or translator 244
9. Selection from an edited book or anthology 244
10. Edition other than the first 245
11. Introduction, preface, foreword, or afterword by a different writer 245
12. Entry in an encyclopedia or dictionary 245
    a. Printed 245
    b. Online 245
13. Multivolume work 245
14. Book in a series 246
15. Sacred text 246
16. Dissertation or thesis 246

Periodicals—Printed and Electronic

17. Article in a scholarly journal 247
    a. Printed 247
    b. Accessed through a database 248
    c. Online 248
18. Article in a magazine 248
    a. Printed 248
    b. Accessed through a database 249
    c. Online 249
19. Article in a newspaper (signed) 249
    a. Printed 249
    b. Accessed through a database 250
    c. Online 250
20. Article or editorial in a newspaper (unsigned) 250
21. Review 250
22. Letter to the editor 251

Other Electronic Sources

23. Website 251
24. Web page or wiki article 252
25. Discussion list or blog posting 252
26. CD-ROM 252

Audio and Visual Sources

27. Motion picture (film, video, DVD) 253
28. Music or other audio recording 253
29. Podcast 253
30. Performance 253
31. Work of art 253

Miscellaneous Sources—Printed and Electronic

32. Government publication 254
33. Interview (published or broadcast) 254
    a. Printed or broadcast 254
    b. Online 254
34. Personal communication 254
    a. Letter 254
    b. E-mail 255
35. Indirect source 255

Here is an example of an actual note:

1. Richard Wrangham, *Catching Fire: How Cooking Made Us Human* (New York: Basic Books, 2011), 96–98.

The basic bibliography entry for a printed book looks like this:

Author's surname, First Name. *Title: Subtitle*. Place of publication: Publisher, date of publication.

Here is an example of an actual bibliography entry:

Wrangham, Richard. *Catching Fire: How Cooking Made Us Human*. New York: Basic Books, 2011.

Chicago Note & Bibliography Entries

1. **One author**
2. Two or three authors
3. More than three authors

The *Chicago Manual* allows for either full publishers' names (the name minus words like *Incorporated* or *Publishers*) or abbreviated versions (*Wiley* instead of *John Wiley & Sons,* for example). Be consistent within your research project. This chapter uses full names.

b. Database

2. W. E. B. Du Bois, *The Souls of Black Folk* (1903; Bartleby.com, 1999), chap. 1, www.bartleby.com/114/.

Du Bois, W. E. B. *The Souls of Black Folk.* Reprint of the 1903 edition, Bartleby.com, 1999. www .bartleby.com/114/.

If the online book is *not* available in print or is not yet in final form and might change by the time your readers seek it out, provide your access date immediately before the DOI or URL. Separate the access date from the surrounding citation by commas in a note and by periods in a bibliography entry.

Chicago Note & Bibliography Entries

1. **One author**
2. **Two or three authors**
3. More than three authors
4. Unnamed (anonymous) author

c. E-book

3. Charles C. Mann, *1491: New Revelations of the Americas before Columbus* (New York: Alfred A. Knopf, 2005), Adobe Reader e-book, chap. 3.

Mann, Charles C. *1491: New Revelations of the Americas before Columbus.* New York: Alfred A. Knopf, 2005. Adobe Reader e-book.

2. Two or three authors

4. Peter Bernstein and Annalyn Swan, *All the Money in the World* (New York: Random House, 2008), 122.

5. William Rick Crandall, John A. Parnell, and John E. Spillan, *Crisis Management: Leading in the New Strategy Landscape* (Thousand Oaks, CA: Sage, 2012), 119.

1st author only listed surname first

Bernstein, Peter, and Annalyn Swan. *All the Money in the World.* New York: Random House, 2008.

Crandall, William Rick, John A. Parnell, and John E. Spillan. *Crisis Management: Leading in the New Strategy Landscape.* Thousand Oaks, CA: Sage, 2012.

3. More than three authors

6. Lawrence Niles et al., *Life Along the Delaware Bay: Cape May Gateway to a Million Shorebirds* (Piscataway, NJ: Rutgers University Press, 2012), 87.

> 1st author plus *et al.* ("and others" in Latin) in note

Niles, Lawrence, Joanna Burger, Amanda Dey, and Jan Van der Kam. *Life Along the Delaware Bay: Cape May Gateway to a Million Shorebirds.* Piscataway, NJ: Rutgers University Press, 2012.

> All authors in bibliography entry

4. Unnamed (anonymous) author   If no author is listed, begin with the title.

7. *Terrorist Hunter: The Extraordinary Story of a Woman Who Went Undercover to Infiltrate the Radical Islamic Groups Operating in America* (New York: Ecco, 2003), 82.

Terrorist Hunter: The Extraordinary Story of a Woman Who Went Undercover to Infiltrate the Radical Islamic Groups Operating in America. New York: Ecco, 2003.

5. Two or more works by the same author   Your note will be the same as for any book by one or more authors. In your bibliography, alphabetize the entries by the first important word in the title, and replace the author's name with three dashes in entries after the first.

Howard, Philip K.. *Life Without Lawyers: Restoring Responsibility in America.* New York: Norton, 2011.

———. *Sacred Cows: How Dead Laws Drag Down Democracy.* New York: Norton, 2012.

6. Group or corporate author

group as author
8. Blackfoot Gallery Committee, *The Story of the Blackfoot People: Nitsitapiisinni* (Richmond Hill, ON: Firefly Books, 2002), 15.

group as author
Blackfoot Gallery Committee. *The Story of the Blackfoot People: Nitsitapiisinni.* Richmond Hill, ON: Firefly Books, 2002.

Chicago Note & Bibliography Entries

> Examples 1–3, 240–43

7. Editor (no author)

9. Robbie B. H. Goh, ed., *Narrating Race: Asia, (Trans)Nationalism, Social Change.* (New York: Ridopi, 2011), 37.

Goh, Robbie B. H., ed. *Narrating Race: Asia, (Trans)Nationalism, Social Change.* New York: Ridopi, 2011.

NOTE When the abbreviation *ed.* appears after a name, it means *editor,* so for more than one editor, change the abbreviation from *ed.* to *eds.*

_____

8. Author and editor or translator

10. John Locke, *The Second Treatise of Government,* ed. Thomas P. Peardon (Indianapolis: Oxford University Press, 1990), 124.

11. Adania Shibli, *We Are All Equally Far from Love,* trans. Paul Starkey (Northhampton, MA: Interlink Books, 2012), 71.

Locke, John. *The Second Treatise of Government.* Edited by Thomas P. Peardon. Indianapolis: Oxford University Press, 1990.

Shibli, Adania. *We Are All Equally Far from Love.* Translated by Paul Starkey. Northhampton, MA: Interlink, 2012.

NOTE When the abbreviation *ed.* appears before a name, it means *edited by,* so do not add an *-s* when there is more than one editor.

_____

9. Selection from an edited book or anthology

selection author	selection title	title of book in which selection appears

12. Rebecca Arnold, "Fashion," in *Feminist Visual Culture,* ed. Fiona Carson and Claire Pajaczkowska (New York: Routledge, 2001), 208.

Arnold, Rebecca. "Fashion." In *Feminist Visual Culture,* edited by Fiona Carson and Claire Pajaczkowska, 207–22. New York: Routledge, 2001.

selection pgs.

Edited by, Translated by, in bibliography

***Chicago* Note & Bibliography Entries**

10. Edition other than the first

> 13. James A. Herrick, *The History and Theory of Rhetoric: An Introduction,* 3rd ed. (Boston: Allyn & Bacon, 2005), 50.

> Herrick, James A. *The History and Theory of Rhetoric: An Introduction.* 3rd ed. Boston: Allyn & Bacon, 2005.

11. Introduction, preface, foreword, or afterword by a different writer

> 14. Mario Andretti, foreword to *Race to Win: How to Become a Complete Champion,* by Derek Daly (Minneapolis: Motorbooks, 2008), 7.

label

> Andretti, Mario. Foreword to *Race to Win: How to Become a Complete Champion,* by Derek Daly, 7–8. Minneapolis: Quayside-Motorbooks, 2008.

12. Entry in an encyclopedia or dictionary For a well-known reference work such as the *American Heritage Dictionary* or the *Encyclopedia Britannica,* a bibliography entry is not necessary.

a. Printed

> 15. *The American Heritage Dictionary,* 2nd college ed., s.v. "plagiarism."

b. Online Unless a "last updated" date appears on the site, include an access date before the URL.

> 16. *Dictionary.com,* s.v. "plagiarism," accessed July 14, 2010, http://dictionary.reference.com/browse/plagiarism.

13. Multivolume work

vol. title

> 17. Robert Caro, *The Years of Lyndon Johnson,* vol. 3, *Master of the Senate* (New York: Alfred A. Knopf, 2002), 4.

> 18. George Brown Tindall and David E. Shi, *America: A Narrative History,* 8th ed. (New York: Norton, 2003), 2:123.

vol. pg.

Chicago Note & Bibliography Entries

8. Author and editor or translator
9. Selection from an edited book or anthology
10. Edition other than the first
11. Introduction, preface, foreword, or afterword by a different writer
12. Entry in an encyclopedia or dictionary
13. Multivolume work
14. Book in a series
15. Sacred text

s.v. Abbreviation of the Latin phrase *sub verbo,* "under the word"

Vols. published in different years with different titles

Vols. published in same year with same title

Caro, Robert. *The Years of Lyndon Johnson.* Vol. 3, *The Master of the Senate.*

New York: Alfred A. Knopf, 2002.

Tindall, George Brown, and David E. Shi. *America: A Narrative History.* 8th ed. 2

vols. New York: Norton, 2003.

14. Book in a series

book title

19. Oleg V. Khlevnyuk, ed., *The History of the Gulag: From*

series title

Collectivization to the Great Terror, Annals of Communism (New Haven,

CT: Yale University Press, 2004), 186–87.

Khlevnyuk, Oleg V., ed. *The History of the Gulag: From Collectivization to the*

Great Terror. Annals of Communism. New Haven, CT: Yale University

Press, 2004.

15. Sacred text

book   lines   version

20. 1 Kings 3:23–26 (King James Version).

verse

21. Qur'an 17:1–2.

Generally, sacred texts are not included in the bibliography.

16. Dissertation or thesis For an unpublished dissertation or thesis, place the title in quotation marks; titles of published dissertations or theses are italicized. Include the type of document (*PhD diss., MA thesis*), the university where it was submitted, and the date of submission.

22. Jessica Davis Powers, "Patrons, Houses and Viewers in Pompeii:

Reconsidering the House of the Gilded Cupids" (PhD diss., University of

Michigan, 2006), 43–57, ProQuest (AAI 3208535).

Example 1, 240

Powers, Jessica Davis. "Patrons, Houses and Viewers in Pompeii:

Reconsidering the House of the Gilded Cupids." PhD diss., University of

Michigan, 2006. ProQuest (AAI 3208535).

Periodicals—Printed and Electronic

A periodical is a publication issued at regular intervals—newspapers are generally published every day, magazines every week or month, and scholarly journals four times a year. For periodicals, include not only the title of the article (in quotation marks) but also the title of the periodical (in italics). The type of publication information you include depends on the type of periodical you are citing.

▷ Annotated visual of where to find author, title, and publication information, on foldouts accompanying tabs 6 and 7

17. Article in a scholarly journal The information you need to create a note and bibliography entry for a printed journal article appears on the cover or title page of the journal and on the first and last page of the article. For articles downloaded from a database, the information appears on the screen listing the articles that fit your search terms, on the full record of the article, or on the first and last page of the file you download. For articles that appear in journals published solely online, you will find the publication information on the website's home page, in the journal's table of contents, or on the first page of the article.

▷ *More about* Formatting author information: Examples 1–6, 240–43

a. Printed The basic note for an article in a printed journal looks like this:

> Ref. No. Author's first name and Surname, "Title of Article," *Title of*
>
> *Journal* Vol. no., issue no. (Year of publication): Pages.

Months (May) or seasons (Winter) may be included before the year of publication, but they are not required. If a journal is paginated by volume—for example, if issue 1 ends on page 175 and issue 2 begins on page 176—the issue number may be omitted. Here are examples of notes and bibliography entries of journals with and without issue numbers.

Paginated by Issue (Issue Number Included)

> 23. Bishupal Limbu, "Democracy, Perhaps: Collectivity, Kinship, and
>
> vol. no.
> the Politics of Friendship," *Comparative Literature* 63, no. 1 (2011): 92.
> issue no.

> Limbu, Bishupal. "Democracy, Perhaps: Collectivity, Kinship, and the Politics of
>
> Friendship." *Comparative Literature* 63, no. 1 (2011): 92.

Paginated by Volume (No Issue Number)

> 24. Sarah Brown, "The Role of Elite Leadership in the Southern Defense
>
> vol. no.
> of Segregation, 1954–1964," *Journal of Southern History* 77 (2011): 832.

> Brown, Sarah. "The Role of Elite Leadership in the Southern Defense of
>
> Segregation, 1954–1964." *Journal of Southern History* 77 (2011): 827–64.

Chicago Note & Bibliography Entries

15. Sacred text
16. Dissertation or thesis
17. **Article in a scholarly journal**
18. Article in a magazine
19. Article in a newspaper (signed)

HTML Hypertext markup language, the coding system used to create websites and web pages

PDF Portable document format, a method for sharing documents without losing formatting

DOI Digital object identifier, a permanent identifier given to electronic sources

b. Accessed through a database Most researchers locate journal articles through subscription databases available through their college library. Frequently, articles indexed in such databases are also available in HTML or PDF format through the database. If the article you are citing is available in PDF format, include the page numbers you are citing in your note and the page range in your bibliography entry. If the article is available only in HTML format, add a subhead or paragraph number to your note if this will help readers locate the passage you are citing. To cite an article accessed through a subscription database, add the name of the database and reference number (if any) at the end of your entry, or include the URL if stable. More and more academic journals are also adding digital object identifiers (DOIs); if the article you are citing includes a DOI, add it in place of the database information.

25. Jazmin A. Reyes and Maurice J. Elias, "Fostering Social-Emotional Resilience among Latino Youth," *Psychology in the Schools* 48, no. 7 (2011): 729, doi:10.1002/pits.20580. EBSCOHost (AN6242560).

Reyes, Jazmin A., and Maurice J. Elias. "Fostering Social-Emotional Resilience among Latino Youth." *Psychology in the Schools* 48, no. 7 (2011): 723–37. doi:10.1002/pits.20580.

Chicago Note & Bibliography Entries

c. Online Online journals may not provide page numbers. Provide a subheading or paragraph number (if the article provides them), and include the DOI (if there is one) or the URL for the article (if there is not).

26. Margaret F. Gibson, "Stressing Reproduction: Reading into Parents of Disabled Children." *Disability Studies Quarterly* 32, no. 1 (2012), http://www.dsq-sds.org/article/view/1654/3055.

Gibson, Margaret F. "Stressing Reproduction: Reading into Parents of Disabled Children." *Disability Studies Quarterly* 32, no. 1 (2012), http://www.dsq-sds.org/article/view/1654/3055.

18. Article in a magazine Omit volume and issue numbers, and replace the parentheses around the publication date (month and year or month, day, and year) with commas. Page numbers may be omitted.

a. Printed

27. Marian Smith Holmes, "The Freedom Riders," *Smithsonian,* February 2009, 72.

Holmes, Marian Smith. "The Freedom Riders." *Smithsonian,* February 2009,

70–75.

b. Accessed through a database

28. Jesse Ellison, "The Refugees Who Saved Lewiston," *Newsweek,*

database
January 17, 2009, 69, LexisNexis Academic.

Ellison, Jesse. "The Refugees Who Saved Lewiston." *Newsweek,* January 17,

2009, 69. LexisNexis Academic.

c. Online

29. Alice Karekezi, "The Science of Warp," *Salon,* December 11, 2011,

article URL
www.salon.com/2011/12/11/the_science_of_warp/.

Karekezi, Alice. "The Science of Warp." *Salon,* December 11, 2011. www.salon

.com/2011/12/11/the_science_of_warp/.

19. Article in a newspaper (signed) Because page numbers may differ from
edition to edition, use the edition name and section letter or number (if available) instead. A bibliography entry may be omitted.

a. Printed

30. John M. Broder, "Geography Is Dividing Democrats over Energy,"

edition name   section no.
New York Times, January 26, 2009, national edition, sec. 1.

Broder, John M. "Geography Is Dividing Democrats over Energy." *New York

Times,* January 26, 2009, national edition, sec. 1.

If the city in which the newspaper is published is not identified on the newspaper's masthead, add it in parentheses; if it might be unfamiliar to readers, add
the state, also.

31. Jim Kenneally, "When Brockton Was Home to a Marathon," *Enterprise*

(Brockton, MA), April 20, 2006, sec. 1.

Kenneally, Jim. "When Brockton Was Home to a Marathon." *Enterprise*

(Brockton, MA), April 20, 2006, sec. 1.

For well-known national newspapers (such as the *Christian Science Monitor,
USA Today,* and the *Wall Street Journal*), no city or state is needed. If you are

unsure whether the newspaper is well known, consult your instructor or a reference librarian.

b. Accessed through a database

32. John M. Broder, "Geography Is Dividing Democrats over Energy," *New York Times,* January 26, 2009, late edition, sec. A, LexisNexis Academic.

database

Broder, John M. "Geography Is Dividing Democrats over Energy." *New York Times,* January 26, 2009, late edition, sec. A. LexisNexis Academic.

c. Online

33. Victor Davis Hanson, "Oil-Rich America?," *Chicago Tribune,* December 8, 2011, www.chicagotribune.com/news/politics/sns-201112070900--tms--vdhansonctnvh-a20111208dec08,0,6557873.column

article URL

Hanson, Victor Davis. "Oil-Rich America?" *Chicago Tribune,* December 8, 2011. www.chicagotribune.com/news/politics/sns-201112070900--tms--vdhansonctnvh-a20111208dec08,0,6557873.column

Question mark and
comma

20. Article or editorial in a newspaper (unsigned)   When no author is named, place the newspaper's title in the author position in your bibliography entry. (*Chicago* style does not require a bibliography entry for unsigned newspaper articles or editorials, but your instructor might.)

34. "Health before Ideology," *Los Angeles Times,* January 27, 2009, sec. A.

Los Angeles Times. "Health before Ideology." January 27, 2009, sec. A.

21. Review

35. Anthony Tommasini, review of *Siegfried,* by Richard Wagner, conducted by Fabio Luisi, Metropolitan Opera, New York, *New York Times,* October 29, 2011, sec. C.

Tommasini, Anthony. Review of *Siegfried,* by Richard Wagner, conducted by Fabio Luisi, Metropolitan Opera, New York. *New York Times,* October 29, 2011, sec. C.

22. Letter to the editor Omit the letter's title, page numbers, and the edition name or number.

> 36. John A. Beck, letter to the editor, *Los Angeles Times*, March 16, 2010.

> Beck, John A. Letter to the editor. *Los Angeles Times*, March 16, 2010.

Other Electronic Sources

Although it is usually easy to find citation information for books and articles in periodicals, websites can be a bit trickier. Most of the information you need will appear at the bottom or top of the web page or on the site's home page. Sometimes, however, you may need to look further. Click on links such as "About us" or "More information." Frequently, websites do not provide complete information, so provide as much information as you can. If no author is listed, place the site's sponsor in the "author" position. If key information is missing, include a phrase describing the site, in case the URL changes.

> Annotated visual of where to find publication information, on foldouts accompanying tabs 6 and 7

23. Website The basic note for a website looks like this:

> Ref. No. Website Title, Author, Sponsoring Organization, last update or
> access date if last update not provided, URL.

However, website titles that are the same as book titles or other types of publications should follow the styling for that publication. Here is an example of an actual note for a website that has the same title as a book:

> 37. *Victorian England: An Introduction*, Christine Roth, University of
> Wisconsin–Oshkosh, Department of English, accessed April 2, 2012,
> www.english.uwosh.edu/roth/VictorianEngland.htm.

The bibliography entry for the note above looks like this:

> Roth, Christine. *Victorian England: An Introduction*. University of Wisconsin–
> Oshkosh, Department of English. Accessed April 2, 2012. www.english
> .uwosh.edu/roth/VictorianEngland.htm.

Include an access date only when the publication date or last update is not indicated. *Chicago* style does not require an entry in the bibliography for web content, but if your instructor does, follow the example above.

Chicago Note
& Bibliography
Entries

20. Article or editorial in a newspaper (unsigned)
21. Review
22. Letter to the editor
23. Website
24. Web page or wiki article
25. Discussion list or blog posting

24. Web page or wiki article When referring to a specific page or article on a website or wiki, place that page's title in quotation marks. For a wiki article, begin with the article's title.

> 38. "Centennial Farm and Ranch Program," Montana History Wiki, Montana Historical Society, last modified August 4, 2011, http://montanahistorywiki.pbworks.com/w/page/21639590/Centennial%20Farm%20and%20Ranch%20Program.

> Montana History Wiki, Montana Historical Society. "Centennial Farm and Ranch Program." Last modified August 4, 2011. http://montanahistorywiki.pbworks.com/w/page/21639590/Centennial%20Farm%20and%20Ranch%20Program.

25. Discussion list or blog posting A blog post need not be included in the bibliography.

> blog author · post title · blog title
> 39. Francis Heaney, "The Tie Project, Days 164–173," *Heaneyland* (blog),
> post date
> July 28, 2007, www.yarnivore.com/francis/archives/001900.html#more.

> Heaney, Francis. *Heaneyland* (blog). www.yarnivore.com/francis/archives/001900.html#more.

26. CD-ROM If there is more than one version or edition of the CD-ROM add that information after the title.

> 40. *History through Art: The 20th Century* (San Jose, CA: Fogware Publishing, 2000). CD-ROM, chap. 1.

> *History through Art: The 20th Century.* San Jose, CA: Fogware Publishing, 2000. CD-ROM.

Audio and Visual Sources

The information you need to create notes and bibliography entries for most audio and visual sources appears on the cover, label, or program or in the credits at the end of a film or a television show. Begin with the author, director, conductor, or performer, or begin your citation with the name of the work, depending on what your project emphasizes. The *Chicago Manual* provides few models of audiovisual sources. Those below are based on the principles explained in *Chicago.*

27. Motion picture (film, video, DVD)

41. *Juno,* directed by Jason Reitman, written by Diablo Cody (2007; Los Angeles: Fox Searchlight Home Entertainment, 2008), DVD.

Juno. Directed by Jason Reitman, written by Diablo Cody. 2007. Los Angeles: Fox Searchlight Home Entertainment, 2008. DVD.

28. Music or other audio recording

42. Johannes Brahms, *Piano Concerto no. 1 in D minor, op. 15,* Berliner Philharmoniker, conducted by Claudio Abbado, Philips Classics Productions BMG D153907, 1986, compact disc.

Brahms, Johannes. *Piano Concerto no. 1 in D minor, op. 15.* Berliner Philharmoniker. Claudio Abbado (conductor). Philips Classics Productions BMG D153907, 1986, compact disc.

29. Podcast

43. Melvyn Bragg, host, "The Indian Mutiny," *In Our Time,* BBC Radio 4, podcast audio, February 18, 2010, www.bbc.co.uk/programmes/b00qprnj.

Bragg, Melvyn, host. "The Indian Mutiny." *In Our Time,* BBC Radio 4, February 18, 2010. Podcast audio. www.bbc.co.uk/programmes/b00qprnj.

30. Performance

44. Jay O. Sanders, *Titus Andronicus,* dir. Michael Sexton, Anspacher Theater, New York, November 29, 2011.

Sanders, Jay O. *Titus Andronicus.* Directed by Michael Sexton. Anspacher Theater, New York, November 29, 2011.

31. Work of art
If a reproduction of the work appears in your project, identify the work in a figure caption. If you discuss the work but do not show it, cite it in your notes but do not provide an entry in your bibliography. If the

---

Chicago Note & Bibliography Entries

> **More about**
> Figure captions (*Chicago* style), 255

Example 9, 244

reproduction is taken from a book, follow the model for a selection from an edited book or anthology.

45. Alexander Calder, *Two Acrobats*, 1929, wire sculpture, Menil

Collection, Houston.

Miscellaneous Sources—Printed and Electronic

32. Government publication For documents published by the US Government Printing Office (or GPO), including the publisher is optional. If you omit the publisher, change the colon after the location to a period.

46. US Department of Education, Office of Communications and

Outreach, *Parent Power: Build the Bridge to Success* (Washington, DC: US

Government Printing Office, 2010), 19.

US Department of Education, Office of Communicaitons and Outreach. *Parent*

Power: Build the Bridge to Success. Washington, DC: US Government

Printing Office, 2010.

33. Interview (published or broadcast)

a. Printed or broadcast

47. Barack Obama, interview by Maria Bartiromo, *Closing Bell*, CNBC,

March 27, 2008.

Obama, Barack. Interview by Maria Bartiromo. *Closing Bell*, CNBC, March 27,

2008.

b. Online

48. Barack Obama, interview by Maria Bartiromo, *Closing Bell,* CNBC,

March 27, 2008, www.cnbc.com/id/23832520.

Obama, Barack. Interview by Maria Bartiromo. *Closing Bell*. CNBC, March 27,

2008. www.cnbc.com/id/23832520.

34. Personal communication Unless your instructor requires it, no bibliography entry is needed for a personal communication.

a. Letter

49. Evan Marks, letter to the author, August 13, 2005.

b. E-mail

> 50. Chris M. Anson, e-mail message to the author, November 11, 2011.

35. Indirect source If you do not have access to the original source, mention the author you are citing in your text and include an entry in the bibliography that names both the original source and the source from which you borrowed the material.

> 51. Theophrastus, *The Characters of Theophrastus,* ed. J. M. Evans
>
> and G. E. V. Austen (London: Blackie and Sons, 1904), 48, quoted in Henry
>
> Gleitman, *Psychology,* 5th ed. (New York: Norton, 2000).

> Theophrastus. *The Characters of Theophrastus.* Edited by J. M. Edmonds and
>
> G. E. V. Austen. London: Blackie and Sons, 1904, 48. Quoted in Henry
>
> Gleitman. *Psychology.* 5th ed. New York: Norton, 2000.

27b Using *Chicago* Style for Tables and Figures

The *Chicago Manual* recommends that you number tables and figures in a separate sequence (*Table 1, Table 2, Figure 1, Figure 2*) both in the text and in the table title or figure caption. Tables and figures should be placed as close as possible after the text reference. For tables, provide a brief identifying title and place it above the table. For figures, provide a caption that includes any information about the figure that readers will need to identify it, such as the title of a work of art, the artist's name, the work's location, and a brief description. If the figure or table, or information used to create the figure or table, comes from another source, provide a source note. Source notes for tables generally appear below the table, while source information for figures appears at the end of the figure caption.

27c Formatting a *Chicago*-Style Research Project

The *Chicago Manual* provides detailed instructions about manuscript preparation for authors submitting their work for publication, but it does not offer formatting instructions for college projects. Follow the formatting instructions provided in chapter 8 or tab 6, or consult your instructor.

> *More about*
> MLA-style formatting, 188–200
> Formatting college projects, 56

1. Format notes.

The *Chicago Manual* recommends numbering bibliographic notes consecutively throughout the project, using superscript (above-the-line) numbers.

> While acknowledging that not all scholars agree, Mann observes, "If Monte Verde is correct, as most believe, people were thriving from Alaska to Chile while much of northern Europe was still empty of mankind and its works."[8]

Type the heading "Notes" at the top of a new page following the end of the text, and type the notes below the heading. (You may need to insert a page break if your word processor has automatically created endnotes on the last page of your paper.)

2. Format the bibliography.

More about
Hanging indent,
189, 228

To begin your list of works cited, type the heading "Bibliography," "References," or "Works Cited" at the top of a new page. (Ask your instructor which heading is preferred.) Entries should be formatted with a hanging indent: Position the first line of each entry flush with the left margin, and indent subsequent lines by half an inch. Entries should be alphabetized by the author's surname.

Student Model Research Project: *Chicago* Style

The research project that follows was written by Abrams Conrad for a history course at American University. Conrad fulfills his responsibilities to topic and audience by drawing on a variety of relevant and reliable sources to make his case. He fulfills his responsibility to the writers from whom he borrows information and ideas by citing them in abbreviated notes in the text and by providing a complete entry for each work in the list of works cited at the end of the project. He demonstrates his credibility as a researcher and a writer by providing evidence to support his claims and by revising, editing, and proofreading his project carefully.

Writing
Responsibly Of Deadlines and Paperclips

Instructors expect students to turn in thoughtful, carefully proofread, and neatly formatted papers on time—usually in class on the due date. They also expect writers to clip or staple the pages of the paper *before* submitting. Do justice to yourself by being fully prepared.

to SELF

Abrams Conrad

History 235

Professor Burke

December 15, 2012

Identifying information (double spaced)

If your instructor requires a title page, see the model on p. 231

Title (centered)   Exploration and Empire: James Cook and the Pacific Northwest

Descriptive title

Exploration of the Pacific Northwest begins and ends with Captain James Cook, the first British explorer to reach the area, map it, and study its peoples, and with those who had sailed and trained under his command. While others sailed to the Pacific Northwest, their motivation was largely for trade. Cook's voyage and those of his successors were motivated as much by a desire to understand the region and its peoples as by the desire for financial gain.

Thesis at end of first paragraph to guide reader

In the late 1770s, the Pacific Northwest was the globe's last temperate coast to be explored and mapped, primarily due to its remoteness from Europe. To get there, ships had to sail around Cape Horn at the tip of South America. Cook's third voyage, begun in 1778, was undertaken to discover a Northwest Passage, an inland waterway connecting the Pacific Ocean with the Atlantic that would shorten the sailing time from Europe to Asia. The Admiralty had instructed him "to search for, and to explore, such Rivers or Inlets as may appear to be of a considerable extent and pointing towards Hudsons or Baffins Bay."[1] While his findings were negative—he all but eliminated the possibility of an inland passage—he was the first Briton to make contact with the area and truly to study the geography and culture of the region.

Quotation integrated into text; source in endnote

Cook made anchor in Nootka Sound for most of April 1778 and then ventured north along the Canadian coast, searching for a waterway northeast, until he put in at Prince William Sound.[2] He made a detailed survey of the coast, a portion of which is shown in Figure 1.

Summary in text with bibliographic endnote

Figure callout in text

Cook's third voyage was also politically strategic: to thwart Spanish and Russian claims to the Pacific Northwest.[3] With the Spanish in the south and moving north, and the Russians in the north and moving south, the northwest coast, or "New Albion," was a place where the British could establish a claim and perhaps eventually a colony.[4]

Transition

Another reason for Cook's exploration of the Northwest was the man himself. Cook was the quintessential explorer; he "never missed an opportunity to chart a reef or an island," wrote Ernest Dodge of the Peabody Museum in Salem, Massachusetts.[5] Cook

Signal phrase with background information

Figure 1. A chart of the northwest coast of America and the northeast coast of Asia, explored in the years 1778 and 1779. Prepared by Lieut. Henry Roberts, under the immediate inspection of Capt. Cook. (1794), David Rumsey Map Coll.

stood out because he was so methodical. He was exact in his measurements and never missed an opportunity to learn or write about indigenous peoples.

Cook's explorations of the Pacific Northwest ended with his death in the Hawaiian Islands in early 1779, but his explorations of the Pacific Northwest had direct consequences for traders. James King, who took over command of the expedition after Cook's death, received 800 Spanish dollars in return for twenty sea otter pelts he brought back from the Pacific Northwest—and those were the ragged ones; King received 120 dollars each for pelts in pristine condition,

an immense amount of money at that time.[6] It is doubtful the price ever went that high again,[7] but this sum put the region on the map for traders and spawned a new series of voyages.

What made Cook so important to the Pacific Northwest were the explorations of the area by those who had sailed with him. In this regard, it is interesting to compare the results of those who sailed under Cook with those who did not. Some of the first voyages to the area after Cook's death were the trading voyages of James Hanna, James Strange, and

John Meares. Hanna sailed from Macao to Nootka Sound (in what is now British Columbia) in 1784–86.[8] His voyage produced few results except those of trade, collecting more than

500 skins.[9] Strange sailed from India; his mission was to proceed to the Northwest, trade at

Nootka Sound and Alaska, make discoveries, and sail through the Bering Strait and Arctic Ocean, as far north as the North Pole.[10] While his instructions stated discovery as the primary goal, his investors looked upon trade as the focus of the expedition, and Strange ended up doing neither very well. He brought back barely 600 skins, not enough to offset the costs of the voyage, and though he tried to put together another trip, he was unsuccessful.[11]

John Meares led a voyage in 1785 to the Gulf of Alaska, where he anticipated better trading and finer pelts; he proved ignorant both of Russian control over the area and of the harsh Alaskan climate.[12] Meares lost twenty-three men to disease.[13] He also got his ship stuck in the ice and was released only with warm weather and the help of George Dixon and Nathanial Portlock (both had sailed with Cook), who provided aid if he promised to leave at once.[14] While Meares showed some bad judgment, he was ultimately successful in trade in the Northwest, but he was not committed to exploration of the coast or the discovery and naming of locations.[15] Meares himself refers to his voyages as "commercial" and describes people and geography in terms of "extension of our particular commerce."[16] Compare Meares's voyages with those of Portlock, Dixon, and Vancouver, all students of Cook.

In May 1785, the King George's Sound Company sent Nathanial Portlock out on a mission to control the region where furs came from. Portlock, who had been to the Northwest with Cook, sailed from London in September 1785 with two ships, the *King George* and the *Queen Charlotte,* captained by George Dixon, another Cook disciple.[17] They became the first men to drop anchor in Hawaii, specifically Kealakekua Bay, since Cook's death. Their primary goal was to collect furs and trade them in Macao or Canton on the Chinese coast. While they did return with a surplus, they made no real killing.[18] Their journals, published in 1789, heavily advocated advancement of the fur trade, but their voyage became known for its geographical results.[19] They discovered the Queen Charlotte Islands off what is now British Columbia, and their accounts of the local people ultimately proved more important than whatever furs they sold.[20] In their accounts, Cook's influence is easily seen. Both made detailed observations, were meticulous in their calculations, and proved to be just as interested in who sold them goods as in the goods themselves.

It is in the voyage of George Vancouver where Cook's influence is clearest. Sailing from England in 1791, Vancouver's voyage was one part discovery, one part trade, and one

Example 3

Transition sentence

Example 4

Example 5

Example 6

part diplomacy. He was to chart the coast from Nootka Sound to Cook Sound for traders, investigate the possibility of an inland northwest passage,[21] retrieve the territory taken by the Spanish around Nootka Sound, and, in the winter months, survey all of the Hawaiian Islands.[22] Arriving in the Strait of Juan de Fuca in late April 1792, Vancouver immediately began his survey of the coast north of California, accomplishing much during the summer of 1792. He missed the Columbia River, much to his dismay, but he mapped and named Puget Sound.[23] His survey finally revealed most of the hazards of the Northwest coastline and negated the idea of an inland northwest passage and a large inland sea.[24] In late August, he met with the Spanish to negotiate the restitution of Nootka Sound. Reaching an impasse, he sent his executive officer back to England requesting instructions and sailed for Hawaii, where he surveyed the Islands.[25] There, in February 1794 (in contrast with Cook), he concluded a treaty with the Hawaiian king, actually gaining control of the islands for England, though the treaty was not ratified in London.[26]

Conclusion: Provides summary and explains significance of research

When comparing the voyages of Hanna, Strange, and Meares with those of Portlock, Dixon, and Vancouver, a glaring difference stands out: While all the voyages shared similar objectives, the *approach* to those objectives was vastly different. Hanna, Strange, and Meares were concerned with trade, pure and simple; Cook's men were also concerned with trade, but as Dodge writes, "[t]he drilling of the Master was notable."[27] The men who had served under Cook considered it their duty both to fulfill their trade objectives and to explore, chart, discover, and explain as much of the region as they could. The missions to the Pacific Northwest that were motivated by trade alone yielded only temporary results. The geographic information gained from the exploratory expeditions of Cook's men paid dividends for years to come. Not only did they provide information for those who followed, both traders and scholars, but they also contributed to the British goal of empire building. Empire is not just geography or territory. It is also about having gone somewhere, mapped it, and named the places. In the Pacific, where the British played a major role in discovery, there are British names in every corner of the sea.[28] Cook and his men were letting it be known worldwide that they had been there. Seeing all those vastly different places, all with British names, added to the inquisitive and the imperialistic mindset of the British. It is at least part of the reason they were so ready to go to war over places so distant.

Notes Heading (centered), new page

Short form of notes used with list of works cited

1. Cook, *The Journals,* 220–24.

2. Ibid., 230.

"Ibid." (abbreviation of *ibidem,* Latin for "in the same place") used when source cited in note immediately above

3. Rose, "Captain Cook," 102–9.

4. Schwantes, *The Pacific Northwest,* 41.

5. Dodge, *Beyond the Capes,* 15.

6. Schwantes, *The Pacific Northwest,* 43.

7. Ibid.

8. Blumenthal, *The Early Exploration,* 3.

9. Dodge, *Beyond the Capes,* 43–44.

10. Gough, "India-Based Expeditions," 219.

11. Ibid., 217–19.

12. Ibid., 220.

13. Ibid.

14. Blumenthal, *The Early Exploration,* 4; *Oxford Dictionary of National Biography,* s.v. "Meares, John," accessed December 8, 2012, www.oxforddnb.com/subscribed.

Two citations in same footnote separated with a semicolon

Reference work: no entry in bibliography, full entry here; use "s.v," *sub verbo,* "under the word" (Latin)

15. Blumenthal, *The Early Exploration,* 3.

16. Ibid., 3, 10.

17. Dodge, *Beyond the Capes,* 44.

18. Ibid., 43–58.

19. *Oxford Dictionary of National Biography,* s.v. "Portlock, Nathanial," accessed December 6, 2012, www.oxforddnb.com/subscribed.

20. Dodge, *Beyond the Capes,* 53.

21. Ibid., 135–55.

22. Vancouver, *Voyage of Discovery,* 283–88.

23. Ibid.

24. Ibid., 288.

25. Dodge, *Beyond the Capes,* 135–55.

26. Ibid.

27. Ibid., 43.

28. Dobbie, "Pacific Place Names," 258–65.

Works Cited

Blumenthal, Richard W., ed. *The Early Exploration of Inland Washington Waters: Journals and Logs from Six Expeditions, 1786–1792.* Jefferson, NC: McFarland, 2004.

Cook, James. *The Journals of Captain James Cook on His Voyages of Discovery.* Edited by J. C. Beaglehole. Vol. 3. Cambridge: Cambridge University Press, 1967.

Dobbie, Elliot V. K. "Pacific Place Names and the History of Discovery." *American Speech* 36 (1961): 258–65.

Dodge, Ernest S. *Beyond the Capes: Pacific Exploration from Captain Cook to the* Challenger, *1776–1877.* Boston: Little, Brown, 1971.

Gough, Barry M. "India-Based Expeditions of Trade and Discovery in the North Pacific in the Late Eighteenth Century." *Geographical Journal* 155, no. 2 (1989): 215–23. http://www.jstor.org/stable/635063.

Rose, J. Holland. "Captain Cook and the Founding of British Power in the Pacific." *Geographical Journal* 73, no. 2 (1929): 102–22. http://www.jstor.org/stable/1783522.

Schwantes, Carlos A. *The Pacific Northwest: An Interpretive History.* Lincoln: University of Nebraska Press, 1989.

Vancouver, George. *A Voyage of Discovery to the North Pacific Ocean and Round the World, 1791–1795: With an Introduction and Appendices.* Edited by W. Kaye Lamb. Vol. 1. London: Hakluyt Society, 1984.

Entries arranged alphabetically

Book: Editor, no author

Book: Editor and author; one volume from multivolume work

Book (printed): Popular press

Journal article: Accessed through a database, stable URL provided

Book (printed): Scholarly press

28 Documenting Sources: CSE Style

Writers in the sciences customarily use formatting and documentation guidelines from *Scientific Style and Format: The CSE Manual for Authors, Editors, and Publishers* (7th ed.) published by the Council of Science Editors (CSE). CSE style requires that sources be cited briefly in the text and documented in a reference list at the end of the project. The goal of providing in-text citations and a list of references is to allow readers to locate and read the sources for themselves and to distinguish the writer's ideas from those borrowed from sources.

28a Creating CSE-Style In-Text Citations

In-text citations, which appear in the body of your paper, identify any material borrowed from a source, whether it is a quotation, paraphrase, summary, or idea. The CSE offers three formats for citing sources in the body of the project:

- Name-year
- Citation-sequence
- Citation-name

The ***name-year system*** requires you to include the last name of the author and the year of publication in parentheses whenever the source is cited:

> Advances have clarified the role of betalains and carotenoids in determining
> author   date
> the color of flowers (Groteworld 2006).

If you use the author's name in your sentence, include just the year of publication in parentheses:

> author
> Christoffel (2007) argues that public health officers adopted the strategies
> date
> they did because they were facing a crisis.

More about
Popular academic documentation styles per discipline, 69
MLA style, 149–200 (tab 6)
APA style, 201–38 (tab 7)
Chicago style, 239–62 (ch. 27)

Writing Responsibly — Citing and Documenting Sources

When you cite and document sources, you acknowledge any material from which you have quoted, paraphrased, summarized, or drawn information, and you join the conversation on your topic by adding your own interpretation, data, methods, and results. Simultaneously, you give interested readers (including your instructor) a way to join the conversation. Accurate entries allow your audience to find and read your sources so that they can evaluate your research and learn more about the subject themselves. Accurate entries also demonstrate the care with which you have written your project, which reinforces your credibility, or ethos.

to AUDIENCE

The name-year system tells readers immediately who wrote the source and how current it is, which is particularly crucial in the sciences. This system involves many rules for creating in-text citations (for example, how to create in-text citations for several authors, with organizations as authors, and so on), which can make it difficult to apply the rules consistently.

The **citation-sequence** and **citation-name systems** use a superscript number (the same number for a source each time it is cited) to refer the reader to a list of references at the end of the project.

Place reference numbers before punctuation marks. When drawing information from multiple sources, include multiple citations, separated by commas (no space between commas and reference numbers).

Some testing of the River Invertebrate Prediction and Classification System (RIVPACS) had already been conducted[1]. Biologists in Great Britain then used environmental data to establish community type[2], and two studies developed predictive models for testing the effects of habitat-specific sampling[3,4]. These did not, however, account for the earlier RIVPACS research[1].

When using the citation-sequence system, arrange the sources in your reference list in order of first mention in your research report and then number them. (The first work cited is number 1, the second work cited is number 2, and so on.) When using the citation-name system, alphabetize sources and then number them. (The first work alphabetically is number 1, the second work alphabetically is number 2, and so on.)

The citation-sequence and citation-name systems need no rules about how to form in-text citations, but they do require readers to turn to the reference list to see the name of the author and the source's date of publication. Since the word processor's footnoting system cannot be used, numbering (and renumbering) of notes must be done by hand. To avoid the confusion that can arise during revision and editing, consider using a simplified author-date system while drafting the research project and inserting the numbers for the citation-sequence or citation-name system in the final draft.

Check with your instructor about which system to use, and use it consistently. If your instructor does not have a preference, consider the advantages and drawbacks of each system before making your choice.

Tech   **Creating Superscript Numbers**

The footnoting function in your word processing program will not work for inserting reference numbers for the citation-sequence or citation-name systems because it will only insert the reference marks in sequence (*1, 2, 3, . . .*), whereas the CSE system requires that you use the same superscript number for a source each time you cite it. Instead, insert superscript numbers manually, without using your word processing program's footnote function, and type your list of references separately. (Use the Help Directory function to learn about inserting superscript numbers.)

28b Preparing a CSE-Style Reference List

A research report or project in CSE style ends with a list of cited references. How you format those references depends on the type of source and the system you use.

Books—Printed and Electronic

In a printed book, you can find most or all of the information you need to create a reference list entry on the copyright and title pages at the beginning of the book. In an online or e-book, print and electronic publication information often appears at the top or bottom of the first page or is available through a link.

CSE Reference List Entries

1. **One author**
2. Two or more authors
3. Group or corporate author

1. One author

a. Printed The basic format for a printed book looks like this:

Name-year system

> Author's surname First and Middle Initials. Date of publication. Title: subtitle.
>
> Place of publication: Publisher.

No punctuation between surname and initials and no period or space between initials

Citation-sequence and citation-name systems

> Ref. No. Author's surname First and Middle Initials. Title: subtitle. Place of
>
> publication: Publisher; date of publication.

Lines after the first align with the author's name, not the reference number.

NOTE Book titles are neither italicized nor underlined in CSE style.

Quick

Reference   Examples of CSE-Style Reference List Entries

Here are examples of actual reference list entries:

Annotated visual of where to find author, title, and publication information, on foldouts accompanying tabs 6 and 7

Name-year system

> Wedge, M. 2012. Pills are not for preschoolers: a drug-free approach for
>
> troubled kids. New York (NY): Norton.

Citation-sequence and citation-name systems

> 1. Wedge, M. Pills are not for preschoolers: a drug-free approach for troubled
>
>   kids. New York (NY): Norton; 2012.

b. Online

CSE Reference
List Entries

1. **One author**
2. **Two or more authors**
3. Group or corporate author
4. Edited book

Name-year system

> Stroup A. 1990. A company of scientists: botany, patronage, and community at
>
> the seventeenth-century Parisian Royal Academy of Sciences [Internet].
>
>   print publication information   access date
> Berkeley (CA): University of California Press [cited 2012 Mar 2]. Available from:
>   URL (permalink)
> http://ark.cdlib.org/ark:/13030/ft587006gh/.

Citation-sequence and citation-name systems

> 2. Stroup A. A company of scientists: botany, patronage, and community at
>
>   the seventeenth-century Parisian Royal Academy of Sciences [Internet].
>
>   Berkeley (CA): University of California Press; 1990 [cited 2012 Mar 2].
>
>   Available from: http://ark.cdlib.org/ark:/13030/ft587006gh/.

Period after citation only if it concludes in a forward slash

2. Two or more authors

Name-year system

> Jamieson BGM, Dallai R, Afzelius BA. 1999. Insects: their spermatozoa and
>
> phylogeny. Enfield (NH): Science Publishers.

Follow the order of authors on the title page. No *and* before last author.

Citation-sequence and citation-name systems

> 3. Jamieson BGM, Dallai R, Afzelius BA. Insects: their spermatozoa and
>
>   phylogeny. Enfield (NH): Science Publishers; 1999.

If the source has more than ten authors, list the first ten; after the tenth author, insert the words *et al.*

3. Group or corporate author

Name-year system

> Institute of Medicine Committee on the Use of Complementary and Alternative Medicine by the American Public. 2005. Complementary and alternative medicine in the United States. Washington (DC): National Academies Press.

Citation-sequence and citation-name systems

> 4. Institute of Medicine Committee on the Use of Complementary and Alternative Medicine by the American Public. Complementary and alternative medicine in the United States. Washington (DC): National Academies Press; 2005.

4. Edited book

Name-year system

> Whelan CT, Mason NJ, editors. 2005. Electron scattering: from atoms, molecules, nuclei, and bulk matter. New York: Kluwer Academic/Plenum.

Citation-sequence and citation-name systems

> 5. Whelan CT, Mason NJ, editors. Electron scattering: from atoms, molecules, nuclei, and bulk matter. New York: Kluwer Academic/Plenum; 2005.

5. Selection from an edited book or conference proceedings

Name-year system

> selection author   selection title
> Berkenkotter C. 2000. Scientific writing and scientific thinking: writing the
> book title
> scientific habit of mind. In: Goggin MD, editor. Inventing a discipline:
> rhetoric scholarship in honor of Richard E. Young. Urbana (IL): National
> selection pages
> Council of Teachers of English. p. 270–284.

Citation-sequence and citation-name systems

> 6. Berkenkotter C. Scientific writing and scientific thinking: writing the scientific habit of mind. In: Goggin MD, editor. Inventing a discipline: rhetoric scholarship in honor of Richard E. Young. Urbana (IL): National Council of Teachers of English; 2000. p. 270–284.

To cite a paper published in the proceedings of a conference, add the number and name of the conference, the date of the conference, and the location of the conference (separated by semicolons and ending with a period) after the title of the book and before the publication information.

> 48th Annual American Society for Cell Biology Conference; 2008
>
> Dec 13–17; San Francisco.

6. Dissertation For dissertations published by University Microfilms International (UMI), include the access number.

Name-year system

> Song LZ. 2003. Relations between optimism, stress and health in
>
> Chinese and American students [dissertation]. Tucson: University of Arizona.
>
> access information   location   access no.
> Available from: UMI, Ann Arbor, MI; AAI3107041.

Citation-sequence and citation-name systems

> 7. Song LZ. Relations between optimism, stress and health in Chinese and
>
> American students [dissertation]. Tucson: University of Arizona; 2003.
>
> Available from: UMI, Ann Arbor, MI; AAI3107041.

> **More about**
> Formatting author information: Examples 1–5, 265–68

If the location of the college is not listed on the title page of the dissertation, place square brackets around this information: [Tucson].

> Annotated visual of where to find author and publication information, on foldouts accompanying tabs 6 and 7

Periodicals—Printed and Electronic

The information needed to document a printed journal article is on the cover or table of contents of the journal and the first and last page of the article. For articles downloaded from a database, the information you need appears on the screen listing the articles that fit your search terms, on the full record of the article, or on the first (and last) page of the file you download. For journal articles published online, the information you need appears on the website's home page, on that issue's web page, or on the first screen of the article.

7. Article in a scholarly journal
a. Printed The basic citation for an article in a scholarly journal looks like this:

Name-year system

> Author's surname First and Middle Initials. Year of publication. Title: subtitle.
>
> Abbreviated Journal Title. Vol. number(Issue number):page numbers.

Citation-sequence and citation-name systems

> Ref. No. Author's surname First and Middle Initials. Title:subtitle. Abbreviated
>
> Journal Title. Year of publication;Vol. number(Issue number):page
>
> numbers.

Here is an actual citation of each type:

Name-year system

> Cox L. 2007. The community health center perspective. Behav Healthc.
>
> 27(3):20–21.

Citation-sequence and citation-name systems

> 8. Cox L. The community health center perspective. Behav Healthc.
>
> 2007;27(3):20–21.

Journal titles: Omit punctuation, articles (*an, the*), and prepositions (*of, on, in*), and abbreviate most words longer than 5 letters (except 1-word titles like *Science* and *Nature*).

b. Accessed through a database   Most researchers locate journal articles through subscription databases available through their college library. Frequently, articles indexed in such databases are available in HTML or PDF format through a link from the database. As yet, the CSE does not provide a model for an article accessed through an online database, but since most library databases are by subscription, readers will probably find the URL of the database's home page more useful than a direct link to the article itself. If a DOI is available, include it.

DOI   Digital object identifier, a permanent identifier assigned to electronic articles

Name-year system

> Yuan F, Mayer B. 2012. Chemical and isotopic evaluation of sulfur
>
> sources and cycling in the Pecos River, New Mexico, USA. Chem Geol
>
> medium   access date   database
>
> [Internet]. [cited 2012 Aug 7];291(1–2):13–22. In: Science Direct. Available
>
> URL (database home page)   DOI
>
> from: www.sciencedirect.com doi:10.1016/j.chemgeo.2011.11.014

No period after URL (unless it concludes with a forward slash) or DOI

Citation-sequence and citation-name systems

> 9. Yuan F, Mayer B. Chemical and isotopic evaluation of sulfur sources and
>
> cycling in the Pecos River, New Mexico, USA. Chem Geol [Internet]. 2004
>
> [cited 2012 Aug 7];291(1–2):13–22. Available from: www.sciencedirect.com
>
> doi:10.1016/j.chemgeo.2011.11.014

CSE Reference
List Entries

6. Dissertation

7. Article in a scholarly journal

8. Article in a magazine

c. Online   Omit page numbers for online articles. When a subscription is not required to access the article, provide a direct permalink URL to the article;

otherwise, provide the URL to the journal's home page. If a DOI is provided, include it.

Name-year system

> Patten SB, Williams HVA, Lavorato DH, Eliasziw M. 2009. Allergies and major depression: a longitudinal community study. Biopsychosoc Med [Internet]. [cited 2012 Feb 5];3(3). Available from: www.bpsmedicine .com/content/3/1/3 doi:10.1186/1751-0759-3-3

URL (permalink)

DOI

No period after
URL or DOI

Citation-sequence and citation-name systems

> 10. Patten SB, Williams HVA, Lavorato DH, Eliasziw M. Allergies and major depression: a longitudinal community study. Biopsychosoc Med [Internet]. 2012 [cited 2009 Feb 5];3(3). Available from: www .bpsmedicine.com/content/3/1/3 doi:10.1186/1751-0759-3-3

CSE Reference
List Entries

8. Article in a magazine

a. Printed

Name-year system

> Gladwell M. 2006 Oct 16. The formula. New Yorker. 138–149.

Citation-sequence and citation-name systems

> 11. Gladwell M. The formula. New Yorker. 2006 Oct 16;138–149.

b. Accessed through a database

Name-year system

> Gladwell M. 2006 Oct 16 [cited 2012 Apr 23]. The formula. New Yorker [Internet]:138–149. Available from: www.ebscohost.com/.

Citation-sequence and citation-name systems

> 12. Gladwell M. The formula. New Yorker [Internet]. 2006 Oct 16 [cited 2012 Apr 23]:138–149. Available from: www.ebscohost.com/.

c. Online

Name-year system

Coghlan A. 2007 May 16 [cited 2012 May 19]. Bipolar children—is the

US overdiagnosing? NewScientist.com [Internet] Available from:

~~URL (permalink)~~

www.newscientist.com/channel/health/

mg19426043.900-bipolar-children--is-the-us-overdiagnosing.html/.

Citation-sequence and citation-name systems

13. Coghlan A. Bipolar children—is the US overdiagnosing? NewScientist

.com [Internet]. 2007 May 16 [cited 2012 May 19]. Available from:

www.newscientist.com/channel/health/

mg19426043.900-bipolar-children--is-the-us-overdiagnosing.html/.

9. Article in a newspaper

a. Printed

Name-year system

LaFraniere S. 2009 Feb 6. Scientists point to possible link between dam

edition   section   col. no.

and China quake. New York Times (Late Ed.). Sect. A:1 (col. 3).

_1st pg._

Citation-sequence and citation-name systems

14. LaFraniere S. Scientists point to possible link between dam and China

quake. New York Times (Late Ed.). 2009 Feb 6;Sect. A:1 (col. 3).

b. Accessed through a database

Name-year system

LaFraniere S. 2009 Feb 6 [cited 2009 Feb 28]. Scientists point to possible link

between dam and China quake. New York Times [Internet]. Sect. A:1. Available

from: www.lexisnexis.com/.

Citation-sequence and citation-name systems

15. LaFraniere S. Scientists point to possible link between dam and China

quake. New York Times [Internet]. 2009 Feb 6 [cited 2011 Feb 28];Sect. A:1.

Available from: www.lexisnexis.com/.

c. Online

Name-year system

> LaFee S. 2006 May 17. Light can hold fatal attraction for many nocturnal
>
> animals. San Diego Union-Tribune [Internet] [cited 2011 May 20] [about
>
> length
>
> 11 paragraphs]. Available from: www.signonsandiego.com/news/science/.

Include permalink URL if available; if not, use URL of home page.

Citation-sequence and citation-name systems

> 16. LaFee S. Light can hold fatal attraction for many nocturnal animals.
>
> San Diego Union-Tribune [Internet]. 2006 May 17 [cited 2011 May 20]
>
> [about 11 paragraphs]. Available from: www.signonsandiego.com/news/
>
> science/.

Miscellaneous Sources—Printed and Electronic

> Annotated visual of where to find author, title, and publication information, on foldouts accompanying Tabs 6 and 7

The information needed to document a website or web page usually appears at the top or bottom of the home page or web page. You may also need to look for a link to a page labeled "About us" or "Contact us." Frequently, information needed for a complete reference list entry is missing, in which case provide as much information as you can.

10. Website

Name-year system

In the name-year system, a sample reference entry for a website looks like this:

> Author. Title of website [Medium (Internet)]. Publication date [Access date].
>
> Available from: URL (home page)

CSE Reference List Entries

Here is an example of an actual entry:

> MIT news [Internet]. 2009 Feb 9 [cited 2012 Mar 10]. Available from: http://web
>
> .mit.edu/newsoffice/index.html/.

The site has no author, so the reference list entry begins with the name of the site's sponsor.

Citation-sequence and citation-name systems

When referencing an entire website, the only difference between the name-year system and the citation-sequence and citation-name systems is that the citation-sequence and citation-name entries add a reference number at the beginning of the entry.

11. Web page When documenting a web page or a document on a website, provide the URL for the web page, not the site's home page.

Name-year system

article author · article title
Schorow S. 2009 Feb 5. Aliens at sea: anthropologist Helmreich studies
· website
researchers studying ocean microbes. MIT News [Internet]. [cited 2012 Mar 10].
· · · · · · · · · · · · · · · URL (web page)
Available from: http://web.mit.edu/newsoffice/2009/alien-ocean-0205.html

Citation-sequence and citation-name systems

17. Schorow S. Aliens at sea: anthropologist Helmreich studies

researchers studying ocean microbes. MIT News [Internet]. 2009 Feb 5

[cited 2012 Mar 10]. Available from: http://web.mit.edu/newsoffice/2009

/alien-ocean-0205.html

12. Discussion list or blog posting

Name-year system

· · · · · · · · · · date/time posted
Hall A. 2004 Aug 5, 11:33 am [cited 2012 Jan 30]. Biology of deep Gulf of
· · · · · · · · · · · · · · · · · disc. list · · · · · · · · · medium
Mexico shipwrecks. In: FISH-SCI [Internet discussion list]. [Lulea (Sweden):

National Higher Research and Education Network]. [about 4 paragraphs].

Available from: http://segate.sunet.se/archives/fish-sci.html

Citation-sequence and citation-name systems

18. Hall A. Biology of deep Gulf of Mexico shipwrecks. In: FISH-SCI [Internet

discussion list]. [Lulea (Sweden): National Higher Research and Education

Network]; 2004 Aug 5, 11:33 am [cited 2012 Jan 30]. [about 4 paragraphs].

Available from: http://segate.sunet.se/archives/fish-sci.html

13. E-mail message

Name-year system

e-mail author · · · · · date/time sent · · · · · · · · · subject line
Martin SP. 2012 Nov 18, 3:31 pm. Revised results [E-mail]. Message to:
· · e-mail recipient · · · · · · · · · · · · · · · · · · · length
Lydia Jimenez [cited 2012 Nov 20]. [about 2 screens].

CSE Reference List Entries

9. Article in a newspaper
10. Website
11. Web page
12. Discussion list or blog posting
13. E-mail message
14. Technical report or government document

CSE Reference
List Entries

Citation-sequence and citation-name systems

19. Martin SP. Revised results [E-mail]. Message to: Lydia Jimenez.

2012 Nov 18, 3:31 pm [cited 2012 Nov 20]. [about 2 screens].

14. Technical report or government document If no author is listed, use the name of the governing nation and the government agency that produced the document, and include any identifying number.

Name-year system

Department of Health and Human Services (US). 1985 May. Women's health.

Report of the Public Health Service Task Force on Women's Health Issues.

[publisher unknown]. PHS:85-50206.

Citation-sequence and citation-name systems

20. Department of Health and Human Services (US). Women's health. Report of

the Public Health Service Task Force on Women's Health Issues. [publisher

unknown]; 1985 May. PHS:85-50206.

28c Formatting a CSE-Style Research Project

The CSE does not specify a format for the body of a college research report, but most scientific reports include the following sections:

More about
Writing an ab-
stract, 229
Formatting college
papers, 56
Formatting a paper
in APA style,
227–38

- Abstract
- Introduction
- Methods
- Results
- Discussion
- References

Writing
Responsibly **Of Deadlines and Paperclips**

Instructors expect students to turn in thoughtful, carefully proofread, and neatly formatted papers on time—usually in class on the due date. They also expect writers
to clip or staple the pages of the paper *before* the paper is submitted. Do justice to
yourself by being fully prepared.

to SELF

Ask your instructor for formatting guidelines, refer to the general formatting guidelines provided in chapter 8, or follow the formatting guidelines for APA style in tab 7.

Start a new page for your reference list, and title it "References."

Name-year system List entries in alphabetical order by author's surname. If no author is listed, alphabetize by the first main word of the title (omitting articles such as *the, a,* and *an*). Do not number the entries.

Citation-sequence system Number your entries in order of their appearance in your paper. Each work should appear in your reference list only once, even if it is cited more than once in your project. Double-check to make sure that the numbers in your reference list match the numbers in your text.

Citation-name system Alphabetize the entries in your reference list first (by the author's surname or the first main word of the title if no author is listed). Then number them. Each work should appear in your reference list only once, even if it is cited more than once in your project. Double-check to make sure that the numbers in your reference list match the numbers in your text.

Student Model Research Project: CSE-Style Reference List

The sample reference list on the next page is taken from a laboratory report by Alicia Keefe, University of Maryland. Keefe fulfilled her responsibility to the writers from whom she borrowed information and ideas by supplying a complete citation for each source. She fulfilled her responsibility to her reader by formatting the entries using the name-year system in CSE style, in keeping with her reader's expectations.

References

Geiger P. 2002. Introduction to *Drosophila melanogaster*. Tucson (AZ): University of Arizona, General Biology Program for Teachers, Biology Department [Internet] [cited 2012 Apr 30]. Available from: http://biology.arizona.edu/sciconn/lessons2/geiger/intro.htm

Hoikkala A, Aspi J. 1993 [cited 2012 Apr 28]. Criteria of female mate choice in *Drosophila littoralis, D. montana,* and *D. ezoana.* Evolution [Internet]. 47(3):768–778. Available from: http://web.ebscohost.com

Ives JD. 1921. Cross-over values in the fruit fly, *Drosophila ampelophila,* when the linked factors enter in different ways. Am Naturalist. 6:571–573.

Mader S. 2005. Lab manual. 9th ed. New York (NY): McGraw-Hill.

Marcillac F, Bousquet F, Alabouvette J, Savarit F, Ferveur JF. 2005 [cited 2012 Apr 28]. A mutation with major effects on *Drosophila melanogaster* sex pheromones. Genetics [Internet]. 171(4):1617–1628. Available from: http://web.ebscohost.com doi:10.1534/genetics.104.033159

Service PM. 1991. Laboratory evolution of longevity and reproductive fitness components in male fruit flies: mating ability. Evolution. 47:387–399.

Web page: Date cited and URL of web page provided

Journal article: Accessed through a database, no DOI; URL of database home page provided

Journal article: Printed, title of journal abbreviated

Journal article: Accessed through a database, with DOI

Journal article: Printed, one-word journal title not abbreviated

9

Style
Matters

Writing Engagingly

Use tab 9 to learn, practice, and master these writer's responsibilities:

❏ **To Audience**

Use parallelism to present ideas forcefully to your readers, use sentence openings and closings to highlight important information, choose language appropriate to your context, and hold your readers' attention with compelling words and figures.

❏ **To Topic**

Address your topic concisely but with substance, use coordination and subordination to distinguish primary from secondary information, choose words appropriately for both their meaning and their associations, and choose accurate synonyms.

❏ **To Other Writers**

Use responsible language to avoid misrepresenting others.

❏ **To Yourself**

Write concisely for increased clarity and effectiveness, choose the active voice whenever possible to energize your writing, and convey your thoughts forthrightly, avoiding euphemism and doublespeak.

9

Style
Matters

29 Writing Concisely

Wordy writing is like young children's soccer: The point gets made haltingly if at all. Concise writing, in contrast, is like the play of a World Cup team. Each word, like each player, counts; every point is made forcefully and without duplication of effort.

 Conciseness What one culture considers wordy, another may consider elegant. Not only culture but also context affects what readers expect: In literary contexts and even in some personal writing, US readers sometimes appreciate rich, expansive sentences. In academic and business contexts, however, US readers usually prefer writing that is concise and to the point.

29a Eliminating Wordy Expressions

First-draft writing sometimes contains common but wordy expressions that pad and clutter sentences. As you revise, prune these away.

Empty expressions like *to all intents and purposes, in fact, the fact is,* and *in the process of* carry no information, so you should delete them.

> ▶ The passengers were ~~in the process of~~ boarding the plane when ~~in fact~~ the flight was canceled.

Similarly, intensifiers like *absolutely, actually, definitely, really,* and *totally* add little meaning to the words they modify.

> ▶ The tourists were ~~absolutely~~ thrilled. None of them had ~~actually~~ seen a polar bear before.

Phrases built around words like *aspect, character, kind, manner,* and *type* are also often mere filler.

Quick
| **Reference** Strategies for Writing Concisely |

- Cut wordy expressions. (277)
- Cut ineffective or unnecessary repetition. (279)
- Avoid wordy sentence patterns. (279–80)
- Consolidate phrases, clauses, and sentences. (280)

More about
Sentence length
and variety,
284–94
Crafting a thesis,
22–24
Developing para-
graphs, 31–35,
39–40

Writing Responsibly

Conciseness versus the Too-Short Paper

Effective writing should be concise but not necessarily brief. Concise writing provides readers with all the information they need without distractions, but it does not skimp on essential detail. It may take a long sentence to express a complex thought. Do not shortchange your readers—or your ideas—by omitting necessary detail.

In contrast, a too-short paper may tempt you to pad, but that may make your writing hard (and boring) to read. Instead of adding words, try developing your ideas and searching for facts, statistics, expert testimony, and examples that will bring your paper to life.

to AUDIENCE

> They ~~are the kind of people who~~ have always ~~behaved in a generous manner.~~ been generous.

Some expressions say in many words what is better said with one.

Wordy Expression	Concise Alternative
at the present time	*now* (or delete entirely)
at this point in time	*now* (or delete entirely)
at that point in time	*then* (or delete entirely)
until such time as	*until*
at all times	*always*
at no time	*never*
most of the time	*usually*
in this day and age	*today*
due to the fact that	*because*
in spite of the fact that	*although, even though*
has the ability to	*can*
in the event that	*if*
in the neighborhood of	*around*

> ~~Due to the fact that~~ Because the housing market is weak ~~at this point in time,~~ many homeowners are waiting to sell until ~~such time as~~ conditions improve.

Tech Style Checkers and Wordiness

Although they might occasionally flag an inappropriate wordy construction, computer style checkers are generally unreliable judges of wordiness. Rely on readers—yourself, your instructor, writing center tutors, your friends—to help you determine what is and is not acceptable.

29b Eliminating Ineffective Repetition

As you revise your writing, look for words repeated unnecessarily, whether exactly or in a different form.

DRAFT	The author's informative overview provides particularly revealing information about the Obama administration.
REVISION	The author's overview provides particularly revealing information about the Obama administration.

> **More about**
> Transitions, 29–31
> Repetition for
> emphasis, 293
> Parallelism, 281–84
> Avoiding ambiguity, 375

Also watch for **redundancy,** unnecessary repetition.

▶ The candidate's mistakes during the campaign were ~~few in number,~~ *few,*
but they cost her the election, and she plans ~~for the future~~ never to
repeat them ~~again.~~

29c Avoiding Wordy Sentence Patterns

Certain sentence patterns tend toward wordiness. These include **expletive constructions,** sentences in the **passive voice,** and sentences built around weak verbs.

1. Sentences that begin with *There are . . . , It is . . .*

Expletive constructions are sentences that begin with expressions like *there are, there is,* or *it is.* (Do not confuse *expletive* in this sense with its other sense of *swear word* or *curse.*) Revising to eliminate expletives will often make a sentence more direct and concise.

> **More about**
> Expletive constructions, 396

DRAFT	There are several measures that institutions can take to curb plagiarism.
REVISION	Institutions can take several measures to curb plagiarism.

2. Passive voice

In an **active-voice** sentence, the subject performs the action. In a passive-voice sentence, the subject receives the action.

> **More about**
> Passive versus
> active voice,
> 293–94, 386–87

	subj.	verb	
ACTIVE	Jared photographed the bear.

	subj.	verb	
PASSIVE	The bear was photographed by Jared.

Rewriting to use the active voice usually makes sentences more concise and direct.

DRAFT (PASSIVE)	A motion was proposed by Andrew that concert planning be delayed until the cost of the party could be accurately determined by the treasurer.
REVISION (ACTIVE)	Andrew proposed delaying concert planning until the treasurer could accurately determine the party's cost.

3. Sentences built around weak verbs

If the sentence is built around a weak verb such as *is, are, were,* or *was* (all forms of the verb *to be*), sometimes replacing the verb can produce a more concise and vivid result.

DRAFT	The destruction of the town by the tornado was complete.
REVISION	The tornado destroyed the town.

29d Consolidating Phrases, Clauses, and Sentences

clause A word group with a subject and a predicate
phrase A group of related words that lacks a subject, a predicate, or both

You can often make your writing more concise by reducing *clauses* to *phrases* and clauses or phrases to single words.

DRAFT	Scientists cite glaciers, which have been retreating, and the polar ice caps, which have been shrinking, as evidence of global climate change.
REVISION	Scientists cite retreating glaciers and shrinking polar ice caps as evidence of global climate change.

Sometimes you can also combine two or more sentences into one more concise, effective sentence.

DRAFT	Scientists note that glaciers have been retreating and the polar ice caps have been shrinking. Most of them now agree that these phenomena are evidence of global climate change.
REVISION	Most scientists now agree that retreating glaciers and the shrinking polar ice caps are evidence of global climate change.

30 Using Parallelism

Andy Warhol's silkscreen painting *Marilyn Diptych* (1962) is made up of parallel parts. Its two panels are each divided into 25 copies of the same image of Marilyn Monroe. On both sides, these images vary subtly in color and clarity, suggesting to some viewers life and death, the transitory nature of fame, and the way image obliterates individuality. Warhol uses visual parallelism to convey his message. Similarly, writers use grammatical ***parallelism***—the expression of equally important ideas in similar grammatical form—to increase the clarity of their writing and to emphasize important points. Here are some examples, with the parallel structures highlighted:

Andy Warhol, *Marilyn Diptych*, 1962

> Greed, for lack of a better word, is good. Greed is right. Greed works. Greed clarifies, cuts through, and captures, the essence of the evolutionary spirit.
> —speech by Gordon Gekko in the movie *Wall Street*

> I don't want to achieve immortality through my work; I want to achieve immortality by not dying.
> —Woody Allen

30a Expressing Paired Items and Items in a Series in Parallel Form

More about
Coordinating conjunctions, 325, 421–22

Readers expect paired ideas and items in a series to be parallel.

1. Items paired with a conjunction such as *and* or *but*

Make paired items linked by coordinating conjunctions (*and, but, for, nor, or, so,* and *yet*) parallel.

> ▶ Girls learn at a young age to be passive and ~~that they should be~~ deferential.

The original uses *and* to pair an infinitive phrase (*to be passive*) with a subordinate clause (*that they should be deferential*); the revision uses *and* to join a pair of adjectives (*passive and deferential*).

> ▶ The course always covers the twentieth century through World War II but sometimes ~~touching~~ *also touches* on the beginning of the Cold War ~~is possible also~~.

In the revision, the verbs *covers* and *touches on* are in parallel form.

281

Deceptive Parallelism Parallel structure is found in most languages, so you are probably familiar with the concept. Use caution, however, to ensure that items that seem parallel are all grammatically equivalent. For example, in "He spoke only positively and friendly about his previous professor," *positively* and *friendly* appear parallel, but *positively* is an adverb, whereas *friendly* is an adjective. To be parallel, the sentence requires revision along these lines: "He had only positive and friendly things to say about his previous professor."

2. Items paired with a correlative conjunction such as *both ... and* or *neither ... nor*

Conjunctions such as *both ... and, either ... or, neither ... nor,* and *not only ... but also* are **correlative conjunctions.** They come in pairs, and they link ideas of equal importance. Readers expect items linked by a correlative conjunction to be parallel. To be parallel, however, the items linked by the correlative conjunctions must have the same grammatical form.

> **More about**
> Correlative con-
> junctions, 325

FAULTY PARALLELISM	The defense attorney convinced the jury not only that her client had no motive for committing the crime, but also was nowhere near the scene of the crime when it occurred.

A clause beginning with *that* follows *not only,* so a clause beginning with *that* should follow *but also.*

REVISED	The defense attorney convinced the jury not only that her client had no motive for committing the crime but also that he was nowhere near the scene of the crime when it occurred.

FAULTY PARALLELISM	According to the prosecutor, the accused both had the opportunity and a motive.

In the original, a verb (*had*) follows *both,* but a noun (*motive*) follows *and.* In the revision, nouns follow both parts of the conjunction.

REVISED	According to the prosecutor, the accused had both the opportunity and a motive.

3. Items in a series

Like paired items, three or more equivalent items in a series should be in parallel form.

FAULTY PARALLELISM	The detectives secured the crime scene, examined it for clues, and the witnesses were then called in for questioning.

REVISED	The detectives secured the crime scene, examined it for clues, and then called in the witnesses for questioning.

Tech **Parallelism and Computer Style Checkers**

A computer style checker cannot identify ideas that merit parallel treatment in an otherwise grammatical sentence.

30b Maintaining Parallelism in Comparisons

When you compare two items with *than* or *as,* the items should be in the same grammatical form.

> ▶ Getting into debt is unfortunately much easier than ~~to get~~ out of it.
>   *getting*

More about
Clear comparisons, 379–80, 393–94
Including function words, 392–93

30c Including All Words Needed to Maintain Parallelism

Words such as articles (*a, an, the*), conjunctions (*and, but, or*), and preposi-tions (*on, in, under*) indicate the relationships among other words in a sen-tence. They should be included or repeated as needed in linked items for clarity and grammar as well as for parallelism.

> ▶ The trail leads over high mountain passes and dense forests.
>   *through*
>
> Trails lead *over* passes but *through* forests.

30d Using Parallelism for Emphasis

Placing ideas in parallel form highlights their differences and similarities.

> ▶ In Andy Warhol's painting *Marilyn Dipytch,* all the images are copies of the same original, the same size, and ~~they have equal~~
>   *all are*   *all are equally spaced*
>
> ~~space between them~~ within a grid of rows and columns.

More about
Parallelism and emphasis, 293

Writing Responsibly | Using Parallelism to Clarify Relationships among Ideas

An important component of the writing process is figuring out the *relationships* among your ideas and making those relationships clear to your read-ers. As you revise, ask yourself questions like these: What is the cause and what is the effect? What items are truly a part of the group and what items are not? Which ideas are important and which ideas provide supporting information? Using parallelism can help you emphasize for your reader that ideas are of equal importance. (Coordination and sub-ordination, discussed in the next chapter, can also help you emphasize that ideas or information are of equal or unequal importance.) Experimenting with some of the techniques you are learning in this chapter, and in other chapters in this tab, can lead to new insights about your topic.

to AUDIENCE

As the following passage from a speech by President Barack Obama shows, parallelism can be a forceful tool for emphasizing important ideas. Notice how Obama's parallelisms (and the parallelisms from the Declaration of Independence that he quotes) generate an almost musical rhythm that drive home the president's point.

> Two hundred and thirty-four years later, the words are just as bold, just as revolutionary, as they were when they were first pronounced: "We hold these truths to be self-evident, that all men are created equal, that they are endowed by their Creator with certain inalienable rights; that among these are life, liberty, and the pursuit of happiness." These are not simply words on aging parchment. They are the principles that define us as a nation, the values we cherish as a people, and the ideals we strive for as a society, even as we know that we constantly have to work in order to perfect our union, and that work is never truly done.
>
> —President Barack Obama, July 4, 2010

31 Engaging Readers with Variety and Emphasis

In this painting, *At the Opera,* artist Mary Cassatt captures our interest with a variety of visual elements, among them the figure of the woman in the foreground; the more sketchily rendered figures in the background; the curving form of the balconies; the bright points of red and white; and the contrasting large, dark areas. Cassatt also structures the painting to emphasize certain elements over others and to direct our attention to a story unfolding within the scene. Our eyes go first to the woman in the foreground; then we follow her gaze through her opera glasses and let the curve of the balcony railing draw our attention to the upper left, where a male figure also is looking through opera glasses—not toward the stage, however, but directly at the woman in the foreground.

Writers also use variety and emphasis. They vary sentence length, sentence structure, and sentence openers to capture and hold their readers' attention, and they use coordination and subordination, strategic repetition, emphatic verbs, and the active voice to highlight key ideas.

31a Varying Sentence Length and Structure

Confronting readers with page after page of sentences of uniform length—short, medium, or long—can make it hard for them to pick out important details. To hold readers' attention and direct it to the points you want to

Quick

Reference   Achieving Variety and Emphasis

- Vary sentence length and structure. (284)
- Use coordination to link or contrast equally important sentence elements. (285)
- Use subordination to distinguish main ideas from supporting ideas. (287)
- Vary sentence openings. (290)
- Use rhythm for emphasis. (291)
- Use strategic repetition. (293)
- Use emphatic verbs and favor the active voice. (293)

emphasize, vary the length of your sentences and include a mix of sentence types: *simple, compound, complex,* and *compound-complex.*

Short sentences deliver information concisely and dramatically. They are most emphatic, however, when they are mixed with longer sentences. In the following passage, too many short sentences in a row create a choppy effect, leaving the reader with the impression that each point is equally important. The revision combines most of the short sentences into longer sentences that clarify the relationship among the ideas the writer wants to convey. The writer's main point is now dramatically isolated in the one short sentence that remains.

> **simple sentence**
> One independent clause and no subordinate clauses
> **compound sentence** Two or more independent clauses and no subordinate clauses
> **complex sentence** One independent clause with at least one subordinate clause
> **compound-complex sentence** Two or more independent clauses with one or more subordinate clauses

DRAFT   The whole planet is at risk. We need to put a stop to the wild spread of this disease. The key is education. First, we should educate the victims. Then we should let them educate the world. They can help us win this war against AIDS. They can help other people understand that everyone is vulnerable.

REVISION   With the whole planet at risk, we need to put a stop to the wild spread of this disease. The key is education. First, we should educate the victims; then we should let them educate the world. They can help us win this war against AIDS by helping other people understand that everyone is vulnerable.

31b Using Coordination to Link or Contrast Equally Important Ideas

Coordination is the joining of elements of equal importance in a sentence. When you coordinate parts of a sentence—whether words, phrases, or clauses—you give them equal emphasis.

To coordinate terms and phrases use either a coordinating conjunction (*and, but, for, nor, or, so,* or *yet*) or a correlative conjunction (*both . . . and, either . . . or,* or *neither . . . nor*). Usually no punctuation separates a pair of coordinated words or phrases.

> **phrase** A group of related words that lacks a subject, a predicate, or both
> **clause** A word group with a subject and a predicate. An *independent clause* can stand alone as a sentence; a *subordinate clause* cannot.

More about
Coordinating and correlative conjunctions, 325

▶ Both <u>Steven Spielberg</u> and <u>George Romero</u> attended the New York Film Academy.

▶ London's Theatre Royal in Drury Lane has staged performances <u>by the Shakespearean actor Edmund Kean</u> and <u>by the Monty Python comedy troupe.</u>

More about
Commas with series, 423–24

Use commas to separate more than two terms or phrases in a coordinated series.

▶ My roommate's favorite directors are <u>Steven Spielberg</u>, <u>the Coen brothers</u>, and <u>James Cameron.</u>

More about
Punctuating coordinated independent clauses, 341–46
Semicolons, 430–32

Use a comma and a coordinating conjunction, a semicolon, or a semicolon and a conjunctive adverb such as *for example, however, in addition,* or *therefore* to coordinate a pair of independent clauses (clauses that can stand alone as a sentence).

▶ <u>Today we consider Shakespeare to be the greatest English playwright</u>, but <u>his contemporaries regarded him as just one among many.</u>

▶ <u>Adele's debut CD was a huge success</u>; <u>it sold millions of copies.</u>

▶ <u>The play received glowing reviews and won a Tony award</u>; however, <u>it closed after only a short run.</u>

1. Conjunctions and their meaning

Conjunctions differ in meaning. The coordinating conjunction *and,* for example, suggests addition (*Jack <u>and</u> Jill went up the hill*), *or* suggests choice (*Jack <u>or</u> Jill fetched a pail of water*), and *but* suggests contrast (*Jack fell down, <u>but</u> Jill managed to keep her balance*). Make sure the meaning of the conjunction matches the relationship between the coordinated elements. In the following sentence, for example, changing *and* to *but* emphasizes the contrast between Spain's accomplishment and Paraguay's.

▶ Paraguay played well, ~~and~~ ^{*but*} Spain won and advanced to the semifinals.

2. Inappropriate coordination

Coordination is inappropriate when it combines elements that are not of equal importance. The following sentence, for example, puts a minor bit of information—Spielberg's year of birth—on an equal footing with a statement about his early accomplishments. The revision subordinates the minor information.

INAPPROPRIATE COORDINATION	Steven Spielberg was born in 1946, and by 1975 he had achieved box office success with *Jaws.*
REVISED	Steven Spielberg, born in 1946, achieved box office success in 1975 with *Jaws.*

Tech	**Style Checkers and Coordination and Subordination**

Using coordination and subordination requires you to figure out the logical relationships among the ideas you want to express and to decide on their relative importance, so that you can make these relationships clear to your audience. A computer style checker cannot do that for you.

3. Excessive coordination

In everyday speech, people often coordinate long strings of sentences with *and* and other conjunctions. What is acceptable in speech, however, quickly becomes tedious, even confusing, in writing. As you edit, look for such *excessive coordination.*

EXCESSIVE COORDINATION	Steven Spielberg graduated from Saratoga High School, in Saratoga, California, in 1965, and he applied to the University of Southern California's film school three times, but he was rejected each time, so he finally decided to attend California State University at Long Beach, and while he was at Cal State he started an unpaid internship at Universal Studios, and an executive was impressed by his talent, so in 1969 he was allowed to direct a television episode there, and by 1975 he was directing films like *Jaws,* and that was his first big hit as a movie director, so perhaps in the end he was lucky to have been rejected by USC.
REVISED	Steven Spielberg, who graduated in 1965 from Saratoga High School in Saratoga, California, applied to the University of Southern California's film school three times and was rejected each time. Finally, he decided to attend California State University at Long Beach. While he was at Cal State, he started an unpaid internship at Universal Studios. An executive there was impressed by his talent, so in 1969 he was allowed to direct a television episode there. By 1975, he was directing films like *Jaws,* his first big hit as a movie director. Perhaps, in the end, he was lucky to have been rejected by USC.

31c Distinguishing Main Ideas from Supporting Ideas with Subordination

Coordination allows you to link equally important ideas. Subordination, in contrast, allows you to emphasize main ideas and de-emphasize supporting examples, explanations, and details.

```
|——— main idea ———| |——— main idea ———|
```
▶ The evidence is conclusive; my client is innocent.

Coordination gives each idea equal weight.

|———————— subordinated idea ————————|——————— main idea ———————|
▸ As the evidence proves conclusively, my client is innocent.

The emphasis is on the client.

|———————————— main idea ——————————————|———— subordinated idea ————|
▸ The evidence proves conclusively that my client is innocent.

The emphasis is on the evidence.

Subordination can also clarify the relationship among a series of ideas. The revised version of the following passage clarifies the chronological relationships and emphasizes that comic books did not become widely popular until 1938.

DRAFT	The first comic books appeared in the early 1920s. Nearly four decades earlier, comic strips had begun appearing in the major newspapers. Comic books did not gain widespread popularity until June 1938. Writer Jerry Siegel and artist Joe Shuster debuted their character Superman in June 1938.
REVISED	Although comic books first appeared in the 1920s, which was nearly four decades after comic strips had begun to appear in the major newspapers, they did not gain widespread popularity until June 1938, when writer Jerry Siegel and artist Joe Shuster debuted their character Superman.

> **More about**
> Subordinating
>   conjunctions,
>   325
> Relative pronouns,
>   322

1. Subordinating terms and their meaning

Subordinating terms include subordinating conjunctions such as *after, although, as, because, before, since, so that, unless, whereas,* and *while* and relative pronouns such as *that, where, which,* and *who.* As with coordinating terms, be sure the meaning of the subordinating term you use matches the relationship you intend to convey. The following sentence uses a term referring to cause in a context that calls for a term referring to purpose. Revising requires either changing the term or rewording the clause.

DRAFT	He ran for mayor because he could bring the town's budget under control.
REVISED	He ran for mayor so that he could bring the town's budget under control.
	or
	He ran for mayor because he wanted to bring the town's budget under control.

Be particularly careful with the subordinating conjunctions *as* and *since,* which can refer ambiguously to both cause and time.

DRAFT	As she was applying the last coat of varnish, Lisa declared the restoration complete.

REVISED   While she was applying the last coat of varnish, Lisa declared the restoration complete.

or

Because she was applying the last coat of varnish, Lisa declared the restoration complete.

2. Illogical subordination

State key ideas in an independent clause, and put illustrations, examples, explanations, and details in subordinate structures. Illogically subordinating a main idea to a supporting idea can confuse readers.

ILLOGICAL
SUBORDINATION   Jodie Foster was only fourteen, although she was already a movie star.

REVISED   Although she was only fourteen, Jodie Foster was already a movie star.

3. Excessive subordination

Excessive subordination—stringing together too many subordinate structures—can make a sentence hard to read.

EXCESSIVE
SUBORDINATION   San Francisco, although generally an ideal habitat for peregrine falcons, is not entirely so, as became clear recently when rescuers had to remove falcon eggs from a nest on the Bay Bridge, despite the parents' protests, because once hatched, the fledglings would probably have drowned while learning to fly.

REVISED   San Francisco, although generally an ideal habitat for peregrine falcons, is not entirely so. Rescuers had to remove falcon eggs from a nest on the Bay Bridge recently, despite the parents' protests, because once hatched, the fledglings would probably have drowned while learning to fly.

 Coordination and Subordination Mastery of subordination is considered a sign of sophistication in American academic writing, but this is not true of all languages or cultures. If academic style in your native language or your style in other contexts favor coordination over subordination, you may need to make a conscious effort to use more subordination in your writing. If academic style in your native language or your native style favors subordination over coordination, you may tend to oversubordinate your sentences in academic English. Your goal should be to strike a balance between coordination and subordination.

> *More about*
Sentence struc-
ture, 325–35,
395–99

31d Varying Sentence Openings

In the default structure of an English sentence, the subject comes first, then the verb, and then the direct object if there is one. Reflecting this structure, most sentences start with the subject. However, a long string of subject-first sentences can make your text monotonous. Use modifying clauses and phrases to vary your sentence openings and to emphasize important information.

> **adverb** A word that modifies a verb, adjective, other adverb, or entire phrase or clause and that specifies how, where, when, and to what extent or degree

Adverbs and adverbial phrases and clauses Where you place an *adverb,* and the phrases and clauses that function as adverbs, affects the rhythm of a sentence and the information it emphasizes.

ADVERBIAL SUBORDINATE CLAUSE

Stocks can be a risky investment because they can lose value.

Because they can lose value, stocks can be a risky investment.

Stocks, because they can lose value, can be a risky investment.

ADVERBIAL PREPOSITIONAL PHRASES

We eat pancakes for breakfast on Sundays.

On Sundays, we eat pancakes for breakfast.

For breakfast, we eat pancakes on Sundays.

NOTE Moving an adverb can sometimes alter the meaning of a sentence. Consider these two examples:

▶ The test was surprisingly hard.

▶ Surprisingly, the test was hard.

In the first, *surprisingly* modifies *hard,* suggesting that the writer found the test harder than expected; in the second, *surprisingly* modifies the whole clause that follows it, suggesting that the writer expected the test to be easy.

> **adjective** A word that modifies a noun or pronoun with descriptive or limiting information

> **participial phrase** A phrase in which the present or past participle acts as an adjective

Adjectival phrases The placement of *adjectives* and most adjectival phrases and clauses is less flexible than the placement of adverbs. However, participles and *participial phrases,* which act as adjectives, can often come at the beginning of a sentence as well as after the terms they modify.

> **subject complement** An adjective, pronoun, or noun phrase that follows a linking verb and describes or refers to the subject of the sentence

▶ New York City's subway system, flooded by torrential rains, shut down at the height of the morning rush hour.

▶ Flooded by torrential rains, New York City's subway system shut down at the height of the morning rush hour.

An adjective phrase that functions as a *subject complement* can also sometimes be repositioned at the beginning of a sentence.

▶ The Mariana Trench is almost seven miles deep, making it the lowest place on the surface of the earth.

▶ Almost seven miles deep, the Mariana Trench is the lowest place on the surface of the earth.

Appositives and absolute phrases An *appositive* is a noun or noun phrase that renames another noun or noun phrase. Because they designate the same thing, the appositive and the original term can switch positions.

More about
Placement of adjectives, 412

▶ The governor, New York's highest official, ordered an investigation into the subway system's failure.

▶ New York's highest official, the governor, ordered an investigation into the subway system's failure.

An *absolute phrase,* consisting of a noun or pronoun with a participle, modifies an entire independent clause. It can often fall either before or after the clause it modifies.

▶ The task finally completed, the workers headed for the parking lot.

▶ The workers headed for the parking lot, the task finally completed.

Transitional expressions A *transitional expression* relates the information in one sentence to material that precedes or follows. Its placement affects the emphasis that falls on other parts of the sentence. The second passage below, for example, calls more attention to Superman's distinctiveness than the first does.

More about
Transitional expressions, 29–31

▶ Most comic book characters from the 1930s quickly fell into obscurity. However, Superman was not one of them.

▶ Most comic book characters from the 1930s quickly fell into obscurity. Superman, however, was not one of them.

31e Using Sentence Rhythm to Emphasize Important Information

Sentences, like music, have rhythm, and within that rhythm, some beats get more stress than others. Readers readily notice the beginning of a sentence, where they usually find the subject, and they notice the end, where everything wraps up. Take advantage of readers' habits by slotting important or striking information into those positions. In the following example, the writer changed the subject of the sentence from *ready availability* to the more significant *free news* and moved *financial ruin* to the end, dramatically underscoring the seriousness of the challenge newspapers face.

DRAFT   The ready availability of free news on the Internet threatens finan-
             cial ruin for traditional newspapers.

REVISED   Free news, readily available on the Internet, threatens traditional
             newspapers with financial ruin.

A common way to organize information in longer sentences is with a cumulative or loose structure. A ***cumulative sentence*** begins with the subject and
verb of an independent clause and accumulates additional information in subsequent modifying phrases and clauses.

> That's the news from Lake Wobegon, where all the women are strong, all the
> men are good-looking, and all the children are above average.
> —Garrison Keillor, tag line from the radio show
> *A Prairie Home Companion*

A ***periodic sentence,*** in contrast, reserves the independent clause for the
end, preceded by modifying details. The effect is to build suspense that highlights key information when it finally arrives.

> Through the center of town, up the strip, past the housing developments and
> shopping malls, street lights giving way to the thin streaming illumination of
> the headlights, trees crowding the asphalt in a black unbroken wall: that was
> the way to Greasy Lake.
> —T. Coraghessan Boyle, "Greasy Lake"

An interrupted periodic sentence begins with the subject of the independent
clause but leaves the conclusion of the clause to the end, separating the two
parts with modifying details. In the following example, the subject of the sentence is highlighted in yellow, and the predicate is highlighted in blue.

> The archaeologist Howard Carter, peering through the small opening to
> the main chamber of Tutankhamen's tomb at treasures hidden from view
> for more than three millennia, when asked what he saw, replied "wonderful
> things."

An ***inversion*** is a sentence in which, contrary to normal English word order, the verb precedes the subject. Inverted sentences call attention to themselves. Used sparingly, they can help you emphasize a point or create a sense of
dramatic tension.

> ▸ Into the middle of town rode the stranger.
> _verb_   _subj._

Developing an Ear for Sentence Variety Many of the sentence structures that
add variety to written English are uncommon in conversation and as a result
may not come naturally to you even if you are fluent in conversational English.
To develop an ear for sentence variety in your academic writing, try imitating
some of the structures in this chapter. Ask an instructor or another skilled writer
of English to check your work to see if you have produced effective sentences.

31f Using Strategic Repetition

Redundancy and other forms of unnecessary repetition clutter writing and distract readers. Repetition is sometimes necessary, however, to add clarity, to maintain parallelism, or to call attention to important ideas, as the repetition of the word *grotesque* does in the following passage.

> I doubt if the texture of Southern life is any more grotesque than that of the rest of the nation, but it does seem evident that the Southern writer is particularly adept at recognizing the grotesque; and to recognize the grotesque, you have to have some notion of what is not grotesque and why.
> —Flannery O'Connor, talk delivered at Notre Dame University

Repetition for emphasis works especially well within parallel structures, as in this sentence from a paper by Syracuse University student Jessica Toro.

> **More about**
> Parallelism, 281–84

> Some children are never told that they are adopted, never given the opportunity to search for their biological parents.

Toro could have used *or* instead of the second *never,* but the repetition dramatically underscores her concern about the consequences for adopted children of not telling them that they are adopted.

31g Creating Emphasis with Emphatic Verbs

Verbs that describe an action directly are often more emphatic than verbs like *be, have,* or *cause* that combine with nouns or adjectives to describe an action indirectly.

> **More about**
> Weak verbs and wordiness, 280

> ▸ Many economists ~~have a belief~~ *believe* that higher gasoline taxes would ~~be beneficial to~~ *benefit* the economy in the long run. The increased costs would ~~have a stimulating effect on~~ *stimulate* research into alternate energy sources and eventually ~~cause a reduction in~~ *reduce* both carbon emissions and our dependence on oil.

31h Distinguishing the Active from the Passive Voice

In an active-voice sentence, the subject performs the action of the verb; in a passive-voice sentence, the subject receives the action of the verb. Sentences in the active voice are usually more emphatic, direct, and concise than sentences in the passive voice.

> **More about**
> Passive voice and wordiness, 279–80

ACTIVE VOICE: EMPHATIC
Rising oil prices stimulate research into alternate energy sources.

PASSIVE VOICE: UNEMPHATIC
Research into alternate energy sources is stimulated by rising oil prices.

Writing Responsibly

Voice and Responsibility

Because the passive voice allows the agent of an action to remain unnamed, it lends itself to misuse by people evading responsibility for their mistakes and misdeeds. Consider, for example, the classic dodge of the cornered politician or bureaucrat: "Mistakes were made."

Be on the lookout for this evasive use of the passive voice in your own writing and the writing of others. It is a usage that comes all too readily when we need to convey unflattering or damaging information about ourselves or those we represent.

to TOPIC

If the performer of the action is unknown or unimportant, however, the passive voice can be appropriate.

▶ According to the coroner, the victim had been murdered between 3 and 4 in the morning.

The identity of the murderer is unknown.

▶ *Harry Potter and the Philosopher's Stone,* the first book in the Harry Potter series, was published in 1997.

The focus is on the date of publication, not the identity of the publisher.

Similarly, in science writing, the passive voice allows the description of procedures without constant reference to the individuals who carried them out.

▶ The effects of human activities on seagrasses were studied at Sandy Neck and Centerville beaches from 31 March 2011 to 30 March 2012.

32 Choosing Appropriate Language

During a job interview, both the applicant and the interviewer need to dress appropriately, behave appropriately, and use language appropriately. Neither would be likely to show up in a bathing suit, jump up and down on a couch, or use language that might offend the other. Such issues of appropriateness apply to your writing as well. In every document you write, use language that is appropriate to the context and avoids bias.

32a Matching Your Language to the Context

We all adjust our language to suit our audience and purpose. No form of the language is intrinsically better or more correct than another, but certain forms have become standard for addressing an academic or business audience. In business and academic writing, using appropriate language usually means the following:

- Avoiding nonstandard dialects
- Avoiding regionalisms, colloquialisms, and slang
- Avoiding overly technical terminology (neologisms and jargon)
- Adopting a straightforward tone, one that is neither overly formal nor informal

1. Nonstandard dialects

A *dialect* is a variant of a language with its own distinctive pronunciation, vocabulary, and grammar. A linguist once quipped that the only difference between the standard form of a language and its other dialects is that the standard form has an army and a navy. The standard form, in other words, became standard because it is the dialect of the elite and powerful.

Nonstandard dialects of English are not "bad" English, as many mistakenly believe. If you speak a dialect like Appalachian English or African American Vernacular English and you are addressing an audience of peers from your community, then your home dialect *is* appropriate. If you are addressing a broader audience or writing in an academic or workplace context, however, the dialect known as Standard American English, or Edited English, is usually the appropriate choice.

> **More about**
> Standard American English grammar, 319–35

2. Regionalisms, colloquialisms, and slang

Regionalisms are expressions that are characteristic of particular areas. Saying the car "needs washed" might be acceptable in Pittsburgh but not in Boston. The expression "I might could do it" might be acceptable in Pikeville, Kentucky, but not in Des Moines, Iowa. Regionalisms can be appropriate in conversation or informal writing but are usually out of place in formal academic writing.

> ▶ Many scientists believe that we might ~~could~~ *be able to* slow global warming if we can reduce carbon emissions.

Colloquialisms are informal expressions common in speech but usually out of place in formal writing.

> ▶ An R rating designates a movie that is not appropriate for ~~kids~~ *children* under seventeen who are not accompanied by ~~a grown-up.~~ *an adult.*

Used judiciously, however, the occasional colloquialism can add spice to your writing.

> ▶ The musicians were only kids, none of them more than ten years old, but they played like seasoned professionals.

Writing Responsibly / **Online Shortcuts**

Users of text messaging, instant messaging, and social networking sites have developed a host of acronyms and abbreviations—like *BTW* for "by the way" and *IMO* for "in my opinion"—that save typing time and space on the tiny screens of mobile phones. With the possible exception of informal e-mail, these expressions are almost never appropriate in other contexts, particularly not in academic or business writing. The same applies to emoticons like :-) and :-(and to other shortcuts such as writing entirely in lowercase without punctuation, as in *i saw her this am.*

to SELF

Slang is the extremely informal, inventive, often colorful (and sometimes off-color) vocabulary of a particular group. In general, slang is inappropriate in formal writing, but as with colloquial language, when used sparingly and judiciously, it can enliven a sentence and help emphasize an important point.

3. Neologisms and jargon

The world changes. Technology advances, new cultural trends emerge, and new research alters our understanding of ourselves and gives rise to new fields of study. As these changes occur, people necessarily invent new words and expressions—*neologisms.* Some neologisms become widely used and establish themselves as acceptable vocabulary for formal writing. Other neologisms, however, soon disappear or never move from informal to formal usage. When you consider using a neologism, ask yourself whether a more familiar synonym might serve as well. If the neologism is necessary but you are not sure your audience will be familiar with it, define it.

> *, websites that allow a group of users to create and edit content collectively,*
> ▸ Some instructors use wikis as tools for teaching collaborative writing.

The term *jargon* refers to the specialized vocabulary of a particular profession or discipline. Doctors speak of *adenomas* and *electroencephalograms.* Automobile mechanics speak of *camber angles* and *ring-and-pinion gears.* Lawyers speak of *effluxions of time* and *words of procreation.* For an audience of specialists, this kind of insider vocabulary can efficiently communicate complex ideas that might otherwise take several sentences, even paragraphs, to explain. If you are addressing other specialists, jargon may be appropriate. If you are addressing a general audience, however, it is usually inappropriate. In most cases, avoid it. When a specialized term is needed, define it.

> *when their lease expired.*
> ▸ The tenants lost the apartment ~~due to the effluxion of time on their lease.~~

4. Appropriate formality

When you speak or write to close friends from your own age group, your language will probably—and appropriately—be relaxed and informal, sprinkled with dialect, slang, and colloquial expressions. Writing for most college courses or in the workplace, however, calls for a formal tone and clear, straightforward language free of slang and colloquialisms. Clear and straightforward, however, should not mean simpleminded or condescending. Use challenging vocabulary if it aptly expresses your meaning, but do not try to impress your readers by inflating your writing with fancy words mined from a thesaurus.

More about
Using a thesaurus, 309

INAPPROPRIATELY INFORMAL	Tarantino is always ripping scenes from earlier flicks to use in his own.
INFLATED	It is a characteristic stylistic mannerism of the auteur Quentin Tarantino to allusively amalgamate scenic quotations from the repertory of his cinematic forebears in his own oeuvre.
APPROPRIATE	In his movies, the director Quentin Tarantino routinely alludes to scenes from earlier movies.

32b Avoiding Biased or Hurtful Language

Biased or *hurtful language* unfairly or offensively characterizes a particular group and its members. It can be as blatant as a slur that targets a specific group, such as *wetback,* for people of Mexican descent, or *guido,* for Italian American men. It can also be subtle and unintentional, as in thoughtless stereotyping or an inappropriately applied label.

A *stereotype* is a simplified, uncritical, and often negative generalization about an entire group of people: *Blondes are ditzy; athletes are weak students; lawyers are unscrupulous; politicians are dishonest.* Even when they seem positive, stereotypes lump people together in ways that offensively ignore their individuality. In an article in the *New York Times,* for example, Chinese American writer Vivian S. Toy remembers among her "painful experiences of being different" that a college adviser once recommended that she switch her major to biology "since Chinese are better suited for the sciences."

More about
Stereotyping, 80

Writing Responsibly   Euphemisms and Doublespeak

We use **euphemisms** in place of words that might be offensive or emotionally painful. We speak to mourners about a relative who has *passed away,* and we excuse ourselves saying we have to go to *the bathroom* without referring to specific bodily functions.

The polite or respectful use of euphemisms, however, can easily shade into an evasive reluctance to address harsh realities. Why use *correctional institution,* for example, when what you mean is *prison*? Why use *ill-advised* when what you mean is *foolish* or *rash*?

Euphemisms that are deliberately deceptive, used to obscure bad news or sanitize an ugly truth, are called **doublespeak.** A company that announces that it is *downsizing,* not that it is about to lay off half of its workforce, is using doublespeak.

When reading, ask yourself: Does this word obscure or downplay the truth? When writing, think carefully about your motives: Are you using a euphemism (or doublespeak) to avoid hurting someone's feelings or to avoid confronting an uncomfortable truth?

to AUDIENCE

We label people whenever we call attention to a particular characteristic about them. ***Labeling*** is appropriate when it is relevant.

▶ Barack Obama is the first African American president.

It is inappropriate, and usually offensive, when it is irrelevant.

▶ President Obama, an African American, is an articulate debater.

To appreciate how irrelevant the label "African American" is in that last sentence, consider the following:

▶ Senator John McCain, who is of Scots-Irish and English descent, is an articulate debater.

1. Gender bias

English has no third-person pronouns that designate an individual person without also designating that person's gender (*she, he, her, him, hers, his, herself, himself*). This lack creates problems when a writer uses the singular to refer to people in general.

▶ The sensible student is careful what [*he? she?*] posts about [*himself? herself?*] on social networking sites like Facebook and Twitter.

Until about the 1970s, the conventional solution to this problem was to use the masculine pronoun as the generic pronoun. In other words, depending on context, *he* referred either to a particular male human or to a generic human of either gender. On the other hand, *she* always meant "female." Similarly, the terms *man* and *mankind* could refer generically to humanity as a whole, but *woman* and *womankind* only to women. Since the 1970s, writers have been replacing this usage—together with other vocabulary that reinforces gender stereotypes—with gender-neutral alternatives.

***Avoid the generic* he** One way to avoid the generic *he*—and often the most graceful way—is to rewrite the sentence using plural nouns, pronouns, and verbs.

▶ ~~The sensible student is~~ careful what ~~he posts~~ about ~~himself~~ on social
  Sensible students are ∧ *they post* ∧ *themselves* ∧
networking sites like Facebook and Twitter.

Another alternative is to use *he or she* (or *she or he*).

▶ The sensible student is careful what he or she posts on social networking sites.

Be sparing with *he or she* (*she or he*), however; used many times in quick succession, it becomes awkward.

AWKWARD   The sensible student is careful what <u>he or she</u> posts about <u>himself or herself</u> on the social networking sites <u>he or she</u> frequents.

NOTE The use of *they* as a generic pronoun for singular antecedents is common in speech, and some people consider it an acceptable alternative to the generic *he* in writing as well. Many readers consider this usage ungrammatical, however, so it is best to avoid it.

More about
Pronoun-antecedent agreement, 354–57

▸ ~~The sensible student is~~ _{Sensible students are} careful what they post about themselves.

***Avoid generic* man** Replace terms like *man, men,* and *mankind* used to represent all human beings with gender-neutral equivalents such as *humanity, humankind,* or *humans.*

▸ _{Humans are the only animals} ~~Man is the only animal~~ to have ventured into space.

Replace occupational names that include the term *man* with gender-neutral alternatives.

▸ _{Members of Congress} ~~Congressmen~~ have excellent health insurance.

Avoid gender stereotypes and inappropriate gender labeling Some occupations with gender-neutral names are stereotypically associated with either men or women. Avoid perpetuating those stereotypes with inappropriate gender labeling.

▸ Nursing is an ancient, honorable profession. _{People} ~~Women~~ who choose it

can expect a rewarding career.

2. Racial, ethnic, and other labels

Racial and ethnic labels are appropriate only when race or ethnicity is relevant to the topic under discussion. The same is true for references to disabilities, sexual orientation, or other personal characteristics. When you do use labels, avoid terms that may give offense; instead, call people what they want to be called. The term *African American* is now widely accepted as a designation for Americans of African descent. People from Asia are *Asians,* not *Orientals* (a term many find disparaging). Be as specific as context permits. If what you mean is *Vietnamese,* or *Japanese,* or *Inuit,* or *Lakota,* or *Catalan,* or *Sicilian,* then use those terms, not the more general *Asian,* or *Native American,* or *European.*

Writing **Responsibly**

Blending Voices in Your Text

Make It Your Own! Good researched writing is more than collecting the ideas of others; it is instead an exploration of how the sources have helped researchers develop their own ideas. You will produce better work if, as you draft your project, you let your readers see *your* thinking.

Whenever you write from sources, you are blending the voices of your sources with one another and with your own. Although *voice* sometimes refers to the difference between passive and active voice, it also refers to who is talking in the text—the writer or the source.

Your audience wants to know whose voice it is "hearing." When you quote, it knows you are importing the voice of the source. When you **paraphrase** (rewrite the information in fresh language), your audience hears you talking. But when you **patchwrite** (copy from sources and make minor changes to its language, but not actually paraphrase), you lead your audience to the mistaken belief that it is hearing you when in fact it is neither your voice nor the source's, but rather an inappropriate mixture of the two. To blend voices successfully, you need to avoid patchwriting and show the beginning and end of your use of sources.

Most readers consider it plagiarism when a writer patchwrites. Regardless of whether he or she classifies it as plagiarism, no reader considers patchwriting good writing. The following passage from a source discussing the history of child psychology, followed by a student's first-draft writing from that source, illustrates the issue:

Passage from source

> In the 1910s and later, as child psychology became an academic discipline, teachers increasingly looked to educational researchers rather than librarians as the central experts in children's reading.

Patchwriting

> From the 1910s on, child psychology became a discipline, and teachers more and more thought that educational researchers rather than librarians were the main experts in children's reading (248).

The patchwriting follows the original sentence, deleting a few words and substituting some others, but still dependent on the language and arrangement of the source sentence. Not knowing that this is a blend of two voices—the writer's and the source's—the reader is misled to think this is the student's voice.

Paraphrase

> Child psychology emerged as an academic discipline in the early twentieth century, prompting teachers to look to researchers for expertise about children's reading. Librarians were no longer the primary authority on the topic (248).

The paraphrase appropriately uses keywords from the original, such as *discipline* and *child psychology,* but it otherwise uses fresh language and fresh sentence arrangement to restate the source.

Ground your own writing in paraphrase and summary, include some quotation, and avoid patchwriting altogether. This will allow your voice, rather than those of your sources, to dominate your text. This strategy requires your conscious effort and practice. Writing true paraphrase is an advanced skill that many college writers do not practice (see chart), but those who master this skill write the most successful research projects.

To let your readers know when you are paraphrasing or summarizing, use a signal phrase at the beginning of the source use and a parenthetical citation at the end. If your use of sources is lengthy, you can also occasionally mention the source or the author as you write, just to remind your readers that they are reading your summary or paraphrase of a source:

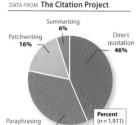

Students' Use of Sources
DATA FROM **The Citation Project**

- Summarizing 6%
- Direct quotation 46%
- Patchwriting 16%
- Paraphrasing 32%

Percent (n = 1,911)

Researchers found that while most college research writers use quotation and patchwriting, the best projects were by those who use summary and paraphrase.

Marking where the source use begins and ends

Signal phrase at beginning of source use	McDowell explains that the academic discipline of child psychology, which emerged in the early twentieth century, looked to researchers for expertise about children's reading. Librarians were no longer the leading authorities on the topic. Both librarians and child psychologists were interested in children's reading patterns, but for different reasons. The
Signal phrase within the source use	librarians, McDowell says, wanted to understand what sorts of texts would interest children so they could get them into the library. Child psychologists, in contrast, wanted to understand the children themselves. Both groups collected information about children's reading, but they did it in different ways. The librarians observed children's reading and reported on their observations, while the child psychologists conducted scientific research (248–49).

- **Paraphrase of a sentence from the source**
- **Summary of two pages in the source**
- **Parenthetical citation at end of source use**

Source: McDowell, Kathleen. "Toward a History of Children as Readers, 1890–1930." *Book History* 12 (2009): 240–65. Print.

Self Assessment

Review your work with each source, revising as necessary, to be sure you:

- ☐ Use paraphrase and summary where possible. Did you avoid overreliance on quotations? ▸ *Summarizing, 127–31; paraphrasing, 127–31; patchwriting, 125*
- ☐ Paraphrase while avoiding patchwriting. Did you restate source material in fresh language and fresh sentences? ▸ *Taking notes and avoiding plagiarism, 126–27*
- ☐ Use signal phrases and parenthetical citations. Did you let your audience know where your paraphrase and summary begins and ends? ▸ *Voice, 143–45; signal phrases, 141–42*

33 Choosing Effective Words

Words have both a literal meaning and emotional associations. ***Diction,*** or the choice of words to best convey an idea, requires attention to both.

33a Denotation and Connotation: Finding the Right Word

More about
Commonly confused words, 311–18

The literal meaning of a word, its dictionary definition, is its ***denotation.*** When you use a word, be sure its denotation matches your intended meaning. Be particularly careful, for example, not to misuse words that are similar in pronunciation or spelling.

> ▶ The name of the *Harry Potter* character Minerva McGonagall ~~eludes~~ *alludes*
>
> to Minerva, the Roman goddess of wisdom.
>
> To *elude* is to evade or escape; to *allude* is to make an indirect reference.

Be careful, too, with words that differ in meaning even though they are otherwise closely related.

> ▶ Many people owe their lives to the ~~heroics~~ *heroism* of volunteer firefighters.
>
> *Heroics* are melodramatic, excessive acts; *heroism* is courageous, potentially self-sacrificing behavior.

The secondary meanings of a word—the psychological or emotional associations it evokes—are its ***connotations.*** The word *walk,* for example, has many synonyms, including *amble, saunter, stride,* and *march.* Each of these, however, has distinctive connotations, as their effect in the following sentence suggests:

> ▶ The candidate *walked* to the podium to address her supporters.
> *ambled*
> *sauntered*
> *strode*
> *marched*
>
> The verb *walk* in this context is emotionally neutral, but the others all have connotations that suggest something about the candidate's state of mind.

Tech **Word Choice and Grammar and Style Checkers**

The grammar and style checkers in most word processing programs offer little help with effective word choice. They often cannot distinguish an incorrectly used word from a correctly used one—*affect* from *effect,* for example—nor can they differentiate between the emotional associations of words whose literal meaning is similar.

Writing Responsibly · Word Choice and Credibility

The denotation and connotation of the words you choose can powerfully influence the tone of your writing, the effect you have on your readers, and what your readers conclude about you. Highly charged vocabulary, as in the following examples, might lead readers to question the writer's objectivity:

> Hippie tree huggers are threatening the jobs of thousands of hardworking loggers.

> Conscientious activists are trying to protect endangered forests from rapacious, tree-murdering logging companies.

In academic writing, you will enhance your credibility if you describe conflicting positions in even-toned language:

> Environmentalists discuss their conflict with the logging industry in terms of the threat industry practices pose to a critical resource; the logging companies, contending that they are responsible forest stewards, describe the conflict in terms of their contribution to local economies.

Once you have looked at the issue fairly, nothing prevents you from then supporting one of these positions and challenging the other.

to AUDIENCE

Amble suggests a relaxed aimlessness, whereas *saunter* suggests a jaunty self-confidence. *Stride* and *march* both suggest purposefulness, but *march,* with its military associations, also carries a hint of aggressiveness.

A word's connotations can vary from reader to reader. To some people, for example, the word *wilderness* evokes a place of great danger; to others, a place of excitement; and to still others, a treasure to be preserved.

> *More about*
> Objectivity, 117–18

33b Choosing Compelling Words and Figures

Some words are general, some specific, and others fall between:

← more general	————————	more specific →
consume	eat	devour
fruit	apple	Granny Smith
mountain	California peak	Mt. Whitney

In addition, some words are concrete, designating things or qualities that can be seen, heard, felt, smelled, or touched; others are abstract, designating concepts like *justice, capitalism,* or *democracy.*

1. Compelling words

Bring your writing to life by combining general and abstract language with the specific and concrete. Use general and abstract language to frame broad issues, and specific, concrete language to capture readers' attention and help them see things through your eyes. Using general language without specifics leaves readers to fill in the blanks on their own, and using specific language without the general and abstract leaves readers wondering what the point is.

The first of the two following descriptions of the Badwater ultramarathon lacks specific language that can tell us how long the race is, why it is challenging, or exactly where it takes place. The second fills in those details with concrete words—like "hottest spot in America," "stinking water hole," "135 miles," "Death Valley," "piney oasis," "8,300 feet up the side of Mt. Whitney," and "asphalt and road gravel." With these specifics, the writer David Ferrell evokes the challenges of the race without recourse to the abstract word "challenging."

GENERAL AND ABSTRACT	Badwater is a long, physically challenging race over a partially paved course that begins in a geological depression and ends partway up a mountain.
CONCRETE AND SPECIFIC	Badwater is a madman's march, a footrace through the summer heat of the hottest spot in America. It extends 135 miles from a stinking water hole on the floor of Death Valley to a piney oasis 8,300 feet up the side of Mt. Whitney. The course is nothing but asphalt and road gravel. Feet and knees and shins ache like they are being whacked with tire irons. Faces turn into shrink-wrap.

—David Ferrell, "Far Beyond a Mere Marathon"

2. Figures of speech

In the example above, notice how Ferrell, in addition to providing concrete specifics, also uses striking comparisons and juxtapositions to paint a vivid picture of the rigors of the race and to suggest the mind-set required to compete in it. He calls the race "a madman's march," for example, and conjures up a beating with a tire iron and an image of a shrink-wrapped face to convey the physical punishment contestants endure. These are examples of *figurative language,* or *figures of speech,* the imaginative use of language to convey meaning in ways that reach beyond the literal meaning of the words involved.

Among the most common figures of speech are similes and metaphors. A *simile* is an explicit comparison between two unlike things, usually expressed with *like* or *as:* "Feet and knees and shins ache like they are being whacked with tire irons." A *metaphor* is an implied comparison between two unlike things stated without *like, as,* or other comparative expressions: "Faces turn into shrink-wrap." (A list of common figures of speech appears in the Quick Reference box on the next page.)

3. Inappropriate figures of speech and mixed metaphors

Used well, figures of speech can spice up your writing. Used in the wrong context, they can be jarring, even silly.

▶ The new high-speed train, like a champion ~~pole vaulter,~~ made it from
                                                        thoroughbred,
Boston to Washington in record time.

Mixed metaphors—which combine multiple, conflicting images for the same concept—confuse readers.

Quick

Reference | Figures of Speech

Figure and Definition	Examples
simile: An explicit comparison between two unlike things, usually expressed with *like* or *as*	Feet and knees and shins ache like they are being whacked with tire irons. —*David Ferrell* Only final exams, like the last lap of a long race, lay between the members of the senior class and their diplomas.
metaphor: An implied comparison between unlike things stated without *like, as,* or other comparative expressions	Faces turn into shrink-wrap. —*David Ferrell* After crossing the finish line of their last exams, seniors looked forward to that moment on the victory stand when the president of the college would bestow a diploma on them.
analogy: An extended simile or metaphor, often comparing something familiar to something unfamiliar (well-constructed analogies can be particularly effective for explaining difficult concepts)	What that means [that the universe is expanding] is that we're not at the center of the universe, after all; instead, we're like a single raisin in a vast lump of dough that is rising in an oven where all the other raisins are moving away from each other, faster and faster as the oven gets hotter and hotter. —*David Perlman, "At 12 Billion Years Old, Universe Still Growing Fast"*
personification: The attribution of human qualities to nonhuman creatures, objects, ideas, or phenomena	The plague that rampaged through Europe in the fourteenth century selected its victims indiscriminately, murdering rich and poor in equal proportion.
hyperbole: Deliberate exaggeration for emphasis	That little restaurant on Main Street makes the best pizza on the planet.
understatement: The deliberate use of less forceful language than a subject warrants	The report of my death was an exaggeration. —*Mark Twain, clearly alive and well, responding to an obituary about him in a London paper*
irony: The use of language to suggest the opposite of its literal meaning or to express an incongruity between what is expected and what occurs	I come to bury Caesar, not to praise him. —*Mark Antony, in Shakespeare's play* Julius Caesar, *in a speech that praises the murdered leader effusively*

MIXED METAPHOR   Confronted with the tsunami of data available on the Internet, researchers, like travelers caught in a blinding desert sandstorm, may have trouble finding the nuggets of valuable information buried in a mountain of otherwise worthless ore.

This sentence confusingly invokes tsunamis, sandstorms, mountains, and mining. The revision (on the next page) works with a single metaphor that compares finding useful information online to mining for precious minerals.

REVISED   As they mine the mountain of data available on the Internet, researchers may have trouble identifying the nuggets of valuable information buried with the otherwise worthless ore they dig up.

33c Mastering Idioms

Idioms are expressions whose meaning does not depend on the meanings of the words that compose them. Each idiom is a unified package of meaning with its own denotations and connotations. The following sentence, for example, would make no sense if you tried to interpret it based on the literal meaning of the words *call, on,* and *carpet:*

▶ The directors called the CEO on the carpet for the company's poor sales in 2012.

Of course, the expression *call on the carpet* has nothing to do with calls or carpets. It is an idiom that, understood as a whole, means *to reprimand* or *scold.*

> **More about**
> Specialized dictionaries, 103–04, 308–11

Most dictionaries list idiomatic uses of particular words. The entry for *call* in the *Merriam-Webster Online Dictionary,* for example, provides definitions for the idioms *call for, call forth, call into question, call it a day,* and *call it quits,* among others. For more detailed information on the history and meaning of particular idioms, consult a specialized dictionary such as the *American Heritage Dictionary of Idioms.*

Idioms, Prepositions, and Phrasal Verbs Non-native speakers of English have to learn idioms just as they must learn an unfamiliar word. If you are an English language learner, pay particular attention to the way prepositions combine with other words in idiomatic ways. A **phrasal verb,** for example, is a combination of a verb with one or more prepositions that has a different meaning than the verb alone.

> **More about**
> Prepositions, 324, 416–20
> Phrasal verbs, 361, 406–07

Raisa *saw* the flat tire on her car. [She looked at it.]

Raisa *saw to* the flat tire on her car. [She had it repaired.]

33d Avoiding Clichés

A *cliché* is a figure of speech, idiom, or other expression that has grown stale from overuse (see the Quick Reference box on the next page for some examples). Clichés come quickly to mind because they encapsulate common wisdom in widely recognized phrases. For the same reason, they provide an easy substitute for fresh expression. They may help you frame a subject in the early drafts of a project, but they can also make your writing sound trite and unimaginative. As the following example indicates, writing that is loaded with clichés is often also loaded with mixed metaphors.

CLICHÉ LADEN	As the campaign pulled into the home stretch and the cold, hard fact of the increasingly nip-and-tuck polls sank in, the candidates threw their promises to stay on their best behavior to the wind and wallowed in the mire of down-and-dirty attack ads.
REVISED	As Election Day neared and the polls showed the race tightening, the candidates abandoned their promises of civility and released a barrage of unscrupulous attack ads.

 What Is the Difference between an Idiom and a Cliché? The only thing that separates an idiom from a cliché is the frequency with which it is used. If you are a native English speaker, be alert to idioms that appear often in popular sources and in conversation, and try to avoid those in academic and professional writing. If you are not a native English speaker, you may not recognize an idiom as a cliché if you have not encountered it often in your reading. If you have questions about clichés and idioms, ask your instructor or consult a dictionary of idioms, such as *McGraw-Hill's Dictionary of American Idioms and Phrasal Verbs* or the *Longman American Idioms Dictionary*.

Quick **Reference**   **Dodging Deadly Clichés**

When you encounter clichés like these in your writing, delete them or replace them with fresher images of your own.

best thing since sliced bread	hit the nail on the head	smart as a whip
beyond a shadow of a doubt	a hundred and one percent	straight and narrow
cold, hard fact	in the prime of life	think outside the box
cool as a cucumber	just desserts	throw [something] to the wind
down and dirty	nip and tuck	tried and true
down the home stretch	no way, shape, or form	wallow in the mire
easier said than done	on their best behavior	without a moment's hesitation
face the music	one foot out the door	zero tolerance
faster than greased lightning	plain as the nose on your face	
green with envy	slow as molasses	

34 Using the Dictionary and Thesaurus

Samuel Johnson's *Dictionary of the English Language* (1755) established many of the conventions still found in dictionaries today. Johnson identified a core vocabulary of some 43,500 words, labeled each word's part of speech, briefly traced its origins, provided a concise, elegant (and sometimes humorous) definition of the word in all its senses, and accompanied each definition with an illustrative quotation. Johnson hoped to define and fix a standard of proper spelling and usage, but his dictionary, like those that have followed it, also reflects the state of the language in the time and place in which it was created.

34a Choosing a General-Purpose or a Specialized Dictionary

Dictionaries today come in a variety of forms, both printed and electronic, large and small, general purpose and specialized. Abridged dictionaries, sometimes referred to as "desk dictionaries," contain information on approximately 200,000 words. Examples include the following:

> *American Heritage College Dictionary* (available online at Yahoo! Education)
>
> *Merriam-Webster's Collegiate Dictionary* (available online as the *Merriam-Webster Online Dictionary*)
>
> *Random House Webster's College Dictionary*

Most word processing programs also include a built-in dictionary with many features of an abridged dictionary.

Unabridged dictionaries contain detailed entries for most English words, some half a million in total. The most comprehensive unabridged dictionary is the twenty-volume *Oxford English Dictionary* (known as the *OED*). Others

More about
Denotation and connotation,
17–18, 302–03

Writing Responsibly / Choosing Accurate Synonyms

When you consult a thesaurus, be sure to check both the meanings (*denotations*) and the associations (*connotations*) of the words you find there. A carelessly chosen synonym can distort the information you intend to convey. Suppose, for example, that you wanted to replace *intimidate* in the sentence "The professor's brilliance intimidated her students." Looking in a thesaurus, you might find both *overawe* and *bludgeon* listed as synonyms. *Overawe* is an appropriate substitute, probably more precisely reflecting the effect of the professor on her students than *intimidate*. *Bludgeon*, in contrast, inappropriately conjures visions of a bloody crime scene.

to TOPIC

include *Random House Webster's Unabridged Dictionary* and *Webster's Third New International Dictionary, Unabridged.*

Both the *OED* and *Webster's Third New International* are available online for a fee. You should be able to find an unabridged dictionary in the reference section of any library, however, and many libraries provide free access to online versions.

 Dictionaries for Second-Language Learners In addition to translation dictionaries and standard abridged and unabridged dictionaries, you may also want to consult an all-English dictionary tailored for the second-language learner, such as *Heinle's Newbury House Dictionary of American English,* the *Longman Dictionary of American English,* or the *Oxford Dictionary of American English.* To understand American slang and idioms, consult a dictionary such as *McGraw-Hill's Dictionary of American Slang and Colloquial Expressions.* Since slang and idioms change rapidly, you should also consult native-speaking and/or American peers.

Specialized dictionaries focus on a particular aspect of English vocabulary.

- Dictionaries of usage provide guidance about the use of particular words or phrases. Examples include the *American Heritage Book of English Usage* (available online at Bartleby.com) and *Right, Wrong, and Risky: A Dictionary of Today's American English Usage.* The *New Fowler's Modern English Usage* provides guidance on British and American usage.

- Subject-specific dictionaries explain the specialized terminology of particular fields and professions. Examples include the *Dictionary of Anthropology, Black's Law Dictionary,* and *A Dictionary of Business and Management.* For links to subject-specific dictionaries and glossaries available online, try Glossarist and YourDictionary.com.

> *More about*
> Finding subject-
>   specific diction-
>   aries, 103–04

34b Consulting a Thesaurus

Thesauruses and synonym dictionaries provide lists of words that are equivalent to or that overlap in meaning with one another (**synonyms**), as well as words that have contrasting meanings (**antonyms**). They can help you find just the right word for a particular context or an alternative to a word you have overused. Examples include *Merriam-Webster's Dictionary of Synonyms* and the *New American Roget's College Thesaurus.* Note also that most word processing programs have a built-in thesaurus.

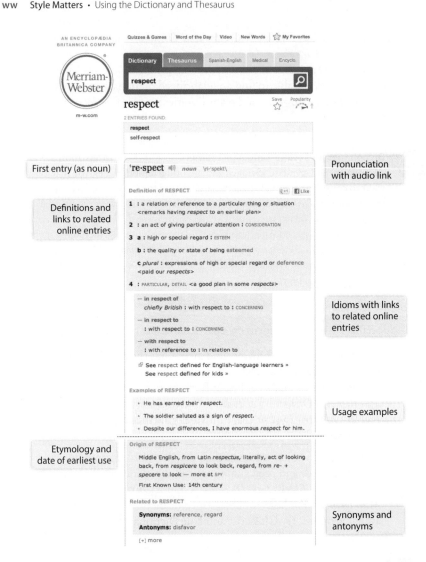

First entry (as noun)

Pronunciation with audio link

Definitions and links to related online entries

Idioms with links to related online entries

Usage examples

Etymology and date of earliest use

Synonyms and antonyms

FIGURE 34.1 The entry for *respect* in the *Merriam-Webster Online Dictionary*

34c Learning to Read a Dictionary Entry

Figure 34.1 shows the entry for the word *respect* in the *Merriam-Webster Online Dictionary,* the online counterpart to the eleventh edition of *Merriam-Webster's Collegiate Dictionary.* Although most online and printed abridged dictionaries present the same kinds of information, each has its own format and system of abbreviations.

More about
Hyphenation,
468–70

Spelling, word division, and pronunciation The main entry begins with the word correctly spelled, followed by acceptable variant spellings, if any. Dots show the division of the word into syllables, indicating where to put a hyphen if you must break the word between lines of text. Next, the pronunciation of the word is given. The print version has a key to pronunciation symbols; the online version has a link to this key, but it also gives the pronunciation in an audio link.

Grammatical functions and forms Labels indicate the part of speech and other grammatical aspects of a word. Most dictionaries specify the forms of irregular verbs (*draw, drew, drawn*) but not of regular verbs like *respect,* and they provide irregular plurals (*woman, women*) but not regular plurals (*dogs*).

More about
Regular and irregular verbs, 346–47, 358–59
Regular and irregular plurals, 467–68

Definitions and examples If a word has more than one definition, each is numbered, and any additional distinctions within a definition are labeled with a letter. Several definitions in the entry for *respect* as a noun include examples of the word used in context. The entry shown in Figure 34.1 includes a definition of the plural form *respects* because it has a usage that does not apply to the singular form. At the end of the entry are the definitions of several idiomatic expressions that include *respect.*

More about
Idiomatic expressions, 306

Synonyms and usage Most dictionaries list synonyms for the entry word; in online dictionaries, clicking on a synonym takes you to the full entry for that word. Usage labels offer guidance on how to use the word appropriately.

More about
Usage, 311–18

35 Glossary of Usage

This usage glossary includes words that writers often confuse (*infer, imply*) or misuse (*disinterested, uninterested*) and expressions that are nonstandard and sometimes even pretentious. Strive to avoid words and expressions that will confuse or distract your readers or that will undermine their confidence in you. Of course, not all words and expressions that cause writers problems are listed here; if a word or expression with which you have trouble is *not* included, check the index, review chapters 32 and 33 ("Choosing Appropriate Language" and "Choosing Effective Words"), consult the usage notes in a dictionary, or check another usage guide, such as *Fowler's Modern English Usage,* the *New York Times Manual of Style and Usage, 100 Words Almost Everyone Confuses and Misuses,* or the *American Heritage Book of English Usage.*

a, an *A* and *an* are indefinite articles. Use *a* before a word that begins with a consonant sound: *a car, a hill, a one-way street.* Use *an* before a word that begins with a vowel sound: *an appointment, an hour, an X-ray.*

accept, except *Accept* is a verb meaning "agree to receive": *I accept the nomination. Except* is a preposition that means "but": *Everyone voted for me except Paul.*

adapt, adopt *Adapt* means "to adjust": *Instead of migrating, the park's ducks adapt to the changing climate. Adopt* means "to take as one's own": *I adopted a cat from the shelter.*

adverse, averse *Adverse* means "unfavorble" or "hostile"; *averse* means "opposed": *She was averse to buying a ticket to a play that had received such adverse criticism.*

advice, advise The noun *advice* means "guidance"; the verb *advise* means "to suggest": *I advised her to get some sleep. She took my advice and went to bed early.*

affect, effect As a verb, *affect* means "to influence" or "to cause a change": *Study habits affect one's grades.* As a noun, *affect* means "feeling or emotion": *The defendant responded without affect to the guilty verdict.* As a noun, *effect* means "result": *The decreased financial aid budget is an effect of the recession.* As a verb, *effect* means "to bring about or accomplish": *Submitting the petition effected a change in the school's policy.*

aggravate, irritate *Aggravate* means "to intensify" or "worsen": *Dancing until dawn aggravated Giorgio's bad back.* *Irritate* means "to annoy": *He was irritated that his chiropractor could not see him until Tuesday.* Colloquially, *aggravate* is often used to mean *annoy,* but this colloquial usage is inappropriate in formal contexts.

agree to, agree with *Agree to* means "to consent to": *Chris agreed to host the party.* *Agree with* means "to be in accord with": *Anne agreed with Chris that a party was just what everyone needed.*

ain't *Ain't* is a nonstandard contraction for *am not, are not,* or *is not* and should not be used in formal writing.

all ready, already *All ready* means "completely prepared"; *already* means "previously": *They were all ready to catch the bus, but it had already left.*

all right, alright *All right* is the standard spelling; *alright* is nonstandard.

all together, altogether *All together* means "as a group": *When Noah's family gathered for his graduation, it was the first time they had been all together in years.* *Altogether* means "completely": *Noah was altogether overwhelmed by the attention.*

allude, elude, refer to *Allude* means "to refer to indirectly"; *elude* means "to avoid" or "to escape": *He eluded further questioning by alluding to his troubled past.* Do not use *allude* to mean "refer directly"; use *refer to* instead: *The speaker referred to [not alluded to] slide six of her PowerPoint presentation.*

allusion, illusion An *allusion* is an indirect reference: *I almost missed the author's allusion to* Macbeth. An *illusion* is a false appearance or belief: *The many literary quotations he drops into his speeches give the illusion that he is well read.*

almost, most *Almost* means "nearly"; *most* means "the majority of": *My roommate will tell me almost anything, but I talk to my sister about most of my own problems.*

a lot, alot *Alot* is nonstandard; always spell *a lot* as two words.

among, amongst *Amongst* is a British alternative to *among;* in American English, *among* is preferred.

among, between Use *among* with three or more nouns or with words that stand for a group composed of three or more members; use *between* with two or more nouns: *I'm double majoring because I could not decide between biology and English. Italian, art history, and calculus are among my other favorites.*

amoral, immoral *Amoral* means "neither moral nor immoral" or "indifferent to moral standards"; *immoral* means "violating moral standards": *While secularists believe that nature is amoral, religionists often view natural disasters as punishments for immoral behavior.*

amount, number Use *amount* with items that cannot be counted (noncount or mass nouns); use *number* with items that can be counted (count nouns): *The dining hall prepares the right amount of food based on the number of people who eat there.*

an See *a, an.*

and/or *And/or* is shorthand for "one or the other or both." It is acceptable in technical and business writing, but it should be avoided in most academic writing.

ante-, anti- The prefix *ante-* means "before," as in *antebellum,* or "before the war"; the prefix *anti-* means "against," as in *antibiotic* ("against bacteria").

anxious, eager *Anxious* means "uneasy": *Dan was anxious about writing his first twenty-page paper.* *Eager* indicates strong interest or enthusiasm: *He was eager to finish his first draft before spring break.*

anybody, any body; anyone, any one *Anybody* and *anyone* are singular indefinite pronouns: *Does anybody [or anyone] have an extra pen? Any body* and *any one* are a noun and pronoun (respectively) modified by the adjective *any: She was not fired for making any one mistake but, rather, for making many mistakes over a number of years.*

anymore, any more *Anymore* means "from now on": *She does not write letters anymore. Any more* means "additional": *I do not need any more stamps.* Both are used only in negative contexts, for example, with *not* or other negative terms such as *hardly* or *scarcely.*

anyplace   *Anyplace* is an informal way of saying *anywhere*. *Anywhere* is preferable in formal writing.

anyways, anywheres   *Anyways* and *anywheres* are nonstandard; use *anyway* and *anywhere* instead.

as   *As* should not be used in place of *because, since,* or *when* if ambiguity will result: *As people were lining up to use the elliptical machine, the management posted a waiting list.* Does this sentence mean that management posted the sign *while* people were lining up, or does it mean that management posted the sign *because* there was such demand for the machine?

as, as if, like   Use *as,* or *as if,* not *like,* as a conjunction in formal writing: *The president spoke as if* [not *like*] *he were possessed by the spirit of Martin Luther King, Jr. Like* is acceptable, however, as a preposition that introduces a comparison: *The president spoke like a true leader.*

at   *At* is not necessary to complete *where* questions: *Where is Waldo?* not *Where is Waldo at?*

averse, adverse   See *adverse, averse.*

awful, awfully   In formal writing, use *awful* and *awfully* to suggest the emotion of fear or wonder, not as a synonym for *bad* or to mean *very. The high priest gave forth an awful cry before casting the captive from the top of the pyramid toward the crowd below.*

awhile, a while   *Awhile* is an adverb: *They talked awhile before going to dinner. A while* is an article and a noun, and should always follow a preposition: *Rest for a while between eating and exercising.*

bad, badly   In formal writing, use the adjective *bad* to modify nouns and pronouns and after linking verbs (as a subject complement): *Because I had a bad day, my husband feels bad.* Use the adverb *badly* to modify verbs, adjectives, and adverbs: *Todd's day went badly from start to finish.*

being as, being that   *Being as* and *being that* are nonstandard substitutes for *because: Because* [not *being as*] *Marcus did well as a teaching assistant, he was asked to teach a class of his own the next year.* Avoid them.

beside, besides   *Beside* is a preposition that means "next to" or "along side of": *You will always find my glasses beside the bed. Besides* is an adverb meaning "furthermore" or a preposition meaning "in addition to": *Besides, it will soon be finals. Besides chemistry, I have exams in art history and statistics.*

between, among   See *among, between.*

bring, take   Use *bring* when something is coming toward the speaker and *take* when it is moving away: *When the waiter brought our entrees, he took our bread.*

burst, bursted; bust, busted   *Burst* is a verb meaning "to break apart violently"; the past tense of *burst* is also *burst,* not *bursted. Bust* is slang for *to burst* or *to break* and should be avoided in formal writing: *The boiler burst* [not *bursted* or *busted*] *in a deadly explosion.*

can, may   Use *can* when discussing ability: *I know she can quit smoking.* Use *may* when discussing permission: *The server told her that she may not smoke anywhere in the restaurant.*

capital, capitol   *Capital,* a noun, can mean "funds," or it can mean "the city that is the seat of government": *The student council did not have enough capital to travel to Harrisburg, Pennsylvania's capital.* The word *capitol* means "the building where lawmakers meet": *The state's capitol is adorned with a golden dome.* When capitalized, *Capitol* refers to the building in Washington, DC, where the US Congress meets.

censor, censure   *Censor* means both "to delete objectionable material" (a verb) and "one who deletes objectionable material" (a noun): *The bedroom scenes, but not the battle scenes, were heavily censored. Clearly, the censors object more to sex than to violence. Censure* means both "to reprimand officially" (verb) and "an official reprimand" (noun): *The ethics committee censured the governor for lying under oath. Members of his party were relieved that a censure was all he suffered.*

cite, sight, site   *Cite,* a verb, means "to quote" or "mention": *Cite your sources following MLA format. Sight,* a noun, means "view" or "scene": *The sight of a field of daffodils makes me think of Wordsworth. Site,* a noun, means "location" or "place" (even online): *That site has the best recipes on the Internet.*

climactic, climatic   *Climactic* is an adjective derived from the noun *climax* and means "culminating" or "most intense"; *climatic* is an adjective derived from the noun *climate: The climactic moment of a thunderstorm occurs when the center of the storm is overhead. Tornados are violent climatic phenomena associated with thunderstorms.*

complement, compliment   *Complement* is a noun meaning "that which completes or perfects something else"; it can also be used as a verb meaning "the process of completing or making perfect." *Compliment* means either "a flattering comment" or "the act of paying a compliment": *My* husband *complements* me and makes me whole; still, it annoys me that he rarely *compliments* me on my appearance.

conscience, conscious   *Conscience* is a noun meaning "sense of right and wrong": *Skipping class weighed heavily on Sunil's conscience. Conscious* is an adjective that means "aware" or "awake": *Maria made a conscious decision to skip class.*

continual(ly), continuous(ly)   *Continual* means "repeated frequently": *The continual request for contributions undermined her resolve to be more charitable. Continuous* means "uninterrupted": *The continuous stream of bad news forced her to shut off the television.*

could care less   *Could care less* is an illogical, and nonstandard, substitute for *could not care less:* If one *could* care less, then one must care, at least a little, and yet this is not the intended meaning.

could of, must of, should of, would of   These are misspellings of *could have, must have, should have,* and *would have.*

criteria, criterion   *Criteria* is the plural form of the noun *criterion,* Latin for "standard": *His criteria for grading may be vague, but I know I fulfilled at least one criterion by submitting my paper on time.*

data, media, phenomena   *Data, media,* and *phenomena* are plural nouns (*datum, medium,* and *phenomenon* are their singular forms): *The data suggest that the economy will rebound by the time you graduate. The news media raise the alarm about public corruption, but it is the voters who must take action. The aurora borealis is one of many amazing natural phenomena.* (*Data* is increasingly used as a singular noun, but continuing to use it as a plural is never wrong.)

differ from, differ with   *Differ from* means "to lack similarity": *Renaissance art differs greatly from art of the Middle Ages. Differ with* means "to disagree": *Martin Luther's forty-nine articles spelled out the ways in which he differed with the Catholic Church.*

discreet, discrete   *Discreet,* an adjective, means "tactful" or "judicious": *Please be discreet—don't announce that you saw Ada crying in the bathroom. Discrete* means "distinct" or "separate": *The study revealed two discrete groups, those who can keep a secret and those who cannot.*

disinterested, uninterested   *Disinterested* means "impartial": *A judge who cannot be disinterested should recuse him- or herself from the case. Uninterested* means "indifferent": *The book seems well written, but I am uninterested in the topic.*

don't, doesn't   *Don't* is a contraction of *do not;* it is used with *I, you, we, they,* and plural nouns: *I don't want to drive, but the trains don't run very often. Doesn't* is a contraction of *does not;* it is used with *he, she, it,* and singular nouns: *It doesn't matter whether you're a little late; Fred doesn't mind waiting.*

each and every   *Each and every* is a wordy substitute for *each* or *every;* use one or the other but not both.

eager, anxious   See *anxious, eager.*

effect, affect   See *affect, effect.*

e.g., i.e.   *E.g.* is an abbreviation of a Latin phrase meaning "for example" or "for instance"; *i.e.* is an abbreviation of a Latin phrase meaning "that is." In formal writing, use the English equivalents rather than the Latin abbreviations; the Latin abbreviations are acceptable in tables, footnotes, and other places where space is at a premium.

elicit, illicit   *Elicit,* a verb, means "to draw out": *Every week,* American Idol *contestants try to elicit enough support to avoid elimination. Illicit,* an adjective, means "illegal" or "impermissible": *In 2003,* American Idol *contestant Frenchie Davis was disqualified for posing in illicit photos.*

elude, allude, refer to   See *allude, elude, refer to.*

emigrate from, immigrate to   *Emigrate from* means "to leave one's country and settle in another": *Jake's grandmother emigrated from Poland in 1919. Immigrate to* means "to move to and settle in a new country": *Jake's grandmother immigrated to the United States in 1919.*

eminent, imminent, immanent   *Eminent* means "renowned": *The university hosts lectures by many eminent scientists. Imminent* means "about to happen" or "looming": *By January 2008, many felt that a recession was imminent. Immanent* means "inherent" or "pervasive throughout the world": *Many religions teach that God's presence is immanent.*

enthused   *Enthused* is a colloquial adjective meaning "enthusiastic." In formal writing, use *enthusiastic: Because of the team's excellent record, Eric was enthusiastic [not enthused] about joining.*

etc.   *Etc.* is an abbreviation of the Latin phrase *et cetera,* meaning "and others." Because *et* means "and," adding the word *and* before *etc.* is redundant. In a series, include a comma before *etc.*: *A great deal of online media are used in classes today: blogs, wikis, Blackboard, Facebook, etc.* In most formal writing, concluding with a final example or *and so on* (the English equivalent of *etc.*) is preferable.

everybody, everyone; every body, every one   *Everybody* and *everyone* are interchangeable singular indefinite pronouns: *Everybody [or everyone] who went to the concert got a free T-shirt. Every body* and *every one* are a noun and a pronoun (respectively) modified by the adjective *every: Coroners must treat every body they examine with respect.*

except, accept   See *accept, except.*

expect, suppose   *Expect* means "to anticipate": *I expect to be home when she arrives. Suppose* means "to presume": *I suppose she should have a key just in case.*

explicit, implicit   *Explicit,* an adjective, means "overt" or "stated outright": *The rules are explicit: "No running." Implicit* is an adjective that means "implied": *Implicit in the rules is a prohibition against skipping.*

farther, further   Use *farther* with distances: *I'd like to drive a hundred miles farther before we pull over for dinner.* Use *further* to mean "more" or "in addition": *I have nothing further to add.*

fewer, less   Use *fewer* with items that can be counted (count nouns). Use *less* with items that cannot be counted (noncount or mass nouns): *This semester, I am taking three fewer classes than I took in the fall, but because I have a job now, I have less time to study.*

first, firstly   *Firstly* is used in Britain, but it sounds overly formal in the United States. *First* (and *second* and *third*) is the standard form in the United States.

flaunt, flout   *Flaunt* means "to parade" or "show off"; *Ivan flaunted his muscular torso on the quad. Flout* means "to disobey" or "ignore": *He flouted school policy by parading about without his shirt on.*

further, farther   See *farther, further.*

get   Many colloquial expressions with *get* should not be used in formal writing. Avoid expressions such as *get with the program, get your act together, get lost,* and so on.

good, well   *Good* is an adjective; *well* is an adverb: *Playing well in the tournament made Lee feel good.* In references to health, however, *well* is an adjective: *She had a cold, but now she is well and back at work.*

hanged, hung   Use the past-tense verb *hanged* only to describe a person executed by hanging. Use the past-tense verb *hung* to describe anything else (pictures, clothing) that can be suspended.

hardly   Use *can hardly* instead of *can't hardly,* a double negative: *I can hardly keep my eyes open.*

he, she; he/she; s/he   Historically, the pronoun *he* was used generically to mean *he or she;* in informal contexts, writers avoid bias by writing *he/she* or *s/he.* In formal writing, however, revise your sentence to avoid a gendered pronoun: *Sensible students are careful what they post about themselves on social networking sites [not The sensible student is careful what he posts about himself on social networking sites].*

hisself   *Hisself* is a nonstandard substitute for *himself.* Avoid it.

i.e., e.g.   See *e.g., i.e.*

if, whether   Use *whether,* not *if,* when alternatives are offered: *If I must go out, I insist that we go to a decent restaurant. I do not care whether we eat Chinese food or Italian, but I refuse to eat at Joe's.*

illicit, elicit   See *elicit, illicit.*

illusion, allusion   See *allusion, illusion.*

immigrate to, emigrate from   See *emigrate from, immigrate to.*

imminent, eminent, immanent   See *eminent, imminent, immanent.*

immoral, amoral   See *amoral, immoral.*

implicit, explicit   See *explicit, implicit.*

imply, infer   *Imply* means "to suggest indirectly": *The circles under Phillip's eyes implied that he had not slept much. Infer* means "to conclude": *From the way he devoured his dinner, I inferred that Raymond was famished.*

incredible, incredulous   *Incredible* means "unbelievable": *Debbie told an incredible story about meeting the Dalai Lama. Incredulous* means "unbelieving": *I am incredulous of everything that the tabloids print.*

infer, imply   See *imply, infer*.

in regards to   *In regards to* is nonstandard. Use *in regard to, as regards,* or *regarding* instead.

irregardless   *Irregardless* is nonstandard; use *regardless* instead.

irritate, aggravate   See *aggravate, irritate*.

is when, is where   Avoid these phrases in definitions: *An oligarchy is a system of government in which the many are ruled by a few,* or *Oligarchy is government of the many by the few [*not *An oligarchy is when the many are ruled by a few].*

it's, its   *It's* is a contraction of "it is" or "it has," and *its* is a possessive pronoun: *It's been a long time since the ailing pigeon flapped its wings in flight.* One trick for distinguishing the two is to recall that contractions such as *it's* are often avoided in formal writing, while possessive pronouns like *its* are perfectly acceptable.

kind, kinds   *Kind* is a singular noun: *This kind of weather is bad for asthmatics. Kinds* (a plural noun) is used only to denote more than one kind: *Many kinds of pollen can adversely affect breathing.*

kind of, sort of   *Kind of* and *sort of* are colloquial; in formal writing, use "somewhat" or "a little" instead: *Julia was somewhat [*not *kind of] pleased to be going back to school.* Use *kind of* and *sort of* in formal writing only to mean "type of": *E.E. Cummings's poetry creates a new kind of grammar.*

lay, lie   *Lay* means "to place"; it requires a direct object. Its main forms are *lay, laid,* and *laid: She laid her paper on the professor's desk. Lie* means "to recline"; it does not take a direct object. Its main forms are *lie, lay,* and *lain: She fell asleep as soon as she lay down.*

leave, let   *Leave* means "to go away"; *let* means "to allow." *If I leave early, will you let me know what happens?*

less, fewer   See *fewer, less*.

like, as, as if   See *as, as if, like*.

loose, lose   The adjective *loose* means "baggy" or "not securely attached": *I have to be careful with my glasses because one of the screws is loose.* The verb *lose* means "to misplace": *I am afraid I will lose the screw and have to attach the earpiece with duct tape.*

lots, lots of   *Lots* and *lots of* are colloquial and should be avoided in academic writing; use terms like *much, many,* and *very* instead.

may, can   See *can, may*.

maybe, may be   The adverb *maybe* means "possibly" or "perhaps"; the verb phrase *may be* means "have the possibility to be": *Maybe I'll apply for an internship next semester, but if I wait too long, all of the positions may be filled.*

may of, might of   *May of* and *might of* are misspellings of *may have* and *might have*.

media   See *data, media, phenomena*.

moral, morale   *Moral* means "ethical lesson": *Aesop's fables each have a moral, such as "don't judge others by their appearance." Morale* means "attitude" or "spirits": *April's warm weather significantly raised student morale.*

most, almost   See *almost, most*.

must of   See *could of, must of, should of, would of*.

myself, himself, herself, etc.   Use pronouns that end with *-self* to refer to or intensify other words: *Obama himself made an appearance.* Do not use them when you are unsure whether to use a pronoun in the nominative case (*I, she, he, we, they*) or the objective case (*me, her, him, us, them*): *This conversation is between him and me [*not *himself and myself].*

nohow, nowheres   *Nohow* and *nowheres* are nonstandard forms of *anyway, in any way, in any place, no place,* and *nowhere.* Avoid them.

number, amount   See *amount, number*.

off of   Omit *of: Sarah took the pin off [*not *off of] her coat.*

OK, O.K., okay   These are all acceptable spellings, but the term is inappropriate in formal writing. Choose a more specific word instead: *Food served in the dining hall is mediocre [*not *okay].*

phenomena   See *data, media, phenomena*.

plus   Avoid using *plus* as a substitute for the coordinating conjunction *and* or the transition *moreover*.

precede, proceed   *Precede* means "come before"; *proceed* means "continue": *Despite warnings from those who preceded me, I proceeded to take six classes in one semester.*

principal, principle   *Principal,* a noun, refers to the leader of an organization. *Principal,* used as an adjective, means "main." *Principle,* used as a noun, means "belief" or "standard": *The school principal's principal concern is the well-being of her students. She runs the school on the principle that fairness is essential.*

proceed, precede   See *precede, proceed.*

raise, rise   The verb *raise* means "lift up" or "move up" and takes a direct object: *Joseph raised the blinds.* The verb *rise* means "to go upward" and does not take a direct object: *We could see the steam rise as the solution started to boil.*

real, really   Do not use *real* or *really* as a synonym for *very: Spring break went very [not real or really] fast.*

reason is because, reason why   To avoid redundancy and faulty predication, choose either *the reason is that* or *because: The reason Chris fell is that he is uncoordinated. It is not because his shoe was untied.*

refer to, allude, elude   See *allude, elude, refer to.*

relation, relationship   Use *relation* to refer to a connection between things: *There is a relation between the amount one sleeps and one's overall health.* Use *relationship* to refer to a connection between people: *Tony has always had a close relationship with his grandfather.*

respectfully, respectively   *Respectfully* means "with respect": *Ben treats his parents respectfully.* *Respectively* means "in the given order": *My mother and father are 54 and 56, respectively.*

rise, raise   See *raise, rise.*

set, sit   The verb *set* means "to place" or "to establish," and it takes a direct object. *The professor set the book on the desk.* The verb *sit* means "to assume a sitting position," and it does not take a direct object: *You can sit in the waiting room until the doctor is ready.*

shall, will   In the past, *shall* was used as a helping verb with *I* and *we,* and *will* was used with *he, she, it,* and *they: I shall go on dancing,* and *they will go home.* Now *will* is generally used with all persons: *I will go on singing, and they will all cover their ears. Shall* is used mainly with polite questions (*Shall we invite your mother?*) and in rules and regulations (*No person shall enter these premises after dusk.*).

should of   See *could of, must of, should of, would of.*

since   *Since* can mean "because" or "from that time," so use it only when there is no chance that readers will infer the wrong meaning. In the sentence that follows, either meaning makes sense: *Since I moved to the country, I have had no trouble sleeping.* Revise to make your meaning clear: *Since January, when I moved to the country . . .* or *Because I moved to the country, . . .*

sit, set   See *set, sit.*

site, sight, cite   See *cite, sight, site.*

somebody, someone   *Somebody* and *someone* are interchangeable singular indefinite pronouns: *Someone [or somebody] is at the door.*

sometime, sometimes   *Sometime* is an adverb meaning "at an indefinite time"; *sometimes* is an adverb meaning "on occasion," "now and then": *Sometimes I wish my future would come sometime soon.*

somewheres   *Somewheres* is nonstandard; use *somewhere* instead.

stationary, stationery   *Stationary* means "not moving"; *stationery* means "writing paper." (Thinking of the *e* in "stationery" as standing for *envelope* may help.)

supposed to, used to   *Supposed to* means "should"; *used to* means "did regularly in the past." In speech, the final *-d* is often dropped, but in writing, it is required: *I was supposed [not suppose] to practice piano daily; instead, I used [not use] to play hockey.*

sure and, sure to; try and, try to   *Sure to* and *try to* are standard; *sure and* and *try and* are not.

take, bring   See *bring, take.*

than, then   *Than* is a conjunction used in comparisons; *then* is an adverb of time: *If Betsy is already taller than I, then I will be impressed.*

that, which In formal writing, *that* is generally used with essential (or restrictive) clauses and *which* with nonessential (nonrestrictive) clauses: *The project that I am working on now is due on Monday, which is why I really have to finish it this weekend.*

that, who In formal writing, use *who* or *whom*, not *that*, to refer to people: *I. M. Pei is the architect who [*not *that] designed this building.*

their, there, they're *Their* is a possessive pronoun, *there* is an adverb of place, and *they're* is a contraction of "they are": *They're always leaving their dishes in the sink. Why must they leave them there instead of putting them in the dishwasher?*

theirself, theirselves, themself *Theirself, theirselves,* and *themself* are nonstandard. Use *themselves* instead.

them In colloquial speech, the pronoun *them* is sometimes used in place of the demonstrative adjective *those;* avoid this nonstandard usage: *Those [*not *them] are the books I need for class.*

then, than See *than, then.*

this here, these here, that there, them there *This here, these here, that there,* and *them there* are nonstandard for *this, these, that,* and *them.*

to, too, two *To* is a preposition, *too* is an adverb, and *two* is a number: *To send two dozen roses to your girlfriend for Valentine's Day is too expensive.*

try and, try to See *sure and, sure to; try and, try to.*

uninterested, disinterested See *disinterested, uninterested.*

unique *Unique* means "the one and only thing of its kind," so it is illogical to modify it with words like *somewhat* or *very* that suggest degrees: *Your approach to the issue is unique [*not *somewhat unique].*

usage, use The noun *usage,* which means a "customary manner, approach," should not be used in place of the noun *use: The use [*not *usage] of cell phones in this restaurant will not be tolerated.*

use, utilize The verb *utilize,* which means "to use purposefully," should not be used in place of *use: Students must use [*not *utilize] parking lots D, E, and F, not those parking lots reserved for faculty and staff.*

wait for, wait on Although *wait on* is sometimes used colloquially as a substitute for "wait for," it is nonstandard. Use *wait on* to mean "serve" and *wait for* to mean "await": *I am waiting for [*not *waiting on] my mother, who is always late.*

ways *Ways* is sometimes used colloquially as a substitute for "distance." Avoid this usage in formal writing: *We still have quite a distance [*not *ways] to go before we get to a rest area.*

weather, whether *Weather,* a noun, means "the state of the atmosphere"; *whether,* a conjunction, indicates a choice between alternatives: *It does not matter whether you prefer rain or snow; the weather will be what it will be.*

well, good See *good, well.*

whether, if See *if, whether.*

which, that See *that, which.*

who, that See *that, who.*

who, whom Use *who* for the subject of clauses; use *whom* for the object of clauses: *Who will be coming to the party? Whom did you ask to bring the cake?*

who's, whose *Who's* is a contraction of "who is" or "who has"; *whose* is a possessive pronoun: *Who's at the door? Whose coat is this?*

will, shall See *shall, will.*

would of See *could of, must of, should of, would of.*

you *You* (the second-person singular pronoun) should be used only to refer to the reader, not to refer to people in an indefinite sense (to replace *one): In medieval society, subjects [*not *you] had to swear an oath of allegiance to the king.*

your, you're *Your* is a possessive pronoun; *you're* is a contraction of "you are": *You're as stubborn as your brother.*

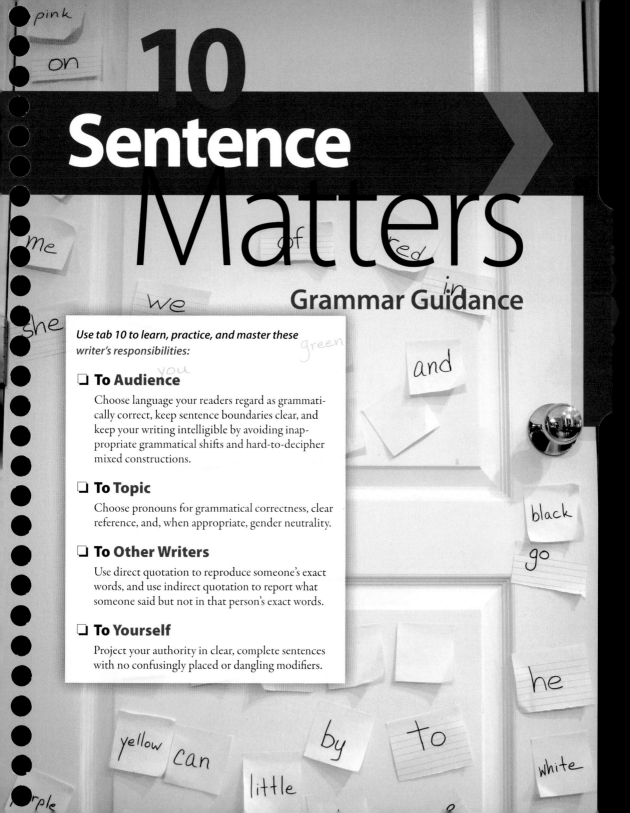

10

Sentence
Matters

Grammar Guidance

Use tab 10 to learn, practice, and master these writer's responsibilities:

❏ **To Audience**

Choose language your readers regard as grammatically correct, keep sentence boundaries clear, and keep your writing intelligible by avoiding inappropriate grammatical shifts and hard-to-decipher mixed constructions.

❏ **To Topic**

Choose pronouns for grammatical correctness, clear reference, and, when appropriate, gender neutrality.

❏ **To Other Writers**

Use direct quotation to reproduce someone's exact words, and use indirect quotation to report what someone said but not in that person's exact words.

❏ **To Yourself**

Project your authority in clear, complete sentences with no confusingly placed or dangling modifiers.

Sentence Matters

Recognizing and Correcting Fused (Run-On) Sentences (341–46)

In a fused (or run-on) sentence, one independent clause incorrectly follows another with no punctuation or joining words between them.

fs   Practices among higher education students are not much ~~better according to~~ research by Donald
            better. According to

L. McCabe, a professor at Rutgers University who has done extensive work on cheating, 38% of

college students admitted to committing forms of plagiarism in the previous year (Rimer 7).

Recognizing and Correcting Comma Splices (341–46)

In a comma splice, two independent clauses are incorrectly joined by a comma alone, without a coordinating conjunction such as and or but.

cs   It is late at night, a student sits staring at a computer.
          and

Using Irregular Verb Forms Correctly (357–62)

Regular verbs form the past tense and past participle by adding -ed to the base form; irregular verbs do not.

vb   A paper is due the following morning, and research needs to be done, notes need to be took,
                     taken,
    and, in the end, an essay needs to be ~~wrote~~ and edited.
                      written

Avoiding Unclear Pronoun Reference (374–76)

Pronoun reference is clear when readers can effortlessly identify a pronoun's antecedent (the word the pronoun replaces).

ref   Undeniably, some ~~of it~~ occurs because students find it easier than simply doing the work required.
        plagiarism   *plagiarizing*

              the main cause of plagiarism, however, is
    The argument that laziness is ~~its main cause, however, is~~ at best incomplete and seems,
                    students
    moreover, to be fed by unfair stereotypes of ~~them~~ as bored by academic rigor, more interested

in video games or their *MySpace* pages than the hard work of learning.

Avoiding Confusing Shifts in Tense and Voice (386–89)

Shifts from one tense to another or from the active to the passive voice are confusing when they occur for no clear reason.

shift Students who view writing papers as hoops they must jump through to graduate, for
  are   *download*
instance, were more likely simply to ~~have downloaded~~ a paper from an online "paper
      ^   ^

mill" than to write one themselves.

_____

Students draw a distinction between their interests and their academic assignments,
  and they rationalize plagiarism
and plagiarism is rationalized by them as a way to escape an "unfair" academic obligation.
        ^

Avoiding Incomplete Constructions (392–94)

A phrase or clause is incomplete if it is missing any words required for idiomatic and grammatical clarity.

                                                                to
inc Websites such as *essaytown.com,* which will write a paper to order, cater students like
                                                                    ^

these, who consider at least some aspects of academia essentially useless.

Avoiding Mixed Constructions (389–92)

A mixed construction is a sentence with parts that do not fit together grammatically or logically.

          students who recognize
mix Even recognizing the importance of citation may not know how to cite their sources
          ^

correctly.

Distinguishing Adjectives and Adverbs (376–80)

Adjectives modify nouns or pronouns; adverbs modify verbs, adjectives, other adverbs, and entire phrases and clauses.

                                  the rapid movement of
ad The Internet is a place of free exchange and information ~~movement rapidly~~ from
                                              ^

computer to computer.

Why Students Cheat:
The Complexities and Oversimplifications of Plagiarism (Draft 1)

frag

su agr

The system of American higher education. It is founded on principles of honesty and academic integrity. For this reason, nearly everyone invested in this system—students, instructors, and administrators—recognize that plagiarism cannot be tolerated. People also agree that a lot of plagiarism is occurring. Reducing the incidence of plagiarism among college students will be difficult, however. Without an understanding of its causes that goes beyond simplistic explanations.

frag

su agr

That plagiarism and related misconduct has become all too common is beyond dispute. A survey published in *Who's Who among American High School Students* (reported by Newberger) indicated that 15 percent of top-ranked high schoolers plagiarize. Practices among higher education students are not much better according to research by Donald L. McCabe, a professor at Rutgers University who has done extensive work on cheating, 38% of college students admitted to committing forms of plagiarism in the previous year (Rimer 7). A recent study by Hand, Conway, and Moran showed that plagiarism was common among the 411 students who participated in their research.

fs

There is a commonly held myth about how most plagiarism occurs. It is late at night, a student sits staring at a computer. A paper is due the following morning, and research needs to be done, notes need to be took, and, in the end, an essay needs to be wrote and edited. The student, overwhelmed, succumbs to the temptations of plagiarism—"cutting and pasting" from sources, downloading an essay from the Internet, or simply buying a paper from another student. In this myth, the student is too apathetic and slothful to finish their assignments on their own; instead, they cheat.

cs

vb

pn agr

Undeniably, some of it occurs because students find it easier than simply doing the work required. The argument that laziness is its main cause, however, is at best incomplete and seems, moreover, to be fed by unfair stereotypes of them as bored by academic rigor, more interested in video games or their *MySpace* pages than the hard work of learning.

ref

ref

ref

In fact, some plagiarism grows from the opposite of these characteristics. High-achieving students, for example, fear what a bad grade will do to their otherwise stellar GPA. Such students may treat the attainment of impressive marks as a necessity and will betray the very academic system he or she reveres in order to sustain his or her average.

pn agr

For the final draft of this paper, see pp. 83-86.

shift

Other students plagiarize more from lack of interest in a particular course than general idleness. Students who view writing papers as hoops they must jump through to graduate, for instance, were more likely simply to have downloaded a paper from an online "paper mill" than to write one themselves. For them, a college writing class is something to be endured rather than an opportunity for learning.

shift

inc

Students draw a distinction between their interests and their academic assignments, and plagiarism is rationalized by them as a way to escape an "unfair" academic obligation. Websites such as *essaytown.com,* which will write a paper to order, cater students like these, who consider at least some aspects of academia essentially useless.

case

Many other instances of plagiarism are committed by students whom it turns out have honest intentions but are ignorant of citation methods. Michael Gunn, a British student, copied quotations from Internet sources in numerous papers over several years and was shocked to learn that this qualified as plagiarism (Baty).

mix

case

Even recognizing the importance of citation may not know how to cite their sources correctly. A student who omits the source of a paraphrase in a paper would probably be surprised to learn that him or her is often considered as guilty of plagiarism as the student who downloads an essay.

ad

mm

dm

The Internet has compounded confusion with regard to citation. The Internet is a place of free exchange and information movement rapidly from computer to computer. In this environment, ownership and citation become hazy. As John Leland, a reporter for the *New York Times*, writes, "Culture's heat now lies with the ability to cut, paste, clip, sample, quote, recycle, customize, and re-circulate." Many students—for example by highlighting it, copying it, and pasting it into a word processing document—find it easy and "natural" to take text from an online source. Having trouble keeping track of everything they have read, however, the chances increase of students accidentally plagiarizing by forgetting to cite a copied text. So, too, does the likelihood of "patchwriting," the substitution of synonyms or the shuffling of sentences in a borrowed text without putting the information fully into the writer's own words (Howard 233). Finally, some students will also be tempted to commit intentional plagiarism, choosing to leave a block of copied text uncited.

For the final draft of this paper, see pp. 83-86.

He, She, Who or *Him, Her, Whom*? Matching Pronoun Case to Function (369–74)

A case problem occurs when the form of a pronoun—subjective, objective, or possessive—does not correspond to its grammatical role in a sentence.

case Many other instances of plagiarism are committed by students whom it turns out have honest

      who, it turns out,

intentions but are ignorant of citation methods.

—————————————————————————

A student who omits the source of a paraphrase in a paper would probably be surprised to learn

    he or she

that ~~him or her~~ is often considered as guilty of plagiarism as the student who downloads an essay.

Avoiding Misplaced Modifiers (381–83)

A misplaced modifier is an ambiguously, confusingly, or disruptively placed modifying word, phrase, or clause.

    find it easy and "natural" to take text from an online source—for

mm Many students—~~for~~ example by highlighting it, copying it, and pasting it into a word processing

document—find it easy and "natural" to take text from an online source.

Avoiding Dangling Modifiers (384–85)

A dangling modifier does not clearly modify the subject or any other part of a sentence, leaving it to the reader to infer the intended meaning.

    Because students can have

dm ~~Having~~ trouble keeping track of everything they have read, however,

               that they will plagiarize accidentally

the chances increase ~~of students' accidentally plagiarizing~~ by

forgetting to cite a copied text.

Recognizing and Correcting Fragments (335–41)

A fragment is an incomplete sentence punctuated as if it were complete.

frag   The system of American higher ~~education. It is~~ founded on principles of
education is
honesty and academic integrity.

Reducing the incidence of plagiarism among college students will be difficult,
however, without
however. Without an understanding of its causes that goes beyond simplistic explanations.

Maintaining Subject-Verb Agreement (346–54)

A verb and its subject agree when they match each other in person (first, second, or third) and number (singular or plural).

su agr   For this reason, nearly everyone invested in this system—students, instructors, and
recognizes
administrators—recognize that plagiarism cannot be tolerated.

have
That plagiarism and related misconduct ~~has~~ become all too common is beyond dispute.

Maintaining Pronoun-Antecedent Agreement (354–57)

A pronoun agrees with its antecedent (the word the pronoun replaces) when they match each other in person (first, second, or third), number (singular or plural), and gender (masculine, feminine, or neuter).

students are
pn ag   In this myth, the student is too apathetic and slothful to finish their assignments on their
own; instead, they cheat.

Such students may treat the attainment of impressive marks as a necessity and will betray
they revere   *their*
the very academic system ~~he or she reveres~~ in order to sustain ~~his or her~~ average.

36 Understanding Grammar

The rules of baseball, which give the game meaning and structure, have become second nature to proficient players. Most of these rules are inflexible: A player who ran around the bases carrying the ball would not be playing baseball. Some rules vary, however: In the American League but not in the National League, teams can designate another player to bat instead of the pitcher.

Languages, too, have rules—*grammars*—that structure words so that they can convey meaning. Just as baseball players have internalized the rules of the game, so have we all internalized the grammar of our native language. Most rules of grammar are inflexible. Any English speaker, for example, would recognize a statement like *throw Maria ball the base first to* as ungrammatical. Some aspects of grammar, however, can vary over time, from region to region, and from group to group.

The form of English accepted today in academic settings and in the workplace in the United States is known as **Standard American English.** Although it is not better or more correct than other varieties, Standard American English is what readers expect to encounter in academic and business writing in the United States. This chapter reviews the rules of Standard American English grammar, and the chapters that follow it in tab 10 focus on aspects of grammar and usage that many writers find troublesome.

PARTS OF SPEECH

The term *parts of speech* refers to the roles words play in a sentence. English has eight parts of speech:

- nouns
- pronouns
- verbs
- adjectives
- adverbs
- prepositions
- conjunctions
- interjections

Writing Responsibly / Why Grammar Matters

Writers have a responsibility to use language their readers regard as grammatically correct. A shared standard of grammar eases communication, and when you follow it, you show respect for your readers. In contrast, when you use language your readers regard as grammatically incorrect, you distract and confuse them, raising questions about the quality of your writing.

to AUDIENCE

The same word can have more than one role, depending on the context in which it appears.

▶ Many students work to help pay for college. [*Work* is a verb.]

▶ Mastering calculus requires hard work. [*Work* is a noun.]

36a Nouns

Nouns name ideas (*justice*), things (*chair*), qualities (*neatness*), actions (*judgment*), people (*Steven Spielberg*), and places (*Tokyo*). They fall into a variety of overlapping categories:

- ■ *Proper nouns* name specific places, people, or things and are usually capitalized: *Nairobi, Hudson Bay, Hillary Rodham Clinton, the Taj Mahal.* All other nouns are ***common nouns,*** which name members of a class or group: *turtle, sophomore, skyscraper.*

- ■ *Collective nouns* name a collection that can function as a single unit: *committee, administration, family.*

- ■ *Concrete nouns* name things that can be seen, touched, heard, smelled, or tasted: *planet, liquid, symphony, skunk, pepper.* ***Abstract nouns*** name qualities or ideas that cannot be perceived by the senses: *mercy, wisdom.*

- ■ *Countable* (or *count*) *nouns* name things or ideas that can be counted. They can be either ***singular*** or ***plural:*** *cat/cats, assignment/assignments, idea/ideas.*

- ■ *Uncountable* (or ***noncount***) *nouns* name ideas or things that cannot be counted and do not have a plural form: *homework, knowledge, pollution.*

> **More about**
> Count and non-
> count nouns,
> 400–05

 Countable and Uncountable Nouns In many languages, the classification of nouns as countable or uncountable affects the way they combine with articles (*a, an, the*) and other determiners (*my, your, some, many, this, those*). Awareness of the effect of this aspect of nouns on sentence grammar will help you avoid errors.

> **More about**
> Noun plurals,
> 467–68

Most nouns form the plural with the addition of a final *-s* or *-es: book/ books, beach/beaches, country/countries.* A few have irregular plurals: *woman/ women, life/lives, mouse/mice.* For some nouns, the singular and the plural forms are the same: *deer/deer, fish/fish.*

> **More about**
> Apostrophes and
> possession,
> 432–35

Nouns indicate possession with a final *s* sound, marked in writing with an apostrophe: *Rosa's idea, the students' plan.*

36b Pronouns

Pronouns rename or take the place of nouns or **noun phrases.** The noun that a pronoun replaces is called its **antecedent.** The Quick Reference box on page 322 summarizes pronoun types and their functions.

> **noun phrase** A noun and its modifiers

> **More about**
> Pronouns, 350,
> 352, 354–57,
> 369–76

36c Verbs

Verbs express action (*The quarterback throws a pass*), occurrence (*The play happened in the second half*), or state of being (*The fans are happy*).

Two kinds of verbs combine to make up a **verb phrase: main verbs** and **helping** (or **auxiliary**) **verbs.** Main verbs carry the principal meaning of a verb phrase. Almost all verb forms other than the present and past tense, however, require a combination of one or more helping verbs with a form of the main verb. Some helping verbs (forms of *be, have,* and *do*) also function as main verbs. Others, called **modal verbs** (*can, could, may, might, must, shall, should, will, would,* and *ought to*), function only as helping verbs.

> **More about**
> Verb forms, 357–68

 Modal Auxiliaries Modal auxiliaries can pose special challenges for multilingual students because other languages use very different grammatical strategies to express intention, possibility, or expectation. For more on their meaning and use, see pages 410–11.

Helping verbs always precede the main verb in a verb phrase.

```
           |— verb phrase —|
           main
           verb
▸ The studio  produced         a successful movie.

           helping    main
           verbs      verb
▸ The movie  may have broken    a box office record.
```

NOTE Do not confuse **verbals** with complete verbs. Verbals are verb forms that act as nouns, adjectives, or adverbs, not as verbs.

> **More about**
> Verbals, 331–32,
> 338

▸ The potters *fired* the vessels in their kiln. [*Fired* is a verb.]

▸ The *fired* clay is rock hard. [*Fired* is a verbal, in this case an adjective modifying *clay.*]

36d Adjectives

Adjectives modify nouns or pronouns with descriptive or limiting information. They answer questions such as *What kind? Which one?* or *How many?*

> **More about**
> Adjectives, 376–80

Quick Reference | Pronouns and Their Functions

Type and Function	Forms	Examples
Personal pronouns take the place of specific nouns or noun phrases.	**Singular:** *I, me, you, he, him, she, her, it* **Plural:** *we, us, you, they, them*	Yue bought the tickets for Adam, and she gave them to him before the concert.
Possessive pronouns are personal pronouns that indicate possession.	**Singular:** *my, mine, your, yours, his, her, hers, its* **Plural:** *our, ours, your, yours, their, theirs*	Adam gave one of the tickets to his roommate.
Reflexive pronouns refer back to the subject of a sentence.	**Singular:** *myself, yourself, himself, herself, itself, oneself* **Plural:** *ourselves, yourselves, themselves*	Laetitia reminded herself to return the books to the library.
Intensive pronouns rename and emphasize their antecedents.	Same as reflexive pronouns	Dr. Collins herself performed the operation.
Demonstrative pronouns rename and point to nouns or noun phrases. They can function as adjectives as well as nouns.	**Singular:** *this, that* **Plural:** *these, those*	Yameng visited the Forbidden City. That was his favorite place in China. That place was his favorite.
Relative pronouns introduce subordinate clauses that describe the pronoun's antecedent.	*who, whom, whoever, whomever, what, whose, whatever, whichever, that, which*	I. M. Pei is the architect who designed the East Wing of the National Gallery.
Interrogative pronouns introduce questions.	*who, whoever, whom, whomever, what, whatever, which, whichever, whose*	Who designed the East Wing of the National Gallery?
Indefinite pronouns do not refer to specific people or things.	**Singular:** *anybody, anyone, anything, each, either, everybody, everyone, everything, much, neither, nobody, no one, nothing, one, somebody, someone, something* **Singular or plural:** *all, any, more, most, some* **Plural:** *both, few, many, several*	Everybody talks about the weather, but nobody does anything about it. —Attributed to Mark Twain
Reciprocal pronouns refer to the individual parts of a plural antecedent.	*each other, one another*	The candidates debated one another many times before the primary.

	adj. noun
WHAT KIND?	a warm day
WHICH ONE?	the next speaker
HOW MANY?	twelve roses

Adjectives most commonly fall before nouns in a noun phrase and after *linking verbs* as *subject complements.*

> adj. noun adj. noun
> ▶ The young musicians played a rousing concert.

> ▶ They were enthusiastic.
> pro- link. adj.
> noun verb

Possessive, demonstrative, and indefinite pronouns that act as adjectives—as well as the articles *a, an,* and *the*—are known as ***determiners*** because they point to or indicate the amount of the nouns they modify. Determiners always come before other adjectives in a noun phrase. Some, like *all* and *both,* also come before any other determiners.

> det. adj. noun det. noun dets. adj. noun
> ▶ The new gym is in that building with all those solar panels on
> det. noun
> the roof.

 The Ordering of Adjectives The ordering of adjectives in noun phrases and the use of articles and other determiners in English can be challenging for multilingual writers. English sentences tend to place adjectives before nouns, while adjective placement in other languages varies and some languages do not use articles at all. For more on these topics, see pages 401–05 and 412.

> **linking verb** A verb that conveys a state of being linking a subject to its complement
> **subject complement** An adjective, pronoun, or noun phrase that follows a linking verb and describes or refers to the sentence subject

36e Adverbs

Adverbs modify verbs, adjectives, and other adverbs, as well as entire phrases and clauses. They answer such questions as *How? Where? When?* and *To what extent or degree?*

> **More about**
> Adverbs, 376–80

	adverb verb adv.
HOW?	Embarrassingly, my cell phone rang loudly.
	The adverb *loudly* modifies the verb *rang.* The adverb *embarrassingly* modifies the whole sentence.
	adv. adj.
WHEN?	Dinner is finally ready.
	The adverb *finally* modifies the adjective *ready.*

Quick

Reference **Common Conjunctive Adverbs**

accordingly	finally	instead	nonetheless	subsequently
also	for example	likewise	now	suddenly
anyway	furthermore	meanwhile	otherwise	then
as a result	hence	moreover	similarly	therefore
besides	however	nevertheless	specifically	thus
certainly	indeed	next	still	

verb adv. adv.

WHERE?
EXTENT? Stop right there!

The adverb *right* modifies the adverb *there,* which modifies the verb *stop.*

> **More about**
> Adjective and
> adverb phrases,
> 330–32
> Adjective and
> adverb clauses,
> 333–35

A ***conjunctive adverb*** is a transitional expression that links one independent clause to another and indicates how the two clauses relate to each other. A period or semicolon, not a comma, should separate independent clauses linked with a conjunctive adverb.

▶ Writers have several options for joining independent clauses; however, a comma alone is not one of them.

36f Prepositions

Prepositions relate nouns or pronouns to other words in a sentence in terms of time, space, cause, and other attributes.

▶ The lecture begins at noon in the auditorium.

> **More about**
> Prepositions,
> 416–20

As the Quick Reference box below indicates, prepositions can consist of more than one word.

Quick

Reference **Common One-Word and Multiword Prepositions**

about	at	far from	near	past
above	because of	for	near to	since
according to	before	from	next to	through
across	behind	in	of	to
after	below	in addition to	off	toward
against	beneath	in case of	on	under
ahead of	beside	in front of	on account of	underneath
along	between	in place of	on behalf of	until
among	by	inside	onto	up
around	by means of	inside of	on top of	upon
as far as	close to	in spite of	out of	with
aside from	down	instead of	outside	within
as to	during	into	outside of	without
as well as	except	like	over	

Quick Reference Common Subordinating Conjunctions

after	*before*	*since*	*when*
although	*even if*	*so that*	*where*
as	*even though*	*though*	*while*
as if	*if*	*unless*	
because	*once*	*until*	

36g Conjunctions

Conjunctions join words, phrases, and clauses to other words, phrases, or clauses and indicate how the joined elements relate to each other. *Coordinating conjunctions* (*and, but, or, for, nor, yet,* and *so*) join similar elements, giving them each equal significance.

▶ Ingenious **and** energetic entrepreneurs can generate effective **but** inexpensive publicity. [The conjunction **and** pairs two adjectives; the conjunction **but** contrasts two adjectives.]

Correlative conjunctions are pairs of terms that, like coordinating conjunctions, join similar elements. Common correlative conjunctions include *either . . . or, neither . . . nor, both . . . and, not only . . . but also,* and *whether . . . or.*

> **More about**
> Independent and subordinate clauses, 332–34

▶ Fred Thompson has been **both** an actor **and** a presidential candidate.

Subordinating conjunctions link subordinate clauses to the independent clauses they modify.

▶ The party could not begin **until** the guest of honor had arrived.

36h Interjections

Interjections are words like *alas, bah, oh, ouch,* and *ugh* that express strong feeling—of regret, contempt, surprise, pain, or disgust, for example—but otherwise serve no grammatical function.

▶ **Ugh!** That's the worst coffee I ever tasted.

SENTENCE STRUCTURE

All sentences have two basic parts: a subject and a predicate. The *subject* is the thing the sentence is about. The *predicate* states something about the subject.

|———— subject ————||———————— predicate ————————|

▶ Digital technology transformed the music industry.

Sentences fall into one of four categories:

- ***Declarative sentences*** (the most common type) make a statement.
  - ▶ Digital technology transformed the music industry.
- ***Imperative sentences*** give a command.
  - ▶ Join the digital bandwagon to survive in today's competitive media marketplace.
- ***Interrogative sentences*** ask a question.
  - ▶ Will digital technology make printed books obsolete?
- ***Exclamatory sentences*** express strong or sudden emotion.
  - ▶ How I hate updating software on my computer!

36i Subjects

The ***simple subject*** of a sentence is a noun or pronoun. The ***complete subject*** consists of the simple subject plus any modifying words or phrases.

|— complete subject —|
simple
subject

- ▶ *Two robotic <u>vehicles</u>* have been exploring Mars since January 2004.

A ***compound subject*** contains two or more simple subjects joined by a conjunction.

|————————— compound subject —————————|
　　　　ss　　conj　　　　　　　　ss

- ▶ *The six-wheeled, solar-powered* <u>Spirit</u> *and the identical* <u>Opportunity</u> landed within three weeks of each other.

In imperative sentences (commands), the subject, *you,* is unstated.

- ▶ [*You*] Learn about space exploration at www.nasa.gov.

In interrogative sentences (questions), the subject falls between a helping verb and the main verb or, if the main verb is a form of *be* alone, after the verb.

helping　　　　　　main
verb　|—subject—|　verb

- ▶ Did　the rovers　find evidence of water on Mars?

verb |———— subject ————|

- ▶ Were *Spirit* and *Opportunity* more durable than expected?

▶ **More about**
Word order and
emphasis,
284–92

Writers occasionally invert normal word order and place the subject after the verb for emphasis.

verb　　|———— subject ————|

- ▶ Out of the swirling dust emerged the hardy Mars rover.

Quick

Reference Finding the Subject

The complete subject of a sentence is the answer to the question "Who or what did the action or was in the state defined by the verb?"

├— complete subject —┤ verb

▶ Two robotic vehicles landed safely on Mars in January 2004.

What landed on Mars in January 2004? Two robotic vehicles did. The subject is *two robotic vehicles.*

├————————— complete subject —————————┤ verb

▶ The scientists and engineers who designed the rovers cheered.

Who cheered? The scientists and engineers who designed the rovers did. The subject is *the scientists and engineers who designed the rovers.*
 The subject usually precedes the verb, but it is not always the first element in a sentence. In the following sentence, for example, the phrase *in July 2007* modifies the rest of the sentence but is not part of the subject.

├——— subject ———┤ verb

▶ In July 2007, Martian dust storms restricted the activity of the rovers.

The subject also follows the verb in sentences that begin with *there* followed by a form of *be.* In these **expletive constructions,** the word *there* functions as a placeholder for the delayed subject.

v ├— subject —┤

▶ There are two vehicles roaming the surface of Mars.

English Word Order In English, word order is less flexible than in many other languages, and the position of a word often affects its grammatical role and meaning. English sentences tend to place subjects before verbs and verbs before their objects. English readers expect this order, so using other word orders can cause confusion.

> **More about**
> English word order,
> 395–99

36j Predicates

The **simple predicate** of a sentence is the main verb and any helping verbs. The **complete predicate** is the simple predicate together with any objects, complements, and modifiers.

├——— complete predicate ———┤
simple
pred.

▶ Polynesian mariners *settled the Hawaiian Islands.*

├————— complete predicate —————┤
simple pred.

▶ The first settlers *may have arrived as early as the fourth century CE.*

A ***compound predicate*** is a complete predicate containing two or more simple predicates joined by a conjunction.

```
                                    |———————————————————————— complete
                      simple pred.
```
▸ Polynesian mariners *navigated thousands of miles of open ocean and*
```
   predicate —————————————————————————|
      sp
```
settled the islands of the South Pacific.

36k Verb Types and Sentence Patterns

There are three kinds of verbs, *intransitive, linking,* and *transitive,* and they combine with other elements in the predicate in five basic sentence patterns.

1. Subject → intransitive verb

Intransitive verbs require no object and can stand alone as the only element in a predicate. They are often modified, however, by adverbs and adverbial phrases and clauses.

```
                     intrans.
    |——subj.——|   verb
```
▸ The volcano *erupted.*

```
                     intrans.
    |——subj.——|   verb   |————————————— adverbial modifiers —————————————|
```
▸ The volcano *erupted suddenly in a powerful blast of ash and steam.*

Quick

Reference   Five Sentence Patterns

1. subject → intransitive verb
   ```
          s       iv
   ```
   ▸ The lights dimmed.

2. subject → linking verb → subject complement
   ```
            s    lv   sc
   ```
   ▸ The audience fell silent.

3. subject → transitive verb → direct object
   ```
            s      tv       do
   ```
   ▸ The orchestra played the overture.

4. subject → transitive verb → indirect object → direct object
   ```
            s    tv      io      do
   ```
   ▸ The show gave the audience a thrill.

5. subject → transitive verb → direct object → object complement
   ```
            s     tv     do    oc
   ```
   ▸ The applause made the actors happy.

2. Subject → linking verb → subject complement

A *subject complement* is an adjective, pronoun, or noun phrase that describes or refers to the subject of a sentence. A *linking verb* connects the subject to its complement. Linking verbs express states of being rather than actions. The verb *be,* when used as a main verb, is always a linking verb. Other verbs that can function as linking verbs include *appear, become, fall, feel, grow, look, make, prove, remain, seem, smell, sound,* and *taste.*

```
                    link.
    |—subj.—|       vb.     |—subj. comp.—|
```
▸ The Oscar   is   a coveted award.

▸ The patient felt   better.

3. Subject → transitive verb → direct object

Transitive verbs have two *voices:* active and passive. *Transitive verbs* in the *active voice* require a *direct object*—a pronoun or noun phrase that receives the action of the verb.

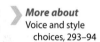
More about
Voice and style
choices, 293–94

```
                         active
    |——— subject ———|  trans. vb.  |——— do ———|
```
▸ The undersea volcano created   a new island.

The *passive voice* reverses the role of the subject, making it the recipient of the action of the verb. An active-voice sentence can usually be changed into a passive-voice sentence of the same meaning. The subject of the passive-voice version is the direct object of the active-voice version.

```
                        passive
    |— subject —|     trans. verb
```
▸ A new island   *was created*   by the undersea volcano.

In the passive voice, the agent of the action can be left unstated.

▸ A new island *was created.*

NOTE Many verbs can be either transitive or intransitive.

TRANSITIVE   My sister *won* the Scrabble game.

INTRANSITIVE   My sister always *wins.*

When in doubt about the usage of a verb, check a dictionary.

----

4. Subject → transitive verb → indirect object → direct object

Some transitive verbs can take an *indirect object* as well as a direct object. The indirect object, which comes before the direct object, identifies who or what benefits from the action of the verb.

> ├── s ──┤ ├── tv ──┤ ├── io ──┤ ├──────── do ────────┤
> ► Juan   lent   Ileana   his notes.

> ► The donor bought the library a new computer center.

Often, the indirect object can also be stated as a prepositional phrase that usually begins with *to* and follows the direct object.

> ► Juan lent his notes *to Ileana.*

Verbs that can take an indirect object include *ask, bring, buy, call, find, get, give, hand, leave, lend, offer, pass, pay, promise, read, send, show, teach, tell, throw,* and *write.*

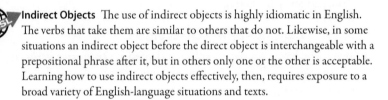

> **More about**
> Indirect objects,
> 397–98

Indirect Objects The use of indirect objects is highly idiomatic in English. The verbs that take them are similar to others that do not. Likewise, in some situations an indirect object before the direct object is interchangeable with a prepositional phrase after it, but in others only one or the other is acceptable. Learning how to use indirect objects effectively, then, requires exposure to a broad variety of English-language situations and texts.

5. Subject → transitive verb → direct object → object complement

An ***object complement*** is an adjective or noun phrase that follows the direct object and describes the condition of the object or a change that the subject has caused it to undergo.

> ├──── s ────┤ ├──── tv ────┤ ├──── do ────┤ ├──── oc ────┤
> ► The fans   considered the umpire's call mistaken.

> ► The manager named   David Ortiz   designated hitter.

36l Phrases

A ***phrase*** is a group of related words that lacks a subject, a predicate, or both. Phrases function in various ways within sentences but cannot function as sentences by themselves. A phrase by itself is a ***fragment,*** not a sentence.

> **fragment** An incomplete sentence punctuated as if it were complete

1. Noun phrases

A ***noun phrase*** consists of a noun together with any modifiers. Noun phrases function as subjects, objects, and complements within sentences.

> ├──── noun phrase/subject ────┤
> ► *Sam's mouth-watering apple pie* emerged piping hot from the oven.

> ├──── noun phrase/direct object ────┤
> ► The guests devoured *Sam's mouth-watering apple pie.*

> ├──── noun phrase/subj. comp. ────┤
> ► The high point of the meal was *Sam's mouth-watering apple pie.*

An ***appositive phrase*** is a noun or noun phrase that renames a noun or noun phrase and is grammatically equivalent to it.

|——————— appositive ———————|

▸ The high point of the meal, *Sam's mouth-watering apple pie,* emerged piping hot from the oven.

2. Verb phrases

A ***verb phrase*** consists of a main verb and all its helping verbs. Verb phrases act as the simple predicates of sentences and clauses.

|——————— verb phrase ———————|

▸ By Election Day, the candidates *will have been campaigning* for almost two years.

3. Prepositional phrases

A ***prepositional phrase*** is a preposition followed by the ***object of the preposition:*** a pronoun or noun and its modifiers. Prepositional phrases function as adjectives and adverbs.

▸ The train arrives <u>in an hour</u>. [The prepositional phrase *in an hour* functions as an adverb modifying the verb *arrives.*]

▸ She recommended the article <u>about Spielberg</u>. [The prepositional phrase *about Spielberg* acts as an adjective modifying the noun *article.*]

4. Verbal phrases

Verbals are verb forms that function as nouns, adjectives, or adverbs. Although they may have objects and complements, verbals lack all the information required of a complete verb. A ***verbal phrase*** consists of a verbal and any modifiers, objects, or complements. There are three kinds of verbal phrases: gerund phrases, infinitive phrases, and participial phrases.

Gerunds A ***gerund*** is the present participle (or *-ing* form) of a verb used as a noun. Like nouns, gerunds and gerund phrases can act as subjects, objects, and complements.

|——————— gerund phrase/subject ———————|

▸ *Increasing automobile fuel efficiency* will reduce carbon emissions.

|——————— gerund phrase/dir. obj. ———————|

▸ The mayor recommends *improving the city's mass transit system.*

Infinitives An ***infinitive*** is the *to* form of the verb (*to decide, to eat, to study*). Infinitives and infinitive phrases can act as adjectives and adverbs as well as nouns.

▶ The goal of the law is *to increase fuel efficiency.*

▶ Congress passed a law *to increase fuel efficiency.*

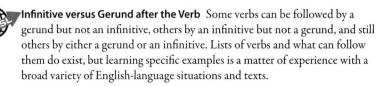

▶ *To reduce traffic congestion,* the city improved its mass transit system.

More about
Infinitive versus
gerund after
verbs, 408–09

Infinitive versus Gerund after the Verb Some verbs can be followed by a gerund but not an infinitive, others by an infinitive but not a gerund, and still others by either a gerund or an infinitive. Lists of verbs and what can follow them do exist, but learning specific examples is a matter of experience with a broad variety of English-language situations and texts.

Participial phrases In a ***participial phrase,*** the present participle or past participle of a verb acts as an adjective. The present participle ends in *-ing.* The past participle of regular verbs ends in *-ed,* but some verbs have irregular past participles.

More about
Irregular past par-
ticiples, 357–61

▶ *Surveying the disheveled apartment,* Grace wondered whether it would be possible to room with Maritza.

▶ *Deeply concerned,* she asked, "How long have you lived alone?"

5. Absolute phrases

Absolute phrases modify entire sentences rather than particular words within sentences. They usually consist of a pronoun or noun phrase followed by a participle. Set off by commas, they can often fall flexibly before, after, or within the rest of the sentence.

▶ *All our quarrels forgotten,* we sat before the fire and talked quietly.

36m Clauses

A ***clause*** is a word group with a subject and a predicate. An ***independent*** (or ***main***) ***clause*** can stand alone as a sentence.

├── independent clause ──┤
▶ Sam's pie won first prize.

A ***subordinate*** (or ***dependent***) clause is a clause within a clause.

├────── independent clause ──────┤
├── sub. clause ──┤
▶ Sam baked the pie that won first prize.

That is, a subordinate clause functions inside an independent clause (or another subordinate clause) as a noun, adjective, or adverb but cannot stand alone as a sentence. A subordinate clause by itself is a *fragment.* A subordinating word—either a *subordinating conjunction* (see the Quick Reference box on p. 325) or a *relative pronoun* (see the Quick Reference box on p. 322)—usually signals the beginning of a subordinate clause.

More about
Subordinate clause fragments, 340
Punctuating subordinate clauses, 422, 424–27

1. Adjective clauses

Like adjectives, *adjective clauses* (also called *relative clauses*) modify nouns or pronouns. They usually begin with a relative pronoun that immediately follows the word the clause modifies and refers back to it.

> Sam baked the pie *that won first prize.*

> The donor *who paid for the library's new computer center* is a recent graduate.

In both these examples, the relative pronoun is the subject of the subordinate clause, and the clause follows normal word order, with the subject before the verb. When the relative pronoun is the direct object, however, it still comes at the beginning of the clause, reversing normal word order.

> The candidate *whom we supported* lost the election.

More about
Who versus whom, 373–74

Adjective clauses can also begin with the subordinating conjunctions *when* and *where.*

> Tupelo, Mississippi, is the town *where Elvis Presley was born.*

It is sometimes acceptable to omit the relative pronoun that introduces an adjective clause when the meaning of the clause is clear without it.

> The candidate [*whom*] *we supported* lost the election.

2. Adverb clauses

Adverb clauses usually begin with a subordinating conjunction, which specifies the relation of a clause to the term it modifies. Like adverbs, adverb clauses can modify verbs, adjectives, and adverbs as well as whole phrases and clauses.

More about
The meaning of subordinating conjunctions, 288–89

> The baby boom began *as World War II ended.*
> The adverb clause modifies the verb *began.*

▶ The 1990s were an affluent decade, *although the general prosperity did not benefit everyone.*

The adverb clause modifies the preceding independent clause.

3. Noun clauses

Noun clauses replace noun phrases as subjects, objects, or complements within an independent clause. Noun clauses can begin with a relative pronoun as well as with certain subordinating conjunctions, including *how, if, when, whenever, where, wherever, whether,* and *why.*

|— subject —|

▶ *Whoever crosses the finish line first* wins the race.

|— subject comp. —|

▶ Home is *where the heart is.*

|— direct object —|

▶ The evidence proves *that the defendant is not guilty.*

36n Sentence Types

Sentences fall into four types depending on the combination of independent and subordinate clauses they contain.

1. Simple sentences

A *simple sentence* has only one independent clause and no subordinate clauses.

|— independent clause —|

▶ Lance Armstrong won the Tour de France seven times.

A simple sentence need not be short or even uncomplicated. A sentence with a compound subject, a compound predicate, or both is still a simple sentence as long as it has a single complete subject, a single complete predicate, and no subordinate clauses.

2. Compound sentences

A *compound sentence* has two or more independent clauses but no subordinate clauses. A comma and a coordinating conjunction, a semicolon, or a semicolon and a conjunctive adverb usually join the clauses in a compound sentence.

|— independent clause —|

▶ Lance Armstrong won the Tour de France seven times, and

|— independent clause —|

in 2002, *Sports Illustrated* named him Sportsman of the Year.

> **More about**
> Punctuating
> compound sen-
> tences, 341–46

3. Complex sentences

A *complex sentence* consists of a single independent clause with at least one subordinate clause.

▶ The Tour de France, which is the world's longest cycling race, covers nearly 2,000 miles in 22 days.

4. Compound-complex sentences

A *compound-complex sentence* has two or more independent clauses with one or more subordinate clauses.

▶ The Tour has long been plagued by allegations of doping among contestants, but the 2007 race, which saw three riders disqualified for doping-related offenses, was particularly scandal ridden.

37 Avoiding Sentence Fragments

An open drawbridge is not a complete bridge; it is two bridge fragments, neither of which, by itself, will get travelers all the way across a river. Similarly, a *sentence fragment* is not a complete sentence. It may begin with a capital letter and end with a period (or a question mark or an exclamation point), but it lacks all the elements of a complete sentence. It takes readers only partway through the writer's thought, leaving them searching for the missing pieces. Although writers may use them intentionally in certain contexts, fragments are almost always out of place in academic and business writing.

37a Recognizing Fragments

A sentence must have at least one *independent clause,* which is a group of related words that has a *complete verb* and a *subject* but does not start with a subordinating term such as *although, because, who,* or *that.* If a word group does not satisfy these conditions but is punctuated like a sentence, it is a fragment, not a sentence.

> **subject** A noun or pronoun that names the topic of a sentence
> **complete verb** A main verb together with any helping verbs needed to indicate tense, voice, and mood

Assessment   Identifying Fragments

To determine whether a word group is a fragment or a sentence, ask yourself the following questions, then make any necessary corrections to your work.

☐ Does it have a complete verb?
   ▶ If the answer is no, it is a fragment.
☐ Does it have a subject?
   ▶ If the answer is no, it is a fragment.
☐ Does it begin with a subordinating word but otherwise stand alone?
   ▶ If the answer is yes, it is a fragment.

> *More about*
> Verbs, 357–68

No verb A *complete verb* consists of a main verb together with any helping verbs needed to express tense, mood, and voice. If a word group lacks a complete verb, it is a *phrase,* and if that phrase is punctuated like a sentence, it is a phrase fragment.

FRAGMENT   Her beautiful new sports car.
(NO VERB)

                                      subj. complete verb

SENTENCE   Her beautiful new sports car was smashed beyond repair.

No subject The subject of a sentence is the answer to the question "Who or what did the action defined by the verb?" If a word group lacks a subject, it is a phrase. If the phrase is punctuated like a sentence, it is a phrase fragment.

              verb

FRAGMENT   Serves no purpose.

              subject   verb

SENTENCE   The breadmaker in my cupboard serves no purpose.

Including a Stated Subject Unlike in most other languages, all sentences in formal English except commands always require an explicitly stated subject. See chapter 46, "Understanding English Word Order and Sentence Structure," page 395.

> *More about*
> Subordinate
> clauses, 332–34

Begins with a subordinating term A subordinate clause, like a sentence, has a subject and a predicate. However, a subordinate clause begins with a subordinating term that links it to another clause. Subordinating terms include subordinating conjunctions and relative pronouns (see the Quick Reference box on the next page). A subordinate clause cannot be a sentence on its own. If it is punctuated like a sentence, it is a subordinate clause fragment.

              subordinator

FRAGMENT   When the drawbridge closes.

                                  subordinator

SENTENCE   We will cross the river when the drawbridge closes.

Quick

Reference   Subordinating Terms

Subordinating Conjunctions

after	before	since	unless	whereas
although	even if	so that	until	while
as	even though	than	when	why
as if	if	that	whenever	
because	once	though	where	

Relative Pronouns

that	whatever	whichever	whoever	whomever
what	which	who	whom	whose

FRAGMENT   *subordinator*
Which made driving hazardous.

SENTENCE   The storm left a foot of snow, *subordinator*
which made driving hazardous.

Note that many relative pronouns can also act as interrogative pronouns to introduce questions. Questions beginning this way are complete sentences.

> **More about**
> Different types of pronouns, 322

FRAGMENT   *relative pronoun*
Who will be attending.

SENTENCE   *interrogative pronoun*
Who will be attending?

37b   Editing Fragments

Once you have identified a fragment, you have two options for correcting it:

1. Connect the fragment to a related independent clause.

   ▶ The first mission to Pluto was launched in 2006. ~~Will arrive~~ *and will arrive* in 2015.

   ▶ He made 5,000 songs available over the university's server. ~~Which~~ *, which* prompted the record companies to threaten legal action.

2. Convert the fragment into an independent clause.

   ▶ The first mission to Pluto was launched in 2006. ~~Will~~ *It will* arrive in 2015.

   ▶ He made 5,000 songs available over the university's server. ~~Which~~ *In response,* prompted the record companies ~~to threaten~~ *threatened* legal action.

Writing Responsibly | **Sentence Fragments and Context**

Although writers sometimes use them deliberately in certain contexts (see 37c), for a variety of reasons you should avoid sentence fragments in your academic or business writing. One is that fragments can create ambiguities, as in the following example:

▶ Our small town has seen many changes. Some long-time stores went out of business. Because the new mall opened. There are now more options for family entertainment.

Did the new mall put stores out of business, provide new entertainment options, or both? To clarify this ambiguity, the writer would need to attach the fragment to the preceding or the following sentence or rewrite these sentences in some other way.

Another reason to avoid fragments is that readers may interpret them as carelessness or a lack of competence, which would undermine your efforts to present yourself authoritatively.

to TOPIC

These options apply to both phrase fragments and subordinate clause fragments. Either option can fix a fragment; deciding on the best one is a stylistic choice that depends on the context in which the fragment occurs.

1. Phrase fragments

As you edit your writing, watch in particular for fragments based on certain kinds of phrases, including prepositional phrases, verbal phrases, appositive phrases, the separate parts of compound predicates, and items in lists and examples. A ***prepositional phrase*** consists of a preposition (such as *as, at, for, from, in addition to, to,* or *until*) followed by a pronoun or noun and its modifiers. You can usually correct a prepositional phrase fragment by attaching it to an adjacent sentence.

More about
Prepositions and prepositional phrases, 324, 331, 416–20

▶ The Kenyon College women won the NCAA Division III title again. For the seventeenth consecutive year.
for

More about
Verbals, 321, 331–32

Verbals are words that look like verbs—they are derived from verbs—but they lack the information about tense required of a complete verb. ***Verbal phrases*** can function as adjectives, adverbs, or nouns within a sentence but not as sentences on their own. In the following example, *stranding* is a verbal.

▶ The car had run out of gas. Stranding us in the middle of nowhere.
gas, stranding

Tech | **Grammar Checkers and Sentence Fragments**

The grammar checkers in word processing programs may miss some fragments and, in some cases, may incorrectly flag imperatives (commands) as fragments.

Although your grammar checker can help you, you will still need to edit your prose carefully for fragments.

An *appositive phrase* renames a preceding noun or noun phrase. Appositives become fragments when they are separated by a period from the phrases they rename.

> **More about**
> Appositives, 331

▶ In her acceptance speech, the Academy Award winner thanked her
biggest ~~fan. Her~~ *fan, her* mother.

> **noun phrase** A noun together with any modifiers

A *compound predicate* consists of two or more complete verbs, together with their objects and modifiers, that are joined by a coordinating conjunction (such as *or, and,* or *but*) and that share the same subject. A fragment results when the last part of a compound predicate is punctuated as a separate sentence.

> **More about**
> Compound predicates, 328

▶ By the end of May, the band members hated one another. ~~But~~ *but* still had

six weeks left on the tour.

Lists become fragments when they are separated from the sentence to which they belong. To correct list fragments, link them to the sentence by rephrasing the passage or replacing the period with a colon or a dash.

FRAGMENT Three authors are most commonly associated with the Beat movement. Allen Ginsberg, Jack Kerouac, and William Burroughs.

REVISED The three authors most commonly associated with the Beat movement are Allen Ginsberg, Jack Kerouac, and William Burroughs.

or

> **More about**
> Punctuation for lists, 446–49

Three authors are most commonly associated with the Beat movement: Allen Ginsberg, Jack Kerouac, and William Burroughs.

Examples or explanations that begin with transitional words such as *for example, in contrast,* and *in addition* can be sentences. They are fragments, however, if they are punctuated like a sentence but lack a subject or a complete verb or otherwise consist of only a subordinate clause. In the following example, the writer corrected a phrase fragment by rephrasing and attaching it to the preceding sentence.

▶ People today have access to many sources of news and ~~opinion. For~~ *opinion, including, for*

example, the Internet and cable television as well as broadcast

television and print newspapers and magazines.

The writer of the next example corrected a subordinate clause fragment by deleting the subordinating word *that,* which turns the fragment into a sentence.

▶ Certain facts underscore the rapid growth of the Internet. For

example,
~~example that~~ web browsers did not become widely available until
     ∧

the mid-1990s.

More about
Subordination and
subordinating
conjunctions,
287–89

2. Subordinate clause fragments

When you correct a subordinate clause fragment, be sure to consider the relationships among the ideas you are expressing before deciding whether to
transform the subordinate clause into an independent clause or to connect
it to a related independent clause. Subordinating conjunctions, for example,
specify the relationship between the information in a subordinate clause and
the clause it modifies. If that relationship is important, you will probably want
to correct the fragment by connecting it to the independent clause to which it
relates.

▶ Twitter continues to gain popularity as a source of information. ~~Because~~
                                                              because
                                                                  ∧

it can publish late-breaking news as soon as it occurs.

The correction retains the subordinating conjunction *because* and with it important information about the cause-and-effect relationship between the two
parts of the sentence.

In other cases, revising a subordinate clause fragment into a separate sentence by deleting the subordinating word can produce a clearer, less awkward
result than would attaching it to another sentence.

▶ Horses and camels have something in common. ~~That the~~ ancestors
                                                       The
                                                        ∧

of both originated in the Western Hemisphere and migrated to the

Eastern Hemisphere.

37c Thinking Carefully before Using an Intentional Fragment

Writers sometimes use fragments not in error but intentionally for emphasis or
to reflect how people actually speak. Exclamations and the answers to questions
often fall into this category.

▶ Another loss! Ouch!

▶ What caused this disaster? The collapse of our running game.

Intentional fragments are also common in advertising copy, and many writers
use them for effect when the context makes their full meaning clear.

▸ All science. No fiction.
> —Toyota advertisement

▸ Man is the only animal that blushes. Or needs to.
> —Mark Twain, *Following the Equator*

Consider your writing situation, your context and genre, and especially your audience before deliberately deciding to use a sentence fragment. In academic or business writing, where clarity of expression is highly prized, fragments are frowned upon and can undermine your authority. On the other hand, if your purpose is expressive or you are writing in an informal context or genre (for example, in a blog or a text message), the occasional intentional fragment can be highly effective.

38 Avoiding Comma Splices and Fused Sentences

If not properly joined with a coupling mechanism, railway cars would either pull apart when the locomotive accelerated or crash into each other when the locomotive braked. Like railway cars, two independent clauses joined in a compound sentence need a proper coupling mechanism. If the clauses are incorrectly joined with a comma alone in a *comma splice,* they may seem to readers to pull apart confusingly. If the clauses crash into one another with no separating punctuation in a *fused* (or *run-on*) *sentence,* readers will not know where one clause ends and the other begins.

38a Joining Independent Clauses Correctly

An *independent clause* can stand on its own as a sentence. Related independent clauses can follow one another as separate sentences, each ending in a period.

> *More about*
> Clauses, 332–34

▸ Richard Harris played Dumbledore in the first two Harry —————— independent
clause ———— Potter movies. Michael Gambon played the role after Harris's ———— independent
clause ———— death in 2002.

> **More about**
> Coordination,
> 285–87

Alternatively, you can join (or *coordinate*) independent clauses in a compound sentence with a variety of coupling mechanisms that let readers know one clause is ending and another beginning. Of these, two are the most common:

- A comma and a coordinating conjunction (*and, but, or, nor, for, so, yet*)
  - ▶ Richard Harris played Dumbledore in the first two Harry Potter movies, but Michael Gambon played the role after Harris's death in 2002.

- A semicolon
  - ▶ Richard Harris played Dumbledore in the first two Harry Potter movies; Michael Gambon played the role after Harris's death in 2002.

You can also use a colon or a dash between independent clauses when the first clause introduces the second or the second elaborates on the first. (The colon is usually more appropriate in formal writing.)

- ▶ Two actors have played Dumbledore: Michael Gambon succeeded Richard Harris in the role after Harris's death in 2002.

38b Recognizing Comma Splices and Fused Sentences as Improperly Joined Independent Clauses

When a writer improperly joins two independent clauses with a comma alone, the result is a *comma splice*.

|——————— independent clause ———————|| |———

COMMA SPLICE   Ronald Reagan was originally an actor, he turned

independent clause ———|
to politics in the 1960s.

When a writer runs two independent clauses together with no punctuation between them, the result is a *fused sentence* (also called a *run-on sentence*).

|——————— independent clause ———————||———

FUSED   Politics and acting have something in common they
SENTENCE

——————— independent clause ———————|
both require a willingness to perform in public.

Writing Responsibly   Clarifying Boundaries

Comma splices and fused sentences obscure the boundaries between linked ideas. If you leave these errors uncorrected in your writing, you burden readers with tasks that should be yours: identifying where one idea ends and another begins and specifying how those ideas relate to each other.

to AUDIENCE

Reference Identifying Comma Splices and Fused Sentences

When two independent clauses are joined by . . .	The result is . . .
A comma and coordinating conjunction	**Not** a comma splice or fused sentence
A semicolon	**Not** a comma splice or fused sentence
A colon or dash	**Not** a comma splice or fused sentence
A comma alone	A **comma splice—revise**
No punctuation at all	A **fused sentence—revise**

38c Recognizing When Comma Splices and Fused Sentences Tend to Occur

To avoid comma splices and fused sentences in your own work, pay attention to situations in which they are particularly likely to occur:

1. When the second clause begins with a conjunctive adverb (such as *for example, however,* or *therefore*) or other transitional expression

   COMMA SPLICE   In the first two Harry Potter movies, Richard Harris played Dumbledore, however, after Harris's death in 2002, Michael Gambon played the role.

   REVISED   In the first two Harry Potter movies, Richard Harris played Dumbledore; however, after Harris's death in 2002, Michael Gambon played the role.

2. When the subject of the second clause is a pronoun that refers to the subject of the first clause

   COMMA SPLICE   Ronald Reagan was originally an actor, he turned to politics in the 1960s.

   REVISED   Ronald Reagan was originally an actor, but he turned to politics in the 1960s.

3. When the first clause introduces the second or the second explains or elaborates on the first

   FUSED SENTENCE   Politics and acting have something in common both require a willingness to perform in public.

   REVISED   Politics and acting have something in common: Both require a willingness to perform in public.

4. When one clause is positive and the other negative

   COMMA SPLICE   We were not upset that the exam was postponed, we were relieved.

   REVISED   We were not upset that the exam was postponed; we were relieved.

Quick **Reference**　Ways to Correct Comma Splices and Fused Sentences

1. Use a period to divide the clauses into separate sentences. (344)
2. Join the clauses correctly with a comma and a coordinating conjunction. (345)
3. Join the clauses correctly with a semicolon. (345)
4. Join the clauses, when appropriate, with a colon or dash. (345)
5. Change one independent clause into a subordinate clause or modifying phrase. (345)

38d Editing Comma Splices and Fused Sentences

The Quick Reference box above lists five strategies for correcting comma splices and fused sentences. The strategy you choose should depend on the logical relationship between the clauses and the meaning you intend to convey.

1. Separate sentences

Correcting a comma splice or fused sentence by dividing the independent clauses into separate sentences makes sense when one or both of the clauses are long or when the two clauses do not have a close logical relationship.

▶ My friends and I began our long-anticipated trip to Peru in early July <del>we</del> . We

arrived in Lima on Saturday morning and flew to Cuzco that same day.

Use a period also when the second clause is a new sentence that continues a quotation that begins in the first clause.

▶ "We must not be enemies," Abraham Lincoln implored the South in

his first inaugural address, "Though passion may have strained, it

must not break our bonds of affection."

Writing Responsibly　Is a Comma Splice Ever Acceptable?

Comma splices often show up in compound sentences composed of two short independent clauses in parallel form, particularly when one is negative and the other positive or when both are commands. This usage is common, for example, in advertising:

　Buy one, get one free.

It can crop up, too, in the work of experienced writers, who may use it deliberately because they feel a period, semicolon, or comma and coordinating conjunction would be too disruptive a separation in sentences like these:

You're not a man, you're a machine.

—George Bernard Shaw,
Arms and the Man

Go ahead, make my day.

—Joseph C. Stinson, screenplay
to *Sudden Impact*

However, this usage is best avoided in academic writing.

to TOPIC

Tech   **Comma Splices, Fused Sentences, and Grammar Checkers**

Grammar checkers in word processing programs do not reliably identify comma splices or fused sentences. They catch some, but they miss many more. One word processor, for example, failed to identify this fused sentence: *We had not had lunch we were hungry.*

---

2. Coordinating conjunction

When you join independent clauses with a comma and a coordinating conjunction (*and, but, or, nor, for, so,* or *yet*), choose the conjunction that best fits the logical relationship between the clauses.

> ▸ We needed to adjust to the altitude before we began hiking in the
>
>   Andes we spent three days sightseeing in Cuzco.
>   , so

> **More about**
> The meaning of coordinating conjunctions, 286

3. Semicolon

Join two independent clauses with a semicolon when they have a clear logical relationship of contrast, example, or explanation.

> ▸ More than sixty people have won two or more Academy Awards in a
>
>   single year, only one person, Walt Disney, has yet won four in a year.
>   ;

> **More about**
> Coordinating with a semicolon, 286

Using a semicolon in combination with a conjunctive adverb or other transitional expression can clarify the relationship between the clauses.

> ▸ More than sixty people have won two or more Academy Awards in a
>
>   single year, only one person, Walt Disney, has yet won four in a year.
>   ; however,

4. Colon or dash

You can use a colon or, less commonly, a dash to join independent clauses when the first clause introduces the second or the second explains or elaborates on the first. This usage can create a more emphatic separation between the clauses than would a semicolon.

> ▸ The message is clear, smoking kills.
>   :

> ▸ Don't get kicked out of school, learn to study effectively.
>   —

> **More about**
> Colons, 448–50
> Dashes, 446–47

5. Subordinate clause or modifying phrase

You can correct a comma splice or fused sentence by turning one of the independent clauses into a subordinate clause or a modifying phrase. Note,

> **More about**
> Subordination and emphasis, 287–89

however, that putting information in subordinate clauses and phrases usually de-emphasizes it in relation to the information in the independent clause it modifies.

COMMA SPLICE	Spanish, like French and Italian, is a Romance language, it derives from Latin, the language of the Romans.
REVISED: SUBORDINATE CLAUSE	Spanish, like French and Italian, is a Romance language ⊢————— subordinate clause —————⊣ because it derives from Latin, the language of the Romans.
REVISED: MODIFYING PHRASE	⊢————— modifying phrase —————⊣ Spanish, a Romance language like French and Italian, derives from Latin, the language of the Romans.

39 Maintaining Agreement

In many languages, the grammatical form of some words in a sentence must match the form of other words. When the forms match, the reader can easily understand the sentence; when they do not, the effect can be like trying to force a square peg into a round hole, leaving the reader distracted or confused. In English, subjects and verbs require this kind of matchup, or *agreement,* as do pronouns and the words to which they refer.

SUBJECT-VERB AGREEMENT

> **More about**
> Identifying sentence subjects, 326–27

A verb and its subject have to agree, or match each other, in person and number. *Person* refers to the form of a word that indicates whether it corresponds to the speaker or writer (*I, we*), the person addressed (*you*), or the people or things spoken or written about (*he, she, it, they, Alice, milkshakes*). *Number* refers to the form of a word that indicates whether it is singular, referring to one thing (*a student*), or plural, referring to more than one (*two students*).

39a Understanding How Subjects and Verbs Agree

1. Agreement in the present tense with third-person subjects

With just a few exceptions, it is only in the present tense that verbs change form to indicate person and number. Even in the present tense, they have only two forms. One form, which ends in *-s,* is for third-person singular subjects; the other is for all other subjects.

Tech　**Grammar Checkers and Subject-Verb Agreement**

Grammar checkers in word processing programs can alert you to many subject-verb agreement problems, but they can also miss errors and can flag some construc-tions as errors that are not. Make your own informed judgment about any changes the computer might recommend.

	Singular		Plural	
	subject	verb	subject	verb
First Person	*I*	vote	*we*	vote
Second Person	*you*	vote	*you*	vote
Third Person	*he, she, it, the student*	vote<u>s</u>	*they, the students*	vote

> **More about**
> The forms of regular and irregular verbs, 357–59

Most nouns form the plural with the addition of an *-s* (*dog, dogs*) or *-es* (*coach, coaches*). In other words, an *-s* on a noun makes the noun plural; an *-s* on a present-tense verb makes the verb singular.

> **More about**
> Regular and irregular plural nouns, 467–68

	Noun	Verb
Singular	The dog	bark<u>s</u>
Plural	The dog<u>s</u>	bark

2. Agreement with *be* and with helping verbs

Unlike any other English verb, *be* has three present-tense forms (*am, are, is*) and two past-tense forms (*was, were*). In **verb phrases** that begin with a form of *be, have,* or *do* as a helping verb, the subject agrees with the helping verb.

> **verb phrase** A *main verb* together with any **auxiliary** (or **helping**) **verbs.** The main verb carries the principal meaning of the phrase; the auxiliaries provide information about tense, voice, and mood.

	⊢——— subject ———⊣	⊢——— verb phrase ———⊣
SINGULAR	The *price* of oil	*has* been fluctuating.
PLURAL	Commodity *prices*	*have* been fluctuating.
SINGULAR	The *price*	*was* fluctuating.
PLURAL	*Prices*	*were* fluctuating.

> **More about**
> Forms of *be, have,* and *do,* 360–61

Quick **Reference**　**Avoiding Subject-Verb Agreement Pitfalls**

1. Ignore words that intervene between the subject and the verb. (348)
2. Distinguish plural from singular compound subjects. (349)
3. Distinguish singular from plural indefinite pronouns. (350)
4. Find agreement with collective-noun and numerical subjects. (350)
5. Recognize that some nouns that end in *-s* are singular. (351)
6. Treat titles, words as words, and gerund phrases as singular. (352)
7. Match the number of a relative pronoun subject (*who, which, that*) to its antecedent. (352)
8. Match the verb to the subject when the subject follows the verb. (353)
9. Match a linking verb with its subject, not its subject complement. (353)

More about
Modal auxiliaries,
411

The modal helping verbs—*can, could, may, might, must, shall, should, will, would,* and *ought to*—have only a single form; they do not take an *-s* ending for third-person singular subjects.

	├ subject ┤	├ verb phrase ┤
SINGULAR	The *price*	*can* change.
PLURAL	*Prices*	*can* change.

39b Ignoring Words That Intervene between the Subject and the Verb

In English, the subject of a sentence is usually near the verb. As a result, writers sometimes mistakenly treat words that fall between the subject and the verb as if they were the subject. The writer of the following sentence mistook the singular noun phrase *Order of the Phoenix* for the true subject, the plural noun *members.* The revision corrects the agreement error.

FAULTY　The members of the Order of the Phoenix is dedicated to thwarting Voldemort.

REVISED　The members of the Order of the Phoenix are dedicated to thwarting Voldemort.

NOTE When a singular subject is followed by a phrase that begins with *as well as, in addition to, together with,* or some similar expression, the verb is singular, not plural.

▸ Harry Potter, together with the other members of the Order of the
　　　　　　　　　is
　Phoenix, ~~are~~ determined to thwart Voldemort.

Writing Responsibly　Dialect Variation in Subject-Verb Agreement

The rules of subject-verb agreement are not the same in all dialects of English. In various communities in the English-speaking world, you might hear people say things like *"The cats is hungry," "We was at the store," "That coat needs washed,"* or *"She be walking to school."* In the contexts in which they occur, these variations are not mistakes; they reflect rules, but those rules are different from those of Standard American English. Still, the subject-verb agreement rules of Standard American English are what most readers in the United States expect to encounter in academic and business writing.

to AUDIENCE

39c Distinguishing Plural from Singular Compound Subjects

A *compound subject* consists of two or more subjects joined by a *conjunction* (*Jack* _and_ *Jill, one* _or_ *another*).

> **conjunction** Part of speech that joins words, phrases, or clauses to other words, phrases, or clauses and specifies the way the joined elements relate to each other

1. Compounds joined by *and* or *both ... and*

Most compound subjects joined by *and* or *both ... and* are plural.

▶ Pinterest *and* Facebook _are_ two popular social networking websites.

▶ *Both* Pinterest *and* Facebook _allow_ users to include photos and videos in their profiles.

A compound subject joined by *and* is singular, however, if the items in the compound refer to the same person or thing.

▶ The winner *and* next president _is_ the candidate with the most electoral votes.

A compound subject joined by *and* is also singular if it begins with *each* or *every*.

▶ *Each* paper *and* exam _contributes_ to your final grade.

However, if it is followed by *each,* a compound joined by *and* is plural.

▶ The research paper *and* the final exam *each* _contribute_ 25 percent toward your final grade.

2. Compounds joined by *or, nor, either ... or, neither ... nor*

When a compound subject is joined by *or, nor, either ... or,* or *neither ... nor,* the verb agrees with the part of the compound that is closest to the verb.

▶ *Neither* the coach *nor* the players _were_ worried by the other team's early lead.

The second part of the compound is plural, so the verb is plural.

Applying this rule can produce an awkward result when the first item in a compound is plural and the second is singular. Reversing the order often resolves the problem. Sometimes the rule produces a result so awkward, however, that the only solution is to reword the sentence. This happens particularly when the subject includes the pronoun *I, we,* or *you* and the verb is a form of *be.*

AWKWARD	*Neither* Carla *nor* I *am leaving* until the job is finished.
REVISED	Carla *and* I *are not leaving* until the job is finished.
	or
	Neither Carla *nor* I *will leave* until the job is finished.

39d Distinguishing Singular and Plural Indefinite Pronouns

Indefinite pronouns refer to unknown or unspecified people, quantities, or things. Most indefinite pronouns always take a singular verb. These include *anybody, anyone, anything, each, either, everybody, everyone, everything, much, neither, no one, nothing, one, somebody, someone,* and *something.*

▶ *Everybody talks* about the weather, but *nobody does* anything about it.

—Attributed to Mark Twain

Some indefinite pronouns (*both, few, many, others, several*) always take a plural verb.

▶ *Many* of us *make* New Year's resolutions, but *few* of us *keep* them.

Some indefinite pronouns (*all, any, more, most, none, some*) are either singular or plural, depending on context.

▶ *Some* of these questions *are* hard.

▶ *Some* of this test *is* hard.

In the first sentence, *some* takes a plural verb because it refers to the plural noun *questions;* in the second sentence, *some* takes a singular verb because it refers to the singular noun *test.*

39e Finding Agreement When the Subject Is a Collective Noun or a Number

A *collective noun* designates a collection, or group, of individuals: *audience, chorus, committee, faculty, family, government.* In US English, a collective noun is singular when it refers to the group acting as a whole.

▶ The *faculty is* revising the general education requirements.

The group acts as a whole.

A collective noun is plural when it refers to the members of the group acting individually.

▶ The *faculty are* unable to agree on the new requirements.
  The individual members of the group disagree among themselves.

If this usage sounds odd to you, however, you can reword the sentence with a clearly plural subject.

▶ The *members* of the faculty *are* unable to agree on the new requirements.

Numbers, fractions, and units of measure take a singular verb when they refer to an undifferentiated mass or quantity.

▶ *One-fourth* of the world's oil *is* consumed in the United States.

Numbers, fractions, and units of measure take a plural verb when they refer to a collection of individual people or things.

▶ *About a third* of the citizens naturalized in 2007 *were* immigrants from Asia.

The word *number* is plural when it appears with *a* but singular when it appears with *the*.

▶ *A number* of voters *are* in favor of the transportation bond.

▶ *The number* of voters in favor of the transportation bond *is* low.

39f Recognizing Nouns That Are Singular Even Though They End in -s

Some nouns that end in *-s* are singular. Examples include diseases like *diabetes* and *measles*.

▶ *Measles is* a contagious disease.

Words like *economics, mathematics,* and *physics* are singular when they refer to an entire field of study or body of knowledge but plural when they refer to a set of individual traits related to the field of study.

▶ *Economics is* a popular major at many schools.

▶ *The economics* of the music industry *are* changing rapidly.

39g Treating Titles, Words as Words, and Gerund Phrases as Singular

The titles of books, articles, movies, and other works; the names of companies and institutions; and words treated as words are all singular even if they are plural in form.

▶ *Harry Potter and the Order of the Phoenix is* the fifth of J. K. Rowling's seven Harry Potter books.

▶ *The Centers for Disease Control and Prevention helps* protect the nation's health.

▶ *Fungi is* one of two acceptable plural forms of the word *fungus;*

funguses is the other.

> **gerund** The present participle (-*ing* form) of a verb used as a noun

The -*ing* form of a verb used as a noun (a **gerund**) is also always singular.

▶ *Conducting excavations is* just one part of an archaeologist's job.

39h Matching a Relative Pronoun (*Who, Which,* or *That*) to Its Antecedent When the Pronoun Is the Subject of a Subordinate Clause

> **More about**
> Pronouns and their antecedents,
> 354–57, 373–76

A relative pronoun (*who, which,* or *that*) that functions as the subject of a subordinate clause is singular if its **antecedent** (the word it refers to) is singular, but it is plural if its antecedent is plural.

▶ People *who live* in glass houses should not throw stones.

▶ The cactus is a plant *that thrives* in a hot, dry environment.

Be careful with antecedent phrases that include the expressions *one of* or *only one of. One of* usually signals a plural antecedent; *only one of* signals a singular antecedent.

▶ Bill Clinton is *one of several presidents* of the United States *who were elected* to two terms.

> Several presidents were elected to two terms, and one of them was Clinton. The pronoun *who* refers to the plural noun *presidents.*

▶ Franklin D. Roosevelt is *the only one* of those presidents *who was elected* to more than two terms.

> Only one president, Roosevelt, was elected to more than two terms. The pronoun *who* refers to that particular one and is singular.

39i Finding Agreement When the Subject Follows the Verb

If you reverse normal order and put the subject after the verb for emphasis or dramatic effect, be sure the verb agrees with the actual subject, not a different word that precedes the verb.

More about Inverted word order, 292

▶ Onto the tennis court *stride the defending champion and her challenger.*

> The subject is the plural compound *the defending champion and her challenger,* not the singular term *tennis court.*

The subject also follows the verb in sentences that begin with *there* followed by a form of *be* (*there is, there are, there was, there were*).

▶ *There are*
~~There's~~ more people registered to vote than actually vote on Election Day.

> The subject, *people,* is plural, so the verb should be plural.

39j Matching a Linking Verb with Its Subject, Not Its Subject Complement

A *linking verb* (such as *was* or *were*) connects the subject of a sentence to a *subject complement,* which describes or refers to the subject. When either the subject or the subject complement is singular but the other is plural, make sure the verb agrees with the subject.

More about Linking verbs and subject complements, 329

▶ One influential voting bloc in the election *was*
~~were~~ young voters.

> The subject is the singular noun *bloc,* not the plural noun *voters.*

| **Tech** | **Grammar Checkers and Pronoun-Antecedent Agreement** |

Grammar checkers in word processing programs cannot identify pronoun-antecedent agreement errors.

PRONOUN-ANTECEDENT AGREEMENT

Pronouns rename or take the place of nouns, noun phrases, or other pronouns. The word or phrase that a pronoun replaces is its *antecedent.* Pronouns and their antecedents must agree in person (first, second, or third), number (singular or plural), and gender (neuter, feminine, or masculine). The antecedent usually appears before the pronoun but sometimes follows it. The two pronouns in the following example have the same antecedent—*Emma*—which follows the first pronoun and precedes the second.

▶ In *her* haste, *Emma* shut down the computer without saving *her* work.

A Possessive Pronoun Agrees with Its Antecedent, Not the Word It Modifies In English, a possessive pronoun (such as *his, hers,* or *its*) agrees with its antecedent, not the word it modifies. In the following example, *father* is the antecedent, so the pronoun should be masculine.

▶ The father beamed joyfully at ~~her~~ *his* newborn daughter.

More about
Singular and plural indefinite pronouns, 350

39k Matching Pronouns Appropriately with Indefinite Pronoun and Generic Noun Antecedents

Antecedents that are singular but have a plural sense are among the most common sources of pronoun-antecedent confusion. These include the following:

- *Indefinite pronouns* such as *each, everybody,* and *everyone* that are singular even though they refer to groups.

- *Generic nouns*—that is, singular nouns used to designate a whole class of people or things rather than a specific individual: *the typical student, the aspiring doctor.*

| Quick **Reference** | **Avoiding Pronoun-Antecedent Agreement Pitfalls** |

1. Match pronouns appropriately with indefinite pronoun and generic noun antecedents. (354)
2. Match pronouns appropriately with collective-noun antecedents. (356)
3. Match pronouns appropriately with compound antecedents. (357)

1. Singular indefinite pronoun or generic noun antecedents

A pronoun with a singular indefinite pronoun or generic noun antecedent should be singular. Do not let the plural sense of the antecedent distract you.

> ▸ The dog is a domesticated animal, unlike ~~their~~ *its* cousins the wolf and coyote.
>
> The antecedent is the singular generic noun *dog,* so the pronoun should be singular too.

This rule creates a problem, however, when the indefinite antecedent refers to both women and men. Correct agreement requires a singular pronoun, but using *he* as a substitute for either *man* or *woman* results in gender bias.

> **More about**
> Avoiding gender bias, 297–99, 355–56

GRAMMATICALLY CORRECT BUT GENDER-BIASED AGREEMENT

> In past downturns, *the affluent consumer* continued to spend, but now even *he* is cutting back.

Writers often try to avoid this conflict with a gender-neutral plural pronoun such as *they,* resulting in faulty pronoun-antecedent agreement.

UNBIASED BUT GRAMMATICALLY INCORRECT AGREEMENT

> In past downturns, *the affluent consumer* continued to spend, but now even *they* are cutting back.

This usage is common in everyday speech, but it is inappropriate for formal writing (although, as the Writing Responsibly box on p. 356 suggests, some language experts think differently).

You can avoid both gender bias and faulty agreement by rephrasing according to one of these strategies:

1. Make both the antecedent and the pronoun plural.

> ▸ In past downturns, ~~the affluent consumer~~ *affluent consumers* continued to spend, but now even ~~he is~~ *they are* cutting back.

2. Rephrase the sentence without the pronoun.

> ▸ ~~In past downturns, the~~ *Even the* affluent consumer continued to spend *, who* ~~but now even he~~ is cutting back *in past downturns, now*.

3. Use *he or she* or the appropriate variant (for example, *him or her* or *her or him*), but sparingly.

> ▸ In past downturns, the affluent consumer continued to spend, but even *she or* he is now cutting back.

Writing Responsibly | Using a Plural Pronoun with a Singular Antecedent

The use of a plural pronoun with singular indefinite antecedents is common in everyday speech, and many language experts maintain that it should be acceptable in formal writing, too. It is a usage, after all, that some of the finest writers in the English language have seen fit to employ:

> God send everyone their heart's desire!

—Shakespeare, *Much Ado About Nothing*, 3.4

Everybody who comes to Southampton finds it either their duty or pleasure to call upon us. . . .

—Jane Austen, from a letter

Nonetheless, many readers find the usage grating, so it is best to avoid it when you are writing for a general audience in an academic or business context.

to AUDIENCE

CAUTION Avoid overusing the phrases *he or she* and *his or her.* They can make your text sound stuffy and strained.

2. Plural or variable indefinite pronoun antecedents

Although most indefinite pronouns are singular, some (*both, few, many, others, several*) are always plural.

▸ *Both* of the candidates released *their* income tax returns.

Others (*all, any, more, most, some*) are singular or plural depending on the context.

▸ When the teacher surprised the *students* with a pop quiz, she discovered that *most* had not been doing *their* homework.

▸ Although some of the river's *water* is diverted for irrigation, *most* still makes *its* way to the sea.

391 Matching Pronouns with Collective Noun Antecedents

Collective nouns (for example, *audience, chorus, committee, faculty, family, government*) are singular when they refer to a group acting as a whole.

▸ *My family* traces *its* roots to West Africa.

Collective nouns are plural when they refer to the members of a group acting individually.

▸ *The billionaire's family* fought over *their* inheritance.

39m Matching Pronouns with Compound Antecedents

Compound antecedents joined by *and* are usually plural and take a plural pronoun.

▶ *Clinton and Obama* were the leading candidates for *their* party's nomination.

Pronouns with compound antecedents joined by *or, nor, either . . . or,* or *neither . . . nor* agree with the nearest antecedent. To avoid awkwardness when one of the antecedents is plural and the other is singular, put the plural antecedent second. When the antecedents differ in gender or person, however, the results of the "nearest antecedent" rule can be so awkward that the only solution is to reword the sentence.

AWKWARD   It was clear after the New Hampshire primary that either Barack Obama or Hillary Clinton would find herself the Democratic Party's nominee for president.

REVISED   It was clear after the New Hampshire primary that either Barack Obama or Hillary Clinton would be the Democratic Party's nominee for president.

40 Using Verbs

Verbs are the driving force in a sentence. They specify the action (*Sylvia won the race*), occurrence (*She became a runner in high school*), or state of being (*She was tired after the meet*) that affects the subject.

VERB FORMS

40a Understanding the Basic Forms of Verbs

With the exception of the verb *be,* all verbs have five forms: base, *-s* form, past tense, past participle, and present participle.

	Base Form	-s Form	Past Tense	Past Participle	Present Participle
Regular Verb	campaign	campaigns	campaigned	campaigned	campaigning
Irregular Verb	choose	chooses	chose	chosen	choosing

- The *base form* is what you find when you look up a verb in the dictionary.

  ▶ Presidential candidates *campaign* every four years.

  ▶ I usually *choose* candidates based on their policies.

More about
Verb tenses,
362–66
Voice, 279–80,
293–94

- The *-s form* is the base form plus *-s* or *-es.*

  ▶ My favorite senator always *campaigns* in our town.

  ▶ She *chooses* positive messages instead of negative ones.

- The past-tense form of regular verbs such as *campaign* is the base form plus *-d* or *-ed,* but the past-tense forms of irregular verbs such as *choose* vary.

  ▶ The mayor *campaigned* downtown yesterday.

  ▶ Some people *chose* to protest his appearance.

- The past participle is the same as the past tense in most verbs but varies in some irregular verbs.

  ▶ The candidate *has campaigned* nonstop.

  ▶ The candidate *has chosen* our town for his last campaign stop.

More about
Voice, 279–80,
293–94

- The present participle of all verbs, regular and irregular, is formed by adding *-ing* to the base form.

  ▶ Senator Brown *is campaigning* here today.

  ▶ They *are choosing* a running mate.

40b Using Regular and Irregular Verb Forms Correctly

The vast majority of English verbs are ***regular,*** meaning that their past-tense and past-participle forms end in *-d* or *-ed.*

Base	Past Tense	Past Participle
climb	climb**ed**	climb**ed**
analyze	analyze**d**	analyze**d**
copy	cop**ied**	cop**ied**

However, about two hundred English verbs are ***irregular,*** with past-tense and past-participle forms that do not follow one set pattern and are easy to confuse.

▶ My wool shirt ~~shrunk~~ *shrank* when I washed it in hot water.

Tech **Grammar Checkers and Verb Problems**

Grammar checkers in word processing programs will spot some errors that involve irregular or missing verbs, verb endings, and the subjunctive mood, but they will miss other errors and may suggest incorrect solutions. You must look for verb errors yourself and carefully evaluate any suggestions from a grammar checker.

If you are unsure whether a verb is regular or irregular or what form you should use in a particular situation, consult a dictionary or the following list. In the dictionary, you will find any irregular forms listed in the entry for the base form of a verb.

Quick

Reference   Common Irregular Verbs

Base Form	Past Tense	Past Participle	Base Form	Past Tense	Past Participle
arise	arose	arisen	leave	left	left
be	was/were	been	lend	lent	lent
bear	bore	borne, born	let	let	let
beat	beat	beaten	lie (recline)†	lay	lain
become	became	become	lose	lost	lost
begin	began	begun	make	made	made
bid	bid	bid	mean	meant	meant
bite	bit	bitten, bit	pay	paid	paid
blow	blew	blown	prove	proved	proved, proven
break	broke	broken	quit	quit	quit
bring	brought	brought	read	read	read
build	built	built	ride	rode	ridden
burst	burst	burst	ring	rang	rung
buy	bought	bought	rise	rose	risen
catch	caught	caught	run	ran	run
choose	chose	chosen	say	said	said
come	came	come	see	saw	seen
cost	cost	cost	send	sent	sent
cut	cut	cut	set	set	set
dig	dug	dug	shake	shook	shaken
dive	dived, dove	dived	shoot	shot	shot
do	did	done	shrink	shrank	shrunk
draw	drew	drawn	sing	sang	sung
drink	drank	drunk	sink	sank	sunk
drive	drove	driven	sit	sat	sat
eat	ate	eaten	sleep	slept	slept
fall	fell	fallen	slide	slid	slid
feel	felt	felt	speak	spoke	spoken
fight	fought	fought	spend	spent	spent
find	found	found	spread	spread	spread
flee	fled	fled	spring	sprang, sprung	sprung
fly	flew	flown	stand	stood	stood
forget	forgot	forgotten, forgot	steal	stole	stolen
freeze	froze	frozen	strike	struck	struck, stricken
get	got	gotten, got	swim	swam	swum
give	gave	given	swing	swung	swung
go	went	gone	take	took	taken
grow	grew	grown	teach	taught	taught
hang (suspend)*	hung	hung	tear	tore	torn
have	had	had	tell	told	told
hear	heard	heard	think	thought	thought
hold	held	held	throw	threw	thrown
hide	hid	hidden	wake	woke, waked	waked, woken
hit	hit	hit	wear	wore	worn
keep	kept	kept	win	won	won
know	knew	known	wind	wound	wound
lay	laid	laid	write	wrote	written
lead	led	led			

*Hang is regular—hang, hanged, hanged—when used to mean "kill by hanging."
†Lie is regular—lie, lied, lied—when used to mean "to be untruthful."

40c Combining Main Verbs with Helping Verbs to Form Complete Verbs

Almost all verb constructions other than the present and past tenses require the combination of a ***main verb*** with one or more ***helping verbs*** (or ***auxiliary verbs***) in a ***verb phrase.*** The most common helping verbs are *be, have,* and *do,* all three of which can also function as main verbs (*they* <u>are</u> *hungry; she* <u>had</u> *lunch; they* <u>did</u> *the dishes*). *Be,* unlike any other English verb, has eight forms.

FORMS OF *BE*

Base		*be*
Present Tense	I	*am*
	we, you, they	*are*
	he, she, it	*is*
Past Tense	I, he, she, it	*was*
	we, you, they	*were*
Past Participle		*been*
Present Participle		*being*

FORMS OF *HAVE* AND *DO*

Present Tense (Base and -s Form)	I, you, we, they	*have*	*do*
	he, she, it	*has*	*does*
Past Tense		*had*	*did*
Past Participle		*had*	*done*
Present Participle		*having*	*doing*

The ***modal verbs***—*can, could, may, might, must, shall, should, will, would,* and *ought to*—function only as helping verbs. Modals indicate ability, intention, permission, possibility, desire, and suggestion. They do not change form to indicate number or tense.

> **More about**
> Modals, 411

Modal Verbs English modal verbs have a range of meanings and unusual grammatical characteristics that you may find challenging. For example, they do not change form to indicate number or tense.

▶ In a close election, one vote ~~cans~~ make a difference.

The main verb carries the principal meaning of the verb phrase; the helping verbs, if any, carry information about tense and voice. A ***complete verb*** is a verb phrase with all the elements needed to determine tense, voice, and mood. Main verbs can stand alone as complete verbs only in their present-tense and past-tense forms.

|—— complete verb ——|
main verb

▶ The candidates   campaigned   until Election Day.

Main verbs in other forms (past or present participles) require helping verbs.

|———— complete verb ————|
helping
verbs   main verb

▶ The candidates   have been campaigning   for almost two years.

Sometimes in informal speech you can drop needed helping verbs, and some dialects allow certain constructions as complete verbs that Standard English does not allow. Helping verbs can sometimes be contracted (*they've voted already, we'll register tomorrow*) but in formal writing should never be omitted entirely.

▶ The candidates *have* been campaigning for almost two years.

CAUTION Do not use *of* for *have* in a verb phrase with a modal. When you use informal contractions like *could've* or *might've* in speech, remember that they mean *could have* and *might have.*

40d Including *-s* or *-es, -d* or *-ed* Endings When Required

Sometimes when speaking informally, you can omit the verb endings *-s, -es, -d,* or *-ed* or blend the sound of an ending inaudibly with the initial sound of the following word. Some dialects do not always require these endings. In formal writing, include them, or not, as standard usage requires.

▶ My dad ~~say~~ *says* I am ~~suppose~~ *supposed* to mow the lawn. I also ~~needs~~ *need* to trim the hedges. Before he ~~move~~ *moved* to Phoenix, my brother ~~use~~ *used* to do the mowing.

> **More about**
> Subject-verb
> agreement,
> 346–54

 Phrasal Verbs Phrasal verbs, such as *ask out* and *give in,* combine a verb with one or more prepositions or adverbs known as *particles.* The verb and particle combination of a phrasal verb has a distinct meaning, one that is different from the stand-alone words that form it. Because phrasal verbs are idiomatic, native English speakers are usually comfortable using them spontaneously. But that does not mean they can explain why one "gets on" a plane but "gets in" a boat.

> **More about**
> Phrasal verbs,
> 406–07

40e Distinguishing *Rise* from *Raise, Sit* from *Set, Lie* from *Lay*

The forms of *rise* and *raise, sit* and *set,* and *lie* and *lay* are easily confused. One verb in each pair (*rise, sit,* and *lie*) is **intransitive,** meaning that it does not take a

> **More about**
> Transitive and in-
> transitive verbs,
> 328–30

direct object. The other verb in each pair (*raise, set,* and *lay*) is **transitive,** meaning that it does take a direct object (underlined in the following examples).

- *Rise* means "to move or stand up." *Raise* means "to cause something (the direct object) to rise."

  ▸ The plane *rises* into the air. The pilot *raises* <u>the landing gear</u>.

- *Sit* means "to be seated." *Set* means "to place or put something (the direct object) on a surface."

  ▸ The passengers in coach *sit* in cramped seats. The attendants *set* <u>drinks</u> on their trays.

- *Lie* means "to recline." *Lay* means "to place or put something (the direct object) on a surface."

  ▸ The passengers in first class *lie* in fully reclining seats. During the landing, the pilot *lays* <u>the plane</u> gently on the runway.

A further difficulty with *lie* and *lay* is their confusing overlap of forms: The past tense of *lie* is *lay,* whereas the past tense of *lay* is *laid.* Changing the previous example to the past tense illustrates the issue.

  ▸ The passengers in first class ~~laid~~ *lay* in fully reclining seats. During the landing, the pilot ~~lay~~ *laid* the plane gently on the runway.

TENSE

40f Using Appropriate Verb Tenses

Verb **tenses** provide information about the time in which an action or event occurs—past, present, or future—about whether the action is ongoing or completed, and about the time of one action relative to another.

Reference Distinguishing *Rise* from *Raise, Sit* from *Set,* and *Lie* from *Lay*				
Base Form	**-s Form**	**Past Tense**	**Past Participle**	**Present Participle**
rise (to get up)	rises	rose	risen	rising
raise (to lift)	raises	raised	raised	raising
sit (to be seated)	sits	sat	sat	sitting
set (to place)	sets	set	set	setting
lie (to recline)	lies	lay	lain	lying
lay (to place)	lays	laid	laid	laying

Quick

1. Simple tenses

Use the ***simple present tense*** for current or habitual actions or events and to state general truths. Accompanied by a reference to a future event, the simple present can also indicate a future occurrence (also see *section 40h,* pp. 365–66).

CURRENT ACTION	Hernando *opens* the door to his classroom.
HABITUAL ACTION	He *enjoys* teaching second-graders.
GENERAL TRUTH	Earth *is* the third planet from the sun.
FUTURE OCCURRENCE	Winter *ends* in two weeks.

Use the ***simple past tense*** for completed actions or occurrences.

▶ The bell *rang.* Hernando *asked* his students to be quiet.

Use the ***simple future tense*** for actions that have not yet occurred.

▶ He *will give* them a spelling test this afternoon.

2. Perfect tenses

The perfect tenses generally indicate the completion of an action before a particular time. Use the ***present perfect tense*** for an action that started in the past but is now completed or for an action that started in the past but is ongoing.

COMPLETED ACTION	I *have read* all the Harry Potter books.
ONGOING ACTION	I *have read* books all my life.

Use the ***past perfect tense*** for actions completed by a specific time in the past or before another past action.

▶ Because the students *had studied* hard for their test, they knew most of the spelling words.

   The studying—*had studied* (past perfect)—came before the knowing—*knew* (simple past).

Use the ***future perfect tense*** for an action that will be completed by a definite time in the future.

▶ By the time the semester ends, Hernando's students *will have improved* their spelling grades.

3. Progressive tenses

The progressive tenses indicate ongoing action. Use the ***present progressive tense*** for an action that is ongoing in the present.

▶ Matilda *is learning* Spanish.

Use the ***past progressive tense*** for an action that was ongoing in the past.

▶ Last night, Yue *was practicing* for her recital.

Quick

Reference An Overview of Verb Tenses and Their Forms

Simple Tenses

Simple present	base or -s form	I *learn* something new every day.
Simple past	past-tense form	I *learned* Spanish many years ago.
Simple future	*will* + base form	I *will learn* to ski next winter.

Perfect Tenses

Present perfect	*has/have* + past participle	I *have learned* to water ski already.
Past perfect	*had* + past participle	I *had learned* to water ski by the time I was nine.
Future perfect	*will have* + past participle	I *will have learned* how to skydive by September.

Progressive Tenses

Present progressive	*am/is/are* + present participle	I *am learning* about Japanese food.
Past progressive	*was/were* + present participle	I *was learning* to make sushi yesterday.
Future progressive	*will be* + present participle	I *will be learning* new skills next week.
Present perfect progressive	*have/has been* + present participle	I *have been cooking* seriously since I was a teenager.
Past perfect progressive	*had been* + present participle	I *had been preparing* simple dishes even before then.
Future perfect progressive	*will have been* + present participle	I *will have been enjoying* this hobby for two decades by the end of the year.

Use the *future progressive tense* for an ongoing action that will occur in the future.

▶ Elena *will be working* as a publishing company intern next summer.

Use the *present perfect progressive tense* for an ongoing action that began in the past.

▶ Hernando *has been working* on his master's degree in education since 2008.

Use the *past perfect progressive tense* for an ongoing past action that is now completed.

▶ Until this semester, he *had been taking* education courses at night.

Use the *future perfect progressive tense* for an ongoing action that will be finished at a definite time in the future.

▶ By the end of August, Hernando *will have been studying* education for more than six years.

Do Not Use the Progressive Tenses with All Verbs Certain verbs, typically those that convey a mental process or a state of being, are not used in the progressive tenses. Examples include *appreciate, belong, contain, envy, fear, know, like, need, owe, own, remember, resemble, seem,* and *want.*

▸ She ~~is seeming~~ angry with her boyfriend. He ~~was owing~~ her

    an apology.

<small>seems</small> <small>owed</small>

40g Following Conventions for Use of the Present Tense

The present tense is conventionally used for describing works of art, for describing events in literary works, and for stating scientific facts.

▸ In his 2007 novel *Bridge of Sighs,* Richard Russo ~~told~~ an engrossing

    story about the Lynch family, who ~~lived~~ in a small town in upstate

    New York.

<small>tells</small> <small>live</small>

▸ Watson and Crick discovered that DNA ~~had~~ a double helix structure.

    Although the discovery was in the past, it remains true.

<small>has</small>

In most cases, use the present tense to introduce a quotation, paraphrase, or summary.

▸ As Harriet Lerner ~~noted,~~ "Anger is neither legitimate nor illegitimate,

    meaningful nor pointless. Anger simply is."

<small>notes,</small>

EXCEPTION The APA documentation style calls for the use of the past tense or the past perfect tense for reporting findings or introducing cited material.

▸ Chodoff (2002) ~~claims~~ that in their efforts to put a diagnostic label

    on "all varieties and vagaries of human feelings," psychiatrists ~~risk~~

    medicalizing "the human condition itself."

<small>claimed</small> <small>risked</small>

> *More about*
> APA documen-
> tation style,
> 201–38

40h Using Tense Sequence to Clarify Time Relationships

When a sentence contains two separate actions, readers need a clear idea of the time relationship between them, which writers communicate by their choice of tenses, or **sequence of tenses.** Do not shift tenses unnecessarily.

> *More about*
> Inappropriate
> shifts in tense,
> 386

In a sentence with two past actions, for example, use the simple past tense for both verbs if the actions occurred simultaneously.

▶ When he *arrived* at the station, the train *departed*.

The arrived and the train departed at the same time.

If the actions happened at different times, use the past perfect tense for the action that occurred first.

▶ By the time he *arrived* at the station, the train *had departed*.

The train departed before he arrived.

1. Infinitives and tense sequence

An ***infinitive*** consists of *to* followed by the base form of the verb (*to listen, to go*). Use this form, the *present infinitive,* for an action that occurs after or simultaneously with the action of the main verb.

▶ Ivan is known to be a good student.

The knowing and the being happen together.

▶ Everyone expects Ivan to get an *A* on the exam.

The expectation is about Ivan's future performance on the exam.

Use the *perfect infinitive—to have* and the past participle (*to have listened, to have gone*)—for an action that happened before the action of the main verb.

▶ Ivan is said to have studied all weekend.

The studying took place before the talk about it.

2. Participles and tense sequence

Use the present participle (*listening, going*) to express action that happens simultaneously with the action of the main verb, regardless of the tense of the main verb.

▶ *Handing* her son Robbie a cup of coffee, Mona offered him some brownies.

Use the past participle (*listened, gone*) or the present perfect participle (*having listened, having gone*) to express action that happens before the action of the main verb.

▶ *Discouraged* by her daughter's aloofness, Mona asked her son to help.

Mona was discouraged before she asked.

▶ *Having mediated* their disagreements for years, Robbie refused to intervene.

Robbie mediated before he refused.

MOOD

40i Understanding Verb Mood

The **mood** of a verb indicates whether a speaker or writer views what is said as a fact, a command, or a possibility. Most English sentences are in the **indicative mood,** which states facts or opinions and asks questions.

▶ Our research papers *are* due tomorrow morning.

▶ *Did* you *say* the deadline had changed?

The **imperative mood** issues commands, gives instructions, or makes requests. The subject of an imperative sentence (*you*) is usually left unstated.

▶ *Hand in* your papers by Friday afternoon.

▶ *Turn* left at the third stoplight.

▶ Please *pass* the salt.

The **subjunctive mood** expresses possibility (or impossibility), as in hypothetical situations, conditions known to be untrue, wishes, suggestions, and requirements.

▶ If I *were* finished, I could go to bed.

▶ The doctor suggests that he *get* more exercise.

40j Using the Subjunctive Mood Correctly

The subjunctive has three tenses: present, past, and past perfect. The present subjunctive is always the base form of the verb, regardless of the person or number of the subject: *Ramon asks that his teacher <u>give</u> (not gives) him an extension.* The past subjunctive of *be* is *were: I wish I <u>were</u> (not was) finished.* For all other verbs, the past subjunctive is identical to the past tense. Similarly, the past perfect subjunctive is identical to the past perfect indicative.

Clauses with verbs in the subjunctive are always subordinate clauses. They include **conditional clauses** that begin with *if, as if,* or *as though* and describe

Writing
Responsibly   **Using the Subjunctive in Formal Writing**

Because the subjunctive has been fading from everyday usage, the indicative may seem more acceptable to you. Most readers, however, still expect to find the subjunctive used in formal writing.

▶ I wish that I ~~was~~ *were* finished.

to AUDIENCE

a condition known to be untrue. Conditional clauses put forward a set of circumstances and modify a main clause that states what follows from those circumstances.

▶ If I *were* taller, I would try out for basketball.

▶ The candidate acts as though he *were* already the winner.

When the main clause includes a modal auxiliary such as *would, could,* or *should,* do not use a similar construction instead of the subjunctive in the *if* clause.

▶ If I ~~would have been~~ taller, I would try out for basketball.
  (*were*)

Verbs in the main clause that express a wish, request, recommendation, or demand also require the subjunctive in the subordinate clause.

▶ The hikers wished their campground ~~was~~ not so far away.
  (*were*)

▶ Citizens are demanding that the government ~~fixes~~ the economy.
  (*fix*)

▶ Senators have requested that the president ~~is~~ more responsive to
  the middle class.
  (*be*)

▶ Alicia's adviser recommended that she ~~takes~~ calculus.
  (*take*)

NOTE When an *if* clause states something that is factual or probable, use the indicative mood, not the subjunctive.

If Susan *is* at the convention, she won't know about the accident.

Her brother hasn't heard about the accident if he *is* on his way to Atlanta.

The indicative mood is called for in these examples because the writer knows that Susan is at a convention and that her brother is traveling to Atlanta.

41 Understanding Pronoun Case and Reference

In an online multiplayer game like World of Warcraft or Halo, you may be interacting with dozens of other players who could be located almost anywhere in the world. Instead of being physically present in the game, all players have virtual stand-ins—avatars. Your avatar acts on your orders and may even change form—from human to animal or student to soldier, for example—depending on the way in which you want it to function in a particular environment.

Like avatars, pronouns are stand-ins. They represent other words—their *antecedents*—from one place to another in speech or writing. Also like avatars, pronouns sometimes change form depending on the role you want them to play within a sentence.

PRONOUN CASE

Nouns and pronouns can play various roles within a sentence. They can be subjects.

	subject	
NOUN	**The Steelers**	lost.
PRONOUN	**They**	lost.

More about
Subjects and objects, 326–30

They can be objects (including direct objects, indirect objects, and objects of prepositions).

	subject		direct object
NOUN	The Bears	beat	**the Steelers.**
PRONOUN	We	beat	**them.**

They can indicate possession.

	possessive			possessive	
NOUN	**Chicago's**	team	beat	**Pittsburgh's**	team.
PRONOUN	**Our**	team	beat	**their**	team.

More about
Indicating possession with apostrophes, 432–35

Case refers to the different forms a noun or pronoun takes—*subjective, objective,* or *possessive*—depending on which of these roles it serves. Nouns have

personal pronouns
Pronouns that take
the place of nouns or
noun phrases
relative pronouns
Pronouns that intro-
duce subordinate
clauses that describe
the pronoun's
antecedent
**interrogative pro-
nouns** Pronouns that
introduce questions

the same form as subjects that they do as objects, and they indicate possession
with an *s* sound that is marked in writing with an apostrophe (*Chicago's team*).
In contrast, most ***personal pronouns*** and some ***relative*** and ***interrogative***
pronouns have distinct forms for each of their roles.

		Subjective Case	Objective Case	Possessive Case
Personal Pronouns				
Singular	1st person	*I*	*me*	*my, mine*
	2nd person	*you*	*you*	*your, yours*
	3rd person	*he*	*him*	*his*
		she	*her*	*her, hers*
		it	*it*	*its*
	1st person	*we*	*us*	*our, ours*
Plural	2nd person	*you*	*you*	*your, yours*
	3rd person	*they*	*them*	*their, theirs*
Case-Variant Relative and		*who*	*whom*	*whose*
Interrogative Pronouns		*whoever*	*whomever*	

For native speakers of English, some case errors are easy to detect because
they sound wrong.

▸ Hermione is one of Harry's best friends, and ~~her~~ often gives ~~he~~
⌃*she* ⌃*him*

sound advice.

However, in situations like those discussed in the following sections, the ear
can be an unreliable guide to proper case usage.

41a Using the Subjective Case for Subject Complements

**subject comple-
ment** An adjective,
pronoun, or noun
phrase that follows
a linking verb and
describes or refers to
the sentence subject

A pronoun that functions as a ***subject complement*** should be in the subjective
case, not the objective case.

▸ Asked who spilled the milk, my sister confessed that the guilty one

was ~~her.~~
⌃*she.*

If this usage sounds overly formal, try reversing the subject and subject
complement.

▸ Asked who spilled the milk, my sister confessed that the guilty
⌃*she was*

~~one was her.~~
⌃*one.*

41b *She and I* or *Her and Me*? Keeping Track of Case in Compounds

Pronouns that are part of compound subjects or subject complements should be in the subjective case.

compound subject

► My friends and ~~me~~ *I* chat online while we play computer games.

Pronouns that are part of compound objects should be in the objective case.

compound dir. obj.

► My parents call my brothers and ~~I~~ *me* every weekend.

Pronouns that are part of compound possessives should be in the possessive case.

compound possessive

► My father often gets ~~me~~ *my* and my brother's names confused.

41c Keeping Track of Pronoun Case in Appositives

The case of a pronoun in an ***appositive phrase*** should reflect the role of the phrase the appositive renames: subjective for a subject or subject complement,

> **appositive phrase**
> A noun or noun phrase that renames a preceding noun or noun phrase and is grammatically equivalent to it

---

Quick **Reference**   **Editing for Case in Compounds**

To determine the correct case of a pronoun in a compound, isolate the pronoun from the rest of the compound; then read the result aloud to yourself. If the pronoun is clearly wrong, replace it with the correct one.

Faulty   [My friends and] me chat online while we play computer games.
Revised   My friends and I chat online while we play computer games.

Me chat online is clearly wrong. Replacing the objective pronoun *me* with the subjective pronoun *I* corrects the problem.

Faulty   My parents call [my siblings and] I every weekend.
Revised   My parents call my siblings and me every weekend.

My parents call I is clearly wrong. Replacing the subjective pronoun *I* with the objective pronoun *me* corrects the problem.

Faulty   My father often gets me [and my brother's] names confused.
Revised   My father often gets my and my brother's names confused.

My father gets me names confused is clearly wrong. Replacing the objective pronoun *me* with the possessive pronoun *my* corrects the problem.

as in the first of the following examples; objective for an object, as in the second example.

▶ The two most talented actors in our school, Valentino and ~~her,~~ always
  get the best roles in school productions.

  (she,)

▶ The director always wants the best artists, ~~she~~ and ~~I,~~ to work on
  the scenery.

  (her   me)

41d Deciding between *We* and *Us* before Nouns

In expressions that combine *we* or *us* with a noun, use *we* with nouns that are subjects or subject complements and *us* with nouns that are objects. To decide which is which, say the sentence to yourself with the pronoun alone.

▶ ~~Us~~ gamers live vicariously in the game world through our avatars.

  (We)

  Us live vicariously is clearly wrong.

▶ Our avatars act vicariously in the game world on behalf of ~~we~~ gamers.

  (us)

  Avatars act on behalf of we is clearly wrong.

41e Using the Objective Case Both before and after an Infinitive

infinitive The *to* form of a verb (*to decide, to eat, to study*)

Use the objective case for both the subject and the object of an ***infinitive.***

▶ I asked *her* <u>to recommend</u> *me* for the job.

  Both *her,* the subject of the infinitive *to recommend,* and *me,* its direct object, are in the objective case.

41f Deciding on Case with *-ing* Words

More about
Gerunds, 331

In most cases, use the possessive form of a noun or pronoun with a ***gerund*** (the *-ing* form of a verb used as a noun).

▶ Professor Nolan, I appreciate ~~you~~ taking time to advise me.

  (your)

Use the objective form of a noun or pronoun, however, when the *-ing* word functions as a modifier rather than a noun.

PRONOUN IS THE MODIFIER	Debbie is a Derek Jeter fan. She admires *his* playing.

PRONOUN IS MODIFIED	Debbie saw *him* playing in the World Series.

41g Clarifying Case in Comparisons with *Than* or *As*

In comparisons with *than* or *as,* changing a pronoun's case can significantly change the meaning of a sentence.

▶ Amy likes her new car more than <u>I</u>.

▶ Amy likes her new car more than <u>me</u>.

In the first sentence, the subjective case (*I*) signals a comparison between Amy's and the writer's fondness for Amy's car (she likes it more than the writer does). In the second sentence, the objective case (*me*) signals a comparison between Amy's fondness for her car and her fondness for the writer (she likes her car more than she likes the writer). To avoid confusing readers in situations like this, supply any words needed to make the comparison explicit.

▶ Amy likes her new car more than <u>I</u> *do.*

▶ Amy likes her new car more than *she likes* <u>me</u>.

41h Using *Who, Whom, Whoever,* and *Whomever*

The pronouns *who, whom, whoever,* and *whomever* have two jobs. As **relative pronouns** they introduce **subordinate clauses.** As **interrogative pronouns** they introduce questions.

> **subordinate clause**
> A word group with a subject and predicate that cannot stand alone as a sentence but instead functions within a sentence as a noun, adjective, or adverb

- Use *who* or *whoever* for the subject of a subordinate clause or question.

  |———— subordinate clause ————|
  subj.

  ▶ Jackie Robinson, *who* integrated major league baseball, played for the Brooklyn Dodgers.

  |———— question ————|
  subj.

  ▶ *Who* integrated major league baseball?

- Use *whom* or *whomever* for the object of a subordinate clause or question. Notice, however, that contrary to normal word order, in which direct objects follow verbs, *whom* and *whomever* usually come at the beginning of a clause or question.

Writing Responsibly   Case and Tone

Many people now ignore the distinction between *who* and *whom,* using only *who.* In academic and business writing, however, many readers will assume that you do not understand correct usage if you use *who* when *whom* is called for. So, even if *whom* and *whomever* sound inappropriately formal, even old-fashioned, to your ear, consider what your reader's expectations are and adjust your usage accordingly.

to AUDIENCE

⊢───── subordinate clause ─────⊣
dir. obj.
▸ Robinson, *whom* the Dodgers hired in 1947, retired in 1956.

⊢────── question ──────⊣
dir. obj.
▸ *Whom* did the Dodgers hire in 1947?

- The case of a relative pronoun is determined by its role in a clause, not the role of the clause in the sentence. The relative pronoun in the following example is the subject of its clause and so should be in the subjective case—*whoever*—even though the clause as a whole is the object of the preposition *to.*

  whoever
  ▸ In professional golf, the winner's prize goes to ~~whomever~~ com-
  ∧
  pletes the course in the fewest strokes.

- Match the pronoun to its verb, not to the verb of an intervening clause. In the following example, the pronoun should be the subjective case *who* because it is the subject of *was,* not the object of *know.*

  who
  ▸ Thomas Edison, ~~whom~~ many people know was the inventor of the
  ∧
  lightbulb, was also the inventor of the phonograph.

CLEAR PRONOUN REFERENCE

Pronoun reference is clear when readers can easily identify a pronoun's antecedent.

▸ Mario talked to his sister Roberta about her career plans.

The pronoun *his* clearly refers to Mario; the pronoun *her* clearly refers to Mario's sister.

Pronoun reference is unclear when readers cannot be certain what a pronoun's antecedent is.

▸ Mario talked to Paul about his career plans.

Did Mario and Paul talk about Mario's career plans or Paul's? Without more information, readers will be uncertain.

41i   Revising for Clear Reference

The reference of a pronoun is ambiguous when it has two or more equally plausible antecedents.

▶ Mario talked to Paul about his career plans.

One way to resolve ambiguous reference is to replace the pronoun with the appropriate noun.

▶ Mario talked to Paul about Paul's career plans.

To avoid repeating the noun, rephrase the sentence in a way that eliminates the ambiguity.

▶ Paul talked about his career plans with Mario.

> The position of the pronoun *his* associates the plans clearly and unambiguously with Paul, not Mario.

41j   Revising for Specific Reference with *It, This, That,* and *Which*

When pronouns such as *it, this, that,* and *which* refer broadly to an entire clause, sentence, or series of sentences, readers may be uncertain about what specific information the pronouns cover.

▶ Who owns Antarctica? Several countries, including Argentina, Australia, Chile, France, New Zealand, Norway, the United Kingdom, and the United States, all claim or reserve the right to claim all or part of the continent. ~~This makes it~~ difficult to answer.
     These competing claims make the question of ownership

> The revision specifies what information the writer meant by *this* and *it*.

41k   Avoiding Implied Reference

A pronoun should have a clearly identifiable antecedent—not, as with *they* in the following example, an unstated, or implied, antecedent.

DRAFT   From her stories of her small-town childhood, they seem like great places to grow up.

REVISED   Her stories of her childhood make small towns seem like great places to grow up.

Similarly, in the next example, the antecedent to *they*—*the researchers*—is implied, confusingly, in the possessive form *researchers'.*

❯ **More about**
Citing sources,
149–200

▶ According to the researchers' study, ~~they found that~~ access to high speed Internet connections at home might reduce students' test scores (Vigdor and Ladd 1).

41l **Avoiding the Indefinite Use of *They, It,* and *You***

In formal writing, the pronouns *they* and *it* need specific antecedents. Avoid using these pronouns to refer to unnamed people or things.

▶ At Hogwarts School of Witchcraft and Wizardry, *students* ~~they~~ use owls, not texting, for sending messages.

▶ *The* ~~In the~~ beginning of the chapter, ~~it~~ compares pronouns to computer-game avatars.

Likewise in formal writing, reserve the pronoun *you* (and the implied *you* of commands) to address the reader directly, as in "you, the reader." Do not use *you* as a substitute for indefinite words such as *anybody, everybody,* or *people.*

▶ Before computers and the Internet, ~~you~~ *people* got ~~your~~ *their* news mostly from newspapers, radio, and television.

42 Using Adjectives and Adverbs

The clothing, jewelry, and hairstyles we choose—our modifiers—send a message to others about how we want them to perceive us. A flamboyant dress, a tattoo, eye-catching jewelry, and flowing hair send one impression; a tailored business suit sends another. Similarly, we send readers a message about how we want them to understand our words by our choice of adjectives and adverbs to modify them.

42a **Learning the Difference between Adjectives and Adverbs**

Adjectives modify (or describe) nouns and pronouns, answering questions such as *What kind? Which one?* or *How many? Adverbs* modify verbs, adjectives, other adverbs, and entire phrases, clauses, and sentences; they answer questions such as *How? Where?* or *When?*

Although many adverbs end in the suffix *-ly,* many do not (*later, often, quite, seldom*), and dozens of adjectives do (*elderly, lowly, scholarly*). The only reliable way to distinguish an adjective from an adverb is not from its form but from its function.

> **More about**
> Modifier placement, 381–85

42b Using Adjectives, Not Adverbs, as Subject Complements after Linking Verbs

Linking verbs express a state of being rather than an action or occurrence. They link the subject to a ***subject complement,*** which describes or refers to the subject. The subject complement, in other words, modifies the subject, not the verb; it can be an adjective or a noun, but not an adverb.

The verb *be,* when used as a main verb, is always a linking verb.

▶ The *food* is *delicious.*

The adjective *delicious* modifies the subject, *food.*

Other verbs, such as *appear, become, feel, look, prove, sound,* and *taste,* may function as linking verbs in one context and action verbs in another. A word following one of these verbs should be an adjective if it modifies the subject and an adverb if it modifies the verb.

> **More about**
> Linking verbs and subject complements, 329

▶ *Maria* looked *anxious* to the dentist.

Looked is a linking verb, and the adjective *anxious* is a subject complement that describes Maria's state of mind as the dentist perceived it.

▶ Maria *looked anxiously* at the dentist.

Looked is an action verb modified by the adverb *anxiously,* which describes how Maria did the looking.

42c Is It *Bad* or *Badly, Good* or *Well?*

In casual speech, we commonly confuse adjectives and adverbs. In writing, however, you should use adjectives to modify nouns and pronouns and adverbs

---

Tech   **Grammar Checkers and Adjective-Adverb Problems**

Grammar checkers in word processing programs catch some adjective and adverb errors but miss many others. A grammar checker, for example, missed errors such as *The Patriots played bad, the boat rocked gentle,* and *Tomás looked well in his tuxedo.*

to modify verbs, adjectives, or other adverbs. Do not confuse *bad* with *badly,* *good* with *well,* or adverbs that end in *-ly* with adjectives that do not.

- *Bad* is an adjective; *badly* is an adverb.

  > ► The Patriots played ~~bad~~ ^badly^ in the fourth quarter.

    Badly modifies the action verb *played.*

  > ► The quarterback feels ~~badly~~ ^bad^ about the loss.

    Feels is a linking verb; *bad* modifies *quarterback.*

- *Good* is an adjective, and *well* is its adverb counterpart. *Well* is an adjective, however, when it is used to mean "healthy."

  > ► Leah did ~~good~~ ^well^ on her final exams.

    The adverb *well* modifies the verb *did.*

  > ► Jalil looks ~~well~~ ^good^ in his tuxedo.

    Looks is a linking verb; the adjective *good* modifies *Jalil.*

  > ► After a late-night graduation party, Leah is not feeling ~~good~~ ^well.^

    Well is used as an adjective because it refers to health.

- Do not confuse adverbs that end in *-ly* with their adjective counterparts that do not.

  > ► You should play ~~gentle~~ ^gently^ with small children.

    The adverb *gently* modifies the verb *play.*

Order of Adjectives in a Series　When more than one adjective modifies a noun, the adjectives usually need to follow a specific order.

> ► a ~~European~~ *stunning* ^European^ racehorse

For guidance on ordering multiple adjectives, see page 412.

42d Using Negatives Correctly

In Standard American English, when two negative modifiers describe the same word, they cancel each other out and the message becomes positive. The sentence *It is not unlikely that the volcano will erupt soon,* for example, means that the volcano is likely to erupt soon. Although some dialects allow the use

---

Quick Reference   **Forming Comparatives and Superlatives**

Regular Forms

	Positive	Comparative	Superlative
Adjectives	bold	bolder/less bold	boldest/least bold
	helpful	more/less helpful	most/least helpful
Adverbs	far	farther	farthest
	realistically	more/less realistically	most/least realistically

Irregular Forms

	Positive	Comparative	Superlative
Adjectives	bad	worse	worst
	good	better	best
	little	less (quantity)/littler (size)	least (quantity)/littlest (size)
	many/much/some	more	most
Adverbs	badly	worse	worst
	well	better	best

---

of double (and more) negatives to emphasize a negative meaning, and many people use them that way in casual speech, you should avoid using them that way in formal writing.

Remember that contractions such as *couldn't* and *shouldn't* include the negative word *not,* and that words like *barely, hardly,* and *scarcely* have a negative meaning.

▶ Students ~~shouldn't~~ never park in a faculty-only lot.
     should

▶ The children ~~can't~~ hardly wait to open their presents.
     can

42e Using Comparative and Superlative Adjectives and Adverbs Correctly

Most adjectives and adverbs have three forms for indicating the relative degree of the quality or manner they specify: positive, comparative, and superlative. The *positive form* is the base form—the form you find when you look the word up in the dictionary.

POSITIVE   Daryl is *tall.*

The *comparative form* indicates a relatively greater or lesser degree of a quality.

COMPARATIVE   Daryl is *taller* than Ivan.

The *superlative form* indicates the greatest or least degree of a quality.

SUPERLATIVE   Daryl is the *tallest* player on the team.

Regular adjectives and adverbs form the comparative and superlative with either the suffixes *-er* and *-est* or the addition of the words *more* and *most* or *less* and *least*. A few adjectives and adverbs have irregular comparative and superlative forms (see the Quick Reference box on page 379). If you are not sure whether to use *-er/-est* or *more/most* for a particular adjective or adverb, look it up in a dictionary. If the entry shows *-er* and *-est* forms, use them. If no such forms are listed, use *more* or *most*.

1. Comparative or superlative

Use the comparative form to compare two things, the superlative to compare three or more.

▶ Between Jon Stewart and Stephen Colbert, I think Colbert is the ~~funniest.~~ *funnier.*

▶ Of all comedians ever, I think Buster Keaton was the ~~funnier.~~ *funniest.*

2. Redundant comparisons

Do not combine the comparative words *more/most* with adjectives or adverbs that are already in comparative form with an *-er* or *-est* ending.

▶ Trains in Europe and Japan are ~~more~~ faster than trains in the United States.

More about
Complete comparisons, 393–94

3. Complete comparisons

Make sure your comparisons are logical and that readers have all the information they need to understand what is being compared to what.

▶ The nurses' test scores were higher. *than those of the pre-med students.*

The first draft makes us ask, "Higher than what?" The revision clarifies the comparison.

4. Absolute terms

Expressions like *more unique* or *most perfect* are common in everyday speech, but if you think about them, they make no sense. *Unique, perfect,* and other words such as *equal, essential, final, full, impossible, infinite,* and *unanimous* are absolutes, and absolutes are beyond compare. If something is unique, it is by definition one of a kind. If something is perfect, it cannot be improved upon. In formal writing, then, avoid using absolute terms comparatively.

▶ Last night's performance of the play was the ~~most perfect~~ *best* yet.

43 Avoiding Misplaced and Dangling Modifiers

Since 1886 the Statue of Liberty has dominated New York harbor, holding aloft a torch in the hand of her outstretched right arm. In 1876, however, while work on the rest of the statue continued in France, the arm and torch stood incongruously at the Philadelphia Centennial Exhibition, displayed there, and later in New York's Madison Square Park, to help raise funds for the construction of the statue's pedestal. This photograph of the display may strike you as strange because this huge sculpture is supposed to be attached appropriately to the rest of the statue. Similarly, when you misplace modifiers in your sentences, you may inadvertently confuse or surprise your readers.

A modifying word, phrase, or clause is misplaced if readers have to puzzle out what it modifies or if they stumble over it while trying to get from one part of a sentence to the next. Look for such *misplaced modifiers* as you revise your drafts.

43a Placing Modifiers Close to the Words They Modify

A modifier positioned far from its intended target might appear to modify some other part of the sentence instead.

> ▶ The couple moved to a bigger apartment after their first child was born ~~because they needed more space.~~ ^because they needed more space^
>
> The couple's need for space did not cause the birth of their child.

> ▶ For more than four years, the two rovers have been exploring the surface of Mars ~~that landed in January 2004.~~ ^that landed in January 2004^
>
> The rovers landed, not the surface of Mars.

Tech | Misplaced Modifiers and Grammar and Style Checkers

The grammar and style checkers in word processing programs usually cannot tell what a modifier is supposed to modify, so they rarely flag those that are confusingly or ambiguously placed. They do flag most split infinitives and some other disruptive modifiers.

43b Avoiding Squinting Modifiers and Ambiguously Placed Limiting Modifiers

A *squinting modifier* confuses readers by appearing to modify both what precedes it and what follows it.

DRAFT   People who study hard <u>usually</u> will get the best grades.

Do people who make a practice of studying hard get the best grades, or do the best grades usually (but not always) go to people who study hard? The sentence can be clarified in two different ways.

REVISION   People who <u>usually</u> study hard will get the best grades.

REVISION   People who study hard will <u>usually</u> get the best grades.

Limiting modifiers include qualifying words such as *almost, even, exactly, hardly, just, merely, only, scarcely,* and *simply.* In the following example, the ambiguous placement of the limiter *just* leaves the reader with a variety of possible interpretations.

AMBIGUOUS   The math department just offers Calculus III at night

on Thursdays.

REVISED   At night on Thursdays, the math department offers just Calculus III. [That is the only math course you can take on Thursday nights.]

REVISED   On Thursdays, the math department offers Calculus III just at night. [That is the only time you can take the class on Thursdays.]

REVISED   The math department offers Calculus III at night just on Thursdays. [That is the only day you can take the class at night.]

43c Moving Disruptively Placed Modifiers

A modifier is disruptive when it awkwardly breaks the flow among grammatically connected parts of a sentence. Long adverbial phrases and clauses tend to be disruptive when they fall between subjects and verbs (as in the first example below), within verb phrases (as in the second example), or between verbs and their objects (as in the third example).

▶ *The Sopranos,* ~~well after its last episode aired in June 2007,~~ continued
   well after its last episode aired in June 2007.
   to elicit admiring commentary and analysis.

Writing Responsibly | Misplaced Modifiers in the Real World

Misplaced modifiers can sometimes cause real distress. A confusing instruction like the one below from the website of the Federal Emergency Management Agency (FEMA) might bewilder a homeowner struggling to recover from a natural disaster.

> You will need your social security number, current and pre-disaster address, phone numbers, type of insurance coverage, total household annual income, and a routing and account number from your bank *if you want to have disaster assistance funds transferred directly into your bank account.* [Emphasis added.]

As written, this statement suggests that an applicant for relief needs all of the listed items in order to have disaster assistance deposited directly into a bank account. Here is what the writer meant to say:

> You will need your social security number, current and pre-disaster address, phone numbers, type of insurance coverage, total household annual income, and, *if you want to have disaster assistance funds transferred directly into your bank account,* a routing and account number from your bank.

to TOPIC

▶ *If it maintains a large following, the*
  ~~The~~ show might, ~~if it maintains a large following,~~ appear in reruns for
  years to come.

▶ The show often jarringly contrasts, ~~leaving the viewer torn between~~
  ~~empathy and revulsion,~~ the mundane events of Tony's family life with
  the callous brutality of the mobster's world. *, leaving the viewer torn between empathy and revulsion.*

43d Avoiding Awkwardly Split Infinitives

An infinitive consists of *to* and the base form of a verb (*to share, to jump, to remember*). An infinitive splits when a modifier is inserted between the *to* and the verb. Although many authorities now consider them acceptable, split infinitives can be awkward and often should be revised, particularly in formal writing.

▶ Grant's strategy was *to ~~relentlessly~~ attack* Lee's army despite the *relentlessly*
  heavy losses the Union army suffered as a result.

Sometimes, however, a modifier is less awkward when splitting an infinitive than in any other spot in a sentence. If the adverb *relentlessly* were placed anywhere else in the following sentence, for example, it would not clearly and unambiguously modify only the word *attack*.

▶ Lincoln urged his generals to *relentlessly* attack retreating enemy forces.

43e Identifying and Correcting Dangling Modifiers

Consider the following sentence:

▶ While paddling the canoe toward shore, our poodle swam alongside.

Who or what is paddling the canoe? Surely not the poodle, yet that is what the sentence seems, absurdly, to suggest. The problem here is that the phrase *while paddling the canoe toward shore* does not actually modify the subject, *poodle,* or anything else in the sentence. It dangles, unattached, leaving it to the reader to infer the existence of some unnamed human paddler. Correcting this **dangling modifier** requires either making the paddler the subject of the sentence (as in the first revision below) or identifying the paddler in the modifier (as in the second revision).

▶ While paddling the canoe toward shore, our poodle ~~swam~~ *I saw* alongside *swimming*.

▶ While ~~paddling~~ *I paddled* the canoe toward shore, our poodle swam alongside.

Dangling modifiers have the following characteristics:

verbal Verb form that functions as a noun, adjective, or adverb

> **More about**
> Phrases and
> clauses, 330–34

- They are most often phrases that include a **verbal** (a gerund, infinitive, or participle) that has an implied but unstated actor.
- They occur most often at the beginnings of sentences.
- They appear to modify the subject of the sentence, so readers expect the implied actor and the subject to be the same.
- They dangle because the implied actor and the actual subject of the sentence are different.

DANGLING INFINITIVE PHRASE

To learn about new products, the company's sales meeting occurs annually in August. [Meetings do not learn.]

DANGLING PARTICIPIAL PHRASE

Hoping to boost morale, an attractive resort hotel is usually selected for the meeting. [Hotels cannot hope.]

DANGLING PREPOSITIONAL PHRASE WITH GERUND OBJECT

After traveling all day, the hotel's hot tub beckoned to the arriving sales reps. [The sales reps traveled, not the hot tub.]

Simply moving a dangling modifier will not correct it.

DANGLING   To learn more about new products, the company's sales meeting occurs annually in August.

STILL
DANGLING   The company's sales meeting occurs annually in August to learn more about new products.

To correct a dangling modifier, first determine the identity of the modifier's unstated actor. You then have two options:

1. Rephrase to make the implied actor the subject of the sentence.
2. Rephrase to include the implied actor in the modifier.

Use the approach that works best given the purpose of the sentence in your draft.

MAKING THE IMPLIED ACTOR THE SUBJECT

To learn about new products, the company's *sales reps attend annual* sales meeting ~~occurs~~

~~annually~~ in August.

Hoping to boost morale, an attractive resort hotel *management usually selects* ~~is usually selected~~ for

the meeting.

In both of these cases, the implied actor—*sales reps* in the first, *management* in the second—was missing entirely from the original sentence.

INCLUDING THE IMPLIED ACTOR IN THE MODIFIER

As the sales reps arrived after
~~After~~ traveling all day, the hotel's hot tub beckoned to ~~the arriving~~ *them.*

~~sales reps.~~

In this case, the implied actor, *sales reps,* appeared in the original sentence but needed to be repositioned.

44 Avoiding Confusing Shifts

When NASCAR drivers round the curves or head into the straightaway, they need to shift gears, but an expert driver shifts only when doing so will provide a clear advantage. Similarly, good writers try not to jar their readers with unnecessary shifts in style or grammar.

44a Avoiding Awkward Shifts in Tense

Verb tenses reveal when events in a sentence happen. Without a corresponding shift in time, shifts from one tense to another confuse readers. Avoid such inappropriate shifts, particularly when you are telling a story or describing a sequence of events.

> The guide waited until we had all reached the top of the pass; then
> she ~~leads~~ *led* the way down to the river and ~~makes~~ *made* sure everybody ~~is~~ *was*
> safe in camp.

More about
Verb tenses,
362–66

It is customary to use the present tense when writing about literary events and characters as well as about films, plays, and other similar works.

> In his movie *Avatar,* director James Cameron ~~presented~~ *presents* a fantastic
> fictional world in rich, convincing detail.

44b Avoiding Awkward Shifts in Mood and Voice

Most sentences are consistently in the indicative mood, which is used to state or question facts and beliefs. It is, however, easy to shift inappropriately between the imperative mood—used for commands, directions, and entreaties—and the indicative mood when explaining a process or giving directions.

> Dig a narrow hole about six inches deep, place the tulip bulb firmly at
> the bottom of the hole, and then ~~you can~~ fill the hole with dirt.

Tech **Catching Confusing Shifts**

The grammar and style checkers in word processing programs do not reliably identify confusing shifts. One style checker, for example, had no objection to this absurd statement: "Yesterday it will rain; tomorrow it snowed two feet." On the other hand, the same style checker flagged every occurrence of the passive voice, regardless of whether it was appropriate to the passage in which it appeared.

The subjunctive mood is used in certain situations to express a wish or demand or to make a statement contrary to fact. Although many of us often replace it with the indicative in everyday speech, readers expect to encounter the subjunctive in formal writing.

> ▶ If the presidential primary ~~was~~ *were* held earlier in the year, our state's
>
>   voters would have a greater voice in the outcome of the race.

More about
Mood, 367–68

Avoid shifting needlessly between the active voice, in which the subject performs the action of the verb (*I wrote the paper*) and the passive voice, in which the subject receives the action (*The paper was written by me*).

> ▶ During the eighteenth century, the British consumed most of their
>
>   carbohydrates in the form of processed sugar. The Italians favored
>
>   pasta, whereas sourdough bread *the French preferred* ~~was preferred by the French.~~

More about
Voice, 92, 279–80,
293–94, 329

44c Avoiding Awkward Shifts in Person and Number

Person refers to the identity of the subject of a sentence and the point of view of the writer. In the first person (*I, we*), the writer and subject are the same. In the second person (*you*), the reader and subject are the same. In the third person (*he, she, it, they, Marie Curie, electrons*), the subject is the writer's topic of discussion, what the writer is informing the reader about. *Number* refers to the quantity (singular or plural) of a noun or pronoun.

More about
Person and number, 346

Arbitrary shifts in person are distracting to readers. The revision to the following passage establishes a consistent first-person point of view.

> ▶ When I get together with my friends in the tech club, we usually
>
>   discuss the latest electronic devices. *We* ~~You~~ tend to forget, though,
>
>   that a garden spade and a ballpoint pen are also technological tools
>
>   and that thousands of nonelectronic items become part of *our* ~~your~~
>
>   technological world every year.

Most academic writing is in the third person. The second person, including commands, is best reserved for addressing readers directly, telling them how to do something or giving them advice. (You have probably noticed that this handbook often addresses you, the reader, in just this way.) Be consistent, however, and avoid shifting arbitrarily between second and third person.

> ▶ To train your dog properly, *you* ~~people~~ need plenty of time, patience, and
>
>   dog biscuits. You should start with simple commands like "sit" and "stay."

More about
Avoiding gender
bias, 297–99,
355–56

Most inappropriate shifts in number are errors in agreement between a pronoun and its antecedent; they are often the result of the writer's desire to avoid gender bias. These kinds of errors can easily happen when the antecedent is a singular generic noun (*person, doctor*) or an indefinite pronoun (*anyone, everyone*).

FAULTY   When a <u>person</u> witnesses a crime, <u>they</u> should report it to the police.

The antecedent of the plural pronoun *they* is the singular generic noun *person.*

Such shifts can be revised in several ways. One is to use the plural throughout. Another is to replace the plural pronoun with *he or she* (although this expression becomes tedious when overused). A third is to rephrase the sentence to avoid the problem entirely.

REVISED:
PLURAL THROUGHOUT   When people witness a crime, they should report it to the police.

REVISED:
HE OR SHE   When a person witnesses a crime, he or she should report it to the police.

REVISED:
REPHRASED   Anybody who witnesses a crime should report it to the police.

44d Avoiding Awkward Shifts from Direct to Indirect Quotations and Questions

More about
Punctuating direct
and indirect quo-
tations, 436–38
Quoting sources,
140–43

Direct quotations reproduce someone's exact words and must always be enclosed in quotation marks: *My roommate announced, "The party will start at 8 p.m." Indirect quotations* report what someone has said but not in that person's exact words: *My roommate announced that the party would start at 8 p.m.*

Abrupt shifts between direct and indirect quotations, like the one in the following example, are awkward and confusing.

AWKWARD SHIFT   Yogi Berra says that you should go to other people's funerals or "otherwise, they won't come to yours."

REVISED:
DIRECT QUOTATION   As Yogi Berra says, "You should always go to other people's funerals. Otherwise, they won't come to yours."

REVISED:
INDIRECT QUOTATION   Yogi Berra says that you should go to other people's funerals because if you don't, they won't come to yours.

More about
Punctuating direct
and indirect
questions,
444–45

Abrupt shifts between direct and indirect questions are also confusing. A *direct question* is stated in question (interrogative) form and ends with a question mark: *When does the library open?* An *indirect question* reports a question in declarative form and ends with a period: *I wonder when the library opens.*

AWKWARD SHIFT	The author asks how much longer can the world depend on fossil fuels and whether alternative sources of energy will be ready in time.
REVISED: DIRECT QUESTION	The author asks two questions: How much longer can the world depend on fossil fuels, and will alternative sources of energy be ready in time?
REVISED: INDIRECT QUESTION	The author asks how much longer the world can depend on fossil fuels and whether alternative sources of energy will be ready in time.

45 Avoiding Mixed and Incomplete Constructions

This disorienting image by artist M. C. Escher shows an impossible building, a mixed construction with a water channel that appears to flow horizontally but somehow ends up two stories higher than it begins, with the water cascading back to its source. As you edit your writing, look for sentences that similarly start in one direction but turn disorientingly in another, leaving readers unsure where you have taken them. Look, too, for sentences that omit words that readers need to grasp fully your intended meaning.

M. C. Escher, *Waterfall*, 1961

45a Recognizing and Correcting Mixed Constructions

When a sentence begins one way and then takes an unexpected turn—in grammar or logic—the result is a ***mixed construction.*** To find and correct mixed constructions in your drafts, make sure every predicate has a grammatically and logically appropriate subject.

Grammatically mixed constructions can occur when a writer uses an introductory phrase or clause—which cannot function as the subject of a sentence—as if it were the subject. The following example starts with a long prepositional phrase (underlined) that the writer erroneously uses as the subject of the sentence. A prepositional phrase, although it can modify the subject or other parts of a sentence, cannot be the subject. The result is a ***sentence fragment,*** not a sentence.

> **sentence fragment**
> An incomplete sentence punctuated as if it were complete

| MIXED | <u>As a justification by American leaders for dropping atomic bombs on Hiroshima and Nagasaki</u> maintained that doing so persuaded the Japanese to surrender without the need for an invasion that might have cost hundreds of thousands of casualties. |

Fixing a sentence like this requires identifying a grammatical subject and isolating it from the introductory phrase. Here is one possible revision (with the subject underlined):

REVISED   As a justification for dropping atomic bombs on Hiroshima and Nagasaki, <u>American leaders</u> maintained that doing so persuaded the Japanese to surrender without the need for an invasion that might have cost hundreds of thousands of casualties.

Here is a more concise revision that eliminates the introductory phrase altogether:

REVISED   <u>American leaders</u> maintained that dropping atomic bombs on Hiroshima and Nagasaki persuaded the Japanese to surrender without the need for an invasion that might have cost hundreds of thousands of casualties.

> **More about**
> Clauses, 332–34
> Relating ideas with subordination, 287–89

In the next example, the writer follows a subordinate clause (*Because the bombings had devastating effects*) with the verb *provoked,* which has no subject. The editing changes the first part of the sentence into a noun phrase subject for *provoked.*

▶ ~~Because the bombings had devastating effects~~ *The devastating effects of the bombings* provoked intense debate over the morality of the military decision.

Mixed constructions also occur when a writer treats a modifying phrase or clause as if it were the predicate of a sentence. Look for this kind of mixed construction, especially in sentences that begin with the phrase *the fact that.* The following example begins with a subject, *the fact,* followed by a long adjective *that* clause that modifies the subject but cannot at the same time be the predicate of the sentence.

MIXED   The fact that Hiroshima and Nagasaki, which were devastated by the bomb, are once again thriving cities.

> **subject complement**
> An adjective, pronoun, noun, or noun phrase that follows a linking verb and refers to the subject of the sentence

One way to revise this sentence is to add the verb *is,* making the *that* clause into a **subject complement.**

REVISED   The fact is that Hiroshima and Nagasaki, which were devastated by the bomb, are once again thriving cities.

> **More about**
> Eliminating wordy expressions, 277–78

Better yet is simply to eliminate the phrase *the fact that,* a wordy expression that adds no information to the sentence.

REVISED   Hiroshima and Nagasaki, which were devastated by the bomb, are once again thriving cities.

45b Recognizing and Correcting Mismatched Subjects and Predicates

The error of *faulty predication* occurs when a subject and predicate are mismatched—when they do not fit together logically. For example, the original subject of the following sentence, *recommendation,* does not work with the verb *insisted.* Recommendations cannot insist; doctors can.

▶ The ~~doctor's recommendation~~ insisted that Joe be hospitalized
                    doctor
                       ^

immediately.

Many instances of faulty predication involve a mismatch between the subject and subject complement in sentences in which the verb is a form of *be* or other ***linking verb.***

> **linking verb** A verb that connects a subject to a subject complement

MISMATCHED   Only <u>students</u> who are absent because of illness or a

family emergency will be <u>grounds</u> for a makeup exam.

REVISED   Only students who are absent because of illness or a family emergency will be permitted to take a makeup exam.

Two forms of expression involving the verb *be* that have become commonplace in everyday speech are examples of faulty predication and should be avoided in formal writing. These are the use of *is where* or *is when* in definitions and the use of *the reason is . . . because* in explanations.

1. *Is where, is when*

Definitions with the expressions *is when* and *is where* usually create logical mismatches because the terms defined involve neither a place (*where*) nor a time (*when*).

▶ A tornado is ~~where~~ high winds swirl around in a funnel-shaped cloud.
              a violent storm in which
                           ^

Because a tornado is a storm, not a place, use "which" instead of "where."

▶ A friend is ~~when~~ someone cares about you and has fun with you.
            who
              ^

A friend is a person, not a time.

The expressions result in grammatical mismatches, too, because *where* and *when* introduce adverb clauses, which cannot function as subject complements.

2. *The reason . . . is because*

Explanations using the expression *the reason . . . is because* are similarly mismatched both logically (*the reason* and *because* are redundant) and grammatically (*because* introduces an adverb clause, which cannot function as a subject complement). The following example shows two simple ways to fix this kind of faulty predication.

▸ ~~The reason~~ I wrote this paper ~~is~~ because my instructor required it.

▸ The reason I wrote this paper is ~~because~~ *that* my instructor required it.

45c Adding Essential Words to Compound and Other Constructions

More about
Writing concisely,
277–80

As you draft sentences, you may unintentionally leave out grammatically or logically essential words. Sometimes these omissions result in sentence fragments. Often, however, they create seemingly minor but nonetheless distracting grammatical or idiomatic bumps. As you proofread and edit your drafts, be especially alert for such missing words in compound and other constructions.

In compound constructions, the omission of *nonessential* repetitions can often help tighten prose.

▸ Abigail needed a new dress to wear to the graduation party and [to] the wedding reception. First she shopped at Macy's and then [she shopped] at Kohl's.

elliptical construction A construction in which otherwise grammatically necessary words can be omitted because their meaning is understood from the surrounding context

Such **elliptical constructions** work, however, only when the stated words in one part of a compound match the omitted words in other parts. When grammar or idiom requires different words—different verb forms, different prepositions, or different articles, for example—those words should be included.

▸ The candidate claimed that she always had *supported* and always would support universal health care coverage.

The word *supported* is needed because *had support* would be ungrammatical.

▸ On the campaign trail and *in* debates, her opponent for the nomination insisted that his plan was better than hers.

In this situation, the word *debates* requires the preposition *in,* not *on.*

More about
Including a stated subject and eliminating redundant subject and object pronouns, 395–97

Obligatory Words and Unacceptable Repetitions in English Unlike some languages, formal written English requires a stated subject in all sentences except commands.

▸ *It rained* ~~Rained~~ all day yesterday.

On the other hand, formal written English does not permit the use of a pronoun to emphasize an already stated subject or direct object.

▸ Maria~~, she~~ forgot to take her umbrella.

▶ A yearning for change, *an* unsettled economy, and *the* character of the
candidates themselves combined to sustain high voter turnout during
the primary season.

> The word *unsettled* requires a different form of the indefinite article (*a, an*)
> than *yearning,* and in this situation the word *character* requires the definite
> article (*the*) rather than the indefinite article.

Occasionally, you may need to repeat a modifier for clarity.

▶ The candidates asked their loyal backers and *their* opponents to support
the winner, whoever that might be.

> The repeated *their* makes clear that the adjective *loyal* applies only to *backers*
> and not to *opponents.*

Although you can often omit the word *that* without obscuring the meaning
of a subordinate clause, sometimes you need to include it to avoid confusion.

▶ I know *that* Sheila, who is a sympathetic person, will not be terribly upset
about the stains on the silk shirt ~~that~~ I borrowed from her.

> In the original, without the first *that, Sheila* could be understood as the object
> of *know* rather than the subject of the long subordinate clause that follows.
> On the other hand, the *that* at the end of the sentence can be eliminated
> because no such ambiguity affects the subject (*I*) of the clause it introduces.

45d Avoiding Incomplete or Ambiguous Comparisons

Comparisons show how two items are alike or different. For comparisons to
be clear, the items they juxtapose must be logically equivalent. The original version of the following sentence confusingly compares a group of people, children, to a process, growing up.

> **More about**
> Comparisons,
> 379–80

▶ Children who grow up on farms are more active than *those who grow* ~~growing~~ up in
big cities.

To be complete, comparisons must fully specify what is being compared
to what.

▶ The Log Cabin Restaurant is better *than Joe's Diner.*

Be careful how you use the terms *any* and *any other* when you compare one
item to others that belong to the same category.

▶ Mount Everest is higher than any *other* mountain in the world.

Mount Everest is a mountain in the world, so without the modifier *other,* the sentence suggests that Mount Everest is higher than itself.

▶ Aconcagua, the highest mountain in South America, is higher than any ~~other~~ mountain in North America.

The sentence compares a mountain in South America to mountains in North America, not to other mountains in South America.

Be sure, also, to include any information you need to avoid ambiguity in your comparisons. In its draft form, the following comparison has two possible interpretations, as the revisions make clear.

DRAFT   Yvette is more concerned about me than my brother.

REVISED   Yvette is more concerned about me than <u>she is about</u> my brother.

REVISED   Yvette is more concerned about me than my brother <u>is</u>.

When you use the word *as* in a comparison, be sure to use it twice.

▶ Stephen King's horror stories are *as* scary as Edgar Allan Poe's.

11

Language
Matters
Issues for Multilingual Writers

Use tab 11 to learn, practice, and master these
writer's responsibilities:

❏ **To Audience**

Address your readers in idiomatic Standard English.

❏ **To Topic**

Communicate your ideas in clear language that
follows the conventions of American academic and
business writing.

❏ **To Other Writers**

Share your knowledge and experience.

❏ **To Yourself**

Present yourself with confidence.

11

Language
Matters

46 Understanding English Word Order and Sentence Structure
by Ted E. Johnston and M. E. Sokolik

English is a word-order language, which means that the position of a word in a sentence often determines its grammatical function. As a result, *The dog chased the cat* means something different from *The cat chased the dog.* This chapter describes and explains word order and related aspects of English sentence structure.

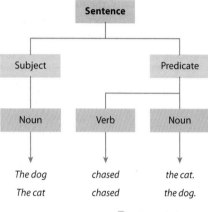

46a Observing Normal Word Order

In English, normal word order is subject-verb-object (or S-V-O). That is, the subject comes first, then the verb, and then the direct object, if there is one, or any other words that make up the predicate.

	v ? ?
FAULTY WORD ORDER	Chased the cat the dog.
	s v o
NORMAL WORD ORDER	The dog chased the cat.

> **More about**
> Sentence types, 325–26
> Word order in questions, 398–99

46b Including a Stated Subject

Except for commands, English sentences and **clauses** require a subject to be stated, even if the identity of the subject is clear from a previous sentence or clause. In the following example, the pronoun *he,* referring to the subject of the first sentence, can serve as the subject of both clauses of the second sentence.

> **clause** A word group with a subject and a predicate. An *independent clause* can stand alone as a sentence; a *subordinate clause* cannot.

▶ Nico has a hard life for a ten-year-old. ^He is^ Is just a boy, but ^he^ is expected to

work like a man.

Similarly, a subordinate clause requires a stated subject even if its subject is a pronoun or another noun phrase that obviously refers to the subject of the clause that comes before it.

├— sub. clause —┤
she
▶ Lucy asked for directions because ^ was lost.

In commands, the subject is unstated but is understood to be "you."

▶ [you] Leave now!

395

46c Managing *There* and *It* Sentences

Expletives are words that are empty of content; that is, they do not refer to anything. In English, the words *there* and *it* are often used as expletives.

There expletives begin with *there* followed by a form of *be,* but *there* is not the subject. Instead, the subject follows the verb, which is singular if the subject is singular or plural if the subject is plural. The expletive *it,* on the other hand, is the subject of the verb and is always singular. *It* expletives often describe an environmental condition (the weather, for example) or some aspect of time. The verb in expletive *it* constructions is often a form of *be,* but can include others, especially those related to process (for example, *start, continue, end*). The expletives *there* and *it* cannot be omitted from these sentences, even though they do not refer to anything.

▶ ~~Are~~ not enough reasons to support your argument.
 There are

▶ Waiter, I am not pleased that is a fly in my soup.
 there

▶ When was almost 3:00 p.m., started hailing really hard.
 it   *it*

In a similar construction, the pronoun *it* is not empty, but refers to content that follows the verb. In the following sentence, for example, *it* refers to *to drive during a snowstorm.* In either case, empty or meaningful, *it* is the subject and cannot be omitted.

▶ ~~Is~~ dangerous to drive during a snowstorm.
 It is

46d Eliminating Redundant Subject and Object Pronouns

Although English requires a stated subject in all clauses except commands, the use of a pronoun to reemphasize an already stated subject is not acceptable in writing, even though it often occurs in informal speech.

 redundant subject
 subj.
▶ Rosalinda, ~~she~~ left early for the airport.

Similarly, when *which* or *that* begins a clause and serves as the clause's subject or direct object, do not also add *it* to serve as the subject or direct object. In the following sentences, for example, both *which* and *it* refer redundantly to the movie *Pan's Labyrinth;* to correct the sentences, eliminate one pronoun or the other.

 redundant subject
 subj.
▶ Last night I saw *Pan's Labyrinth,* which ~~it~~ impressed me very much.

or

▸ Last night I saw *Pan's Labyrinth,* which it impressed me very much.

dir. obj.

redundant object
↓

▸ I liked *Pan's Labyrinth,* which many of my friends liked it too.

or

▸ I liked *Pan's Labyrinth,* which many of my friends liked it too.

46e Observing Standard Word Order with Direct Objects, Indirect Objects, and Object Complements

Direct objects, indirect objects, and object complements can follow a transitive verb.

1. Direct and indirect objects

A *direct object* receives or carries the action of a transitive verb. Certain transitive verbs—such as *ask, find, give, order, send, show, teach, tell,* and *write*—can also take an *indirect object,* which identifies who or what benefits from the action of the verb. The indirect object falls between the verb and the direct object.

> **More about**
> Transitive verbs and direct and indirect objects, 328–30

    s   v   io   do
▸ She sent Michiko a book on Scandinavian cuisine.

Alternatively, the indirect object can be identified in a phrase beginning with a preposition, usually *to,* that follows the direct object.

    s   v   do   alternative phrase
▸ She sent a book on Scandinavian cuisine to Michiko.

When the direct object is a personal pronoun, the pronoun follows the verb and is itself followed by a prepositional phrase containing the indirect object.

to Michiko.
▸ She sent Michiko it.

Several common verbs do not take indirect objects that fall between the verb and the direct object, even though the actions they refer to are similar to those of verbs that do. These verbs include *answer, carry, change, close, complete, deliver, describe, explain, keep, mention, open, propose, put, recommend, repair* (or *fix* when it means *repair*), and *say.* With these verbs, the indirect object can only come after the direct object in a prepositional phrase beginning with *to* (or sometimes *for*).

▶ The doctor explained ~~my father~~ the dangers of secondhand smoke. *to my father.*

▶ The professor opened ~~us~~ the door to understanding. *for us.*

2. Object complements

An *object complement* follows a direct object and describes the condition of the object or a change that the subject has caused the object to undergo.

▶ Some workers here make my <u>job</u> <u>impossible</u>.
  <small>do</small> <small>obj. comp.</small>

Placing an object complement before the direct object will either make a sentence ungrammatical or change its meaning. The following sentence, as originally written, was ungrammatical.

▶ The players have just elected ~~their team captain~~ Paul. *their team captain.*

In contrast, both of the following sentences are grammatical, but they have different meanings.

▶ We need to keep all the <u>happy</u> workers.

▶ We need to keep all the workers <u>happy</u>.

The first sentence, with the adjective *happy* before the direct object, recommends retaining the workers who are already happy, but not necessarily those who are not. The second, with *happy* in the object complement position after the direct object, recommends taking action to make sure that not one of the workers feels unhappy.

46f Observing Word-Order Patterns in Questions

In questions, unlike in other sentences, a verb nearly always precedes the subject.

■ To form a question with one-word forms of the verb *be,* simply invert subject and verb.

<small>s</small> <small>v</small>
The grapes are ripe.

<small>v</small> <small>s</small>
Are the grapes ripe?

---

verb phrase A main verb and all its helping verbs

■ In all other cases, a question requires a helping verb as well as a main verb. The subject goes after the first helping verb in a verb phrase and before the rest of the verb phrase.

<small>s</small> <small>hv</small> <small>mv</small>
They have left for New York.

<small>hv</small> <small>s</small> <small>mv</small>
Have they left for New York?

s   hv mv
The children can go with us.

hv   s   mv
Can the children go with us?

s   hv   hv   mv
The painters should have finished.

hv   s   hv   mv
Should the painters have finished?

- To form a question with one-word verbs other than forms of *be,* use the appropriate form of *do* as the helper.

s   v
The prisoner escaped.

hv   s   mv
Did the prisoner escape?

- Questions that begin with question words like *what, who,* and *why* normally follow the same word order as other questions.

hv   s   mv
What is the engineer saying about the project?

- If the question word is the subject, however, the question follows subject-before-verb word order.

s   v   do
Who is saying these things about the project?

46g Observing Inverted Word Order When Certain Conjunctions or Adverbs Begin a Clause

When certain words and phrases appear at the beginning of a sentence, they require inverted word order similar to that used in questions. These include certain adverbs, adverb phrases, correlative conjunctions (such as *neither . . . nor* and *not only . . . but also*), and the conjunction *nor* by itself.

▶ *Neither* ~~the parents~~ have called the principal, *nor* ~~they~~ have informed
the parents   they
the school board.

▶ The twins don't bowl, *nor* they play tennis.
do

The adverbs *rarely, seldom, no sooner, no longer,* and similar negating or limiting expressions also require inverted word order when they start a sentence or clause. Such sentences have a formal tone.

▶ *Seldom* ~~the dancers~~ have had the opportunity to perform in public.
the dancers

Moving the adverb to the interior of the sentence cancels the inversion.

▶ The dancers have *seldom* had the opportunity to perform in public.

> **More about**
> Adverbs, 376–80,
> 413–15

Usually, this less formal, noninverted version is preferable to the inverted version.

Using Nouns and Noun Determiners
by Ted E. Johnston and M. E. Sokolik

The New Yorker, July 28, 2008. © J. C. Duffy/The New Yorker Collection/cartoonbank.com.

"What can I say? I was an English major."

English nouns rarely appear by themselves. Most of the time they are paired with words such as *a, an, the, my, that, each, one, ten, several, more, less,* and *fewer.* These words are known as **determiners** because they help us figure out—or determine— how a noun works and what it means when we encounter it in a sentence. As this cartoon suggests, learning to use nouns and determiners appropriately can sometimes challenge native speakers as much as it does multilingual students.

47a Identifying Different Types of Nouns

To use a noun properly, you need to know whether it is a *proper noun* or a *common noun,* and, if it is a common noun, whether it is *count* or *noncount.* A **common noun** identifies a general category and is usually not capitalized: *woman, era, bridge, corporation, mountain, war.* A **proper noun** identifies someone or something specific and is usually capitalized: *Hillary Clinton, Middle Ages, Golden Gate Bridge, Burger King, Himalayas, World War II.*

Count nouns name discrete, countable things. **Noncount nouns** (also called **noncountable** or **mass** nouns) usually name things made of a continuous substance or of small, indistinguishable particles, or they refer to a general quality. A *drop,* a *grain,* and a *suggestion,* for example, are count nouns, but *water, sand,* and *advice* are noncount nouns.

> **More about**
> Types of nouns, 320

> **More about**
> Forming noun plurals, 467–68

- Count nouns can be singular (*drop*) or plural (*drops*). Most noncount nouns are singular, even those that end in *-s,* and thus should be matched with singular verbs. Noncount nouns cannot be preceded by a number or any other term that would imply countability (such as *a, an, several, another,* or *many*), nor can they be made plural if they are singular.

  > Aerobics ~~help~~ me to relax.
  >   *helps*
  >   ^

Here are some examples of contrasting count and noncount nouns:

Count	Noncount
car/cars	traffic
dollar/dollars	money
noodle/noodles	spaghetti
pebble/pebbles	gravel
spoon/spoons	silverware

Quick Reference   Some Common Noncount Nouns

Although there is no hard-and-fast way to distinguish noncount from count nouns, most noncount nouns do fall into a few general categories.

Abstractions and emotions	advice, courage, happiness, hate, jealousy, information, knowledge, love, luck, maturity, patriotism, warmth
Mass substances	air, blood, dirt, gasoline, glue, sand, shampoo, water
Food items	beef, bread, corn, flour, gravy, pork, rice, salt, sugar
Collections of related items	cash, clothing, equipment, furniture, graffiti, information, jewelry, luggage, mail, news, traffic
Games and other activities	aerobics, baseball, checkers, homework, news, poker, pool, soccer, tennis, volleyball, yoga
Weather-related phenomena	cold, drizzle, frost, hail, heat, humidity, lightning, rain, sleet, snow, sunshine, thunder
Diseases	arthritis, chicken pox, diabetes, influenza, measles
Fields of study	botany, chemistry, mathematics, physics, sociology

- Many nouns can be noncount in one context and count in another.
  - ▶ While speaking of *love* [noncount], my grandmother recalled the three *loves* [count] of her life.

    In the opening phrase, *love* is an abstraction. In the main clause, *loves* refers to the people the grandmother has loved.

- All languages have count and noncount nouns, but a noun that is count in one language may be noncount in another.

47b Using Nouns with Articles (*a, an, the*) and Other Determiners

The *articles* *a, an,* and *the* are the most common determiners. Other determiners include possessives (*my, your, Ivan's*), numbers (*one, five, a hundred*), and other words that quantify (*some, many, a few*) or specify (*this, those*).

1. Articles with common nouns

The main function of the *indefinite articles, a* and *an,* is to introduce nouns that are new to the reader. The *definite article, the,* usually precedes nouns that have already been introduced or whose identity is known or clear from the context. Noncount nouns and plural count nouns also sometimes appear with no article (or the *zero article*).

- Use *a* before a consonant sound (*a cat*) and *an* before a vowel sound (*an elephant*). Do not be misled by written vowels that are pronounced as consonants (*a European tour*) or written consonants that are pronounced as vowels (*an hour early*). Be especially careful with words that begin with *h* (*a hot stove*, *an honorary degree*) and *u* (*a uniform*, *an upheaval*).

- Use *a* or *an* only with singular count nouns. A singular count noun must be preceded by an article or some other determiner even if other modifiers come between the determiner and the noun.

  ▸ A friend of mine bought an antique car on eBay.

- Never use *a* or *an* with a noncount noun.

  ▸ A good advice is hard to find.
    Good

- Use *a* or *an* when you first introduce a singular count noun if the specific identity of the noun is not yet known to the reader or is not otherwise clear from the context. Use *the* for later references to the same noun.

  ▸ A friend of mine bought an antique car on eBay. She restored the car and sold it for a tidy profit. The profit came in handy when she took a vacation.

    The is appropriate for *car* in the second sentence because it refers to the same car introduced in the first sentence. The word *profit* in the second sentence takes *a* because it is making its first appearance there. The third sentence continues the process.

- Use *the* with both count and noncount nouns whose specific identity has been previously established or is clear from the context.

  ▸ We admired the antique car that my friend bought on eBay.
    The description *that my friend bought on eBay* identifies a specific car.

  ▸ She sold it for a tidy profit and used the money for a vacation.
    The context clearly identifies the money with the profit.

  ▸ My friend is traveling around the world for three months.
    The noun *world* logically refers to the planet we live on—not, say, Mars or Venus.

  ▸ Vicky is the fastest runner on her team.
    The superlative *fastest* refers specifically to one person.

  More about
  Superlatives,
  379–80

- No article is used to introduce noncount nouns or plural count nouns used generically—that is, to make generalizations.

  ▸ Good advice is hard to find.

  ▸ Good teachers can change lives.

- Both the definite and indefinite articles can introduce singular nouns used generically. Sometimes either is appropriate.

  ▸ <u>The</u> good teacher can change lives.

  ▸ <u>A</u> good teacher can change lives.

  Sometimes the generic meaning is clear with only one or the other.

  ▸ Thomas Alva Edison invented a̲ lightbulb.
  　　　　　　　　　　　　　　　the

2. Articles with proper nouns

Proper nouns in English almost never occur with the indefinite article (*a, an*), and most occur with no article.

  ▸ Ruby grew up in Lima, Peru, but now lives in Wichita, Kansas.

There are many exceptions, however:

- Certain place names always occur with *the: the Bronx, the Philippines, the Northeast, the Pacific Ocean.*
- The names of ships (including airships) conventionally occur with *the: the* Queen Mary, *the* Challenger.
- Many product names can be used with *a* or *the* or sometimes both: *the Cheerios, an/the iPad, a/the Honda.*
- Many multiword proper nouns occur with *the: the United States, the Brooklyn Bridge, the Department of State, the War of 1812.* Others do not, however. The city of Chicago, for example, is home to both *the Wrigley Building* (with article) and *Wrigley Field* (no article).
- Most plural proper nouns occur with *the: the Bartons, the Chicago Cubs.*

3. Nouns and other determiners

As with articles, the use of other determiners with nouns depends on the kind of noun in question, particularly whether it is singular or plural, count or noncount. In all cases, determiners precede any other adjectives that modify a noun.

> **More about**
> Order of adjectives, 412

Possessive nouns or pronouns Use possessive nouns (*Julio's*) and possessive pronouns (*my, our, your, his, her, its, their, whose*) with any count or noncount noun.

sing. count	plural count	noncount
Ann's book	*Ann's* books	*Ann's* information
her book	*her* books	*her* information

Quick

Reference   Matching Nouns with Quantifying Words and Phrases

Quantifying Word or Phrase	Singular Count Nouns	Plural Count Nouns	Noncount Nouns	Examples
any, no	✓	✓	✓	You can read <u>any</u> book on the list.
				Have you read <u>any</u> books this summer?
				Do you have <u>any</u> information about the reading list?
another, each, every, either, neither	✓	no	no	I read <u>another</u> book last week.
the other	✓	✓	✓	<u>The other</u> book is a murder mystery.
				I haven't finished <u>the other</u> books on the reading list.
				<u>The other</u> information is the most reliable.
a couple of, a number of, both, few, a few, fewer, fewest, many, several	no	✓	no	The professor assigned <u>fewer books</u> last term.
a lot of, lots of, all, enough, more, most, other, some	no	✓	✓	<u>Some</u> books are inspiring.
				<u>Some</u> information is unreliable.
little, a little, much, a great deal of, less, least	no	no	✓	I need <u>a little</u> information about the course requirements.

This, that, these, those The demonstrative pronouns *this, that, these,* and *those* specify, or single out, particular instances of a noun. Use *this* and *that* only with noncount nouns and singular count nouns. Use *these* and *those* only with plural count nouns.

sing. count	plural count	noncount
this book	*these* books	*this* information
that book	*those* books	*that* information

Quantifying words or phrases Use numbers only with count nouns: *one shirt, two shirts.* See the Quick Reference box above for a list of other quantifying words and how they work with different kinds of nouns in most contexts.

Few *versus* a few *and* little *versus* a little The determiners *few* and *a few* (for count nouns) and *little* and *a little* (for noncount nouns) all indicate a small quantity, but they have significant differences in meaning. *Few* means a negligible amount, whereas *a few* means a small but significant number. Likewise, *little* means *almost none,* whereas *a little* means *some.*

Writing Responsibly

Less versus *Fewer*, or "Do as I Say, Not as I Do"

The quantifier *less* is properly used only with noncount nouns, not count nouns.

> *fewer*
> ▶ The automobile industry sold ~~less~~ cars this year than last year.

As the cartoon that opens this chapter suggests, however, many native English speakers violate this rule, particularly in everyday speech. (*Items* is a count noun.) Try not to follow their example, particularly when writing for an academic audience.

to AUDIENCE

▶ Rhoda has *few* good friends.

   She is almost friendless.

▶ Rhoda has *a few* good friends.

   She has significant companionship.

▶ Pete provided *little* help before the party.

   He didn't do his share.

▶ Pete gave me *a little* help after everyone left.

   He made himself useful.

Indicating extent or amount with noncount nouns   Because a noncount noun is always singular, do not make it plural or add a determiner that implies a plural form. For example, do not use a determiner such as *a large number of, many,* or *several* immediately before a noncount noun. Instead, use a determiner such as *a great deal of, less, little, much,* or *some*—or revise the sentence another way.

> *some*
> ▶ The city is doing ~~researches~~ on the proposal.

   The modifier *some* is appropriate for the noncount noun *research* because it does not imply plurality.

> *loaves of*
> ▶ Gina bought two ~~breads~~ at the store.

   In the edited version, *two* modifies the count noun *loaves.*

> *incidents of violence*
> ▶ We do not have many ~~violences~~ in our neighborhood.

> *great deal*
> ▶ A ~~large number~~ of information is available on your topic.

   A large number of, which suggests plurality, cannot be used with *information,* a noncount noun.

48 Managing English Verbs
by Ted E. Johnston and M. E. Sokolik

Verbs can express an action or occurrence (*The dog jumps for the Frisbee*) or indicate a state of being (*The dog is frisky*). In many languages, verbs can have several forms. For example, they may change to indicate the identity of a subject or object or the time frame in which an event happens. English verbs, in contrast, have only a few forms, but these combine with other words to accomplish the same functions.

48a Understanding Phrasal Verbs

More about
Verbs and verb phrases, 321, 331, 360–61

Phrasal verbs—sometimes called multi-word verbs—consist of a verb and one or two *particles.* The particle takes the form of a preposition or adverb, and it combines with the verb to create a new verb with a new meaning. For example, the verb *throw* means to project something through the air. The phrasal verb *throw out* consists of the verb *throw* and the particle *out;* it means to dispose of something.

> phrasal vb.　　　particle
> ▸ Segundo threw out his old notebook.

> verb
> ▸ Segundo threw his old notebook on his bed.

The meaning of a verb-and-particle combination differs from the meaning of the same words in a verb-and-preposition combination. The phrasal verb *look up,* for example, means to consult or find something in a reference work, which is different from the meaning of *look* followed by a phrase that happens to begin with the preposition *up.*

PHRASAL VERB	phrasal vb. Svetlana looked up the word in the dictionary.
VERB WITH PREPOSITION	verb　prep. Svetlana looked up the steep trail and began to hike.

A transitive phrasal verb is *separable* if its direct object can fall either between the verb and the particle (separating them) or after the particle.

> dir. obj.
> ▸ She looked up the address online.

> dir. obj.
> ▸ She looked the address up online.

If the direct object of a separable phrasal verb is a pronoun, it must come between the verb and the particle.

Quick

Reference   Some Common Phrasal Verbs and Their Meanings

SEPARABLE		INSEPARABLE	
ask out	invite for a date	**add up to**	total
calm down	make calm, become calm	**barge in on**	interrupt unannounced
give up	surrender	**call on**	visit, or ask for a response directly
hand in	submit		
hand out	distribute	**come across**	find accidentally
look up	find something in a reference work	**drop in**	visit unannounced
		get out of	evade an obligation, exit
put back	return to original position	**give in**	surrender
put down	criticize meanly; suppress	**grow up**	mature
		hint at	suggest
take back	return; retract	**look down on**	disdain
take off	remove	**look up to**	admire
take on	assume responsibility for	**put up with**	tolerate
		run into	encounter; collide
take up	begin a hobby or activity	**stand in for**	substitute for
throw out	dispose of	**turn up**	show up, arrive

> ▸ I decided to hand ~~in it.~~ _it in._

A phrasal verb is *__inseparable__* if no words can fall between the verb and the particle.

FAULTY   I came an old photo across in the drawer.

REVISED   I came across an old photo in the drawer.

The meaning of a phrasal verb changes when the particle changes (see the Quick Reference box above). The phrasal verb *take on,* for example, means "to assume responsibility for."

> ▸ She took on the editing of the newsletter.

The phrasal verb *take back,* in contrast, means "return" or "retract."

> ▸ She took all her overdue books back to the library.

48b Learning When to Use Gerunds and Infinitives after Verbs and Prepositions

A *gerund* is the *-ing* form of a verb used as a noun (*listening, eating*). An **infinitive** is the base form of a verb preceded by *to* (*to listen, to eat*).

1. Gerunds and infinitives after verbs

- Only gerunds can follow some verbs, and only infinitives can follow others.

  ▶ The committee recommended ~~to submit~~ the proposal for a vote.
  submitting

  ▶ Rosa Parks refused ~~leaving~~ her seat on the bus.
  to leave

- Some verbs can be followed by either gerunds or infinitives. For some of these verbs, the choice of gerund or infinitive has little effect on meaning, but for a few the difference is significant.

Quick Reference — Gerund or Infinitive after Selected Verbs

Some verbs that can be directly followed by a gerund but not an infinitive

admit	discuss	imagine	practice	risk
avoid	enjoy	mind	quit	suggest
consider	escape	miss	recall	tolerate
deny	finish	postpone	resist	understand

Some verbs that can be directly followed by an infinitive but not a gerund

agree	claim	hope	offer	refuse
appear	decide	manage	plan	wait
ask	expect	mean	pretend	want
beg	have	need	promise	wish

Some verbs that can be directly followed by a gerund or an infinitive with little effect on meaning

begin	hate	love	start
continue	like	prefer	

Some verbs for which choice of gerund or infinitive affects meaning

forget	remember	stop	try

Some verbs that take an infinitive only after an intervening noun or pronoun

advise	command	force	persuade	tell
allow	convince	instruct	remind	urge
cause	encourage	order	require	warn

SAME MEANING	The economy *continued* to grow. The economy *continued* growing.
DIFFERENT MEANINGS	Juan *remembered* to e-mail his paper to his professor. [He didn't forget to do it.]
	Juan *remembered* e-mailing his paper to his professor. [He recalled having done it already.]

- Some verbs that can be followed by an infinitive can also be followed by an infinitive after an intervening noun or pronoun.

  ▶ Yue *wanted* to study the violin.

  ▶ Yue's parents *wanted* her to study the violin.

  Certain verbs, however, take an infinitive only after an object noun or pronoun.

  ▶ The candidate *urged* citizens to vote on Election Day.

A few verbs (for example, *feel, have, hear, let, look at,* and *see*) require an **unmarked infinitive**—the base verb alone, without *to* —after an intervening noun or pronoun.

  ▶ Paolo let his children ~~to go~~ to the movies.
  (go)

  ▶ Jen heard a dog ~~to bark~~ late at night.
  (bark)

2. Gerunds after prepositions

Only a gerund, not an infinitive, can be the object of a preposition.

  ▶ The article is about ~~to travel~~ in South America.
  (traveling)

48c   Understanding the Use of Participles as Adjectives

Both the present participle and the past participle of a verb can act as adjectives, but they convey different meanings, especially if the verb refers to an emotion or state of mind such as anger or boredom. The ***present participle*** (or *-ing* form) usually describes the cause or agent of a state of affairs. The ***past participle*** (the *-ed* form in regular verbs) usually describes the result of the state of affairs.

> **More about**
> Regular and irregular verb forms, 358–62

State of Affairs	Cause	Result
verb Physics class bored me today.	*adj.* The class was boring.	*adj.* I was bored.
verb Dr. Sung's lecture interested me.	*adj.* The lecture was interesting.	*adj.* I was interested.

48d Using Helping Verbs for Verb Formation

More about
Verb forms, 357–68
Subject-verb
agreement,
346–53

Most complete English verbs, other than the present and past tenses, consist of a main verb with one or more helping (auxiliary) verbs. The main verb carries the principal meaning, and the helping verbs carry information about time, mood, and voice. There are two kinds of helping verbs: simple and modal.

- The simple helping verbs—*have, do,* and *be*—also function as main verbs, and like other main verbs, they change form to indicate person and tense.

- The modal helping verbs—including *can, could, may, might, must, ought to, shall, should, will,* and *would*—carry information about attributes of the main verb such as ability, intention, permission, possibility, desire, and suggestion (see the Quick Reference box on the next page). Unlike the simple auxiliaries, the modal auxiliaries do not change form to indicate person and tense.

  ▶ All the contestants at the Olympics can swim fast, but Michael
     can
     Phelps ~~cans~~ swim faster than any of the others.
              ^

                                                    should have worked
  ▶ William should work all day today, and he ~~shoulded work~~
                                                          ^
     yesterday too.

NOTE When you hear such contractions as *should've* or *could've* in speech (or similar contractions with other modals), remember that the contracted word is *have* (*should have, could have*), not *of.*

_____

- In a verb phrase, auxiliaries almost always precede the main verb, and modals precede any other auxiliaries.

                      auxiliaries
                 modal   simple   main verb
  ▶ In June, Chen will   have been   living in Seattle for ten years.

- When forming verbs, include needed auxiliaries.

        is
  ▶ Demetrio taking four courses this term.
            ^

           have
  ▶ My grandparents been visiting Scotland every year.
                  ^

- In general, never follow a modal with another modal, and always follow a modal with the base form of a simple auxiliary or main verb.

          be able to
  ▶ Tomás should ~~can~~ finish his calculus homework before the
              ^
     movie starts.

  ▶ Yuki must ~~to~~ take three more courses to graduate.

Quick

Reference   Modals and Meaning

Modals	Meaning	Examples
can, could	Used to indicate ability, possibility, and willingness and to request or grant permission	Sam can paint wonderful watercolors. [ability]
		You can leave class early today. [grant permission]
		Could we meet at the library? [request permission]
		I'm so tired I could fall asleep standing up. [possibility]
		I could work your shift if you need me to. [willingness]
may, might	Used to request and grant permission and to offer suggestions. For requests, *might* has a more hesitant and polite connotation than *may*, but they are otherwise usually interchangeable.	May I see the comments you wrote? [request permission]
		Might I borrow your car this afternoon? [more polite request for permission]
		It may/might rain this afternoon. [possibility]
		You may/might want to bring an umbrella. [suggestion]
must	Expresses necessity, prohibition (in the negative), and logical probability	Passengers must pass through airport security before boarding. [necessity]
		Passengers must not leave their seats while the seatbelt sign is illuminated. [prohibition]
		We must be on our final approach. [logical probability]
shall, should, ought to	*Should* and *ought to* express advisability and expectation, usually interchangeably. *Shall* expresses intention as well as advisability, but in American English it usually appears only in questions.	Shall/Should we eat in or go out for dinner tonight? [advisability]
		We should/ought to eat out less to save money. [advisability]
		The pizza should/ought to arrive in 20 minutes or so. [expectation]
will, would	*Will* expresses intention, willingness, and expectation. *Would* expresses intention, willingness, typical or repeated action, and logical assumption, and it is also used for polite requests.	I will finish the laundry if you want. [willingness]
		I will apply to graduate school next year. [intention]
		The bus will arrive soon. [expectation]
		Would you mind opening the window? [request]
		Amalia decided she would apply to graduate school. [intention]
		When preparing dinner, he would always clean up as he cooked. [repeated action]
		That alarm you're hearing would be the monthly test of the emergency system. [logical probability]

49 Managing Adjectives and Adverbs

by Ted E. Johnston and M. E. Sokolik

Just as a coat of paint can change our perception of the surface it covers, adjectives and adverbs color our understanding of the words they modify. *Adjectives* modify nouns and pronouns. *Adverbs* modify verbs, adjectives, other adverbs, and entire phrases, clauses, and sentences. This chapter will help you use adjectives and adverbs correctly and place them appropriately in your sentences.

49a Placing Adjectives in the Proper Order

- Most English adjectives have only one form, regardless of whether the noun they modify is singular or plural.

  ▶ Serena wants a <u>white</u> dress, but many of these <u>white</u> dresses are not to her liking.

- English adjectives usually come before a noun (*Serena has a <u>white</u> dress*) or after a ***linking verb*** (*Serena's dress is <u>white</u>*).

- When multiple adjectives cumulatively modify the same noun, the kind of information they convey determines their proper order (see the Quick Reference box below).

> **linking verbs** *Be* and other verbs that express a state of being rather than an action and connect a subject to its subject complement

Quick Reference Putting Cumulative Adjectives in Standard Order

Article or Other Determiner	Overall Evaluation or Opinion	Size	Shape or Other Intrinsic Aspect	Age	Color	Essence: Nationality, Material, or Purpose	Noun
two		big			red	rubber	balls
an	exciting			new		mystery	novel
my		tiny	helpless	newborn			kitten
those	funny			old	black-and-white		sitcoms
the	delicious		round			French	pastry

412

49b Choosing the Correct Prepositions with Adjectives

On a particular day, you might be excited *by* a lecture, mad *at* a friend, or happy *about* the election in Pakistan. As these phrases reveal, you need to be careful when combining adjectives and prepositions. When in doubt, consult a dictionary to make sure you are using the proper idiom. The editing in the following paragraph gives additional examples of idiomatic usage.

More about
Articles and other
    determiners,
    401–03
Cumulative versus
    coordinate ad-
    jectives, 423–24

More about
Prepositions,
    416–20

Ally is delighted ~~in~~ *with* her midterm grades. She had been nervous ~~of~~ *about* flunking biochemistry. Ally is grateful ~~at~~ *to* her instructors. When she struggled, they were not disappointed ~~at~~ *in* her, and they were proud ~~about~~ *of* her when she succeeded. She is dedicated ~~with~~ *to* completing her nursing degree.

49c Placing Adverbs Correctly

- An adverb cannot be located between a verb and its object.

    ▸ Susan plays ~~beautifully~~ the piano. *beautifully.*

    In this sentence, *beautifully* fits correctly only at the end, after *piano,* the direct object.

- Many adverbs, primarily those related to time (such as *often* and *frequently*), may be placed either before the subject or verb or after the direct object.

    ▸ *Recently,* Susan learned ~~recently~~ a new concerto.

    ▸ Susan learned *recently* ~~recently~~ a new concerto.

    ▸ Susan learned ~~recently~~ a new concerto. *recently.*

Writing Responsibly | Too Many Adjectives before a Noun

More than three adjectives in a row can be awkward. Instead, vary your sentences to distribute the adjectives without confusing your readers.

TOO MANY ADJECTIVES	I love to ride my exciting, shiny, new, eighteen-speed bicycle.
REVISED	I love my new eighteen-speed bicycle. It's shiny and exciting to ride.

to AUDIENCE

- When a main verb has no helping verbs, the adverb should precede it. When the main verb has helping verbs, the adverb should usually be placed between the first helper and the main verb.

  ▸ Carla <u>carelessly</u> *wasted* gas by leaving the motor running.

  ▸ Carla ~~carelessly~~ *has been wasting* gas by leaving the motor running.

carelessly

  Some adverbs (but not all) can be placed between the second helper and the main verb.

  ▸ Carla ~~carelessly~~ has been wasting gas by leaving the motor running.

carelessly

- In most instances, place an adverb first if it modifies the entire sentence.

  ▸ <u>Surprisingly</u>, she has decided to change her major to psychology.

More about
Inverted word or-
der when certain
negative adverbs
start a sentence,
399

- When certain negative adverbs or adverb phrases begin a sentence, they require a change in the standard subject-verb order. Included in this group are *at no time, never, not only, rarely,* and *seldom.*

  ▸ Seldom I ~~have~~ been so proud of my brother.

have

49d Distinguishing between Confusing Adverbs

Certain English adverbs seem similar but actually have significantly different connotations and functions. Often-confused words include *too* with *so, too* with *either, not* with *no, hard* with *hardly,* and *such* with *so.*

1. *Too* and *so*

To give an adjective a negative or more negative meaning, use *too* in most instances. To emphasize any adjective, use *so* or *very* or a similar adverb.

  ▸ The professor realized her first test had been ~~so~~ difficult and was

too

  surprised to find us still ~~too~~ excited about the class.

so

2. *Too* and *either*

When following up a statement about one subject's action with a statement about another subject's doing likewise, use *either* after a verb that is grammatically negative (as with *not* or *never* or *won't* or *hasn't*), and use *too* after a verb that is grammatically positive. Remember that unless verbs such as *avoided* or *refused* are used with a negative adverb (such as *not*), they are grammatically positive, even though by themselves they have negative meanings.

- Floyd <u>didn't join</u> the fraternity, and I <u>didn't, either</u>.
  Neither one joined.

- Floyd <u>joined</u> the fraternity, and I <u>did, too</u>.
  Both joined.

- Floyd <u>refused to join</u>, and I <u>did, too</u>.
  Neither one joined.

- Floyd <u>didn't refuse to join</u>, and I <u>didn't, either</u>.
  Both were willing to join.

3. *Not* and *no*

Because *no* is an adjective, it can only modify a noun. The adverb *not*, however, can modify an adjective, a verb, or another adverb. The expression *not a (an)* can replace the adjective *no* in front of a noun.

- Keith is ~~no~~ *not* friendly. Because he will ~~no~~ *not* talk to me, he is ~~not~~ *no (or: not a)* friend
  of mine.

4. *Hard* and *hardly*

The word *hard* can be either an adjective or an adverb. As an adverb, it means *intensely* or *with great effort*. The adverb *hardly* means *just a little* or *almost not at all*.

- Juan got an *A* after he studied <u>hard</u> for the exam. Laura got a *D*
  because she <u>hardly</u> looked at her notes.

5. *Such* and *so*

Such a (an), *such*, or *so* can emphasize a type or a quality. Use *such a (an)* before an adjective that precedes a concrete noun: *She is <u>such a</u> wise person.* Use *such* by itself directly in front of an abstract noun: *<u>Such</u> wisdom is rare.* To intensify any freestanding adjective, as in the case of a subject complement, use *so*: *She is <u>so</u> wise.*

50 Using Prepositions
by Ted E. Johnston and M. E. Sokolik

Prepositions are words that specify a relationship between other words or phrases. They usually combine with nouns, pronouns, or noun phrases to form *prepositional phrases*. In the sentence "I found my socks under the washing machine," for example, *under the washing machine* is a prepositional phrase introduced by the preposition *under*.

To help you learn to use prepositions correctly, this chapter explains how to identify prepositions (*section 50a*), how to determine the function they serve (*50b*), and how to use them correctly (*50c and d*).

50a Recognizing Prepositions

Although there are fewer than one hundred single-word prepositions in use in English, many additional multiword prepositions function in similar ways. The Quick Reference below lists some of the most common of both.

Quick Reference — **Common Single-Word and Multiword Prepositions**

Single-Word Prepositions

about	beneath	like	to
above	beside	near	toward
across	between	of	under
after	by	off	underneath
against	down	on	until
along	during	onto	up
among	except	out	upon
around	for	outside	with
at	from	over	within
before	in	past	without
behind	inside	since	
below	into	through	

Multiword Prepositions

according to	by means of	in front of	on account of
ahead of	close to	in place of	on behalf of
as far as	due to	inside of	on top of
aside from	far from	in spite of	out of
as to	in addition to	near to	outside of
as well as	in accordance with	instead of	
because of	in case of	next to	

Quick

Reference   **Learning the Functions of Prepositions**

Common functions of prepositions include the following:

1. To indicate *location* (417)
2. To indicate *time* (418)
3. To indicate *condition* or *degree* (418)
4. To specify *cause* or *reason* (418)
5. To designate *possession, attribute,* or *origin* (419)

50b Learning the Functions of Prepositions

Every preposition has multiple possible functions depending on the context in which it occurs. As a result, it is often easier to understand prepositions in terms of their function than to try to memorize what each one means.

The most basic use for a preposition is to indicate *location*. Other important functions are to indicate *time*, to indicate *condition* or *degree*, to specify *cause* or *reason*, and to designate *possession, attribute,* or *origin*.

1. Location

The most basic prepositions for indicating the location of things are *at, on,* and *in*.

- *At* specifies a general point of orientation.
  - ▸ Meet me at the station.

- *On* specifies contact between two things.
  - ▸ The book is on the table.
  - ▸ The clipboard hangs on the wall.

- *In* specifies that one thing is contained within another.
  - ▸ The solution is in the beaker.
  - ▸ Liz is in San Francisco.

NOTE Many locations operate like *surfaces* or *containers*. Generally, use *in* for locations that seem like containers and *on* for locations that seem like surfaces.

CONTAINER	He sat in his car. [**Not:** *He sat on his car,* which would mean he was on top of it.]
SURFACE	He sat on the bus. [Buses, trains, and airplanes are usually considered surfaces because people can walk around on them.]
CONTAINER	We walked in the hallway.
SURFACE	We walked on the sidewalk.

2. Time

The most common prepositions for relating things to a moment in or period of time are *at, in, on,* and *by.*

- *At* designates a particular point in time.
  - ▶ Let's meet at 4:00.
  - ▶ The party ended at midnight.

- *In* can designate either a future time or a particular period.
  - ▶ I'll leave in 10 minutes.
  - ▶ We'll finish the job in April.

- *On* designates a particular day or date.
  - ▶ His birthday is on Friday.
  - ▶ Her birthday is on the twelfth.

- *By* indicates *no later than.*
  - ▶ Turn in your essay by 3:00 p.m.
  - ▶ They decided to leave by 5:00 a.m. to avoid rush hour.

3. Condition / Degree

Prepositions of condition or degree indicate the state of the object. Some common prepositions in this category are *in, on, of, around,* and *about.*

- *In* or *on* can specify a condition. These uses are often idiomatic.
  - ▶ The house is on fire.
  - ▶ She is on vacation.
  - ▶ Charlie is not in trouble.
  - ▶ Darlene left her desk in perfect order.

- *Of* is used in phrases indicating fractions or portions.
  - ▶ Three of the books are required for the course.
  - ▶ One of those coats is mine.

- *Around* or *about* can indicate approximation.
  - ▶ That book costs around twenty dollars.
  - ▶ I walked about ten miles.

4. Cause / Reason

Prepositions showing cause include *from, for, of,* and *because of.*

- *From* indicates cause or explains a condition.
  - ▶ We were wet from the rain.
  - ▶ We were tired from walking all day.

- *For* often indicates a cause and answers the question *Why?*
  - ▶ Oregon is famous for its forests.
  - ▶ She got an award for selling more cars than anyone else.

- *Of* and *because of* both show a reason.
  - ▶ The patient died of pneumonia.
  - ▶ I sneezed because of my cold.

5. Possession / Attribute / Origin

The most common prepositions showing possession, attribute, or origin are *of,* *with,* and *from.*

- Possession is typically shown with *of.*
  - ▸ That song is one of Wilco's.
  - ▸ The composer of the song is Jay Bennett.

- An attribute can be indicated by *with.*
  - ▸ He was a man with real talent.
  - ▸ He is the one with the red beard.

- *From* can show origin.
  - ▸ Bennett was from Illinois.
  - ▸ The CD came from a website.

NOTE Indicating possession with *of* instead of *'s* or *s'* is often awkward.

AWKWARD	the bike of Maria
PREFERRED	Maria's bike

50c Using Prepositions Correctly

Certain verbs or nouns suggest the use of particular prepositions. It may help to memorize these phrases:

- ▸ *give* something *to* someone
- ▸ *take* something *from* someone
- ▸ *sell* something *to* someone
- ▸ *buy* something *from* someone
- ▸ *lend* something *to* someone
- ▸ *borrow* something *from* someone
- ▸ get *married* or *engaged to* someone
- ▸ *fill* something *with* something
- ▸ *shout to* someone (in greeting)
- ▸ *shout at* someone (in anger)

In addition, some prepositions serve a particular grammatical function. For example, in the passive voice, the preposition *by* identifies who or what did something.

- ▸ The car was repaired by Pat.

> **More about**
> Passive voice, 279–80, 293–94, 329
> Direct and indirect objects, 329–30, 397–98

Similarly, indirect objects, when placed after rather than before a direct object, are usually preceded by *to*.

▶ Theo gave the present to his father.

50d Learning When Prepositions Are Needed

Unfortunately, there is no rule of grammar to tell when a preposition is needed. Consider these examples:

▶ I like to listen ^ to ^ music.

▶ She was looking ^ at ^ the book.

Similarly, there is no rule to tell when one is not needed.

▶ ~~In one~~ ^ One ^ block from the school, there is a coffee shop.

▶ We were discussing ~~about~~ climate change in class.

To make things more complicated, sometimes a phrase is acceptable with or without a preposition.

▶ I've lived here for six years.

▶ I've lived here six years.

One strategy for mastering these usages, some of them idiomatic, is to notice in your reading when you encounter unfamiliar constructions involving prepositions. Some students keep a grammar log or other notebook to help them remember these constructions.

12 Detail
Matters
Punctuation and Mechanics

Use tab 12 to learn, practice, and master these writer's responsibilities:

❏ **To Audience**

Convey your meaning clearly with the appropriate use of commas and other punctuation, avoid contractions in formal writing, confine online abbreviations and other shortcuts to informal communication, and choose italics only sparingly for emphasis.

❏ **To Other Writers**

Use *[sic]* with sensitivity when identifying another writer's error.

❏ **To Topic**

Use quotation marks when you borrow language from a source.

❏ **To Yourself**

Check your punctuation and spelling carefully to demonstrate careful attention to detail.

Detail Matters

12

51 Using Commas

Commas function as dividers within—but not between—sentences. Think of each sentence as a room. If the periods are walls between these rooms, the commas are screens used to make subdivisions within them. Just as a screen might set off a dressing area from a larger bedroom, a comma sets off information within the main sentence. Problems with commas can be caused not only by omitting them but also by inserting them where they are *not* needed: Imagine having a screen in your kitchen between your stove and refrigerator.

51a Using Commas with *and, but, or, nor, for, so,* or *yet* in Compound Sentences

In a ***compound sentence*** a comma and ***coordinating conjunction*** (*and, but, or, nor, for, so,* or *yet*) work together: The comma marks the break between the two ***independent clauses,*** and the coordinating conjunction joins them into a single sentence. When a coordinating conjunction combines two independent clauses, place a comma *before* it (not *after* it).

▶ My heart is in San Francisco, but my body is in New York.

NOTE Unless readers will be confused, the comma can be omitted when the two independent clauses are very short.

▶ I sing in Italian but I speak only English.

> **compound sentence**
> Two or more independent clauses linked by a comma and a coordinating conjunction or a semicolon

> **independent (or main) clause** A clause that can stand alone as a sentence

Writing Responsibly / Commas and Clarity

Incorrect comma use can distort the meaning of a sentence. Consider this example, with and without commas:

This sentence . . .	means . . .
Writing to my mother is a terrible chore.	I find writing to my mother a real pain!
Writing, to my mother, is a terrible chore.	My mother finds writing a real pain!

You have a responsibility to your reader to look carefully at your use of commas when editing a document. Ask yourself, "Does this say what I intended?" If the answer is no, correct your use of commas.

to AUDIENCE

Do not use a comma before the conjunction if the joined parts are not each complete sentences.

> independent clause · · · · · · · · · · · · verb phrase
> ▸ My accountant left the country, and took my bank balance
>
> with him.

> pairs
> ▸ Both my purse, and my bank account are empty.

More about
Semicolons,
430–32
Comma splices,
341–46

When the clauses are long and already contain commas, the sentence will be clearer if you use a semicolon instead of a comma before the coordinating conjunction.

> ▸ Comic books are gradually becoming more respectable as works of serious fiction, with graphic novels such as *Maus* and *Watchmen* earning tremendous critical acclaim; yet many people, including my girlfriend, refuse to take them seriously.

NOTE Without a coordinating conjunction, a comma between two independent clauses creates a ***comma splice.***

---

subordinate clause
A word group with a subject and predicate that acts as a noun or modifier within a sentence but that cannot stand alone as a sentence

51b Using Commas after Introductory Elements

A word, phrase, or subordinate clause introducing an independent clause is usually followed by a comma.

> introductory phrase · · · · · · · · · · independent clause
> ▸ In an unguarded moment, the politician muttered an unprintable
>
> phrase into the live microphone.

> introductory subordinate clause · · · · · · · · ind.
> ▸ Although Boythorn prided himself on his gruff demeanor, he
> clause
> doted on his pet bird.

phrase A group of related words that lacks a subject, predicate, or both; it cannot stand alone as a sentence, but it can function *in* a sentence as a noun, a verb, or a modifier

When an introductory element is very brief, some writers omit the comma. If readers might be confused, even for a moment, include it.

> ▸ Before eating the missionaries said grace.

EXCEPTIONS No comma follows an introductory word group that precedes the verb in an inverted sentence (one in which the subject follows the verb). Likewise, no comma follows an introductory word group that is the subject of the sentence.

> introductory word group · · · · · · verb · · · · subject
> ▸ Into the forbidding jungle marched Dr. Livingston.

> subject · · · · · · · · · · · · verb
> ▸ Exploring forbidding jungles is what he does.

51c Using Commas to Set Off Conjunctive Adverbs and Most Transitional Phrases

Transitional expressions and ***conjunctive adverbs*** are usually set off by commas.

▶ The basking shark, in fact, consumes only zooplankton and

small fish. It may end up as dinner for an orca or tiger shark, however.

When the transitional expression or conjunctive adverb is used to link independent clauses, place a semicolon before it.

▶ The whale shark is the largest fish in today's oceans; nevertheless, it presents no threat to humans.

transitional expressions Words and phrases that link ideas within and between sentences

conjunctive adverb A transitional expression that can link one independent clause to another

51d Inserting Commas to Set Off Interjections, Contrasting Information, Expressions of Direct Address, Parenthetical and Conversational Expressions, and Tag Questions

▶ Wow, that wind farm is gorgeous!
▶ Some people, alas, think the industrial look of a wind farm is ugly.
▶ The current energy situation requires us to revise, not cling to, traditional notions of beauty.
▶ Professor Kinney, how much do you know about offshore wind farming?
▶ The first US offshore wind farm, it turns out, is on Nantucket Sound.
▶ No, wind farming alone isn't the solution to our energy problems.
▶ Wind farms will make a big contribution, won't they?

51e Using Commas to Separate Items in a Series

Place a comma between items in a series of three or more.

▶ Our new house will feature solar panels, a hilltop windmill, and rainwater conversion.

Some writers (particularly British writers) and many publications in the United States omit the comma before the coordinating conjunction (in this case *and*) that precedes the last element in a series. Readers, however, may find the final comma helpful in distinguishing paired and unpaired elements. The managing editor of the *Chicago Manual of Style* likes to quote this hypothetical dedication, which highlights the potential problems that can be caused by omitting the serial comma.

> ▶ I dedicate this book to my parents, Mother Teresa and the Pope.

More about
Using semicolons
in a series, 431

When the items in the series are long or contain internal commas, substituting semicolons for commas can make the sentence easier to read.

> ▶ Phillis Wheatley was born in Senegal in 1753, was sold into slavery
>
> to a Boston, Massachusetts, family, studied Greek, Latin, and English,
>
> and became the first published African American writer.

51f Using Commas to Separate Coordinate, Not Cumulative, Adjectives

Coordinate adjectives separately modify the noun or pronoun they precede and are of equal weight; *cumulative adjectives* modify not only the noun or pronoun they precede but also the next adjective in the series. Hence, changing the order of coordinate adjectives does not change their sense, but changing the order of cumulative adjectives usually results in nonsense.

Consider the following examples:

coordinate adjectives

> ▶ South Korea is a hot, humid country in the summer.
>
> *Hot* and *humid* each equally modifies *country*. Changing their order (*humid, hot country*) or putting *and* between them (*hot and humid country*) does not change their sense.

Quick

Reference — Testing for Coordinate and Cumulative Adjectives

To determine whether two or more adjectives should be separated by a comma, try these two tests:

1. **Place the word *and* between the two adjectives.** If the phrase still makes sense, then the adjectives are coordinate, and you should put a comma between them.

   Yes: sexy and exciting boyfriend
   No: enormous and shoulder bag

2. **Reverse the order.** If the meaning remains the same no matter what order they appear in, then the adjectives are coordinate, and you should insert a comma between them.

   Yes: sexy, exciting boyfriend = exciting, sexy boyfriend
   No: enormous shoulder bag ≠ shoulder enormous bag

cumulative adjectives

▶ His mother is a powerful corporate executive.

Powerful modifies *corporate,* and both modify *executive* together. It makes no sense to say *corporate powerful executive.*

coordinate adjectives

▶ The girl struggled to hide her brooding, moody nature from the

coordinate adjectives

sympathetic, insightful child psychologist she visited weekly.

cumulative adjectives

While you could reverse *brooding* and *moody* or *insightful* and *sympathetic,* you could not reverse *insightful* and *child:* A *child insightful psychologist* does not make sense.

More about
Adjective order,
412

51g Using Commas to Set Off Nonessential Appositives, Phrases, and Clauses

Words, phrases, or clauses that add information to a sentence but do not identify the person, place, or thing being described are **nonessential** (or *nonrestrictive*) **elements** and should be set off by commas from the rest of the sentence. Words, phrases, or clauses that identify the person, place, or thing being described are **essential** (or *restrictive*) and should *not* be set off by commas.

essential   nonessential

▶ My coworker Philip, whom I had never seen without a tie, arrived at the office this morning wearing a toga.

Philip picks out one coworker from among the rest, so that element is essential. *Whom I had never seen without a tie* provides important information about Philip but does not identify him from among the writer's colleagues, so it is nonessential.

Compare the sentence above to this sentence:

nonessential

▶ My coworker, Philip, showed up at work this morning wearing a toga.

In this sentence, *Philip* is set off by commas, suggesting that the writer has only one colleague, so identifying him by name is not essential.

1. Commas with nonessential appositives and other phrases

An **appositive** renames a preceding noun phrase. When the appositive identifies, or specifies, the noun phrase, it is essential and is not set off by commas.

noun phrase   essential
appositive

▶ The Roman emperor Claudius suffered from an ailment that caused him to limp and to stammer uncontrollably.

appositive A noun or noun phrase that renames the noun, pronoun, or noun phrase that precedes it

In this case, *Claudius* distinguishes this Roman emperor from all the other Roman emperors, so it is essential and should not be set off by commas.

When the appositive adds information but does not identify, it is nonessential and is set off by commas.

▶ The fourth Roman emperor, Claudius, suffered from an ailment that caused him to limp and to stammer uncontrollably.

Because there was only one *fourth Roman emperor,* the name *Claudius* is nonessential.

A phrase that acts like an adjective, modifying a noun, pronoun, or noun phrase, can also be essential or nonessential. If it identifies what it is describing, then it is essential and should *not* be set off by commas; if it does not identify, then it is nonessential and *should* be set off by commas.

▶ The girl, asked by her father to behave, said, "I am behaving."

▶ The girl asked by her father to behave is my niece.

2. Commas with nonessential clauses

A subordinate (or dependent) clause can also act like an adjective, modifying a noun, pronoun, or noun phrase. When it identifies the noun, pronoun, or noun phrase, the clause is essential and is *not* set off by commas; when it does not, it is nonessential and *is* set off by commas.

That *clauses versus* which *clauses* Subordinate clauses beginning with the word *that* are always essential and thus never set off by commas.

▶ Produce that has been genetically modified differs from its non–GM counterpart by a human-made alteration to its DNA.

The word *which,* on the other hand, is used today to introduce both essential and nonessential clauses.

▶ Genetically modified produce, which is sold in grocery stores throughout the United States, is still looked on with suspicion by many consumers.

NOTE Some writers (and instructors), especially in the United States, believe *which* should be used exclusively with nonessential clauses.

Adverb clauses If an adverb clause appears at the beginning of a sentence, it is usually set off by a comma. Most adverb clauses are essential and are not set off by a comma when they fall at the end of a sentence.

>   _{nonessential adv. clause}
> <u>Because</u> he found the politics required to win an Academy Award
>   _{noun}
> demeaning, George C. Scott refused to accept an Oscar for his
> performance in the movie *Patton*.

>   _{noun}
> George C. Scott refused to accept an Academy Award for his
>   _{essential adv. clause}
> performance in the movie *Patton* <u>because</u> he found the politics
> required to win an Oscar demeaning.

Adverb clauses beginning with words like *although* and *whereas* that present contrasting information are usually nonessential and are set off by a comma when they fall at the end of a sentence.

51h Using Commas with Quotations

In most cases, separate a ***direct quotation*** from a ***signal phrase*** with a comma.

>   _{signal phrase}
> After learning that he had been appointed poet laureate, Charles Simic exclaimed, "I'm almost afraid to get out of bed—too much good luck in one week."

Exceptions

- When the quotation begins the sentence and ends with a question mark or exclamation point, no comma should be added.

  > "When shall we three meet again, in thunder, lightning, or in rain?" asks the first witch in Shakespeare's *Macbeth* (1.1.1–2).

- When the quotation is integrated into your own sentence, omit the comma.

  > Friar Lawrence warns Romeo that "these violent delights have violent ends" (2.6.9).

- When the signal phrase is incorporated into a complete sentence that makes sense without the quotation, use a colon before the quotation.

  > Hamlet exits the graveyard scene with a veiled threat: "The cat will mew, and dog will have his day" (5.1.298).

Indirect quotations should *not* be set off by commas.

> New poet laureate Charles Simic confessed that/ having so much good luck worried him.

direct quotation The exact words someone has used; direct quotations must be placed in quotation marks to avoid plagiarism

signal phrase A noun or pronoun plus an appropriate verb identifying the writer from whom you are borrowing words or ideas

indirect quotation A quotation that has been paraphrased (put into the writer's own words), instead of taken word-for-word from the source

51i Using Commas with Numbers, Names and Titles, Place Names and Addresses, and Dates

Numbers, names and titles, place names and addresses, and dates are each punctuated according to specialized conventions, some of which vary from one community or discipline to another.

More about
Numbers, 462–64

1. In numbers

The following conventions are standard in most American English usage.

- In four-digit numbers, using a comma to mark divisions of hundreds is optional, except with years, when no comma should be included.

  ▶ The company paid $9347 for those supplies in 2012.

  ▶ The company paid $9,347 for those supplies in 2012.

- In numbers of five digits or more, a comma is used to mark divisions of hundreds.

  ▶ Workers have filed 93,471 unemployment claims since January.

2. Between personal names and titles

Use a comma to separate a personal name from a title that follows it.

  ▶ Send the request to Janet Woodcock, director of the Center for Drug Evaluation and Research.

Use no comma when a title precedes the name or when the "title" consists of Roman numerals.

  ▶ Send the request to Doctor Janet Woodcock.

  ▶ My son will be named Albert Farnsworth IV.

The titles Jr. and Sr. may appear with or without commas.

  ▶ Ken Griffey, Jr., appears in the *Simpsons* episode "Homer at the Bat."

  ▶ Ken Griffey Jr. appears in the *Simpsons* episode "Homer at the Bat."

3. In place names and addresses

Use a comma to separate names of cities from states, provinces, regions, or countries.

  ▶ Boston, Massachusetts, was the birthplace of Benjamin Franklin. Franklin also lived for several years in London, England, and Paris, France. He died at age eighty-four in Philadelphia, Pennsylvania.

Do *not* place a comma between the name of a state and the zip code.

▶ The Franklin Institute, founded to honor Benjamin Franklin, is located at 222 North 20th Street, Philadelphia, Pennsylvania 19103.

4. In dates

Use commas to set off dates in which the day follows the month and when dates include the time of day or the day of the week.

▶ I will never forget that my son was born at 5:17 a.m., Tuesday, March 17, 2009.

No comma is needed in dates when only the month and year are used or when the day *precedes* the month.

▶ My niece was born in February 2000.

▶ Her exact birth date is 13 February 2000.

51j Using Commas to Avoid Ambiguity

A comma can separate ideas that might otherwise be misinterpreted, and it can also mark places where words have been deleted.

1. To separate ideas

When two ideas could be misread as a single unit, add a comma to separate the two.

▶ My friends who can afford to take taxis frequently.

2. To replace omitted words and avoid repetition

Replace a repeated word with a comma after its first use:

▶ I vacationed in the Adirondacks and my brother ~~vacationed~~ in British Columbia.

51k Avoiding Commas between Subjects and Verbs, Verbs and Objects

A single comma should not separate a subject from its verb or a verb from its object unless another rule calls for it.

▶ The Senate Finance Committee, is the focus of much attention.

▶ The committee must explain, its decision to a nervous public.

52 Using Semicolons

Although it has other uses, the semicolon's main function is to link two independent clauses into a single sentence. The semicolon, however, is seldom the only option for this job. You can also usually combine independent clauses with a comma and a coordinating conjunction, you can divide them into separate sentences with a period, or you can revise to make one clause subordinate to the other. What makes the semicolon useful is the signal it sends. It tells the reader that the linked clauses are of equal importance and have a close, logical relationship.

By Gerard Whyman. Reproduced by permission from www.CartoonStock.com.

"I think Lassie is trying to tell us something, ma."

52a Using a Semicolon to Link Closely Related Independent Clauses

independent (or main) clause A clause that can stand alone as a sentence

A semicolon is a good choice for linking two *independent clauses* when both are of equal weight and the second relates closely to the first. For example, the second clause might give a reason for the first, restate its meaning, or introduce a contrast to it.

GIVING A REASON

|———————————— independent clause 1 ————————————|
My grandparents' grandparents immigrated to this country in 1895;
|———————————— independent clause 2 ————————————|
they were seeking a better life for themselves and their children.

RESTATING MEANING

> **More about**
> Parallelism, 281–84
> Commas, 421–29
> End punctuation, 444–45
> Coordinating conjunctions, 286, 345

|———————————— independent clause 1 ————————————
In the more than one hundred years since our immigrant ancestors arrived,
——————————————————| |———— independent clause 2 ————
our family has grown and dispersed; I have dozens of cousins who live in
————————————————|
almost every region of the country.

CONTRAST

|———————————— independent clause 1 ————————————|
My ancestors took months to journey from the land of their birth to
——————————| |———— independent clause 2 ————|
their new home; we can make the return journey in hours.

430

Writing Responsibly

Sending a Signal with Semicolons

Randomly using the semicolon to connect independent clauses can lead readers to see a connection between ideas that the writer did not intend. Consider this sentence: *Angelina is working in New York; Brad has a headache.* The semicolon here suggests that there is a logical relationship between the two clauses, that one is the cause or effect of the other, when, in fact, the two may reflect mere coincidence. Avoid conveying more than you mean; use the semicolon with care.

to TOPIC

52b Using a Semicolon with a Conjunctive Adverb or a Transitional Phrase to Link Two Independent Clauses

> *More about*
> Conjunctive adverbs (list), 324
> Transitional words and phrases (list), 30

A semicolon can also join two independent clauses when the second clause begins with or includes a conjunctive adverb (such as *therefore, however,* and *furthermore*) or a transitional phrase such as *in addition* or *for example.* A comma should follow the conjunctive adverb or transitional phrase when it begins the clause and should set it off on both sides when it falls within the clause.

▶ *Shakespeare in Love* introduced the playwright to a new

semi. + conj. adv. + comma

generation of moviegoers; moreover, it was an entertaining film.

semi.   comma + trans. + comma

▶ Film is a popular form of entertainment; it can be, in addition, a means of exploring literature's classic themes in contemporary contexts.

52c Using a Semicolon to Separate Items in a Series When the Items Have Internal Punctuation

Ordinarily, commas separate items in a series. Use semicolons, however, when the items are especially long or complex or when one or more of the items in the series has internal punctuation.

▶ The architectural firm of Hanover, Harvey, and Witkins recommends

creating an off-grid home by building with straw bales; packing them

tightly, which makes them flame-resistant; utilizing solar power; and

generating additional energy through windmills on the property.

52d Using a Semicolon to Repair a Comma Splice or a Fused Sentence

> *More about*
> Comma splices and fused sentences, 341–46

A semicolon can repair a ***comma splice*** (two independent clauses improperly joined with a comma alone) or a ***fused sentence*** (two independent clauses joined without any punctuation).

> ▶ Reporters without Borders fights restrictions placed on journalists, the group also raises awareness about this increasingly important issue.

52e Avoiding Misusing Semicolons

Do not use a semicolon to link an independent clause to a phrase, subordinate clause, or anything except another, related independent clause.

> ▶ The new Harry Potter film proved successful, grossing $22 million in the first night.

Use a colon, not a semicolon, to introduce a list.

> ▶ On our vacation we visited the following national parks: Yosemite, Grand Teton, and Glen Canyon.

53 Using Apostrophes

Apostrophes, like patches on torn clothing, replace something that is missing: Patches replace missing fabric; apostrophes replace letters in contractions (*can't, ma'am*). Apostrophes also make nouns and indefinite pronouns possessive (*Edward's* or *somebody's horse*).

53a Using an Apostrophe to Indicate Possession

The possessive form of a noun or pronoun indicates ownership. In spoken English, the possessive form of most nouns and indefinite pronouns ends with an *s* sound. Written English marks the possessive form with an apostrophe plus an *-s: Yue's violin, someone's book.*

noun A word that names ideas, things, qualities, actions, people, and places

indefinite pronouns Pronouns that do not refer to specific people or things, such as *all, anybody, either, everybody, few, many, neither, no one, someone*

1. With singular nouns and indefinite pronouns (but not personal pronouns)

Singular **nouns** and **indefinite pronouns** add an apostrophe and an *-s* to indicate possession.

> ▶ The factory's smokestacks belched thick, black smoke.

> ▶ No one's health was unaffected.

Writing Responsibly | **Contractions in Formal Writing**

Contractions and other abbreviations provide useful shortcuts in speech and in informal writing, and they are finding their way into more formal academic and business writing. They are still not fully accepted, however. To determine whether contractions will be acceptable to your audience or undermine your authoritative tone, check with your instructor, look for contractions in academic journals in your field, or consult reports or business letters written by other company employees. If you are in any doubt, spell the words out.

to SELF

Even for most singular nouns that already end in *-s,* add an *-'s.*

▶ Dolores's asthma was particularly aggravated.

Add an apostrophe alone to a singular noun or pronoun only when adding an *-'s* would make the word difficult to pronounce.

▶ Socrates' pneumonia became so serious he had to be hospitalized.

Never use an apostrophe to make a ***personal pronoun*** possessive. The personal pronouns all have their own possessive forms: *my, mine, your, yours, her, hers, his, its, our, ours, their, theirs.*

> **personal pronouns**
> Pronouns that replace specific nouns or noun phrases, such as *I, me, he, him, she, her, it, we, us, you, they, them*

               your   *their*

▶ We regret that ~~you're~~ new power plant will have to close, but ~~they're~~ health is more important.

Be especially careful with *its.*

- *It's (it is)* is a contraction like *don't (do not)* and *can't (cannot).*
- *Its* is a ***possessive pronoun*** like *his* and *hers.*

> **possessive pronouns**
> Pronouns that indicate ownership, such as *my, his, hers, yours, mine, theirs*

If you tend to confuse *it's* and *its,* remember that the contraction always takes an apostrophe, but the personal pronoun never does.

                                 possessive

▶ The restaurant serves Italian cuisine at its best, so

   contraction

     it's a good idea to call ahead for reservations.

2. With plural nouns

To make plural nouns possessive, first form the plural and then the possessive. When the plural form ends in *-s,* just add an apostrophe; when it does not end in *-s,* add an apostrophe and *-s.*

Tech | **Apostrophes and Spelling or Grammar Checkers**

Be wary of apostrophe-related "errors" identified by your word processor's spelling or grammar checker. These programs may mistake *its* for *it's* (or vice versa).	Pay attention to the program's suggestions, but always double-check them for accuracy.

Singular	Plural	Possessive
lady	ladies	ladies'
person	people	people's

▸ By midnight, the ladies' maids were exhausted.

▸ I'm often amazed by people's consideration for the well-being of others.

This rule applies to family names that end in -s, too: Make the name plural and then possessive.

▸ The ~~Williams~~ parties always ended at dawn.
    ^ *Williamses'*

NOTE Just because a word ends with an -s does not mean that it needs an apostrophe. Delete apostrophes from plural nouns and singular verbs.

▸ Your dog's bark wildly, but my cat remain's placid.
       noun (plu.)   *verb (sing.)*

---

3. To indicate joint or individual ownership or possession

First, decide whether the apostrophe indicates *joint* or *individual ownership*. When the nouns share possession, make only the last noun possessive.

▸ We all enjoy Mikel and Laetitia's parties.

   They give the parties collaboratively.

When the nouns each possess the same object, quality, or event, make each noun possessive.

▸ Mikel's and Laetitia's jobs don't leave them much free time.

   They have different jobs.

4. With compound nouns

Although in a compound noun, number (singular or plural) is usually attached to the core noun, the possessive is attached to the last noun.

▸ Jeremiah is driving his sisters-in-law crazy.
                         core (plural)

   Jeremiah has more than one sister-in-law, and he is driving them all crazy. Attach number to the core noun, *sister*.

▸ Jeremiah is driving his sister-in-law's car.
                              last (possessive)

   Jeremiah is using the car belonging to his sister-in-law; attach possession to the last noun, *law*.

▸ Jeremiah has his sisters-in-law's unwavering support.
                    core (plural) last (possessive)

Jeremiah has more than one sister-in-law, and he has their unwavering support; attach the plural to the core noun (*sisters*) and possession to the last noun (*law's*).

53b Using Apostrophes in Contractions and Abbreviated Years

An apostrophe can stand in place of missing letters or numbers in a contraction or in an abbreviated year.

▶ I am	I'm		▶ Cannot	Can't
▶ He is, she is	He's, she's		▶ Could not	Couldn't
			Would not	Wouldn't
▶ It is/has	It's		▶ Let us	Let's
▶ They are	They're		▶ Who is	Who's
▶ You are	You're		▶ 2012	'12

53c Avoiding, in General, Using Apostrophes to Form Plurals of Abbreviations, Dates, Numbers, and Words or Letters Used as Words

Until recently, adding -*'s* was an accepted way to form the plural for abbreviations, dates, and words or characters used as words, but this practice seems to be falling out of fashion. Unless the style guide you use instructs otherwise, do not use apostrophes to form these plurals.

- ▶ My brother has stayed in more YMCA's than anyone else I know.
- ▶ He spent the 1990's traveling around the United States playing music.
- ▶ Now he minds the *p*'s and *q*'s of students in composition classes.
- ▶ His students give him 5's on his evaluations.

You can, however, use an apostrophe to form a plural letter if its absence might cause confusion.

CONFUSING   You've dotted your *i*s and crossed your *t*s.   *may be misread as is*

CLEAR   You've dotted your *i*'s and crossed your *t*'s.

Add the apostrophe to *t*'s for consistency's sake.

NOTE The Modern Language Association (MLA) still recommends the use of an apostrophe with the plurals of letters.

Now he minds the *p*'s and *q*'s of students in composition classes.

54 Using Quotation Marks

Indicating who said what is an important use of quotation marks. Failing to indicate—whether accidentally or on purpose—that words were spoken or written by others opens a writer to charges of plagiarism. Misusing quotation marks can also confuse or annoy readers. Learning when to use—and when *not* to use—quotation marks is an important part of a writer's responsibilities.

54a Setting Off Direct Quotations with Quotation Marks

1. Direct versus indirect quotations

Double quotation marks (" ") indicate the beginning and end of direct quotations (someone's exact words, whether written or spoken).

▶ Of grappling with the unknown, Albert Einstein wrote this: "The most beautiful thing we can experience is the mysterious. It is the source of all true art and all science."

Single quotation marks (' ') indicate quotations within quotations.

▶ Barbara Jordan, the first African American woman to represent a southern state in Congress, felt that when the Constitution was written she "was not included in that 'We, the people.'"

> **More about**
> Paraphrasing,
> 127–29

Indirect quotations, which paraphrase someone's words, do *not* use quotation marks.

▶ Albert Einstein said that ~~"~~the unknown inspires scientists as well as artists.~~"~~

2. Dialog

When quoting dialog, start a new paragraph each time the speaker changes, and put all spoken words in quotation marks.

▶ "Have you brought women here before?" He smiled and kept chewing, so I said, "Do you always use the same tricks?"

"What tricks?" He looked at me like he didn't understand.

—Leslie Marmon Silko, "Yellow Woman"

Quick

Reference   Common Quotation Mark Do's and Don'ts

Do use quotation marks . . .

. . . to set off direct quotations. (436)

▶ Eisenhower once said that any person "who wants to be president is either an egomaniac or crazy."

. . . to indicate irony (use sparingly). (439)

▶ After an unsuccessful stint as president of Columbia University, Eisenhower let himself be "persuaded" to run for the US presidency.

. . . to refer to words as words. (439)

▶ "Popular" is an adjective often attached to Eisenhower's presidency.

(Italics are also widely used for this purpose.)

Do *not* use quotation marks . . .

. . . to set off indirect quotations (paraphrases). (436)

▶ Eisenhower once said that "lunatics or narcissists are the only people who would desire the presidency."

. . . for emphasis. (439)

▶ Eisenhower was a five-star general and "Supreme" Commander of Allied forces in Europe during World War II.

. . . with slang or clichés. (440)

▶ "Snafus" occur regularly in the army, but Eisenhower generally avoided them through careful planning.

In formal contexts, consider recasting to avoid slang. Clichés are rarely appropriate; rewrite to avoid them.

If one speaker continues for more than a paragraph, use quotation marks at the beginning of each paragraph, but omit closing quotation marks until the end of the speech.

3. Long quotations

For lengthy quotations, omit quotation marks, and indent quotations in a block from the left margin.

▶ Lucio Guerrero examines how local Goths feel about their lifestyle's mass-market appeal:

> For some, that suburbanization of Goth may be what saves the subculture. "If someone who identifies as Goth doesn't

Generally, introduce block quotations with a complete sentence plus a colon.

In block quotations, use double quotation marks for quotations within a quotation.

 Quotation Marks in American English Use of quotation marks varies from place to place and culture to culture. In contemporary American English, double quotation marks signal a quotation, and single quotation marks signal a quotation within a quotation:

▶ John complained, "For the third time this month, Mary said, 'I need a few bucks to tide me over till payday.' And it's only June 15!"

British usage is the opposite and would be considered wrong in the US:

▶ John complained, 'For the third time this month, Mary said, "I need a few bucks to tide me over till payday." And it's only June 15!'

More about
Formatting block
quotations, 153,
190 (MLA style),
227 (APA style)

> **Tech**   **Smart Quotes versus Straight Quotes**
>
> Word processing programs usually default to *smart*, or curly, quotation marks ("/"). Smart quotes may look more professional than straight quotes ("/"), but they often turn to gibberish when they are pasted into an online document or uploaded to a web page. If you plan to e-mail or post content that includes quotation marks, change your program's preferences to straight quotation marks. Use the Help function to locate this option.

have easy access to the fashion or accouterments that they feel drawn to, but they do have access to a store like Hot Topic, then it's a positive thing," said Scary Lady Sarah, a local DJ and supporter of Chicago's Goth community.

—Lucio Guerrero, "Like a GOTH," *Chicago Sun-Times*

Lucio Guerrero, "Like a GOTH," *Chicago Sun-Times,* Sept. 16, 2005, p. 53. Reproduced by Courtesy of the Chicago Sun-Times.

4. Quotations from poetry

When quoting one to three lines of poetry, use quotation marks and run the lines into your text. Indicate the end of each line by inserting a slash with a space on each side.

▶ Furthermore, lines 21–22 ("In the pay of a man / From town") and 25–26 ("And here we must draw / Our line") have a marching cadence, a rhythm that reinforces the battlefield symbolism.

When quoting four or more lines, omit quotation marks, set the poetry as a block, and retain the original line breaks.

▶ Gary Snyder's "Front Lines" begins powerfully:

> The edge of the cancer
> Swells against the hill—we feel
> A foul breeze—
> And it sinks back down. (lines 1–4)

Gary Snyder, "Front Lines," from *Turtle Island,* copyright © 1974 by Gary Snyder. Reprinted by permission of New Directions Publishing Corp.

54b Indicating the Titles of Short Works with Quotation Marks

More about
Italicizing titles of
longer works,
456–57

Most American style guides suggest placing titles of short works in quotation marks and titles of long works in italics.

▶ Lahiri's short story "Year's End" appeared in the collection *Unaccustomed Earth.*

▶ "Front Lines," a poem by Gary Snyder, is from his book *No Nature.*

- Ben Brantley's review of *Romeo and Juliet,* "Rash and Unadvis'd Seeks Same," ran in the *New York Times.*

- *Grey's Anatomy* is my guilty pleasure; "I Am a Tree" is my favorite episode.

- The podcast "Of Two Minds, One Consciousness" from the *Scientific American* website uses results from split-brain studies to explore thought.

- "Bleeding Love," from Leona Lewis's album *Spirit,* reached the top of the Billboard charts.

> **More about**
> Citing and documenting sources
> 149–200 (MLA style, tab 6),
> 201–38 (APA style, tab 7),
> 239–62 (*Chicago* style, ch. 27),
> 263–76 (CSE style, ch. 28)

In APA, CSE, and the *Chicago Manual of Style* parenthetical style, omit quotation marks from the titles of short works in bibliographic entries.

54c Using Quotation Marks to Indicate Words Used in a Special Sense

Quotation marks can call attention to words used in a special sense. When talking *about* a word, enclose it in quotation marks to avoid confusion.

- Many people confuse "lay" and "lie."

Italics can also be used for this purpose.

To signal that you are using a word ironically or sarcastically, place it in quotation marks.

- I didn't know that the Indian "problem" on the plains began in the 1860s. . . .

—James Welch, *Killing Custer*

Overusing quotation marks in this way, however, can annoy readers. Your words should usually be able to convey irony on their own.

Set a term to be defined in italics and the definition in quotation marks.

- Many writers don't realize that *e.g.* stands for "for example" in Latin.

54d Avoiding the Misuse of Quotation Marks

- Do not use quotation marks for emphasis.

  - Paul Potts's debut album was "amazing," selling 130,000 copies in its first week alone.

> **More about**
> Using italics for emphasis, 457

- Do not use quotation marks for slang. If slang is acceptable in a particular context, use it without the apology that quotation marks represent; if not, replace it with a more appropriate word or phrase.

  ▶ Daniel Radcliffe "~~beat out~~" *bested* hundreds of competitors to win the role of Harry Potter.

- Do not justify the use of a cliché by enclosing it in quotation marks. Instead, avoid the cliché.

  ▶ I left the party before ~~the "sun was over the yardarm."~~ *drinks were served.*

54e Positioning Quotation Marks Correctly with Punctuation

More about
Periods, 444
Commas, 421–29
Question marks, 444–45
Exclamation points, 445
Dashes, 446–47

Whether punctuation appears before or after the closing quotation mark depends on the punctuation mark.

1. With periods and commas

In American English, commas and periods go *inside* the closing quotation mark, except when a citation follows the quotation.

  ▶ "Sacred cows," said the sixties radical Abbie Hoffman, "make the tastiest hamburger."

  ▶ According to sixties radical Abbie Hoffman, "Sacred cows make the tastiest hamburger" (qtd. in Albert 43).

More about
Citing indirect sources, 160 (MLA), 209 (APA)

Commas and Periods with Quotation Marks In many countries that use the roman alphabet, commas and periods follow rather than precede the closing quotation mark. Since American English requires that commas and periods come before the closing quotation mark, be sure to adjust your usage to meet readers' expectations.

2. With question marks, exclamation points, and dashes

Question marks, exclamation points, and dashes go *inside* the closing quotation mark when they are part of the quotation.

  ▶ In *The Graduate* (1967), a family friend offers Benjamin career advice: "I just want to say one word to you: plastics!"

They go *outside* the closing quotation mark when they are not:

  ▶ Why does Robert Duvall's character in *Apocalypse Now* (1979) say "I love the smell of Napalm in the morning"? He explains that "it smells like victory"!

3. With colons and semicolons

Colons and semicolons go outside the closing quotation mark.

▶ "Love means never having to say you're sorry"; so wrote Erich Segal in *Love Story.*

▶ "Lions and tigers and bears": These are the only problems Dorothy does not encounter on her yellow-brick road to self-knowledge.

54f Introducing and Identifying Quotations

Use a colon to introduce a quotation if the clause preceding the quotation could stand on its own as a sentence and could make sense without the quotation.

> **More about**
> Clauses, 332–34

▶ Darwin's own words clarify the issue: "It is not the strongest of the species that survive . . . but the ones most responsive to change."

Use a comma with signal phrases such as "Darwin said" or "she wrote."

▶ Charles Darwin said, "It is not the strongest of the species that survive . . . but the ones most responsive to change."
    signal phrase

> **More about**
> Using signal phrases, 141–42, 202

Use no punctuation if the quotation is needed to complete the sentence (as when the word *that* precedes it), and do not capitalize the first word in the quotation.

▶ Darwin asserts that "[i]t is not the strongest of the species that survive . . . but the ones most responsive to change."

If a signal phrase interrupts the quotation, insert a comma before the closing quotation mark and after the signal phrase.

▶ "It is not the strongest of the species that survive," Darwin asserts, ". . . but the ones most responsive to change."
    signal phrase

Writing Responsibly   Using Quotations Fairly

You have a responsibility to your reader and other writers to supply quotation marks whenever you borrow language from a source. Omitting quotation marks when they are needed can mislead your readers and undermine your reputation as a writer to be trusted.

to OTHER WRITERS

> **More about**
> Plagiarism, 124–33
> Patchwriting, 127–31

Writing **Responsibly**
Acknowledging Indirect Sources

Make It Your Own! Confusing direct and indirect sources is a common problem. Fortunately, the procedures for correctly representing indirect sources in your research papers are not hard to learn, and following them will subtly enhance your writing.

When you cite sources, you do not just inform your audience about where you obtained your information; you also have a responsibility to let your audience know who is speaking in the source. If your source quotes or uses ideas from another writer, that other writer is for you an indirect source[1]: You are not reading that other writer yourself but are reading what he or she said. If you want to use that material from the indirect source, you should acknowledge the indirect source as well as the source that was talking about it. This is a sophisticated technique that takes practice to master; researchers with the Citation Project discovered that citing indirect sources was a challenge for first-year college writers, separating them from experienced writers.

The following example, from a paper exploring the Graduate Equivalency Diploma (GED) alternative to traditional high schools, shows how the problem occurs:

Student's first draft

Paraphrase of passage in source

Quotation from source

> Nontraditional high school students in the GED Options Pathway program shouldn't be labeled "GED kids"; they should be judged on their individual accomplishments. "This is supposed to be the land of the free and equal opportunity and all that stuff" (Peterson).

In-text citation

Peterson, who is cited in the sample above, is the writer of the newspaper story in which the quotation appears. However, Peterson does not speak the sentence in quotation marks. That sentence is being spoken by another source, whom Peterson is quoting in the following passage:

Passage from source

> The program does use the Graduate Equivalency Degree, or GED, as a tool. The students all have to pass the test's five sections, but when they complete the program they earn a regular high school diploma. This is an important point for Robbins, and she stresses that her students will get to graduate with their classes.
>
> "In fact, I'm trying to get everybody to quit calling them those GED kids," she said.

Quoted passage

> "Number one, they've labeled them. That irritates me. This is supposed to be land of the free and equal opportunity and all that stuff. Don't label my kids. Let them prove what they can do. Let the test scores speak."

[1]The terms *indirect source* and *indirect quotation* are often used interchangeably.

When you are drawing on material from a source that is quoting, paraphrasing, or summarizing another, your citations should accurately indicate who is speaking and should also indicate where you found the material. This can be accomplished in a parenthetical citation, a signal phrase, or a combination of the two:

Parenthetical citation: Name the speaker, write "qtd. in" (quoted in), then name the source's author

Paraphrase of passage in source	Students in the GED Options Pathway program should not be labeled "GED kids"; they should be judged on their individual accomplishments. "This is supposed to be the land of the free and equal opportunity and all that stuff" (Robbins, qtd. in Peterson).
Quotation from source	

(right margin) Parenthetical citation identifies speaker and source

Signal phrase: Name both the speaker and the source in your text

Signal phrase identifies source and speaker

Journalist Erica Peterson reports teacher Anastasia Robbins's beliefs: Students in the GED Options Pathway program should not be labeled "GED kids"; they should be judged on their individual accomplishments. "This is supposed to be the land of the free and equal opportunity and all that stuff," says Robbins.

(right margin) Paraphrase of passage in source

Quotation

Combination of signal phrase and parenthetical citation:

Signal phrase identifies the speaker

Parenthetical citation identifies the source

Teacher Anastasia Robbins believes that students in the GED Options Pathway program should not be labeled "GED kids"; they should be judged on their individual accomplishments. "This is supposed to be the land of the free and equal opportunity and all that stuff" (qtd. in Peterson).

(right margin) Paraphrase of passage in source

Quotation

Source: Peterson, Erica. "W.Va. Program Gives High-Risk Students an Option." *wvgazette.com.* West Virginia Gazette, 24 Apr. 2011. Web. 4 May 2012.

Providing the name of the person being quoted (regardless of whether it is a person who was interviewed or another author) is all you need for acknowledging your indirect source; that name should not be in the list of works cited at the end of your paper, since you did not read the original. The source you were reading, though, should be both cited in your paper and included in your list of works cited.

Self Assessment

Review your work to be sure that whenever you work from an indirect source, you:

☐ Cite the direct source. Did you name the source in which you found the material?
▶ *Direct versus indirect sources, 388–89*

☐ Use parenthetical citation, signal phrases, or a combination of both to acknowledge the name of the speaker in the indirect source and the author of the source in which you found the material. Did you make clear who is speaking? ▶ *Signal phrases, 141–42*

55

Using End Punctuation
Periods, Question Marks, and Exclamation Points

Imagine that each of the people in these photographs has just uttered the words "you're here." Just by looking at their faces, can you guess who was perplexed, thrilled, or neutral? In face-to-face encounters, sight and sound play a huge role in how we interpret tone and meaning, but in a written text, we depend on words and punctuation—especially the punctuation ending the sentence—to signal mood. Think of the question mark as a raised eyebrow, the exclamation point as wide eyes and an open mouth, and the period as the neutral expression we usually wear.

55a Using Periods to End Statements and Mild Commands

Periods end most sentences, including statements (or *declarative sentences*), mild commands, and *indirect* (or reported) *questions*.

STATEMENT	Our library has survived a flood and two fires.
MILD COMMAND/ INSTRUCTION	Please urge the council to situate the new library building on higher ground.
INDIRECT QUESTION	She wondered whether the water had ever risen so fast before.

More about
Using periods with abbreviations, 459–60

Periods are also used with some, but not all, abbreviations.

55b Using Question Marks to End Direct (Not Indirect) Questions

Use a question mark to end a *direct question*.

- What country has the highest life expectancy in the world?

- Did you know that life expectancy at birth in Japan is 82.17 years?

Use a period, not a question mark, to punctuate *indirect* questions, that is, questions that are reported, not asked directly.

- Dr. Wilson asked why life expectancy in Japan is so high.

Use a period, not a question mark, in requests phrased as questions to soften the tone.

> ▶ Would you please find out the life expectancy in the United States.

A question mark in parentheses can also suggest doubt about a date, number, or word.

> ▶ Life expectancy at birth in the United States is 78.24 years (?).

You may also punctuate a series of questions with question marks, even when they are part of the same sentence.

> ▶ What country has the fastest growing economy? the highest average income? the lowest inflation rate?

> Note that capital letters are optional if each question is not a complete sentence.

55c Using Exclamation Points with Strong Commands or to Express Excitement or Surprise

When giving an emphatic command or expressing sudden excitement or surprise, use an exclamation point to end the sentence.

> ▶ Don't go there!

> ▶ "Mom is coming!"

The same sentence, when ended with a period, conveys much less urgency.

> ▶ Don't go there.

> ▶ "Mom is coming."

NOTE Overusing exclamation points, especially in more formal contexts, may undermine your credibility with readers.

Tech — **Using Exclamation Points in E-mail Messages**

Because warmth can be difficult to convey in e-mail, writers often use an exclamation point to soften the tone. Compare:

> ▶ We look forward to seeing you next week.

> ▶ We look forward to seeing you next week!

Writing Responsibly / Question Marks and Exclamation Points

In an e-mail to a friend, you might use a series of question marks or exclamation points to convey surprise or lend emphasis:

> ▶ Isn't it about time Joey got rid of the goatee???!

But such techniques are not appropriate in more formal contexts, such as an e-mail to an instructor:

> ▶ I look forward to studying Indiana government with you next term!!!!

Your responsibility to yourself as an authoritative writer is to use restraint, for overusing exclamation points or other punctuation may undermine your credibility with readers.

to SELF

56 Using Other Punctuation
Dashes, Parentheses, Brackets, Colons, Ellipses, and Slashes

Writers thinking about punctuation typically focus on the comma, the semicolon, the period, and maybe the quotation mark—the star players of the punctuation team. But dashes, parentheses, brackets, colons, ellipses, and slashes also play key roles. Think of these other marks as the special teams of punctuation: While you may call on them in only a limited number of situations, when needed, there is no better punctuation mark for the job.

56a Using Dashes to Set Off and Emphasize Information

Dashes lend emphasis to examples, explanations, and appositives. Use them singly when the information to be set off falls at the end of a sentence or in pairs when it falls in the middle.

▸ In almost every era of Western culture, women's clothing has been decidedly restrictive and uncomfortable—and the garments of the [example] mid–nineteenth century are a prime example.

▸ To be fashionable, women had to wear clothing that hampered their mobility—cumbersome petticoats and long dresses dragged [explanation] in puddles and snagged on stairways, turning even a short walk into a navigational challenge.

▸ In the 1870s another torture device—the bustle—was introduced. [appositive]

Dashes also emphasize contrasts, definitions, and items in a list.

> **More about**
> Apostrophes,
> 432–35

▸ The bustle, which emphasized a woman's backside, was considered erotic in its day—but from a modern perspective, it is quite modest. [contrast]

▸ For both daytime and evening wear, women were strapped into corsets—close-fitting undergarments that laced tightly around the torso. [definition]

▸ The trappings of mid-nineteenth-century dress—six petticoats, a long [list] hem, a bulky bustle, and a tight corset—guaranteed women's discomfort.

Tech **Typing a Dash**

Keyboards do not have a single key for dashes, but you can usually create them with a special series of keystrokes or from the Insert menu. If you cannot find your word processor's combination for typing a dash, type two hyphens (--) instead.

Dashes can also indicate a break in thought, speech, or tone.

▶ Women's dress today ranges from the prim to the promiscuous— break (tone)
anything goes!

CAUTION If you use dashes more than once or twice over several pages, consider replacing one or more with commas: Overuse of dashes undermines their effectiveness.

56b Enclosing Supplementary Information in Parentheses

Use parentheses to set off supplementary information (such as examples, dates, abbreviations, or citations) to avoid distracting readers from the main point. Parentheses also enclose letters or numbers delineating items in a list.

▶ The English word for a trifling flaw or offense, *peccadillo,* comes from the Spanish word for a small sin, but many other borrowings
from Spanish (*barbecue, chocolate, hammock, potato, tomato*) examples
actually originated in languages of the peoples whom the Spanish conquered in the Caribbean, Mexico, and South America.

▶ In 1991, the Spanish government founded the Instituto Cervantes (IC), abbrev.
named for Miguel de Cervantes (1547–1616), the author of *Don Quixote* dates
(1605, 1615). dates

> Unless a complete sentence is enclosed, punctuation goes outside the closing parenthesis.

▶ The goals of the IC are (1) to promote the study of Spanish worldwide, list item 1
(2) to improve the methods of teaching Spanish as a second language, list item 2
and (3) to advance understanding of Spanish and Latin American list item 3
cultures.

▶ The proverb "Make hay while the sun shines" first appeared in *Don Quixote* (vol. 1, ch. 11). citation

More about
Altering quota-
tions with
ellipses and
brackets, 448,
450–51

Capital replaced to
fit quotation into
writer's sentence.

Gutenberg's replaces
his in source for
clarity.

Freshwater added
to explain an
antiquated meaning
of "sweet."

56c Using Brackets in Quotations and within Parentheses

Square brackets have two primary uses—to indicate additions or changes to a quotation and to replace parentheses within parentheses.

▶ Ramo and Burke explain that "[i]n 1456, when the first Bible rolled off [Gutenberg's] press, there were fewer than 30,000 books in Europe."

▶ Only four years after Gutenberg printed his first book, the Spanish explorer Vincente Yanez Pinzón reached the mouth of the Amazon, which he called Río Santa María de la Mar Dulce ("River St. Mary of the Sweet [Freshwater] Sea").

Square brackets are also used to enclose the Latin word *sic,* which means *thus* or *so.* [*Sic*] is inserted into a quotation following an error to make clear that it was the original writer, not the person using the quotation, who made the mistake.

Writer uses [sic] to
point out subject-
verb agreement
error (*are* should
be *is*).

▶ The most compelling review noted that "each of these blockbusters are [sic] flawed in a different, and interesting, way."

NOTE The Modern Language Association (MLA) and the Council of Science Editors (CSE) do not recommend underlining or italicizing *sic*; the *Chicago Manual of Style* and the American Psychological Association (APA), on the other hand, do recommend italicizing this Latin word.

56d Using Colons to Introduce Elaborating Material and Quotations

More about
Independent
clauses, 332–33,
341–42

A colon usually follows an independent clause to introduce and call attention to what follows. Colons are also used to separate titles from subtitles and in other conventional ways.

1. To introduce an example, explanation, appositive, or list

Use a colon following an independent (or main) clause to introduce an example, an explanation, an appositive, or a list.

Writing
Responsibly ⟨ **Using *[sic]*** ⟩

Use *[sic]* cautiously: Calling attention to an error simply to point out another writer's mistake can make you look impolite or even condescending and might undermine your reputation (or ethos) as a respectful writer. When you come across a simple ty-pographical error in a passage you want to quote (the writer typed *teh* instead of *the,* for example), either paraphrase or correct the error.

to SELF

examples

▶ Cervantes was unlucky: At the battle of Lepanto, he lost the use of his left hand, and on the return journey, he was captured by Algerian pirates. When the colon introduces a second independent clause, as here, you can start the second clause with either a capital or a lowercase letter, but whichever you choose, be consistent in other similar situations.

▶ Writing *Don Quixote* gave its impoverished author something more than just satisfaction: the opportunity to make some money.

appositive

▶ A number of important writers died on April 23: Rupert Brooke, William Wordsworth, Miguel de Cervantes, and William Shakespeare.

list

A dash can substitute for a colon in these cases, but a colon is more appropriate in formal writing.

Colons are also used to introduce a list that is preceded by the phrases *as follows* or *the following.*

list

▶ The following writers all died on April 23: Rupert Brooke, William Wordsworth, Miguel de Cervantes, and William Shakespeare.

Do not introduce a list with a colon when the introductory clause concludes with *like, such as,* or *including.*

▶ A number of important writers all died on April 23, including: Rupert Brooke, William Wordsworth, Miguel de Cervantes, and William Shakespeare.

> **More about**
> Using commas in
> quotations, 427

2. To introduce a quotation

Use a colon to introduce a quotation only when it is preceded by an independent clause that would make sense without it, but not when the quotation is introduced by a signal phrase such as *she said* or *Hughes asks.*

ind. clause makes sense without quotation

COLON   In 1918, William Strunk, Jr., gave writers a piece of timeless advice: "Omit needless words."

signal phrase needs quotation to make sense

COMMA   In 1918, William Strunk, Jr., said, "Omit needless words."

3. Other conventional uses

■ Between title and subtitle and between publication date and page numbers (for periodicals) and location and publisher (for books) in bibliographic citations for some documentation styles

More about
MLA style, 149–200
(tab 6),
APA style, 201–38
(tab 7),
Chicago style,
239–62 (ch. 27),
CSE style, 263–76
(ch. 28)

More about
Business letter
formats, 56–59

title   subtitle
Langford, David. "Hogwarts Proctology Class: Probing the End of Harry

Potter." *New York Review of Science Fiction* 20.2 (2007): 1, 8–11. Print.
title   subtitle   city   publisher
Satrapi, Marjane. *Persepolis 2: The Story of a Return.* New York: Pantheon,

2004. Print.

- Following the salutation and following *cc* in formal business
  correspondence

  ▸ Dear Professor Howard:

  ▸ cc: June Carter

- Between chapter and verse in scripture; between hours, minutes, and
  seconds; in ratios

  ▸ Song of Solomon 3:1–11

  ▸ 4:30 p.m.

  ▸ Women outnumber men in college 2:1.

4. Common mistakes with colons

- Do not insert a colon between a verb and its complement or object.

              verb   object
  ▸ Young readers awaited: the next volume in Stephenie

  Meyer's vampire love saga.

- Do not insert a colon between a preposition and its object.

                        prep.   object
  ▸ *Vogue* announced a return to: hippie-style clothing.

56e Using Ellipses to Indicate Deletions in Quotations and Dramatic Pauses in Dialog

An *ellipsis* is a deliberate omission of a portion of a quotation. The word *ellipsis* (plural: *ellipses*) also refers to the punctuation used to mark an omission: a set of three periods—or *ellipsis points*—with a space between each. Ellipses are also sometimes used to indicate a dramatic pause or to suggest that the writer is unable or unwilling to say something.

1. To indicate deletions from quotations

Although it is not acceptable to alter the meaning of a quotation, writers can and do omit words from quotations as needed to delete irrelevant information or to make a quotation fit into their own sentence. The ellipsis alerts readers that a change has been made.

▶ *Don Quixote* begins like a fable: "In a village of La Mancha, comma + ellipsis . . . there lived not long since one of those gentlemen that keep a lance, comma + ellipsis . . . a lean hack, comma + ellipsis . . . and an old greyhound for coursing. period + ellipsis . . ."

> Use four dots—a period plus the ellipsis—if a deletion occurs at the end of the sentence.

With a parenthetical citation, insert the ellipsis before the closing quotation marks and the period after the citation.

▶ "They will have it his surname was Quixada . . ." ellipsis + closing quote (1). citation + period

Quotations of only a few words or that begin with a lowercase letter are obviously taken from a longer original and do not require ellipses. Similarly, a quotation of an entire sentence does not need ellipses to indicate that it comes from within a longer passage.

> **More about**
> Altering quotations, 147–48, 448, 450–51

When quoting poetry, use not a single ellipsis mark (three dots) but a whole line of dots to replace one or more missing lines.

▶ One of the most famous lines in Robert Frost's poem "Mending Wall" is "Good fences make good neighbors," but the speaker's meaning is lost when this line is taken out of context:

> There where it is we do not need the wall:
>
> . . . .
>
> My apple trees will never get across
> And eat the cones under his pines, I tell him.
> He only says, "Good fences make good neighbors." (lines 23–27)

2. To indicate a dramatic pause or interruption in dialog

An ellipsis can indicate an incomplete thought, a dramatic pause, or an interruption in speech.

▶ The disgruntled writer muttered, "The only word to describe my editor is . . . unprintable."

Writing Responsibly   Altering Quotations

Exercise care when changing quotations with brackets or ellipses: Never make a change that might distort the original or that might mislead readers, and always use ellipses and brackets to indicate alterations.

to OTHER WRITERS

56f Using Slashes in Verse, Fractions, and URLs

The slash (or *virgule*) is used to mark the ends of lines in poetry when the poetry is run into a sentence. Insert a space on either side of the slash.

▶ *Don Quixote* opens with some "commendatory verses" that warn the writer "Whoso indites frivolities, / Will but by simpletons be sought" (lines 62–63).

Slashes are also used in fractions and URLs. For this use, do not insert a space around the slash.

▶ 1/2   1/3   3/4

▶ www.unh.edu/writing/cwc/handouts

In informal contexts, the slash is sometimes used to indicate that either of two terms is applicable.

▶ I've got so many courses this semester that I decided to take Spanish pass/fail.

In more formal contexts (such as academic or business writing), replace the slash with the word *or,* or rewrite the sentence.

▶ The test consisted entirely of ~~true/false~~ *true or false* questions.

57 Capitalizing

Like a spire soaring over surrounding rooftops, a capital letter beckons the reader, calling attention to the word it adorns. But just as architecture varies from place to place, so the rules of capitalization vary from language to language. This chapter summarizes the most important rules of capitalization in English.

 Capitalization English capitalization can be confusing to people for whom English is a foreign language. In Spanish, French, and German, the first-person singular pronoun is lowercased (*yo, je, ich*), but in English it is capitalized (*I*), although the other personal pronouns are not. In Spanish and French, the names of months and days of the week are lowercased, but not in English. In German, all nouns are capitalized, but in English only proper nouns are. Languages such as Arabic and Korean have no capital letters at all. Proofread your work carefully to adhere to the conventions of English capitalization, referring to this chapter and a good college dictionary as needed.

Quick

Reference Common Capitalization Do's and Don'ts

Do capitalize . . .

... **the first word of a sentence. (453)**

▶ The day broke gray and dull. —Somerset Maugham, *Of Human Bondage*

... **proper nouns and proper adjectives. (455)**

▶ Aunt Julia, Beijing, Dad (used as a name), Band-Aid, Shakespearean, Texan

... **the first, last, and important words in titles and subtitles. (455)**

▶ *Harry Potter and the Order of the Phoenix*

... **the first-person pronoun *I*. (456)**

▶ I think; therefore, I am. —René Descartes

... **abbreviations and acronyms. (456)**

▶ Eng. Dept., UCLA, NYPD

Do not capitalize . . .

... **common nouns and common adjectives. (454)**

▶ dog, cat, aunt, city, my dad, bandage

... **compass directions. (454)**

▶ north, south, northwest, southeast

... **seasons or academic years and terms. (454)**

▶ spring, freshman, intersession

57a Capitalizing the First Word of a Sentence

Capitalize the first letter of the first word of every sentence.

▶ In response to Franklin Roosevelt's long tenure, the US Congress passed an amendment limiting a president to two terms.

This rule applies even to sentences in parentheses, unless they are incorporated into another sentence.

▶ His vice president, Harry S. Truman, decided not to run for reelection, although the amendment did not apply to him. (The sitting president was exempted.)

▶ Although the amendment did not apply to him (the sitting president was exempted), Truman decided not to run for reelection.

More about Parentheses, 447

Capitalize the first word of a sentence you are quoting, even when it is incorporated into your own sentence.

▶ In response to a question about the amendment, President Eisenhower said, "By and large, the United States ought to be able to choose for its president anybody that it wants, regardless of the number of terms he has served."

Do not capitalize the first word when you are quoting only a phrase.

▶ President Eisenhower's "faith in the long-term common sense of the American people" made him feel the amendment was unnecessary.

When interrupting a quoted sentence, do not capitalize the first word of the second part.

▶ "By and large," Eisenhower said, "the United States ought to be able to choose for its president anybody that it wants, regardless of the number of terms he has served."

More about
Brackets, 448
Altering quotations, 147–48, 448, 450–51

NOTE In MLA style, if you must change a capital to a lowercase letter (or vice versa) to incorporate a quotation into your sentence, place brackets around the letter to alert readers to the change.

Quick Reference **Capitalizing Proper Nouns and Proper Adjectives**

	Proper Nouns and Proper Adjectives	Common Nouns and Common Adjectives
Departments and Disciplines	Political Science Department	political science
Historical Events, Eras, and Documents	Korean War, Roaring Twenties, the Emancipation Proclamation	the war, the twenties, the proclamation
Nations, Ethnic Groups, Races, and Languages	Pakistan, Pakistani, African American, Swahili	her country, his nationality, their language
Organizations, Offices, and Companies	National Wildlife Federation, Government Accountability Office, National Broadcasting Corporation	a conservation group, the legislative branch, the network, the corporation
People and Titles	Lewis and Clark, Senator Robert C. Byrd, Dickens, Dickensian	the expedition leaders, the senator, the author, satirical
Places, Compass Directions	Central Park, Neptune, the Northwest	the park, an outer planet, northwest
Religions, Sacred Texts, and Religious Terms	Buddhism, Presbyterian, Vedas, Bible, God	your religion, denominational, a sacred text, biblical, the gods
Time Periods and Holidays	Tuesday, June, Memorial Day	a weekday, this summer, spring break
Trade Names and Products	Coke, Kleenex, Xerox	a soda, a tissue, a photocopy
Vessels, Vehicles, and Modes of Transportation	U.S.S. *Constitution*, Greyhound, Amtrak	this battleship, a bus, the train

If a colon links two *independent clauses,* the second clause can begin with a capital letter or not. Whichever option you choose, apply it consistently.

independent (or main) clause A clause that can stand alone as a sentence

▸ Our company is at a crossroads: We must adapt to new conditions.

or

▸ Our company is at a crossroads: we must adapt to new conditions.

57b Capitalizing Proper Nouns and Proper Adjectives

Capitalize the first letter of *proper nouns* (the names of specific people, places, and things) and the adjectives derived from them. Do not capitalize common nouns (names for general groups of people, places, and things) or common adjectives. The Quick Reference guide on the previous page provides examples of words in each group.

57c Capitalizing Titles and Subtitles

In general, capitalize the first and last words of titles and subtitles, as well as any other important words: nouns (*Pride, Persuasion*), verbs (*Is, Ran*), pronouns (*It, Their*), adjectives (*Green, Starry*), and adverbs (*Slow, Extremely*). Do not capitalize prepositions (*in, at, to, by*), coordinating conjunctions (*and, but, for, nor, or, so, yet*), *to* in infinitive verbs, or articles (*a, an, the*) unless they begin or end the title or subtitle.

Extremely Loud and Incredibly Close (novel)	"I Kissed a Girl" (song)
"In the Basement of the Ivory Tower" (article)	*The Dark Knight* (movie)
Pokéman XD: Gale of Darkness (game)	Flying Popcorn (software)

Writing Responsibly — Capitalizing in E-mail and IM

The rules of capitalization are usually the same online as they are in print. But while in print a writer may sometimes type a word in all capital letters for emphasis, in e-mail or other online contexts, words typed in all capital letters are interpreted as shouting. When formatting is available, use italics (or boldface type) for emphasis in online writing; when such formatting is unavailable, place an asterisk before and after the word you want to emphasize. Also, although omitting capital letters in e-mail and instant messages may be acceptable in informal contexts, to maintain a professional tone you should follow the rules of capitalization when texting or e-mailing in business or academic settings.

to SELF

More about
MLA style, 149–200
(tab 6)
APA style, 201–38
(tab 7)
Chicago style,
239–62 (ch. 27)
CSE style, 263–76
(ch. 28)

NOTE Style guides may recommend different capitalization for titles and subtitles in reference lists and bibliographies. Check the style guide you are using and follow the rules described there.

57d Capitalizing the First-Person Pronoun *I*

In all formal contexts, capitalize the first-person singular pronoun *I*.

▶ I wish I could meet myself in twenty years.

More about
Abbreviations,
459–62

57e Capitalizing Abbreviations and Acronyms

Abbreviations of proper nouns should be capitalized, and acronyms should be typed in all capital letters.

acronym Word
formed from the first
letter of each major
word in a name

| ABBREVIATIONS | U. of Mich., Anthro. Dept. |
| ACRONYMS | RADAR, NASA, OPEC |

58 Italics and Underlining

Before the computer, writers typed on typewriters and used underlining to emphasize words; to set off the titles of longer works; to distinguish words, letters, and numbers used as words; to set off unfamiliar non-English words; and to call out the names of ships, airplanes, spacecraft, and other vehicles. Now writers type on computers and use italics for these purposes.

58a Italicizing Titles of Long Works

More about
Using quotation
marks with titles
of shorter works,
438–39

Use italics (or underlining) for titles of long works such as books, periodicals (magazines, journals, and newspapers), films, CDs, television series, and websites; use quotation marks for short works, such as stories, articles, songs, television episodes, and web pages.

Annie Proulx's collection *Close Range: Wyoming Stories* includes the story "Brokeback Mountain," which originally appeared in the *New Yorker* magazine. Kenneth Turan, critic for the *Los Angeles Times,* called the 2005 film *Brokeback Mountain* "groundbreaking," and Roger Ebert of the *Chicago Sun-*

Writing Responsibly | **Using Italics for Emphasis**

When using italics for emphasis, consider your reader. Sometimes italics can help convey the writer's feelings, but will readers be interested? In a personal context, the use of italics in the sentence below might be acceptable:

▶ Should *I* call *him,* or should I wait for *him* to call *me*?

But such emphasis on the writer's emotions is usually inappropriate in a business or academic context.

to AUDIENCE

Times gave it two thumbs up. The *Brokeback Mountain* soundtrack on CD includes songs like "He Was a Friend of Mine" by Willie Nelson and "The Devil's Right Hand" by Steve Earle.

In addition, the titles of stand-alone items like court cases and works of art (paintings and sculptures) are italicized.

▶ *Bowers v. Hardwick*   ▶ *Mona Lisa*   ▶ *The Bronco Buster*

In contrast, the titles of major historical documents and religious works are not italicized.

▶ Magna Carta, Mayflower Compact, Kyoto Protocol

▶ Bible, Qur'an, Vedas

58b Italicizing for Emphasis Sparingly

Italics are sometimes used for emphasis.

▶ Rowling wants readers to *identify* with Harry, not merely to *sympathize* with him.

In the sentence above, the italics heighten attention to the contrast. To be effective, italics must be used sparingly for emphasis. Using italics haphazardly or overusing them can annoy or even confuse readers.

58c Italicizing Names of Vehicles

The names of individual trains, ships, aircraft, and spacecraft are all italicized.

▶ *Titanic, Spirit of St. Louis, Challenger*

However, vehicles referred to by company, brand, or model names are not.

▶ Corvette, Boeing 747

Reference **Common Italics Do's and Don'ts**

Do **use italics . . .**

. . . with titles of long works. (456)

▶ We will be discussing the novel *Wuthering Heights* for the next two weeks. By the way, the novel's main character has nothing to do with the comic strip *Heathcliff.*

. . . for emphasis. (457)

▶ I ask you *not* to read beyond the first chapter until we have discussed it in class.

(Use italics for emphasis sparingly in academic prose.)

. . . with words, letters, or numbers used as words. (458)

▶ You will notice that several of the characters' names begin with the letter *h;* this can be confusing.

Do *not* **use italics . . .**

. . . with titles of short works. (456)

"Girl"

▶ Jamaica Kincaid's story ~~Girl~~ is only one page long.
        ^

. . . with historical documents and religious works. (457)

Declaration of Independence   Bible

▶ The ~~Declaration of Independence~~ and the ~~Bible~~ take pride of place on
        ^   ^

my grandmother's bookshelf.

. . . with links to websites and web pages (underline if a hyperlink). (459)

▶ If you do not want to buy the book discussed in Salon.com, you can download it from Project Gutenberg <u>www.gutenberg.org/etext/768</u>.

58d Italicizing Words, Letters, or Numbers Used as Words

When referring to words, letters, or numbers used as words, set them off from the rest of the sentence with italics.

More about
Plurals of letters,
435

▶ My chemistry instructor used the word *interesting* to describe the results I got on my last lab. He told me to be more careful next time to dot all my *i*'s and cross all my *t*'s.

58e Italicizing Unfamiliar Non-English Words and Latin Genus and Species Names

English is an opportunistic language: When encountering new things or ideas, English speakers often adopt words already used in other languages. The word *raccoon,* for example, comes from Algonquian and the word *sushi* from Japanese. Once they are fully absorbed, borrowed words are typed with no special formatting. Until then, borrowings should be italicized.

▶ The review provides a good example of *diegesis* in that it describes the film without making a judgment about it.

To determine whether a non-English word warrants italics, check your dictionary: Words familiar enough to be found in a college dictionary should not be italicized.

Latin genus and species names are also italicized.

▶ The Latin term *Acer saccharum* identifies the genus and species of the sugar maple.

58f Underlining Hyperlinks

In recent years, underlining has taken on a new, specialized meaning: It is used (along with color) to indicate hyperlinks in both printed and online documents. Because many documents today will ultimately appear online, writers are increasingly reserving underlining for hyperlinks and are using italics for all the other purposes outlined in this chapter.

▶ The Library of Congress website (www.loc.gov) has a wealth of digital resources.

59 Using Abbreviations

When you see this familiar symbol, you know at a glance that the object it adorns was made from recycled materials. When they are familiar to an audience, icons like this one communicate information briefly and quickly. Abbreviations accomplish a similar goal in writing: They convey information rapidly but only when readers know what they stand for. Although they are used frequently in business, scientific, and technical contexts, abbreviations are used sparingly in writing in the humanities and for a general audience, except in tables (where space is at a premium) and in bibliographic citations.

When you do abbreviate, use a period with a person's initials and with most abbreviations that end in lowercase letters:

▶ J. K. Rowling   Martin Luther King, Jr.   Blvd.   Ave.

Use a period after each letter with abbreviations of more than one word:

▶ i.e.   e.g.   a.m.   p.m.

Most abbreviations made up of all capital letters no longer use periods:

▸ BS   MA   DVD   UN

59a Abbreviating Titles before and after Names

▸ Mr. Tony Carter   Christopher Aviles, PhD

▸ Ms. Aoife Shaughnessy   Namazi Hamid, DDS

▸ Dr. Jonnelle Price   Robert Min, MD

▸ Rev. Jane Genung   Frederick C. Copelston, SJ

In most cases, avoid abbreviating titles when they are not used with a proper name.

▸ I'm hoping my English ~~prof.~~ *professor* will write me a letter of recommendation.

Academic degrees are an exception.

▸ My auto mechanic comes from a highly educated family: His father has an MS, his mother has an MLS, and his sister has a PhD.

Never use a title both before and after a name: Change *Dr. Hazel L. Cunningham, PhD* to either *Dr. Hazel L. Cunningham* or *Hazel L. Cunningham, PhD*.

59b Using Acronyms and Initialisms Appropriately

Acronyms and *initialisms* are abbreviations made of all capital letters formed from the first letters of a series of words. Acronyms are pronounced as words (*AIDS, CARE, NASA, NATO, OPEC*), while initialisms are pronounced as a series of letters (*DNA, HBO, JFK, USA*). Familiar acronyms and initialisms are acceptable in any context.

▸ The UN Security Council met to discuss a response to North Korea's nuclear tests.

However, if the abbreviation is likely to be unfamiliar to readers, spell out the term on first use and follow it with the abbreviation in parentheses. Subsequently, just use the abbreviation.

▸ The International Olympic Committee (IOC) failed to take action following the arrest of two elderly Chinese women who had applied for permission to protest in the designated protest areas during the Beijing Olympics. A spokesperson claimed that the IOC has no control over the protest areas.

Writing Responsibly   **Using Online Abbreviations Appropriately**

A new breed of initialism has emerged in online discourse. Here are some examples:

BFN (bye for now)	OIC (oh, I see!)
IDK (I don't know)	OTOH (on the other hand)
IMO (in my opinion)	ROTFL (rolling on the floor, laughing)
LOL (laughing out loud)	TMI (too much information!)

The irreverence of some of these initialisms corresponds with the freewheeling characteristics of online discourse. Use them in text messages or on informal networking sites, but avoid them in college and professional writing, including e-mails. While they might establish your online savvy, they might also annoy readers in more formal contexts, undermining your credibility.

to SELF

59c   Using Abbreviations with Specific Years (BC, BCE, AD, CE), Hours (a.m., p.m.), Numbers (no.), and Dollars ($)

▶ The emperor Augustus ruled Rome from 27 BCE until his death in 14 CE.

> AD precedes the year; BC, BCE, and CE follow the year.

▶ The Roman historian Titus Livius (known as Livy) lived from 59 BC until AD 17.

▶ I didn't get home until 11:45 p.m., because the no. 27 bus was so late.

▶ I owe my sister $27.32, and she won't let me forget it.

NOTE The abbreviations BCE (for *before the common era*) and CE (for *common era*) are now generally preferred over BC (*before Christ*) and AD (*anno domini*, "the year of the Lord" in Latin).

59d   Avoiding, in Prose, Abbreviating Names, Words, Courses, Parts of Books, States and Countries, Days and Months, Holidays, and Units of Measurement

▶ In F̶r̶., people receive gifts not on X̶m̶a̶s̶ but on J̶a̶n̶. 6.
   France,   *Christmas*   *January*

▶ On M̶o̶n̶. mornings, P̶s̶y̶c̶h̶. 121 meets in a tiny classroom: It is only ten f̶t̶. wide.
   Monday   *Psychology*   *feet*

▶ My E̶n̶g̶. teacher, E̶l̶i̶z̶. Santos, recommends that we always read the i̶n̶t̶r̶o̶. first.
   English   *Elizabeth*   *introduction*

An exception is the names of businesses, when the abbreviation is part of the official name:

▸ Dun & Bradstreet, Inc., was ~~inc.~~ *incorporated* in New York ~~&~~ *and* is still located there.

59e Replacing Latin Abbreviations with English Equivalents in Formal Prose

Generally, avoid Latin abbreviations, like those below, in formal writing (except in bibliographies).

▸	e.g.	for example	▸	cf.	compare
▸	i.e.	in other words	▸	et al.	and others
▸	etc.	and so forth	▸	N.B.	note especially

NOTE Both *etc.* and *and so forth* are best avoided in formal prose. Instead, include all the items or precede a partial list with *such as* or *for example*. Follow *e.g.* and *i.e.* with a comma if you use them in tables or parenthetical material. Common Latin abbreviations are not italicized or underlined.

60 Using Numbers

Are we "number one" or "#1"? It depends on the context. Rules for deciding whether to use numerals or to spell out numbers vary widely according to context. In business and the news, single-digit numbers are usually spelled out, while numerals are used for numbers over ten. The rules in this chapter are appropriate to an academic audience in the humanities.

60a Spelling Out Numbers When They Can Be Expressed in One or Two Words

Spell out numbers under one hundred and round numbers—numbers that can be expressed in one or two words.

▸ Satchel Paige pitched sixty-four scoreless innings and won twenty-one games in a row.

Writing Responsibly / **Ethos and Convention**

Using numbers and symbols in conventional ways does not normally affect meaning. Yet conventional usage is important, especially in formal contexts like school or the workplace, because it lends support to your ethos, or credibility. The way you use numbers and symbols can subtly affect the way your audience perceives you and thus how seriously they take what you say.

to SELF

More about
Appropriate language, 294–99
Ethos, 76

If your text uses a combination of numbers—some that can be expressed in one or two words and others that cannot—use numerals throughout for consistency's sake.

> ▶ Satchel Paige pitched an estimated ~~two thousand~~ 2,000 baseball games during his career. At his first game, 78,383 fans were in attendance, and at his first game as a starter, 72,434 spectators looked on.

Avoid beginning a sentence with numerals. Instead, spell out the number or revise your sentence.

> ▶ Seventy-eight thousand 78,000 people attended Satchel Paige's first game as a pitcher.

> ▶ Satchel Paige's first game as a pitcher drew 78,000 fans.

Numbers over a million are often best expressed as a combination of words and numerals.

> ▶ More than 10 million fans attended Negro League baseball games in 1930.

60b Following Conventions for Dates, Times, Addresses, Specific Amounts of Money and Other Quantitative Information, and Divisions of Literary Works

- **Dates:** May 4, 2013   the fourth of May   429 BCE
  1066 CE   AD 1066

- **Times, years:** 4:15 p.m.   seven o'clock   1990s   the nineties
  1999–2009   from 1999 to 2009

- **Phone numbers, addresses:** (800) 624-5789
  26 Peachtree Lane   221 W. 34th Street
  Atlanta, GA 30303   New York, NY 10001

- **Exact sums of money:** $10.95 $579.89 $24 million

- **Decimals and fractions:** half   ½   three-quarters   ¾   4⅝   3.95

NOTE MLA style generally recommends using the percent symbol (%) with numerals. The *Chicago Manual* recommends using the word *percent* with numerals in writing for the humanities and the symbol % with numerals in writing for the sciences.

- **Scores, statistics, and percentages:** 5 to 4   42–28
  13.3 percent (or 13.3%)   3 out of 10
- **Measurements:** 55 mph   90–100 rpm   135 pounds   5 feet
  9 liters   41°F
- **Divisions of books, plays, poems:** part 3   book 7   chapter 15
  page 419 or p. 419   act 1   scene 3   lines 4–19

 Punctuating Numbers in American English Conventions for punctuating numbers differ across cultures. In many European countries, for instance, commas separate whole numbers from decimal fractions, where periods mark divisions of thousands. In the United States, the convention is reversed:

▶ 2,541   94.7

61

Mastering Spelling and Hyphenation

In a well-known experiment, psychologists found that people have little difficulty when asked simply to read the words in the box shown here, yet they have a lot of trouble when asked to identify the color of ink each word is printed in. We absorb the meaning of each word alone automatically, but when we try to identify the ink color, we get confused because the color conflicts with the word's meaning. Readers similarly process most correctly spelled words automatically but get distracted or confused by misspelled words. If you want readers to pay attention to your ideas rather than to struggle to decipher your meaning word by word, you should check your spelling carefully.

> **RED**
>
> **GREEN**
>
> **BLUE**

61a Distinguishing Homonyms and Other Problem Words

Many spelling errors result from confusion over homonyms and near-homonyms.

- *Homonyms* are groups of words that sound exactly alike but have different spellings and meanings, such as *to/too/two* and *cite/sight/site*.

- *Near-homonyms* are groups of words such as *personal/personnel* and *conscience/conscious* that are close but not the same in pronunciation. Near-homonyms also include different forms of the same word, such as *breath/breathe* and *advice/advise*.

There is no easy formula for mastering these words. If any of them give you trouble, try to memorize their spellings and meanings, and always check for them as you proofread your writing.

> **More about**
> Confusing words
> and phrases in
> "Glossary of
> Usage," 311–18

Use American Rather Than British Spelling Multilingual writers who began their study of English outside the United States may be accustomed to British spelling, which is often different from American. For example, Americans fly in *airplanes* (not in *aeroplanes*), and they pay bills with *checks* (not *cheques*). Some writers striving for formality mistakenly believe that British spellings are preferable. If you are writing for a US audience, be sure to follow American spelling. When in doubt, consult an American dictionary, which will give the preferred American spelling before any alternatives.

61b Remembering Spelling Rules

Mastering a few key rules—and noting their exceptions—can improve the accuracy of your spelling.

1. The *ie/ei* rule

The traditional rule—"*i* before *e* except after *c* or when sounded like *ay* as in *neighbor* and *weigh*"—will help you spell words like *believe, receive,* and *sleigh* correctly.

I BEFORE *E*	diesel, piece, pier, retrieve, shield, siege
E BEFORE *I* AFTER *C*	ceiling, conceit, conceive, deceit, perceive, receipt
EI SOUNDS LIKE *AY*	beige, deign, eighteen, reindeer, sleigh, veil

Some exceptions: *feisty, forfeit, heifer, height, heir, neither, protein, sovereign, seize, their, weird.*

Writing Responsibly   **Spelling Errors**

A misspelled word is not an important issue when you are texting friends, but in other situations it may signal that you are careless about details. If you misspell *accountant* in a job-application letter to a financial firm, for example, the recipient may wonder how accurate you are about numbers. If you misspell a name, people may interpret it as a sign of indifference or disrespect.

to SELF

2. Suffixes

Suffixes attach to the end of a root word to change its meaning and grammatical form.

Words that end with a silent e In most instances, drop the silent *e* if the suffix starts with a vowel.

observe → observant   response → responsible   revoke → revoked

Retain the silent *e* if the suffix starts with a consonant.

hope → hopeful   love → lovely   polite → politeness

Some exceptions: *advantageous, argument, judgment, serviceable.*

Words that end in y For most words that end in a consonant and *y,* change the *y* to an *i* when you add a suffix.

apology → apologize   deny → denies

heavy → heavier   merry → merriment

Retain the *y* if the suffix is *-ing,* if a vowel precedes the *y,* or if the word ending in *y* is a proper name.

spy → spying   play → playful   McCoy → McCoys

Suffixes -ally versus -ly and -efy versus -ify When a word ends in *ic,* use the suffix *-ally.* In all other instances, use *-ly.*

basic → basically   magic → magically

brisk → briskly   confident → confidently

Only four words use the suffix *-efy: liquefy, putrefy, rarefy, stupefy.* All other such words use the suffix *-ify: beautify, certify, justify, purify.*

Words that end with a consonant Do not double a final consonant if the suffix begins with a consonant (*commitment, fearless, kinship, poorly*). For suffixes that begin with a vowel, follow these guidelines:

- **One-syllable root words.** Double the final consonant if only one vowel precedes it; otherwise, do not double the consonant.

  bit → bitten   chat → chatty   skip → skipping

  chart → charted   droop → drooping   speak → speaker

- **Multisyllable words.** Double the final consonant if only one vowel precedes it and if the final syllable of the root is accented in the new word containing the suffix.

  admit → ad**mit**tance   concur → con**cur**rent

  For multisyllable words that do not meet these criteria, do not double the final consonant.

  devil → devilish   proclaim → proclaiming

61c Forming Plurals Correctly

To form the plural of most English nouns, add an -s.

letter → letters   shoe → shoes   Erickson → the Ericksons

To form the plural of nouns that end in s, sh, ch, x, or z, add -es.

miss → misses   dish → dishes   latch → latches

box → boxes   quartz → quartzes   Davis → the Davises

To form the plural of some nouns that end in f or fe, change the f to a v and add -s or -es.

knife → knives   loaf → loaves

However, words that end in ff or ffe and some words that end in f or fe form the plural just with the addition of an -s.

bluff → bluffs   giraffe → giraffes   safe → safes

To form the plural of nouns that end in o, add -s if the o is preceded by a vowel or if the word is a proper noun. Add -es if the o is preceded by a consonant.

duo → duos   ratio → ratios   video → videos

echo → echoes   potato → potatoes   veto → vetoes

Some exceptions: *autos, ponchos, sopranos, tacos.*

To form the plural of words that end in y, add -s if the y is preceded by a vowel or if the word is a proper noun.

decoy → decoys   essay → essays   Hagarty → the Hagartys

Change the y to i and add -es if the y is preceded by a consonant.

berry → berries   enemy → enemies   family → families

Irregular plurals The only way to learn irregular plurals is to memorize them. Many nouns have irregular plurals that have survived from earlier forms of English.

woman → women   child → children   deer → deer

Tech   **Use Spelling Checkers Cautiously**

Most of today's word processing programs correct some misspelled words while you type, identify other words that may be misspelled, and let you run a manual spelling check whenever you wish. Although these features are helpful, you cannot depend on them alone to guarantee error-free spelling. Spelling checkers, for example, do not differenti-ate homonyms and commonly confused words such as *descent, dissent* or *too, two.* If you type a correctly spelled word that happens not to be correct for the context, a spelling checker will not mark it wrong.

Spelling checkers, then, are a useful tool but not a replacement for a dictionary and careful proofreading. Check the spelling checker.

Other nouns with irregular plurals were borrowed into English from languages such as Greek, Latin, and French and retain the plural form of the original language.

> alumna → alumnae   analysis → analyses   criterion → criteria

Plurals of compound nouns To form the plural of compound nouns composed of separate or hyphenated words, add -s or -es to the main noun in the compound.

> brigadier generals   chiefs of staff   runners-up

An exception: *passersby*.

61d Using Hyphens to Form Compounds

1. Hyphenate compound adjectives.

Hyphenate compound adjectives when they precede the noun but not when they follow it.

> ▸ The well-intentioned efforts by the International Olympic Committee (IOC) to allow peaceful protests were thwarted by the Chinese government.

> ▸ The efforts of the IOC to allow peaceful protests were well-intentioned but ill-conceived.

When an adverb ending in -*ly* is part of a compound adjective, no hyphen is necessary.

> ▸ In China, politically-sensitive websites are blocked by the government.

When two or more parallel compound adjectives share the same base word, avoid repetition by putting a space after the first hyphen and stating the base word only once.

> ▸ Class- and race-based analyses of *To Kill a Mockingbird* show that Harper Lee was not completely able to rise above her social background.

2. Link prefixes and suffixes to root words.

In general, hyphens are not needed to attach prefixes and suffixes to the root word.

> *de*compress   *pre*test   *re*define   *sub*category

But the prefixes *all-*, *ex-*, and *self-* and the suffix *-elect* are always attached to the root word with a hyphen.

> ▶ *all-*star   *ex-*boyfriend   *self-*absorbed   president-*elect*

In most cases, to avoid double or triple letter combinations, add a hyphen.

> ▶ *anti-*inflationary   *multi-*institutional   *re-*education   ball-*like*

Some exceptions: *override, cooperate.*

If the prefix will be attached to a numeral or to a root that begins with a capital letter, insert a hyphen.

> ▶ post-1914   pre-1945   anti-Semite   un-American

Finally, if the prefix-plus-root combination could be misread as another word, add a hyphen to avoid confusion.

> ▶ He finally recovered from a bout of the flu.

> ▶ We re-covered the sofa with a floral fabric.
>   ∧

3. Use hyphens in numbers, number ranges, and scores.

Numbers over twenty and under one hundred are hyphenated when written out.

> ▶ Workaholics would work twenty-four hours a day, seven days a week,
>   ∧
>   fifty-two weeks a year if their bodies would cooperate.
>   ∧

A hyphen can replace the words *from* and *to* with dates.

> ▶ The years from 1919 to 1938 offered a brief respite between the two world wars.
>
>   or
>
> ▶ The years 1919-1938 offered a brief respite between the two world wars.

Tech   **Breaking URLs and E-mail Addresses**

Most word processing programs offer automatic hyphenation of words. However, you must break URLs or e-mail addresses manually. If you are following MLA or CSE style guidelines, break URLs only after a slash. If you are following APA guidelines, break URLs before most punctuation (except the *://* following *http*). If you are following *Chicago Manual* guidelines, break a URL or e-mail address before a period or other punctuation, or after the @ symbol, a single or double slash, or a colon. Do *not* insert a hyphen when a URL breaks to the next line.

But do not combine methods.

> ▸ from 1919~~-~~1938 ^to^   or   ~~from~~ 1919-1938

In sports scores, use a hyphen between numbers instead of *to*.

> ▸ The Vikings lost to the Bengals 23-17.

61e Using Hyphens to Break Words at the Ends of Lines

Most word processing programs automatically move a too-long word from the end of one line to the beginning of the next or break the word between lines with a hyphen. To break words manually or to check words you think your word processor may have broken incorrectly, follow these rules:

- Break words between syllables. (Check your dictionary for syllable breaks.)

  > ▸ CIA operatives in the Middle East have found it impossible to ~~infiltr~~ ^infil-^
  > *trate*
  > ~~ate~~ al Qaeda.

- Break compound words between parts or after hyphens.

  > ▸ Washington, DC's long-standing handgun ban was ~~overturn~~ ^over-^
  > *turned*
  > ~~ed~~ in 2008 by the Supreme Court.

- Do not break one-syllable words or contractions.

  > ▸ To determine surface area, multiply the ~~wid-~~ ^width^
  > ~~th~~ of a room by its length.

- Break words so that at least two letters remain at the end of a line and at least three letters move down to the beginning of the next line.

  > ▸ Increases in the cost of gas and food have ~~reduc-~~ ^re-^
  > *duced*
  > ~~ed~~ discretionary spending.

Glossary of Key Terms

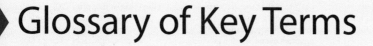

A

absolute phrase (291, 332) A phrase consisting of a noun or pronoun followed by a participle (the -*ing* or -*ed* form of a verb) that modifies an entire clause or sentence: *Our spirits rising, we began our vacation.*

abstract (108, 115, 229) Overview of a text, with a summary of its main claims and most important supporting points.

abstract noun (320) See *noun.*

acronym (460) An abbreviation formed from the first letters of a series of words and pronounced as a word (*AIDS, NASA*). Compare *initialism.*

active voice (328) See *voice.*

adjective (290, 321, 376, 412) A word that modifies a noun or pronoun with descriptive or limiting information, answering questions such as *what kind, which one,* or *how many: a happy camper, the tall building.*

adjective clause (333) A subordinate clause, usually beginning with a relative pronoun (such as *who, whom, which,* or *that*), that modifies a noun or pronoun: *Sam baked the pie that won first prize.* Adjective clauses can also begin with the subordinating conjunctions *when* and *where.*

adverb (290, 323, 376, 412) A word that modifies a verb, adjective, other adverb, or entire phrase or clause, answering questions such as *how? where? when?* and *to what extent or degree? The door opened abruptly.*

adverb clause (333, 426–27) A subordinate clause, usually introduced by a subordinating conjunction such as *although, because,* or *until,* that functions as an adverb within a sentence: *I walk to class because I need the exercise.*

agreement (346–57) The matching of form between one word and another. Verbs must agree with, or match, their subjects in person and number (subject-verb agreement), and pronouns must agree in person, number, and gender with their antecedents (pronoun-antecedent agreement). See also *antecedent, gender, number, person.*

alignment (52) Arrangement in a straight line (vertical, horizontal, or diagonal) of elements on a page or screen to create connections among parts and ideas.

alternating pattern of organization (32) A method of organizing a comparison-contrast paragraph or essay by discussing each common or divergent trait of both items before moving on to the next trait. See also *block pattern.*

analogy (305) An extended comparison of something familiar with something unfamiliar. (See also *figurative language, simile, metaphor.*) An analogy becomes a false analogy (81) when the items being compared have no significant shared traits.

analysis (10, 34, 89) The process of dividing an entity, concept, or text into its component parts to study its meaning and function. Analysis is central to critical reading and is a common strategy for developing paragraphs and essays in academic writing. Also called *classification, division.*

annotated bibliography (100–02) A bibliography that includes not only retrieval information for each source but also information about the source, such as its content, its relevance to the writer's project, or the writer's evaluation of it.

annotation (7–8) The process of taking notes on a text, including writing down definitions, identifying key concepts, highlighting unfamiliar vocabulary and words that reveal tone, and making connections or noting personal responses.

antecedent (321, 352–53, 354, 369) The noun or noun phrase to which a pronoun refers. In the sentence *The pitcher caught the ball and threw it to first base,* the noun *ball* is the antecedent to the pronoun *it.*

antonyms (309) Words with opposite meanings—for example, *good* and *bad.* Compare *synonyms.*

APA style (201–38) The citation and documentation style of the American Psychological Association, used frequently in the social sciences.

appeals (75–77) Efforts to engage the reader. Emotional appeals (**pathos**) engage the reader's feelings; intellectual appeals (**logos**) engage the reader's rational faculties; ethical appeals (**ethos**) engage the reader's sense of fairness and respect for good character.

appositive (291, 331, 339, 371, 425) A noun or noun phrase that renames a preceding noun or noun phrase and is grammatically equivalent to it: *Miguel, my roommate, avoids early morning classes.*

arguable claim (74–75) A claim of judgment or value on which reasonable people might hold differing opinions and that can be supported by evidence.

argument (16) An attempt to persuade others to accept your opinion by providing logical supporting evidence. See also *persuasive argument, purpose.*

article (402–06) The words *a, an,* and *the.* A and an are **indefinite articles;** *the* is a **definite article.** The **zero article** refers to nouns that appear with no article.

asynchronous media (61) Communication media such as e-mail and discussion lists that allow users to participate at their own convenience. Compare *synchronous media;* see also *discussion list.*

audience (17, 51) The intended readers for a writing project or listeners for a presentation.

authority (117) See *expertise.*

B

bar graph (55) An information graphic that compares data in two or more categories using bars of different heights or lengths.

belief (22, 74) A conviction based on values. See also *claim.*

biased or hurtful language (297–98) Language that unfairly or offensively characterizes a group and, by extension, the individual members of that group.

bibliographic notes (187, 226–27) See *informational notes.*

bibliography (100–02) A list of works cited in a text, with full retrieval information (usually including

G1

author, title, publisher, date of publication, and type of publication) for each entry. Bibliographies are usually constructed following a style sheet such as MLA or APA.

block pattern of organization (32) A method of organizing a comparison-contrast paragraph or essay by discussing all the traits of the first item before moving on to traits of the second item. See also *alternating pattern*.

block quotations (153) Exact quotations of longer than four lines (MLA style) or forty words (APA style) in which quotation marks are omitted and the quotation is indented as a block from the left margin of the text.

block style (58) A format for business letters and e-mails in which all text is flush with the left margin and a line space is inserted before paragraphs. In *modified block style,* all text begins flush left except for the return address, date, closing, and signature.

blog (or **weblog**) (59–60) An online journal that chronicles thoughts, opinions, and information often on a single topic. See also *asynchronous media*.

body (63) The portion of a text or presentation that develops and supports the thesis.

Boolean operator (106) The terms *and, not,* and *or* used in databases and search engines for refining keyword searches.

brainstorming (or **listing**) (20) A technique for generating ideas by listing all the ideas that come to you during a fixed amount of time; brainstorming can also take place in groups.

C

case (369–74) The form of a noun or pronoun that corresponds to its grammatical role in a sentence. Many pronouns have three cases: **subjective** (for example, *I, we, he, she, they, who*), **objective** (for example, *me, us, him, her, them, whom*), and **possessive** (for example, *mine, ours, his, hers, theirs, whose*). Nouns change form only to indicate possession.

cause and effect (34) A method of paragraph or essay development that explains why something happened or what its consequences were or will be.

Chicago **style** (239–62) The citation and documentation style recommended in the *Chicago Manual of Style,* used frequently in the humani-

ties (except in literature, composition, and language courses).

chronological organization (33) A pattern of organization in which events are discussed in the order in which they occurred; chronological organization is used when telling a story (*narration*) or explaining a process (*process analysis*).

citation (139, 149, 201) The acknowledgment of sources in the body of a research project, usually tagged to a bibliography, works-cited list, or reference list. See also *in-text citation, parenthetical citation, signal phrase.*

citation-name system (264) In CSE style, a system of acknowledgment for research projects that provides a superscript number in the text and a list of references, numbered in alphabetical order by author's surname at the end of the project.

citation-sequence system (264) In CSE style, a system of acknowledgment for research projects that provides a superscript number in the text and a list of references, numbered in order of appearance, at the end of the project.

claim (74–75) An assertion that is supported by evidence. A *claim of fact* asserts a verifiable piece of information; it can be a central claim in an informative text but not in an argumentative text. A *claim of judgment* is an opinion, a tentative conclusion based on evaluation of available facts. A *claim of value* asserts that one's personal beliefs or convictions should be embraced. Claims of judgment and value are appropriate central claims in argumentative texts.

classical model (78) A model for organizing an argument composed of five parts: introduction, background, evidence, counterclaims and counterevidence, and conclusion. Compare *Rogerian* and *Toulmin models.*

classification (34) See *analysis.*

clause (280, 285, 332, 395) A word group with a subject and a predicate. An **independent clause** can stand on its own as a sentence. A **subordinate** (or **dependent**) **clause** functions within a sentence as a noun, adjective, or adverb but cannot stand as a sentence on its own. See also *predicate, sentence, subject.*

cliché (306–07) A figure of speech, idiom, or other expression that has grown stale from overuse. See also *figurative language, idiom.*

clustering or **mapping** (20) An idea-generating technique for organizing, developing, or discovering connections among ideas by writing a topic in the center of the page, adding related topics and subtopics around the central topic, and connecting them to show relationships.

coherence, coherent (29–30) The quality of a text in which sentences and paragraphs are organized logically and clearly so that readers can move from idea to idea without having to puzzle out the relationships among parts.

collective noun (320, 350) See *noun.*

colloquialism (295) An informal expression common in speech but usually out of place in formal writing.

comma splice (341–46, 431) The incorrect joining of two independent clauses with a comma alone—without a coordinating conjunction.

common knowledge (125–26) Information that is available from three or more sources and that is considered factual and incontestable. Common knowledge does not require documentation.

common noun (400) See *noun.*

comparative form (379–80) See *comparison of adjectives and adverbs.*

comparison-contrast (32) A pattern of paragraph or essay development in which the writer points out the similarities and differences among items. See also *alternating pattern, block pattern.*

comparison of adjectives and adverbs (379–80) The form of an adjective or adverb that indicates the relative degree of the quality or manner it specifies. The **positive form** is the base form of the adjective (for example, *brave*) or adverb (for example, *bravely*). The **comparative form** indicates a relatively greater or lesser degree (*braver, more bravely*). The **superlative form** indicates the greatest or least degree (*bravest, most bravely*).

complement (327–28) See *subject complement, object complement.*

complete predicate (327) See *predicate.*

complete subject (326) See *subject.*

complete verb (335, 360) A main verb together with any helping verbs needed to express tense, mood, and voice.

complex sentence (285, 335) See *sentence.*

compound-complex sentence (285, 335) See *sentence.*

compound predicate (327, 339) See *predicate.*

compound sentence (285, 334, 421) See *sentence.*

compound subject (326, 349) See *subject.*

conciseness (277–80) The statement of something in the fewest and most effective words needed for clarity and full understanding.

conclusion (63–64) The closing paragraph or section in a text. An effective conclusion provides readers with a sense of closure and a sense that their time has been well spent.

concrete noun (320) See *noun.*

conditional clause (369–69) A subordinate clause that begins with *if* and describes a set of circumstances (*conditions*). A conditional clause modifies an independent clause describing what follows from those circumstances.

conjunction (325, 349) A word that joins a word, phrase, or clause to other words, phrases, or clauses and specifies the way the joined elements relate to one another. **Coordinating conjunctions** (*and, but, or, for, nor, yet,* and *so*) join grammatically equivalent elements, giving them each equal significance: *Jack and Jill went up the hill.* **Correlative conjunctions** are pairs of terms (such as *either . . . or, neither . . . nor,* and *both . . . and*) that join grammatically equivalent elements: *Both Jack and Jill fell down.* **Subordinating conjunctions** link subordinate clauses to the clauses they modify. *After Jack and Jill went up the hill, they both fell down.*

conjunctive adverb (324, 423) A transitional expression (such as *for example, however,* and *therefore*) that can relate one independent clause to a preceding independent clause.

connected (37) See *transition.*

connotation (17, 42, 302) The emotional resonance of a word. Compare *denotation.*

content notes (187, 226–27) See *informational notes.*

context (18, 51) The social, rhetorical, and historical setting in which a text is produced or read. The context in which Lincoln's Gettysburg Address was produced is different from the context in which it may be read today, but both are important for fully understanding the text.

contrast (51) In design, differences that call attention to and highlight one element among others. See also *comparison-contrast.*

coordinate adjectives (424–25) Two or more adjectives that separately and equally modify the noun they precede. Coordinate adjectives should be separated by a comma: *an innovative, exciting vocal group.*

coordinating conjunction (421) See *conjunction.*

coordination (285–87) The joining of elements of equal weight or importance in a sentence. See also *subordination.*

correlative conjunction (282, 325) See *conjunction.*

counterevidence (77) Evidence that undermines or contradicts a claim.

count noun (or **countable noun**) (320, 400) See *noun.*

critical reading (7–13) A thoughtful, systematic approach to a text, going below the surface to uncover meaning and draw conclusions. Critical reading begins with reading actively; it requires analysis, interpretation, synthesis, and critique.

critique (12) An evaluation based on evidence accumulated through careful reading, analysis, interpretation, and synthesis. It may be positive, negative, or a bit of both.

CSE style (239–62) The citation and documentation style recommended in *Scientific Style and Format: The CSE Manual for Authors, Editors, and Publishers,* used frequently in the sciences.

cumulative adjectives (424–25) Two or more adjectives that modify not only the noun or pronoun they precede but also the next adjective in the series. Cumulative adjectives should not be separated by commas: *A great American rock band.*

cumulative sentence (292) A sentence that begins with the subject and verb of an independent clause and accumulates additional information in subsequent modifying phrases and clauses: *The mountaineers set off, anticipating the view from the peak but wary of the dangers they faced to get there.*

D

dangling modifier (384–85) A word, phrase, or clause that erroneously does not actually modify the subject or anything else in a sentence,

leaving it to the reader to infer the intended meaning. In the sentence *As your parent, you should put on a sweater when it is cold,* the phrase *as your parent* dangles; it appears illogically to modify the subject, *you,* but actually refers to the speaker, as in *As your parent, I recommend that you put on a sweater when it is cold.*

database (107, 173) A collection of data, now usually available in digital form. In research, databases provide citations to articles in periodicals (academic journals, magazines, and newspapers).

declarative sentence (326) See *sentence.*

deductive logic (10) A form of reasoning that moves from a general principle to a specific case to draw a conclusion; if the premises are true, the conclusion must be true. Compare *inductive reasoning.*

definite article (401–03) See *article.*

definition (34–35) An explanation of the meaning of a word or concept made by including it in a larger class and then providing the characteristics that distinguish it from other members of that class: In the definition *People are reasoning animals, people* is the term to be defined, *animals* is the larger class to which people belong, and *reasoning* is the trait that distinguishes people from other animals. Extended definitions (of a paragraph or more) analyze in detail a term's meaning, using anecdotes, examples, and reasons to demonstrate the term's significance.

demonstrative pronouns (322) The pronouns *this, that, these,* and *those* used as nouns or adjectives to rename and point to nouns or noun phrases: *These are interesting times we live in.*

denotation (42, 302) The literal meaning of a word; its dictionary definition. Compare *connotation.*

dependent clause (332) A subordinate clause. See *clause.*

description (32) In writing, a pattern of paragraph or essay development that draws on specific, concrete details to depict a scene or object in terms of the senses (seeing, hearing, smelling, touching, tasting). Often, descriptive paragraphs are also organized spatially and include indications of place or location (*above, below*).

determiner (323, 400–06) An article (*a, an,* or *the*) or a possessive, demonstrative, or indefinite pronoun that functions as an adjective to specify or quantify the noun it modifies: *a cat, some cats, that cat, her cat.*

development (25, 31–35, 42–43, 137–38) The depth at which a topic or idea is explored.

dialect (295) A variant of a language with its own distinctive pronunciation, vocabulary, and grammar.

diction (302) The choice of words to best convey an idea.

direct object (329, 397) See *object.*

direct question (388) A sentence that asks a question and ends with a question mark. Compare *indirect question.*

direct quotation (388, 427) A copy of the exact words that someone has written or spoken, enclosed in quotation marks or, for longer quotations, indented as a block. Compare *indirect quotation.*

direct source (388, 442–43) A text that you are yourself reading (as contrasted to a source *quoted in* a text you are reading).

discussion (229, 274) In APA and CSE style, the last section of a research project; the Discussion section provides the writer's opinion of the implications of the research.

discussion list (104) An electronic mailing list that enables a group of people to participate in e-mail conversations on a specific topic. See also *asynchronous media.*

division (10, 34, 89) See *analysis.*

documentation (149, 201) Information in a bibliography, reference list, or list of works cited that allows readers to locate a source cited in the text. See also *citation.*

document design (51–66) The arranging and formatting of text elements on a page or screen using proximity (nearness), alignment, repetition, and contrast to indicate their relative importance and their relation to each other.

DOI (211, 218, 222, 242, 248) Digital object identifier, a permanent identifier assigned to print and electronic publications.

domain (120) The ending of the main portion of a URL; the most common domains are *.com* (commercial), *.edu* (educational), *.gov* (governmental), *.net* (network), and *.org* (organization).

doublespeak (297) Euphemisms that are deliberately deceptive, used to obscure bad news or sanitize an ugly truth.

drafting (25, 137–38) The stage of the writing process in which the writer puts ideas on paper in complete sentences and paragraphs.

E

editing (42–43) The stage of the writing process in which the writer fine-tunes the draft by correcting words and sentences to enhance clarity and power.

ellipsis (plural **ellipses**) (450–51) A deliberate omission of a portion of a quotation. Also, the punctuation used to mark such an omission: a set of three periods, or *ellipsis points,* with a space between each. Ellipses are also sometimes used to indicate a dramatic pause or to suggest that the writer is unable or unwilling to say something.

elliptical construction (392) A construction in which grammatically necessary words can be omitted as understood because their meaning and function are otherwise clear from the context: *The movie [that] we saw last night is excellent.*

empty expressions (277–78) Expressions like *in fact, the fact is,* and *in the process of* that carry no information and can be deleted.

endnote (239) A note that appears in a list at the end of the project.

entertaining text (16) See *purpose.*

essential (or **restrictive**) **element** (425–27) A word, phrase, or clause that provides essential information about the word or words it modifies. Essential elements are not set off by commas: *The train that she is on has been delayed.* See also *nonessential element.*

et al. (154) Abbreviation of the Latin phrase *et alia,* "and others."

ethos (76) See *appeals.*

euphemism (297) An inoffensive word or expression used in place of one that might be offensive or emotionally painful.

evaluation (114–21) In research, assessment of sources to determine their relevance and reliability.

evidence (25) The facts, examples, statistics, expert opinions, and other information writers use to support their claims.

excessive coordination (287) The joining of tediously long strings of independent clauses with *and* and other conjunctions.

excessive subordination (289) The stringing together of too many subordinate structures.

exclamatory sentence (326) See *sentence.*

exemplification (33) A pattern of paragraph or essay development that explains by example or illustration.

expertise (117) Special knowledge, training, or experience in a specific field. Someone with expertise is an expert or authority.

expletive construction (279, 327, 396) A kind of inverted construction in which *there* or *it* precedes a form of the verb *to be* and the subject follows the verb: *There are seven days in a week.*

exploratory argument (73–74) An argument in which the author considers a wide range of evidence before arriving at the most plausible position; in exploratory arguments, the thesis is often offered at the conclusion of the text. See also *argument, persuasive argument, purpose.*

expository report (16) See *informative report.*

expressive text (16) See *purpose.*

F

fact (23) A piece of information that can be verified, that is either true or false.

fallacy (80–86) A mistake in reasoning.

faulty predication (391) A logical or grammatical mismatch between subject and predicate.

field research (112–14) The gathering of research data in person rather than from sources. Field research includes interviews, observational studies, and surveys. See also *primary source.*

figurative language or **figures of speech** (304–05) The imaginative use of language to convey meaning in ways that reach beyond the literal meaning of the words involved. See *analogy, hyperbole, irony, metaphor, personification, simile, understatement.*

flaming (62) Writing a scathing response to or personal attack on someone with whom the writer disagrees, usually in e-mail or on Internet forums.

focused freewriting (20) See *freewriting.*

font (52–53) Typeface; fonts may be serif (such as Times New Roman) or sans serif (such as Arial), may be set in **boldface**, *italics,* or <u>underlining,</u> and may be in a larger or smaller size. (The most common sizes are 10 point and 12 point.)

footer (188)   Material (most often a page number, sometimes accompanied by title or author's name) appearing at the bottom of every page of a text.

footnote (239)   A note that appears at the bottom of the page.

formal outline (24–25)   See *outline.*

formalist approach (89)   An approach to literature that focuses on the work itself rather than on the author's life or other theoretical approaches.

format (52–54)   The look of a document created by choice of font and color and use of white space, lists, headings, and visuals. See also *layout.*

fragment (330, 333)   An incomplete sentence punctuated as if it were complete, beginning with a capital letter and ending with a period, question mark, or exclamation point.

freewriting (20)   An idea-generating technique that requires writing nonstop for a fixed period of time (often ten to fifteen minutes); in *focused freewriting,* the writer writes nonstop about a specific topic or idea.

fused sentence or **run-on sentence** (341–46, 431)   A sentence in which one independent clause improperly follows another with no punctuation or joining words between them.

future perfect progressive tense (364)   See *tense.*

future perfect tense (363)   See *tense.*

future progressive tense (364)   See *tense.*

future tense (364)   See *tense.*

G

gender (354)   The classification of nouns and pronouns as feminine (*woman, mother, she*), masculine (*man, father, he*), or neuter (*table, book, it*).

gender bias (298–99)   Stereotyping people according to their gender.

generalization (80)   A broad statement. If not supported by specific details, a generalization becomes a hasty generalization (jumping to conclusions) or a sweeping generalization (application of a claim to all cases when it applies only to a few or none).

generic noun (354)   A noun used to designate a whole class of people or things rather than a specific individual or individuals: *the average <u>child</u>.*

genre (16, 18–19, 51)   A category or type of writing; in literature, genres include poetry, fiction, and drama; in college writing, genres may include analytical essays, case studies, or observational reports.

gerund (331, 372, 408)   The present participle of a verb (the *-ing* form) used as a noun: *<u>Walking</u> is good exercise.*

global revision (39–40)   See *revision.*

grammar (319)   The rules of a language that structure words so they can convey meaning.

grounds (75)   In an argument, the evidence that supports the claim. See *Toulmin model.*

H

header (188)   Material (most often a page number, sometimes accompanied by title or author's name) appearing at the top of every page of a text.

heading (54)   A brief caption describing or labeling a section of text.

helping verb or **auxiliary verb** (320, 321, 360)   A verb that combines with a main verb to provide information about tense, voice, mood, and manner. Helping verbs include forms of *be, have,* and *do* and the modal verbs *can, could, may, might, must, shall, should, will, would,* and *ought to.*

home page (60)   On a website, the page designed to introduce visitors to the site.

homonyms (465)   Words that sound exactly alike but have different spellings and meanings: *their, there, they're.*

HTML (102, 108)   Hypertext Markup Language, a coding system used to format texts for the web.

hyperbole (305)   Deliberate exaggeration for emphasis: *That restaurant makes the best pizza in the universe.* See *figurative language.*

hyperlink (60)   See *link.*

hypertext (60)   An online text that provides links to other online files, texts, images, audio files, and video files, allowing readers to jump to other related sites rather than reading *linearly.*

hypothesis (113)   A tentative answer to a research question that is subject to testing and modification during the research process.

I

idea-generating techniques (19–22)   See *invention techniques.*

idiom (306)   A customary expression whose meaning cannot be determined from the literal meaning of the words that compose it: *They struggled to make ends meet.*

imperative (326, 367)   See *mood, sentence.*

indefinite article (401–03)   See *article.*

indefinite pronoun (322, 350, 354, 432)   A pronoun such as *anybody, anyone, somebody, some,* or *several* that does not refer to a specific person or thing.

independent clause (332, 335, 341, 421, 430, 455)   See *clause.*

indicative (367)   See *mood.*

indirect object (329, 397)   See *object.*

indirect question (388)   A sentence that reports a question and ends with a period: *My teacher asked us if we texted each other even when we're in the same room.* Compare *direct question.*

indirect quotation (388, 427)   A sentence that uses paraphrase or summary to report what someone has said rather than quoting word-forword. Indirect quotations need to be cited but should not be marked with quotation marks or block indenting. Compare *direct quotation.*

indirect source (160, 209, 255, 442–43)   If you read a text that quotes or uses ideas from another source, that other source is for you an "indirect source": You are not reading that other source yourself but are reading about its ideas. If you want to use that material from the indirect source, you should acknowledge the indirect source as well as the source that was talking about it.

inductive logic (10)   A form of reasoning that draws conclusions based on specific examples or facts. Compare *deductive logic.*

infinitive (331, 366, 372, 408)   A verbal formed by combining *to* with the base form of the verb (*to decide, to eat, to study*). Infinitives can function as adjectives and adverbs as well as nouns. See *verbal.*

informal (scratch) outline (24)   See *outline.*

information graphics (55)   Graphics that convey and depict relationships among data; information graphics include tables, bar graphs, line graphs, and pie charts.

informational notes (187, 226–27)   Notes that add supplementary information or acknowledge help or conflicts of interest.

informative (or **expository**) **writing project** (16)   A text in which the main purpose is to explain a concept or report information. See also *purpose*.

initialism (460)   Abbreviation formed from the first letters of a series of words and pronounced as letters (*DNA, HBO*). Compare *acronym*.

inseparable (407)   A transitive phrasal verb whose direct object can fall only after the particle, not before it.

intensive pronoun (322)   A pronoun that renames and emphasizes its antecedent: *Dr. Collins herself performed the operation.*

interesting (28)   Paragraphs and essays that make the audience want to continue reading.

interjections (325)   Words like *alas* and *ugh* that express strong feeling but otherwise serve no grammatical function.

interpret, interpretation (10)   Explain the meaning or significance of a text.

interpretive analysis (87–91)   An in-depth interpretation of the meaning or significance of literary texts.

interrogative pronoun (322, 370, 373)   A pronoun such as *who, whom, whose, what,* or *which* used to introduce a question: *What did she say?*

interrogative sentence (326)   See *sentence.*

in-text citation (140–41, 149, 201, 263)   A citation that appears in the body of the research project. See also *parenthetical citation, signal phrase.*

intransitive verb (328, 361)   A verb that does not require a direct object: *The child smiled.*

introduction (63)   The opening paragraph or section of a text. An effective introduction should identify your topic and your stance toward the topic, establish your purpose, and engage your readers.

invention techniques (19–22)   Prewriting strategies that help you generate and explore ideas. See *brainstorming, freewriting.*

inversion (292)   An inversion is a sentence in which, contrary to normal English word order, the verb precedes the subject, usually to emphasize the point being made.

irony (305)   The use of language to suggest the opposite of its literal meaning or to express an incongruity between what is expected and what occurs. See *figurative language.*

irregular verb (358–59)   A verb that does not form the past tense or past participle by adding *-ed* to the base form.

J

jargon (296)   The specialized vocabulary of a particular profession or discipline; inappropriately technical language.

journal (107–10, 118)   A periodical the articles in which are written and reviewed (in advance of publication) by subject matter experts, usually scholars at colleges and universities. See also *periodical.*

journalists' questions (**plus two**) (21)   Questions that ask *who, what, where, when, why,* and *how* to help you explore a topic. In college writing, also ask yourself about the significance of your topic (*Is it important?*) and its consequences (*What are its effects?*).

K

keyword (103)   (a) A term entered into an Internet search engine, online database, or library catalog to find sources of information. (b) A word or phrase in a text that highlights or is essential to the message of the text.

L

labeling (298)   Applying a word or phrase to describe an entire group, such as *autistic, Cub Scout,* or *Asian American.* When the label does not apply to all group members, or when it unfairly characterizes the group, it contributes to **stereotyping.**

layout (52)   The visual arrangement of text and images using proximity (nearness), alignment, repetition, and contrast. See also *format.*

level of formality (17)   The choice of words to convey a tone (formal or informal) appropriate to the audience. See *tone, connotation.*

linear text (60)   A document, such as a novel or magazine article, that is arranged so that readers begin at page 1 and read through to the end. Compare *hypertext.*

line graphs (55)   A type of information graphic that uses lines and points on a graph to show changes over time.

link (60)   A navigation tool that allows users to jump from place to place on a web page or from web page to web page; links (or hyperlinks) appear as highlighted words or images on a web page.

linking verb (323, 329, 353, 377, 391, 412)   A verb that expresses a state of being rather than an action and connects the subject to its subject complement. The verb *be,* when used as a main verb, is always a linking verb. *They are excited.* See also *subject complement.*

list of works cited (154)   In MLA style, a section at the end of a research project in which the writer provides full bibliographic information for all sources cited in the text.

local revision (42–43)   See *editing.*

logical fallacy (78–80)   See *fallacy.*

logical organization (31)   The arrangement of a sentence, paragraph, or entire text in a way that will seem sensible to readers, that will not confuse or puzzle them. See *organization.*

logos (76)   See *appeals.*

M

main verb (320, 360)   The part of a verb phrase that carries its principal meaning. See *verb phrase.*

mechanics (421–70)   Conventions governing capitalization, italics, abbreviation, numbers, and hyphenation.

menu (59–60)   A list of the main sections of a website.

metaphor (304–06)   An implied comparison between unlike things stated without *like, as,* or other comparative expressions: *Her mind buzzed with original ideas.* See *figurative language, simile.*

methods (113, 229, 274)   In APA and CSE style, the section of a research project that explains the research methods and describes any research participants (such as people interviewed) or data collected.

misplaced modifier (381–83)   An ambiguously, confusingly, or disruptively placed modifying word, phrase, or clause.

mixed construction (389–90)   A sentence with parts that do not fit together grammatically or logically.

mixed metaphor (304–06) A combination of multiple conflicting figures of speech for the same concept. See *figurative language.*

MLA style (149–200) The citation and documentation style of the Modern Language Association, used frequently in literature and languages.

modal verb (321, 360–61) See *helping verb.*

modified block style (58–59) See *block style.*

modifier (290–91) A word, phrase, or clause that functions as an adjective or adverb to qualify or describe another word, phrase, or clause.

mood (367) The form of a verb that indicates how the writer or speaker views what is written or said. The **indicative mood** states facts or opinions and asks questions: *I finished my paper.* The **imperative mood** issues commands, gives instructions, or makes requests: *Hand in your papers by Friday.* The **subjunctive mood** expresses possibility, as in hypothetical situations or wishes: *If I were finished, I could go out with my friends.*

N

name-year system (263–65) In CSE style, a system of acknowledgment for research projects that includes the last name of the author and the year of publication in parentheses in the text and is accompanied by an alphabetical list of references at the end of the project.

narration (33) A pattern of paragraph or essay development that tells a story, usually in chronological (time) order. See also *chronological organization.*

near-homonyms (465) Words that are close but not the same in pronunciation (*moral, morale*) or are different forms of the same word (*breath, breathe*).

neologism (296) A newly coined word or expression.

noncount noun (or **uncountable** or **mass noun**) (320, 400) See *noun.*

nonessential (or **nonrestrictive**) **element** (425–27) A modifying word, phrase, or clause that adds information to the element it modifies but does not identify it. Commas should set off nonessential elements from the rest of the sentence. *My grandfather, who recently retired, worked for the same company for forty-five years.*

noun (320, 432) A word that names an idea (*justice*), thing (*chair*), quality (*neatness*), action (*judgment*), person (*Oprah*), or place (*Tokyo*). **Proper nouns** name specific places, people, or things and are usually capitalized: *Nairobi, George Clooney.* **Common nouns** name members of a class or group: *turtle, skyscraper.* **Collective nouns** name a collection that can function as a single unit: *committee, family.* **Concrete nouns** name things that can be seen, touched, heard, smelled, or tasted: *rainbow, mink, symphony, skunk.* **Abstract nouns** name qualities or ideas that cannot be perceived by the senses: *mercy, fear.* **Count** (or **countable**) **nouns** name countable things and can be either singular or plural: *cat/cats, idea/ideas.* **Noncount** (or **uncountable** or **mass**) **nouns** name ideas or things that cannot be counted and do not have a plural form: *knowledge, pollution.*

noun clause (334) A subordinate clause that functions as a noun. See *clause.*

noun phrase (321, 330) A noun and its modifiers. See *phrase.*

number (346, 387) The form of a word that indicates whether it is singular, referring to one thing (*a student*), or plural, referring to more than one (*two students*).

O

object (331) A noun or pronoun (or a noun phrase or noun clause) that receives or benefits from the action of a transitive verb or that follows a preposition. A **direct object** receives the action of the verb: *My friend wrote a letter.* An **indirect object** benefits from the action of the verb: *My friend wrote me a letter.* The **object of a preposition** usually follows a preposition to form a prepositional phrase. *She sent the letter by mail.*

object complement (330, 398) An adjective or noun phrase that follows the direct object and describes the condition of the object or a change that the subject has caused it to undergo: *The candidate declared his opponent incompetent.*

objective case (369–74) See *case.*

objectivity (74–75, 117) A text is objective when it makes reasonable claims supported by logical evidence; recognizes alternative perspectives; and treats those alternatives respectfully.

object of a preposition (331) See *object.*

opinion (75) The most plausible answer for now, based on an evaluation of the available facts. Opinions are subject to revision in light of new evidence and are often the basis of an argument.

organization (31–35) Arranging the parts of a sentence, paragraph, or essay so that readers can most readily understand and appreciate it.

outline (24–25, 136–37) A method of classifying information into main points, supporting points, and specific details. An **informal** (or **scratch**) **outline** arranges ideas in order of presentation; a **formal outline** uses roman and arabic numerals, upper- and lowercase letters, and indentions to classify information into main points, supporting points, and specific details; a **sentence outline** writes out main points, supporting points, and specific details in complete sentences; a **topic outline** uses words and phrases to indicate the ideas to be discussed.

P

paragraph (28–29) A group of sentences that focus on a single topic or example, often organized around a *topic sentence.*

parallelism (281–84) The expression of equivalent ideas in equivalent grammatical structures.

paraphrase (127) The statement of the ideas of others in one's own words and sentence structures.

parenthetical citation (140, 202) A citation to a source that appears in parentheses in the body of a research paper. Compare *signal phrase;* see also *in-text citation.*

participial phrase (290, 332) A phrase in which the present or past participle of a verb acts as an adjective: *the writing assignment, the written word.*

participles (332, 357–58) Forms of a verb that combine with helping verbs to form certain tenses and that, as verbals, can function as adjectives. The **present participle** is the *-ing* form of the verb. The **past participle** is the *-ed* form in regular verbs (the same as the past tense) but takes various forms in irregular verbs. See *participial phrase, tense, verbal.*

particle (406–07) A preposition or adverb that combines with a verb to create a new verb with a meaning that differs from the verb's meaning on its own—for example, *throw away* versus *throw*.

parts of speech (319–25) The categories in which words can be classified according to the role they play in a sentence. English has eight parts of speech: *adjective, adverb, conjunction, interjection, noun, preposition, pronoun,* and *verb*.

passive voice (279, 329) See *voice*.

past participle (409–10) See *participles*.

past perfect progressive tense (364) See *tense*.

past perfect tense (363) See *tense*.

past progressive tense (363) See *tense*.

past tense (362–65) See *tense*.

patchwriting (125, 127–29) A faulty paraphrase that relies too heavily on the language or sentence structure of the source text. Patchwritten texts may replace some terms from the source passage with synonyms, add or delete a few words, or alter the sentence structure slightly, but they do not put the passage fully into fresh words and sentences. At some colleges and universities, patchwriting is considered *plagiarism*.

pathos (76–77) See *appeals*.

patterns of organization (31–32) See *analysis, cause and effect, comparison-contrast, definition, description, exemplification, narration,* and *process analysis*.

PDF (Portable Document Format) (102, 108, 116) A file format developed by Adobe that allows documents to be opened in different systems without altering their formatting.

peer review (39–40) A revising strategy in which the writer solicits feedback on a text from classmates, colleagues, or friends. See also *revising*.

perfect tenses (363) See *tense*.

periodical (107) A publication, such as a magazine, newspaper, or scholarly journal, that is issued at regular intervals—daily, weekly, monthly, quarterly. See also *journal*.

periodic sentence (292) A sentence that reserves the independent clause for the end, building suspense that highlights key information when it finally arrives.

person (346, 387) The form of a word that indicates whether it corresponds to the speaker or writer (*I, we*), the person addressed (*you*), or the people

or things spoken or written about (*he, she, it, they, Marta, milkshakes*).

persona (6, 42) The personality of the writer as reflected in tone and style.

personal pronoun (322, 370, 433) The pronouns *I, me, you, he, him, she, her, it, we, us, they, them,* which take the place of specific nouns or noun phrases.

personal statement (191) In a portfolio, the writer's description of the contents and explanation for the choice and arrangement of selections. See also *portfolio*.

personification (305) The attribution of human qualities to nonhuman creatures, objects, ideas, or phenomena: *The tornado swallowed the house.* See *figurative language*.

persuasive argument (16, 73) An argument that advocates for a claim. The writer's purpose is to convince readers to agree with or at least to respect a position on a debatable issue. See also *argument, exploratory argument, purpose*.

phrasal verb (406) A verb combined with one or two particles that together create a new verb with a meaning different from that of the original verb alone. See *particle*.

phrase (280, 285, 330, 336, 422) A group of related words that lacks a subject, predicate, or both. A phrase cannot stand alone as a sentence, but it can function *in* a sentence as a noun, a verb, or a modifier.

pie chart (55) An information graphic that depicts the relationship of the parts to the whole; its sections must add up to 100 percent.

plagiarism (20, 100, 121, 124–27) Presenting a work or a portion of a work of any kind—a paper, a photograph, a speech, a web page—by someone else as if it were one's own.

plural (320) Referring to more than one thing. See *number*.

point of view (89) The perspective of the narrator in a work of literature.

portfolio (192) A printed or online collection of a writer's work. A portfolio may contain the writer's best work, a range of types of writing (a proposal, a report, a set of instructions), or a collection of texts from a single project (prewriting, outline, first draft, revised draft). A portfolio usually also includes a table of contents and a personal statement.

positive form (379–80) See *comparison of adjectives and adverbs*.

possessive case (369, 374) See *case*.

possessive pronoun (322, 404, 433) The pronouns *my, mine, your, yours, his, hers, its, our, ours, your, yours, their,* and *theirs,* which indicate possession.

predicate (325–35) The part of a sentence or clause that states (*predicates*) something about the subject. The **simple predicate** consists of a main verb together with any helping verbs: *Marta is writing her parents a long e-mail.* The **complete predicate** consists of the simple predicate together with any objects, complements, and modifiers: *Marta is writing her parents a long e-mail.* A **compound predicate** is a complete predicate with two or more simple predicates joined with a conjunction: *Marta wrote the e-mail but decided not to send it.*

prefix (468–69) A group of letters that attaches to the beginning of a root word to modify its meaning: *act, react.*

prejudice (75) Ascribing qualities to an individual based on generalities about a group, generalities that are often inaccurate. See also *stereotype*.

premise (81) A claim or assumption on which the conclusion of an argument is based.

preposition (324, 416–20) A word or term that relates nouns or pronouns to other words in a sentence in terms of time, space, cause, and other attributes.

prepositional phrase (331, 338) A preposition followed by its object—a noun or pronoun and its modifiers. Prepositional phrases function as adjectives and adverbs: *the cat with gray fur.*

present participle (409–10) See *participle*.

present perfect progressive tense (364) See *tense*.

present perfect tense (363) See *tense*.

present progressive tense (363) See *tense*.

present tense (362–65) See *tense*.

previewing (7) Scanning the title, subtitle, abstract, introduction, conclusion, sidebars, key terms, headings, subheadings, figures, and illustrations of a text to get a sense of its content, organization, and emphases before reading it in full.

primary source (68) Firsthand information, such as an eyewitness account, a research report, a recorded interview, or a work of literature or art. Compare *secondary source*. See also *field research*.

process analysis (33)   A pattern of paragraph or essay development that explains a process step by step. See also *chronological organization*.

progressive tenses (362–65)   See *tense*.

pronoun (321, 354–57)   A word that renames or takes the place of a noun or noun phrase.

pronoun reference (374–76)   The relationship between a pronoun and its antecedent (the word it replaces). Pronoun reference is clear when readers can tell effortlessly what a pronoun's antecedent is.

proofreading (43–44)   Reading a text to identify and correct spelling and typographical mistakes as well as punctuation and mechanical errors.

proper noun (320, 400, 455)   See *noun*.

proximity (51)   In design, the arrangement of content to show relationships. Material that is related should be placed close together; material that is unrelated should be placed at a distance.

purpose (16, 51)   Your main reason for writing: to express your feelings or impressions or to entertain, inform, or persuade your audience.

Q

quantifier (404)   An adjective such as *some, many, much, less,* or *few* that indicates the amount of a noun.

quotation (131–32)   A restatement of what someone else has said or written, either in a *direct quotation* (word for word) or an *indirect quotation* (a report of what was said or written). See *direct quotation, indirect quotation*.

R

reciprocal pronoun (322)   A pronoun that refers to the individual parts of a plural antecedent: *The candidates debated one another*.

redundancy (279)   Unnecessary repetition: *It was a cloudy, overcast day*.

reference list (210–26, 230, 265–74, 275–76)   In APA and CSE style, a section at the end of a writing project in which the writer provides full bibliographic information for all sources cited in the text.

reference work (110)   Sources, such as dictionaries, encyclopedias, bibliographies, almanacs, and atlases, that provide overview and background information on a word or topic. Specialized reference works may be appropriate sources to cite in a college project, but general reference works are not. Use general reference works only for background.

reflection (7, 8)   The process of thinking about, annotating, and writing about a text; reflection is a necessary step for coming fully to terms with the text. See also *annotation*.

reflexive pronoun (322)   A pronoun that refers back to the subject of a sentence: *She helped herself to the buffet*.

regionalism (295)   Nonstandard usage characteristic of people in a particular locality.

regular verbs (358–59)   Verbs whose past-tense and past-participle forms end in *-d* or *-ed*.

relative clause (333)   An adjective clause introduced by a relative pronoun such as *who, whom,* or *that*. See *adjective clause*.

relative pronouns (322, 333, 370, 373)   Pronouns such as *who, whom, whose, that,* and *which* used to introduce a subordinate clause that describes the pronoun's antecedent: *The apartment that I rented is small*.

relevance (28, 115–16)   The extent to which supporting evidence not only addresses the general topic of a text but also contributes to the reader's understanding of or belief in the text's main idea (the *thesis*). A relevant source offers information that will enrich understanding, provide background information or evidence to support claims, or suggest alternative perspectives.

reliability (116–20)   The extent to which a source is accurate and trustworthy.

research hypothesis (113)   See *hypothesis*.

research questions (98–99)   Intriguing questions about a topic that research might answer.

response (7–8)   Your own reactions to and insights about a text. Response occurs while a reader reads, and it often changes and develops as a result of re-reading and studying the text.

restrictive element (425–27)   See *essential element*.

résumé (58–59)   A brief summary of an applicant's qualifications and experience.

revision (138–39)   The stage of the writing process in which the writer assesses global issues such as whether the text fulfills its purpose, addresses its intended audience, is fully developed, and is organized clearly and logically; also the stage in which the writer assesses local issues such as word choice, sentence variety and emphasis, and wordiness. See also *editing, peer review*.

rhetorical appeal (75)   See *appeal*.

rhetorical citation (139)   Naming the source of information, words, or ideas while providing information about the source or your attitude toward it.

Rogerian model (79)   A model for organizing an exploratory argument that discusses evidence and counter-evidence before drawing a conclusion. Compare *classical* and *Toulmin models*.

S

scholarly sources (68)   Peer-reviewed journal articles and books by experts, often published by university presses.

scratch (informal) outline (24, 136)   See *outline*.

secondary source (68)   A source that describes, evaluates, or interprets primary sources or other secondary sources. A textbook is a secondary source. Compare *primary source*.

sentence (284–94)   A word group with a subject and predicate that does not begin with a subordinating expression. A **declarative sentence** makes a statement: *The phone rang*. An **imperative sentence** gives a command: *Answer the phone*. An **interrogative sentence** asks a question: *Did the phone ring?* An **exclamatory sentence** expresses strong or sudden emotion: *How I hate annoying ringtones!* A **simple sentence** has only one independent clause and no subordinate clauses: *The phone rang*. A **compound sentence** has two or more independent clauses but no subordinate clauses: *The phone rang, and I answered it*. A **complex sentence** consists of a single independent clause with at least one subordinate clause: *My cell phone rang while I was in the elevator*. A **compound-complex sentence** has two or more independent clauses with one or more subordinate clauses: *My cell phone rang, but I didn't answer it because I was in a crowded elevator.*

sentence fragment (335, 389)   A word group punctuated like a sentence but lacking one or more of the essential parts of a sentence: an independent clause, a complete verb, and a subject.

sentence outline (24–25, 136–37)   See *outline.*

separable (406)   A transitive phrasal verb is *separable* if its direct object can fall either between the verb and the particle (separating them) or after the particle.

sequence of tenses (365–66)   The choice of tenses that best reflects the time relationship among the events described in the clauses of a sentence.

setting (89)   In works of literature, where and when the action occurs.

signal phrase (141–42, 149, 151, 202, 263, 427)   A phrase that identifies, discusses, or describes the author or source being cited: *"How do I know what I think,"* E. M. Forster asked, *"until I see what I say?"*

simile (304–06)   An explicit comparison between two unlike things, usually expressed with *like* or *as: run like the wind* (see also *figurative language, metaphor*).

simple future tense (363)   See *tense.*

simple past tense (363)   See *tense.*

simple predicate (327)   See *predicate.*

simple present tense (363)   See *tense.*

simple sentence (285, 334)   See *sentence.*

simple subject (326)   See *subject.*

simple tenses (362–63)   See *tense.*

singular (326)   Referring to one thing.

slang (296)   The informal, inventive, often colorful (and off color) vocabulary of a particular group. Slang is usually inappropriate in formal writing.

slash (452)   Punctuation used to mark the ends of lines in poetry when the poetry is run into a sentence.

spatial organization (33)   See *description.*

sponsors (121)   Corporations, agencies, and organizations that are responsible for creating and making available a website's content.

squinting modifier (382)   A modifier that appears confusingly to modify both what precedes it and what follows it.

Standard American English (319)   The dialect of English that prevails in academic and business settings in the United States.

stereotype (297)   A simplified, uncritical, and often negative generalization about an entire group of people. See also *prejudice.*

styles of documentation (149, 201, 239, 263)   A set of specifications for citing and documenting sources. Most of the well-known style sheets, such as MLA, APA, *Chicago,* and CSE, are sponsored and updated by professional organizations or publishers.

subject (325–35)   The part of a sentence that identifies what the predicate is making a statement about. The **simple subject** is a noun or pronoun: *The cat hissed at the dog.* The **complete subject** is the simple subject with any modifying words or phrases: *The excitable gray cat chased the dog.* A **compound subject** is a complete subject with two or more simple subjects joined with a conjunction: *The cat and the dog usually get along.*

subject complement (290–91, 323, 329, 353, 370, 377, 390)   An adjective, pronoun, or noun phrase that follows a linking verb and describes or refers to the sentence subject: *This food is delicious.* See *linking verb.*

subjective case (369–74)   See *case.*

subjunctive mood (367–68)   See *mood.*

subordinate clause, or **dependent clause** (332–33, 373, 422)   See *clause.*

subordinating conjunction (325, 333)   See *conjunction.*

subordination (287–89)   The incorporation of secondary or modifying elements into a sentence or clause: *Although he got a late start, he arrived on time.* See also *coordination.*

suffix (466)   A group of letters that attaches to the end of a root word to change its meaning and grammatical form: *act, action.*

summary (7, 129–31)   A passage restating the main idea and major supporting points of a source in the reader's own words and sentence structures. A summary is usually at least 50 percent shorter than the text it restates.

superlative form (379–80)   See *comparison of adjectives and adverbs.*

s.v. (245)   Abbreviation of the Latin phrase *sub verbo,* "under the word."

symbolism (89)   The use of a character, event, or object to represent something more than its literal meaning.

synchronous media (61)   Communication media such as instant messaging and online chat in which participants discuss topics in real time. Compare *asynchronous media.*

synonyms (309)   Words with similar meanings—for example, *wrong* and *incorrect.* Compare *antonyms.*

synthesis (11)   The process of making connections among ideas in a text, ideas in other texts, and the writer's own ideas and experiences. Synthesis is an important component in critical thinking and reading and is central to successful college writing.

T

table (55)   An information graphic that organizes data into rows and columns.

tense (362–66)   The form of a verb that indicates the time in which an action or event occurs, when it occurred relative to other events, and whether it is ongoing or completed. The three **simple tenses** are the simple present (*I practice*), the simple past (*I practiced*), and the simple future (*I will practice*). The **perfect tenses** generally indicate the completion of an action before a particular time. They include the present perfect (*I have practiced*), the past perfect (*I had practiced*), and the future perfect (*I will have practiced*). The **progressive tenses** indicate ongoing action. They include the present progressive (*I am practicing*), the past progressive (*I was practicing*), the future progressive (*I will be practicing*), the present perfect progressive (*I have been practicing*), the past perfect progressive (*I had been practicing*), and the future perfect progressive (*I will have been practicing*).

tense sequence (365–66)   See *sequence of tenses.*

theme (87)   The main point of a work of literature.

thesis (7, 22–24)   A brief statement (one or two sentences) of a text's main claim.

tone (8)   The attitude of the writer toward the audience, the topic, and the writer her- or himself as conveyed through word choice, style, and content.

topic (17, 51)   The subject of a text.

topic outline (24–25) See *outline.*

topic sentence (28–29) A sentence (sometimes two) that states a paragraph's main idea.

Toulmin model (79) A model for organizing an argument based on *claims* (or assertions), *grounds* (or evidence), and *warrants* (or assumptions linking claims to grounds). Compare *classical* and *Rogerian* models.

transitional expressions (29, 291, 423) Words and phrases, such as *in addition, however,* and *since,* that show the relationship among sentences or paragraphs.

transitive verb (329, 361) A verb that takes a direct object.

U

understatement (305) The deliberate use of less forceful language than a subject warrants: *An A average is pretty good.* See *figurative language.*

unified, unity (28–29) A quality of a text in which all the examples and evidence support the paragraph's topic sentence and in which each of the supporting paragraphs supports the text's thesis statement.

unmarked infinitive (409) The base verb alone, without *to.*

URL (120) Universal resource locator, a website's Internet address. See also *domain.*

V

verb (321) A word that expresses action (*The quarterback throws a pass*), occurrence (*The play happened in the second half*), or state of being (*The fans are happy*). Verbs also carry information about time (tense), as well as person, number, voice, and mood.

verbal (321, 331–32, 338, 384) A verb form that functions as a noun, adjective, or adverb. Verbals may have objects and complements, but they lack the information about tense required of a complete verb: *I don't like mowing the lawn, but I do like the smell of freshly mowed grass.*

verb phrase (321, 331–32, 347, 360, 398) A main verb with any helping (or auxiliary) verbs.

verbal phrase (331, 338) A verbal and any modifiers, objects, or complements.

vested interest (118) A participant or stakeholder who might personally benefit from the results of a decision, event, or process has a vested (not objective) interest in that decision, event, or process and thus might influence it not for the welfare of others but for personal gain.

voice (92, 280, 293–94, 329) In grammar, the form of a transitive verb that indicates whether the subject is acting or acted upon. In the **active voice,** the subject performs the action of the verb: *The dog chased the cat.* In the **passive voice,** the subject receives the action of the verb: *The cat was chased by the dog.* Also, in writing, the sense of the writer's personality as conveyed through the writer's word, style, and content choices. See also *persona, tone.*

W

warrant (78) An unstated assumption that underlies an argument's main claim. See *Toulmin model.*

weblog (or **blog**) (59) See *blog.*

web page (59) A file on a website in addition to the home page; web pages may include text, audio, video, still images, and database files.

website (59) A collection of files located at a single address (URL) on the World Wide Web.

well developed (28) Paragraphs or essays that supply the information readers need to be persuaded of the writer's point.

white space (53) The portion of a page or screen with no text, graphics, or images.

wiki (59) A website designed for collaborative writing and editing.

wordy expression (277–78) An expression that uses many words (*at the present time*) to say what is better said in one (*now*).

working bibliography (100–02) A list of sources a researcher compiles before and during the research process.

working thesis (90) The first version of a thesis that a writer can imagine for the text he or she is writing. Typically the working thesis goes through several revisions as the writer drafts and revises the text.

works-cited list (150–51, 164–86) See *list of works cited.*

writing process (7–50) The process a writer engages in to produce a writing project. The writing process includes reading and thinking critically, analyzing the assignment, planning the project, generating ideas, drafting, revising, editing, designing, and proofreading.

writing situation (16–19) The characteristics of a text, including its purpose, audience, topic, context, and genre.

Z

zero article (401) See *article.*

Credits

Tab Credits

TAB 1

Fig. 1.1 University of Arizona Library website, *Facsimiles of Illuminated Manuscripts: The Kennicott Bible* <http://www.library.arizona.edu/exhibits/illuman/15_01.html>. University of Arizona Libraries, Special Collections. Used by permission.

TAB 2

pp. 8–10 "Tiny Bat Pits Green against Green," By Maria Glod, *The Washington Post,* October 22, 2009. Copyright © 2009 by Maria Glod. Reprinted by permission of The Washington Post. **pp. 29–30** Peter Canby, "The Cat Came Back," *Harper's Magazine,* March 2005. Copyright © 2005 by Peter Canby. Reprinted by permission of International Creative Management, Inc. **p. 30** Tad Friend, "The Harriet-the-Spy Club," *The New Yorker,* July 31, 2000, p. 36. Copyright © 2000 by Tad Friend. Reprinted by permission of International Creative Management. **p. 32** Virginia Morell, "OK, There It Is—Our Mystery Mollusk," from "Monterey Menagerie," *National Geographic,* June 2004. Copyright © 2004 by Virginia Morell. Reprinted by permission of the author. **p. 33** Barbara Ehrenreich, "What I've Learned from Men: Lessons for a Full-Grown Feminist," published in *Ms. Magazine,* 1985. Copyright © 1985. Reprinted by permission. **p. 37** Al Gore, *An Inconvenient Truth: The Planetary Emergency of Global Warming and What We Can Do About It,* (Rodale Books, 2006). Copyright © 2006 by Al Gore. Permission granted by Rodale, Inc., Emmaus PA 18098.

TAB 3

p. 65 PowerPoint presentation of "Holy Underground Comics" by Lydia Nichols. Copyright © Lydia Nichols. Created with the use of Microsoft Office PowerPoint® presentation software.

TAB 4

p. 88 Gary Snyder, "Front Lines," from *Turtle Island.* Copyright © 1974 by Gary Snyder. Reprinted by permission of New Directions Publishing Corp.

TAB 5

p. 107 Screenshot of blog, "Real Men Don't Write Blogs: Exploring Love, Marriage, and other Difficulties," by Mark Sherman, Ph.D., *Psychology Today* Website. Copyright © by Mark Sherman, Ph.D. Reprinted by permission of Sussex Publishers, LLC. **Fig. 14.1** An advanced search on Google: Google screen shot for search of <<history "underground comics" site: .edu, .org, .gov <www.google.com/advanced_search?q=history etc.>>. Copyright © 2009 Google. **Fig. 14.3** Search results for "underground comics AND genre" on EBSCO Host: Academic Search Premier's Webpage. Copyright © and reproduced by permission of EBSCO Host Copyright Agent. **Fig. 14.4** A library website: screenshot of Minnesota State University [Mankato] Library Services <http://lib.mnsu.edu>. Copyright 2005–2009 Minnesota State University, Mankato, MN. **Fig. 14.5** Library "Summit" search for publications on underground comics by call number PN6725. <http://summit.syr.edu.libezproxy2.syr.edu/cgi-bin/Pwebrecon.cgi?Search_Arg=PN6725&SL=None&Search_Code=CALL_&PID=yMeGf8bImyRkd8bbKzP1TyV3W8&SEQ=20090325171711&CNT=50&HIST=1>. SUMMIT Catalog, Libraries of Syracuse University and SUNY Environmental Sciences and Forestry, http://summit.syr.edu. Copyright © 2009 Syracuse University Library. Reproduced by permission. **p. 114** "Do you have this in sheep?" by Marty Bucella. Copyright © by Marty Bucella. Reproduced by permission of www.CartoonStock.com. **Fig. 15.1** Search results for "underground comics AND genre" on EBSCO Host: Academic Search Premier screen shot. Reproduced by permission of EBSCO Host Copyright Agent. **Fig. 15.2** Cover, *South Beach Diet: The Delicious, Doctor-Designed, Foolproof Plan for Fast and Healthy Weight Loss* by Arthur Agatston, MD, (Rodale Books, 2005). Copyright © 2005 by Rodale Books. Reprinted by permission of Rodale, Inc., Emmaus PA 18098. Cover, *Unbearable Weight: Feminism, Western Culture, and the* Body by Susan Bordo, University of California Press. Copyright © 1995, University of California Press. Reprinted by permission.
p. 117 Al Gore, *An Inconvenient Truth: The Planetary Emergency of Global Warming and What We Can Do About It* (Rodale Books, 2006). Copyright © 2006 by Al Gore. Reprinted by permission of Rodale, Inc., Emmaus PA 18098. **Fig. 15.3** Determining reliability by assessing citations screen shot from EBSCO Host Academic Search Premier for "Times cited in this database" featuring authors Cara Laney and Elizabeth F. Loftus. Reproduced by permission of EBSCO Host Copyright Agent. **p. 131** "Webcomics: The Influence and Continuation of the Comix Revolution," by Sean Fenty, Trena Houp, and Laurie Taylor, *ImageTexT* 1.2 [2004]: par. 2. Web, 18 March 2007. Copyright © Sean Fenty, Trena Houp, and Laurie Taylor. Reprinted by permission.

TAB 6

p. 158 Excerpt, "Hanging Fire," by Audre Lorde, from *The Collected Poems of Audre Lorde.* Copyright © 1978 by Audre Lorde. Reprinted by permission of W. W. Norton & Company, Inc. This selection may not be reproduced, stored in a retrieval system, or transmitted in any form or by any means without the prior written permission of the publisher. **p. 159** Excerpt, *Ludlow* by David Mason, published by Red Hen Press, Granada Hills, CA. Copyright © 2007 by David Mason. Reprinted by permission. **p. 189** Microsoft toolbars showing margins and indentation. Created with Microsoft Office Word® software. **Fig 22.1** PowerPoint presentation of "Holy Underground Comics" by Lydia Nichols. Copyright © 2004 by Lydia Nichols. Reprinted by permission. **197** Adrian Tomine, 8-panel cartoon "Optic Nerve #6," p. 22, from *Drawn and Quarterly,* February 1999. Copyright © 1999 by Adrian Tomine. Reproduced by permission.

TAB 7

p. 228 Microsoft toolbars showing ruler feature. Created with Microsoft Office Word® software.

TAB 9

p. 293 Flannery O'Connor, talk delivered at Notre Dame University, 1957,

Photo Credits

Index

ESL Index

A

a, an, 320, 401–03. *See also* Articles
about, 418
Academic expectations, 68
Adjectives, 412–13
    cumulative, 412
    excessive, 413
    linking verbs and, 412
    past participles as, 409
    prepositions with, 413
    present participles as, 409
    unchanging form of, 412
Adverbs, 413–15
    confusing, 414–15
    hard and *hardly,* 415
    inverted word order and, 399
    negative, 414–15
    not and *no,* 415
    in phrasal verbs, 406
    placement of, 413–14
a few, 404
a great deal of, 404, 405
Agreement
    adjectives and, 412
    pronoun-antecedent, 354
a little, 404–05
Amounts, noncount nouns and, 405
answer, 397
Apostrophes, 419
Arguments
    exploratory *vs.* persuasive, 74
    logos and ethos in the United States, 77
around, 418
Articles *(a, an, the),* 401–03
    a or *an* usage, 311, 401–03
    with common nouns, 401–03
    with count and noncount nouns, 320, 400
    definite *(the)* and indefinite *(a, an),* 401–02
    with generic nouns, 402–03
    with proper nouns, 403
    with words starting with *h-* or *u-,* 402
    zero, 401
ask, 397, 408
ask out, 361, 407
at, 417–18
at no time, 414
Attribute, prepositions indicating, 418
Auxiliary verbs. *See* Helping (auxiliary) verbs

B

Base form of verb, 408

be. See to be
because of, 418
Bilingual dictionaries, 17
by, 418, 419

C

can, could, meanings as modals, 410, 411
Capitalization, 452
carry, 397
Cause/reason, prepositions indicating, 418
change, 397
Class discussions, 63
Clauses
    stated subjects in, 336, 395, 396–97
    subordinate, 395
Clichés and idioms, 306–07
close, 397
Code-switching, 2
Commands (imperative sentences), 395
Common nouns, 400, 401–03
complete, 397
Conciseness, 277
Condition/degree, prepositions indicating, 418
Conjunctions, word order and, 399
Connotations, 18
continue, 408
Contractions, 410
Coordination, 289
Correlative conjunctions, 399
could, can, meanings as modals, 411
Count (countable) nouns, 400–05
    articles with, 320, 401–03
    identifying, 400–01
    other determiners with, 403–05
Cumulative adjectives, 412

D

Definite article *(the),* 401–02. *See also* Articles
Degree, prepositions of, 418
deliver, 397
Demonstrative pronouns, 404
Dependent (subordinate) clauses, 395
describe, 397
Determiners, 401–05. *See also* Articles
Diction
    connotations, 18
    idioms, 306, 307, 407, 420
Dictionaries for second language learners, 17, 309
Direct objects
    adverbs and, 413
    object complements and, 398

phrasal verbs and, 406–07
word order and, 397–98
do, 360

E

-ed verb form (past participle), as adjective, 409
either, too, 414–15
e-mail, cultural differences and, 58
end, 396
engaged to, 419
Ethos, 77
explain, 397
Expletive constructions *(there is/there are/it is),* 396
Explicit subjects, requirements for, 336, 395, 396–97
Extent, indicating, 405

F

few, a few, 404–05
fewer, less, 405
find, 330, 397
fix, 397
for, 397–98, 418
Fragments, 336
frequently, 413
from, 418, 419

G

Generic nouns, 402–03
Gerunds, after verbs and prepositions, 332, 408–09
Gestures, during presentations, 66
give, 397
give in, 361

H

h-, a vs. *an* for words beginning with, 402
hard and *hardly,* 415
Helping (auxiliary) verbs
    adverbs and, 406
    contractions of, 410
    modal auxiliaries, 410–11
    in questions, 398–99
    simple auxiliaries, 410
    word order, 410

I

Idea generation, 20
Idioms
    clichés and, 306–07
    indirect objects as, 330

Notes

Notes

Notes

Notes

Notes

Editing and Proofreading Symbols and Abbreviations

Numbers and letters refer to chapters and sections of *Writing Matters*.

abbr	faulty abbreviation 59	*fs*	fused (run-on) sentence 38	*pn agr*	pronoun agreement problem 39k–m
add	add missing word, phrase 45c–d	*gram*	grammar error 36	*prep*	preposition error 36f, 50
adj	misused adjective 42	*hyph*	hyphen problem 61d–e	*proof*	proofreading needed 6e
adv	misused adverb 42	*idiom*	faulty idiom 33c	*quote*	quotation problem 16d, 54
agr	agreement problem (subject-verb, pronoun) 39	*inc*	incomplete construction 45c–d	*ref*	pronoun reference problem 41i–n

abbr   faulty abbreviation 59
add   add missing word, phrase 45c–d
adj   misused adjective 42
adv   misused adverb 42
agr   agreement problem (subject-verb, pronoun) 39
appr   inappropriate language 32
art   incorrect, missing article (*a, an, the*) 47b
aud   attention to audience needed 2a, 4a
awk   awkward phrasing
bias   biased language 32b
cap   capitalization problem 57
case   problem with pronoun case 41a–h
cite   source citation needed 19–20 (MLA), 23–24 (APA), 27a (*Chicago*), 28a–b (CSE)
cliché   overused expression 33d
coh   coherence problem 5c
concl   stronger conclusion needed 5f
coord   coordination problem 31b
crit   critical thinking, reading needed 3
cs   comma splice 38
det   problem with noun determiner 47b
dev   development needed 5d
dic   problem with diction 33
dm   dangling modifier 43e
doc   problem with documentation 19–20 (MLA), 23–24 (APA), 27a (*Chicago*), 28a–b (CSE)
edit   editing needed 6d
emph   problem with emphasis 31
ethos   writer's credibility needs support 2d, 11d
exact   inexact language 33a
exam   example needed 5d
frag   sentence fragment 37

fs   fused (run-on) sentence 38
gram   grammar error 36
hyph   hyphen problem 61d–e
idiom   faulty idiom 33c
inc   incomplete construction 45c–d
intro   stronger introduction needed 5e
ital   italics needed 58
jarg   inappropriate use of jargon 32a
lc   lowercase letter needed 57
mix   mixed construction 45a–b
mm   misplaced modifier 43a–c
mng?   meaning unclear
mood   problem with mood 40i–j, 44b
num   problem with number use 60
org   reconsider organization 4e, 17b
¶   paragraph 5
P   punctuation problem 51–56
˅   apostrophe 53
[ ]   brackets 56c
⟨⟩   colon 56d
∧   comma 51
—   dash 56a
. . .   ellipses 56e
!   exclamation point 55c
( )   parentheses 56b
⊙   period 55a
?   question mark 55b
˅˅   quotation marks 54
;   semicolon 52
/   slash 56f
para   problem with paraphrase 16c
pass   ineffective use of passive voice 31h, 44b
patch   patchwriting 16c

pn agr   pronoun agreement problem 39k–m
prep   preposition error 36f, 50
proof   proofreading needed 6e
quote   quotation problem 16d, 54
ref   pronoun reference problem 41i–n
rele   problem with relevance 5a, 15a
rep   ineffective repetition 29b, 31f
rev   revision needed 6a–c
run-on   run-on (fused) sentence 38
sexist   sexist language 32b
shift   inappropriate shift (mood, point of view, tense, voice) 44
sl   slang 32b
sp   spelling error 61a–c
sub   subordination problem 31c
sv agr   subject-verb agreement problem 39a–j
t   tense problem 40f–h, 44a
thesis   thesis needs revision 4d, 11b, 12b, 17a
topic   topic inappropriate 2b, 4a
trans   transition needed 5c, 5g
usage   usage problem 33a, 35
var   lack of sentence variety 31a–e
vb   verb problem 40
w   wordy 29
wo   word-order problem 46
ww   wrong word 33a–b
⌒   close up
⌿   delete
∧   insert
/ /   parallelism problem 30
add a space
X   obvious error
??   unclear

Contents

Quick Reference *A Menu of Resources*

WRITING MATTERS

Make It Your Own

Writing Matters unites research, reasoning, documentation, grammar, and style into a cohesive whole, helping students see the conventions of writing as a network of **responsibilities** writers have…

…to **other writers**. *Writing Matters* emphasizes the responsibility writers share, whether collaborating online in peer review or conducting research with digital and print sources, to treat information fairly and accurately and to craft writing that is unique and original—their own!

…to the **audience**. *Writing Matters* emphasizes the need to use conventions appropriate to the readership, to write clearly, and to provide readers with the information and interpretation they need to make sense of a topic.

… to the **topic**. *Writing Matters* encourages writers to explore a topic thoroughly and creatively, to assess sources carefully, and to provide reliable information at a depth that does the topic justice.

…to **themselves**. *Writing Matters* encourages writers to take their writing seriously and to approach writing tasks as an opportunity to learn about a topic and to expand their scope as writers. Students are more likely to write well when they think of themselves as writers rather than as error-makers.

---

mcgrawhillconnect.com

Powered by Connect Composition Plus 2.0, *Writing Matters* helps students own their ideas and put responsible writing into practice with four-year subscription access, online peer-review tools, continually adaptive personalized remediation for grammar and mechanics, and unique tools to empower outcomes-based writing assessment.

connect plus+
ICOMPOSITION

ISBN 978-0-07-750597-4
MHID 0-07-750597-2

EAN

9 780077 505974

90000

www.mhhe.com